The Blackwell Guide to
Recorded Jazz

The Blackwell Guide to
Recorded Jazz

Edited by

Barry Kernfeld

Copyright © Basil Blackwell Ltd 1991
Editorial organization © Barry Kernfeld 1991

First published 1991
First published in paperback (with CD supplement) 1992

Blackwell Publishers
108 Cowley Road, Oxford OX4 1JF, UK
238 Main Street, Suite 501, Cambridge, MA 02142, USA

British Library Cataloguing in Publication Data
A CIP catalogue record for this book is available from the British Library.

Library of Congress Cataloging-in-Publication Data
A CIP catalog record of this book is available from the Library of Congress.
ISBN 0–631–18531–3

Typeset in Palatino
by Inforum, Rowlands Castle, Hants
Printed in Great Britain by TJ Press Ltd, Padstow, Cornwall

Contents

Contributors

JAMES LINCOLN COLLIER is an author whose publications include the history *The Making of Jazz* (1978), biographies of Louis Armstrong (1983), Duke Ellington (1987) and Benny Goodman (1989), and the leading article, 'Jazz', in *The New Grove Dictionary of Jazz*.

DIGBY FAIRWEATHER maintains several careers in the music: as a cornet player he was named the BBC Jazz Society's Musician of the Year in 1979, and he is today more active than ever. With Ian Carr and Brian Priestley he wrote *Jazz: the Essential Companion* (1987), and he is a frequent broadcaster.

MARK GARDNER is a veteran interviewer and discographer of bop and hard-bop musicians. From 1962 until their demise his work appeared regularly in *Discographical Forum* and *Jazz Monthly*, and he continues to write for *Jazz Journal*. He contributed extensively to *The New Grove Dictionary of Jazz*.

MARK GILBERT has been deputy editor of *Jazz Journal International* since 1980 and has written about jazz for *Melody Maker*, the *Daily Mail* and *The Stage* as well as contributing to *The New Grove Dictionary of Jazz*. He is also a musician and music teacher.

MIKE HAZELDINE managed tours for New Orleans musicians and produced and distributed some historic recordings during the 1960s. He has organized two Duke Ellington International Conferences and put together wide-ranging jazz concerts for various theatres. He contributed to *The New Grove Dictionary of Jazz* and is currently editor of *New Orleans Music*.

EKKEHARD JOST is professor of musicology at the University of Giessen in Germany and he plays baritone saxophone. His publications include *Free Jazz* (1974), *Sozialgeschichte des Jazz in den USA* (1982), *Jazzmusiker: Materialien zur Soziologie der afro-amerikanischen Musik* (1982) and *Europas Jazz, 1960–1980* (1987).

BARRY KERNFELD is a freelance writer and editor of jazz books. After contributing to *The New Grove Dictionary of American Music* (1986) and *The Harvard Dictionary of Music* (1986) he edited *The New Grove Dictionary of Jazz* (1988). He is presently writing *What to Listen For in Jazz* for Yale University Press.

Preface and Acknowledgements

The foremost aim of *The Blackwell Guide to Recorded Jazz* is to suggest a starter collection as a means for newcomers to gain a grasp of this wonderful music. There are about 125 or 150 selections in the book, depending on how you wish to count double albums and multi-volume sets. These selections are – within particular eras, styles and instrumental genres – among the first and best of jazz. But it must be said at the start that they should not be construed as embracing *all* the best of this vast and ever-expanding music.

The book is up to date in its coverage of relevant issues on compact disc, and indeed in some cases it is positively ahead of itself, offering information on future CD issues of our selections. But given the notoriously rapid rate at which jazz recordings go in and out of press, we recognize the danger of focusing solely on current issues. Instead our approach is a different one, new for this sort of book: for each selection we provide a comprehensive and historical listing of issues on CD, LP and cassette, so that the volume may prove useful both to the owner of nothing but the latest equipment and to someone with access to only well-worn LPs in the local library. Correspondingly, the text focuses on the music itself rather than on a particular recorded object, though we have addressed issues of fidelity when these are significant. (The editor made an across-the-board decision not to include low-fidelity broadcast recordings. While these preserve many of the greatest jazz improvisations, they are somewhat of an acquired taste and, owing to the sound quality, perhaps not the best place for a newcomer to start listening.)

The Blackwell Guide to Recorded Jazz is one in a series of Blackwell Guides, and in particular we have taken account of the coverage of boogie-woogie pianists, blues shouters and classic blues singers in *The Blackwell Guide to Blues Records* (1989) edited by Paul Oliver. These musicians are intimately tied to jazz, but there seemed no point in retracing the same ground; accordingly, the jazz guide defers to the blues guide in these areas. It should also be mentioned that charting the 125 or so selections has proved so complex that there is no room for the secondary lists of additional selections that appear in the other Blackwell Guides.

We have endeavoured to write in plain English (using English spelling and punctuation) but making use of a hybrid style that reflects both the international authorship (English, American and German) and the Americanisms that dominate jazz literature. We avoid jazz jargon whenever possible; those few terms which are absolutely essential are explained parenthetically at their first appearance. A small portion of the text presumes a rudimentary knowledge of music (for example, the identification of an instrument, a minor key blues progression or a syncopated rhythmic pattern). One such item requires systematic explanation: in descriptions of the form of a piece, upper-case italic letters refer to themes, while lower-case italics refer to sections of a single theme.

The discographies were prepared by Mark Gardner, Howard Rye and Barry Kernfeld. In addition to the recorded documents themselves, we have consulted for one reason or another the majority of the general and specialist discographies and catalogues available. It is impossible to list these sources in a non-academic book such as this; instead a blanket acknowledgement of our indebtedness to jazz discographers and an expression of our gratitude must suffice.

This book owes its existence to Peter Clayton, who created its original plan, saw it through the normal stages of proposal and approval at the publisher, and commissioned chapters from contributors before ill-health forced him to withdraw from the project. The book has changed dramatically since then, but three of the contributors and a number of their selections remain as Peter had planned. I offer my thanks to Peter for having cut through so much of the red tape, and I regret that he cannot share more in the rewards of completing the project.

I am also deeply grateful to Alyn Shipton, Reference Publisher at Basil Blackwell, for asking me to edit the book after Peter determined he could not continue. Alyn's penetrating suggestions and criticisms, stemming both from his regular duties as a publisher and from his intense involvement with jazz, have substantially improved the quality of the volume. And it was a delight and privilege to be involved once again with the book's managing editor, Caroline Richmond. Having spent four years working together on a jazz dictionary, we long ago arrived at an easy manner of communicating and a virtually telepathic agreement on matters of style and substance.

It goes without saying that my thanks are due to the six contributors, all of whom took time away from busy schedules to do their part. I also wish to thank Howard Rye, a freelance discographer and the driving force behind *Collector's Items* magazine. Howard checked the recording citations and made literally hundreds of additions and corrections.

Fortunately jazz record stores are friendly places: invariably I was allowed to loiter at those I frequented in London, Oxford, San Francisco and State College, even when I had reached that rude stage of no longer buying recordings, but just copying down titles and numbers of issues closely related to what I had already acquired. I also wish to thank Ralph Kaffel, president of Fantasy, Inc., for providing information on forthcoming issues on his Milestone and Original Jazz Classics labels; Norman Field, head of Neovox Record Co., for providing catalogues of his cassettes; George Avakian and Michael Brooks, for supplying information on the forthcoming final volume in CBS's Jazz Masterpieces series of Billie Holiday recordings; and Bruce Shamma, an employee of my local CD store Blue Train, for helping me keep abreast of the latest discs as the book was going into production.

My father, Bernard Kernfeld, typed the text of Chapter 1 onto the word processor, and thus gave me a much-needed breathing space. This book was nearly completed during my wife's tenure as a Rhodes fellow at St Hilda's College, Oxford, coincidentally but conveniently located close to Blackwell's publishing building; even after returning to her teaching schedule at Penn State University, she has, as always, continued to be supportive of my career as a freelance jazz writer.

In addition to the many people mentioned above who have now aided in the making of an updated paperback edition of the *Guide*, the editor would like to thank Orrin Keepnews, who provided information on new issues on the Milestone, Bluebird and MCA labels.

BARRY KERNFELD
State College, Pennsylvania
June 1992

Discographical Conventions

The discographies proceed as follows:

1) Main selection: its place of issue, title, label name and issue number.
2) Personnel and instrumentation, place, date, individual tracks. (If someone other than the subject of an essay leads a recording, the leader's name appears parenthetically at the head of the personnel.)
3) Equivalent and related recordings. These are separated by recording medium (CD, LP, cassette) and ordered according to the extent to which their contents duplicate the main selection. The phrase 'same contents' implies the same title as well; of course, when this is not the case, the alternative title appears. In addition, many titles of related issues differ from the main selection. These are shown in one of two ways: for recordings issued only in one place, immediately following the name of an individual country or continent; for those issued in more than one place, at the end of the line directly preceding the names of countries or continents. Places are ordered thus: USA, UK, Europe, individual European countries (organized alphabetically), Japan, Australia, elsewhere. The phrase 'tracks x, y, z' indicates that only this material appears; 'incl. tracks x, y, z' means that there is also other material. In general the phrase 'plus additional tracks' is a code for boxed sets and other sorts of multi-volume issues.

Because this is a book for newcomers, we have avoided the compressed style that is standard in jazz discography. Everything is spelt out in full, with two exceptions. First, the tracks of each main selection are referred to by number, rather than by title, in the lists of equivalent and related recordings; for collections of more than ten items, the tracks are numbered at the right-hand side to facilitate matching the titles to the related issues. Second, the normal jazz instruments are abbreviated as follows:

arr	arranger	kbd	keyboard
as	alto saxophone	org	organ
bar	baritone saxophone	p	piano
bb	brass bass	per	percussion
bj	banjo	sb	string bass
bsx	bass saxophone	ss	soprano saxophone

c	cornet	syn	synthesizer
cl	clarinet	tb	trombone
d	drums	tpt	trumpet
elb	electric bass guitar	ts	tenor saxophone
elg	electric guitar	v	vocal
elp	electric piano	vb	vibraphone/vibraharp
fl	flute	vln	violin
g	guitar	wbd	washboard

CHAPTER 1

The First Hot Bands

James Lincoln Collier

It is generally accepted that jazz first developed in New Orleans in the early years of the century, and that all jazz has evolved from the version that was created there. It was an outgrowth or variant of ragtime, differing mainly in a certain rhythmic feel which has come to be called 'swing'. In addition, elements of the blues were added, especially the inflection of notes through the use of pitch bends, mutes of various kinds, and throat-tones to roughen the sound.

This New Orleans music was played by many different combinations of instruments. In the honky-tonks of the New Orleans brothel district, bands were likely to be small, consisting of one or two brass or reed instruments accompanied by one or two rhythm instruments. The new style also found its way into music of the larger marching or brass bands of the city. But in time there developed a jazz dance band of cornet, trombone and clarinet over a rhythm section, which in its fullest form comprised string bass, guitar, drums and piano – although in many if not most instances not all of these rhythm instruments would be present. At times a violin would be added to double the lead. Later, after about World War I, tuba and banjo were usually substituted for string bass and guitar.

The classic New Orleans band played an ensemble music that was frequently interrupted by short solo 'breaks' which were usually two bars in length, but could be longer or shorter. Full-dress solos were relatively rare, and when they did occur they were not improvised, but fairly formal statements of a theme. In the ensemble the cornet played a comparatively simple melody in the middle register, the clarinet wove rising and falling lines through the melody or shrilled on top in imitation of marching fifes, and the trombone provided a bass line, as well as making connecting links between phrases of the melody, often through the use of slurs.

This fairly rigid system of the classic New Orleans style obviously owes a great deal to the band marches which were so popular in America in the years around the turn of the century. It was in place by 1915, certainly, and probably at least five years earlier. It began to spread out from New Orleans from about 1910, carried especially to the West Coast, and then Chicago, by musicians from New Orleans adept at it. These bands played in a variety of situations, but many worked in the dance halls and saloons of the vice districts that were a feature of American cities at that time. Associations with the brothels discredited the music in the eyes of many Americans; nonetheless, it rapidly attracted a nationwide audience, and, with the astounding success of the records of the Original Dixieland Jass [sic] Band in 1917, New Orleans jazz became an important part of American popular music, played for listening as well as dancing. The music was simply called jazz; but as other forms arose, it began to be referred to as 'New Orleans jazz', 'New Orleans' and eventually 'dixieland', after the group which had first made it famous. In time it was supplanted by big dance bands playing arranged music, and then other forms; but dixieland has continued to attract an audience worldwide, and must be honoured as the seminal form of the music.

* * *

Original Dixieland Jazz Band: *The Complete Original Dixieland Jazz Band (1917–1921)*

In 1915, as part of the diaspora from New Orleans, some white New Orleans musicians were brought to Chicago to play in the city's clubs and dance halls. Two of these groups were led by drummer Johnny Stein and trombonist Tom Brown. After some switching of personnel the Stein group, without Stein and now called the Original Dixieland Jass Band, was brought east. In January 1917 it opened at a famous restaurant in New York called Reisenweber's, where it quickly became something of a popular sensation. Reisenweber's was one of the lobster palaces catering to middle-class New Yorkers and tourists. The introduction of jazz to such a locale signalled that it was now acceptable to mainstream Americans. The group's Victor records made that year and after were best-sellers and were important in making jazz a national phenomenon. Its first hit paired *Barnyard Blues* (better known as *Livery Stable Blues*) and *At the Jazz Band Ball*. Besides these, perhaps the best known of the Victor Original Dixieland Jass Band sides were *Bluin' the Blues*, *Ostrich Walk*, *Sensation Rag*, *Clarinet Marmalade*, *Fidgety Feet* and *Tiger Rag*, which became virtually the theme song for early jazz.

Because there was little true improvising, early jazz musicians were not as individually distinctive as later jazz musicians would be. LaRocca played a bright, relatively simple, punchy line, with the notes sharply attacked, and the tone clean and muscular. Shields frequently began his figures on a high note, which he would then let fall off in a descending slur which would break into a downward cascade. His tone was somewhat shrill in the upper register, as was generally the case with early New Orleans players, but was liquid and clean in the mid-range. Edwards played almost invariably in the mid to low range, to stay out of the way of the other instruments. As was typical of New Orleans trombonists, he introduced a great many slurs; the slide trombone had only recently supplanted the valve trombone in general use in popular music, and trombonists were, at the period, over-using the potential for slurs. None of these musicians developed along with the music to become important individual soloists. In 1936 the group was reassembled to make a documentary film and to re-create its earlier performances on record. The musicians played in much the same manner as they had in 1917, although with an inevitable loosening of the rhythm.

The tunes made famous by the Original Dixieland Jass Band were typical of New Orleans jazz vehicles, usually consisting of two, three or even more strains, like the rags and marches from which they were derived. The strains often modulated to another key, usually up a fourth. The famous *Tiger Rag*, for example, consists of strains in B flat, E flat and A flat. Some strains were linked by interludes, as in *Clarinet Marmalade Blues*. At times its music, and that of other New Orleans bands, was not melodic, but consisted of collections of devices rather arbitrarily strung together: slurs, growls, sudden outbursts of drumming. Particularly important was the break, where the band ceased briefly – usually for two or four measures – in order to allow one instrument to parade alone. These breaks were often comical in intent: early jazz had one foot in vaudeville, and there were always elements of humour in the music, for example, the imitation of the whinnying horse and the crowing rooster in *Barnyard Blues* and the trombone's downward octave plop, meant to imitate the roar of the tiger, in the last strain of *Tiger Rag*.

The Original Dixieland Jass Band has never been considered a truly great jazz band. But it was a good one, which played with verve and infectious swing, and, considering that the musicians were mostly untutored, with surprising accuracy and good intonation. It may have been typical of the New Orleans bands of the day, though we have no idea how typical, because it was in any case the first jazz band to record. As the first to have not only national, but – through its work in London in 1919 – international success, it played a seminal role in teaching the world about this exciting new music, and became the early model for thousands of young musicians who were attempting to play it, among them Bix Beiderbecke and Benny Goodman.

CD

France: *The Complete Original Dixieland Jazz Band (1917–1921)*,
RCA PD 90026

Nick LaRocca (c), Eddie Edwards (tb), Larry Shields (cl), Henry Ragas (p), Tony Sbarbaro (d)

New York	26 Feb 1917	**Livery Stable Blues**	
		Dixie Jass Band One-Step	
	18 March 1918	**At the Jazz Band Ball**	
		Ostrich Walk	
	25 March 1918	**Skeleton Jangle**	5
		Tiger Rag	
	25 June 1918	**Bluin' the Blues**	
		Fidgety Feet	
		Sensation Rag	
	17 July 1918	**Mournin' Blues**	10
		Clarinet Marmalade Blues	
		Lazy Daddy	

add Benny Krueger (as); J. Russel Robinson (p) replaces Ragas

	1 Dec 1920	**Margie**	
	4 Dec 1920	**Palesteena**	
	30 Dec 1920	**Broadway Rose**	15

add Clifford Cairns, Eddie King, band (v)

		Sweet Mamma	

omit (v)

	28 Jan 1921	**Home Again Blues**	
		Crazy Blues	

Frank Signorelli (p) replaces Robinson

	3 May 1921	**Jazz Me Blues**	

add Al Bernard (v)

	25 May 1921	**St Louis Blues**	20
		Royal Garden Blues	
	7 June 1921	**Dangerous Blues**	

omit Bernard and Sbarbaro

	1 Dec 1921	**Bow Wow Blues**	

Other CDs

incl. tracks 1–2, 6–9, 11–13:
   UK: *Sensation!*, Living Era CD AJA 5023

LPs

plus 1936 tracks cited below:
   France: *Original Dixieland Jazz Band*, vols.1–2, RCA 730703 and 730704;
   RCA NL 90026
incl. tracks 1–4, 6, 8–10, 15, 17, 20–21, plus 1936 tracks cited below:
   Italy: *Original Dixieland Jazz Band*, RCA NL 42745
incl. tracks 1–2, 6–9, 11–13:
   UK: *Sensation!*, Living Era AJA 5023
incl. tracks 1–11:
   Japan: *Jazz from New Orleans*, RCA 5328
tracks 1–2, 6, 9, 11–15, 17, plus 1936 tracks cited below:
   The Original Dixieland Jazz Band
   USA: RCA Victor LPV 547
   UK: RCA RD 7919

Cassettes

plus additional tracks:
   UK: *Original Dixieland Jazz Band: 70th Anniversary*, vol.1, 1917–18,
   Neovox 828; vol.2, 1918–20, Neovox 831; vol.3, 1920–23, Neovox 834
incl. tracks 1–2, 6–9, 11–13:
   UK: *Sensation!*, Living Era ZC AJA 5023

LP

USA: *The Original Dixieland Jazz Band*, RCA Victor LPV 547
tracks cited above, plus:
LaRocca (c), Edwards (tb), Shields (cl), Robinson (p), Sbarbaro (d)

New York	25 Sept 1936	**Skeleton Jangle**
	10 Nov 1936	**Clarinet Marmalade**
		Bluin' the Blues
		Tiger Rag
		Barnyard Blues
		Original Dixieland One-Step

Other LPs

same contents:
   UK: RCA RD 7919
plus additional tracks:
   France: *The Complete Original Dixieland Jazz Band*, vols.1–2, RCA 730703
   and 730704, RCA NL 90026
incl. tracks 2, 3, 4:
   Italy: *Original Dixieland Jazz Band*, RCA NL 42745

New Orleans Rhythm Kings: *New Orleans Rhythm Kings and Jelly Roll Morton*

The success of the Stein and Brown bands in Chicago, followed by the national celebrity of the Original Dixieland Jass Band, led cabaret and dance-hall managers to search for similar New Orleans groups. Over the years after 1917 more New Orleans musicians, both singly and in groups, began to move northward, encouraged to do so in no little part by the pay scale, which was substantially higher in places such as New York, Chicago and San Francisco than it was in New Orleans. In the years after about 1916 or so, Chicago in particular came to be seen as the center of jazz activity, supplanting New Orleans, in considerable measure because most of the best New Orleans musicians had come north. Even in New York, through much of the 1920s, it was recognized that the western musicians in Chicago were playing a hotter, stronger version of jazz than was to be heard in the East.

One of the most influential of the New Orleans bands to arrive in Chicago was the group that came to be called the New Orleans Rhythm Kings, although its initial recordings were issued as by the Friar's Society Orchestra, after the Friar's Inn, where the band was playing. This group was not brought intact from New Orleans, as some of the earlier groups had been, but was put together piecemeal out of combinations of New Orleans musicians who had drifted north, with midwesterners who, by the early 1920s, were playing the new music. The group which made the first and very influential recordings included four New Orleanians: Paul Mares, cornet; George Brunies, trombone; Leon Roppolo, clarinet; and Steve Brown, bass. To them were added midwesterners Jack Pettis, saxophones; Elmer Schoebel, piano; Lou Black, banjo; and Frank Snyder, drums. Through the relatively brief career of the group the personnel shifted as saxophonists came and went, and changes were made to the rhythm section. For a period Ben Pollack, considered by other musicians to be one of the finest drummers of the time, was in the band. But the key figures were the front line of Mares, Brunies and Roppolo, who were on all of the early, influential cuts.

Like the ODJB, the New Orleans Rhythm Kings was a typical New Orleans group, playing the classic contrapuntal style with cornet lead, clarinet weaving upwards and downwards through the melody in the flute or fife-like marching band style, and the trombone providing connecting links. The saxophones that appear on some of these sides were a concession to a fad for the instrument: in 1919 the Art Hickman band, a jazz-based dance group which featured a saxophone duet, had become widely popular, and the saxophone had become, during the early 1920s, a vogue instrument.

As was the case with the Original Dixieland Jass Band, the New Orleans Rhythm Kings did not improvise, in the main, but played set-pieces with carefully worked out parts, which they might embellish or vary to some extent in the course of playing. This was true even of the solos: George Brunies plays his famous solo on *Tin Roof Blues* more or less the same on three takes of the tune, and he continued to play it thus for the remainder of his career. This was still primarily an ensemble jazz band in the old New Orleans style, with the solos scattered sparsely through the performance and meant mainly to provide variety rather than to act, as happened a few years later, as the central point of the music. On *Eccentric*, for example, the solos consist of sets of two-bar breaks by clarinet, trumpet and trombone for a total of 22 bars; the rest of the cut is played by the ensemble.

The band performs with less of the hokum that had helped to make the Original Dixieland Jass Band famous, and there is nothing like the obvious horseplay of that group's *Livery Stable Blues*. But touches of comedy remain in, for example, some of the breaks on *Eccentric*.

The New Orleans Rhythm Kings is clearly a superior jazz band to its predecessor. It is generally assumed by jazz historians that it owed a good deal to the influence of the black New Orleans bands, and especially to King Oliver's Creole Jazz Band, which was working in Chicago at the same moment. Paul Mares's breaks on *Bugle Call Blues* are played with the plunger mute, a device believed to have been developed by Oliver, and employ mainly quarter, rather than eighth, notes, a characteristic of Oliver's style. Taken as a whole, the New Orleans Rhythm Kings plays with a looser, more supple swing than the Original Dixieland Jass Band, as is evident in the very driving lead of Mares on the aforementioned *Bugle Call Blues*. Note also on the last ride-out chorus of this piece the drum 'backbeat' (accents on the second and fourth beats), a device which would become a cliché in jazz playing, providing here the classic rocking two-beat swing.

Although Mares and Brunies were influential as far as the young jazz players in Chicago and elsewhere were concerned, the most admired member of the group was clarinettist Leon Roppolo. To some extent this was owing to his early madness and death, which cast a romantic aura around him, but there is no denying the liquid quality of his tone, evident in the breaks on *Eccentric*, and the easy swing he achieved. His playing is less shrill than that of many of the early jazz clarinettists, especially in the upper register.

Just as the Original Dixieland Jass Band brought into the repertory a number of classic tunes, such as *Tiger Rag* and *Clarinet Marmalade*, so too the New Orleans Rhythm Kings added at least three famous ones – *Bugle Call Blues* (better known as *Bugle Call Rag*), *Farewell Blues* and *Tin Roof Blues*, possibly the most frequently played of any of the New Orleans pieces. It should not be thought that these numbers were composed in their entirety by these musicians: although the evidence is not firm, it is probable that they were put together out of musical oddments familiar to many players. But they have remained classics.

(A footnote to this collection: during the course of extensive interviews with Tom Thibeau, a Connecticut businessman who had been a professional pianist in Chicago, the latter explained that Kyle Pierce had sent him as a substitute for the session of 17 July 1922, a session attributed to Pierce and Jelly Roll Morton. Thibeau definitely identified himself as the soloist on *Marguerite* and also claimed to be on *Sobbin' Blues*. He did not remember Morton being on the date, though no one challenges Morton's presence on *Mr Jelly Lord* and two tracks from the next day.)

LP
USA: *New Orleans Rhythm Kings and Jelly Roll Morton*, Milestone
M 47020

(Friar's Society Orchestra:) Paul Mares (tpt), George Brunies (tb), Leon Roppolo (cl), Jack Pettis (C-melody sax, ts), Elmer Schoebel (p), Lou Black (bj), Steve Brown (sb), Frank Snyder (d)

Richmond, IN	29 Aug 1922	Eccentric	
		Farewell Blues	
		Discontented Blues	
		Bugle Call Blues	
	30 Aug 1922	Panama	5
		Tiger Rag	
		Livery Stable Blues	
		Oriental	

Mares (tpt), Brunies (tb), Roppolo (cl), Mel Stitzel (p), Ben Pollack (d)

	12 March 1922	Sweet Lovin' Man	
		Sweet Lovin' Man (take A)	10
		That's a Plenty	
		That's a Plenty (take A)	
		Shimmeshawabble	
		Weary Blues	
	13 March 1922	Da Da Strain	15
		Wolverine Blues (take A)	
		Wolverine Blues (take B)	
		Maple Leaf Rag	
		Tin Roof Blues	
		Tin Roof Blues (take A)	20
		Tin Roof Blues (take B)	

Mares (tpt), Brunies (tb), Roppolo (cl), Pettis (C-melody sax), Glenn Scoville (as, ts), Don Murray (cl, ts), Tom Thibeau (p), Bob Gillette (bj), Chink Martin (bb), Pollack (d)

17 July 1923	**Sobbin' Blues**	
	Marguerite	

also incl. Thibeau ?	**Angry**	
	Clarinet Marmalade	25
	Clarinet Marmalade (take A)	

Jelly Roll Morton replaces ? (p)	**Mr Jelly Lord** (take A)	
	Mr Jelly Lord (take C)	
18 July 1923	**London Blues**	
	Milenberg Joys (take C)	30

Kyle Pierce (p) replaces Morton	**Mad**

Other LPs

same contents:
  France: Milestone 2C178-96405/06
plus additional takes: *New Orleans Rhythm Kings*, vol.1 (1922–23) and vol.2
  (1923)
  Italy: Kings of Jazz NLJ 18009 and NLJ 18010
  Sweden: Classic Jazz Masters CJM 12 and CJM 13
  Australia: Swaggie S 829 and S 830
tracks 1–10, 12–17:
  Italy: *New Orleans Rhythm Kings*, BYG 19
tracks 18–31, plus additional takes:
  UK: *New Orleans Rhythm Kings featuring Jelly Roll Morton*, Rhapsody
  RHA 6022
  Italy: *New Orleans Rhythm Kings*, BYG 27
tracks 1–8, 12, 18, 20, 31: *New Orleans Rhythm Kings*
  USA: Riverside RLP 12–146; Orpheum ORP 102 (fake stereo version)
  France: BYG 529.057
  Italy: Joker SM 3092
tracks 9, 13–16, 22–5, 27, 29–30: *New Orleans Rhythm Kings*
  USA: Riverside RLP 12-102
  France: BYG 529.069

Cassettes

tracks 1–10, 12–27 or 28, 29–31:
  UK: *New Orleans Rhythm Kings, Gennetts Complete*, vols.1–2, 1922–1923,
  Neovox 139 and 140

tracks 1–9, 12–15, 17–18, 21–4, 26–7, 29–31, plus additional tracks:
  UK: *The Complete New Orleans Rhythm Kings*, vol.1, 1922–23, and vol.2,
  1923–25, Neovox 797 and 799

* * *

King Oliver: *The Complete King Oliver Creole Jazz Band*

By 1920, with the enormous success of the Original Dixieland Jass Band and
its imitators, New Orleans jazz had become a national fad. Everywhere
young musicians were attempting to learn the new music, and they were
looking to established New Orleans players to provide a lead. One effect of
the vogue for jazz was to draw out of New Orleans many of the best
musicians. Among these was King Oliver, who from about 1919 was playing
in Chicago with his Creole Jazz Band. The group very quickly became the
primary model for the jazz musicians of Chicago and, as its first records
appeared, elsewhere.

The personnel of the group shifted over time, as was generally the case
with early jazz bands, but most of its recordings were made with Oliver,
cornet; Honore Dutrey, trombone; Johnny Dodds, clarinet; Baby Dodds,
drums; Bill Johnson, banjo; Lil Hardin, piano; and, at times, various saxophone players. And in 1922 Oliver added Louis Armstrong on second
cornet. All the recordings of this important early Oliver group were made in
1923 for four different companies: Gennett, Paramount, Okeh and Columbia. The Gennett and Okeh series are longer, and are considered the heart of
Oliver's recordings.

Like most New Orleans bands, the group worked out its music in advance, even including the solos – as is indicated, for example, by the different masters of *Riverside Blues*, which contain virtually identical solos by
Armstrong. Rhythmically, the group achieves an easy two-beat rock, somewhat different from the four-beat swing that would evolve during the 1920s.
Oliver did not want a frantic, hard-driving band. He believed in a controlled, well-organized performance which swung but did not press. As a
consequence the three main melody instruments work at keeping their lines
distinct and clean; it is this ensemble sound for which we listen in the work
of this band. This is also dance music, as was most early jazz. Tempos are
necessarily moderate, in the range of 140 to 190 beats per minute. The music
is not without flaws: structurally there is a tendency for the pieces simply to
alternate two strains, an acceptable practice for dancing, but too predictable
for music meant to be listened to. The saxophones add nothing, and at times
simply muddy the sound.

Paradoxically, the band's best-known tune was a solo feature for Oliver, employing his specialty, mutes. This was *Dippermouth Blues*, known in some later versions as *Sugar Foot Stomp*. Oliver's solo shows the deep influence of the blues on early jazz. The opening note is the blue third slurring down to the tonic and shaded by the opening and closing of the plunger mute. It bears an uncanny resemblance to the whine of a blues guitar, especially one played with a bottleneck, as it was undoubtedly meant to do. We can also hear in this solo the way that Oliver has placed the notes around the beat, rather than on them, an important characteristic of jazz. Indeed, in many cases it is actually difficult to determine where the notes come, so ambiguous are they.

Although it was not realized at the time, in retrospect we see *Chimes Blues* and *Froggie Moore* are equally important, for they contain Louis Armstrong's first two recorded solos. *Chimes Blues* is so thoroughly worked out that the musicians could have been reading it from written scores, and it is characterized by the easy rock that the band frequently achieved. Typically, Armstrong's solo is played straight, presumably on Oliver's instructions. One of Oliver's trademarks was the use of figures which displace accents from their normal spots, thus contradicting the prevailing metre. The main figure in Armstrong's solo is one of this type, and it confuses Armstrong, so that he turns the beat around in the middle of the solo and has to take a quick skip to find his place again.

Armstrong's solo on *Froggie Moore*, a Jelly Roll Morton tune, can be considered the first important recorded jazz solo. From the moment Armstrong enters we feel a difference in the rhythm from the way the rest of the band is playing. Through a use of terminal vibrato (a vibrato increasing in intensity during a held note), shifting accents, uneven division of the beat and placement of his notes around the beat, rather than on it, Armstrong defines what would come to be called 'swing'.

At the time, however, Oliver, and not Armstrong, was seen by other musicians as the key figure in the group. One device that impressed them was the use of duet breaks featuring the two cornets, who appeared to improvise a break together spontaneously in correct harmony. In fact, according to Armstrong, at an appropriate moment ahead of time Oliver would play for Armstrong the figure he intended to use; it would be no problem for a trained musician to improvise a harmony to the line. These duet breaks appear on a number of the Creole Jazz Band cuts, especially *Snake Rag*, in which they are featured.

The Creole Jazz Band is considered by many jazz authorities to be the most influential of the early jazz bands. By 1922 young musicians, including many white ones, were visiting Lincoln Gardens to hear the group. In fact, in time the management began putting on special 'for whites only' musical nights for the benefit of white musicians when they came off their jobs.

Musicians were also buying the records as they came out. By the mid-1920s King Oliver was well known not merely to jazz musicians and fans, but to the wider audience for hot dance music. In 1924 a show business newspaper could say, 'King Oliver, Negro jazz trumpeter, is the "hottest" jazz musician of his kind in the business. He has set the pace which all the jazz cornetists with the crack bands follow' (Abel Green in *The Clipper*, 10 April 1924, 14).

The reissue on Milestone also contains some cuts by a group called the Red Onion Jazz Babies. By the mid-1920s a black composer named Clarence Williams, a New Orleanian, was in New York, building what would become a small musical empire. Williams was, among other things, organizing recording sessions for various companies, employing New Orleans players when he could. He frequently used Louis Armstrong, who was working with the Fletcher Henderson band in New York, as well as the brilliant but bristly New Orleans clarinet and soprano saxophone player Sidney Bechet. These two giants of early jazz appear together on several of these items. The most important is *Cake Walking Babies (from Home)*, a blazing hot version of the tune which Bechet dominates, in part because he was over-recorded. This is not the disciplined ensemble work of the Oliver group, but it may have been more representative of the way jazz was played in New Orleans honky-tonks.

CD

France: *The Complete King Oliver Creole Jazz Band*, **Music Memoria 30.295**

King Oliver, Louis Armstrong (c), Honore Dutrey (tb), Johnny Dodds (cl), Lil Hardin (p), Bill Johnson (bj), Baby Dodds (d)

Richmond, IN	5 April 1923	**Just Gone**	
		Canal Street Blues	
		Mandy Lee Blues	
		I'm Going Away to Wear You off my Mind	
		Chimes Blues	5
	6 April 1923	**Weather Bird Rag**	
add Johnson (v break)		**Dippermouth Blues**	
omit (v break)		**Froggie Moore**	
		Snake Rag	
Bud Scott (bj, v) replaces Johnson			
Chicago	22 June 1923	**Snake Rag**	10
omit (v)		**Sweet Lovin' Man**	
		High Society Rag	

add Armstrong (slide whistle)   **Sobbin' Blues**

omit (slide whistle)
                        23 June 1923   **Where Did You Stay Last Night?**
add Scott (v)   **Dipper Mouth Blues**   **15**

omit (v)   **Jazzin' Babies' Blues**

add Stump Evans (C-melody sax); Johnny St Cyr (bj) replaces Johnson
                        5 Oct 1923   **Alligator Hop**
                                         Zulu's Ball
                                         Working Man's Blues
                                         Krooked Blues   **20**

*Oliver, Armstrong (c), Eddie Atkins (tb), Jimmie Noone (cl), Hardin (p), Johnny
St Cyr (bj), Baby Dodds (d)*
                        15 Oct 1923   **Chattanooga Stomp**

Buster Bailey (cl) replaces Noone
                        16 Oct 1923   **London (Cafe) Blues**
                                         Camp Meeting Blues
                                         New Orleans Stomp

*Oliver (c), Armstrong (c, slide whistle), Dutrey (tb), Johnny Dodds (cl), Hardin (p),
St Cyr (bj), Charlie Jackson (bass sax), Baby Dodds (d)*
                        c25 Oct 1923   **Buddy's Habit**   **25**

omit (slide whistle)   **Tears**
                                         I Ain't Gonna Tell Nobody
                                         Room Rent Blues
                        c26 Oct 1923   **Riverside Blues**
                                         Sweet Baby Doll   **30**
                                         Working Man Blues
                                         Mabel's Dream

omit St Cyr, add Jackson (bb)
Chicago   c24 Dec 1923   **Mabel's Dream** (take 1)
                                         Mabel's Dream (take 2)
                                         The Southern Stomps (take 1)   **35**
                                         The Southern Stomps (take 2)
                                         Riverside Blues

(Butterbeans and Susie:) Oliver (c), Clarence Williams (p), Josie and Susie Edwards (v)

New York   12 Sept 1924   **Kiss Me Sweet**
                                                  Construction Gang

Oliver (c), Jelly Roll Morton (p)
Chicago   cDec 1924   **King Porter**   40
                                                  Tom Cat

Other CDs

incl. tracks 1–9, 17, 20:
  France: *The Jazz Collection: Louis Armstrong, vol.1, 1923–1925*, BYG
  9299.432

LPs

tracks 1–37:
  Italy: *The Saga of King Oliver's Creole Jazz Band*, Kings of Jazz NLJ
  18003 and NLJ 18004
tracks 1–9, 17–20, 33–7, 40–41, plus Red Onion Jazz Babies, cited below:
  USA: *King Oliver – Louis Armstrong*, Milestone M 47017
  France: *King Oliver – Louis Armstrong*, Milestone M 47017; Milestone
  2C178-96402/03
  Italy: *Louis Armstrong and King Oliver*, Milestone HB 6028
tracks 1–9, 17–20, 33–7:
  UK: *King Oliver's Creole Jazz Band*, VJM VLP 49
tracks 1–9, 17–20, 33–4, 36 twice (not 35–6), 37:
  UK: *King Oliver and his Creole Jazz Band 1923*, Riverside RLP 8805
  France: *King Oliver's Creole Jazz Band: Classic Jazz Masters 1923*,
  Mercury 6332.995; *King Oliver's Creole Jazz Band 1923*, Pierre Cardin PC
  93508; *King Oliver and his Creole Jazz Band 1923*, S.F.P. 5502
  Germany: *King Oliver and his Creole Jazz Band 1923*, Classic Jazz Masters
  22023
  Italy: title unknown, Music Parade LEL 187
  Netherlands: *King Oliver and his Creole Jazz Band 1923*, Classic Jazz
  Masters 88502, Riverside RM 8805
  Argentina: *La Creole Jazz Band de King Oliver 1923*, Philips 82131 PL
tracks 1–9, 17–20:
  USA: *King Oliver: the Great 1923 Gennetts*, Herwin H 106
  UK: *King Oliver: Gennett Sides of April and October 1923*, Rhapsody RHA
  6023
  Italy: *King Oliver*, I Grandi del Jazz GDJ 65
tracks 1–9, 17–19:

Italy: *King Oliver's Original Creole Jazz Band*, BYG 12
tracks 1–9, 17, 20:
  USA: *The King Oliver Creole Jazz Band – 1923, featuring Louis Armstrong*,
  Olympic OL 7133; *The Great Louis Armstrong 1923*, Orpheum ORP 105
  France: *Archive of Jazz vol.1: Louis Armstrong*, BYG 529.051
  Italy: *La Storia del Jazz: King Oliver 1923*, Joker SM 3089
tracks 1–9, 36, 40:
  Germany: *Classic Jazz*, Jazz Story 40002
tracks 1–3, 5–9, 34, 36–7 (last two titles reversed): *Louis Armstrong 1923*
  USA: Riverside RLP 12-122
  Europe: Riverside 12-122
  Netherlands: Riverside 122
  Japan: Riverside R 5019
  Australia: *Louis Armstrong 1923 with King Oliver's Creole Jazz Band*, Top
  Rank International TRL 8569
incl. tracks 10–16, 21–32, 38–9:
  USA: *King Oliver's Jazz Band 1923*, Smithsonian R 001
tracks 10–16, 25–32:
  UK: *King Oliver's Jazz Band: the OKeh Sessions 1923*, Parlophone PC 7032;
  The OKeh Sessions 1923, EMI-Retrospect EG 26-0579-1; *The OKeh Sessions
  1923*, World Records SH 358
  Italy: *King Oliver's Jazz Band: the OKeh Sessions 1923*, Parlophone
  C 054-05639
  Netherlands: *Early Jazz Moments, vol.1: King Oliver's Jazz Band*, Odeon
  OPXH 1016
  Japan: *King Oliver's Jazz Band*, Odeon OR 8075
  Australia: *King Oliver's Jazz Band: the OKeh Sessions 1923*, Parlophone
  PMCO 7032; *King Oliver's Jazz Band 1923*, Swaggie S 1257; *The OKeh
  Sessions 1923*, World Record Club R 08417
tracks 10–13, 15, 22–3, 27–8, 30–32:
  USA: *King Oliver*, Epic LN 3208; Epic LA 16003
  UK: *King Oliver*, Philips BBL 7181
  Europe: *King Oliver*, Philips B 07435 L
  France: *King Oliver*, Epic LA 16003; *King Oliver and his Orchestra*, Epic LN
  24255
  Japan: *King Oliver*, Epic NL 1012
  Argentina: *King Oliver and his Orchestra*, CBS 8.615
tracks 10–13, 22–3, 27–32:
  USA: *Lincoln Gardens*, Jazz Panorama 1205
incl. tracks 17–20, 34, 36:
  Germany: *Young Satchmo*, Jazz Story 40031
incl. tracks 2, 5, 9, 21, 23, 29, 40:
  Italy: *King Oliver*, Giants of Jazz LPJT 21

incl. tracks 20, 33–7:
  Italy: *Riverside Blues*, BYG 25

Cassettes

tracks 1–18:
  UK: *King Oliver's Jazz Band, vol.I, 1923*, Neovox 792
tracks 19–33, 35, 37, 40–41:
  UK: *King Oliver's Jazz Band, vol.II: Oliver – Jelly Roll Morton 1923–24*,
  Neovox 796
tracks 1–9, 17–20, 33–4, 36 twice (not 35–6), 37:
  Netherlands: *King Oliver and his Creole Jazz Band 1923*, Classic Jazz
  Masters 88502 C
tracks 10–13, 25–32: *The OKeh Sessions 1923*
  UK: EMI-Retrospect EG 26-0579-1; World Records TCSH 358
  Italy: Parlophone C 234-05639
  Australia: World Record Club C 08417
incl. tracks 10–13, 21, 24, 29, 32:
  UK: *An Introduction to Classic Jazz 1923/1925*, Neovox 120
incl. tracks 2, 5, 9, 21, 23, 29, 40:
  Italy: *King Oliver*, Giants of Jazz MCJT 21

LP

USA: *King Oliver – Louis Armstrong*, **Milestone M 47017**
some tracks cited above, plus:

(Alberta Hunter and the Red Onion Jazz Babies:) Louis Armstrong (c), Aaron Thompson (tb), Buster Bailey (cl), Lil Armstrong (p), Buddy Christian (bj), Hunter (v)

New York	8 Nov 1924	**Texas Moaner Blues**

(Red Onion Jazz Babies:) omit Hunter

		Of All the Wrongs You Done to Me
	26 Nov 1924	**Terrible Blues**
		Santa Claus Blues

(Hunter and Red Onion Jazz Babies:) Louis Armstrong (c), Charlie Irvis (tb), Sidney Bechet (cl, ss), Lil Armstrong (p), Christian (bj), Hunter (v)

22 Dec 1924   **Nobody Knows the Way I Feel**
                     'dis Mornin'
                     Early Every Morn

(Red Onion Jazz Babies:) Eva Taylor (v) replaces Hunter; add Clarence Todd (v)
                     Cake Walking Babies (from
                     Home)

Other LPs
plus additional Red Onion Jazz Babies track: *Louis Armstrong / Freddie
   Keppard*
   UK: Fountain FJ 107; Retrieval FJ 107
   Australia: Swaggie 804

* * *

Original Memphis Five: 'The Sounds of New York', vol.1

Of all the groups that set out to imitate the Original Dixieland Jass Band, far
and away the most successful was the one generally known as the Original
Memphis Five. Primarily a recording band, it made dozens of discs under
that name and dozens more under a variety of pseudonyms, among them
the Cotton Pickers, Jazz-bo's Carolina Serenaders and Ladd's Black Aces,
the last for records aimed at the market for black groups. The personnel
shifted frequently, but was built around Phil Napoleon, cornet; Jimmy
Lytell, clarinet; either Miff Mole or Charlie Panelli, trombone; Jack Roth,
drums; and Frank Signorelli, piano. Other musicians who recorded with the
group included pianist (and comic) Jimmy Durante; the obscure clarinettist
Doc Behrendson, a major influence on Benny Goodman; drummer Ray
Bauduc, a star with Bob Crosby's orchestra in the swing band era; and
bigger names such as Red Nichols and the Dorsey brothers.
   Initially the band frankly imitated the Original Dixieland Jass Band and
others of the New Orleanian bands becoming known after about 1919 or so.
Lytell was very much influenced by Larry Shields, and employed the same
eighth-note ensemble style, which rambled through the cornet lead. Their
Tin Roof Blues, recorded in October 1923, is adapted from the New Orleans
Rhythm Kings' version made a few months earlier, and includes George
Brunies's famous trombone solo, in this instance played by Miff Mole.
   In general the Memphis Five musicians were influenced more by white
groups such as the New Orleans Rhythm Kings, and various ensembles

including Bix Beiderbecke, than by black New Orleans bands such as Oliver's, which New Orleans and Chicago musicians were hearing first-hand. The style is lighter, somewhat drier, perhaps more controlled and more precise in intonation. These New York musicians were not using the rapid terminal vibrato that was characteristic of New Orleans players and many of their imitators, traces of which could be found even in the playing of Benny Goodman decades later. Phil Napoleon's lead on *Who's Sorry Now?*, for example, employs notes held out to their full value, which was rare with New Orleans players, and on the same recording trombonist Charlie Panelli plays the melody virtually uninflected, using the very minimum of vibrato.

A more important trombonist with the group was Miff Mole. His playing, relatively clipped and exact, with a bright, clean tone, can be heard to advantage on *I've Got a Song for Sale*. It was a style contrasting markedly with the blurry, slurred playing of New Orleanian trombonists, and this lighter, cleaner approach sounded more modern and advanced than the older dixieland style. As a consequence, through the mid-1920s Mole was perhaps the most influential trombonist in jazz, until Jack Teagarden and others appeared with a more legato, rougher manner.

Although the Memphis Five groups play cleanly and with better intonation than had some of the earlier groups, *Snake Hips* (1923) presents a band that is relatively stiff rhythmically, lacking the easy swing of the Oliver band or the driving intensity of the New Orleans Rhythm Kings. But by the time of the 1926 recording *Off to Buffalo*, the music had changed. As the influence of Chicago players, especially Armstrong and the Oliver group, became felt in New York, a hotter, less carefully worked out style became evident. There are in *Off to Buffalo* true solos, and the ensemble is hard driving, led by a Phil Napoleon who is far more abandoned in his playing than he was on the 1923 cut.

The Original Memphis Five, in its many guises, recorded some 400 sides, and, because these records sold well, it was one of the most generally influential jazz bands of the time with jazz fans and the dance-band audience. To many Americans in the mid-1920s this, more than the Oliver or Armstrong sound, was what jazz was all about.

LP
France: 'The Sounds of New York', vol.1, RCA 741.115

Phil Napoleon (tpt), Charlie Panelli (tb), Jimmy Lytell (cl), Frank Signorelli (p), Jack Roth (d)

New York   22 March 1923   **Snake Hips**
                                     Who's Sorry Now?

Miff Mole (tb) replaces Panelli

4 Oct 1923	**I've Got a Song for Sale**
	Tin Roof Blues

Panelli (tb) replaces Mole

1 Oct 1924	**How Come You Do Me Like You Do?**	**5**
	Meanest Blues	
4 Feb 1925	**Throw Down Blues**	
12 Feb 1925	**Sob Sister Sadie**	

add Napoleon (bb); Mole (tb) replaces Panelli

17 Sept 1925	**Bass Ale Blues**

omit (bb)

	Military Mike	**10**
16 April 1926	**Static Strut** (take 2)	
	Static Strut (take 5)	

add ?Roth (second p)

	Tampeekoe

add Lytell (as); Ray Bauduc (d) replaces Roth

28 Dec 1926	**A Blues Serenade**	
	Off to Buffalo	**15**

Cassettes

incl. tracks 1–13:
  UK: *Original Memphis Five, 1922–1926*, Neovox 825
incl. tracks 1–6:
  UK: *Original Memphis Five and Cotton Pickers, 1922–1924*, Neovox 102

* * *

Jelly Roll Morton: *The Gennett Piano Solos; The Pearls*

Jelly Roll Morton was one of the most fascinating characters in jazz history. A braggart who fancied himself a pool shark and pimp, he was nevertheless a brilliant musician, one of the three or four greatest of the early jazz pioneers. Born in New Orleans, where he served his apprenticeship, he followed the migration of jazz out of the South to the West Coast, and eventually to Chicago. By the early 1920s it was clear that he was one of the pre-eminent pianists in jazz, playing in an individual style he had manufactured for himself, with blues as the important element. Eventually Morton's supremacy would be challenged by Earl Hines, the stride players such as Fats Waller, and the swing players who followed. But in the early 1920s he was dominant. He began his recording career in 1923 with some band sides, but the most important recordings he made during these first years were a series of piano solos, among them his classics *Wolverine Blues*, *The Pearls*, *Kansas City Stomp* and *King Porter* (which would be a hit during the swing period in a Benny Goodman version arranged by Fletcher Henderson).

Morton's piano pieces, like much jazz of the time, were based on rags. They all have two or more strains, usually with transitional interludes between them, as had rags and the marches from which they were derived. For example, *Wolverine Blues* has an interlude modulating up a fourth. The first two choruses of the following strain are particularly interesting: the first chorus is played in whole notes with no rhythmic accompaniment and comes as close to being arhythmic as anything in early jazz; the second is a fancy variation on the same theme using trills and ornaments of various kinds, typical of ragtime playing. The right-hand figures in the opening strain of *Grandpa's Spells* are pure ragtime.

However, we must remain aware that Morton undergirds his music with a four beat, instead of the two beat that was almost invariable in ragtime. This shift was crucial in making the jump from ragtime to jazz – indeed it may have been the single critical change. Morton claimed that he was the first to employ this device, and it is even possible that he is correct. For another thing, Morton had grown up hearing the blues and utilized them more in his playing than did the stride players of the Northeast: note the seventh chord which ends *New Orleans Joys*, a characteristic blues device, and the eccentric 'tone clusters' in the second strain of *Grandpa's Spells*, which suggest the microtonality of blue notes. Finally, Morton believed that the piano ought to imitate a band, and he used trills to suggest woodwind and in particular trombonistic figures in the bass, very evident in *New Orleans Joys*.

Had Jelly Roll Morton recorded nothing but his piano solos, especially this early series, he would have had a secure place in jazz history. However, during the years when he was at his peak of fame and influence, he worked and recorded primarily with a classic New Orleans jazz band, utilizing the standard cornet–trombone–clarinet front line with a rhythm section, known as Jelly Roll Morton's Red Hot Peppers. Many of the numbers played by this group were improvised in the ordinary manner of New Orleans ensembles, but, for recording, Morton usually made careful arrangements of the tunes, guided the musicians and rehearsed them in advance. His arrangements are often quite elaborate and are true compositions, in the sense that Duke Ellington's arrangements are usually thought of as compositions. From this point of view, Morton can be considered the first significant jazz composer.

The care with which Morton went about presenting his music is evident in the attention to detail. Individual brass and reed melodies are accompanied by riffs, introduced by propelling figures and carefully taken out with other figures. Many of these solos are not freely improvised, but were worked out in advance or guided by Morton, as, for example, the clarinet solo which precedes the piano solo on *Black Bottom Stomp*. For *Sidewalk Blues* Morton brought into the studio two extra clarinets just to play one chorus of a clarinet trio. Nothing was left to chance.

Particularly striking is the variety Morton brings to his music with this limited orchestra, frequently using the most basic materials. *Sidewalk Blues*, for example, opens with the honking of an auto horn and some patter; there are brief breaks by the horns in sequence to provide an introduction. There follows a cornet melody accompanied by the band's backbeat rhythm, a second blues chorus of collective playing and a clarinet solo with the same backbeat rhythm. An interlude built on a descending scale leads from the blues into a harmonized dirge, during the middle of which the raucous auto horn suddenly intrudes. As the new second strain concludes and repeats there is more collective playing, then the clarinet trio and a last jammed ensemble, this time with a plunger mute in the trumpet. To close, we have the auto horn again and a final bit of patter. This constant shifting of tone colour, key, theme and orchestration is basic to Morton's method. The introduction of the auto horn in the middle of the recording is particularly felicitous, for it integrates into the piece what in other hands would have been simple hokum, making it a genuine thread in the composition – no different from the mechanical sounds woven into pieces by the avant-garde composers of the same period.

In these sides Morton carried the New Orleans style a step further; they were certainly New Orleans in feeling, but, inventing new devices and drawing others from around him, Morton raised the older form to a new level of musical sophistication. In fact, the Jelly Roll Morton Hot Peppers sides brought the New Orleans style – which was then dying – to an apogee.

In 1939 Morton was in obscurity, forgotten by a new generation of jazz fans and many of the older ones as well. However, as a historical interest in jazz began to assert itself, he found his way back to the studio that same year with a band drawn from some of the best of the musicians working both in the old style and in the more modern, swing manner. These recordings are basically in the mode that he had established for himself 15 years earlier. The ensemble work is not improvised but generally worked out, with arranged passages that may actually have been scored, as, for example, the figures behind Sidney Bechet's solo on *I Thought I Heard Buddy Bolden Say* and again behind the trombone lead on *Winin' Boy*. On this latter passage Bechet is given an obbligato against the lead; typically he plays too loud for a proper balance. The trombone line, too, is executed in a modern swing band style that is not entirely in keeping with the general New Orleans tone of these recordings. Morton sings the famous words on both these cuts. His voice has lost some of its old power and confidence, and he suffers from intonation problems, particularly on *Winin' Boy*. But, taken all in all, they show that he was still capable of putting together first-rate jazz performances.

LP

Australia: *The Gennett Piano Solos,* **Swaggie 801**

Jelly Roll Morton (p)

Richmond, IN	17 July 1923	King Portor – a Stomp [*sic*]	
		New Orleans (Blues) [*sic*] Joys	
		New Orleans (Blues) [*sic*] Joys (take A)	
	18 July 1923	Grandpa's Spells	
		Kansas City Stomp	5
		Wolverine Blues	
		The Pearls (a Stomp)	
	9 June 1924	Tia Juana	
		Shreveport Stomps	
		Mamamita	10
		Jelly Roll Blues	
		Big Foot Ham	
		Bucktown Blues	
		Tom Cat Blues	
		Stratford Hunch	15
		Perfect Rag	

Other LPs

plus additional tracks:
   Italy: *The Jelly Roll Morton's First Recordings Thesaurus*, Kings of Jazz
   NLJ 18007 and NLJ 18008
incl. tracks 1–2, 4–16:
   UK: *Ferd 'Jelly Roll' Morton*, Fountain FJ 104; Retrieval FJ 104
incl. tracks 1–2, 4–12, 14–16: *Jelly Roll Morton*
   USA: Milestone M 47018
   France: Milestone 47018; Milestone 2C 178-96.407 and 2C 178-96.408
incl. tracks 1–2, 4–10:
   Italy: *Jelly Roll Morton*, BYG 14

incl. tracks 1–2, 4–6, 9, 11–16: *Classic Piano Solos*
  USA: Orpheum ORP 103; Riverside 12-111
  France: BYG 529.056
  Italy: Joker SM 3091; Penny REL-ST 19324
incl. tracks 1–2, 4–6, 9, 11, 13, 15–16:
  USA: *Jelly Roll Morton Plays Jelly Roll*, Olympic OL 7131
incl. tracks 2, 4–5, 8–16:
  USA: *Thirty-six Minutes with Jelly Roll Morton*, Jazz Panorama 1206
incl. tracks 3–5, 7–8, 10: *The Incomparable Jelly Roll Morton*
  UK: Riverside RLP 8816
  France: BASF 10-29842-6; Mercury 6332 986; Pierre Cardin PC 93.512
  Netherlands: Riverside RM 8816

Cassettes

incl. tracks 1–2, 4–16:
  UK: *The 1923–24 Piano Solos*, Retrieval CFJ 104

CD

USA: *The Pearls*, Bluebird 6588-2 RB (takes not identified)

George Mitchell (c), Kid Ory (tb), Omer Simeon (cl), Morton (p), Johnny St Cyr
(bj), John Lindsay (sb), Andrew Hilaire (d)
Chicago   15 Sept 1926   **Black Bottom Stomp**
                                       Smoke-House Blues
                                       The Chant

add Morton, St Cyr (dialogue), Barney Bigard, Darnell Howard (cl), Marty Bloom
(sound effects)
                   21 Sept 1926   **Sidewalk Blues**
                                       Dead Man Blues   5

add Simeon (bass cl); omit Bigard, Howard
                                       Steamboat Stomp

omit (dialogue), omit (bass cl); add St Cyr (g)
                   16 Dec 1926   **Grandpa's Spells**
                                       Original Jelly-Roll Blues

add Morton (v)   **Doctor Jazz**

omit (v)   **Cannon Ball Blues**   10

Mitchell (c), Gerald Reeves (tb), Johnny Dodds (cl), Stump Evans (as), Morton (p), Bud Scott (g), Quinn Wilson (bb), Baby Dodds (d)

10 June 1927	**The Pearls**

Johnny Dodds (cl), Morton (p), Baby Dodds (d)

Wolverine Blues
Mr Jelly Lord

Ward Pinkett (tpt), Geechie Fields (tb), Simeon (cl), Morton (p), Lee Blair (bj), Bill Benford (bb), Tommy Benford (d)

New York   11 June 1928   **Georgia Swing**
                                        Kansas City Stomps   15

Simeon (cl), Morton (p), Benford (d)

Shreveport

add Fields (tb)   **Mournful Serenade**

Ed Anderson, Edwin Swayze (tpt), William Kato (tb), Russell Procope (cl, as), Paul Barnes (ss), Joe Garland (ts), Morton (p), Blair (g), William 'Bass' Moore (bb), Manzie Johnson (d)

                          6 Dec 1928   **Red Hot Pepper**
                                              Deep Creek

Morton (p)
Camden, NJ   8 July 1929   **Freakish**   20

Boyd 'Red' Rosser, Walter Briscoe (tpt), Charlie Irvis (tb), George Baquet (cl), Barnes (ss), Joe Thomas (as), Foots Thomas (ts), Morton (p), Barney Alexander (bj), Harry Prather (bb), William Laws (d)

                          12 July 1929   **Tank Town Bump**

Sidney De Paris (tpt), Claude Jones (tb), Albert Nicholas (cl), Sidney Bechet (ss), Happy Caldwell (ts), Morton (p, v), Lawrence Lucie (g), Wellman Braud (sb), Zutty Singleton (d)

New York   14 Sept 1939   **I Thought I Heard Buddy Bolden**
                                            Say
                                        Winin' Boy Blues

Other CDs

same contents:
  Europe: RCA ND 86588

plus additional tracks:
   USA: *The Jelly Roll Morton Centennial: His Complete Victor Recordings*,
   Bluebird 2361-2 RB
incl. tracks 1, 3, 5, 7–8, 15, 19:
   UK: *Jazz Classics in Digital Stereo*, BBC 604

LPs

plus additional tracks:
   Jazz Tribune no.9: the Complete Jelly Roll Morton, volumes 1/2,
   Jazz Tribune no.11: the Complete Jelly Roll Morton, volumes 3/4, and
   Jazz Tribune no.38: the Complete Jelly Roll Morton, volumes 7/8
   Europe: RCA NL 89768, NL 89769, NL 89748
   France: RCA PM 42405, PM 43170, PM 45372
incl tracks 1–19, 21–3:
   Japan: title unknown, RCA RA 9/10/11/12
incl. tracks 1–17, 21–3:
   Italy: *The Saga of Mr Jelly Lord*, vols.1–3, 5–6, Joker SM 3550 (also
   RIS R.10.550), SM 3551, SM 3552, SM 3554, SM 3555
incl. tracks 1–15, 20–21:
   Japan: title unknown, RCA RA 9019-9120
   title unknown, Victor SHP 5693 M and 5694 M
incl. tracks 1–15, 17: *The Pearls*
   USA: Bluebird 6588-1 RB
   Europe: RCA NL 86588
incl. tracks 1–15: *King of New Orleans Jazz*
   USA: RCA LPM 1649
   UK: RCA RD 27113
   Germany: RCA LPM 1649c
   Italy: RCA LPM 1649
   Japan: Victor LS 5151
   Australia: RCA L 10654
   Argentina: RCA LPM 1649; Argentina AVS 4466
incl. tracks 1, 3–17:
   France: *Jelly Roll Morton*, vol.3, RCA 731.059, vol. 4, RCA 741.040
incl. tracks 1, 3, 6–12, 14–20:
   France: *Jelly Roll Morton*, vol.1, RCA 430.268, vol.2, 430.269
incl. tracks 1–10, 12, 15–17:
   Japan: title unknown, RCA RPM 5104
incl. tracks 1–3, 5–11, 14–15:
   Europe: *King of New Orleans Jazz*, RCA NL 89015
incl. tracks 1–5, 8–9, 11, 15, 18:
   UK: *Doctor Jazz*, RCA CL 89808

incl. tracks 1, 5, 8–9, 12–13, 15, 17, 20:
  Italy: title unknown, RCA NL 47359
incl. tracks 1, 5, 8, 9, 12–13, 15, 17, 20–21:
  USA: *Giants of Jazz: Jelly Roll Morton*, Time-Life STL J07
incl. tracks 1, 3, 5, 7–8, 15, 19:
  UK: *Jazz Classics in Digital Stereo*, BBC REB 604

Cassettes

plus additional tracks:
  Europe: *Jazz Tribune no.9: the Complete Jelly Roll Morton, volumes 1/2,
  Jazz Tribune no.11: the Complete Jelly Roll Morton, volumes 3/4*, and
  Jazz Tribune no.38: the Complete Jelly Roll Morton, volumes 7/8,
  RCA NK 89768, NK 89769, NK89748
incl. tracks 1–15, 17: *The Pearls*
  USA: Bluebird 6588-4 RB
  Europe: RCA NK 86588
incl. tracks 1–15:
  Argentina: *King of New Orleans Jazz*, RCA APMS 4466
incl. tracks 1–21:
  UK: *The Essential Jelly Roll Morton*, vol.1, 1926–27, Neovox 716, vol.2,
  1927–29, Neovox 731, vol.3, 1929–30, Neovox 750
incl. tracks 1–3, 5–11, 14–15:
  Europe: *King of New Orleans Jazz*, RCA NK 89015
incl. tracks 1, 3, 5, 7–8, 15, 19:
  UK: *Jazz Classics in Digital Stereo*, BBC ZCF 604

* * *

Louis Armstrong: *The Hot Fives and Hot Sevens, vols.1–3; Louis Armstrong and Earl Hines*, vol.4

Louis Armstrong is considered by the majority of jazz critics to be one of the most profoundly influential of all jazz musicians. Others, especially Charlie Parker and John Coltrane, drastically reshaped the music by their example, but Armstrong established its course in the early days. When he came to prominence, jazz was an ensemble music; within five years he had turned it into a soloist's art. Armstrong served his apprenticeship in New Orleans, came to Chicago to work with Oliver's Creole Jazz Band, and then went to New York as the jazz specialist in Fletcher Henderson's orchestra. With Henderson's group he had the opportunity to solo frequently, and it quickly became clear that he was a special talent. In 1925 he returned to Chicago, where he began to record under his own name the series generally known as the Hot Fives, although that included varying combinations of musicians.

The Hot Fives are critical to jazz history. Listening to them chronologically reveals two things. The first is the development of Armstrong's style. At first rather sunny and happy-go-lucky, it deepens emotionally as the series goes on, until we reach the climactic moments in the deeply sad *Tight Like This* and *West End Blues*. The second tendency through these recordings is the emergence of Armstrong as a soloist. In the earlier sides he functions primarily as the cornet lead in a classic New Orleans ensemble. As it became clear to the record producers that Armstrong was the draw, and the other members of the group only a supporting cast, Louis was brought more and more to the front, both as a singer and a jazz soloist, until by the end of the series he was taking a good half of many of these recordings for himself. From this moment on it was the jazz solo, not the ensemble, that mattered, and by 1928, when the last of the Hot Fives was made, the old New Orleans style was moribund.

The personnel for the first of the Hot Fives was Armstrong, cornet; Johnny Dodds, clarinet; Kid Ory, trombone; Johnny St Cyr, banjo; and Armstrong's wife, Lil, piano. At times other musicians were added or replaced the originals, most notably pianist Earl Hines and drummer Zutty Singleton, and Armstrong himself switched from cornet to trumpet in the midst of the series.

The first important issue is *Heebie Jeebies*, a novelty tune with an aimless lyric. It was not Armstrong's first vocal recording, but it was the first one to attract attention. In particular, Armstrong, rather that sticking to the lyric, sang in nonsense syllables ('scat singing') during the second half of the chorus, and the novelty of the scatted vocal helped to make the record a big hit for that time, selling perhaps 40,000 copies fairly quickly. (There is a legend that Armstrong dropped the lyric sheet halfway through the vocal and was forced to scat the rest, but as the switch to scatting takes place at a natural division in the song, the tale is open to question.)

Immediately after *Heebie Jeebies* was cut, the band made *Cornet Chop Suey*, a tune conceived as a feature for Armstrong. The high point of the recording is a 16-bar stop-time chorus which amounts to a series of breaks exhibiting many of the devices intrinsic to his style. Note that he never proceeds for very long in one direction, but is constantly turning the line back on itself. Note also the great rhythmic variety, with many rhythmically indefinable figures regularly mixed in. *Cornet Chop Suey* astonished musicians, and fans, and was learned and imitated by trumpet players all over the country.

Another recording which excited the musicians was *Big Butter and Egg Man*, a tune that Armstrong played and sang at the Sunset Café, where he was then appearing. The solo is taken in an easier, less impassioned mood than was usual with Armstrong, and consists of a series of related figures each of which is by itself a melodic gem. By now Armstrong had grown confident of his power and was ready for what would come. From this point on the masterpieces followed in what seemed an unending stream.

It is impossible to touch on more than a few in a short space. Of particular importance is *Hotter Than That*, considered by some critics Armstrong's finest fast number from this period. He plays it with a breakneck dash and confidence, beginning with a fiery eight-bar introduction which leaps directly into what is putatively a New Orleans ensemble, but is in reality a solo with accompanying musicians. Note especially the figure which begins in the second bar; a less imaginative musician would have finished it off logically in the next bar, but Armstrong unwinds out of it a related extension which carries it further. *Hotter Than That* also contained a scatted vocal featuring a series of notes in a polyrhythmic passage of two against three over the ordinary 4/4 time, today a cliché, but fresh and exciting when Armstrong first spun it out.

By 1928 the pretence that this was a New Orleans ensemble had been dropped. Don Redman was brought in to work out arrangements, using for the most part journeyman musicians, and the recordings were now showcases for Armstrong. Among the best-known of these is *Muggles*. It opens as a slow blues, and then Armstrong leaps in with a break to double the tempo up, a masterful example of an ambiguous tempo finally resolving to the new time. He follows this with a solo built around a reiterated tonic, which he fills in with rapid phrases, always returning to the repeated note as a point of reference.

Even more celebrated than *Muggles* is *Tight Like This*. The high point is the final passage in which Armstrong plays a sequence of passionate figures running up and down the instrument, ending with a series of high notes which finally winds down to a melancholy conclusion.

The best-known of Armstrong's recordings is *West End Blues*, considered by some critics to be the greatest of all jazz recordings. It opens with a famous elaborate cadenza introduction, which falls, rises and falls, followed by a very simple blues chorus, which grows more complex as it proceeds. There are solos by other instruments and a moody, introspective scat chorus by Armstrong. Then comes the great final chorus. Armstrong opens it with a long held note, then breaks into a succession of falling figures which finally wind down into a mood of quiet resignation; there is a brief piano interlude, and a quiet ending by Armstrong. *West End Blues* is a masterpiece of construction, a complete, if small, drama with a beginning, a middle and an end. It is filled with movement and variety, but proceeds relentlessly to the climactic last chorus and then the quiet denouement, so that the piece does not merely end, as so many jazz performances do, but finishes.

Although Armstrong came in the end to dominate the Hot Fives, the personnel included a number of the best jazz musicians of the day, among them trombonist Kid Ory, who was possibly the best of those playing in the old, slurred style, and clarinettist Johnny Dodds. Dodds has always been seen as a particularly fine player of the blues. In *Gut Bucket Blues* he executes a much more imaginative obbligato over the cornet lead than was typical of the New Orleans players, filled with high-register splashes and rising and falling lines. His solo on the piece again employs held notes in the upper register which slur downwards to produce the smeary effect characteristic of the early blues.

Yet another musician who made important contributions to this series was Earl Hines, who, unlike the stride pianists, had heard a lot of blues as a youth and played in a less pianistic style, using octaves and single-finger runs in the right hand, and jagged, broken figures in the left hand. His best-known piece with Armstrong is *Weather Bird*, a duet which, while not strictly one of the Hot Fives, is usually classified with the series. In Hines's solo which follows the opening chorus we hear all of these devices: the right-hand octaves, the irregular bass patterns, and passages where right and left hand even appear to be quarreling with each other.

But regardless of the virtues of the other players, it was Louis Armstrong who mattered. The Hot Five series is at the heart of any study of jazz, playing a role in jazz history akin to that of the masterpieces of Bach in classical music.

CDs

USA: *The Hot Fives and Hot Sevens*, **vol.1–3,** *Louis Armstrong and Earl Hines*, **vol. 4, Columbia Jazz Masterpieces CK 44049, CK 44253, CK 44422, CK 45142**

Louis Armstrong (c), Kid Ory (tb), Johnny Dodds (cl), Lil Armstrong (p), Johnny St Cyr (bj)

Chicago	12 Nov 1925	**My Heart**
		Yes! I'm in the Barrel

add Louis Armstrong (speech) **Gut Bucket Blues**

omit (speech); add Dodds (as)

	22 Feb 1926	**Come Back, Sweet Papa**

add Louis and Lil Armstrong (v)

	26 Feb 1926	**Georgia Grind**	5

omit Lil Armstrong (v) **Heebie Jeebies**

omit (v)	**Cornet Chop Suey**	
	Oriental Strut	
	You're Next	
	Muskrat Ramble	10

add Louis Armstrong (v); Dodds (as, not cl)
16 June 1926   **Don't Forget to Mess Around**

Dodds (cl, not as)   **I'm Gonna Gitcha**
Dropping Shucks

omit (v); add Louis Armstrong (slide whistle)
Whosit

omit (slide whistle); add Louis and Lil Armstrong, Clarence Babcock (speech)
23 June 1926   **The King of the Zulus**   15

omit (speech); add Louis Armstrong (v)
Big Fat Ma and Skinny Pa
Lonesome Blues

omit (v)   **Sweet Little Papa**
16 Nov 1926   **Jazz Lips**

add Louis Armstrong (v)   **Skid-dat-de-dat**   20

add May Alix (v)   **Big Butter and Egg Man**

omit Armstrong (v)   **Sunset Cafe Stomp**

Louis Armstrong (v) replaces Alix; probably Henry Clark (tb) replaces Ory
27 Nov 1926   **You Made Me Love You**
Irish Black Bottom

Louis Armstrong (c), John Thomas (tb), Johnny Dodds (cl), Lil Armstrong (p), St Cyr (bj), Pete Briggs (bb), Baby Dodds (d)
7 May 1927   **Willie the Weeper**   25
Wild Man Blues

Armstrong, Bill Wilson (c), Honore Dutrey (tb), Boyd Atkins (cl, ss, as), Joe Walker (as, bar), Albert Washington (ts), Earl Hines (p), Rip Bassett (bj, g), Briggs (bb), Tubby Hall (d), Carroll Dickerson (director)
9 May 1927   **Chicago Breakdown**

as **Willie the Weeper**

10 May 1927	**Alligator Crawl**	
	Potato Head Blues	
11 May 1927	**Melancholy Blues**	30
	Weary Blues	
	Twelfth Street Rag	

add Louis Armstrong (v)

13 May 1927	**Keyhole Blues**	
	S. O. L. Blues	
14 May 1927	**Gully Low Blues**	35

add Lil Armstrong (v)

That's When I'll Come Back to You

Louis Armstrong (c, v), Ory (tb), Johnny Dodds (cl), Lil Armstrong (p), St Cyr (bj, g)

2 Sept 1927	**Put 'em Down Blues**

omit (v)

Ory's Creole Trombone

add Louis Armstrong (v)

6 Sept 1927	**The Last Time**

omit (v)

9 Dec 1927	**Struttin' with Some Barbecue**	40
	Got No Blues	
10 Dec 1927	**Once in a While**	

add Louis Armstrong (v), Lonnie Johnson (g); St Cyr (bj, not g)

	I'm not Rough
13 Dec 1927	**Hotter Than That**

omit (v)

Savoy Blues   45

Armstrong (tpt), Fred Robinson (tb), Jimmy Strong (cl, ts), Earl Hines (p), Mancy Carr (bj), Zutty Singleton (d)

27 June 1928	**Fireworks**	
	Skip the Gutter	

add Armstrong, Hines (v)

A Monday Date

omit (v)

28 June 1928	**Don't Jive Me**

add Armstrong (v)		**West End Blues**	**50**
		Sugar Foot Strut	
omit (v)	29 June 1928	**Two Deuces**	
add Armstrong, Hines, Carr (v)		**Squeeze Me**	
*as **Fireworks**, but Strong (cl)*		**Knee Drops**	

(Dickerson:) Armstrong, Homer Hobson (tpt), Robinson (tb), Bert Curry, Crawford Wethington (as), Strong (cl, ts), Hines (p), Carr (bj), Briggs (bb), Singleton (d)

	5 July 1928	**Symphonic Raps**	**55**
		Savoyageurs' Stomp	

*as **Fireworks**, but add Hines (celeste)*

	4 Dec 1928	**No (No, Papa, No)**

add Armstrong, Hines, Carr (v)   **Basin Street Blues**

Armstrong (tpt, v), Robinson (tb), Don Redman (cl, as), Hines (p), Dave Wilborn (bj), Singleton (d)

	5 Dec 1928	**No One Else But You** (arr Redman)	
		Beau Koo Jack (arr Alex Hill)	**60**
		Save it, Pretty Mama (arr Redman)	

Armstrong (tpt), Hines (p)   **Weather Bird**

*as **Fireworks***	7 Dec 1928	**Muggles**

add Armstrong (speech), Redman (cl, as), Strong (cl, ts)

	12 Dec 1928	**Heah Me Talkin' to Ya**	
omit (speech), but Armstrong (v)		**St James Infirmary**	**65**

omit (v), but Armstrong, Redman, Hines (speech)   **Tight Like This**

Other CDs

same contents:
  Europe: CBS Jazz Masterpieces 460821-2, 463052-2, 465189-2, 466308-2

details unknown:
   UK: *Louis Armstrong: vol.2: Hot Fives and Sevens*, JSP CD 313

LPs

same contents:
   USA: Columbia Jazz Masterpieces CJ 44049, CJ 44253, CJ 44422, CJ 45142
   Europe: CBS Jazz Masterpieces 460821-1, 463052-1, 465189-1, 466308-1
same contents: *His Greatest Years*, vols.1–4
   UK: Parlophone PMC 1140, PMC 1142, PMC 1146, PMC 1150
   France, Germany: Odeon 2C.152-05166-2C.152-05169
   Japan: Odeon OR 8002-OR 8005
   Australia: Swaggie S 1230, S 1233, S 1236, S 1239
plus additional tracks:
   UK: *The Louis Armstrong Legend 1925–26*, World SH 404; . . . *1926–27*,
   World SH 405; . . . *1927–28*, World SH 406; . . . *1928–29*, World SH 407
plus additional tracks: *Very Special Old Phonography*
   France: CBS 64270-64274; CBS 8800-88003; Odeon XOC-170P-XOC-174P
tracks 2–3, 6–7, 10, 20, 25–36, 38–41, 43–4, 47, 49, 50–53, 57–8, 62–3,
   65–6: *The Louis Armstrong Story*, vols.1–3
   USA: Columbia CL 851, CL 852, CL 853

Cassettes

same contents:
   USA: Columbia Jazz Masterpieces CJT 44049, CJT 44253, CJT 44422, CJT
   45142
   Europe: CBS Jazz Masterpieces 460821-4, 463052-4, 465189-4, 466308-4
plus additional tracks:
   UK: *The Louis Armstrong Legend 1925–26*, World TC-SH 404; . . . *1926–27*,
   World TC-SH 405, World EG26 0458 4; . . . *1927–28*, World TC-SH 406;
   . . . *1928–29*, World TC-SH 407
   The Essential Louis Armstrong, vol.1, '25–6 Hot Five, Neovox 704, . . *vol. 2,
   1926–1927*, Neovox 715, . . . *vol.3, Hot Fives '27–8*, Neovox 727, . . . *vol.4,
   1928–29*, Neovox 737

* * *

Johnny Dodds: *Johnny Dodds, 1926–1928*

Johnny Dodds, almost from the moment he opened with the Creole Jazz
Band at Lincoln Gardens, was seen as the quintessential New Orleans clarinettist. With the Creole orchestra he was featured more than anybody,

except Oliver, playing brief breaks on almost every one of the band's record-ings and extended solos on many of them. He then became the primary clarinettist for Armstrong's critically important and widely admired Hot Five series. He thus achieved greater exposure on important recordings than any of the New Orleans clarinettists, if we except Shields with the best-selling Original Dixieland Jass Band. The sound of Dodds's clarinet came to be almost intrinsic to New Orleans jazz.

Dodds, like many New Orleans clarinettists, studied with Lorenzo Tio Jr, and, like many of the clarinettists with some formal training, his playing is replete with long passages of fairly evenly played notes. However, Dodds proved by nature to be a more driving, fiery player than clarinettists more in the creole tradition, such as Jimmie Noone and Barney Bigard, and it was this relentless forward motion, more than anything, that attracted so many jazz fans, both then and now.

Johnny Dodds left Oliver along with some of the other regulars in a fight over money. He quickly took over a band at Kelly's Stables, which he led for six years and which gave him yet more exposure, at least to the musicians and jazz fans haunting Chicago's night spots. This regular job made him available for a lot of freelance recordings, among them the Hot Fives. In addition, between 1926 and 1929 he made a long series of recordings under his own name – including sessions by the Black Bottom Stompers – and as a member of the New Orleans Wanderers, the New Orleans Bootblacks and the Chicago Footwarmers. Some of these are with standard dixieland instru-mentation, some are duets or trios featuring Dodds and some are quartets with two horns and rhythm. These Dodds sides, with cornetist George Mitchell or Natty Dominique, have always held a special place in the hearts of followers of New Orleans jazz.

A good example of Dodds's hot style is on the up-tempo *Grandma's Ball* with Dominique on cornet. Dodds is almost constantly in motion, barely pausing to breathe as he rolls long chains of eighth notes up and down through the cornet line. This busy, swirling style was typical of Dodds on fast passages. On the blues, however, he adopted a different course. He plays the introduction to the minor-key opening strain of *Perdido Street Blues* with a sequence of glissandos – long, deep swoops which have always been characteristic of blues playing. In his solo on the major-key strain he uses the fast terminal vibrato that was a staple part of the New Orleans style on long held notes, suddenly interrupting them, usually to cascade downwards in a shower of fast notes. This practice of breaking off a held note in the upper register in a downward plunge was a standard New Orleans clarinet device, evident on recordings in the playing of Larry Shields on the earliest of the Original Dixieland Jass Band's sides.

Dodds was certainly the prototype New Orleans musician, and the style he choose for his recordings reflects this. *Gate Mouth* is played almost entirely by the whole ensemble, except for a brief saxophone solo and characteristic breaks, including one trio break in the last chorus. The piece is stitched together with long slurs by Ory's trombone, and features a spare lead by Mitchell, who at times uses the plunger mute very much in the Oliver manner.

But the most highly regarded of Dodds's sides are the quartets issued as the first of the sessions by the Chicago Footwarmers, which had cornet, piano, washboard and the leader's clarinet. Such groups frequently worked in the honky-tonks of New Orleans, where the music would be tough and hot. Typical is the up-tempo *Ballin' a Jack*, on which cornetist Dominique uses the plunger mute when he re-enters after Dodds's solo. In a small group of this kind, where there is less aural competition, a clarinettist is able to use the lower register in a more normal fashion, and even on the ensembles we hear Dodds playing extended figures which frequently move into the mid-range, or below.

These recordings were popular at the time they were issued and continued to be important to later generations of fans of New Orleans music. As a consequence it was Dodds's manner of playing on which much of the New Orleans revival was based. His influence on jazz clarinet playing was immense.

CD

UK: *Johnny Dodds, 1926–1928*, JSP CD 319

(*New Orleans Wanderers:*) *George Mitchell (c), Kid Ory (tb), Johnny Dodds (cl), Lil Armstrong (p), Johnny St Cyr (bj)*

Chicago	13 July 1926	**Perdido Street Blues**	
add Joe Clark (as)		**Gate Mouth**	
add St Cyr (speech)		**Too Tight**	
omit (speech)		**Papa Dip**	

(*New Orleans Bootblacks:*) *as **Gate Mouth***

	14 July 1926	**Mixed Salad** 5
		I Can't Say
		Flat Foot
		Mad Dog

(*Johnny Dodds's Black Bottom Stompers:*) *Mitchell, Natty Dominique (c), John*

Thomas (tb), Johnny Dodds (cl), Charlie Alexander (p), Bud Scott (bj), Baby Dodds (d)   8 Oct 1927   **Come on and Stomp, Stomp, Stomp**

add unknown (v)   **After You've Gone**   10

omit (v)   **After You've Gone**
                                                          Joe Turner Blues
                                                          When Erastus Plays his Old Kazoo

(Chicago Footwarmers:) Dominique (c), Johnny Dodds (cl), Jimmy Blythe (p), Baby Dodds (washboard)

                          3 Dec 1927   **Ballin' a Jack**
                                                Grandma's Ball   15
                          15 Dec 1927   **My Baby**
                                                Oriental Man

add Ory (tb), Bill Johnson (sb)
                          2 July 1928   **Get 'em Again Blues**
                                                Brush Stomp
                                                My Girl   20

Honore Dutrey (tb) replaces Ory
                          4 July 1928   **Sweep 'em Clean**
                                                Lady Love
                                                Brown Bottom Bess

Other CDs

incl. tracks 1, 6, 14–15: *Jazz Classics in Digital Stereo: Johnny Dodds*
  UK: BBC CD 603
  Australia: ABC CD 38556; ABC 836.202-2

LPs

tracks 1–8, 14–23:
  UK: *The Immortal Johnny Dodds*, VJM VLP 48
  Australia: *Johnny Dodds, 1926–1928*, Swaggie 807
incl. tracks 1–3, 14–15, 17–18, 22:
  Italy: *The Myth of New Orleans*, Giants of Jazz LPJT 47
incl. tracks 1–8, 16–17, 22–3: *Johnny Dodds with Kid Ory*
  USA: CSP JLA 16004; Epic LN 3207; Epic LA 16004; Jazz Panorama 1203
  UK: Philips BBL 7181

France: Epic LN 24255; Philips 07872 RF
Netherlands: Philips B 07428 L
incl. tracks 1, 6, 14–15: *Jazz Classics in Digital Stereo: Johnny Dodds*
  UK: BBC REB 603
  Australia: ABC L 38556; ABC 836.202-1

Cassettes

incl. tracks 1–8, 10–18, 22–3
  UK: *The Best of Johnny Dodds, 1926–1927, vol.I*, Neovox 717; *Johnny Dodds, 1927–29, vol.II*, Neovox 739; *Johnny Dodds, vol.III: '27–9*, Neovox 798
incl. tracks 1–3, 14–15, 17–18, 22:
  Italy: *The Myth of New Orleans*, Giants of Jazz MCJT 47
incl. tracks 1, 6, 14–15: *Jazz Classics in Digital Stereo: Johnny Dodds*
  UK: BBC ZCF 603
  Australia: ABC C 38556; ABC 836-202-4

* * *

Jimmie Noone: *At the Apex Club*

There has been some tendency on the part of jazz scholars to separate out from the New Orleans clarinets a school of creole clarinettists. Actually, the term 'creole' is subject to some confusion. What is really meant is a New Orleans subculture of mixed-blood people, who descended from the French-speaking old settlers of New Orleans and elsewhere in the Caribbean. Musically, their interests lay in the so-called French Opera House and in classical music generally, and they studied 'legitimate' technique. The consequence was that the creole clarinettists tended to approach jazz music in a somewhat classically oriented manner. They tended to use a purer sound, eschewing to an extent the bent notes and growls common in the playing of the black clarinettists; they played their eighth notes more evenly, instead of emphasizing the first of pairs of putative eighths; and their intonation was often better than that of self-taught clarinettists.

Jimmie Noone studied at least briefly with the creole Sidney Bechet and perhaps more formally with Lorenzo Tio Jr, a classically trained Mexican player who taught many of the New Orleanian clarinettists. He was thus given early in his career a symphonic approach to the instrument. He was one of the musicians who began drifting away from New Orleans around the time of World War I, and he eventually landed with one of the early versions of the famous Creole Jazz Band – whose members were not, in the main, Creoles. With this group Noone made a few recordings in 1923 which show him playing with the liquid sound and more evenly played eighth notes characteristic of the creole style.

At about this time, Noone began to study with a classical clarinettist, Franz Schoepp, a remarkable man who not only taught many of the reed players with the Chicago Symphony Orchestra but, probably out of social conscience, worked with immigrant and black youngsters, among them Benny Goodman, Buster Bailey and Noone. Schoepp gave Noone one of the best foundations of any clarinettists in jazz of the time, and it is no accident that Noone and Goodman were the most technically proficient players in the music.

With this background, in 1928, and with a band he was leading at the Apex Club, Noone made the series of recordings that has given him his place in jazz history. The personnel was Joe Poston, alto saxophone; Bud Scott, banjo; Johnny Wells, drums; and Earl Hines, piano. Hines was about to become, as a consequence of his work with Armstrong's Hot Fives and a series of solo performances he would make later that same year for QRS, a major figure in jazz. Poston was never highly regarded, but he played the lead lines accurately and with considerable swing, and made an excellent foil for Noone.

Noone, however, is the important figure on these sessions. The best known of the Apex Club Orchestra's cuts is *I Know That You Know*. The tune is somewhat idiosyncratic in its avoidance of the tonic for much of its length. After an opening statement of the melody, Noone takes a full chorus, utilizing long passages of relatively even eighth notes which rise and fall through the chord changes. This is followed by a solo by Earl Hines in his typically choppy style with the broken bass line, which is neither true stride nor simple chording, but a mix of both. Then, after an ensemble chorus built on a repeated riff, Noone returns with a low-register chorus again consisting principally of fast eighth notes. In the final chorus Noone breaks out into driving upper-register quarter notes which contrast with the general tenor of the rest of his playing on this recording; just after the middle of this chorus, he executes a sequence of descending eighths as precisely as a symphonic musician would.

Another of the best of this series is *Sweet Sue – Just You*. It is taken at a very slow, almost lugubrious tempo. The whole second chorus is played straight by the alto saxophone and clarinet in harmony, the interest being supplied by Hines's highly rhythmic right hand behind the horns. For the last chorus Noone plays a series of long, looping, rubato figures over the melody by Poston. This kind of easy, measured delivery was typical of the New Orleans creole style, which contrasted with the far hotter manner of a clarinettist like Johnny Dodds.

The contrast is even more marked in Noone's approach to the blues. In

Apex Blues, which employs a very simple riff as a theme, Noone plays far fewer of the bent notes that were typical of the standard blues style, and entirely avoids the rasps and throat-tones that were almost a *sine qua non* of the blues. Note how evenly played are his eighth notes, especially in the liquid, low-register ending to his first solo chorus. But Noone did not entirely dismiss the characteristic traits of the blues: he leads into the down beat of the last chorus of the recording with a long high note which rises in pitch and then drops off again, one of those twisted notes that give the blues much of their emotional force.

A Monday Date again shows the band in its hot, driving mode. The tune was written by Hines, and his solo evinces all the trademarks of his style: the choppy bass figures, the octaves, the tremolos in the right hand. Noone, particularly in the last choruses, demonstrates a characteristic of the creole style, a tendency to play scalar runs rather than the saw-toothed half-step up, step down, pattern more typical of jazz clarinet playing. (Note that the first clarinet solo chorus, after the piano solo, is by Joe Poston.)

Noone's Apex Club Orchestra is in format a long way from the standard New Orleans dixieland band, but it carries with it a certain easy, relaxed swing that was typical of the best New Orleans bands. These recordings by the Apex Club Orchestra are among the finest small-group recordings in jazz. Noone influenced a whole school of clarinettists, among them Buster Bailey with Fletcher Henderson, and Barney Bigard with Duke Ellington. Contrary to what has often been said, he did not directly influence Benny Goodman, whose style was forming before he heard Noone. But Goodman did employ devices which Noone featured, such as the fast, low-register passages; and Goodman's quartet version of *Sweet Sue – Just You* is taken at the same kind of deliberate tempo as Noone's.

LP

USA: *At the Apex Club*, **MCA 1313**

Jimmie Noone (cl), Joe Poston (cl, as), Earl Hines (p), Bud Scott (bj), Johnny Wells (d)

| Chicago | 16 May 1928 | **I Know That You Know** |
| | | **Sweet Sue – Just You** |

| *add Noone, Poston (v)* | | **Four or Five Times** (take B or C?) |

| *omit (v)* | | **Every Evening (I Miss You)** |
| | | (take B) |

| | | **Every Evening (I Miss You)** (take C) | **5** |

add Noone, Poston (v)

| 14 June 1928 | **Ready for the River** |

omit (v)

| **Forevermore** |

add Lawson Buford (bb)

23 Aug 1928	**Apex Blues**
	A Monday Date (My Monday Date)
	Blues my Naughty Sweetie Gives to Me **10**
25 Aug 1928	**Oh, Sister! Ain't That Hot?**
	King Joe
	Sweet Lorraine (take A)
	Sweet Lorraine (take B)

Other LPs

same contents:
    USA: Decca 79235
    France: MCA 510.039
plus additional tracks:
    Australia: *Jimmie Noone's Apex Club Orchestra, vol.1, 1928* and
    Jimmie Noone's Apex Club Orchestra, vol.2, 1928–1929, Swaggie
    S 841 and S 842
incl. tracks 1–5, 8–14:
    Italy: *The Amazing Soft World of Jimmie Noone,* Kings of Jazz NLJ 18005
incl. tracks 2–4, 8–14:
    UK: *Apex Club Blues*, Affinity AFS 1023
incl. tracks 1–10
    Sweden: *Jimmie Noone*, vol.1, CJM 29
incl. tracks 1–2, 4 or 5, 8, 10–12, 13 or 14:
    Italy: *Jimmie Noone 1928–1940*, Giants of Jazz LPJT 75
incl. tracks 3, 4 or 5, 6–7, 9:
    UK: *Jazz at the Apex Club*, Ace of Hearts AH 84

Cassettes

same contents:
    USA: MCA MCAC 1313
incl. tracks 1–4, 8–12, 14:

UK: *The Best of Jimmy Noone, vol.1, 1928/29*, Neovox 786
incl. tracks 1–2, 4 or 5, 8, 10–12, 13 or 14:
  Italy: *Jimmie Noone 1928–1940*, Giants of Jazz MCJT 75

* * *

Bix Beiderbecke: *Bix Beiderbecke, vol.1: Singin' the Blues*

Bix Beiderbecke is generally considered to be the most significant jazz musician, after Louis Armstrong, from the 1920s period. Like Armstrong, he astonished musicians and jazz fans with the clarity of his bell-like cornet sound, the freshness of his conception and the intensity of his feeling. A whole school of players, both black and white, followed in his path, providing an alternative approach to jazz playing that differed significantly from Armstrong's. Where Armstrong was broad in his conception, Beiderbecke hewed to a narrow spectrum; where Armstrong employed the whole range of his instrument, Beiderbecke played mainly in the middle register; where Armstrong was at times ornate, even showy, Beiderbecke was consistently modest. Few deny that Armstrong was, finally, the greater musician, in part because of his more sweeping, romantic approach, but Beiderbecke was not far behind.

Like many of the jazz players of the day, Beiderbecke was self-taught. His first important recordings were made with the Wolverines, a dixieland group typical of the time. He moved on to work with the large dance orchestras of Jean Goldkette and Paul Whiteman, with whom he was the star soloist. Unhappily, he suffered from alcoholism, and died from the effects in 1930.

Despite the excellence of the solos he made with Whiteman, Beiderbecke's best-known recordings were a series he made from 1924 to 1928 with pick-up groups under his own name, with others under pseudonyms such as the Sioux City Six and the Chicago Loopers, and with yet others under the leadership of Frankie Trumbauer. The sessions were rather haphazardly put together. The personnel was usually drawn from the bands Beiderbecke happened to be working with at the moment, and owed as much to friendship as to musical skill. Some of the men on these dates were excellent jazz musicians, some were merely adequate. As a consequence, the accompaniment is less good than it might have been had Beiderbecke taken firm charge of the musical aspects of the sessions.

The most important of these players was C-melody saxophonist Frankie Trumbauer, known as Tram. Trumbauer was not a great improvising jazz player, but a skilled technician who often worked out his solos in advance, and was much admired by other musicians of the day. He undoubtedly helped to give Bix the thoughtful approach to improvising that was characteristic of his playing. The partnership produced some of Bix's finest work.

One of Beiderbecke's best-known solos is on *Royal Garden Blues* (on vol.2 of the series); this opens with a rising and falling line built on triplets, which is then repeated. This deliberateness carries over to his often very subtle, but thoughtful placement of notes around the beat, as, for example, the opening quarter notes to his solo on *Way Down Yonder in New Orleans*, which are placed slightly differently against the beat each time. Again, in bars 9 and 10 of this chorus he plays a variation of the same idea.

Beiderbecke's masterpieces are *I'm Coming, Virginia* and especially *Singin' the Blues*, which was learned by young musicians all over the United States: Fletcher Henderson had the entire piece orchestrated for his band, with Rex Stewart playing Beiderbecke's famous chorus. Beiderbecke thought more deeply about improvising methods than did many other jazz musicians. In particular, he devised the concept of the 'correlated chorus', in which, let us say, two bars of a given idea are followed by two or more of a related one, after which the whole four-bar segment is re-examined in the following four bars. We can see this method at work in the opening part of his solo on *Singin' the Blues*, in which the second figure is a reflection of the first, and the following one re-examines the previous two; the four bars which follow amplify what has gone on before. His *I'm Coming, Virginia* is not so precisely worked out, but figures are constantly related to each other. Many of them are built around alternations of notes a third apart and feature sudden reversals of direction. But Beiderbecke was capable of less introspective, more driving work. In the ride-out chorus of *Goose Pimples* (also on vol.2) he plays one hard, hot figure three times, slightly varied, and then suddenly twists it into a new shape and stretches it out to twice its length.

Bix was also admired at the time for his piano playing, in particular a group of rambling compositions which drew from modernists such as Debussy and Ravel. Bix played these differently at each performance, but he recorded one, *In a Mist*, which thus took on a comparatively fixed form and became quite celebrated: he once played it at Carnegie Hall. Today we tend to see these pieces as pastiches; it is his cornet playing that matters.

CD

USA: *Bix Beiderbecke, vol.1: Singin' the Blues,* **Columbia Jazz Masterpieces CK 45450**

(Frankie Trumbauer:) Bix Beiderbecke (c), Bill Rank (tb), Jimmy Dorsey (cl, as), Trumbauer (C-melody sax), Paul Mertz (p), Eddie Lang (bj, g), Chauncey Morehouse (d)

New York   4 Feb 1927   **Trumbology** (arr Mertz)

add Doc Ryker (as)   **Clarinet Marmalade**
                                            Singin' the Blues

Don Murray (cl, bar) replaces Dorsey, Itzy Riskin (p) replaces Mertz
                9 May 1927   **Ostrich Walk** (arr Bill Challis)
                                            Riverboat Shuffle (arr Challis)   5
                13 May 1927   **I'm Coming, Virginia** (arr Riskin)
                                            'Way Down Yonder in New
                                              Orleans (arr Murray)

(Trumbauer:) Beiderbecke (c, p), Trumbauer (C-melody sax), Lang (g)
                                            For No Reason at All in C

(Trumbauer:) Beiderbecke (c), Rank (tb), Murray (cl, bar), Ryker (as), Trumbauer
(C-melody sax), Adrian Rollini (bass sax), Riskin (p), Lang (g), Morehouse (d)
                25 Aug 1927   **Three Blind Mice** (arr Trumbauer,
                                              Murray)

add Seger Ellis (v)   **Blue River**   10
                                            There's a Cradle in Caroline

(Beiderbecke:) Beiderbecke (p)
                9 Sept 1927   **In a Mist**

(Trumbauer:) Beiderbecke (c, p), Trumbauer (C-melody sax), Lang (g)
                17 Sept 1927   **Wringin' and Twistin'**

(Trumbauer:) Beiderbecke (c), Rank (tb), Murray (cl, bar), Bobby Davis (as), Trum-
bauer (C-melody sax), Rollini (bass sax), Joe Venuti (vln), Frank Signorelli (p),
Lang (g), Morehouse (d)
                28 Sept 1927   **Humpty Dumpty** (arr Fud
                                              Livingston)
                                            Krazy Kat (arr Murray)   15
                                            Baltimore

(Broadway Bell Hops:) Beiderbecke (c), Hymie Farberman (tpt), Rank (tb), Murray
(cl), Davis (as), Trumbauer (C-melody sax), Venuti (vln), Signorelli (p), John Cali
(bj), Joe Tarto (bb), Vic Berton (d), Irving Kaufman (v)
                29 Sept 1927   **There Ain' No Land Like**
                                              Dixieland
                                            There's a Cradle in Caroline

(Trumbauer:) as **Humpty Dumpty***, but Lang (bj) and add Sylvester Ahola (tpt),
Kaufman (v)*

30 Sept 1927   Just an Hour of Love

I'm Wonderin' Who   **20**

Other CDs

same contents:
   Europe: CBS Jazz Masterpieces 466309-2
tracks 1–11, 13–20:
   UK: *Bix Beiderbecke and Frankie Trumbauer,* JSP CD 316

LPs

same contents:
   USA: Columbia Jazz Masterpieces CJ 45450
   UK: CBS Jazz Masterpieces 466309-1
plus additional tracks:
   USA: *Sincerely Bix Beiderbecke,* BIX1-BIX20 (20-volume set)
   Italy: *The Bix Beiderbecke 'Records Story' in Chronological Order,* Joker
   SM 3557 through SM 3570
   UK: *The Studio Groups 1927,* EMI EG 260527-1; World Records SH 413;
   The Studio Groups, late 1927, World Records SH 414
incl. tracks 1–9, 11, 13, 15, 20:
   Australia: *Bix & Tram 1927,* Swaggie S 1242
incl. tracks 10, 14, 16–19: *The Rare Bix*
   UK: Parlophone PMC 1237
   Australia: Swaggie S 1218
incl. tracks 2–7, 9–11, 14–16, 19–20:
   UK: *Bix and Tram 1927,* Parlophone PMC 7064
incl. tracks 1, 3, 5–7, 12, 14, 16, 20:
   UK: *The Golden Age of Bix Beiderbecke, 1927,* Golden Age TC-GX 2513
incl. tracks 2–8, 13: *The Bix Beiderbecke Story, vol.1–3*
   USA: Columbia CL 844, CL 845, CL 846
   Europe: CBS 62373, 62374, 62375
   France: CBS 66367
incl. tracks 2–8, 13:
   UK: *Young Man with a Horn,* CBS 22179
incl. tracks 2–7:
   UK: *'The Beiderbecke File' (Featuring the Real Bix),* Saville SVL 201
incl. tracks 3, 6–8, 12:
   Italy: *Bix Beiderbecke,* Giants of Jazz LPJT 25

Cassettes

same contents:
   USA: Columbia Jazz Masterpieces CJT 45450
   UK: CBS Jazz Masterpieces 466309-4
tracks 1–16, 19–20:
   UK: *Bix: the Essential Bix Beiderbecke*, vol.1, Neovox 713
incl. tracks 1, 3, 5–7, 12, 14, 16, 20:
   UK: *The Golden Age of Bix Beiderbecke, 1927*, EMI TC-MFP 5828; Golden
   Age TC-GX 2513
incl. tracks 2–8, 13:
   UK: *Young Man with a Horn*, CBS 40-22179
incl. tracks 2–7:
   UK: *'The Beiderbecke File' (Featuring the Real Bix)*, Saville CSVL 201
incl. tracks 3, 6–8, 12:
   Italy: *Bix Beiderbecke*, Giants of Jazz MCJT 25

* * *

Red Nichols: *Red Nichols, vol.1*

Red Nichols had the misfortune to become a jazz star playing in a style
similar to Bix Beiderbecke's at a time when Beiderbecke was little known.
When it became apparent that Beiderbecke was the greater of the two men,
there was a tendency on the part of romantically inclined jazz fans to see
Nichols as a usurper who built a major reputation in jazz, and the dance-
band world in general, on the work of another man. Making matters worse,
in the years after World War II Nichols had some popularity with a rather
slick dixieland band which featured his own technically adroit, but somewhat empty playing, and this did not add to his reputation as a great jazz
musician. Nonetheless, in the 1920s he was one of the best cornetists in jazz,
a player with a bell-like tone, exceptionally clean execution and a good, if
not great, conception. He deserves more consideration than he has received
from jazz critics.

   In 1926 Nichols began to record with a group under his own name, which
at times included Miff Mole and Jimmy Dorsey, both also among the technically most proficient musicians in jazz, and both capable of excellent hot
playing. Given the high quality of this front line, it is hardly surprising that
this early Nichols group rapidly became vastly admired by both jazz musicians and closer observers of dance-band music. Over the next several years
Nichols made scores of recordings with various combinations, some using
arrangements, others primarily improvising in the dixieland style. Although

Nichols's groups were generally known as Red Nichols and his Five Pennies, the band recorded under a number of pseudonyms.

The first of his recordings were basically in the older, dixieland mode, and contained a good deal of ensemble jamming. However, Nichols's players were musically more sophisticated than most of the early jazzmen, and this shows in the little arranged passages found throughout the cuts, and in the use of unusual instruments, such as the mellophone and timpani, the latter of which the group's primary drummer, Vic Berton, was trained to play.

All these tendencies may be noted in *Boneyard Shuffle* (1926), which has little arranged passages, a solo by guitarist Eddie Lang and timpani splashed in here and there. The solos on the old New Orleans tune *Buddy's Habits* are particularly fine. The playing of these white New Yorkers was much more clipped than was the case with the New Orleans players – Mole in particular used a more staccato manner than any other important trombone player in jazz. Nichols's solo on *Buddy's Habits* is replete with devices associated with Beiderbecke, which can be heard clearly in his opening break, in bars 3 and 4 and in the break at mid-chorus. Nichols's debt to Beiderbecke, which he readily admitted, is also obvious – for example, in the upward rip he plays going into the middle of his solo on *Alabama Stomp*. But, as this solo shows, his ringing tone was his own and can stand comparison with Beiderbecke's sound. This recording also features a fine solo by Miff Mole in his bright, clipped style, which had become firmer and more confident since the days of the Original Memphis Five; by now Mole was, perhaps, the most admired trombone player among jazz musicians. *Alabama Stomp* ends with a quick splash of timpani played by Berton.

One of the best in this series is *Hurricane*. It is essentially a string of solos, with relatively brief ensemble passages to open and close the cut. Particularly under the influence of Armstrong, jazz was rapidly becoming a soloist's music. The dixieland style was already being pushed aside by the big bands when *Hurricane* was made, and when dixieland was later revived it took this form, with ensembles limited in the main to opening and closing choruses and the rest of the space given over to solos. Furthermore, the careful assignment of roles to cornet, clarinet and trombone was breaking down. For example, in the final ensemble, although Mole stays out of the upper register, he is not playing the slurs that had been typical of the dixieland style, but rather extended passages of eighth notes, to produce a more truly contrapuntal effect than had been typical of the form.

By the late 1920s it was apparent that the popularity of the improvising dixieland ensemble was rapidly waning: the public preference was now for the big 10- or 12-piece hot dance band playing arranged music, with a good deal of jazz soloing throughout. Nichols added musicians and made the change, and his later recordings continue to offer first-rate jazz, including solos by himself and premier jazz players such as Benny Goodman, Jack

Teagarden and many others. This tendency was already apparent in the 1927 recording *Cornfed*, which has brief arranged passages – probably *ad hoc* arrangements worked out in the studio – and the solos in many cases cut back to four or eight bars.

Red Nichols today is seen as a minor figure in jazz, but in fact the influence of his groups was substantial during the late 1920s. Many of the musicians who would become important figures in the swing-band movement a decade later served apprenticeship with Nichols, and it was this approach to the music, rather than the heavy, hot, blues-oriented style, that came to dominate jazz.

LP

Sweden: *Red Nichols, vol.1*, CJM 24

Red Nichols (c), Jimmy Dorsey (cl, as), Arthur Schutt (p), Eddie Lang (g), Vic Berton (d, timpani)

New York	8 Dec 1926	Washboard Blues	
		Washboard Blues	
		That's No Bargain	
		That's No Bargain	

add Miff Mole (tb)

	20 Dec 1926	Buddy's Habits	5
		Boneyard Shuffle	
		Boneyard Shuffle	
	12 Jan 1927	Alabama Stomp	
		Alabama Stomp	
		Alabama Stomp	10
		Hurricane	
		Hurricane	

add Joe Venuti (vln)

	3 March 1927	Bugle Call Rag	
		Back Beats	

Adrian Rollini (bass sax) replaces Venuti (vln)

	20 June 1927	Cornfed	15
		Cornfed	

CDs

incl. tracks 5–6, 8, 11, 16:
  UK: *Rhythm of the Day*, Living Era CD AJA 5025

Other LPs

same contents:
    Australia: *Red Nichols and his Five Pennies, vol.1*, Swaggie S 836
incl. tracks 1, 3, 5–6, 13:
    UK: *Feelin' No Pain*, Affinity AFS 1038
incl. tracks 2, 4, 5–6, 13:
    Germany: *Red Nichols 1926–1928*, Coral COPS 6795
incl. tracks 5–6, 8, 11, 16:
    UK: *Rhythm of the Day*, Living Era AJA 5025

Cassettes

incl. tracks 5–6, 8, 11, 16:
    UK: *Rhythm of the Day*, Living Era ZC AJA 5025
incl. one take of each title:
    UK: *The Essential Red Nichols, vol.1, 1926–27*, Neovox 710, and
    The Essential Red Nichols, vol.2, 1927, Neovox 721

* * *

Joe Venuti and Eddie Lang: *Jazz Classics in Digital Stereo: Joe Venuti / Eddie Lang*

The earliest true New Orleans jazz bands frequently included a violin, which roughly doubled the lead with the cornet. It owed its presence, for one reason, to the fact that it was one of the basic instruments in dance bands, and was therefore carried over into the early jazz bands. For another, violinists were generally trained to read music and could therefore teach the new tunes to the wind players, who were often non-readers. However, as the jazz band developed in New Orleans and elsewhere, the violin, unable to match the volume of the horns, began to drop out. One of the few early players to make a specialty of the instrument was Joe Venuti. He became well known to the dance-band public for the long series of recordings he made with a schoolboy friend, guitarist Eddie Lang, who had also started as a violinist. They worked together as a duo and in small groups.

Duets can put a considerable burden on both the rhythm player and the melody instrument, and the musicians are likely to be unnerved by the responsibility of carrying the whole load. But Venuti and Lang flew through theirs with vigour and aplomb. A fine example of their skill with the form is *Stringing the Blues*, a thinly disguised version of *Tiger Rag*. Both musicians play continuously throughout the cut. Venuti's playing is typically flamboyant and heedless, without frills. He bows double-stops (two notes simultaneously) only rarely and then mainly to accentuate the line during the breaks the piece provides. Lang, who must supply both the harmonies and the ground beat, perforce plays full chords constantly. So impeccable is his time that he holds the beat almost exactly from beginning to end.

But, typically, Lang was a single-string soloist, using chords only infrequently. A fine example of this style is *Eddie's Twister*, an original composition. An important strain in jazz of the period was the attempt to marry classical music with jazz. *Eddie's Twister* is by no means classical music, but its advanced harmonies and somewhat formal quality reflect Lang's early training as a violinist playing the classical repertory, as well as the devices from classical music which arrangers such as Bill Challis and Ferde Grofé were bringing to jazz.

Lang was seen as cool-headed and businesslike by his colleagues, but Venuti was the reverse – hot-headed, earthy, and a notorious practical joker around whom anecdotes clustered. Another musician who recorded with Venuti and Lang frequently, Adrian Rollini, was quixotic. Given these temperaments it is not surprising that there is a comic, or even fey, quality to some of their recordings. In part this was to enhance audience appeal in a day when having fun was the spirit of the time; but it also suggests the attitude of first-rate musicians throwing together in the studio something light for their own pleasure. *Put and Take*, which is credited to Venuti, but is in reality just improvising on three unrelated strains strung together for no apparent reason, is certainly that.

Lang and Venuti play excellent and wholly typical solos, and Rollini is featured on bass saxophone and hot fountain pen (a small clarinet with a limited range), one of the home-made instruments he liked to devise. Rollini was an excellent musician with a rather precise conception, good intonation, a crisp attack and a considerable ability to swing. Besides the bass saxophone and the home-made instruments, Rollini, who had trained as a pianist as a boy, played vibraphone, then a rare instrument. Had he chosen to take up one of the more standard instruments, for example, alto saxophone, he would today have a major reputation.

The small Venuti–Lang combinations were popular with jazz fans and with the general public. However, in retrospect it was a recording session with a somewhat larger group which appears more significant. Issued in 1931 as by Venuti–Lang and their All-Star Orchestra, it included trombonist Jack Teagarden, clarinettist Benny Goodman, and Teagarden's brother Charlie playing trumpet. Goodman, Jack Teagarden, Lang and Venuti were perhaps the best jazz musicians on their respective instruments at that moment, and the others were above average. The results were felicitous.

The BBC anthology includes one of the four tracks from the session, *Beale Street Blues*. It opens with a carefully thought-out introduction by Venuti and Lang in sequence. Charlie Teagarden leads a quiet, relaxed ensemble; in later years the trumpeter could be rather mechanical in approach, but here he strikes a note of ease. Jack Teagarden then sings the famous lyric, accompanied by Goodman, always excellent at accompanying singers. At times he plays no more than a single, unobtrusive note which acts like a finger pointing briefly at Teagarden's musical phrase. Taken altogether, *Beale Street Blues* is a relaxed, almost tender performance. Even the usually impassioned Venuti catches the easy-going mood. This session with these jazz giants is one of the little gems from the period.

CD
UK: *Jazz Classics in Digital Stereo: Joe Venuti/Eddie Lang*, BBC CD 644

(Venuti:) Joe Venuti (vln), Eddie Lang (g)
New York   29 Sept 1926   **Stringing the Blues**

(Red Nichols:) Nichols (c), Miff Mole (tb), Jimmy Dorsey (cl, as), Venuti (vln), Arthur Schutt (p), Lang (g), Vic Berton (d)
                              3 March 1927   **Bugle Call Rag**
(Lang:) Schutt (p), Lang (g)
                              1 April 1927   **Eddie's Twister**

(Frankie Trumbauer:) Bix Beiderbecke (c), Bill Rank (tb), Trumbauer (C-melody sax), Don Murray (cl, bar), Bobby Davis (as), Adrian Rollini (bass sax), Venuti (vln), Frank Signorelli (p), Lang (g), Chauncey Morehouse (d)
                              28 Sept 1927   **Krazy Kat**

(Venuti:) Murray (cl, bar), Venuti (vln), Signorelli (p), Lang (g), ?Justin Ring (cymbal)
                              15 Nov 1927   **Four String Joe**   5

(Red McKenzie:) Venuti (vln), Lang (g), Eddie Condon (bj), McKenzie (comb, v)
                              28 May 1928   **My Baby Came Home**

(Venuti:) Dorsey (cl, as, bar), Venuti (vln), Rube Bloom (p, v), Lang (g), Paul Graselli (d)
                              27 Sept 1928   **Sensation**

(Blind Willie Dunn:) Signorelli (p), Lang (g), Ring (chimes)
                              5 Nov 1928   **Church Street Sobbin' Blues**

(Lang:) Leo McConville (tpt), Tommy Dorsey (tb), Jimmy Dorsey (cl, as), Schutt (p), Lang (g), Joe Tarto (sb), Stan King (d)

22 May 1929   **Hot Heels**

(Trumbauer:) Charlie Margulis (tpt), Andy Secrest (c), Bill Rank (tb), Charles Strickfaden (as), Trumbauer (C-melody sax), Izzy Friedman (cl, ts), Min Leibrook (bass sax), Venuti (vln), Lennie Hayton (p), Lang (g), George Marsh (d)
22 May 1929   **Shivery Stomp**   10

(Venuti:) Trumbauer (bassoon), Venuti (vln), Hayton (p), Lang (g)
18 Oct 1929   **Runnin' Ragged (Bamboozlin'**
                          the Bassoon)

(Venuti:) Rollini (bass sax, hot fountain pen), Venuti (vln), Itzy Riskin (p), Lang (g)
7 May 1930   **Put and Take**

(Venuti:) Pete Pumiglio (cl, bar), Venuti (vln), Signorelli (p), Lang (g)
7 Oct 1930   **The Wild Dog**

(Nichols:) Nichols (tpt), Jimmy Dorsey (cl, as), Venuti (vln), Fulton McGrath (p), Eddie Lang (g), Vic Berton (d)
16 Sept 1931   **Oh! Peter (You're so Nice)**

(Venuti–Lang:) Charlie Teagarden (tpt), Jack Teagarden (tb), Benny Goodman (cl), Venuti (vln), Signorelli (p), Lang (g), Ward Lay (sb), Neil Marshall (d)
22 Oct 1931   **Beale Street Blues**   15

(Venuti:) Jimmy Dorsey (tpt, cl, as), Rollini (vb, sound effects), Venuti (vln, sb), Phil Wall (p), Dick McDonough (g), unknown (kazoo)
8 May 1933   **Vibraphonia**

Other CDs
incl. tracks 1, 5, 7, 11-13:
   UK: *Joe Venuti and Eddie Lang*, JSP CD 309 and CD 310

LPs
same contents:
   UK: BBC REB 644
incl. tracks 1, 7-8, 10, 15:
   USA: *Stringing the Blues*, Columbia C2L 24; Columbia Special Products
   JC2L 24
   UK: CBS BPG 62143 and BPG 62144
   France: CBS 88142

incl. tracks 1, 10-12:
  Australia: *Joe Venuti and Eddie Lang*, Swaggie S 817
incl. 1931 all-star session:
  USA: (Benny Goodman and others:) *A Jazz Holiday*, MCA 2-4018
  Australia: *Joe Venuti and Eddie Lang*, Swaggie S 819

Cassettes

same contents:
  UK: BBC ZCF 644
incl. tracks 1, 7-8, 10, 15:
  USA: *Stringing the Blues*, CBS Special Products BT 1927
incl. tracks 1, 3, 8, 11-13, 15-16, plus 1931 all-star session:
  UK: *The Essential Venuti--Lang, vol.I, 1926-1927*, Neovox 718,
  . . . *vol.II, 1927-29*, Neovox 719, . . . *vol.III: 1929-31*, Neovox 767; . . . *vol.IV: 1931-1933*, Neovox 793

* * *

Eddie Condon: 'Chicago Style'

The presence in Chicago of some of the best of the New Orleans bands, both black and white, for long stays – especially after 1920 – worked as a training school for young white musicians, many of them still adolescents, who were being drawn to the new jazz music. These youngsters spent as much time as they could listening to King Oliver at the Lincoln Gardens and the Plantation Café, the New Orleans Rhythm Kings at Friar's Inn, Louis Armstrong at the Dreamland Café and the Sunset Café, Jimmie Noone at the Apex Club, and others elsewhere. They set out frankly to copy their heroes: Muggsy Spanier followed Oliver; Gene Krupa, Baby Dodds; the clarinettists, Johnny Dodds, Noone and Leon Roppolo; and everybody, Armstrong.

The core of this cadre of young white musicians was a group who were attending Chicago's Austin High School, including cornetist Jimmy McPartland, his brother, guitarist Dick McPartland, bassist Jim Lanigan and clarinettist Frank Teschemacher. They jammed together after school, began to play at local dances and attracted like-minded youngsters, among them tenor saxophonist Bud Freeman, pianist Joe Sullivan, drummers Krupa and Dave Tough, clarinettist Benny Goodman and eventually others from the Midwest outside Chicago, such as drummer George Wettling, cornetist Wild Bill Davison, clarinettist Pee Wee Russell and banjoist Eddie Condon, an outgoing, witty Irishman who eventually became the catalyst for the group. These musicians developed a way of playing that came to be called

'Chicago style'. Their music grew directly out of the New Orleans style and can best be seen as a sub-genre of dixieland. It tended to be more impassioned, less relaxed, than the dixieland of Oliver and Noone. By the late 1920s it was attracting many followers.

Probably the most important of the recordings from this sub-genre are four cuts made in Chicago in December 1927: *Sugar*, *China Boy*, *Nobody's Sweetheart* and *Liza* (not George Gershwin's *Liza*, but a tune written by Condon). The sides were issued as by McKenzie and Condon's Chicagoans, the first leader being Red McKenzie, a rough singer and comb player who had made a public reputation with novelty groups, the best known of which was the Mound City Blue Blowers. He had, however, little to do with these recordings, which set the mould for the Chicago style. There is a tenor saxophone instead of a trombone. There are substantially more arranged passages than was customary in the New Orleans system. Following the first chorus of *Sugar* and in the opening chorus of the other three titles, Teschemacher and Freeman mainly play harmonies parallel to the cornet lead, rather than creating the opposite motion usual with the dixieland clarinet and trombone. There is a good deal more soloing than took place in New Orleans music. And the final 'ride-out' chorus was raised a notch in intensity, which was not always the case with the New Orleans bands.

Not all of this music was intense: some of the slower numbers, such as *Sugar*, are relatively relaxed, but even this title picks up steam at the end. More typical is the thoroughly hot *China Boy*. It was this recording which especially excited young listeners at the time. Issued at the moment when Duke Ellington was beginning to attract serious attention, when Louis Armstrong was in the midst of making the great Hot Five series and when Bix Beiderbecke was producing some of his most important recordings, *China Boy* offered something different – a way of playing that was at a considerable remove from the expressionistic colouring of Ellington, the sweeping conception of Armstrong or the carefully carved sculptures of Bix. This was heedless, hot playing, full speed ahead and damn the torpedos.

The solos were not meant to be thoughtful. Sullivan, clearly influenced by Earl Hines, plays driving, rhythmic piano, and there is a rough and equally driving solo by Freeman, who inflects his lines with growls and swirls more expressive of heated passion than of cogitation. Teschemacher is generally regarded as the quintessential Chicago player. *China Boy* shows him using a broad vibrato, a shrill whining timbre as well as vocalized tones, descending saw-toothed figures, a division of the beat into more equal eighth notes than was customary with players like Goodman or Armstrong, and a very hot approach to playing. Despite questionable intonation and many blatant clinkers (for example, the wrong note repeated five times in the last part of his solo), he was much admired by the musicians who worked with him, some of whom said that he would have proved to be one of the great clarinettists in jazz had he not been killed in an automobile accident in 1932.

Like most of the geographic definitions that were popular in early jazz writing, the term 'Chicago' was a loose one. Many of the musicians associated with the school were from elsewhere, and some did not even work much in Chicago during the period. A case in point is Jack Teagarden, who was born and raised in the Southwest, where he acquired his early musical experience, and was based in New York during the heyday of the Chicago style. But his classic *Makin' Friends* was recorded under Condon's name and included many of the Chicagoans. The high point of the recording is the concluding minor-key passage for trombone. Teagarden here uses a stunt he made into a feature: removing the bell of the trombone, he slips an ordinary water glass over the open end of the slide and proceeds to play. It is a trick which requires some practice, for the slide positions are completely altered, but it produces a cold, smoky sound eminently suitable for the minor mode.

Another of the best-known recordings from the Chicago school was *The Eel*, written by Bud Freeman and used by him as a set-piece to display his virtuosity. It is built around strings of eighth notes. Freeman races through the idiosyncratic melody, then improvises a hot solo on it. After an ensemble interlude he improvises two more choruses on the blues. Other members of the band also solo on the blues, and then Freeman plays the theme again for a finale. Freeman handles the fast passages adroitly and swings hard in the typical Chicago helter-skelter style on the improvised passages. The recording was something of a *tour de force* and gave Freeman the start of his reputation with jazz musicians and fans.

LP

UK: 'Chicago Style', VJM VLP 55

(McKenzie and Condon's Chicagoans:) Jimmy McPartland (c), Frank Teschemacher (cl), Bud Freeman (ts), Joe Sullivan (p), Eddie Condon (bj), Jim Lanigan (bb, sb), Gene Krupa (d)

Chicago	8 Dec 1927	**Sugar**
		China Boy
	16 Dec 1927	**Nobody's Sweetheart**
		Liza

(Chicago Rhythm Kings:) Muggsy Spanier (c), Teschemacher (cl), Mezz Mezzrow (ts), Sullivan (p), Condon (bj), Lanigan (bb), Krupa (d), Red McKenzie (v)

	6 April 1928	**There'll Be Some Changes Made**

5

omit (v)   **I've Found a New Baby**

(McKenzie:) Joe Venuti (vln), Eddie Lang (g), Condon (bj), McKenzie (v)
New York   28 May 1928   **My Baby Came Home**
                                        From Monday on

(Miff Mole:) Red Nichols (tpt), Mole (tb), Teschemacher (cl), Sullivan (p), Condon (bj), Krupa (d)
                        6 July 1928   **One Step to Heaven**
                                          Shim-me-sha-wabble   10

(Condon:) Teschemacher (cl), Sullivan (p), Condon (bj), Krupa (d)
                        28 July 1928   **Oh! Baby**

omit (v)   **Indiana**

McPartland (c), Jack Teagarden (tb), Mezzrow (cl), Sullivan (p), Condon (bj, v),
Art Miller (sb), Johnny Powell (d)
                        30 Oct 1928   **I'm Sorry I Made You Cry**

add Mezzrow (speech), Teagarden (v) replaces Condon (v)
                                          Makin' Friends

Leonard Davis (tpt), Teagarden (tb, v), Mezzrow (cl), Happy Caldwell (ts), Sul-
livan (p), Condon (bj), George Stafford (d)
                        8 Feb 1929   **I'm Gonna Stomp, Mr Henry Lee**
                                          (take 1)   15
                                          That's a Serious Thing (take 2)

Max Kaminsky (tpt), Floyd O'Brien (tb), Pee Wee Russell (cl), Freeman (ts), Alex
Hill (p), Condon (bj), Artie Bernstein (sb), Sid Catlett (d)
                        21 Oct 1933   **The Eel**
                                          Tennessee Twilight (take A)
                                          Madame Dynamite (take A)
                                          Home Cooking   20

Other LPs

incl. tracks 1-4, 9-14: 'That Toddlin' Town'
  UK: Parlophone PMC 7072
  Italy: Parlophone 3C054.05641
  Australia: Swaggie S 1256
incl. tracks 1-4:

USA: (with Paul Mares and others:) *Chicago Jazz*, Columbia CL 632
incl. tracks 5–6, 17:
Australia: *Chicago Jazz*, Swaggie S 809
incl. tracks 17–20:
Italy: Eddie Condon 1929–1933, Family SFRDP 697
Sweden: (Bud Freeman:) *Home Cooking*, Tax M 8019
Australia: *Chicago Styled*, vol.2, Swaggie S 1358

Cassettes

incl. tracks 1–6, 11–12, 15–20:
UK: *Chicago Style Jazz: Formative Years*, Neovox 728; *Chicago Style Jazz, vol.III, 1933–36*, Neovox 819

* * *

Sidney Bechet: *Bechet of New Orleans*

A substantial number of the first generation of jazz musicians, and some of the best of them, were Creoles. Jelly Roll Morton was one. Another was Sidney Bechet. In the early years of jazz recording, these two musicians, together with Louis Armstrong, were mostly playing what would come to be called 'swing'.

Bechet was originally a clarinettist. He studied to an extent with Lorenzo Tio Jr and others, but was basically self-taught. Early in the 1920s he took up the soprano saxophone, then more in use than it would be later on. Although he continued to play clarinet throughout his career and made some excellent recordings with it, including his moving blues *Blue Horizon*, he is thought of primarily as a soprano saxophonist. He was a ferocious player who tended to dominate any musical circumstance he was in. He liked to work out figures and practise them, and as a result his solos tend to be more regular and patterned than is frequently the case in jazz. Most important in his playing, however, is the characteristic drive, the sharply attacked notes followed by slurs, and the pronounced terminal vibrato.

All these effects can be heard on *Maple Leaf Rag*, recorded in 1932. The tune, of course, is the most famous of all rags, intended by its composer, Scott Joplin, to be played with delicacy at a moderate speed. Bechet instead takes it at a breath-taking tempo, roaring through at a mad dash which leaves the other musicians sitting in the dust. Aside from a brief piano solo, Bechet carries the whole piece, flinging patches of phrases out with abandon one after the other. We are now a long way from the New Orleans format, despite the fact that Bechet and trumpeter Tommy Ladnier, who worked with Bechet frequently, are both New Orleanians. Armstrong had just finished refashioning jazz as a soloist's music, and this is a solo *par excellence* – one of the rare examples in jazz where one player solos for virtually the full length of a three-minute 78 rpm record.

Bechet liked to play 'oriental' set-pieces – supposed oriental music was popular with the American public in the teens and 1920s. *Egyptian Fantasy* is one of these, a piece with a slightly spooky theme in a minor key, opening out into a second strain in the major. On this and on *Wild Man Blues*, a tune originally cut by Armstrong as part of the Hot Five series, Bechet reverts to his first instrument, the clarinet. Although Bechet was a Creole, his approach was closer to that of Dodds than Noone. It is true that this clarinet sound has the liquid, fluid quality associated with creole players, and it is also true that Bechet uses a narrower vibrato on clarinet than on soprano saxophone. But where Noone tended to use a clear, clean, more 'legitimate' tone throughout, Bechet's sound is enormously varied – at times liquid, at times shrill, at times even capturing some of the quality of a cornet played with a plunger mute.

Bechet occasionally played both soprano and clarinet on the same recording. He does that on *Texas Moaner Blues*, a tune he had originally cut in 1924 under Clarence Williams's leadership, with Louis Armstrong on cornet. Allowing for the way the music had developed, it is classic New Orleans blues, played much the way it would have been for the whores and their customers to dance the slow-drag in the New Orleans honky-tonks. Bechet switches to the soprano midway through, at the unprepared modulation to a new key; his playing on the saxophone is stronger, less delicate than it sometimes is on the clarinet. This recording includes trumpeter Charlie Shavers, usually associated with bravura big-band playing, but here working in the narrower, more perfervid blues style.

One other cut of interest is the famous one-man band version of *The Sheik of Araby*, on which Bechet plays all the instruments – clarinet, soprano and tenor saxophones, bass and drums. It is not great jazz, but it is a technical triumph of sorts at a time before tape recording.

Sweetie Dear was recorded at the same session as *Maple Leaf Rag*, and the two were issued as a coupling. It is one of the great couplings in jazz. Bechet was in superb form that day. He plays clarinet here, and with the softer instrument does not dominate the music as he did on *Maple Leaf Rag* – trumpeter Ladnier just manages to stay on top of things. The piece ends with a series of riffs, again typical of Bechet, who, however impassioned he might be, liked a certain orderliness in what he played. These riffs signal, if nothing else had, that the New Orleans style was gone, or was at least going.

LP
USA: *Bechet of New Orleans*, **RCA LPV 510**

(New Orleans Feetwarmers:) Tommy Ladnier (tpt), Teddy Nixon (tb), Sidney Bechet (cl), Hank Duncan (p), Wilson Myers (sb) Morris Morland (d)
New York   15 Sept 1932   **Sweetie Dear**

as Sweetie Dear, but Bechet (ss)

Maple Leaf Rag

(Ladnier:) Ladnier (tpt), Bechet (cl, ss), Mezz Mezzrow (cl), Cliff Jackson (p), Teddy Bunn (g), Elmer James (sb), Manzie Johnson (d)
                    28 Nov 1938   **Weary Blues**

(Jelly Roll Morton:) Sidney De Paris (tpt), Claude Jones (tb), Albert Nicholas (cl), Bechet (ss), Happy Caldwell (ts), Morton (p, v), Lawrence Lucie (g), Wellman Braud (sb), Zutty Singleton (d)
                    14 Sept 1939   **I Thought I Heard Buddy Bolden Say**

(Bechet:) De Paris (tpt), Sandy Williams (tb), Bechet (ss), Jackson (p), Bernard Addison (g), Braud (sb), Sid Catlett (d)
                    4 June 1940   **Shake it and Break it** (take 1)   **5**

as Shake it and Break it, but Bechet (cl)   **Wild Man Blues** (take 1)

Rex Stewart (c), Bechet (cl, ss), Earl Hines (p), John Lindsay (sb), Baby Dodds (d)
Chicago   6 Sept 1940   **Save it, Pretty Mama**

(Henry Levine:) Levine (tpt), Jack Epstine (tb), Alfie Evans (cl), Bechet (ss), Rudolph Adler (ts), Mario Janarro (p), Tony Colucci (g), Harry Patent (sb), Nat Levine (d)
New York   11 Nov 1940   **Muskrat Ramble**

(Bechet:) Henry 'Red' Allen (tpt), J. C. Higginbotham (tb), Bechet (cl), James Tolliver (p), Braud (sb), J. C. Heard (d)
                    8 Jan 1941   **Egyptian Fantasy**

as Egyptian Fantasy, but Bechet (ss)   **Baby, Won't You Please Come Home?**   **10**

Bechet (cl, ss, ts, p, sb, d)
                    18 April 1941   **The Sheik of Araby** (take 4R)

Gus Aiken (tpt), Williams (tb), Bechet (ss), Lem Johnson (ts), Jackson (p), Myers (sb), Arthur Herbert (d)

28 April 1941	**When it's Sleepy Time Down South** (take 2)
	I Ain't Gonna Give Nobody None of This Jelly Roll

Charlie Shavers (tpt), Bechet (ss), Willie 'the Lion' Smith (p), Everett Barksdale (elg), Braud (sb), Johnson (d)

13 Sept 1941	**Georgia Cabin** (take 1A)

add Bechet (cl)   **Texas Moaner**   **15**

*as **Georgia Cabin**, but Bechet (cl), Catlett (d) replaces Johnson*

24 Oct 1941	**12th Street Rag**

CDs
plus additional tracks: *Sidney Bechet 1932–1943: The Bluebird Sessions*
   Europe: Bluebird ND 90317
incl. tracks 2–3, 5–8, 10, 11–12 (alternate takes), 16: *The Legendary Sidney Bechet, 1932–1941*
   USA: Bluebird 6590-2 RB
   Europe: Bluebird ND 86590

Other LPs
same contents:
   UK: RCA RD 7696
   Germany: RCA LPM 510
plus additional tracks: *Sidney Bechet 1932–1943: The Bluebird Sessions*
   Europe: Bluebird NL 90317
incl. tracks 1–3, 5–16: *Jazz Tribune no.10: The Complete Sidney Bechet, vol.1/2* and *Jazz Tribune no.18: The Complete Sidney Bechet, vol.3/4*
   Europe: RCA NL 89760 and NL 89759
   France: RCA PM 42409 and PM 43262
incl. tracks 1–3, 5–7, 9–16:
   USA: *Master Musician*, Bluebird AXM 2-5516
incl. tracks 2–3, 6, 8, 11–12 (alternate takes), 16: *The Legendary Sidney Bechet, 1932–1941*
   USA: Bluebird 6590-1 RB
   Europe: Bluebird NL 86590
incl. tracks 1–2, 5–7, 13, 15:

France: *Sidney Bechet, vol.2*, RCA 730.593
incl. tracks 8–10, 12, 16:
   France: *Sidney Bechet, vol.1*, RCA 730.560; *Horizons du Jazz no.2:*
   Blues in the Air, RCA 430.216
   Italy: *Sidney Bechet, vol.1*, Vik KLPV 181
   Australia: *Sidney Bechet, vol.1*, Victor LPV 1001
incl. tracks 11, 14:
   France: *Sidney Bechet, vol.3*, RCA 430.639; RCA 741.069
incl. tracks 1–2, 5–9, 11 (take 3):
   USA: title unknown, RCA LPM 9885

Cassettes

plus additional tracks: *Sidney Bechet 1932–1943: The Bluebird Sessions*
   Europe: Bluebird NK 90317
incl. tracks 1–3, 5–16:
   Europe: *Jazz Tribune no.10: The Complete Sidney Bechet, vol.1/2* and
   Jazz Tribune no.18: The Complete Sidney Bechet, vol.3/4, RCA NK 89760
   and NL 89759
incl. tracks 2–3, 6, 8, 11–12 (alternate takes), 16: *The Legendary*
   Sidney Bechet, 1932–1941
   USA: Bluebird 6590-4 RB
   Europe: Bluebird NK 86590

* * *

Billy Banks: *The Rhythmakers*

The series of recordings issued under the name of Billy Banks and his Orchestra, The Rhythmakers and Jack Bland and the Rhythmakers holds a special place in the history of jazz. They are perhaps the hottest jazz recordings ever made – if we define hot as meaning music played with perfervid, reckless abandon. Billy Banks was a singer and general entertainer of no great talent who specialized in falsetto, a device employed commonly by black entertainers. The recordings were meant to feature his singing, but so hot were the instrumental sections that the singing is today seen as merely an intrusion. These groups included some of the finest jazz players of the day, both black and white, and are among the earliest important bands to mix racially in the recording studios. Among the musicians were trumpeter Henry 'Red' Allen, who also sings on some of the items, pianist Fats Waller, clarinettist and tenor saxophonist Pee Wee Russell, pianist Joe Sullivan, banjoist Eddie Condon and even trombonist Tommy Dorsey. Drummer

Zutty Singleton is on all but the first session, which has Gene Krupa, and Singleton's New Orleans compatriots Al Morgan and Pops Foster are on bass. Perhaps the least known among the other participants was guitarist Jack Bland, who became the nominal leader on a few tracks made without Banks.

These cuts were recorded in 1932, at a time when the New Orleans style was virtually dead and the big bands were taking over. They are not classic New Orleans jazz – among other things, most of them have no trombone. But Allen and the aforementioned rhythm players were New Orleanians, and Russell, Sullivan and some of the other supporting cast had been weaned on New Orleans music. This is what came to be called Chicago style – hot, driving playing with the New Orleans flavour, filled with the blues and unconcerned with form.

The playing here is rhythmic, not melodic. The musicians again and again resort to the simplest of phrases, frequently repeating a two- or three-note figure several times with slightly varied rhythm. In many instances the music becomes even more basic, as, for example, when clarinettist Russell repeats a single note several times after the break in the fifth chorus of *Bugle Call Rag*. If that were not basic enough, at times the players hold one note for long stretches, varying it in pitch and intensity as it goes along: Tommy Dorsey holds a single note, with very broad lip vibrato, for over half his solo on *Who Stole the Lock?*, and Russell plays almost the entire last 16 bars of *Bugle Call Rag* on a held note. Even Fats Waller, ordinarily a very busy player, catches the mood: his introduction to *Mean Old Bed Bug Blues* is atypically sparse and punchy.

Among the occasional solos on these recordings, Russell plays tenor sax on *I Would Do Anything for You*, *Mean Old Bed Bug Blues* and *Yellow Dog Blues*; he frequently worked in saxophone sections of commercial dance bands, but his recorded solos on the instrument are very rare. The solo offerings are outnumbered by a lot of hard-driving ensemble playing, with Allen banging away at the top of his range and the clarinet and tenor saxophone swirling along in his wake.

In addition, the pieces are built on the simplest of material. About half are blues, and the rest are pop tunes or comic material (such as *Yes, Suh!* and *Who Stole the Lock?*) on the most basic chord changes. The Rhythmaker sides do not call for extended musical analysis. They are simply superb jazz at its hottest, made by some of the finest players of the day. If the New Orleans format was gone, there remained the lusty, heedless swing of that good-time city.

There is a bizarre footnote to these recordings: Billy Banks ended his career as an entertainer in Tokyo, where he was discovered by *Life* magazine, and where he died in 1967.

LP

USA: *The Rhythmakers*, IAJRC 4

(Billy Banks and his Orchestra:) Henry Allen (tpt), Pee Wee Russell (cl, ts), Joe Sullivan (p), Eddie Condon (bj), Jack Bland (g), Al Morgan (sb), Gene Krupa (d)
New York   18 April 1932   **Bugle Call Rag**

add Allen (v)   **Oh Peter** (take 1)

Banks (v) replaces Allen (v)   **Margie**

*as **Margie**, but Zutty Singleton (d) replaces Krupa*
                      23 May 1932   **Oh Peter** (take 3)
                                           Spider Crawl   5
                                           Who's Sorry Now?
                                           Take it Slow and Easy
                                           Bald-headed Mama

(The Rhythmakers:) Allen (tpt), Jimmy Lord (cl), Russell (ts), Fats Waller (p), Condon (bj), Bland (g), Pops Foster (sb), Singleton (d), Banks (v)
                      26 July 1932   **I Would Do Anything for You**
                                           (takes 1–2)

add second (v), probably Waller   **Mean Old Bed Bug Blues** (takes
                                           1–2)   **10**

omit second (v)   **Yellow Dog Blues** (takes 2–3)

add band (v)   **Yes, Suh!** (take 1)

(Jack Bland and his Rhythmakers:) Allen (tpt, v), Tommy Dorsey (tb), Russell (cl), Happy Caldwell (ts), Frank Froeba (p), Condon (bj), Bland (g), Foster (sb), Singleton (d), band (v)
                      8 Oct 1932   **Who Stole the Lock?** (take 1)

Other LPs

same contents:
   UK: CBS Realm Jazz 52732
plus additional tracks:
   UK: *The Rhythmakers 1932*, VJM VLP 53
master takes only:
   Denmark: *The Rhythmakers*, Collectors Classics CC 14

alternate takes only:
 Denmark: *Henry Allen, vol.5*, Collectors Classics CC 55

Cassettes
incl. tracks 1–9, 12–14, 15 (alternate take), 16, plus additional tracks:
 UK: *1932: Billy Banks, The Rhythmakers, Chicago Rhythm Kings*, Neovox 768

CHAPTER 2
Solo Stride and Swing Pianists

Barry Kernfeld

At the same time that the hot combos and the big bands developed, pianists began to stake out a separate realm of unaccompanied playing. From time to time solo guitarists offered a challenge to the pianists, and since the 1970s other possibilities have emerged, as in the extended unaccompanied musings of tenor saxophonist Sonny Rollins and the many solo free-jazz concerts and albums on just about any instrument imaginable. But as jazz ends its first century, the piano has remained dominant for a straightforward reason: a pianist could outdo anyone else in the ability to produce single-handedly the explicit beat, bass, chords and melody essential to so many styles of jazz. Only the Hammond B-3 organ, with its bass pedals and two keyboards, might have offered jazz a more versatile solo instrument, but in practice this machine has rarely appeared in settings smaller than a trio. The wide variety of electronic keyboards available in the 1990s has now seriously begun to challenge the supremacy of the piano, but an assessment of their role remains speculative.

As an introduction to the field, this chapter surveys three of the pianists who created the unaccompanied stride and swing styles – James P. Johnson, Fats Waller and Earl Hines – and two who carried these styles to extremes – Art Tatum and Thelonious Monk. Jelly Roll Morton's solo playing has been discussed in Chapter 1. Other formidable pianists of the era are present in this book for their crucial contributions to groups – Joe Sullivan in various rhythm sections with Eddie Condon; Teddy Wilson with Benny Goodman and Billie Holiday; Nat 'King' Cole and Erroll Garner leading trios; Count Basie leading combos and his big band; Duke Ellington leading his big band – but it should be noted that Sullivan, Wilson and Garner also made fine unaccompanied recordings, and there is a good dose of stride and swing soloing in the midst of Basie and Ellington's band work.

(The equally important early piano style of boogie-woogie has no proper representation here, simply because it receives a full chapter of its own in a companion volume in this series, *The Blackwell Guide to Blues Records*, ed. Paul Oliver, Oxford, 1989.)

James P. Johnson: *From Ragtime to Jazz*

At the end of World War I James P. Johnson, Luckey Roberts and Willie 'the Lion' Smith were at the centre of an informal group of Harlem-based stride pianists. They were soon joined by Fats Waller, who became Johnson's protégé after he had learnt Johnson's *Carolina Shout* by copying the action of the version recorded on a piano roll. Whereas he had begun to make such rolls while still playing in a ragtime style, Johnson was immersed in the jazzy stride style by the time of his recording the earliest discs in the CBS collection, which date from 1921. Easiest to hear, and thus most readily identified with the style, is the recurring motion of the left hand. Spread apart, the hand would 'stride' repeatedly back and forth between an interval (comprising a bass note in the little finger and another note above in the thumb) in the lower register and a chord (comprising several notes) in the middle register. This method of using the left hand comes directly from ragtime, but differs subtly in the use of intervals (generally tenths) rather than single bass notes, and in the practice of striking those intervals top to bottom ('backward tenths'), with the thumb hitting slightly before the little finger, so as to impart a special rhythmic drive.

There is more to stride than just this motion. Broadly speaking, Johnson developed a virtuoso, percussive, swinging adaptation of ragtime piano forms and figurations. In some ways his work represents an orchestral and formal approach which stands in opposition to the folk-like boogie-woogie blues style. (This view is supported indirectly by his personal goals: he aspired to write symphonies and the like.) He had a formidable classical technique, enabling him to present sophisticated accompaniments while negotiating twisted right-hand figures effortlessly. His use of harmony, though tinged by the blues, is generally straightforward, following the fundamental progressions of Western art music, as did ragtime. And the crucial early pieces, *The Harlem Strut*, *Keep off the Grass* and *Carolina Shout*, all his own compositions, follow typical ragtime structures in presenting several distinct 16-bar themes symmetrically divided into eight-bar antecedent and consequent phrases: Johnson states an idea, it continues without resolving, he restates the idea, and a varied continuation resolves it. (The second theme of *Keep off the Grass* is 32 bars long, rather than 16.)

Yet for Johnson, more than for any of the other leading stride players, classification as an orchestral rather than a folk-like pianist may be misleading. The overall sensation of these performances is one of percussive attack. He strikes the piano as if it were a drum set. *The Harlem Strut* is nearly a perpetual motion piece, and *Keep off the Grass* is only slightly less frenetic. *Carolina Shout* is more relaxed, but this is on account of the slower tempo rather than any change in approach. Regularly in these pieces, Johnson imparts a feeling of swing in his right hand through the subtle differentiation of duration (making the notes alternately a bit longer and a bit shorter) and articulation (the manner in which he strikes those notes). His striding left hand is never continuous. Following ragtime composers like Scott Joplin and such jazzy ragtime pianists as Eubie Blake, Johnson erratically but purposefully breaks up the pattern, inserting successive bass notes or successive chords. These jerky off-beat accents, which became a universal part of stride playing, supply great energy to the performances. (This is most readily heard on a later recording, *Toddlin'*.) Both *The Harlem Shout* and *Carolina Shout* have sequences of stabbing alternations as the hands rock between beats and off-beats. In both *Keep off the Grass* and *Carolina Shout*, and on many of the later recordings, he smashes two adjacent pitches simultaneously; on pieces such as *Weeping Blues* and *Worried and Lonesome Blues* this device might be interpreted as a simulation of blue notes (which the piano cannot produce literally), but in the many instances on non-blues tracks Johnson can only be described as obscuring pitch in favour of accentuation. It is revealing that when he includes a popular song, *If Dreams Come True*, among his solo recordings of 1939, he obliterates the melody, first in a stream of smashing dissonances and next with florid ornamentation; he then discards it in favour of another perpetual motion figure and a cascading riff; when the melody returns, again in a rhythmically charged form, it gives way to other essentially rhythmic ideas. Another piece, *Riffs*, recorded a decade earlier (1929), carries these various rhythmic tendencies still further, offering a zany demonstration of unpredictable accentuation. At one climactic point Johnson drops in sparkling trebly off-beat chords, and at another he moves fleetingly into a stride waltz, repeating oom pah pahs.

This anthology focuses on Johnson's greatest contribution to jazz, his exuberant stride performances, but he was a great musician in other genres as well. He accompanied blues and vaudeville singers, including Bessie Smith and Ethel Waters, and during a long career in musical theatre he composed many popular songs, among them *The Charleston*, *Old Fashioned Love* and *If I Could Be with You One Hour Tonight*. To a lesser extent these talents find expression in this collection. *All That I Had is Gone* (1927) explores other approaches in addition to stride, including a bass movement reminiscent of boogie-woogie and an elegant passage of interweaving independent lines. The appropriately titled *Feelin' Blue* (1929) follows stride techniques, but the performance is emotionally introspective. (By contrast, the inappropriately titled *Snowy Morning Blues*, from 1927, is cheery and not a blues.) Finally, there are two vaudeville dialogues recorded with Clarence Williams in 1930. The jokes quickly grow tiresome, but they are supported and framed by more fine examples of stride playing, especially at the end of *I've Found a New Baby*. I can scarcely hear the two pianos which are ostensibly present on these two tracks with Williams. The lower lines are clear throughout, as if one man were playing, and the upper ones are only a bit muddy. Did Williams understand that he was not a pianist of Johnson's stature, and hold back, staying out of the way?

CD

Europe: *From Ragtime to Jazz*, **CBS 465651-2**

James P. Johnson (p)

New York	Aug 1921	**The Harlem Strut**	
	18 Oct 1921	**Keep off the Grass**	
		Carolina Shout	
	28 June 1923	**Weeping Blues**	
		Worried and Lonesome Blues	5
	8 Aug 1923	**Scouting Around**	
		Toddlin'	
	25 Feb 1927	**All That I Had is Gone**	
		Snowy Morning Blues	
	29 Jan 1929	**Riffs**	10
		Feelin' Blue	

Johnson and Clarence Williams (p)

| New York | 31 Jan 1930 | **How Could I be Blue?** | |
| | | **I've Found a New Baby** | |

Johnson

New York	14 June 1939	**If Dreams Come True**	
		Fascination	15
		A-Flat Dream	
		The Mule Walk	
		Lonesome Reverie	
		Blueberry Rhyme	

LPs

same contents:
   Europe: CBS 85387
incl. tracks 8–11:
   UK: *Feelin' Blue*, Halcyon HDL 107

Fats Waller: *Fats Waller Piano Solos (1929–1941)*

Fats Waller wore many hats, as composer, songwriter, pianist, organist, bandleader, singer and entertainer in diverse combinations for musical theatre, popular music and jazz. The Bluebird double album gathers together his finest unaccompanied jazz piano recordings. Before discussing these, I should mention that two tracks are not solos, but duets with Bennie Payne. Unlike the collaborations between James P. Johnson and Clarence Williams, or Waller's duets with Johnson in 1928, or Waller's big band battle with his second pianist Hank Duncan in a 1935 version of *I Got Rhythm*, these are ponderous performances, with numerous clashes over harmony, melody and rhythm.

Having studied with Johnson, Waller thoroughly absorbed and extended the latter's left-hand stride technique, the backbone of these recordings. His version of Johnson's *Carolina Shout*, recorded in 1941, keeps close to the original. Among Waller's own compositions here, *Valentine Stomp, Smashing Thirds* (both from 1929) and *Russian Fantasy* imitate Johnson's percussive stride style. *Smashing Thirds* is based on 16-bar themes in different keys, in the pattern *AABABBBA*, and there are the usual introductory and transitional passages. (Unusually, ascending and descending scales in block chords extend the first *B* to 24 bars.) As Johnson might do, Waller composes a rhythmic melody and moves it up an octave, and then up another, in successive presentations of the first theme. There are moments of chordal accompaniment in the first two *A*s and a syncopated walking bass line during the third, but stride techniques predominate, with Johnson-like rhythmic surprises in the second half of the piece.

In this collection of recordings, when Waller leaves Johnson's approach behind the result is not for the better. *Clothes Line Ballet* (1934) is a frivolous pastiche, presenting in sequence a trill; four bars of slow quasi-blues juxtaposed with four of fast riffs and stride; a sentimental light romantic ballad played chordally in free rhythm; a 32-bar *aaba* riff theme; and the quasi-blues.

On his best-known stride composition, *Handful of Keys* (1929), as well as on *Gladyse* (1929), *African Ripples, Alligator Crawl* and *Viper's Drag* (all from 1934), he finds a happy medium between innovation and tradition. All have two strongly contrasting themes, but with the exception of the second one in *Handful of Keys* each theme is based on *aaba* popular song form rather than on antecedent and consequent ragtime phrases; this is hardly surprising, given Waller's other activities. There are also contrasts in volume (most dramatically in *Gladyse* and *Viper's Drag*), tempo (*Viper's Drag*) and in the manner of accompaniment. In *Gladyse* and *African Ripples* we can hear Waller working out versions of the same piece. A dancing motif (which also recurs in *Valentine Stomp*) is supported in the first theme by smooth, gentle swing chords, with one note oscillating up and down. Cleverly and deceptively, this chordal motion also serves as the introduction, eliding with the theme proper so that its first appearance and its return is not 16, but 18 (in *Gladyse*) or 20 (in *African Ripples*) bars long. As this theme recurs, Waller increases the intensity by replacing the legato chords with a stride motion. Both pieces also use a four-bar transition to the new key of their 32-bar *B* themes, and leave the latter with an abrupt plonk, but here the relationship ends. In *Gladyse*, the earlier version, conventional stride predominates, supporting a heavily syncopated melody and then a return of the dancing motif. In *African Ripples* Waller invents a tuneful melody and loosens up the rhythm, playing at a free and generally slow tempo.

The Bluebird collection includes three 12-bar blues. *Numb Fumblin'*, *My Feelin's Are Hurt* (both from 1929) and *E Flat Blues* (1935) are delicate, elegant performances, stressing musicality rather than the emotional depth of the blues. This playing serves as a reminder that Waller may have learned as much from Willie 'the Lion' Smith as from Johnson. (Later, in 1939, Smith recorded his own series of solos, bringing together stride and French impressionism.) In the last chorus of *Numb Fumblin'* is one of Waller's great moments, as a breathlessly cascading 10-bar-long high register line moves in and out of phase with the stride bass.

Waller also interprets popular songs. Sessions from 1929 include routine readings (routine, at least, if you are Fats Waller!) of his and others' songs, with a regular stride motion accompanying fairly straightforward presentations of tunes. Representative are his own *Sweet Savannah Sue* and *Ain't Misbehavin'*. With the exception of *Rockin' Chair* (1941), in later years he took more liberties. In *Keepin' out of Mischief Now* and *Star Dust* (both from 1937) a good deal of pianistic filagree ornaments the melody. Both also include choruses of block chords, shouting and whispering above a rolling bass line. In *Basin Street Blues* (1937), taken at a bouncy tempo, unusually Waller pays little attention to melody and instead concentrates on rhythmic bass lines and chords. *Tea for Two* (1937) and *Honeysuckle Rose* (1941) are playful. The former begins with overly dramatic comical pauses throughout the opening statement of the tune, while the latter is completely fragmented, demonstrating how this familiar melody by Waller may be phrased, ornamented and harmonized in styles ranging from furiously paced stride to a romantic waltz. In a thoughtful rendition of *I Ain't Got Nobody* (1937) the opening phrases include a striking contrapuntal line in the middle register, more prominent than the melody; later, blues passages dissolve as Waller gracefully suspends a tinkling motif against a decelerating stride accompaniment. *Ring Dem Bells* (1941) is Waller's most radical recasting of existing material, his stark moody rendition standing in sharp contrast to high-spirited versions by Duke Ellington (1930) and subsequent remakes by, among others, Lionel Hampton (1938) and Andy Kirk (earlier in 1941). This performance suggests that Waller was dramatically furthering his creativity as a pianist during the last years of his life.

LP

USA: *Fats Waller Piano Solos (1929–1941)*, **Bluebird AXM2-5518**

Fats Waller (p)

New York	1 March 1929	**Handful of Keys**	
		Numb Fumblin'	
Camden, NJ	2 Aug 1929	**Ain't Misbehavin'**	
		Sweet Savannah Sue	
		I've Got a Feeling I'm Falling	5
		Love Me or Leave Me	
		Gladyse	
		Valentine Stomp	
	29 Aug 1929	**Waiting at the End of the Road**	
		Baby, oh! Where Can You Be?	10
New York	11 Sept 1929	**Goin' About**	
		My Feelin's Are Hurt	
	24 Sept 1929	**Smashing Thirds**	
	4 Dec 1929	**My Fate is in your Hands**	
		Turn on the Heat	15

Waller and Bennie Payne (p)

	21 March 1930	**St Louis Blues**	
		After You've Gone	

Waller

	16 Nov 1934	**African Ripples**	
		Clothes Line Ballet	
		Alligator Crawl	20
		Viper's Drag	
	11 March 1935	**Russian Fantasy**	
		E Flat Blues	
	11 June 1937	**Keepin' out of Mischief Now**	
		Star Dust	25
		Basin Street Blues	
		Tea for Two	
		I Ain't Got Nobody	
	13 May 1941	**Georgia on my Mind**	
		Rockin' Chair	30
		Carolina Shout	
		Honeysuckle Rose	
		Ring Dem Bells	

CDs

tracks 1–13, plus alternate takes:
   France: *Piano Masterworks, vol.1: Hot 'n Sweet*, FDC 5106 (vol.2 planned)
incl. tracks 1–3, 13, 18, 20–21, 27–8, 31: *The Joint is Jumpin'*
   USA: Bluebird 6288-2-RB
   UK: Bluebird ND 86288
incl. tracks 1–2, 8, 18, 21, 24, 31:
   Denmark: *Fats Waller*, Official 83030-2

Other LPs

same contents:
   Germany: *Masters of Jazz, vol.2*, RCA CL 42343DP
not incl. **Russian Fantasy**
   France: *Piano Solos*, RCA PM 43270
not incl. 1937 tracks: *Jazz Tribune no.23: Fats Waller Piano Solos*
   France: RCA NL 89471; RCA PM 43270
plus additional tracks:
   France: *Fats Waller Complete Recordings*, on these vols.: RCA 730.570, 730.660, 731.054, 731.057, 731.058, 741.076, 740.086, 741.094, 741.112, FXM1-7074
incl. tracks 1–3, 13, 18, 20–21, 27–8, 31: *The Joint is Jumpin'*
   USA: Bluebird 6288-1-R
incl. tracks 1–2, 8, 18, 21, 24, 31:
   Denmark: *Fats Waller*, Official 3030-1

Cassettes

same contents:
   USA: Bluebird AXK 2-5518
not incl. 1937 tracks: *Jazz Tribune no.23: Fats Waller Piano Solos*
   France: RCA NK 89471
incl. tracks 1–3, 13, 18, 20–21, 27–8, 31: *The Joint is Jumpin'*
   USA: Bluebird 6288-4-R

* * *

Earl Hines: *Paris Session*

A few days after recording the competitive duo *Weather Bird* with Louis Armstrong in December 1928, Earl Hines began recording under his own name by performing as a soloist for three remarkable sessions of piano rolls and discs. These had little effect on his studio career, which included only the occasional solo recording between 1929 and 1956, and evidently none whatsoever on his performing career. In 1964 David Himmelstein and Dan Morgenstern 'discovered that Hines had never played a concert as a featured pianist' and invited him to the Little Theater in New York (Morgenstern, 'Today's Life with Fatha Hines', *Down Beat*, xxxii, 26 Aug 1965, 25). His three concerts there were a rousing success, and for the remainder of his life Hines interspersed solo performances and recordings among his activities leading groups.

The **Paris Session** dates from a European tour in 1965, by which time James P. Johnson, Fats Waller and Art Tatum were dead. In addition to the remarkable music and the way in which the rich sound of the piano has been captured, the album offers the advantage of being available on an American reissue at the time of writing. In the event it disappears from circulation, it is worth noting that the late solo albums are consistently wonderful; substitutes will do.

By the 1960s Hines was a veteran of continuous work in bands ranging stylistically from traditional jazz to bop, and all essential elements of his piano style were fully formed. He was consequently puzzled and a bit irritated by the hoopla surrounding his 'rediscovery'. Yet the late period piano work deserves to be singled out, because these tracks strike a fine balance between control and impetuosity which his earlier recordings as a bandleader cannot match, and because one gets nothing but Hines, who after all is a greater soloist than most of the sidemen on his decades of studio recordings as a leader. Moreover, Hines resists the temptation to pull out his most blatant applause-seeking tricks, such as the droning right-hand tremolo (which, even if amazing for his technique and endurance, is a bit crass). He does sing one chorus of *I Can't Give You Anything but Love* in a pleasant, laid back, but unremarkable voice resembling Doc Cheatham's; his radical recasting of the melody, especially in the substitution of repeated pitches for moving lines, is indebted to Louis Armstrong's famous version.

All the tunes are based on 32-bar popular song forms, including Hines's own composition *Sixty-Five Faubourg* (named after the address of Hugues Panassié, who produced the session). He had co-written *Second Balcony Jump* during his years leading big bands. (My copy of the LP, the Italian issue, credits Hines and 'O. Wilson' as co-composers of *Blue Because of You*, but Fats Waller's 1935 recording of the same tune has it by 'Carpenter, Dunlap, and Wilson'.) All the rest are familiar tunes by others, and Hines spends little time stating their melodies plainly. But he spends time building recognizable paraphrases, and regularly during his inspired improvisations he returns to fragments of tunes; the wildest instance occurs in *Somebody Loves Me*, where the ascending motif expressing the title words precedes and follows an upwardly screaming treble flourish at the beginning of the fourth 32-bar chorus.

A tremendous sense of swing permeates these performances. In achieving it, Hines subscribes to no fixed method. From one moment to the next we hear a walking bass and a running melody, stabbing off-beat single-note and chordal punctuations, a two-beat, a bit of stride, the hands locked together in block chords, the fingers chasing one another in octaves, a burst of classically inspired arpeggiation. Somehow amidst this seeming discontinuity there are always enough pounding bass notes and well-placed chordal attacks to keep the implicit beat at least firmly in place on such relaxed tunes as *I Cover the Waterfront* and *Blue Because of You*, if not positively charging ahead on such as *I Surrender Dear* and *Sweet Sue*. On better than half the LP, in pieces taken at medium to fast tempos, we can hear Hines's shoe making a metronomic click. Though by no means essential, I wonder if this little sound doesn't provide a useful anchor, as if a drummer were tapping out the beat lightly on a closed hi hat cymbal. Hines was not yet accustomed to playing without the support of bass and drums (although, of course, the results were already quite spectacular), and so he might have been using his shoe as a drumstick. (He also grunts along with some of his playing, contributing to the ambience of the session albeit in a less directly musical way.) On this album, the only exceptions to Hines's argument that solo piano playing ought to swing are the jarring yet still tasteful introduction to *I Cover the Waterfront*, the rhapsodic opening statement and ending of *A Pretty Girl is Like a Melody*, the extended out of tempo ending to *Blue Because of You* and the second *a* section of the fourth 32-bar *aaba* chorus of *Sweet Sue*, where the tempo (by my reckoning, at least) temporarily disintegrates under the force of Hines's torrent of accentuations.

LP

France: *Paris Session*, Ducretet Thomson 300V140

*Earl Hines (p and *v)*

Paris	27 May 1965	I Surrender Dear	
		I Cover the Waterfront	
		Second Balcony Jump	
		A Pretty Girl is Like a Melody	
		I Can't Give You Anything but	
		Love (*v)	5
		Blue Because of You	
		Somebody Loves Me	
		Sixty-Five Faubourg	
		On the Sunny Side of the Street	
		Sweet Sue	10

Other LPs

same contents:
  USA: Inner City IC 1142
  UK: Columbia 33SX6030
  France: Dux 40262; Emidisc C 048-50756; Pathé 1552611
  Italy: *Europe Session*, Ducretet Thomson KTLP 158

* * *

Art Tatum: *Art Tatum Solos 1940*

Appreciation of Art Tatum, the most technically gifted of all jazz pianists, tends to run into either/ors, ifs and buts. First comes the problem of the legendary Tatum and the available Tatum. The legendary Tatum – one of jazz's most astounding improvisers, a man who at a party would spend hours disintegrating and reconstructing American popular songs – remains, well, mostly legendary. Only glimpses are available, mainly on very low fidelity recordings which require a considerable amount of wishful thinking to bring you to the party. The available Tatum – who recorded prolifically for major labels in good studios – was a more cautious man, who by no means avoided improvisation, but whose recorded legacy does not provide the wildly imaginative playing to which his respected colleagues testified again and again in interviews.

Listening to the studio recordings, one encounters the next roadblock, combo performances. The need for Tatum and his fellow players to be in some sort of agreement about rhythm and harmony undercut his fondness for varying the tempo and reharmonizing a chord progression without a moment's notice, and his busy style could get in the way of the others. This is especially a problem in his trios with Slam Stewart (whose own solos with Tatum, in his invariable style of humming while bowing the string bass, are not the best of his career and quickly wear thin). In his uncharacteristic combo sessions with blues shouter Joe Turner and in his mid-1950s albums with all star swing musicians this is less of a problem, but still the chemistry is not always right.

Among Tatum's unaccompanied studio recordings, again a problem appears. On late recordings for Capitol and for Norman Granz's labels Clef and Verve, the dazzle and flash of his early solos have given way to a deeper musicality on some titles, but more often have yielded to dullness and a lack of swing. And so there remain the dazzle and flash: the Decca solo recordings which many have criticized for shallowness. These sides are wonderful. Listen to *Get Happy*. How could anyone play the piano that well? And the examples of jazzing the classics are not offensive. Usually the idea is insipid and the results appalling, but by proceeding from such lightweight fare as Jules Massenet's *Elegie* and Antonin Dvořák's *Humoresque*, Tatum could scarcely do them terrible damage. Actually, this material is improved considerably by his arrangements, especially in the adaptation of *Humoresque* to Fats Waller's stride style.

For a jazz musician of his era, Tatum has an unusual conception of rhythm, in that for considerable stretches he plays out of tempo. Flexibly slow rhapsodic passages, interrupted by swoops up and down the keyboard, come directly from European romantic piano music and feed directly into the jazzy cocktail piano style which he inspired. But Tatum also has a manner of hurtling quickly through a melody, as in the opening statement of *Emaline*. This sensation of speed uncoupled from tempo seems more directly in the jazz tradition, but it had no direct impact; only later, separately, did free-jazz musicians develop the concept of rhythmic 'energy' freed from the beat.

Tatum also plays in jazz time, sometimes from the start, but at other times in the middle of a piece, the steady beat providing a structural contrast to the rhapsodic sections. On *Sweet Lorraine* sweeping bursts interrupt a stride motion, but the implicit beat remains steady and the performance swings wonderfully. On *Indiana*, also taken at a relaxed swing tempo, there is less stride motion and more of Tatum's left hand slithering through his chromatically coloured version of the tune's harmonies. *Get Happy* is also steady, but frantic; left-hand drones and trills alternate with a rapid stride motion. *Tiger Rag* is positively hysterical. If this is too fast for good taste, forget taste and marvel at technique. In a continuous outburst – as in the discontinuous swoops which ornament other performances – he shows an extraordinary touch, bringing out lines in either hand at lightning speed with great clarity. He effectively imitates the tailgate trombone plops in the 'hold that tiger' strain of the piece and then, for a breathless last chorus, moves into the fastest possible stride version.

The other great achievement of Tatum's playing is subtle – indeed well beyond the scope of this book; his ability to reharmonize songs can be demonstrated only through elaborate music examples. But perhaps a couple of the more blatant occurrences will provide some insight into this. In the late 1950s and early 1960s the notion of playing 'outside' came into jazz improvisation, especially through the work of Eric Dolphy, who intentionally emphasized pitches which were not in accord with the accompanying harmonies. Tatum was already a master at it. In the last chorus of *Indiana* he breaks out of the key on the first three phrases, then each time works his way back in. The same thing happens at the start of the second and third stride choruses of *Emaline*, where Tatum, having hurtled through the theme, now momentarily hurtles out of the key.

CD
USA: *Art Tatum Solos 1940*, **MCA MCAD 42327**

Art Tatum (p)

Los Angeles	22 Feb 1940	**Elegie**	
		Humoresque	
		Sweet Lorraine	
		Get Happy	
		Lullaby of the Leaves	5
		Tiger Rag	
		Sweet Emaline, my Gal (take A)	
		Sweet Emaline, my Gal (take B)	
		Emaline	
		Moonglow	10
		Love Me	
		Cocktails for Two	
	26 July 1940	**St Louis Blues**	
		Begin the Beguine	
		Rosetta	15
		Indiana	

LPs
incl. tracks 1–7, 9, 11–16:
  USA: MCA MCA 42327
incl. tracks 1–6, 9, 11–16:
  USA: *Art Tatum Masterpieces*, MCA 2-4019
  France: *The Art of Tatum*, vol.2, MCA 510082
  Germany: *The Art of Tatum*, Brunswick LPBM 87507
  Italy: title unknown, MCA MAPD 7028
  Japan: title unknown, MCA 3073-3075
incl. tracks 1–6, 9, 11, 13–16
  UK: *Pure Genius*, Affinity AFF 118
incl. tracks 1–6, 9, 11–12, 16: *The Art of Tatum*
  USA: Decca DL 8715
  UK: Ace of Hearts AH 133; Brunswick LAT 8375; Coral CP 62 (some jackets have EMI CRLM 1044 instead of CP 62)
  France: MCA MAP 2686
  Germany: Coral COP 2686
  Australia: Swaggie S1223
incl. tracks 5–6, 9, 11–13:
  France: title unknown, Cathala BLP 100.005

Cassettes

incl. tracks 1–7, 9, 11–16:
  USA: MCA MCAC 42327

* * *

Thelonious Monk: *Solo Monk*

Why place Thelonious Monk in the midst of stride and swing pianists? He was, after all, one of the most important bop musicians and most of his recordings were made with bop groups (see Chapter 7). As a composer and improviser he contributed new melodic shapes, which in turn grew out of his untraditional notions of rhythmic placement, accentuation, piano voicings (how individual chords might be expressed at the keyboard) and harmonic progressions (how chords follow one another). All of these elements were incorporated into definitive bop recordings. At the same time, Monk remained a traditional melodist, above all in the very fact of his preference for repeating memorable tunes rather than spinning out ever-changing complex lines. On the album **Solo Monk** this concern comes to the fore, as do other features which show his fondness for earlier jazz styles.

The album de-emphasizes Monk's great bop writing. There are two blues based on repeated figures: the theme of *North of the Sunset* takes up a jagged boppish motif better known from his composition *Well You Needn't*, and *Monk's Point* uses adjacent pitches which are attacked and released in such a way as to simulate a blue note. There are two ballads, *Ruby, my Dear* and *Ask Me Now*, the latter belonging to neither his best-known nor his most distinctive work. The remaining eight tracks are popular songs. While this in itself marks some diversion from his usual approach, still more important is the way in which he treats the material. Bop performers frequently use the structures of pop songs as a basis for improvisation, downplaying, ignoring or rewriting the melodies. Here Monk doesn't merely borrow structures, he plays the songs themselves. Captivated by their melodies, he can hardly bear to move away from them. Characteristically, he ornaments a melody only a bit and slightly displaces its relation to the beat; for a clear example, listen to the first phrase of *Dinah*, beginning on beat 1 at the start and on beat 2 at its repetition eight bars later. He never improvises for long before returning to the tune, and showy pianistic gestures (the cascading and climbing runs at the end of *I Surrender Dear*) are rare. This is true not only of the pop songs, but also of his own ballads. *Ruby, my Dear* is essentially a meditation on his theme, the second half of which he repeats over and over again.

To help bring out these melodies, Monk plays mainly at slow (and sometimes elastic) tempos, and he never goes beyond a relaxed walking pace. By avoiding speedy performances and the temptation to go into double time, he takes up a rhythmic conception that harks back to the earliest southern traditions in jazz. In an equally strong way he invites comparison with the Harlem-based pianists and their followers. Steady stride rhythms crop up throughout the album, from the delightful and straightforward readings of *Dinah*, *I'm Confessin'* and *These Foolish Things* to the two blues, which would exemplify his bop playing were it not for his breaking into a stride motion as he begins to improvise. There are also moments of old-fashioned tremolos (a trademark of Earl Hines's playing) in several wry endings to tunes and in the last statement of the melody of *Sweet and Lovely*.

Other aspects of Monk's playing invariably stand apart from established styles, old or new. He prefers stark, dissonant, colourful combinations of pitches. A typical example occurs in *Sweet and Lovely*. Without disrupting the melody, he reharmonizes the first phrase so that the accompaniment slithers downwards in parallel minor sevenths (moving step-by-step from B flat with an A flat above, down to C with a B flat above). The touch of his right hand is hard and crisp, producing a bell-like sound; paradoxically, he likes to obscure this clarity by striking clusters of notes, which may, through his use of the foot pedal, ring on in an echoing mass of sound. Fine examples occur in his deliberate and freely metred version of *I Should Care*, where dense chords alternate with stark individual pitches, and overlapping sounds break into silence as he releases the pedal; and in the high-pitched thicket of notes which he punches out just before the end of *Ask Me Now*. In these respects his playing was intensely personal and has scarcely been imitated successfully.

LP

USA: *Solo Monk*, **Columbia CL 2349 and CS 9149**

Thelonious Monk (p)

Los Angeles	31 Oct 1964	I Surrender Dear	
		Sweet and Lovely	
		Everything Happens to Me	
		I Should Care	
		North of the Sunset	5
	11 Nov 1964	These Foolish Things	
		I Hadn't Anyone Till You	
		Dinah	
		I'm Confessin'	
		Monk's Point	10

New York   23 Feb 1965   **Ask Me Now**
                    2 March 1965   **Ruby, my Dear**

CDs

probably same contents:
  Japan: CBS 32 DP 666

Other LPs

same contents:
  Europe: CBS 62549 and S 62549
  Japan: CBS Sony 149; CBS Sony 20 AP 1497

CHAPTER 3
Big Bands

Barry Kernfeld

The leaders of the first important jazz big bands were pragmatic men. They established their orchestras somewhat haphazardly during the mid-1920s, expanding their small groups into big bands more to meet the demands of nightclub and dance-hall operators than from any inner musical impulse towards a new jazz style suitable for large ensembles. It was the 'jazz age'. Audiences were big. Music often had to fill vast spaces, without the aid of amplification. So each man augmented his number of instrumentalists, adding brass and reeds. But quickly a new music resulted. While drawing in many ways from that of the hot bands, it now treated brass and reeds not only as individuals, but also as members of a section; and when, a few years later, the brass split into two sub-sections, the big band had settled into its long-lived form: trumpets, trombones, reeds (saxophones and clarinets) and rhythm section (piano; banjo or guitar; tuba or string bass; drums). These developments immediately afforded a special status to the composer or arranger who could feature and combine the four sections in the most imaginative ways.

The idea of sections (but with a string section prominent) and the importance of a good writer had already made their mark in popular dance music, beginning at the end of the 1910s, and jazz-orientated leaders had not missed noting how much money this approach generated, above all when the baton was in Paul Whiteman's hand. Less than a decade later, though, the new idea of blending gutsy jazz with dignified control had proved so successful that the much tamer 'symphonic jazz' of Whiteman had fallen out of fashion. It was no longer enough just to hire a few hot soloists – whole bands were beginning to learn how to swing. Soon big-band jazz would reach its widest audience, as American popular music and jazz temporarily merged into one, blurring distinctions among dance big bands, swing big bands and jazz big bands.

This chapter surveys the most innovative and creative jazz big bands from the 1920s into the 1950s, a period governed by the principle of brass and reed sections. It concludes, exceptionally, with the most original and successful departure from this tradition, an example of Gil Evans's orchestral collaborations with Miles Davis. Chapter 10 surveys the very different tradition of free-jazz orchestras, dating from the mid-1960s onwards and involving such leaders as John Coltrane, Don Cherry, Sun Ra and Alexander von Schlippenbach. Concurrently there began a resurgence of conventional jazz big bands, although by this time the potential of this approach had been pretty well worn out, and even the very best orchestra (led by Thad Jones and Mel Lewis) had none of the significance of a Gillespie or a Herman, yet alone of an Ellington or a Basie.

* * *

Fletcher Henderson: *First Impressions, 1924-1931; Swing's the Thing, 1931-1934*

Fletcher Henderson's orchestra was at the vanguard of the jazz scene in New York, helping to develop a stylistic vocabulary for big bands at two crucial points: when such bands began to form, and, later, just before big-band swing became the popular music of its day. Among the many and varied reissues of Henderson's prolific recordings, the Decca/MCA anthology, despite its rather poor sound quality, best covers these points in the decade that it spans. At the time of the first recording in this collection, October 1924, Louis Armstrong was one month into his 13-month stay as the group's principal soloist. At the time of the last, September 1934, Henderson's drastically changed group was two months from disbanding, and in the next year their music, a good deal of it arranged by Henderson himself, would provide the central material for Benny Goodman's big band.

This collection presents an orchestra that remained heavily indebted to early jazz traditions, both black and white, well into the 1930s. The New Orleans and dixieland influences are of several types. Apart from the playing of the rhythm section (described below), there are many passages of collective improvisation. In a sense Henderson's brass and reed men outdo their predecessors. When seven (and later eight) musicians are improvising, where formerly three, four or five might have done, the result can be just too massive, as for example in *Clarinet Marmalade* (1926), after the tenor saxophone solo. But usually they succeed in creating a wonderfully chaotic and exciting sound, heard intermittently through the otherwise formal arrangement of *Copenhagen* (1924) and at the 'all in' endings to *Fidgety Feet* (1927) and *Hop Off* (1928).

In addition to the use of this device, there is the repertory itself. The group's recorded legacy includes plenty of pop songs (*I'm Crazy 'bout my Baby*) and such atmospheric instrumentals as *Radio Rhythm* (both from 1931). But it is no accident that the Decca/MCA set includes, in the years from 1924 to 1931, *Copenhagen*, earlier recorded by the Wolverines (with Bix Beiderbecke); *Clarinet Marmalade*, *Fidgety Feet* and *Sensation*, all borrowed from the Original Dixieland Jazz Band; *Sugar Foot Stomp*, made famous under its original title, *Dippermouth Blues*, by King Oliver's Creole Jazz Band; *The House of David Blues*, recorded by the Original Memphis Five; and *Singin' the Blues*, recorded by Frankie Trumbauer (again with Beiderbecke). This last title most literally pays homage to the past. An arranged passage for saxophones parallels Trumbauer's line, and cornetist Rex Stewart copies Beiderbecke's pretty solo, though he cannot avoid 'blueing' a few notes and attacking the final phrases in a manner more characteristic of black New Orleans brassmen.

What ultimately drove the music far from its New Orleans basis was the search for effective ways to use all the wind instruments. Collective improvising among large numbers of players worked for only a few seconds at a time. (The sustained free collective improvising heard on John Coltrane's *Ascension* was still 40 years away, and that was geared to a specialized audience.) One solution was to have nearly everyone sit silent, effectively reducing the orchestra to a combo comprising a soloist and the rhythm section. This happened frequently at the start. Gradually, though, the winds came more and more into play as accompanists during solos, perhaps holding sustained chords, or jabbing out a riff, or presenting a contrapuntal melody, although in Henderson's orchestra the soloist was never pushed completely into the background (as happened with some of his more popularly oriented imitators).

Another solution was to focus attention on groups of winds, arranging themes and riffs for the whole ensemble in rhythmic unison, or breaking it into sections: reed players (saxophonists and clarinettists, with individuals regularly doubling on two or more reeds); and the brass, subdividing into trumpeters (sometimes two trumpets and one cornet, although this sort of distinction is not terribly important when speaking of sectional playing) and a trombonist (later two trombonists). In dealing with sections in this manner, Don Redman, Henderson's first important arranger, was particularly fond of trios – trumpet trios, saxophone trios, clarinet trios – which may be heard throughout the early recordings. For the most part this was simply a matter of using what instruments he had. The band kept three trumpeters. The saxophone trio disappeared as the saxophone section grew, but, oddly, the clarinet trio persisted as a stylistic device long after its sound had become old fashioned and Redman had left the orchestra. It pops out in one of the most unlikely places, the last chorus of *Down South Camp Meetin'* (1934), which in all other respects is one of the archetypal recordings of big-band swing. Composed by Henderson, *Down South Camp Meetin'* became one of the arrangements on which Benny Goodman built his successful orchestra when Henderson's group failed and the leader was hired by Goodman. Nearly everything has a compelling energy: the driving four beat; the tight sax and brass riffs, traded back and forth; trumpeter Henry 'Red' Allen's solo, over sax chords and riffs; the fancier sax line, taken up by the brass in the following chorus. Only the anachronistic clarinet trio takes the steam out of the performance, although perhaps this is because of sloppy playing at the end rather than because of the clarinet trio *per se*.

Although Henderson's rhythm section was never the best of its day, this two-volume anthology provides a tidy summary of the development of jazz rhythm sections over the decade. In the 1920s the beat is crisp and clipped, carried by the tuba playing a two beat (on beats 1 and 3) and the banjo playing on all four beats. The piano seems to support the banjo, though it can scarcely be heard. Drummer Kaiser Marshall has little responsibility for keeping time. He may occasionally maintain some steady drum clicks or cymbal crashes, but more often he either participates as a soloist, providing ornamental accents (on *Fidgety Feet* and *Sensation*, for example), or seemingly he does not play at all. The beat gets particularly thin on *Hot Mustard* (1926) and *Have it Ready* (1927). Both arrangements treat the tuba as a member of the brass section rather than as the bass instrument; Henderson plays a brief blues piano solo on *Hot Mustard* and a brief stride solo on *Have it Ready*, but when the rest of the band is playing his left hand cannot possibly cover for the tuba.

Since 1930 John Kirby had been using string bass intermittently on Henderson's recordings, but on all the selections here from 1931 his tuba two-beat rhythm is still present. Now it is set against steady chords from the smooth rhythm guitar (not banjo) and a more prominently recorded piano, all underpinned by Walter Johnson's soft, slightly stiff cymbal patterns. The drummer has fallen much more into the role of a time-keeper, and on *Low Down on the Bayou* (which, incidentally, juxtaposes antiphonal swing riffs and a clarinet trio) Johnson drives the beat as much as Kirby does. The exception in this collection is *Just Blues*, on which the tuba and the chordal instruments pound out the beat, with no drums audible.

The sessions from 1934 offer, with the switch to string bass, a nearly full-blown swing rhythm section. The remaining link to past styles is Elmer James. He has a hard attack, which regularly crosses over into the New Orleans 'slap-bass' technique, but apparently he could not quite handle fast tempos. On *Limehouse Blues*, *Happy as the Day is Long*, *Wild Party* (based on Duke Ellington's recording *Old Man Blues*) and *Hotter Than 'ell* (recorded a year earlier as *Yeah Man!*), James steadfastly maintains a two beat against the ensemble's furious four beat, thus preventing the volcanic energy of these pieces from completely erupting. A comparison with Al Morgan's or Pops

Foster's four-beat playing on the Rhythmakers sides (discussed in Chapter 1) will show what might be done on pieces like these.

Henderson's soloists are always prominent. On the evidence of this collection of recordings, Buster Bailey is the best of the reeds, playing clarinet in a cheery, perpetual motion style that does not change significantly between the mid-1920s and his return to the band in 1934. Hilton Jefferson and Russell Procope's alto saxophone solos are hesitant, polite, unswinging. Coleman Hawkins plays brittle, jerky lines; only his plaintive contribution to *The House of David Blues* in 1931 hints at his coming stature. As a tenor saxophone soloist with the band in 1934, Ben Webster was still young, still trying to hit the right notes.

If the reed soloists are sometimes only passable, the brass are always glorious. The first soloist is Louis Armstrong, playing cornet in 1924, and it is instructive to compare the two versions of *Shanghai Shuffle* – recorded first in 1924, when Armstrong in his muted solo was the only band member who knew how to swing, and then again in 1934, when the whole performance builds upon sectional and ensemble swing rhythms. Apart from Armstrong's contribution, there are longstanding questions of attribution involving Henderson's brass players. For example, over a period of two years Charlie Green, Jimmy Harrison and Benny Morton literally played musical chairs, the three trombonists moving in and out of the two trombone seats. Green, a rough-toned trombonist who may be heard playing in a traditional sliding 'tailgate' manner on *Copenhagen* and in a more melodic fashion on the first *Shanghai Shuffle*, should easily be distinguished from Harrison, a major innovator who preferred higher-pitched, fluid lines. But Morton was capable of striking a middle ground between the two men, and being confused with either. Typifying the resulting abundant argument and confusion is the French MCA reissue, which credits the first trombone solo on *Stockholm Stomp* (1927) to Green, who was not in the band at the time (according to Walter C. Allen's book *Hendersonia: the Music of Fletcher Henderson and his Musicians: a Bio-discography*, Highland Park, NJ, 1973). But it should be remembered that in many instances the brassmen were filling established roles rather than trying to express their individuality. In any event, the solos in question account for only a small percentage of the whole, and generally the liner notes here and on all the other issues I have examined give a reasonable guide to the individual contributions of these three men, as well as those of other related pairs: trombonists Morton and Claude Jones, Jones and Keg Johnson, trumpeters Tommy Ladnier and Joe Smith, trumpeter Bobby Stark and cornetist Rex Stewart, trumpeters Irving 'Mouse' Randolph and Henry 'Red' Allen. It would be easy to get hung up trying to identify the questionable tracks for each one and to miss the point of how great all these players are. Nor would I care, or dare, to list the best brass solos in this collection: there are too many.

LP

USA: *First Impressions, 1924–1931*, **Decca DL9227 and DL79227**

Elmer Chambers, Howard Scott (tpt), Louis Armstrong (c), Charlie Green (tb), Buster Bailey (cl, as), Don Redman (as, cl), Coleman Hawkins (ts, cl), Fletcher Henderson (p), Charlie Dixon (bj), Bob Escudero (bb), Kaiser Marshall (d)
New York   30 Oct 1924   **Copenhagen** (arr Redman)

as **Copenhagen**, *but Buster Bailey (cl, as, ss)*
                    7 Nov 1924   **Shanghai Shuffle** (arr Redman)

as **Copenhagen**, *but Russell Smith, Joe Smith, Tommy Ladnier (tpt) replace Scott, Chambers, Armstrong; June Cole (bb) replaces Escudero*
                    8 Dec 1926   **Clarinet Marmalade** (arr
                                        ?Redman)
                                        Hot Mustard (arr ?Redman)

Benny Morton, Jimmy Harrison (tb) replace Green
                    22 Jan 1927   **Stockholm Stomp**   5
                                        Have it Ready (arr Ken
                                        Macomber)

omit Morton   19 March 1927   **Fidgety Feet**
                                        Sensation

Russell Smith, Joe Smith, Bobby Stark (tpt), Morton, ?Green (tb), Bailey (cl, as), Redman (as), Hawkins (ts), Henderson (p), Dixon (bj), Cole (bb), Marshall (d)
                    14 Sept 1928   **Hop Off**

Russell Smith, Stark (tpt), Rex Stewart (c), Claude Jones, Morton (tb), Russell Procope, Harvey Boone (as, cl), Hawkins (ts), Henderson (p), Clarence Holiday (g), John Kirby (bb), Walter Johnson (d)
                    10 April 1931   **I'm Crazy 'bout my Baby**   10
                                        Sugar Foot Stomp (arr
                                        Henderson)
                                        Just Blues (arr probably
                                        Henderson)
                                        Singin' the Blues (arr probably
                                        Bill Challis)

as **I'm Crazy 'bout my Baby**, *but Edgar Sampson (as, cl, vln) replaces Boone; Hawkins (ts, cl)*
                    17 July 1931   **Low Down on the Bayou**

Other LPs

same contents:
   USA: MCA 1310
   France: MCA 510.035
   Uruguay: Decca DUSL 80503
not incl. **Hop Off** and **Low Down on the Bayou:**
   Germany: *First Impressions*, Coral COPS 3450; MCA Coral 6.21852 AG
incl. tracks 4–6, 8, 10–14, plus tracks cited below:
   UK: *Fletcher Henderson with the Connie's Inn Orchestra*, Ace of Hearts
   AH 41

Cassettes

same contents:
   USA: MCA MCAC 1310
incl. tracks 3–4, 7–14, plus first 2 tracks cited below:
   UK: *Fletcher Henderson Classics*, vol.1, 1925–27, Neovox 709, vol.2,
   1927–31, Neovox 748, vol.3, 1931, Neovox 778

LP
USA: *Swing's the Thing, 1931–1934*, Decca 9228 and 79228

*Russell Smith, Stark (tpt), Rex Stewart (c), Claude Jones, Morton (tb), Russell
Procope, Sampson (as, cl), Hawkins (ts, cl), Henderson (p), Clarence Holiday (g),
John Kirby (bb), Walter Johnson (d)*

New York   17 July 1931   **The House of David Blues**
                                      Radio Rhythm (arr Nat Leslie)

*Russell Smith, Irving 'Mouse' Randolph, Henry 'Red' Allen (tpt), Jones, Keg
Johnson (tb), Bailey (cl), Procope, Hilton Jefferson (as), Ben Webster (ts), Henderson (p), Lawrence Lucie (g), Elmer James (b), Johnson (d)*

              11 Sept 1934   **Limehouse Blues** (arr Benny
                                        Carter)

Horace Henderson replaces Fletcher Henderson (p)
                                 Shanghai Shuffle (arr Fletcher
                                        Henderson)
                               Big John's Special (arr Horace
                                      Henderson)   5
                               Happy as the Day is Long (arr
                                      Carter)

as previous track, but Procope, Jefferson (as, cl), Fletcher Henderson (p)
              12 Sept 1934   **Tidal Wave** (arr Russ Morgan)

> **Down South Camp Meetin'** (arr
> Fletcher Henderson)

Procope, Jefferson (as); Horace replaces Fletcher (p)

> **Wrappin' it up** (arr Fletcher
> Henderson)
> **Memphis Blues** (arr Fletcher
> Henderson)   **10**

25 Sept 1934 **Wild Party** (arr ?Morgan)

Fletcher replaces Horace (p)

> **Rug Cutter's Swing** (arr Horace
> Henderson)
> **Hotter Than 'ell** (arr Horace
> Henderson)

add Benny Carter (as); Fletcher and Horace Henderson alternate (p)

> **Liza**

Other LPs

same contents:
  USA: MCA 1318
  France: MCA 510.060
  Italy: Coral COPS 1912
  Uruguay: Decca SUDL 80512
incl. tracks 1–2, plus some tracks cited above:
  UK: *Fletcher Henderson with the Connie's Inn Orchestra*, Ace of Hearts
  AH 41
tracks 3–14:
  UK: *Fletcher Henderson 1934*, Ace of Hearts AH 61; Wild Party!, Hep 1009
incl. tracks 1–2:
  UK: *Yeah Man!*, Hep 1016; *Blue Rhythm July 1931 to March 1932*, VJM VLP
  64

Cassettes

same contents:
  USA: MCA MCAC 1318

Duke Ellington: *Early Ellington; The Blanton–Webster Band*

In 1924, while Henderson was working at the Roseland Ballroom and, owing to Louis Armstrong's presence in the band, almost immediately making a huge impact, Duke Ellington settled in a couple of blocks away at the Kentucky Club. There, somewhat more gradually, he organized what would soon become, and remain, the greatest of the big bands. His orchestra's rich and substantial legacy of recordings spanned a half century, and the selections here are drawn from his two best series of studio sessions, both made for the Victor label. The first captures the band while it was playing at the Cotton Club and traces its growth into the mid-1930s. The second dates from the early 1940s, when the swing era was in full bloom.

From the start of its tenure at the Cotton Club, Ellington's then ten-piece big band was not, like Henderson's, playing mainly for patrons to dance to. Instead the group supplied music for shows, and out of these shows there developed an unforgettable style of pseudo-Africana known as 'jungle music'. The pivotal figure in this new style was trumpeter Bubber Miley, who may be heard on these early Victor recordings playing in a distinctive 'growl-and-plunger' blues style: it involved a vocal growl to intensify the instrument's tone, and a toilet plunger mute to achieve wa-wa effects.

Miley's manner of using this technique yielded the first of the extraordinary sounds that helped make Ellington's orchestra so special, and it spread into the band's performances in other ways. Tricky Sam Nanton transferred the technique directly to the trombone, and using it he remained one of the orchestra's principal soloists for many years. Nanton may be heard, for example, on *Black and Tan Fantasie*, between Ellington's nimble stride piano solo and Miley's striking, stuttering return. Fleetingly, Adelaide Hall duplicated Miley as well. After Ellington heard her impromptu imitation, he organized *Creole Love Call*, on which the first 'instrument' is Hall's voice. (Hall's other piece in this collection, *The Blues I Love to Sing*, is unimportant, yet interesting, if only to remind us of how far her normal vaudeville voice was from this marvellous and freakish blues sound.) Later, when Miley left the band, his successors were expected to adopt some version of the growl-and-plunger approach. It is worth noting that there has been some dispute over the identity of the soloist who begins and ends *The Mooche*. Apparently Miley was absent, and at the session of 30 October 1928 Freddie Jenkins was in his chair. Whoever the soloist is, if it is not Miley, he is imitating Miley.

There were other elements to jungle music, though none as essential as Miley's contribution. These include a heightened emphasis on minor harmonies, as in the opening strains of *Black and Tan Fantasie*, *East St Louis Toodle-oo* and *The Mooche*; Harry Carney's dark, cutting baritone saxophone, which leads his section mates from below on *East St Louis Toodle-oo*; and such 'exotic' sounds as the mysterious chord that ends *Creole Love Call*, the clarinet trio's harmonized descent from a screaming chord on *The Mooche* and, also on *The Mooche*, the combination of Barney Bigard's low-register clarinet and Sonny Greer's temple blocks (a 'clip-clop' sound). The blocks, incidentally, were but one of the vast array of items found in Greer's drum kit, which he designed to contribute visually as well as aurally to the jungle shows.

Separate from these features, but equally crucial to the band's early success, was Wellman Braud's string bass playing, which the Victor engineers recorded extremely well. Braud took two approaches, neither of which proved to be the preferred manner of bop bassists, but nonetheless in his hands the results were impressive. On *Black and Tan Fantasie* he bows the instrument, which ends up sounding much like a tuba, though slightly smoother. On *Washington Wobble* he plucks it, using the hot and driving slap-bass technique associated with New Orleans players (of which Braud was one). His solo bass breaks on *Black Beauty* foreshadow later developments, discussed below.

On the earliest of these pieces, Ellington and his men were still feeling their way towards a command of formal elements, so that all these marvels would hang together. *Creole Love Call* ducks the issue by presenting the jungle sounds over a beautifully expressed but utterly simple blues riff, which passes through the orchestra. But both *Black and Tan Fantasie* and *East St Louis Toodle-oo* attempt to juxtapose greatly varied themes. While in principle this need not be a drawback, in these instances the juxtapositions are jolting. With *The Mooche*, Ellington achieved for the first of many times a perfect balance between composition and improvisation, ensemble and individual, repetition and contrast. This piece rewards listening not only for all of the details already mentioned, but also for its formal gracefulness and logic. And it introduces yet another mainstay of the orchestra, Johnny Hodges, here playing alto saxophone in a dialogue with the Mileyesque trumpeter.

As the 1930s arrived, the band was gradually growing in size, its long stand at the Cotton Club was coming to an end and the 'jungle' star, Miley, had been gone for over a year – Cootie Williams having taken over that chair. All three pieces from the decade's beginning – *Ring dem Bells*, *Old Man Blues* and *Mood Indigo* – exemplify strong, well-conceived, satisfying big-band compositions. The last, *Mood Indigo*, is another landmark in the band's history, as a muted trumpet, muted trombone and clarinet present a deliberate, velvety, sad theme in phrases of magically inspired orchestration and harmony. The anthology closes in 1934 with *Solitude*, which marries the feeling and orchestration of *Mood Indigo* to one of the most complex popular ballad melodies in the jazz repertory.

The next and even greater burst of masterpieces came in the years 1940–

42. These have been comprehensively reissued in a large anthology, **The Blanton–Webster Band**. At this point the band had 15 musicians, including cornetist Rex Stewart (whose mid-1930s achievements should not be missed, although with these two collections they fall between the cracks), as well as Williams, Nanton, Bigard, Hodges, Carney and Greer. Alongside them were string bassist Jimmy Blanton and tenor saxophonist Ben Webster. In the less than two years that Blanton remained a member, before succumbing to tuberculosis, he set new standards for the jazz bass, not only by filling roles that would previously have been given to a more conventionally melodic instrument, but more importantly by combining for the first time a fullness of tone, an ability to sustain pizzicato notes, a firmness of rhythm, an assured command of harmonically correct bass lines and a tuneful manner of executing those lines. Webster, no longer the halting voice heard on Henderson's big-band sides from 1934, had become one of the music's greatest soloists. A serious rival to Coleman Hawkins and Lester Young, he combined the former's intensity and arabesques with the latter's gentleness and melodiousness.

By 1940, long-term show work was years in the past, and it was touring that supported and would continue to support Ellington for the remainder of his career. But the jungle-music style had not died along with the shows. In fact, it reached its highest peak in *Ko-Ko*, a moody, seething piece. *Ko-Ko* begins with Carney's baritone sax and Greer's tom-tom droning together against a trombone riff. The body of the piece is a progression of increasingly urgent minor-key blues choruses. First, ascending saxophone chords and du-wah plunger-muted brass support Nanton's 'ya-ya' mute and plunger solo. Nanton yields to weird, atonal flourishes from Ellington's piano, and then the brass take over the sax riff, building to a series of breaks for Blanton's solo bass, and then to a climactic full ensemble chorus.

Concerto for Cootie was a feature for Williams at a time when he was about to end his lengthy first stay with Ellington. (He re-joined in the 1960s and 1970s.) If the melody seems familiar it may be because it reached a wider audience three years later, when it was regularized and popularized, with lyrics, as *Do Nothin' Till You Hear from Me*. The complex original composition, recorded shortly after *Ko-Ko* in March 1940, is noteworthy above all as a study in jazz trumpet timbres and effects. The introduction has Williams using his plunger, pressed tightly over a small straight mute. He plays the first theme (unusually, ten bars long, not eight or 12) with the plunger partially open, but on the theme's repetitions he pushes it back in tightly. Initially, on held notes, he adds a rapid, quivering effect that lies somewhere between vibrato and a 'shake' (a trill between non-adjacent pitches), and for the contrasting section of the first theme he adds a growl. Then, as Ellington moves the piece into a new key, presenting a bright new theme, Williams plays mainly with an open tone, though he also squeezes out notes in expressive upward glides. The first theme, with its characteristic timbres, returns to end the number.

Having once absorbed Williams's achievement, the listener might focus on Blanton. Regularly the bassist leaves aside a conventional walking rhythm to participate instead as a companion to the brass and reeds. He plays along exactly with their arranged lines and riffs, and he adds a little solo that bridges the movement from the bright second theme back to the first.

Shortly after recording these two demonstrations of big-band jazz as a high art, Ellington's orchestra showed that it was also a force to be reckoned with for earthy jazz. Certain artistic elements of *Cotton Tail* should not be missed, especially the careful way in which Ben Webster crafts his solo to build in intensity and to interlock with the brass punches, and also the virtuosic sax chorus he wrote. But the real point of the piece is its tremendous, toe-tapping swing, in which Blanton and Greer play no small part.

Never No Lament, recorded at the same session as *Cotton Tail*, started life earlier, as a counter-melody to a piece Ellington had recorded in 1938, *I Let a Song Go out of my Heart*. By 1940 it had taken on a life of its own, and, as with *Concerto for Cootie*, the instrumental *Never No Lament* was popularized and rereleased with lyrics a couple of years later, under the new title *Don't Get Around Much Any More*. The highlight of the 1940 Victor recording is Johnny Hodges's luscious alto saxophone chorus, in which he gently paraphrases the melody.

Harlem Air Shaft is yet another brilliantly orchestrated piece. It dances between swinging simplicity and arty complexity, both in its form and its accompanimental figures. Deceptively, the theme sounds as if it is a blues, but it breaks off after eight bars, which then prove to be the first eight of a standard 32-bar *aaba* song form (not a 12-bar blues). As often in Ellington's music, the accompanimental figures seek a balance between repeated riffs and arranged lines. These figures introduce and support a succession of greatly contrasting solos that typify the band's personalities: Nanton, presenting his du-wah effects with mute and plunger; alternately Williams, dominating with his open trumpet sound while Greer's drums kick him along, and Bigard, weaving his clarinet around reed riffs; Williams again, now muted and almost underneath the quiet ensemble; and finally Bigard, wailing away in his highest register.

These marvels, from *Ko-Ko* through *Harlem Air Shaft*, had been recorded in the space of four and a half months. The band's prolific sessions for Victor continued, and if, understandably, neither this orchestra nor any other ever matched this flurry of big-band jazz masterpieces, there would still be plenty of outstanding sides, of which the most important from the Blanton–Webster period are *In a Mellotone*, *Take the 'A' Train* and *Perdido*, the last dating from January 1942, not long after Blanton's illness had forced him to resign. On all three of these, Carney's rollicking baritone sax takes charge of laying out the melody, either with the section, or alone. These melodies are catchy, and the harmonies of *Take the 'A' Train* and *Perdido* made both of these into perennial jam session favourites. But, as usual with Ellington's recordings, casual jamming is not the point of the originals, which pay great attention to detail – as, for example, in the ornate, harmonized trombone lines that serve as a commentary on the melody of *In a Mellotone*. The memorable ensemble writing in *Take the 'A' Train* includes a transitional passage that momentarily moves into a waltz rhythm and – towards the end of Ray Nance's widely imitated trumpet solo – a fleeting, dissonant pyramid of sound that announces the melody's return. *Take the 'A' Train* caused Ellington some good-humoured grief in later years, because it became closely associated with him, probably more so than any other piece. But – as he was quick to point out – he did not write it. It is the work of Billy Strayhorn, a quiet, devoted man who from 1939 until his death in 1967 served as Ellington's second pianist and associate arranger and composer.

These two anthologies include neither such landmarks as singer Ivie Anderson's rendition of *It Don't Mean a Thing if it Ain't Got That Swing* (recorded in 1932) and Mary Lou Williams's tremendously exciting arrangement of *Blue Skies*, titled *Trumpets No End* (recorded in 1946), nor the dozens of 'lesser' masterpieces which might head the list were we listening to any other big band. Indeed, while making sure not to miss Count Basie's big band of 1937–8, one might take a different route into big-band jazz from the approach detailed in this chapter: just go out and buy 15 or 20 Duke Ellington collections.

CD
USA: *Early Ellington*, **Bluebird 6852-2 RB**

Bubber Miley, Louis Metcalf (tpt), Tricky Sam Nanton (tb), Otto Hardwick (ss, as, bar), Harry Carney (cl, as, bar), Rudy Jackson (cl, ts), Duke Ellington (p), Fred Guy (bj), Wellman Braud (sb), Sonny Greer (d), Adelaide Hall (v)

| Camden, NJ | 26 Oct 1927 | **Creole Love Call** |
| | | **The Blues I Love to Sing** (take 2) |

omit (v)		**Black and Tan Fantasie**
		Washington Wobble
New York	19 Dec 1927	**East St Louis Toodle-oo** (take 2) 5

Arthur Whetsol (tpt) replaces Metcalf, Barney Bigard (cl, ts) replaces Jackson

| | 26 March 1928 | **Black Beauty** |

Whetsol, Freddie Jenkins (tpt), Nanton (tb), Johnny Hodges (cl, ss, as), Carney (cl, as, bar), Bigard (cl, ts), Ellington (p), Guy (bj), Braud (bb), Greer (d)

	30 Oct 1928	**The Mooche**	

add Miley (tpt); Braud (sb, not bb)

	16 Jan 1929	**Flaming Youth** (take 2)	
		Saturday Night Function	

Cootie Williams (tpt) replaces Miley

	3 May 1929	**Cotton Club Stomp**	10

add Williams (v), Juan Tizol (valve tb), Charlie Barnet (chimes)

Hollywood	20 Aug 1930	**Ring dem Bells** (take 3)	

omit (v) and (chimes)

	26 Aug 1930	**Old Man Blues** (take 6)	
New York	10 Dec 1930	**Mood Indigo**	
	16 Jan 1931	**Rockin' in Rhythm** (take 1)	
Camden, NJ	11 June 1931	**Creole Rhapsody**	15
	16 June 1931	**Echoes of the Jungle**	

add Louis Bacon (tpt); Lawrence Brown (tb) replaces Tizol; add Hardwick (cl, as, bass sax)

Chicago	4 Dec 1933	**Daybreak Express**	
	9 Jan 1934	**Delta Serenade**	
		Stompy Jones	

add Tizol (valve tb)

	10 Jan 1934	**Solitude**	20

Other CDs

same contents:
   Europe: RCA Bluebird ND 86852
   Japan: Victor B20D-47007

LPs

plus additional tracks:
   France: *The Works of Duke Ellington*, vol.1–3, 5–6, 8, RCA 731.043,
   741.028, 741.029, 741.048, 741.068, 741.114
plus additional tracks:
   Jazz Tribune no.21: The Indispensable Duke Ellington, vols.1/2 and
   Jazz Tribune no.28: The Indispensable Duke Ellington, vols.3/4
   Europe: RCA NL 89749 and NL 89762

France: RCA PM 43687 and PM 43696
plus additional tracks, with take 6 of track 11:
  Japan: *Duke Ellington Story, vol.I*, RCA RA 30-RA 35
tracks 1, 3, 5–8, 11–17, 19–20: *Early Ellington*
  USA: Bluebird 6852-1 R
  Europe: RCA Bluebird NL 86852
incl. tracks 1–2, 5, 8, 10–11, 14:
  France: *Duke Ellington et son Orchestre, 1927–1931*, RCA 430666
incl. tracks 1–2, 5–9:
  Japan: *Flaming Youth*, Victor RA 5299
incl. tracks 3–7, 10–11, 14–15:
  USA: *Mood Indigo*, Camden ADL 2-0152
incl. tracks 1–3, 5–8: *Flaming Youth*
  USA: RCA LPV 568
  UK: RCA RD 8089
  Germany: RCA LPM 568
  Italy: RCA LPM 34049
incl. tracks 1–7, 10–13 (some different versions):
  Italy: *Duke Ellington and His Orchestra, 1927–1930*, Giants of Jazz LPJT 35
incl. tracks 1, 3, 5, 7, 11 (take 6), 13, 18, 20, plus tracks cited below:
  This is Duke Ellington
  USA: RCA VPM 6042 and VPS 6042-1/2
  Germany: RCA 26.28036 DP; RCA NL 89234
incl. tracks 1, 3, 6, 11 (take 6):
  USA: *Giants of Jazz: Duke Ellington*, Time-Life STL J02
incl. tracks 16–20: *Daybreak Express*
  USA: RCA LPV 506
  Germany: RCA LPM 506
  Italy: RCA LPM 34078

Cassettes

plus additional tracks:
  Europe: *Jazz Tribune no.21: The Indispensable Duke Ellington, vols.1/2*
  and *Jazz Tribune no.28: The Indispensable Duke Ellington, vols.3/4*,
  RCA NK 89749 and NK 89762
tracks 1, 3, 5–8, 11–17, 19–20: *Early Ellington*
  USA: Bluebird 6852-4-R
  Europe: RCA Bluebird NK 86852
incl. tracks 1–9:
  UK: *The Early Classics*, vol.1, Neovox 725
incl. tracks 1–7, 10–13 (some different versions):
  Italy: *Duke Ellington and His Orchestra, 1927–1930*, Giants of Jazz MCJT 35

CD

USA: *The Blanton–Webster Band,* **Bluebird 5659-2 RB**

Wallace Jones, Williams (tpt), Rex Stewart (c), Nanton, Brown (tb), Tizol (valve tb), Bigard (cl), Hodges (cl, ss, as), Carney (cl, as, bar), Hardwick (as, bass sax), Ben Webster (ts), Guy (g), Ellington (p), Jimmy Blanton (sb), Greer (d), Herb Jeffries (v)

Chicago	6 March 1940	**You, You Darlin'**	
omit (v)		**Jack the Bear**	
		Ko-Ko	
		Morning Glory	
Add Ivie Anderson (v)		**So Far, So Good**	5
omit (v)	15 March 1940	**Conga Brava**	
		Concerto for Cootie (Do Nothin' Till You Hear from Me)	
add Anderson (v)		**Me and You**	
omit (v)			
Hollywood	4 May 1940	**Cotton Tail**	
		Never No Lament (Don't Get Around Much Any More)	10
Chicago	28 May 1940	**Dusk**	
		Bojangles (A Portrait of Bill Robinson)	
		A Portrait of Bert Williams	
		Blue Goose	
New York	22 July 1940	**Harlem Air Shaft (Rumpus in Richmond)**	15
add Anderson (v)		**At a Dixie Roadside Diner**	
omit (v)		**All too Soon**	
		Rumpus in Richmond (Brasserie)	
	24 July 1940	**My Greatest Mistake**	
		Sepia Panorama (Night House)	20
add Jeffries (v)			
Chicago	5 Sept 1940	**There Shall Be No Night**	

omit (v)		In a Mellotone	
add Anderson (v)		Five O'Clock Whistle	
omit (v)	17 Oct 1940	Warm Valley	
		The Flaming Sword	25
	28 Oct 1940	Across the Track Blues	
		Chloe (Song of the Swamp)	
add Jeffries (v)		I Never Felt This Way Before	

Ray Nance (tpt, vln) replaces Williams

	28 Dec 1940	Sidewalks of New York	

Billy Strayhorn (p) replaces Ellington; add Jeffries (v)

		Flamingo	30

Ellington (p) replaces Strayhorn

		The Girl in my Dreams Tries to Look Like You	

omit (v)			
Hollywood	15 Feb 1941	Take the 'A' Train	
		Jumpin' Punkins	
		John Hardy's Wife	
		Blue Serge	35

Strayhorn (p) replaces Ellington   After All

Ellington (p) replaces Strayhorn

	5 June 1941	Bakiff	
		Are You Sticking?	
		Just a-Settin' and a-Rockin'	
		The Giddybug Gallop	40

add Anderson (v)

	26 June 1941	Chocolate Shake	
		I Got it Bad and That Ain't Good	

omit (v)	2 July 1941	Clementine	
add Jeffries (v)		The Brown Skin Gal (in the Calico Gown)	
		Jump for Joy	45

omit (v)		**Moon over Cuba (Puerto Rican Gal)**
	26 Sept 1941	**Five O'Clock Drag**

Strayhorn (p) replaces Ellington; add Anderson (v)
Rocks in my Bed

Ellington (p) replaces Strayhorn, Nance (v) replaces Anderson
Bli-Blip

Strayhorn (p) replaces Ellington, Junior Raglin (sb) replaces Blanton; omit (v)
2 Dec 1941   **Chelsea Bridge**   50

Ellington (p) replaces Strayhorn   **Raincheck**

Strayhorn (p) replaces Ellington; add Jeffries (v)
What Good Would it Do?

Ellington (p) replaces Strayhorn   **I Don't Know What Kind of Blues I Got**

omit (v)
Chicago   21 Jan 1942   **Perdido**
                                     The 'C' Jam Blues   55
                                     Moon Mist (Atmosphere)
New York   26 Feb 1942   **What Am I Here For?**

add Anderson (v)   **I Don't Mind**

omit (v)   **Someone (You've Got my Heart)**

Strayhorn (p) replaces Ellington; add Jeffries (v)
Hollywood   26 June 1942   **My Little Brown Book**   60

Ellington (p) replaces Strayhorn; omit (v)
Main Stem (Altitude)

Strayhorn (p) replaces Ellington   **Johnny Come Lately**

Chauncey Haughton (cl) replaces Bigard, Ellington (p) replaces Strayhorn; Add Anderson (v)
Chicago   28 July 1942   **Hayfoot, Strawfoot**

omit (v)   **Sentimental Lady (Someone)**

add Nance (v)   **A Slip of the Lip (Me and my**
                                              Wig)   **65**

omit (v)   **Sherman Shuffle (Fussy Puss)**

Other CDs

same contents:
   Europe: Bluebird PD 85659

LPs

same contents:
   USA: Bluebird 5659-1 RB
   Europe: Bluebird PL 85659
plus additional tracks:
   France: *The Works of Duke Ellington*, vol.9–12, 14–18, RCA FPM 1-7002,
   FPM 1-7047, FXM 1-7072, FXM 1-7094, FXM 1-7134, FXM 1-7135, FXM
   1-7201, FXM 1-7274, FXM 1-7301
incl. tracks 2–4, 6–7, 9–18, 20, 22–4, 26–7, 29: *Jazz Tribune no.33: the*
   Indispensible Duke Ellington, vols.5/6, 1940
   Europe: RCA NL 89750
   France: RCA PM 45352
tracks 32–6, 38–45, 47–51, 53–66:
   Europe: *Jazz Tribune no.55: the Indispensible Duke Ellington, vols.*
   7/8, 1941–1942, RCA NL 89274
tracks 9, 13, 17–18, 20, 22, 25, 32, 35, 39, 42, 48, 53–4, 57, 61: *In a*
   Mellotone
   USA: RCA LPM 1364
   UK: RCA RD 27134; RCA LSA 3069
   Germany: RCA LPM 1364 C
   Australia: RCA L 10020
tracks 4, 11, 34, 37–8, 40, 43, 46–7, 50, 55–6: *The Duke and his Men*
   USA: LPM 1092
   France: RCA 430.227
incl. tracks 2–3, 7, 15, 24, 26–7: *At his Very Best*
   USA: RCA LPM 1715
   UK: RCA RD 27133; RCA LSA 3071
incl. tracks 4, 10, 12, 50–51, 64 (alternate take): *The Indispensible Duke*
   Ellington
   USA: RCA LPM 6009
   UK: RCA RD 27258 and RD 27259

incl. tracks 2–3, 7, 9–10, 15, 22, 24, 32, 42, 54–5:
USA: *Giants of Jazz: Duke Ellington*, Time-Life STL J02
incl. tracks 6–7, 9–10, 13, 22, 24, 32, 54–5:
Italy: *Duke Ellington and his Orchestra: the Fabulous Forties*, Giants of
Jazz LPJT 66
incl. tracks 7, 9–10, 32, 42, 54–5, plus tracks cited above:
This is Duke Ellington
USA: RCA VPM 6042 and VPS 6042-1/2
Germany: RCA 26.28036; RCA NL 89234

Cassettes

incl. tracks 2–4, 6–7, 9–18, 20, 22–4, 26–7, 29:
Europe: *Jazz Tribune no.33: the Indispensible Duke Ellington, vols.
5/6, 1940*, RCA NK 89750
tracks 32–6, 38–45, 47–51, 53–66:
Europe: *Jazz Tribune no.55: the Indispensible Duke Ellington, vols.
7/8, 1941–1942*, RCA NK 89274
incl. tracks 6–7, 9–10, 13, 22, 24, 32, 54–5:
Italy: *Duke Ellington and his Orchestra: the Fabulous Forties*, Giants of
Jazz MCJT 66

* * *

Bennie Moten: *Bennie Moten's Kansas City Orchestra: Basie's Beginnings*; Count Basie: *The Best of Count Basie; Lester Leaps In; April in Paris*

While New York served as the base of operations for two of the three most innovative jazz big bands – those of Duke Ellington and Fletcher Henderson – the third, Count Basie's, developed gradually out of territory bands based in southwestern and midwestern states. In the late 1920s the principal rivals were Walter Page's Blue Devils and Bennie Moten's Kansas City Orchestra. Moten settled the contest by raiding Page's ranks. By the time of the 1929 sessions for Victor, he had hired Basie. (He had also hired two past Blue Devils and future Basie sidemen: trombonist, guitarist and arranger Eddie Durham and saxophonist Jack Washington.) By the 1930 recordings, he had acquired trumpeter Hot Lips Page (no relation to Walter or to Vernon Page, the tuba player on these sessions) and singer Jimmy Rushing. Finally, by 1932 he had hired Walter himself, whose string bass replaced the tuba.

These recordings look forward not only to future affiliations under Basie's name, but also to aspects of Basie's future style, most notably through Rushing's blues singing, the role played by Hot Lips Page, and the interlocking sectional riffs and relaxed swing of the 1932 session. They also point, in two unusually successful formal designs and in some details of arranging, in directions Basie would never pursue. But the main attraction of Moten's recordings is their sheer delightfulness, in which old-fashioned and simple elements play just as big a role as forward-looking and complex ones. I have even come to love the quirky bits: Buster Moten's hot accordion, with a tone like a thin version of a calliope on a merry-go-round; clarinettist Woodie Walder's violently clipped notes; Rushing's vaudeville style, with a heavy, fast vibrato, on the non-blues numbers. (Incidentally, Buster Moten should not be confused with bandleader Bennie, who may have been Buster's brother or uncle.)

On the sessions from 1929 and 1930, the rhythm section is like a gracefully dancing fat man, somehow chunky and light at the same time, the tuba and bass drum's two beat rocking back and forth against the banjo and cymbal, with Basie's striding left hand supporting them all. (When I'm Alone has a tuba four beat rollicking through much of it.)

The best of the soloists are Hot Lips Page, Basie and Rushing. Page is by far the most consistent and mature instrumentalist in the band, creating unhurried, swinging lines. He plays mainly muted, bluesy wa-wa melodies (as does the lesser-known trumpeter Booker Washington at the opening sessions, on *The Jones Law Blues* and *New Vine Street Blues*). Basie at the time remained strongly under the influence of the busy stride piano style he had learned in New York, as heard on *Small Black* (some issues present a composite of two takes, spliced together to extend the piano solo) and also on *Rit-Dit-Ray*. Rushing's voice is slightly thinner than it would become, but at the time of this date he was already a great blues shouter, in touch with the inflections, urgency and emotion of down-home blues singing and yet comfortable with its translation into jazz. When he sings 'Good morning blues, blues how do you do?' and 'Sent for you yesterday, baby here you come today' in his two choruses on *That Too, Do*, everything that would be heard in Basie's orchestra is already in place.

Two unusual formal designs work well. *The Jones Law Blues* is made of three parts: a 'jungle-style' section built almost entirely on two minor chords; 12-bar blues solos by alto saxophonist Harlan Leonard and trombonist Thamon Hayes, each followed by a four-bar interlude; and a 16-bar spiritual, with a chord progression resembling that of *When the Saints Go Marching in*. The parts then repeat in reverse order, with the four-bar interlude preceding Basie's florid blues solo. *That Too, Do* is a 12-bar blues, but each of the first two choruses are followed by an eight-bar contrasting section, for Buster Moten's accordion solo and then for Basie.

There are also many clever touches of the arranger's hand. *Won't You be my Baby?* includes imitation between Hayes's trombone and the other brass (following Rushing's vocal), and the surprising sound of a vibraphone on the last note of the piece. *Oh! Eddie* has a similar imitation between accordion and brass (after Basie's solo); this leads to a single line chopped into pieces and divided between the saxophones and the brass, and then to the tremendous ending, which tosses about a three-beat figure played by the full ensemble (twice), then piano, reeds, brass, tuba, reeds again and full ensemble once more. *That Too, Do* uses the baritone sax as a bass instrument, playing an ostinato line against the rhythm section at the introduction and the ending; and Rushing makes his voice a part of the band's punctuation of Hot Lips Page's stop-time blues chorus.

The session in 1932 followed numerous changes in personnel, and it was made in the midst of a debilitating tour east and back home, by the end of which the band had begun to disintegrate. In spite of these circumstances the first three of ten titles recorded that day are marvels of big band swing, setting the model for the rhythm, riff and solo style of Basie's future group. *Toby*, *Moten Swing* and *The Blue Room* focus on riffs, which alternate with, support and sometimes bury the soloists, this last effect being not necessarily a fault, since the good, but less than consistently outstanding, quality of the soloists (excepting trumpeter Page) is one thing that *does* separate Moten's band from Basie's. Driven by Walter Page's four-beat string bass lines, the rhythm section is clean and flowing even at the very rapid tempo of *Toby*, and the saxophones are equally comfortable with their florid riffs set against brass punches. There is an incredible kick, another of the great moments in jazz, when, after Basie's stride piano solo on *Toby*, Page's bass and the riffs re-enter. Other exhilarating moments include, on *The Blue Room*, the smooth swing supporting Hot Lips Page's solo, with Basie's piano plinking away, and the coordinated effect of riffs and a strong cymbal backbeat at the end.

Basie did not record again for nearly four years, during which a pool of a few dozen musicians formed and re-formed under several leaders before crystallizing, a year after Moten's death in 1935, into a band which under Basie's leadership presented the Kansas City jazz style in its fullest glory. Because the myriad issues of Basie's recordings present *ad hoc* small combo sessions together with the regular work of the big band, and because Basie's style transferred effortlessly from one size of group to the other, it seems best to break the pattern of the book and discuss both together in this chapter. (Other swing combos, some including Basie's sidemen, appear in subsequent chapters.)

After signing a disadvantageous contract with Decca, Basie brought an instrumental quintet, plus Rushing, into a Vocalion studio in November 1936 to record under the conveniently anonymous pseudonym Jones–Smith Inc. The former was drummer Jo Jones, who, with Basie and Page, made up the rhythm section. The latter was trumpeter Carl Smith (substituting for Buck Clayton), who was joined in the front line by the big band's star soloist, tenor saxophonist Lester Young (yet another former member of Page's Blue Devils). Among the results was *Lady be Good*, which has one of Lester Young's finest solos, if not the finest. Holding nothing back, the big band then made a string of great recordings for Decca from 1937 to February 1939; towards the end were a couple of less significant combo sessions. The anthologies conclude with recordings for Vocalion and Okeh (which became subsidiaries of Columbia), including a renowned session by Basie's Kansas City Seven. By the time of an uninspired remake of *Moten Swing*, the compositional weight of the group's performances had switched from an emphasis on improvised solos and casually made (though spectacularly played) riffs to a less successful emphasis on formal arrangement.

On these recordings Basie's groups carry the rhythm, riff and solo style developed under Moten to its highest possible level. The orchestra's *Swingin' at the Daisy Chain* represents a distinctive tune type, an *aaba* form with the *a* section built on top of a bass line that repeatedly walks down through a portion of a minor scale. But, otherwise, the formal bases of these performances are not meant to be interesting in themselves, since they draw their life from a flexible simplicity. Invariably the best tracks are built on conventional pop song forms and blues progressions.

The rhythm section is the best of its era, its understated approach generating tremendous propulsion and swing. Occasionally – as in his solo on *Swingin' the Blues* – Jones shows his command of the extroverted school of swing drumming. Still less often he goes in for special effects, as in the phrases played on temple blocks at the end of Clayton's muted wa-wa solo on *Swingin' at the Daisy Chain* and again during the intentionally corny statement of the theme of *Twelfth Street Rag*. In the main he is a subtle drummer, concentrating on coaxing a metronomical, dancing beat from his cymbals. It is Jones's sensitive musicality that allows this band to produce many shades of volume, with sudden shifts from a roar to softness, and with endings that gradually fade away. Page is the same steady bass player he had been all along. He is supported beat by beat by guitarist Freddie Green, whose strumming, more felt than heard, comes through fairly clearly at the start of *Swingin' the Blues*. Repeatedly, Basie begins tunes alone; indeed, this was one of his most important functions, for he was acclaimed for his ability always to set the perfect tempo. As an accompanist he still provides moments of stride playing, as he had done with Moten, but now, four years later, he prefers to drop intermittent chordal accents into the rhythmic flow set up by the other three men. He carries this restraint to such an extent that, on some performances (especially the latter part of the combo recording *Lester Leaps in*), what might be construed as a piano solo is actually just a rhythmic groove focusing on the beat, not on making a melody.

The riffs work well enough in the combo performances, and on *Shoe Shine Boy* Young's subtone riff (produced in the lowest range of the instrument) is so compelling that it distracts attention from Smith's trumpet solo. But no individual instrument can match the sectional riffing in the big band. *One O'Clock Jump* exemplifies this approach, in which repeated tidbits of swinging melody either serve as accompanimental figures or interlock with other tidbits to form themes in and of themselves. It begins with Basie's boogie-woogie piano setting the tempo, with firm but quiet support from the rhythm section. After two choruses of blues, an abrupt change of key marks the beginning of the riffs. These have been carefully chosen to provide timbral contrast to the soloist: muted brass against Herschel Evans's tenor sax, saxes against trombonist George Hunt, biting brass against Young's tenor sax, saxes against trumpeter Clayton. Basie sets up the rhythmic groove once again, to place in relief the final three blues choruses of band riffs, in which trombone and trumpet punctuations repeat against a saxophone part that changes with each new chorus. The equally famous *Jumpin' at the Woodside*, which finds Young at the top of his form, shows how the band applied the same approach to a popular song form rather than blues. Typically, the musicians invent an outstanding series of riffs which change chorus by chorus, but this effort is concentrated on the *a* sections of the *aaba* structure. They do not bother to come up with riffs for the *b* sections, but instead give these over for contrast to a soloist alone with the rhythm. Then, at the end, the riffs continue to keep up the level of excitement; during the second half of the first chorus of Herschel Evans's clarinet solo this last section of the piece includes as one of the trombone riffs a startlingly violent upward gliss, like an elephant trumpeting.

With this rhythmic, riffing support, a stream of star instrumentalists, and Rushing, walk up to the microphone. The most original and creative is Lester Young. Apart from noting that in its upper range his clarinet tone on *Blue and Sentimental* and *Texas Shuffle* is screechy (as is Evans's clarinet on *Jumpin' at the Woodside*), there is not much point in citing his best solos. As a tenor saxophonist he is consistently great. His soft, vibratoless sound and tunefully melodic approach offered the first significant alternative to Coleman Hawkins's conception of the instrument. An endlessly imaginative improviser, Young – just like the rhythm section – swings madly in a subtle way. With the aim of propelling the rhythm forward, at times he simplifies his melodies, perhaps oscillating between two notes, or changing the timbre of one, or starting emphatically and unexpectedly right on a down beat; towards that same goal, he made complex, asymmetrical melodies, weaving his lines through conventional phrase divisions with a fluency that few other soloists have ever matched. (Many players did, though, copy his patented use of false fingerings to alter a note's timbre, heard for example at his entrance on *Jumpin' at the Woodside* and in the midst of his equally great improvisation on *Lester Leaps in*.)

By reputation Young engaged in battles with Herschel Evans, a player influenced by Hawkins. But on these recordings there are none of the phrase-by-phrase confrontations which would appear in later battles of the tenors in bop and hard bop (see Chapter 7). For example, Evans is the only tenor soloist on *Swingin' at the Daisy Chain*, *Sent for You Yesterday* and *Texas Shuffle*. He plays separately from and before Young on *One O'Clock Jump*, *John's Idea* and *Doggin' Around*, separately from and after him on *Swingin' the Blues*. Moreover, on his ballad feature, *Blue and Sentimental*, Evans shows an individual sound falling between that of Hawkins and Young in his use of a slow, soft vibrato and a tone which is gentle but still has a slight edge. Nor – during Evans's last illness – were there immediate head-to-head battles with his temporary replacement Chu Berry, who plays before the trumpet solo on *Lady be Good* (Young follows trumpeter Shad Collins), or – after Evans's death early in 1939 – with his replacement Buddy Tate. The latter plays his first and best solo with the band on *Rock-a-Bye Basie*, is the first tenor heard in the trade with band riffs (*not* a trade between tenors) on *Taxi War Dance*, and again plays alone on *Jump for Me*, this time sounding more like Young than Hawkins!

With the strong tenors, there is little room left for baritone saxophonist Jack Washington. Among his infrequent but excellent solos, the best is *Topsy*.

Earle Warren, an accomplished lead alto saxophonist, takes occasional undistinguished solos. There is a devastating contrast between his attempt to create ideas at the rapid tempo of *Clap Hands, Here Comes Charlie* and Lester Young's following demonstration of how it is done. (On the other hand, not even Young dared try the *b* section of *Cherokee*, which is omitted altogether during the second half of this two-part, six-minute performance; at the time of Basie's recording, Charlie Parker was just beginning to work out the definitive route through that labyrinth.)

In the trumpet section, the principals are Buck Clayton and Harry 'Sweets' Edison (who joined in 1938). Like their predecessor Hot Lips Page, both are polished, tuneful, bluesy, swinging improvisers, and both are fluent in the use of mutes, though they do not use these in the 'jungle style' that Page borrowed from Ellington's band. This is most evident in *Blues in the Dark*, where Clayton chooses not to join in with the growling, wa-wa trombones in the minor-key strain that precedes and follows Rushing's blues choruses, but instead plays with his typically delicate muted sound; the beginning of *Topsy* provides a similar example, though here Clayton aims for a tone that is a little bit nastier. Neither Clayton's nor Edison's playing could be mistaken for the overly ambitious work of trumpeter Bobby Moore, who hits quite a few clinkers on *Out the Window*. They play in a manner less clipped than Shad Collins's muted work on *Lady be Good*, though there is less obvious difference in Collins's solo on the preceding combo date, *You Can Depend on Me*. And distinguishing between the two principals, Clayton and Edison, is not a simple matter. I would only be copying from the definitive source (Chris Sheridan: *Count Basie: a Bio-discography*, New York, 1986) if I pretended to be able to do so. Even more than with the tenor saxes, Basie avoids setting up Clayton and Edison in head-to-head confrontations. According to Sheridan, on *Sent for You Yesterday* Clayton's muted trumpet embroiders Rushing's singing, while Edison's open sound follows Rushing's last blues verse; on *Swingin' the Blues* Clayton's muted solo follows Young, and after the interlude Edison's open and closed wa-wa solo follows Evans.

The band's trombonists soloed infrequently until mid-1938, when Dicky Wells replaced Eddie Durham, whose brass work was less prominent than his solo guitar playing and far less important than his arranging. Benny Morton had been in the band since September 1937, but he had few solos on studio recordings; presumably Basie found Morton's approach (as heard on *Out the Window*, from his first date with the band) somewhat old-fashioned and kept him out of the spotlight. Morton improvises nimbly on *Shorty George*, recorded in November 1938, and a few months after that was given the unpleasant assignment of being the only man in the band to try to solo over the *b* section of *Cherokee*, near the start of part 1. Wells, a widely acclaimed player, is not a personal favourite of mine. I find his tone cloying and his approach heavy-handed, as, for example, when he solos after Morton in *Cherokee*, on the comparitively easy *a* section of the theme. One of the most compelling arguments for following the band past the period of the tracks discussed here is the opportunity to hear the dry, witty, vibratoless trombone playing of Vic Dickenson, who joined in February 1940 and left with Lester Young at the end of that same year.

Alongside Rushing (whose talent and approach to the blues are unchanged, except for an even bigger sound than before), Young, Evans, Clayton and Edison, the other star is Basie, though he is erratic. Sometimes he falls back into thoughtless patterns, with a strong emphasis on sing-song, four-square, on-the-beat, right-hand figures, grating against the rhythm section's gliding swing. Sometimes he plays traditional stride and boogie-woogie figures. When he wished, he could bring forth one of the most original jazz piano styles, playing exceedingly sparse, perfectly placed progressions of riff-like motifs. The big band's *Texas Shuffle* and the septet's *Lester Leaps in* provide two of the best examples of this.

A third landmark in Basie's career came when, after the declining big-band business forced him to lead an octet from 1950 to 1951, he founded a new big band. Until roughly the late 1960s the group always had many fine soloists, and included on the album **April in Paris**, from the years 1955–6, are trumpeters Thad Jones and Joe Newman, trombonists Henry Coker,

Benny Powell and Bill Hughes, tenor saxophonist Frank Foster, saxophonist and flautist Frank Wess (who, despite the liner notes on the original issue, plays alto, not tenor, sax on *Magic*) and of course Basie. But the main reason to listen to the band lies elsewhere, in its well-rehearsed and swinging execution of a single concept: melodies harmonized in block chords. Often these melodies build from riff-like patterns which repeat sequentially at different pitches. This sound pervades the album, and it would be misleading to pay too much attention to the individual arranging styles of Wild Bill Davis (on the title tune), Frank Foster (who as a composer does deserve special praise for contributing *Shiny Stockings* to the repertory), Ernie Wilkins, Neal Hefti and Freddie Green.

In playing in this manner, the group shows the same sensitivity to many shades of volume found in the earlier band, but on average this is more of a powerhouse ensemble than before. Regularly there are grand climaxes, headed by a screaming lead trumpet and by Sonny Payne's exuberant drum kicks; adding to the excitement are perfectly coordinated shakes (slow, wide trills between two notes). Rather than citing examples of all this, it seems more efficient to mention the exception: on Wilkins's arrangement of *Sweetie Cakes* the richly harmonized saxophone theme is not just in block chords, but instead moves through contrapuntal lines, with a prominent part for the baritone sax and with moments of unison playing. (The album also has a sextet performance, *Midgets*, featuring Newman's tightly muted trumpet alongside Wess's pure-toned flute.)

None of the soloists from this era had the same stature among their contemporaries as did the late 1930s soloists in their era, excepting Basie and an intermittent sideman, tenor saxophonist Eddie 'Lockjaw' Davis. But the group deserves consideration alongside Basie's earlier efforts for its single-minded achievement of a level of ensemble cohesiveness which has never been surpassed.

CD

USA: *Bennie Moten's Kansas City Orchestra: Basie's Beginnings*, **Bluebird 9768-2 RB**

Ed Lewis, Booker Washington (tpt), Eddie Durham, Thamon Hayes (tb), Harlan Leonard (cl, ss, as), Woodie 'Hots' Walder (cl, ts), Jack Washington (cl, ss, bar), Count Basie (p), Buster Moten (accordion), Leroy Berry (bj), Vernon Page (bb), Mack Washington (d)

Chicago	23 Oct 1929	**The Jones Law Blues** (take 3)
add Durham (g)		**Small Black** (take 2)
		Every Day Blues

omit (g), add Mack Washington (v)
        24 Oct 1929   **Rit-Dit-Ray** (take 2)

add Durham (g), omit (v)   **New Vine Street Blues** (arr
                                             Durham)   5
                                     Sweetheart of Yesterday (arr
                                             Bennie Moten)

*Lewis, Booker Washington, Hot Lips Page (tpt), Durham, Hayes (tb), Leonard (cl,
ss, as), Walder (cl, ts), Jack Washington (cl, ss, bar), Basie (p), Buster Moten
(accordion), Berry (bj), Vernon Page (bb), Mack Washington (d, vb), Jimmy Rushing (v)*
Kansas City   27 Oct 1930   **Won't You be my Baby?**

omit (vb) and (v)
        28 Oct 1930   **Oh! Eddie** (arr Durham)

add Durham (g), Rushing (v), Buster or Bennie Moten (p solo)
                                     That Too, Do (arr Basie and
                                             Durham; take 2)

omit (g) and (v); Buster Moten (accordion only)
        29 Oct 1930   **The Count**   10

add Durham (g), Mack Washington (vb), Rushing (v)
                                     Liza Lee (arr Basie and Durham;
                                             take 1)

*as **That Too, Do**, but Buster or Bennie Moten (second p)*
        30 Oct 1930   **When I'm Alone**

omit (second p) and (v)   **New Moten Stomp** (arr Basie and
                                             Durham)

omit (g), add Basie (v)
        31 Oct 1930   **Somebody Stole my Gal**

omit Basie (v), add Rushing (v)   **Now that I Need You**   15

*Joe Keyes, Hot Lips Page, Dee Stewart (tpt), Durham (tb, g), Dan Minor (tb), Eddie
Barefield (cl, as), Ben Webster (ts), Jack Washington (as, bar), Basie (p), Berry (g),
Walter Page (sb), Mack Washington (d)*
Camden, NJ   13 Dec 1932   **Toby** (arr Barefield)

Moten Swing (arr Basie and
   Durham)

as **Toby**, *but Durham (tb)*   **The Blue Room** (arr ?Barefield)

as **Toby**, *but add Rushing (v)*   **New Orleans**

as **Toby**, *but Durham (tb)*   **Milenberg Joys** (arr ?Durham)   **20**
                                      Lafayette (arr Durham)
                                      Prince of Wails (arr Durham)

Other CDs
same contents:
   Europe: RCA ND 90403

LPs
plus additional tracks:
   France: *Bennie Moten's Kansas City Orchestra*, vol.3–5, RCA 741.108,
   FPM1-7004 and FXM1-7062
   Jazz Tribune no.31: The Complete Bennie Moten, vol.3–4 and
   Jazz Tribune no.40: The Complete Bennie Moten, vol.5–6, RCA NL 89616
   and NL 89617; PM 43693 and PM 45688
   Japan: *The Big Band Era*, pt.1, RCA RA 45–53
   tracks 1–2, 4–5, 8–11, 14–19, 21–2: *Bennie Moten's Kansas City Orchestra:
   Basie's Beginnings*
   USA: Bluebird 9768-1 RB
   Europe: RCA NL 90403
   tracks 1 (take 2), 2 (composite take), 5, 7–9, 12, 14, 16–22: *Count Basie in
   Kansas City*
   USA: RCA LPV 514
   UK: RCA RD 7904
   Germany: RCA LPM 514
   Japan: RCA VRA 5008
   Count Basie: Kansas City Style
   USA: RCA AFM 1-5186
   tracks 1 (take 2), 2, 5, 7–9, 12, 14, 16–22: *Treasury of Jazz no.59:
   Bennie Moten*
   France: RCA 430.690

Cassettes
tracks 1–2, 4–5, 8–11, 14–19, 21–2: *Bennie Moten's Kansas City Orchestra:*

Basie's Beginnings
USA: Bluebird 9768-4 RB
Europe: RCA NK 90403
tracks 1 (take 2), 2 (composite take), 5, 7–9, 12, 14, 16–22: *Count Basie: Kansas City Style*
USA: RCA AFK 1-5186
incl. tracks 1 (take 2), 2 (take 3), 3–17, 19:
UK: *Essential Bennie Moten, vol.3, '29–30*, Neovox 790, *Essential Bennie Moten, vol.4, 1930–32*, Neovox 830

LP

USA: *The Best of Count Basie*, Decca DXB 170 and DXSB 7170

Buck Clayton, Joe Keyes, Carl Smith (tpt), George Hunt, Dan Minor (tb), Caughey Roberts (as), Herschel Evans, Lester Young (ts), Jack Washington (bar, as), Basie (p), Claude Williams (g), Walter Page (sb), Jo Jones (d)

New York	21 Jan 1937	**Honeysuckle Rose**
		Swingin' at the Daisy Chain (arr ?Buster Smith)
		Roseland Shuffle (arr Fletcher Henderson)

Ed Lewis and Bobby Moore (tpt) replace Keyes and Smith, Freddie Green (g) replaces Williams; add Jimmy Rushing (v)

| | 26 March 1937 | **Boogie Woogie** |

Earle Warren (as, bar) replaces Roberts; omit Rushing (v)

| | 7 July 1937 | **One O'Clock Jump** (arr Eddie Durham and Buster Smith)   5 |
| | | **John's Idea** (arr Durham) |

Clayton, Lewis, Moore (tpt), Hunt, Minor (tb), Warren (as), Evans, Young (ts), Washington (bar, as), Basie (p), Green (g), Durham (elg), Page (sb), Jones (d)

| | 9 Aug 1937 | **Time Out** (arr Durham) |

*as **Time Out**, but Durham (tb)*

| | | **Topsy** (arr Durham) |

Benny Morton replaces Hunt

| | 13 Oct 1937 | **Out the Window** (arr Durham) |

Karl George (tpt) replaces Moore; add Rushing (v)

3 Jan 1938	**Blues in the Dark** (arr Clayton)
	10

Harry 'Sweets' Edison (tpt) replaces George
16 Feb 1938   **Sent for You Yesterday**

Clayton, Edison, Ed Lewis (tpt), Durham, Minor, Morton (tb), Warren (as), Evans,
Young (ts), Washington (bar, as), Basie (p), Green (g), Page (sb), Jones (d)
Every Tub (arr Durham)
Swingin' the Blues (arr Durham)

as Every Tub, but Young (ts, cl)
6 June 1938   **Blue and Sentimental** (arr
Durham)

as Every Tub, but Evans (ts, cl)   **Doggin' Around** (arr Edgar Battle
and Evans)   **15**

as Every Tub, but Dicky Wells (tb) replaces Durham; Young (ts, cl)
22 Aug 1938   **Texas Shuffle** (arr Evans)

as Texas Shuffle, but Evans (ts, cl), Young (ts)
Jumpin' at the Woodside

omit (cl)   16 Nov 1938   **Shorty George** (arr Andy Gibson)
Panassié Stomp

Shad Collins (tpt), Young (ts), Basie (p), Green (g), Page (sb), Jones (d), Rushing
(v)
2 Feb 1939   **You Can Depend on Me**   **20**

Clayton, Collins, Edison, Lewis (tpt), Minor, Morton, Wells (tb), Warren (as), Chu
Berry, Young (ts), Washington (bar, as), Basie (p), Green (g), Page (sb), Jones (d)
3 Feb 1939   **Cherokee** (arr Jimmy Mundy)

add Helen Humes (v)   **Blame it on my Last Affair**

Clayton, Collins, Edison (tpt), Wells (tb), Young (ts), Washington (bar), Basie (p),
Green (g), Page (sb), Jones (d)
4 Feb 1939   **Jive at Five** (arr Edison)

as Cherokee   **Lady be Good**

CDs

plus additional tracks:

Europe: *The Chronological Count Basie and his Orchestra 1936–38*, Classics 503; . . . *1938–39*, Classics 504; . . . *1939*, Classics 513

incl. tracks 1–19:

UK: *'Listen . . . You Shall Hear'*, Hep CD 1025, and *Do You Wanna Jump . . .?*, Hep CD 1027

incl. tracks 1–18:

USA: *One O'Clock Jump*, MCA MCAD 42324

Other LPs

same contents:

USA: MCA 2-4050

France: MCA MAPS 1979 and MAPS 1980

Germany: Coral COPS 1788 D/1-2

Japan: Decca AS 2; Decca DL 15–16

same contents: *The Best of Basie, Vol.1, The Best of Basie, vol.2*

France: MCA 510.013 and 510.019

plus additional tracks:

USA: *Count Basie in Discographical Order*, vols.1–5, Ajax LP 126, LP 129, LP 137, LP 143, LP 150

France: *The Best of Count Basie and his Orchestra*, MCA 251.212; *Early Count*, MCA 510.167-510.170

Japan: *The Best Collection of Count Basie*, MCA 3059-3062; *The Golden Age of Count Basie*, MCA VIM 5501-5504

not incl. track 4:

Europe: *Count Basie: 28 Golden Memories*, MCA 301.393-370

incl. tracks 1–19:

UK: *'Listen . . . You Shall Hear'*, Hep 1025, and *Do You Wanna Jump . . .?*, Hep 1027

incl. tracks 6–9, 11–20, 23–4:

UK: *Swingin' the Blues*, Affinity AFS 1010

incl. tracks 1–2, 5–6, 10, 13–14, 16, 19, 23: *Count Basie and his Orchestra*

USA: Decca DL 8049

UK: Decca BKL 8028; Decca LAT 8028

France: CID UMT 263.137

Japan: JDL 5006

incl. tracks 1–2, 5–6, 11, 13–14, 18–19, 23:

Europe: *The Count Swinging the Blues*, Decca BLK 87014 P

France, Germany: *Swinging the Blues*, Brunswick 87.036 LPBM

incl. tracks 1, 4–6, 11, 13, 16–17, 19, 22, 24: *Rendezvous with Count Basie*

Belgium: MCA 4C0456-96715

France: MCA MAPS 8021
incl. tracks 2, 5–6, 8, 11–17, 19, 23:
  USA: *Giants of Jazz: Count Basie*, Time-Life STL J22
incl. tracks 2–3, 5–6, 9–14, 19:
  Germany: *Count Basie and his Orchestra*, Coral PCO 8263; Coral 6.22420 AK
incl. tracks 1, 3–6, 8, 10, 13–15, 17, 21, 23–4:
  Japan: *One O'Clock Jump: the Best of Count Basie*, MCA 7034; MCA VIM 7505
incl. tracks 1, 3–6, 8, 10, 13–15, 17, 21:
  Japan: *The Best of Count Basie*, Decca SDL 18
incl. tracks 12, 15, 17–18, plus others cited below:
  Denmark: *Lester Young*, Official 3035-2

Cassettes

same contents:
  USA: MCA 2-4050
not incl. track 4:
  Europe: *Count Basie: 28 Golden Memories*, MCA 501.393-372
incl. tracks 6–9, 11–20, 23–4:
  UK: *Swingin' the Blues*, Affinity TC-AFS 1010

LP

USA: *Lester Leaps In*, Epic LN 3107

(Jones–Smith Inc:) Carl Smith *(tpt)*, Young *(ts)*, Basie *(p)*, Page *(sb)*, Jones *(d)*
Chicago   9 Nov 1936   **Shoe Shine Boy** (take 1)

add Rushing (v)   **Boogie Woogie**

as Shoe Shine Boy   **Lady be Good**

Clayton, Collins, Edison, Lewis *(tpt)*, Minor, Morton, Wells *(tb)*, Warren *(as)*, Buddy Tate, Young *(ts)*, Washington *(bar, as)*, Basie *(p)*, Green *(g)*, Page *(sb)*, Jones *(d)*
New York   19 March 1939   **Rock-a-Bye Basie** (arr Mundy)
                                         Taxi War Dance   5
                  20 March 1939   **Jump for Me** (arr Gibson)
                  5 April 1939   **Twelfth Street Rag**
                  4 Aug 1939   **Song of the Islands** (arr ?Clayton)
                                         Clap Hands, Here Comes Charlie
                                            (arr Mundy)

Clayton (tpt), Wells (tb), Young (ts), Basie (p), Green (g), Page (sb), Jones (d)
5 Sept 1939   **Dickie's Dream** (take 4)   **10**
                     Lester Leaps in (take 2)

Clayton, Al Killian, Edison, Lewis (tpt), Minor, Vic Dickenson, Wells (tb), Tab Smith (as), Tate, Young (ts), Washington (bar), Basie (p), Green (g), Page (sb), Jones (d)

8 August 1940   **Moten Swing**

CDs
incl. tracks 4–7, 9–11: *The Essential Count Basie*, vol.1–2
   USA: Columbia Jazz Masterpieces CK 40608 and CK 40835
   Europe: CBS Jazz Masterpieces 460061-2 and 460828-2

Other LPs
plus additional tracks:
   USA: *Count Basie in Discographical Order*, vols.1, 5–7, 9, Ajax LP 126, LP
   150, LP 157, Ajaz [sic] LP 163, LP 208
   Europe: *The Complete Count Basie, vol.1–10: 1936–41*, CBS 66101
plus additional tracks:
   Europe: *Count Basie vol.1, 1936 and 1939: 'the Count & the President'*,
   CBS 88667; *Count Basie vol.2, 1939–40: 'Lester Leaps In'*, CBS 88668;
   Count Basie vol.3, 1940–1941, CBS 88672
incl. tracks 1, 3, 5, 10–11, plus others:
   Denmark: *Lester Young*, Official 3035-2
incl. tracks 4–7, 9–11: *The Essential Count Basie*, vol.1–2
   USA: Columbia Jazz Masterpieces CJ 40608 and CJ 40835
   Europe: CBS Jazz Masterpieces 460061-1 and 460828-1

Cassettes
plus additional tracks:
   France: *Count Basie vol.1, 1936 and 1939: 'the Count & the President'*,
   CBS 44-88667; *Count Basie vol.2, 1939–40: 'Lester Leaps In'*, CBS
   44-88668; *Count Basie vol.3, 1940–1941*, CBS 44-88672
incl. tracks 1–6, 8–12:
   USA: *Lester Young Memorial Album*, Epic LN 3576 and LN 3577; Epic SN
   6031
   Lester Young–Count Basie, Epic EE 662121
   UK: *Lester Young Memorial Album*, Fontana TFL 5064 and TFL 5065
   France: *Count Basie with Lester Young*, Columbia FPX 244 and FPX 260

Netherlands: *Lester Young Memorial Album*, Fontana 682.175 TL and 682.176 TL
Japan: *Lester Young Memorial Album*, Nippon Columbia SL 1243/4
incl. tracks 1–3, 5, 7–11:
Japan: *Lester Young Memorial*, Epic SONP 50426/7
incl. tracks 1–3, 5, 9–11:
Europe: *The Immortal Lester Young*, Philips B 07521 L
Japan: *Lester Young, 1936–40*, CBS/Sony 20 AP 1448
incl. tracks 1, 3, 5, 10–11:
USA: *Giants of Jazz: Lester Young*, Time-Life STL J13
incl. tracks 4, 6, 8:
USA: *Giants of Jazz: Count Basie*, Time-Life STL J22
incl. tracks 4–7, 9–11: *The Essential Count Basie*, vol.1–2
USA: Columbia Jazz Masterpieces CJT 40608 and CJT 40835
Europe: CBS Jazz Masterpieces 460061-4 and 460828-4

CD

Germany: *April in Paris*, Verve 825.575-2

Wendell Culley, Reunald Jones, Thad Jones, Joe Newman (tpt), Henry Coker, Bill Hughes, Benny Powell (tb), Marshall Royal, Bill Graham (as), Frank Wess, Frank Foster (ts), Charlie Fowlkes (bs), Count Basie (p), Freddie Green (g), Eddie Jones (sb), Sonny Payne (d)

New York	26 July 1955	**April in Paris** (arr Wild Bill Davis)	
		Corner Pocket (arr ?Greene)	
		Did'n You? (arr Foster)	
		Sweetie Cakes (arr Ernie Wilkins)	

*as **April in Paris**, but Wess (as, ts)*

	4 Jan 1956	**Shiny Stockings** (arr Foster)	5
		What am I Here for? (arr Foster)	
		Magic (arr ?Foster)	

Newman (tpt), Wess (fl), Basie (p), Green (g), Jones (sb), Payne (d)
Midgets

*as **April in Paris**, but Green (g, per); add José Mangual, Ubaldo Nieto (per)*

	5 Jan 1956	**Mambo Inn** (arr Foster)

*as **April in Paris***

		Dinner with Friends (arr Neal Hefti)
		Hefti) **10**

LPs

same contents:
USA: Verve MGV 8012
UK: Columbia 33CX 10088
Europe: Verve 711.117
France: Blue Star GLP 3596; Verve 2304.408
Japan: Verve MV 2641; Verve 18MJ 9022; Verve 20MJ 0023; Verve 23MJ 3233
not incl. **Mambo Inn:**
Germany: *The King of Jazz*, Historia DLP 2-770
not incl. **Dinner with Friends:**
UK: *April in Paris*, Encore ENC 153

Cassettes

not incl. **Mambo Inn:**
Germany: *The King of Jazz*, Historia DMC 42-770

* * *

Chick Webb: *A Legend, vol.1 (1929–1936); King of the Savoy, vol.2 (1937–1939)*

The central core of studio recordings by Chick Webb's big band is collected on two albums issued in 1967 on Decca and widely reissued on MCA. Above all, the point of listening to these tracks is to hear Webb, one of the great swing drummers. Even with the best of mid-1930s technology, it can be hard to pick out of a big band's sound the individual drums, cymbals, blocks, bells and other accessories of the drum kit. Decca's dubbings, not the best, make this a greater challenge than it need be, and so it seems worth mentioning a rival album, even though it is long out of print: **Midnite in Harlem**, an LP issued on the Ace of Hearts label, would be worth looking for in a second-hand store. Its dozen tracks from the years 1934–9 include ten of the best found on the Decca set, and the sound is much crisper.

Decca's anthology begins in 1929, when Webb's then three-year-old group recorded two titles as the Jungle Band, emulating Duke Ellington's orchestra (some 78 rpm labels issued the discs falsely under Ellington's name). *Dog Bottom* is a kaleidoscopic compendium of techniques of arranging for contemporary big bands, in which Elmer James's chunky two-beat tuba playing and John Trueheart's bright banjo strumming are never allowed to establish a foothold for any length of time. Highlights include the saxophone trio break, Webb's hot cymbal breaks, brass and reeds in overlapping pyramids of sound, Elmer Williams's tenor saxophone solo, and Ward Pinkett's wildly energetic scat singing. In the contrasting *Jungle Mama*, simple, traditional blues riffs serve as a theme and also as the background for a succession of solos, beginning with a trumpet muted and growling after the manner of Ellington's Bubber Miley. Webb is inaudible, except for a steady, soft bass-drum beat and a trace of snare drum at the very end.

In 1931 Webb led his first session under his own name. The best of the three titles recorded that day (two of which are included here) is Benny Carter's arrangement of *Heebie Jeebies*, a tune which Louis Armstrong had made popular. The performance has a lilting rhythm which is not at all hurt by James's having switched to string bass. In addition to excellent solos from tenor saxophonist Williams (whose playing here and on *Soft and Sweet* is unusually free rhythmically, floating away from the beat), pianist Don Kirkpatrick and trombonist Jimmy Harrison, *Heebie Jeebies* offers (following Kirkpatrick) an early example of one of Carter's characteristic devices, a twisting melody arranged for the saxophone section playing in chords.

Webb's band had played at New York's Savoy Ballroom occasionally since 1927, and late in 1931 it began regular long engagements there. But it was another two years before Webb recorded steadily. The Decca collection picks up the story yet another year later, in the autumn of 1934. The last of the preliminary material in this collection consists of two numbers featuring Taft Jordan. *It's Over Because We're Through* is a blatant copy of Armstrong's sweet muted and dramatic open trumpet playing, and of his singing. *That Rhythm Man* is a joyful performance which also pays homage to Armstrong (who recorded the same piece five years before). It has a fine muted solo by trombonist Sandy Williams and a striking ending that gradually grows softer.

The central features of the band's mature style are Edgar Sampson's writing, Ella Fitzgerald's singing and Webb's drumming. In addition to Fitzgerald and Webb, there are numerous strong soloists on these tracks, of whom the most creative are the two Williamses (tenor saxophonist Elmer and trombonist Sandy) and trumpeter Bobby Stark. The band plays tightly, and John Kirby (on bass) and Trueheart (now on guitar) help Webb drive the rhythm. Trueheart is most prominent on *Blue Minor*, *It's Over Because We're Through* and the scratchiest of Decca's dubbings, *Blue Lou*.

Sampson had written *Stomping at the Savoy* (not on this collection) and *Don't Be That Way* in 1933 for Rex Stewart's band, and these later became anthems of the swing era in modified arrangements recorded by Benny Goodman. In the interim, Webb recorded both in performances faster and livelier than Goodman's. *Don't Be That Way* has the essence of the mainstream big-band style, presenting themes and accompanimental figures which straddle the boundary between repeated riffs and arranged melodies. *Blue Minor* shows Sampson writing in another vein. This is a two-part piece, setting Ellington-style jungle music with muted wa-wa brass playing in a minor key against a jauntier theme in a major key; one phrase of the minor theme returns to end the piece.

Ella Fitzgerald joined the band in 1935 and recorded with it from 1936 to 1942, having taken over the leadership after Webb's death in 1939. Her big hit was *A-tisket, A-tasket*, but there's just no room in my cruel heart for jazz versions of nursery rhymes. (Jimmy Rushing's version of *London Bridge is Falling Down*, recorded by Count Basie's big band, is equally dreadful.) *Undecided*, adapted from trumpeter Charlie Shavers's composition for John Kirby's sextet, suffers from undecided rhythm, tottering back and forth between the fast-tempoed feel of the band's playing and the half-time feel of Fitzgerald's singing. The best of her tracks here is *A Little Bit Later On*, which captures her irrepressible swing. Still, it is hard not to make invidious comparisons between Billie Holiday's contemporary accounts of shattered love and this girlish account ('cryin' boo-hoo-hoo').

Finally, the star of these performances, Webb: he plays prominent drum fills in the last part of *Don't Be That Way*, ending with a neatly constructed series of breaks which slow from triplets to a duple division of the beat to a series of strokes on the beat, these last accented in such a way as to superimpose a fragment of waltz rhythm on the swing beat; in the context, this seemingly un-hip idea – playing on the beat, and in waltz time – provides the perfect climax to his solo. *Facts and Figures* (composed and arranged by Sampson) ends with Webb playing a break on temple blocks. On *Go Harlem* (a riff tune arranged by Sampson), Webb is in the foreground from the start. He supplies another effective 'un-hip' idea, simply playing right on the beat for eight straight beats (drums and block, drums and cymbal) at the end of Teddy McRae's brief tenor saxophone solo. At the end he takes a series of solo breaks, exploring timbral contrasts as he moves constantly about the drum kit; rarely does he take more than two consecutive strokes at any one piece of it. The same may be said for the fast swing version of *Clap Hands! Here Comes Charley* (again arranged by Sampson), with drum breaks at the start and following the solos by Jordan and Sandy Williams. In contrast to these high-energy performances, in a sultry version of *Squeeze Me*, Webb appropriately plays relaxed, 'striptease' drum patterns and fills. *Harlem Congo* ends with a 24-bar drum solo on which the leader concentrates on dynamic snare-drum syncopations. In this collection, Webb's only bad moment occurs on *Spinnin' the Webb*. The *a* section of this *aaba* theme has the feel of rhythm and blues. Stark takes his best solo over it, spinning out a relaxed melody which contrasts a biting open tone with a growling one; but Webb's drum break breaks the groove, and the band members seem unsure where to place their punctuated notes. *Liza* (arranged by Benny Carter), however, has four solo segments featuring Webb at his energetic best.

The Decca collection also includes a track by one of the less important instances of a band within a band: the quintet Chick Webb and his Little Chicks. Their cute and dainty version of *I Got Rhythm* is notable only as proof that the pioneering jazz flautist Wayman Carver did not succeed in his effort to be the first to make that a convincing solo instrument in the swing style.

LP
USA: *A Legend, vol.1 (1929–1936)*, Decca DL 9222 and DL 79222

(the Jungle Band:) Ward Pinkett (tpt, v), Edwin Swayze (tpt), Robert Horton (tb), Hilton Jefferson, Louis Jordan (as), Elmer Williams (ts), Don Kirkpatrick (p), John Trueheart (bj), Elmer James (bb), Chick Webb (d)
New York   14 June 1929   **Dog Bottom**

*as **Dog Bottom**, but Jefferson, Jordan, Williams (cl), Trueheart (g); omit (v)*
                                 Jungle Mama

Shelton Hemphill, Louis Hunt, Louis Bacon (tpt), Jimmy Harrison (tb), Benny Carter, Hilton Jefferson (as), Williams (ts), Kirkpatrick (p, celeste), Trueheart (g), James (sb), Webb (d)
            30 March 1931   **Heebie Jeebies** (arr Carter)

*as **Heebie Jeebies**, but Carter, Jefferson (cl, as), Williams (cl, ts), Kirkpatrick (p)*
                                 Soft and Sweet (arr Carter)

Mario Bauza, Bobby Stark (tpt), Taft Jordan (tpt, v), Sandy Williams, Claude Jones (tb), Pete Clarke, Edgar Sampson (as), Elmer Williams, Wayman Carver (ts), Kirkpatrick (p), Trueheart (g), John Kirby (sb), Webb (d)
            10 Sept 1934   **That Rhythm Man**   5

*as **That Rhythm Man**, but Jordan (tpt), Clarke (cl, as)*
                                 Blue Minor (arr Sampson)

*as **That Rhythm Man***
            19 Nov 1934   **It's Over Because We're Through**

*as **That Rhythm Man**, but Jordan (tpt)*
                                 Don't Be That Way (arr Sampson)
                                 What a Shuffle (arr Sampson)
                                 Blue Lou (arr Sampson)   10

as **That Rhythm Man**, *but Jordan (tpt), Clarke (cl, as), Carver (fl, ts), Elmer Williams (ts, ?bass cl)*
12 June 1935   **Down Home Rag** (arr Carver)

as **Down Home Rag**, *but omit (bass cl); Bill Thomas (sb) replaces Kirby*
12 Oct 1935   **Facts and Figures** (arr Sampson)

Bauza, Stark, Jordan (tpt), Sandy Williams, Nat Story (tb), Clarke (as, cl), Sampson (as), Teddy McRae, Carver (ts), Kirkpatrick (p), Trueheart (g), Thomas (sb), Webb (d)
2 June 1936   **Go Harlem** (arr Sampson)

as **Go Harlem**, *but Clarke (as), Ella Fitzgerald (v)*
A Little Bit Later On

CDs
incl. tracks 1–10:
   Europe: *The Chronological Chick Webb and his Orchestra 1929–1934*, CD Classics 502

Other LPs
same contents:
   USA: MCA 1303
   France: MCA 510.014
   Germany: Coral COPS 3453
incl. tracks 5–7, 11, 12, 14, plus others cited below:
   UK: *Spinning the Webb*, Coral CP3; Coral CRLM 1021
incl. tracks 8, 10, plus others cited below:
   USA: *The Best of Chick Webb*, MCA 2-4107
incl. tracks 6, 8–10, 13, plus others cited below:
   UK: *Midnite in Harlem*, Ace of Hearts AH 32
incl. tracks 8–10, 13, plus others cited below:
   UK: *In the Groove*, Affinity AFS 1007

Cassettes
same contents:
   USA: MCA MCAC 1303

LP
USA: *King of the Savoy, vol.2 (1937–1939)*, Decca DL 9223 and DL 79223

*Bauza, Stark, Taft Jordan (tpt), Williams, Story (tb), Clarke (cl, as), Louis Jordan
(as), McRae, Carver (ts, bar), Tommy Fulford (p), Trueheart (g), Beverly Peer (sb),
Webb (d)*

New York 24 March 1937 **Clap Hands! Here Comes Charley**
That Naughty Waltz (arr Charlie
Dixon)

Chauncey Haughton (cl), Carver (fl), Fulford (p), Peer (sb), Webb (d)
21 Sept 1937 **I Got Rhythm**

*as **Clap Hands! Here Comes Charley**, but Haughton (cl, as) replaces Clarke,
?Carver (?bar or bass sax), Bobby Johnson (g) replaces Trueheart*
1 Nov 1937 **Squeeze Me**
Harlem Congo (arr Dixon) 5

*Bauza, Stark, Jordan (tpt), Williams, Story (tb), Garvin Bushell (cl, as), Jordan (as),
McRae, Carver (ts), Fulford (p), Johnson (g), Peer (sb), Webb (d), Fitzgerald (v)*
17 Dec 1937 **The Dipsy Doodle**

*as **The Dipsy Doodle**, but Carver (fl, ts)*
Hallelujah

*as **The Dipsy Doodle**, but Bushell (as); omit Fitzgerald*
**Midnite in a Madhouse (Midnite
in Harlem)**

add George Matthews (tb), Fitzgerald (v)
2 May 1938 **A-tisket, A-tasket**

omit Fitzgerald 3 May 1938 **Spinnin' the Webb** (arr Benny
Carter) 10
Liza (arr Carter)

*Bauza, Stark, Jordan (tpt), Williams, Story, Matthews (tb), Bushell (as, cl), Hilton
Jefferson (as), McRae (ts), Carver (fl, ts), Fulford (p), Johnson (g), Peer (sb), Webb
(d)*
18 Aug 1938 **Who ya Hunchin'?**

add Fitzgerald (v)
17 Feb 1939 **Undecided**

*as **Who ya Hunchin'?***
In the Groove at the Grove

Other LPs

same contents:
  France: MCA 510.020
  Italy: Coral COPS 1921
incl. tracks 2–3, 5–7, 9–10, 12–13, plus others cited above:
  UK: *Spinning the Webb*, Coral CP3; Coral CRLM 1021
incl. tracks 3–7, 9–11, 13–14, plus others cited above:
  USA: *The Best of Chick Webb*, MCA 2-4107
incl. tracks 1, 4, 8, 11, 14, plus others cited above:
  UK: *Midnite in Harlem*, Ace of Hearts AH 32
incl. tracks 4, 9–11, 13–14, plus others cited above:
  UK: *In the Groove*, Affinity AFS 1007

* * *

Jimmie Lunceford: *Strictly Lunceford*

Sweet and hot, old and modern, simple and complex, stiff and swinging, mannered and unrestrained, sentimental and bluesy, imitative and original, funny and serious, naive and hip, Jimmie Lunceford's orchestra presented all these qualities in ever changing combinations. Numerous great performances guarantee the group's inclusion in any discreet selection of big-band jazz, but it is necessary to jump around quite a bit to find these. Accordingly, my selection is a reissue on Affinity (licensed from MCA), rather than one of the albums from the series on the Decca and MCA labels or from the higher fidelity series on the Hep label, because it collects together several fine tracks within a representative sample of recordings made between 1934 and 1944, while giving less emphasis to the slighter performances (especially the lightweight singing) that fill large portions of the multi-volume series. Before discussing these, I should note that Lunceford's name will not appear again. He founded the band in 1927, rehearsed and directed it until his death two decades later, occasionally played alto sax, trombone, flute or guitar, and contributed compositions, but he neither performed on nor arranged any of the tracks in this particular collection.

   Sophisticated Lady is a bold reworking of Duke Ellington's ballad arranged by the orchestra's lead alto saxophonist and strongest soloist, Willie Smith (who shouldn't be confused with the stride pianist Willie 'the Lion' Smith). Adding complex, unusual lines, Smith first has the clarinet playing the melody against muted brass punctuations and then, after a piano solo, pitted in the muted brass against a bizarre, old-fashioned passage of massed saxophones, sharply articulating every note. Drummer Jimmy Crawford's few notes on the vibraphone announce an interlude, and there follows a well polished (if somewhat stilted) passage which no other big-band saxophone section of the mid-1930s could have pulled off so cleanly. (Immediately following this track, on the session of 4 September 1934, the orchestra recorded Smith's even more successful reworking of Ellington's ballad *Mood Indigo*, which may be found on volume 1 of the Decca, MCA and Hep LP collections and on the Classics CD collection.)

The orchestra's rhythm section was known for its ability to generate a bouncing rhythmic feeling, as on the aptly named *Rhythm is our Business* (1934) and on *Four or Five Times* (1935). Generally speaking, Moses Allen would play a two-beat bass line, while guitarist Al Norris and pianist Ed Wilcox contributed four-beat chords (perhaps emphasizing beats 2 and 4 more than 1 and 3) and drummer Crawford provided discreet swing patterns. But nothing was constant with this orchestra! They take a different approach on the sometimes dainty, sometimes jazzy version of *My Blue Heaven* (1935). At one point a stiff, 'boom-chuck' drum pattern is married to the two-beat bass line, but at another everyone plays with a bouncy four-beat feeling; above this are, successively, a passage of sweet, smooth Lombardoish saxophones, Smith's biting baritone saxophone solo as counterpoint to the brass melody, and then Norris's undistinguished violin lines weaving around a corny vocal trio modelled after Paul Whiteman's slick Rhythm Boys.

On this album all of the tracks from 1935 to 1938 were arranged by Sy Oliver, whose eclecticism and sense of humour were well suited to the band. He had no qualms about scoring strange material. I wonder how the band *really* felt about it. Is the intentionally overdone, corny piano solo on *Swanee River* (1935) supposed to be funny, or was Wilcox just expressing his embarrassment?

Oliver's most famous pieces are *Organ Grinder's Swing* (1936) and *For Dancers Only* (1937). The first is, like *My Blue Heaven*, a study in changing textures. For the organ grinder's theme, Oliver places a clarinet, trombone and muted trumpet (the same instrumentation which Ellington's orchestra used for *Mood Indigo*), a celeste, and finally the three winds again, over temple blocks played by Crawford; this elides with a blues progression involving a four-beat swing feeling and solos first from Oliver (whose growling, muted trumpet also recalls Ellington's music) together with Earl Carruthers (baritone sax), then Smith (on clarinet), Norris (on guitar), Paul Webster (playing trumpet without a mute) and again Oliver and Carruthers. Another appropriately titled piece, *For Dancers Only*, follows a completely different path. It is a straightforward dance tune, devoted to a strong beat and to riffs traded among the horn sections. The main riff is modelled after that of *Christopher Columbus*, recorded by Benny Goodman, Fletcher Henderson and Fats Waller the previous year. This is the sort of piece that could easily be opened up for extended improvisation while dancers stayed on the floor, but in the studio there was time only for solos from Smith (playing alto sax this time) and Webster (screaming in the trumpet's upper register).

Oliver's arrangement of *Annie Laurie* was an attempt to cash in on Maxine Sullivan's hit version of *Loch Lomond*, recorded earlier that same year, 1937. There is a striking incongruity between the basic material, a Scottish song, and the solo taken by Joe Thomas, whose growling, emotive tenor saxophone style helped set the stage for future rhythm-and-blues tenor players. Oliver's *Margie*, made the following year, introduces Trummy Young's laidback singing and trombone playing.

The best moments on later recordings in this collection are the solos on *Blue Prelude*, *Blues in the Night* and *Strictly Instrumental*. On *Blues in the Night*, Harold Arlen's hit song from a movie the orchestra helped make in 1941, Smith models his alto saxophone playing after Johnny Hodges, scooping up to the notes of the melody, and Webster plays a muted, growling solo; at the end the group achieves a sound that anticipates that of Basie's band of the 1950s. *Strictly Instrumental* is a good example of what was by 1942 the generic riffs-and-solos swing style, with the emotive solos by Thomas and Smith pointing more than ever towards rhythm and blues; Norris makes the connection even stronger by playing electric guitar. In its decline later that same decade, Lunceford's group became a rhythm-and-blues band.

LP
UK: *Strictly Lunceford*, Affinity AFS 1003

Eddie Thompkins, Tommy Stevenson, Sy Oliver (tpt), Henry Wells, Russell Bowles (tb), Willie Smith (as, cl), Laforet Dent (as), Joe Thomas (ts, cl), Earl Carruthers (bar), Eddie Wilcox (p), Al Norris (g), Moses Allen (sb), Jimmy Crawford (d, vb)
New York   4 Sept 1934   **Sophisticated Lady** (arr Smith)

as **Sophisticated Lady**, *but Smith (as, v), Crawford (d), band (v)*
          18 Dec 1934   **Rhythm is our Business** (arr
                              Wilcox)

Thompkins, Paul Webster (tpt), Oliver (tpt, v), Bowles, Elmer Crumbley, Eddie Durham (tb), Smith, Dent, Dan Grissom (as), Thomas (ts), Carruthers (bar), Wilcox (p), Norris (g), Allen (sb), Crawford (d)
          29 May 1935   **Four or Five Times** (arr Oliver)

as **Four or Five Times**, *but Oliver (tpt)*
          23 Sept 1935   **Swanee River** (arr Oliver)

as **Four or Five Times**, *but Norris (g, vln), Smith (bar, v), Grissom (v)*

23 Dec 1935	**My Blue Heaven** (arr Oliver) **5**

as **Four or Five Times**, *but Oliver (tpt), Smith (cl), Wilcox (celeste)*
| | | |
| 31 Aug 1936 | **Organ Grinder's Swing** (arr Oliver) |

as **Four or Five Times**, *but Oliver (tpt); Ed Brown (as) replaces Dent*
| | | |
| 15 June 1937 | **For Dancers Only** (arr Oliver) |

Thompkins, Webster, Oliver (tpt), Bowles, Crumbley, Trummy Young (tb), Smith, Ted Buckner, Dan Grissom (as), Thomas (ts), Carruthers (bar), Wilcox (p), Norris (g), Allen (sb), Crawford (d)
Los Angeles   5 Nov 1937   **Annie Laurie** (arr Oliver)

add Young (v)
New York   6 Jan 1938   **Margie** (arr Oliver)

Grissom (v); omit Young (v)
| | | |
| 12 April 1938 | **Down by the Old Mill Stream** (arr Oliver)   **10** |

Snooky Young, Webster, Gerald Wilson (tpt), Bowles, Crumbley, Trummy Young (tb), Smith, Buckner (as), Thomas (ts), Carruthers (bar), Wilcox (p), Norris (g), Allen (sb), Crawford (d), Grissom (v)
| | | |
| 26 March 1941 | **Blue Prelude** (arr Roger Segure) |

as **Blue Prelude**, *but Trummy Young (v, tb), Grissom (as), band (v)*
Twenty-four Robbers (arr Segure)

as **Blue Prelude**, *but Smith (cl, as); omit (v)*
Los Angeles   23 June 1941   **Siesta at the Fiesta**

as **Blue Prelude**, *but Smith (as, v), Grissom (as), band (v)*
New York   22 Dec 1941   **Blues in the Night**

as **Blue Prelude**
| | | |
| 14 April 1942 | **I'm Gonna Move to the Outskirts of Town** (arr Wilcox)   **15** |

Freddy Webster, Paul Webster, Bob Mitchell, Harry Jackson (tpt), Fernando Arbello, Bowles, Trummy Young (tb), Smith, Benny Waters, Grissom (as), Thomas (ts), Carruthers (bar), Wilcox (p), Norris (elg), Truck Parham (sb), Crawford (d)

Los Angeles   26 June 1942   **Strictly Instrumental** (arr Edgar
                                           Battle)

*Melvin Moore, Ralph Griffin, William 'Chiefie' Scott, Russell Green (tpt), Arbello,
Earl Hardy, John 'Streamline' Ewing (tb), Omer Simeon (cl, as), Chauncey Jarret
(as), Thomas, Ernest Purce (ts), Carruthers (bar), Wilcox (p), Norris (g), Parham
(bs), Joe Marshall (d)*
New York   8 Feb 1944   **Back Door Stuff** (arr Segure)

Other LPs

plus additional tracks: *vol.1: Rhythm is our Business (1934–1935),
    vol.2: Harlem Shout (1935–1936), vol.3: For Dancers Only (1936–1937),
    vol.4: Blues in the Night (1938–1942), vol.5: Jimmie's Legacy (1934–
    1937), vol.6: The Last Sparks (1941–1944)*
    USA: Decca DL 9239 and DL 9240, DL 79239 and DL 79240 (vols.1–2 only);
    MCA 1302, 1305, 1307, 1314, 1320, 1321
    France: MCA 510.012, 510.018, 510.032, 510.040, 510.066, 510.067
incl. tracks 1–6:
    UK: *Stratospheric*, Hep 1011; *Rhythm Business*, Hep 1013; *Oh Boy*, Hep
    1017; *Harlem Shout*, Hep 1022
incl. tracks 6–7, 9, 12, 14–15, 17:
    Italy: *Jimmie Lunceford and His Orchestra: Masterpieces*, Giants of Jazz
    LPJT 22

CDs

incl. tracks 1–6:
    Europe: *The Chronological Jimmie Lunceford and His Orchestra, 1930–1934*,
    Classics 501; . . . *1934–1935*, Classics 505, . . . *1935–1937*, Classics 510

Cassettes

plus additional tracks: *vol.1: Rhythm is our Business (1934–1935),
    vol.2: Harlem Shout (1935–1936), vol.3: For Dancers Only (1936–1937),
    vol.4: Blues in the Night (1938–1942), vol.5: Jimmie's Legacy (1934–
    1937), vol.6: The Last Sparks (1941–1944)*
    USA: MCA MCAC 1302, 1305, 1307, 1314, 1320, 1321
incl. tracks 6–7, 9, 12, 14–15, 17:
    Italy: *Jimmie Lunceford and His Orchestra: Masterpieces*, Giants of Jazz
    MCJT 22

Artie Shaw: *Begin the Beguine*

The recorded legacy of white swing orchestras is, for me, problematic in two significant ways. First, in their studio work during the heyday of swing-era sessions – from 1935 up to the recording ban set by the American Federation of Musicians in 1942 – none of the important white ensembles were any-where near as orientated towards jazz as those of Henderson, Moten, Ellington, Webb, Earl Hines and Basie. Listening in depth to the orchestras of Charlie Barnet, Bunny Berigan, Bob Crosby, Tommy Dorsey, Benny Goodman, early Woody Herman, Harry James, Gene Krupa, Glenn Miller, Artie Shaw, reveals a repertory dominated by popular singers, whose sounds – unlike those of Louis Armstrong, Cab Calloway, Ella Fitzgerald, Billie Holiday and Fats Waller – were often distantly removed from, if not diametrically opposed to, sounds derived from jazz traditions. Second, a sift through these sessions for jazz tracks, and for the jazzy portions of pop tracks, brings out entirely different obstacles. While there are plenty of fine soloists to hear, including Berigan (who also worked with Dorsey), Good-man, James (initially with Goodman) and Shaw, many of the rhythm sec-tions are uninspiring and many of the arrangements depend on scores already recorded by the black big bands. These particular faults of dull rhythm and unoriginal scoring are especially true of the most jazz-orientated of the bunch, Goodman's orchestra.

Against this backdrop, Crosby's orchestra stands out for its successful union of swing and dixieland styles (discussed together with his small group, the Bob Cats, in Chapter 5), and Artie Shaw's looks to be the most adventuresome and creative of the white big bands of the swing era. Selec-tions of its successes and failures have been issued on several RCA an-thologies, including **Begin the Beguine**, which gathers together tracks from several stops along Shaw's ever-changing and tumultuous career, during which he moved back and forth between a conventional big band and a bigger (not better) big band, while also maintaining a small group within the band, his Gramercy Five.

It would be a nice story if the collection showed the orchestra struggling its way towards success, but life was not so obliging. Shaw's first hit, *Begin the Beguine*, was his best one and, to undercut the drama further, the best note of the piece was the first one. There was nothing unusual about a brass punch coordinated with a snare-drum shot, but this device would usually be used by big-band arrangers as an answer to some gentler sound that had come before; here, in a brilliant stroke, arranger Jerry Gray begins the be-guine with the punch and shot right on the downbeat of the first bar, the result being one of the most exhilarating starts in all of jazz. The hard accents continue, set against a catchy, swinging riff, which in turn becomes the background for Shaw's entrance on the melody. The remainder of the piece not only continues to highlight Gray's skill, but more generally provides an extreme example of the importance of the big-band arranger: it is made entirely of statements and restatements of the theme, played variously by the leader, the full ensemble, the saxes, the trombones, and tenor saxophonist Tony Pastor. The whole thing is underpinned by a jaunty, four-beat swing which drummer Cliff Leeman holds together. In addition to his rim shots, the special effect of his splash cymbal is worth noting – it is heard most clearly behind Pastor's solo. Leeman was one of a succession of first-rate drummers who worked for Shaw, helping set the band apart from the pack.

Following examples set by Barnet's big band and Goodman's combo, Shaw had brought into his orchestra a black musician, none other than Billie Holiday, who had used Shaw as a sideman on her own recordings earlier, and who here recorded his song *Any Old Time* at the same session as *Begin the Beguine*. The result is a demonstration of how far below Holiday's normal level of performance the band could be. Perhaps out of courtesy to the composer and leader, she stays closer to the shape of Shaw's melody than she might have done with her own and Teddy Wilson's groups, but she gives its rhythm her usual treatment, floating across and around the beat. In the process she shows up the band's plodding pulse, which not even Leeman could rescue. A detail worth noting in Gray's arrangement is that the interlude (just before Holiday enters) has the kernel of the theme of Glenn Miller's A *String of Pearls*, which Gray composed and arranged three years later.

Nightmare, again written by Shaw, was the orchestra's theme, and the sort of eccentricity it exemplified was another distinctive feature of the band. The composition, such as it is, consists of nothing but a slow, unrelenting, droning brood on a couple of bluesy minor chords, with Shaw's clarinet set against muted brass.

Holiday's roughly ten-month stay with Shaw ended in November 1938. By March, when *Deep Purple* was recorded, the unenviable task of filling her place had been given to Helen Forrest, who comes through admirably under the circumstances. Neither she nor anyone else could match Holiday's tone and improvisatory flair, but she had a reasonable sense of swing, which isn't hurt at all by having drummer Buddy Rich marking time behind her. More importantly, on this track at least, a cutting edge to her tone and an avoidance of a corny sentimental vibrato separated her approach from that heard on many white big-band vocal tracks, including some of her own work with Shaw, Goodman and James.

Rich is more prominent on other tracks, though, to my ear, less satisfying. On *Serenade to a Savage* he moves back and forth between an 'exotic' section (with a tom tom beat obviously meant to capitalize on Krupa's popular drumming on Goodman's *Sing, Sing, Sing*), and much more compelling swing segments, including a good muted wa-wa trumpet solo from Bernie Privin. On *Traffic Jam* Rich adopts a swing style which is so far on top of the beat that the beat accelerates: some listeners like this type of jazz drumming, feeling that the forward rush adds to the excitement of the performance, but it is not an approach that I find satisfying. Similarly, on the band's interpretation of *Oh! Lady be Good*, I think he pushes unnecessarily.

Two of the best solos that Shaw recorded may be heard on the aforementioned *Deep Purple* and on *Star Dust*, recorded in October 1940. On both he fashions deliberate, perfectly executed lines which bounce back and forth between a paraphrase of the melody and the invention of a new melody. Like his rival Benny Goodman, Shaw seems to have left in the rehearsal room whatever struggle he might have had, presenting for public view a finished, polished product of great originality. Far more than Goodman, he favoured a pure tone, without the vocalized effects of New Orleans clarinettists, and not coincidentally he was a much less convincing blues player. His tone in the lower register, best heard on *Frenesi*, could take on a gorgeous, woody, round quality, but this disappeared as he ascended through the instrument's range, and in the highest register his tone was positively shrill.

In the interim between the quasi-Caribbean exotica of *Carioca* and the quasi-Mexican exotica of *Frenesi*, Shaw had disbanded briefly and then re-formed the group on the strength of an unfortunate idea: he would add a string section, and sometimes orchestral winds as well, to the big band. This walk in the footsteps of Paul Whiteman's symphonic jazz resulted in some unbelievable juxtapositions of smarminess and swing. In addition to the sharp contrasts between the string lines and Shaw's playing on these tracks, there are great incongruities between the strings' rhythmic feel and drummer Nick Fatool's relaxed swing on *Moon Glow*. Also, the strings break up Billy Butterfield's glorious presentation of the melody of *Star Dust*; playing with his open but slightly burnished tone, he re-enters with a jolt by smacking a high note and holding on to it, as if to ask the strings to go away.

CD

USA: *Begin the Beguine*, Bluebird 6274-2 RB

Chuck Peterson, Johnny Best, Claude Bowen (tpt), George Arus, Harry Rogers, Ted Vesely (tb), Artie Shaw (cl), Les Robinson, Hank Freeman (as), Tony Pastor, Ronnie Perry (ts), Les Burness (p), Al Avola (g), Sid Weiss (sb), Cliff Leeman (d)

New York   24 July 1938   **Begin the Beguine** (arr Jerry Gray)

add Pastor and band (v)   **Indian Love Call**

omit (v)   **Back Bay Shuffle** (arr Teddy
                                        McRae)

add Billie Holiday (v)
                                        Any Old Time (arr Gray)

Russell Brown (tb) and George Koenig (as) replace Vesely and Robinson; omit (v)
                27 Sept 1938   **Nightmare** (arr Shaw)   **5**
                                        What is This Thing Called Love?

Peterson, Best, Bernie Privin (tpt), Arus, Rogers, Les Jenkins (tb), Shaw (cl),
Robinson, Freeman (as), Pastor, Georgie Auld (ts), Bob Kitsis (p), Avola (g), Weiss
(sb), Buddy Rich (d), Helen Forrest (v)
                12 March 1939   **Deep Purple** (arr Gray)
Hollywood   12 June 1939   **Comes Love**

omit Forrest   **Traffic Jam** (arr McRae)
                22 June 1939   **Serenade to a Savage**   **10**

Harry Geller (tpt) replaces Best
New York   19 Aug 1939   **Carioca** (arr Gray)
                27 Aug 1939   **Oh! Lady be Good**

Dave Barbour (g) replaces Avola, add Forrest (v)
                11 Nov 1939   **Moon Ray**

Charlie Margulis, Manny Klein, George Thow (tpt), Randall Miller, Bill Rank,
Babe Bowman (tb), Jack Cave (french horn), Shaw (cl), Blake Reynolds, Bud Carl-
ton, Jack Stacey (as), Dick Clark (ts), Joe Krechter (bass cl), Morton Ruderman (fl),
Phil Nemoli (oboe), Mark Levant, Harry Bluestone, Peter Eisenberg, Robert Barene,
Sid Brokaw, Dave Cracov, Alex Law, Jerry Joyce (vln), David Sturkin, Stanley
Spiegelman, Jack Gray (viola), Irving Lipschultz, Jules Tannenbaum (cello), Stan
Wrightman (p), Bobby Sherwood (g), Jud DeNaut (sb), Carl Maus (d)
Hollywood   4 March 1940   **Frenesi** (arr William Grant Still)

Billy Butterfield (tpt), Shaw (cl), Johnny Guarnieri (harpsichord), Al Hendrickson
(elg), DeNaut (sb), Nick Fatool (d)
                3 Sept 1940   **Special Delivery Stomp**   **15**
                                        Summit Ridge Drive

Butterfield, George Wendt, Jack Cathcart (tpt), Jack Jenney, Vernon Brown (tb),
Shaw (cl), Bus Bassey, Neely Plumb (as), Les Robinson, Jerry Jerome (ts), E. Lamas,
T. Klages, Bob Morrow, B. Bower, Al Beller (vln), A. Harshman, K. Collins (viola),
F. Goerner (cello), Guarnieri (p), Hendrickson (elg), DeNaut (sb), Fatool (d)

7 Sept 1940	**Temptation**	
7 Oct 1940	**Star Dust** (arr Lennie Hayton)	
4 Dec 1940	**Blues** (arr Still)	

add Ray Conniff (tb)

23 Jan 1941	**Moon Glow**	**20**

Other CDs

same contents:
  Europe: Bluebird ND 86274
  Japan: RCA R32J 1073

LPs

plus additional tracks:
  USA: *The Complete Artie Shaw*, vols.1–4 (1938–41), Bluebird AXM 2-5517,
  AXM 2-5533, AXM 2-5556, AXM 2-5572
details unknown; probably same contents:
  USA: *Begin the Beguine*, Bluebird 6274-1 RB
incl. tracks 1–2, 5, 9–10, 12, 14, 17–18, 20:
  USA: *Moonglow*, RCA LPM 1244
  UK: *The Best of Artie Shaw*, RCA Starcall NL 11089
incl. tracks 1–4, 6–7, 11 (different version), 14, 16–18, 20:
  This is Artie Shaw
  USA: RCA VPM 6039 and VPM 6062
  Europe: RCA NL 89411
  Germany: 26.28034 DP
incl. tracks 1, 3–5, 7, 9, 11–12, 14, 18:
  UK: *Concerto for Clarinet*, RCA DPM 2028
incl. tracks 1, 3–5, 7, 9, 11, 14, 18:
  Europe: *The Best of Artie Shaw*, RCA NL 89104
incl. tracks 1–2, 5, 10, 11 (different version), 12, 17, 20:
  Italy: *Artie Shaw*, Giants of Jazz LPJT 6

Cassettes

tracks 1–3, 5–10, 12, 14–18, 20:
  Germany: *Jazz Collector Edition: Artie Shaw*, Laserlight 79713
incl. tracks 1, 3–5, 7, 9, 11, 14, 18:
  Europe: *The Best of Artie Shaw*, RCA NK 89104
incl. tracks 1–2, 5, 10, 11 (different version), 12, 17, 20:
  Italy: *Artie Shaw*, Giants of Jazz MCJT 6

Woody Herman: *The Thundering Herds 1945–1947*

Over the years a succession of reissues has presented the glorious work of Woody Herman's First and Second Herds for the Columbia label. With one exception, these big-band tracks require none of the equivocating appreciation with apologies given to Artie Shaw's orchestra. The compositions, arrangements, soloists and rhythm are consistently first-rate, and the only drag on the proceedings is Herman's unbearably bad singing. While countless white instrumentalists have rendered the blues convincingly, scarcely any white singers have grasped its language, tone and inflections. Jack Teagarden was one. Herman was not. The leader had the further handicap of an almost toneless voice, so that his ballad singing was even more dreadful than his blues. Enough said.

Before forming the First Herd (heard on all but two tracks on the CD) Herman led 'the band that plays the blues', and, as the First Herd was about to disband, in December 1946 it remade the earlier group's biggest hits, *Woodchopper's Ball* and *Blue Flame* (first recorded in 1939 and 1941 respectively). Although the Herds developed very much their own styles, not surprisingly these earlier compositions owe a debt to the fountainheads of big-band jazz, and they indicate in some sense the direction Herman followed – that of Count Basie – and the one he did not – that of Duke Ellington. *Woodchopper's Ball* is in Basie's mould, a blues built on the principle of riffs, swing rhythms and solos. The simple, toe-tapping ideas remind us what a short step it could be from swing, to rhythm and blues, to rock and roll, to rock. (Indeed, the rhythmically uncontrollable rock guitarist Alvin Lee made *Woodchopper's Ball* his theme song.) *Blue Flame*, Herman's theme song, is also a blues, but in the Ellingtonian 'jungle music' style, with a bass-register trombone du-wah and a deliberate tom-tom rhythm forming the background for a moody sax riff, Herman's bluesy clarinet, Bill Harris's trombone and Chuck Wayne's somewhat too cheery electric guitar.

The bulk of the recordings on this CD were new to the First Herd. They show a creative approach that provides to some extent a swing-era parallel to the relationship between the restrained New Orleans style and the no-holds-barred Chicago style. If Basie's work was a starting point for the First Herd, the group transformed that approach by injecting it with a high-powered intensity in the brass and rhythm. *Goosey Gander*, for example, has (after Harris's solo) wild three-part interlocking riffs which are repeated with trumpeter Pete Candoli screaming over the top. In the last chorus of *Panacea* a blaring Harris and a screaming Candoli play together over an ensemble riff, all supported by the rhythm of bassist Chubby Jackson and Chicagoan drummer Dave Tough, who enthusiastically takes the beat into double time for the first eight bars to kick the intensity up another notch. There are high-register brass riffs in *Wild Root*, a great performance marred by an annoyingly resonant droning pitch (perhaps emanating from the drums), and also in *Backtalk*, which in addition features brassy fanfares, Herman's clarinet riding above or alongside the brass and Dòn Lamond's forceful drumming. It is worth noting that the relationship came full circle a few years later, when one of the principal arrangers on these sessions, Neal Hefti, began writing for Basie; *The Good Earth* is a close cousin of his later scores for Basie, who adopted, together with Hefti's cute themes, a power-house brassy style in combination with Sonny Payne's extroverted drumming.

Adventuresome ideas went hand in hand with this energetic approach. The wildest ones include the ending to *Apple Honey*, as the band slithers upwards to an abrupt halt; the ending to *Goosey Gander*, where the saxophones' honks and slides in the 'Shortnin' Bread' theme are interrupted by overlapping downward glisses tossed around the brass; and the last chorus of *Your Father's Moustache*, where, eight bars after a wild brass break, Herman painstakingly bends a clarinet note against soft sax and muted brass riffs, and some combination of instruments (I cannot identify it) makes a low-pitched glowering sound. The First Herd also took conventional poses, as for example in the themes of *Northwest Passage* and *Backtalk*, reminiscent of Benny Goodman's combos in their velvety blend of vibraphone, electric guitar and reeds.

Three principal soloists return again and again throughout these tracks from 1945 and 1946: clarinettist Herman, tenor saxophonist Flip Phillips and trombonist Harris. Herman and Phillips, though never innovators on their instruments, nonetheless had the tone, time, taste and technique to justify their prominence. Harris was an outrageously innovative trombonist who married old-fashioned sounds – a heavy-handed vibrato and an overdriven, brash timbre – to highly original improvised melodies. Among other soloists, there is veteran swing vibraphonist Red Norvo, at his best on *Backtalk* (which he wrote in collaboration with Shorty Rogers). Candoli, as mentioned, filled the screaming trumpet solo chair until the band's last session, when it was handed over with poorer results to Al Porcino; the latter, on *Non-Alcoholic* at least, comes across as more a squealer than a screamer. Trumpeter Sonny Berman, though not a high-note specialist, takes his place alongside Candoli and Porcino in supplying a soloist's equivalent to the 'Chicago style' parallel drawn above: like Frank Teschemacher, Berman places enthusiasm over polish in his solo on *Your Father's Moustache*; having begun to hit clinkers in the second half of his improvisation, he stays with them, creating an original but completely 'out to lunch' melody. This band was not bashful.

Herman's intended retirement on Christmas Eve, 1946, did not last long. Soon he was back in the studios with a combo, a medium-sized band and a big band, and in September 1947 he formed his renowned Second Herd. It is represented on the CD by two tracks: *The Goof and I*, a carefully wrought, delightfully swinging piece composed and arranged by Al Cohn, and *Four Brothers*, Herman's greatest recording.

Four Brothers was written by Jimmy Giuffre, whose inspiration dated back to the previous year, when he was a member of a four-tenor-saxophone section in a rehearsal band that Gene Roland was leading in Los Angeles. Now, in December 1947, three of the same tenor players – Stan Getz, Zoot Sims and Herbie Steward – were sitting beside Herman's new favourite soloist, baritone saxophonist Serge Chaloff. Giuffre set their mellow sounds, modelled after Lester Young's style, against crisp brass and Lamond's sensational playing on drums. The theme has the four brothers gliding along in tightly packed harmony, with trebly brass punches and snappy drum accents articulating the smooth, cool sounds. Each man takes a solo – Sims, Chaloff, Steward and Getz – and the honours go to the first and last, who with this recording began to push Flip Phillips into the background in the larger history of outstanding tenor saxophonists in Herman's Herds. The contrast of hot brass and drums and cool saxes continues, moving through a powerful riff (to which lyricist and singer Jon Hendricks later conveniently set the words 'four brothers') and a series of loud, exhilarating, perfectly executed stop-time breaks for the saxes playing individually (Getz, Sims, Steward, Chaloff) but with a single conception, and then collectively in harmony.

One other extremely important recording, *Early Autumn*, with Getz's definitive cool ballad playing, is not in the collection for the simple reason that it was recorded for Capitol, to which label Herman switched at the conclusion of the second recording ban by the American Federation of Musicians in 1948. But it seems a shame that the compilers of the CD set chose the rightfully rejected, painful rendition of *A Jug of Wine* rather than the warm-up for *Early Autumn*, Ralph Burns's *Summer Sequence (part iv)*, which is on several of Columbia's LP anthologies of Herman's sessions. In addition to giving a good taste of Getz's future achievement, *Summer Sequence (part iv)* beautifully captures Herman's alto saxophone playing, modelled after Johnny Hodges's sensuous style. Also, the earliest tracks on this CD are not the master takes, which generally do appear on the LPs.

CD

USA: *The Thundering Herds 1945–1947*, Columbia Jazz Masterpieces CK 44108

Sonny Berman, Chuck Frankhouser, Ray Wetzel, Pete Candoli, Carl Warwick (tpt), Ralph Pfeffner, Bill Harris, Ed Kiefer (tb), Woody Herman (cl), Sam Marowitz, John LaPorta (as), Flip Phillips, Pete Mondello (ts), Skippy DeSair (bar), Marjorie

Hyams (vb), Ralph Burns (p), Billy Bauer (elg), Chubby Jackson (sb), Dave Tough (d)

New York   19 Feb 1945   **Apple Honey** (take 3) (arr Burns)

1 March 1945   **Goosey Gander** (take 2) (arr Burns)

Northwest Passage (take 1) (arr Burns)

Berman, Conte Candoli, Pete Candoli, Irv Lewis, Neal Hefti (tpt), Pfeffner, Harris, Kiefer (tb), Herman (cl), Marowitz, LaPorta (as), Phillips, Mondello (ts), DeSair (bar), Tony Aless (p), Bauer (elg), Jackson (sb), Tough (d)

10 Aug 1945   **The Good Earth** (take 2) (arr Hefti)

20 Aug 1945   **Bijou** (arr Burns)   5

add Ray Linn (tpt), Red Norvo (vb), Herman and band (v); Buddy Rich (d) replaces Tough

5 Sept 1945   **Your Father's Moustache** (arr Hefti and Harris)

Berman, Pete Candoli, Lewis, Hefti, Shorty Rogers (tpt), Pfeffner, Harris, Kiefer (tb), Herman (cl), Marowitz, LaPorta (as), Phillips, Mickey Folus (ts), Sam Rubinowich (bar), Aless (p), Bauer (elg), Jackson (sb), Don Lamond (d)

16 Nov 1945   **Wild Root** (arr Hefti)

Berman, Candoli, Marky Markowitz, Conrad Gozzo, Rogers (tpt), Pfeffner, Harris, Kiefer (tb), Herman (cl, v), Marowitz, LaPorta (as), Phillips, Mickey Folus (ts), Sam Rubinowich (bar), Red Norvo (vb), Aless (p), Bauer (elg), Jackson (sb), Don Lamond (d)

17 Feb 1946   **A Jug of Wine**

Panacea (arr Burns)

add Neal Reid (tb); Cappy Lewis (tpt), Jimmie Rowles (p), Chuck Wayne (g), Joe Mondragon (sb) replace Markowitz, Aless, Bauer, Jackson; omit (v)

Los Angeles   20 Sept 1946   **Backtalk** (arr Rogers)   10

Al Porcino, Lewis, Gozzo, Chuck Peterson, Bob Peck (tpt), Pfeffner, Harris, Kiefer (tb), Herman (cl), Marowitz, LaPorta (as), Phillips, Mickey Folus (ts), Sam Rubinowich (bar), Rowles (p), Wayne (elg), Mondragon (sb), Don Lamond (d)

Chicago   10 Dec 1946   **Woodchopper's Ball** (take 1) (arr Hefti)

Blue Flame (arr Jiggs Noble)

add Herman (v)   **The Blues are Brewin'**

omit (v)   **Non-Alcoholic** (arr LaPorta)

Ernie Royal, Bernie Glow, Stan Fishelson, Markowitz, Rogers (tpt), Earl Swope, Ollie Wilson, Bob Swift (tb), Herman (cl), Marowitz, Herbie Steward (as), Stan Getz, Zoot Sims (ts), Serge Chaloff (bar), Fred Otis (p), Gene Sargent (g), Walt Yoder (sb), Lamond (d)
Los Angeles   24 Dec 1947   **The Goof and I** (arr Al Cohn)   **15**

omit Marowitz; Steward (ts)
                     27 Dec 1947   **Four Brothers**

Other CDs
same contents:
  Europe: CBS Jazz Masterpieces 460825-2
incl. tracks 1–5, 15–16:
  UK: *Blowin' up a Storm*, CD Charly 100; Big Band Era 2601.822

LPs
same contents:
  USA: Columbia Jazz Masterpieces CJ 44108
  Europe: CBS Jazz Masterpieces 460825-1
incl. tracks 1–7, 9–14:
  USA: *Woody Herman Complete in Discographical Order*, vol.16, Ajax 231,
    vol.17, Ajax 239, vol.18, Ajax 247, vol.22, Ajax 277
incl. tracks 1–7, 9–11, 14–16 (incl. alternate takes): *The Thundering Herds*
  USA: Columbia C3L 25
  UK: CBS BPG 62158, BPG 62159, BPG 62160
  France: CBS 66378
incl. tracks 1, 3–7, 11–12, 16 (incl. alternate takes):
  USA: *Woody Herman's Greatest Hits*, Columbia CL 2491 and CS 9291;
  The Three Herds, Columbia Special Products JCL 592
incl. tracks 1–3, 5–7, 9, 11 (incl. alternate takes):
  USA: *Bijou*, Harmony HL 7013
incl. tracks 1–3, 5, 15–16:
  UK: *Blowin' up a Storm*, Affinity AFS 1043

Cassettes
same contents:
  USA: Columbia Jazz Masterpieces CJT 44108
  Europe: CBS Jazz Masterpieces 460825-4

Dizzy Gillespie: 'Shaw 'Nuff'; Jazz Tribune no.2: Dizzy Gillespie vol.1/2 (1946–1949)

Jazz history tells us that singer Billy Eckstine formed the first bop big band in 1944, and indeed its roster of sidemen reads like a who's who of the music: Dizzy Gillespie, Charlie Parker, Fats Navarro, Gene Ammons, Dexter Gordon, Sonny Stitt and Art Blakey, all in its first year. But with little exception the group's studio recordings focused on the leader's romantic ballads, light years away from the then new style. Path-breaking big-band bop recordings came not from Eckstine, but from Gillespie. The innovative trumpeter first led his own large ensemble in 1945, but it failed, and the start of his studio sessions had to wait until the following year, when he successfully re-established the orchestra and began recording for Musicraft. In 1947, with RCA Victor, he moved the group in a new and even more unusual direction, bringing swing, bop and Latin music together into a style that came to be known as Afro-Cuban jazz. The unifying factor among all these recordings is that the band was designed to feature Gillespie as its principal soloist, and for good reason: from start to finish his improvising is consistently nothing short of spectacular.

The fanciest modern equipment cannot do much for the Musicraft material, which was not well recorded. And, naturally, some of Gillespie's experiments did not come off. But these faults are outweighed by the music's greatness and its historical importance: excepting the Afro-Cuban idea, the Musicraft sessions lay out the directions Gillespie was to pursue for RCA and with subsequent big bands. One of the many innovations which came directly out of bop combos was Gillespie's dismissal of the guitar from the big band. He did not want that chugging chomp in his rhythm section. From the list of instruments, it may seem that Gillespie simply replaced the guitar with Milt Jackson's vibraphone. But the leader evidently required Jackson to leave aside his considerable ability as an accompanist and instead use the vibraphone strictly as a solo melody instrument.

Among these performances, *Things to Come* is technically the most difficult and conceptually the most simplistic, aiming to create bop big-band music by having everyone play as if they were in a giant bop combo, an assignment which the massed brass cannot possibly handle at a tempo resembling that of Bennie Moten's *Toby*. During his solo the leader's display of effortless originality at high speed underlines, by comparison, the unrelaxed, frenetic, sloppy ensemble work. Things hadn't come together yet. Of greatest interest, after Gillespie's trumpeting, are Jackson's bop vibraphone solo (partially drowned out by the brass) and a characteristic emphasis on weakly functional, suspended harmonies, culminating in the mysterious and unresolved final chords that lead to a glissando down and back up.

One Bass Hit no.2 is a follow-up to a combo version that Gillespie made two months earlier. Both versions are meant to feature bassist Ray Brown, but the poor fidelity is especially hard on Brown's instrument, and in any event on both it is Gillespie who steals the show. Apart from in the solos, the bop style makes its presence felt in the rapid-fire licks that the trumpets trade around as an introduction to Gillespie's solo, in the complexity of the line arranged for saxophones, and generally – as with *Things to Come* and many pieces to follow – in the emphasis on strange, tense harmonies. The next year, RCA's far superior technology afforded Brown an opportunity to stand out on *Two Bass Hit*, particularly in the unaccompanied solo on blues harmonies that he takes at the end, but again he is upstaged by Gillespie's trumpeting as well as by the writing, credited to Gillespie and pianist John Lewis. Outstanding are the stuttering but catchy theme and the slithering chromatic dissonant lines accompanying Gillespie in his third blues chorus.

Our Delight, the first title recorded for Musicraft, marks the start of arranger Tadd Dameron's contributions to the band, which continued on RCA with *Stay on it*, *Cool Breeze* and *Good Bait*. These are the most swing-orientated of Gillespie's recordings. All four have a tunefulness, a cheeriness, a wholesome brightness which immediately mark them as Dameron's, and which belie the circumstances of his turbulent life.

Good Dues Blues, devoted mainly to an absolutely dreary vocal by Alice Roberts, is rescued at the end by one of the most perfect blues improvisations that Gillespie ever recorded. Often he sacrificed polish for wildly creative ideas, but here he has both. The solo demonstrates how he combined traditional licks with his special sense of harmony, twisting familiar phrases in surprising directions. A few months later Roberts redeemed herself on *He Beeped when He Shoulda Bopped*, a joyful, tongue-in-cheek pop song about a musician who was 'draggin' them out of the groove' by beeping when he should have bopped. The tune confirms, and pokes fun at, the status of bop as an insider music, not for just anyone.

Also making a less than auspicious start was singer Kenny Hagood, who performs the tricky ballad *I Waited for You* out of tune and with a heavy, quivering vibrato inappropriate to the bop style. But the arrangement is interesting, showing the obvious influence of Thelonious Monk in its suspenseful harmonies and in the stark accompanimental lines that emphasize colourful elements of chords. With the switch to RCA, Hagood sings duets with Gillespie. On *Oop-pop-a-da*, the churning introductory rhythms and harmonies relax into Lewis's piano, which sets up the bop blues vocal theme, sung in unison by Hagood and Gillespie and punctuated variously by brass glisses moving slowly upwards, by Lewis's piano obbligato and by Gillespie's wacky vocal fills. A four-bar duo vocal break is repeated twice, with each man filling out the rest of the chorus as a soloist. The contrast is illuminating: Gillespie sings just like he plays. His tone is much thinner than Hagood's, but his ideas and his choice of scat singing syllables are much hipper. After the instrumental solos the riff theme returns, cleverly spread out with Hagood in his low range and Gillespie in falsetto. Dameron's blues *Cool Breeze*, on which the two men trade phrases, and Gil Fuller's blues *Ool-ya-koo*, on which they sing the riff theme together and then take solos (Hagood first), show in Gillespie the same contrasts of thinner tone and better ideas. Fuller's piece has a great ending: Kenny Clarke's brief drum solo leads to a return of the theme, this time not sung, but played in combination with loud, energetic counter-riffs; the last time around, Gillespie tops it off with screaming trumpet licks and the title words, shouted.

Despite the presence of Sonny Stitt and Leo Parker in the band, one weakness on its recordings was the lack of a saxophone soloist talented enough to stand up against the leader. The problem was relieved late in 1946, when Cecil Payne joined. Payne's was a straight bop style, modelled after Charlie Parker's, and his was no small achievement in transferring the nimble-fingered requirements of bop melody to the large and cumbersome fingering of the baritone saxophone. Gillespie wasted no time in featuring Payne, who appears on the first track for RCA, *Ow!*, both as a soloist and in the lead of the riff theme played by the sax section. He is also the first soloist on *Stay on it*.

The Afro-Cuban element came into the band with the hiring of conga drummer Chano Pozo in 1947. Pozo was murdered in 1948, which happened to be the year of the second recording ban imposed by the musicians' union, and so his studio career was brief. It was nonetheless tremendously influential. On some tracks, his rhythmic contribution juxtaposes Latin-style even subdivisions of the beat against everyone else's swing-style uneven subdivisions, with the result that the rhythm seems to pulsate in and out of phase. This is most evident on Dameron's pieces *Cool Breeze* and *Good Bait*. Gillespie's composition *Algo Bueno* (better known as *Woody 'n You*) more convincingly incorporates Pozo's rhythmic conception, though the result is still a jazz-Latin hybrid, not a jazz-Latin fusion. It begins with stuttering syncopated saxophone lines, which are coordinated with the conga beat, and with bassist Al McKibbon playing a syncopated pattern rather than a walking line. But the *b* section of the *aaba* theme comes straight out of Duke Ellington's *Satin Doll* and cries out for a swing feel rather than the even-eighth treatment it gets. The band breaks into swing for the alto sax solo; Pozo leaps back to Latin rhythm for his solo break. The following ensemble passage swings; the restatement of the theme returns to the Latin beat.

The two-sided 78 rpm recording of George Russell's *Cubana Be* and *Cubana Bop* (also known as *Cubano Be* and *Cubano Bop*, because this is what the band members actually sing) is the famed art piece of Afro-Cuban jazz. While it convincingly presents the voodoo roots of Pozo's percussion playing, it does not hang together well at all, being composed of part lumbering elephantine ensemble hockets (i.e., a succession of sounds and silences resulting from the introduction of rests), part self-consciously 'different' and dissonant lines, part overly tame, old-fashioned sentimental melody.

Instead the really memorable recording, and the masterpiece of these collections, is *Manteca*, credited to Gillespie and Pozo. The opening gradually builds up into an interlocking collection of repeated, two-bar Latin riffs, with the string bass on the one hand and baritone sax and trombone on the other playing rollicking lines, either of which alone would have been enough to carry the piece forward; together the effect is irresistibly propulsive. The theme emerges seamlessly out of the interlocking riff, but then there is a clear break into a swing-bop feel, with a walking bass line rather than the syncopated pattern. The cycle begins again as the introductory Latin riffs return, but this time the theme presents itself in the guise of swing, with the bass walking in support of Big Nick Nicholas's tenor sax solo; Nicholas even quotes from a swing standard, *Blue Moon*, to begin the second half of his solo. After Gillespie's solo the Latin rhythms return, and then the opening vamp moves in reverse, reducing down to bass and conga drum as Gillespie shouts out the title of this euphoric performance.

(On reissues, Gillespie's essential big-band tracks appear in tandem with his bop combo recordings. Although the combo work is described in Chapter 7, for convenience all details on reissues appear below and are fully duplicated in that later chapter. Note also that, on Prestige's double album **In the Beginning**, the titles on side 3 are out of order on the jacket, but correct on the label.)

CD

USA: 'Shaw 'nuff', Musicraft MVSCD 53

Dizzy Gillespie (tpt), Dexter Gordon (ts), Frank Paparelli (p), Chuck Wayne (elg), Murray Shipinski (sb), Irv Kluger (d)
New York   9 Feb 1945   **Blue 'n Boogie**

Gillespie (tpt), Charlie Parker (as), Clyde Hart (p), Remo Palmieri (elg), Slam Stewart (sb), Cozy Cole (d)
                  28 Feb 1945   **Groovin' High**
                                       All the Things You Are
                                       Dizzy Atmosphere

Gillespie (tpt, v), Parker (as), Al Haig (p), Curly Russell (sb), Sid Catlett (d)
                  11 May 1945   **Salt Peanuts**   5

omit (v)   **Shaw 'nuff**

add Sarah Vaughan (v)   **Lover Man**

omit (v)   **Hot House**

Gillespie (tpt), Sonny Stitt (as), Milt Jackson (vb), Haig (p), Ray Brown (sb), Kenny Clarke (d)

                15 May 1946   **One Bass Hit no.1**

add Gillespie, Gil Fuller (v)   **Oop Bop Sh'bam**   10
                                         That's Earl, Brother

Gillespie, Dave Burns, Raymond Orr, Talib Daawud, John Lynch (tpt), Alton Moore, Charles Greenlea (tb), John Brown, Howard Johnson (as), Ray Abrams, Warren Luckey (ts), Pee Wee Moore (bar), Jackson (p), Ray Brown (sb), Clarke (d)

                10 June 1946   **Our Delight**

add Roberts (v)   **Good Dues Blues**

Gillespie, Burns, Daawud, Kenny Dorham, Lynch, Elmon Wright (tpt), Leon Com-egeys, Gordon Thomas, Moore (tb), Johnson, Stitt (as), Abrams, Luckey (ts), Leo Parker (bar), John Lewis (p), Brown (sb), Clarke (d)

                9 July 1946   **One Bass Hit no.2**
                                         Ray's Idea   15

add Jackson (vb)   **Things to Come**

add Roberts (v)   **He Beeped when He Shoulda**
                                         Bopped

Gillespie, Burns, Lynch, Wright, Matthew McKay (tpt), Thomas, Alton Moore, Taswell Baird (tb), John Brown, Scoops Carry (as), James Moody, Bill Frazier (ts), Pee Wee Moore (bar), John Lewis (p), Ray Brown (sb), Joe Harris (d), Kenny Hagood (v)

                12 Nov 1946   **I Waited for You**

add Jackson (vb)   **Emanon**

Other CDs
incl. tracks 2, 4–6, 12, 16, plus others cited below
Denmark: *Dizzy Gillespie*, Official 83056-2

LPs

plus additional tracks:
USA: *In the Beginning*, Prestige 24030
incl. tracks 1–11:
USA: *The Small Groups*, Phoenix LP 2
incl. tracks 12–18:
USA: *Dizzy's Delight*, Phoenix LP 4
tracks 1–5, 8–13, 14–16, 19: *Groovin' High*
USA: Savoy MG 12020
France: BYG 529.145; Savoy-Musidisc 30 SA 6037
incl. tracks 1–4, 9–11:
USA: *Dizzy Gillespie: the Development of an American Artist, 1940–1946*,
Smithsonian R004
tracks 1–4, 8, 10–13, 15–16, 19:
UK: *The Dizzy Gillespie Story*, Ember EMB 3344
tracks 1, 3–4, 8–17, 19:
USA: *Blue 'n Boogie*, Allegro LP 3083
incl. tracks 1, 4–5, 9–10, 12, 15–16, 19, plus others cited below:
Italy: *Dizzy Gillespie: Small Combos*, Giants of Jazz LPJT 32, and
Dizzy Gillespie and His Orchestra, Giants of Jazz LPJT 37
tracks 2–5, 8, 10–12, 14, 16–17, 19:
UK: *Dizzy Gillespie and His Orchestra*, Saga ERO 8017
incl. tracks 2, 4–6, 12, 16, plus others cited below
Denmark: *Dizzy Gillespie*, Official 3056–2

Cassettes

incl. tracks 1, 4–5, 9–10, 12, 15–16, 19, plus others cited below:
Italy: *Dizzy Gillespie: Small Combos*, Giants of Jazz MCJT 32, and
Dizzy Gillespie and His Orchestra, Giants of Jazz MCJT 37

LP

Europe: *Jazz Tribune no.2: Dizzy Gillespie, vol.1/2 (1946–1949)*,
RCA NL 89763

Gillespie (tpt), Don Byas (ts), Jackson (vb), Haig (p), Bill DeArango (elg), Brown
(b), J. C. Heard (d)

New York	22 Feb 1946	**52nd Street Theme** (take 1)	
		52nd Street Theme (take 2)	
		A Night in Tunisia	
		Ol' Man Rebop	
		Anthropology (take 1)	5
		Anthropology (take 2)	

Gillespie, Burns, Wright, McKay, Raymond Orr (tpt), Baird or Ted Kelly?, Bill Shepherd (tb), John Brown, Johnson (as), Moody or Big Nick Nicholas?, Joe Gayles (ts), Cecil Payne (bar), Lewis (p), Ray Brown or Al McKibbon? (sb), Harris or Clarke? (d)

22 Aug 1947	**Ow!**	

add Gillespie, Hagood (v)   **Oop-pop-a-da**

omit (v)   **Two Bass Hit**

                                   Stay on it   10

Gillespie, Burns, Elmon Wright, Lammar Wright Jr, Benny Bailey (tpt), Kelly, Shepherd (tb), John Brown, Johnson (as), Nicholas, Joe Gayles (ts), Payne (bar), Lewis (p), McKibbon (sb), Clarke (d), Chano Pozo (conga drum)

           22 Dec 1947   **Algo Bueno (Woody 'n You)**

add Gillespie, Hagood (v)   **Cool Breeze**

Pozo and band (v) replace Gillespie, Hagood

                                   Cubana Be

                                   Cubana Bop

*as **Algo Bueno**, but Gillespie (v)*

           30 Dec 1947   **Manteca**   15

omit (v)   **Good Bait**

add Gillespie, Hagood (v)   **Ool-ya-koo**

omit (v)   **Minor Walk**

Gillespie, Burns, Elmon Wright, Willie Cook (tpt), Andy Duryea, Sam Hurt, Jesse Tarrant (tb), Brown, Ernie Henry (as), Gayles, Budd Johnson (ts), Payne (bar), James Forman (p), McKibbon (sb), Teddy Stewart (d), Harris (conga drum), Sabu Martinez (bongo)

           29 Dec 1948   **Guarachi Guaro**

                                   Duff Capers   20

                                   Lover Come Back to Me

add Gillespie (v)   **I'm Be Boppin' Too** (take 1)

                                 I'm Be Boppin' Too (take 2)

(Metronome All Stars:) Gillespie, Miles Davis, Fats Navarro (tpt), J. J. Johnson, Kai Winding (tb), Buddy DeFranco (cl), Charlie Parker (as), Charlie Ventura (ts), Ernie

Caceres (bar), Lennie Tristano (p), Billy Bauer (elg), Eddie Safranski (sb), Shelly Manne (d)

| 3 Jan 1949 | **Overtime** | |
| | **Victory Ball** | **25** |

Gillespie, Little Benny Harris, Wright, Cook (tpt), Duryea, Hurt, Tarrant (tb), Brown, Henry (as), Gayles, Yusef Lateef (ts), Al Gibson (bar), Forman (p), McKibbon (sb), Stewart (d), Vince Guerro (conga drum)

14 April 1949	**St Louis Blues**
	Swedish Suite
6 May 1949	**Katy (Dizzier and Dizzier)**

add Gillespie, Joe 'Bebop' Carroll (v)

Jump Did-le-ba

Charles Greenlea, J. J. Johnson (tb) replace Hurt and Tarrant

| 6 July 1949 | **Hey Pete, Let's Eat Mo' Meat**   **30** |

omit (v)   **Jumpin' with Symphony Sid**

add Carroll (v)   **In the Land of Oo-bla-dee**

CDs

incl. tracks 7, 9, 11, 13–16, 19, 28, 31:
   Europe: (various artists:) *The Bebop Revolution*, Bluebird ND 82177
incl. tracks 3, 7, 11, 28, plus others cited above:
   Denmark: *Dizzy Gillespie*, Official 83056-2

Other LPs

same contents:
   France: RCA PM 42408
tracks 2–5, 9, 13–16, 18, 26, 28: *The Greatest of Dizzy Gillespie*
   USA: RCA LPM 2398
   UK: RCA RD 27242; RCA SF 5123
tracks 2–5, 7–10, 11 (alternate take), 12–22, 26–31:
   France: *Horizons du Jazz: Dizzy Gillespie Orchestra*, RCA 430.215, and
   title unknown, RCA 430.207
incl. tracks 1, 3–5, 8–16, 18, 21, 24–5, 27, 30, 32:
   France: *Dizzy Gillespie, vol.1*, RCA 731.676 and *Dizzy Gillespie, vol.2*,
   RCA 731.068
tracks 1, 3 (alternate take), 4, 11, 17, 19–21, 23, 27, 30–32: *Dizzy
   Gillespie*

USA: RCA LPV 530
UK: RCA RD 7827
incl. tracks 3, 7–10, 11 (alternate take), 12–17, 31, plus others cited above:
Italy: *Dizzy Gillespie: Small Combos*, Giants of Jazz LPJT 32, and *Dizzy Gillespie and His Orchestra*, Giants of Jazz LPJT 37
incl. tracks 2–3, 5–12, 15–17:
Europe: *Diz Delights*, RCA CL 89804
tracks 7, 9, 11 (alternate take), 13–15, 20, 22, 26–8, 30–32:
USA: *Dizzier and Dizzier*, RCA LJM 1009
incl. tracks 7–8, 10, 12, 29: (various leaders:) *The Be-bop Era*
USA: RCA LPV 519
UK: RCA RD 7827
incl. tracks 17, 19–23, 27–32:
France: *When Be-bop Meets the Big Band (Dizzy Gillespie, vol.1, 1947–49)* RCA 741.095
incl. tracks 3, 7, 11, 28, plus others cited above:
Denmark: *Dizzy Gillespie*, Official 3056-2

Cassettes

same contents:
Europe: RCA NK 89763
incl. tracks 2–3, 5–12, 15–17:
Europe: *Diz Delights*, RCA CK 89804
incl. tracks 3, 7–10, 11 (alternate take), 12–17, 31, plus others cited above:
Italy: *Dizzy Gillespie: Small Combos*, Giants of Jazz MCJT 32, and *Dizzy Gillespie and His Orchestra*, Giants of Jazz MCJT 37

* * *

Miles Davis: *Porgy and Bess*

In 1957, seven years after concluding their leading roles in the 'birth of the cool' (see Chapter 7), arranger Gil Evans and trumpeter and flugelhorn player Miles Davis began to make a series of albums presenting by far the most successful new conception of how a jazz big band might sound. The second of these collaborations, recorded in 1958, is Evans's adaptation, without vocal parts, of selections from George Gershwin's opera *Porgy and Bess*.

From the first phrases of *The Buzzard Song*, with screaming trumpets blending directly into trilling flutes, Evans's originality shines through. In part the newness results automatically from the unusual instrumentation, which expands the orchestral palette developed in their earlier cool-jazz nonet: there is no piano in the rhythm section; french horns and a tuba join the conventional brass sections of trumpets and trombones; flutes join the saxophones. But mainly it comes from the imaginative, ever-changing colours that Evans draws from these instruments. In *The Buzzard Song* and again just before Davis enters with the melody to the title line of *Bess, You is my Woman Now*, the string bass of Paul Chambers and tuba of Bill Barber are paired together, but not as bass instruments; instead they play a jumpy low-pitched melody. On the same track Evans uses massed winds in constantly changing textures of chordal accompaniment to Davis's mellow flugelhorn, such that the overall texture is one of soft colours, but forceful trumpets or dissonant accompanimental lines fleetingly intrude and retreat. On *Gone*, powerful block chords, in unpredictable combinations with and without Davis, provide a framework for Philly Joe Jones's drum solo and a hard-bop trio improvisation (Davis, Chambers and Jones) on an obliquely stated 12-bar blues progression. This provides a strong contrast to *Gone, Gone, Gone*, where the same block chords return in a gentle guise, against which Davis provides a stabbing version of Gershwin's music. On *Summertime* Evans brings an unusual twist to notions of big-band riffs, by having french horns and then flutes lead the riff that accompanies Davis. On *Prayer*, again there are wondrous combinations of sound in the orchestra's 'congregational shouts' accompanying Davis's bluesy 'preaching'. And halfway through *I Loves You, Porgy*, which threatens to coagulate into a sugary gel through its too-heavy reliance on orchestral winds, Evans brings Davis's intense trumpet back in to set the mood to a slow burn.

A good deal of rhythmic ambiguity goes hand in hand with Evans's diverse colouristic effects. *Bess, You is my Woman Now* deviates from being exclusively a slow ballad through arranged changes of tempo and metre. The block chords of *Gone, Gone, Gone* proceed at a slow, free tempo. On the slow ballad *Bess, oh Where's my Bess?* an undercurrent of double time in the brushwork of drummer Jimmy Cobb breaks through into true double time in portions of the second half of the track. *Prayer* has no explicit beat at all, and near the end Cobb's cymbals are there to provide tone, not rhythm. *My Man's Gone Now* moves back and forth between a slow and double-time pace. Finally, at the start of both *It Ain't Necessarily So* and *I Loves You, Porgy*, Evans devises rhythmic swirls; on the former the bass and on the latter the flutes play triplet figures, obscuring what turns out to be the true metre of each piece.

Rivalling this *tour de force* in colouristic and rhythmic orchestration is the quality of Davis's improvisations. He plays in a restrained, spacious manner, swinging devilishly in the trio passages and always keeping closely in touch with the blues through his use of bent notes, through the toughness of his attack, and through the plaintive quality of his open and muted timbres. He is not afraid to repeat ideas, and in doing so he has few peers in his ability to restate phrases in a microscopically varied continuum of positions around the beat. On the whole he avoids light witticisms, though he does paraphrase a snippet of *It's All Right with Me* in the fourth blues chorus of the trio's segment of *Gone*. Don't miss the sarcastic kiss he throws into his horn at the last instant of *It Ain't Necessarily So*, as if to underscore the meaning of the title.

This special big band also took up a path usually associated only with Davis's sextet, though it was in fact a general concern of his at the time: segments of three pieces provide examples of what came to be known as 'modal jazz', in which improvisation takes place over static harmony rather than over fast-moving chord progressions. These are the main section of *The Buzzard Song* (beginning at the move from a waltz rhythm into a swinging four beat); the oscillating accompaniment in *Prayer* (resembling a slow version of the title track of Davis's album **Milestones**, recorded by his sextet four months earlier) and the main section of *It Ain't Necessarily So* (closely resembling *Milestones*).

CD

USA: *Porgy and Bess*, **Columbia Jazz Masterpieces CK 40647**

Miles Davis (tpt, flugelhorn), Louis Mucci, Ernie Royal, Johnny Coles, Bernie Glow (tpt), Jimmy Cleveland, Joseph Bennett, Dick Hixon, Frank Rehak (tb), Willie Ruff, Julius Watkins, Gunther Schuller (french horn), Bill Barber (tuba), Cannonball Adderley (as), Danny Banks (sax), Phil Bodner, Romeo Penque (fl), Paul Chambers (sb), Philly Joe Jones (d), Gil Evans (arr)

New York	22 July 1958	**My Man's Gone Now**
		Gone
		Gone, Gone, Gone

Jimmy Cobb (d) replaces Jones

	29 July 1958	**Here Come de Honey Man**
		Bess, You is my Woman Now 5
		It Ain't Necessarily So
		Fisherman, Strawberry and Devil Crab

Jerome Richardson (fl) replaces Bodner

	4 Aug 1958	**Prayer (Oh Doctor Jesus)**
		Bess, oh Where's my Bess?
		The Buzzard Song 10

18 Aug 1958   **Summertime**
There's a Boat that's Leaving
    Soon for New York
I Loves You, Porgy

Other CDs
same contents:
Europe: CBS Jazz Masterpieces 480985-2
Japan: CBS 32 DP 512

LPs
same contents:
USA: Columbia CL 1274; Columbia CS 8085, KCS 8085, PC 8085;
Columbia Jazz Masterpieces CJ 40647
UK: CBS 32188; Fontana TFL 5056; Fontana STFL 507
Europe: CBS BPG 62108 and SBPG 62108; CBS Jazz Masterpieces 450985-1;
Fontana 682044 TL; Fontana 885109 TY

Cassettes
same contents:
USA: Columbia Jazz Masterpieces CJT 40647
UK: CBS 40-32188
Europe: CBS Jazz Masterpieces 450985-4

CHAPTER 4
Swing Combos

Barry Kernfeld

As the 1930s rolled along, hot bands gave way to swing combos, not in the manner of the seemingly abrupt emergence of bop in the early 1940s, nor in that of the much more abrupt emergence in the late 1950s of free jazz, but rather in a seamless transition in which certain tendencies of early jazz received less prominence, while others came to the fore. There was less collective improvisation, though countless examples still remained, especially in the climactic last choruses of pieces (the 'ride out'). Instead, there were greater proportions of space given over to soloists; greater proportions of themes stated alone, or in unison, or in arranged block harmonies; greater proportions of simple repeated snippets of melody ('riffs') used as both themes and accompanimental figures. In the core repertory, multithematic pieces (rags, marches, multi-part blues) took a back seat to pop song forms, while the 12-bar blues remained as crucial as ever, and hand in hand with this simplification of the repertory came a greater complexity of its interpretation, in that for both accompanists and soloists the underpinning of fundamental three- and four-note harmonies became less transparent. The roles of instruments shifted somewhat. The saxophone began to push the trumpet out of its position as the foremost jazz instrument. In the completion of a years-long process that saw the rhythm grow smoother, guitar replaced banjo, string bass replaced tuba, and the drums more often simply kept time rather than participating actively as the main percussive element in collective improvisation. More generally, whole combos began to grasp 'swing', that rhythmic propulsion which such individuals as Jelly Roll Morton, Sidney Bechet and, above all, Louis Armstrong, already had under their control in recordings made in the previous decade.

Swing was so basic to the first 40 years of jazz recording that swing combos absorbed, or combined with, hot and bop combos in every imaginable way, with the result that sometimes their separate identity seems to depend as much on period and affiliation as on distinct sound. Thus it is that swing combos are the subject of three chapters in this book. This chapter and the one that follows begin with combos that flourished from the mid-1930s into the 1940s, the height of the swing era. Some were fairly stable groups, both dependent and independent. The former, such as Benny Goodman's combo and Bob Crosby's Bob Cats, were affiliated with a big band, from which they partially, if not entirely, drew their personnel, and through such an affiliation they reached audiences far larger than the jazz community. The latter, such as the combo Sid Catlett led on 52nd Street in New York and the quintet Django Reinhardt and Stephane Grappelli led in Paris, generally did not reach out beyond jazz, and in this respect two groups, Fats Waller and his Rhythm and Nat 'King' Cole's trio, are atypical, since both entered segments of the popular market-place. Other types of swing combos made their way into the recording studios on an *ad hoc* basis, perhaps to accompany a soloist, as in the ever-changing all-star combos heard on Billie Holiday's sessions, or perhaps just to get away from big-band arrangements and let off some steam, as on the informal 'jam session' recorded by Roy Eldridge and Chu Berry.

The present chapter then leaps abruptly to a selection from 1964 in which swing-era star Ella Fitzgerald – still at the height of her powers – leads a concert performance in which the musical style remains close to the central stream. Chapter 5, which surveys combos presenting a blend of swing and dixieland, moves into the 1950s to trace analogous continuations of that hybrid. Chapter 8 surveys a different hybrid, those combos blending swing and bop.

* * *

Benny Goodman: *Trio–Quartet–Quintet*; Charlie Christian: *The Genius of the Electric Guitar*

While leading the ensemble which from 1935 was *the* most popular big band (giving way to Glenn Miller only as the decade ended), Benny Goodman also directed a swing combo. Anthologies recorded for the Victor and Columbia labels document his small group's growth from a trio to six, seven, and – for one recording session – eight pieces (all of the latter curiously called 'sextets'). These afford plenty of opportunity to hear Goodman's immaculate clarinet playing. Furthermore, the combo sessions, in comparison with the big-band ones, are far less heavily indebted to borrowings from other ensembles.

There is a sprinkling of significant performances by racially mixed groups to be found among early jazz recordings. Examples include Jelly Roll Morton with the New Orleans Rhythm Kings in 1923, Eddie Lang (masquerading as Blind Willie Dunn) with King Oliver and Lonnie Johnson in 1929, Billy Banks's Rhythmakers in 1932. But it was one thing to hold *ad hoc* sessions for a specialized buying public and quite another for America's most popular musician to follow up a jam session with pianist Teddy Wilson and drummer Gene Krupa by incorporating Wilson into his regular group, first in recording sessions and then in live performances, the mixed combo being presented as an adjunct to the white big band. Later other great black players joined, including vibraphonist Lionel Hampton (who in mid-1939 doubled as a drummer with the big band), guitarist Charlie Christian and trumpeter Cootie Williams (who also played with the big band); pianist Count Basie made several guest appearances.

These recordings testify to Goodman's sensitivity to instrumental sounds. There had only occasionally been jazz trios of clarinet, piano and drums (notably Morton again, with Barney Bigard and Zutty Singleton in 1929). The combination became still more unusual with the addition of vibraphone, with which Hampton produced a shimmering sound, setting the instrument's mechanically rotating discs to produce a vibrato at the fastest possible speed. The addition of string bass, tenor sax and trumpet moved the combo's overall sound towards the conventional, but at the same time along came Charlie Christian, playing electric guitar as if it were a wind instrument.

The first album dates from Goodman's association with Victor. Most issues of these recordings are large anthologies, including undistinguished singing, jazz versions of wedding and bar mitzvah music, and second-but-not-enlightening takes of several tunes. I am therefore focusing on the contents of the classic LP, which contains the best sample of the group's work.

On the trio tracks, Krupa is far less heavy handed than he is with the big band. He keeps time on the snare drum, adding accents on other drums and cymbals as the more energetic pieces move along, and playing a solo on *Tiger Rag*. Wilson, while maintaining a striding left hand, improvises florid new melodies both in solos and in filling the spaces around Goodman's melodies. Wilson is a gentle player, and even when he is inventing a rhythmically charged solo, as in the second chorus of *Oh, Lady be Good!*, he does not hit the keyboard hard (as, say, Earl Hines would do). Goodman produces a beautiful sound, playing with a light, fast vibrato, yet he also distorts his sound when appropriate; in the same way, he moves freely between playing perfectly in tune and sliding around to produce blue notes. Within the context of these general approaches, the three men produce a varied sound, especially on *Tiger Rag*, which for contrast includes a chorus of Goodman's woody low-register playing and a series of stop-time solo choruses.

When Hampton joins to make the trio a quartet, he fully exploits the possibilities of his instrument. A second striking feature of these tracks, aside from the mere fact of the particular instruments played, is the multitude of ways in which the instruments combine. If the repertory and rhythms are weighted towards swing, other aspects of these performances are more closely related to Morton's goals for small-band jazz – to achieve a carefully rehearsed balance between composition and improvisation and to pull greatly varied textures out of a small number of players – than to the notion of a free-wheeling swing-era combo jam session. Examples include the dixieland ending to *Dinah*, in which clarinet, piano and vibes improvise as if there were a trumpeter anchoring the proceedings; in *Runnin' Wild*, the fast line played in harmony by clarinet and vibraphone at the beginning and ending and a vibes solo accompanied by a steady drum beat but a stop-time clarinet and piano riff; piano and vibraphone striking chords heavily against Goodman's sombre rendition of the melody of *The Man I Love*; and the riffing call and response between Goodman and Hampton that opens and ends *Smiles* (essentially big-band sectional playing translated to individual instruments). The most complex of these meticulous arrangements is *Opus ½*, a multi-thematic piece comprising an introduction, a first theme in a minor key, and a succession of blues choruses sandwiched between a second theme which returns at the end with its middle section omitted. *Opus ½* and a straightforward rendition of *Sweet Georgia Brown* were recorded in October 1938, by which time Krupa had left to form his own big band, thereby initiating a period of rapid personnel turnover in Goodman's group. Dave Tough replaces Krupa on these tracks, but he has no opportunity to show off his great drumming, both performances demanding restraint. The only dull track on the classic collection is the final one, *Pick-a-Rib* (1939), a two-part blues and boogie tune with Buddy Schutz in Tough's chair and John Kirby's string bass added, somewhat redundantly, against Wilson's left hand.

By the time of the Columbia recordings featuring Charlie Christian (1939–41), Goodman's six- and seven-piece 'sextets' had moved completely into the mould of the free-wheeling swing-era combo jam session. The emphasis is on riffs and improvisation, with arrangement kept to a minimum. Among the principal soloists, Count Basie plays in the sparse style by then already well known from his work with his own big band. Cootie Williams keeps on his Duke Ellington mask, playing growling, muted 'jungle music' solos; the only exception is *Waitin' for Benny*, which he did not realize was being recorded. Tenor saxophonist Georgie Auld plays in a manner heavily indebted to Ben Webster. Goodman's playing complements what we have already heard on the Victor sessions, and he has an opportunity on *Wholly Cats*, *Gone with 'What' Wind* and *Breakfast Feud* to show what a fine blues soloist he is. But the main point of having this collection is to hear Christian.

Christian's period in the spotlight extended only a couple of months on either side of these recordings, from September 1939, when he joined Goodman, to June 1941, when tuberculosis caused him to be confined in a sanatorium permanently. In these two years he established an enormously influential approach to jazz electric guitar-playing. He was not the first jazz electric guitarist, but he was the first brilliant electric-guitar soloist. He preferred a clean, round tone, and this aspect of his playing had a stifling effect upon jazz; only 30 years later, after blues and rock musicians showed the way, did jazz electric guitarists stop imitating Christian's sound and begin exploring the sort of timbral variety that wind, brass and percussion players had been exploring all along. Christian balanced this single-minded approach to tone with his fertile imagination for melody. He effortlessly tossed out new swinging riffs and running lines, and in this respect he put his instrument on an equal footing with winds and brass. All of the commercial recordings have consistently creative guitar solos; possibly the best are on *Rose Room*, *Boy Meets Goy* (the offensive title was changed to *Grand Slam* early on), *Breakfast Feud* (on many issues as a composite of two takes to extend Christian's solo) and *I Found a New Baby*. To show off his ability in the freest possible jam session, the Columbia collections also include informal warm-ups: *Blues in B* and *Waitin' for Benny* were test recordings, subsequently released because of Christian's great playing. On *Blues in B* someone asks Charlie to play a blues in B. (Is this the recording engineer, who perhaps did not know the difference between B and B flat?) The horn players are flustered, this being a difficult key for them, and in the background you can hear 'what the hell . . . in B!' as they noodle about, but for guitar this is one of the easiest keys, and Christian plunges right in. *Waitin' for Benny* begins as a one-chord jam without piano and bass, then segues into a fast version of *A Smoo-o-o-oth One* with pianist Johnny Guarnieri joining in. (The authorized version of *A Smoo-o-o-oth One*, recorded after Benny arrived, is much slower, more restrained, and more formal; it is included on many of the LPs but is on a different set in the Columbia Jazz Masterpieces series: **The Benny Goodman Sextet 1939–41 Featuring Charlie Christian**).

Christian generally did not play with Goodman's big band, which kept its own rhythm guitarist. Among his occasional recordings with it, the best known is *Solo Flight*, which, except for a brief solo by Goodman, pits Christian's fluid lines against a busy succession of swing riffs and sustained chords, as arranged by Jimmy Mundy.

LP
USA: *Trio–Quartet–Quintet*, **RCA LPM 1226**

Benny Goodman (cl), Teddy Wilson (p), Gene Krupa (d)

New York	13 July 1935	**Body and Soul** (take 1)
Chicago	27 April 1936	**Oh, Lady be Good!**

Goodman (cl), Wilson (p), Krupa (d), Lionel Hampton (vb)

Hollywood	26 Aug 1936	**Dinah**

| New York | 18 Nov 1936 | **Sweet Sue – Just You** | |

Goodman, Wilson, Krupa
| | 2 Dec 1936 | **Tiger Rag** | 5 |

Goodman, Wilson, Krupa, Hampton
	2 Dec 1936	**Whispering**	
	3 Feb 1937	**Runnin' Wild**	
Hollywood	30 July 1937	**The Man I Love**	
	2 Aug 1937	**Smiles**	

Goodman (cl), Wilson (p), Dave Tough (d), Hampton (vb)
| Chicago | 12 Oct 1938 | **Opus ½** | 10 |
| | | **Sweet Georgia Brown** | |

Goodman (cl), Wilson (p), John Kirby (sb), Buddy Schutz (d), Hampton (vb)
| New York | 29 Dec 1938 | **Pick-a-Rib** | |

CDs

incl. tracks 1–7: *After You've Gone: the Original Trio & Quartet Sessions vol.1*
  USA: Bluebird 5631-2 R
  Europe: RCA ND 85631

Other LPs

same contents:
  France: *Trio, Quartet, and Quintet*, RCA 430 230
plus additional tracks: *Jazz Tribune no.13: 'The Complete Small Combinations' vols.1/2 (1935–1937)* and *Jazz Tribune no.22: 'The Complete Small Combinations' vols.3/4 (1937/1939)*
  Europe: RCA NL 89753 and NL 89754
  France: RCA PM 43176 and PM 43684
plus additional tracks, with alternate take of pt.2 of **Pick-a-Rib:**
  USA: *The Complete Benny Goodman* vols.1–4, 6, 7, Bluebird AXM2-5505, AXM2-5515, AXM2-5532, AXM2-5537, AXM2-5566, AXM2-5567
  Japan: title unknown, RCA RA 72, RA 73, RA 74
incl. tracks 1–7: *After You've Gone: the Original Trio & Quartet Sessions vol.1*
  USA: Bluebird 5631-1 R
  Europe: RCA NL 85631
incl. tracks 2, 3, 5, 6, 8, 10, 11:

France: *Trio and Quartet vol.2*, RCA 730629

Cassettes

plus additional tracks:
Europe: *Jazz Tribune no.13: 'The Complete Small Combinations' vols. 1/2 (1935–1937)* and *Jazz Tribune no.22: 'The Complete Small Combinations' vols.3/4 (1937/1939)*, RCA NK 89753 and NK 89754

CD

USA: Charlie Christian: *The Genius of the Electric Guitar*, Columbia Jazz Masterpieces CK 40846

Goodman (cl), Fletcher Henderson (p), Christian (elg), Artie Bernstein (sb), Nick Fatool (d), Hampton (vb)

New York	2 Oct 1939	**Rose Room**	
	22 Nov 1939	**Seven Come Eleven**	

Count Basie replaces Henderson

	7 Feb 1940	**Till Tom Special**
		Gone with 'What' Wind

Johnny Guarnieri replaces Basie

	16 April 1940	**Boy Meets Goy (Grand Slam)**	5

Dudley Brooks replaces Guarnieri

Los Angeles	20 June 1940	**Six Appeal**

Cootie Williams (tpt), Goodman (cl), Georgie Auld (ts), Basie (p), Christian (elg), Bernstein (sb), Harry Jaeger (d)

New York	7 Nov 1940	**Wholly Cats**	
		Royal Garden Blues	
		As Long as I Live	
		Benny's Bugle	10

Jo Jones replaces Jaeger

	15 Jan 1941	**Breakfast Feud**
		I Found a New Baby

Goodman (cl, dir), Alec Fila, Jimmy Maxwell, Williams, Irving Goodman (tpt), Lou McGarity, Cutty Cutshall (tb), Skippy Martin, Gus Bivona (as), Auld, Pete Mondello (ts), Bob Snyder (bar), Johnny Guarnieri (p), Christian (elg), Bernstein (sb), Tough (d), Jimmy Mundy (arr)

4 March 1941	**Solo Flight**	

Williams, Auld, Guarnieri, Christian, Bernstein, Tough
13 March 1941	**Blues in B**	

omit Bernstein	**Waitin' for Benny**	15

add Goodman and Bernstein	**Good Enough to Keep (Air Mail Special)**	

Other CDs
same contents:
  Europe: CBS Jazz Masterpieces 460612-2
contents unknown:
  Japan: *Charlie Christian with Benny Goodman Sextet and Orchestra,*
  CBS 25 DP 5301

LPs
same contents:
  USA: Columbia Jazz Masterpieces CJ 40846
  Europe: CBS Jazz Masterpieces 460612-1
plus additional tracks:
  Japan: *Charlie Christian Album*, CBS Sony SOPZ 4-6; CBS Sony 56AP 674-6
incl. alternate and composite takes: *The Genius of Charlie Christian: Solo Flight*
  USA: Columbia G 30779
  Europe: CBS 67233
incl. tracks 2–4, 6, 7, 11, 13–16, with alternate and composite takes:
  Charlie Christian with the Benny Goodman Sextet and Orchestra
  USA: Columbia CL 652
  Europe: CBS Realm Jazz Series RM 52538; Philips B 07247 L; Philips BBL 7172
  France: CBS 62387
  Japan: CBS Sony SOPM 155; CBS Sony XM 4
  Australia: Coronet KPL 510

Cassettes
same contents:
  USA: Columbia Jazz Masterpieces CJT 40846
  Europe: CBS Jazz Masterpieces 460612-4

Fats Waller: *Jazz Tribune no.32: The Indispensable Fats Waller, vols.3/4 (1935–1936)*

The sextet Fats Waller and his Rhythm was formed in 1934 and recorded steadily for the Victor label and its subsidiary Bluebird until the recording ban of 1942, shortly before Waller's death. Of various chronological slices of this large body of work, the best is from the early period, 1935–6. It focuses on the sextet's regular format with the leader singing and playing piano. It also includes two tracks with him on organ, four with piano and celeste or celeste alone, two without song lyrics (but with plenty of jiving chatter), and three with the big band that he led intermittently from the time of these recordings.

Strictly, as an instrumental swing combo, the Rhythm does not deserve a place in this book. Most of the horn solos are weak; the best of Waller's brass and reed players, trumpeter Bill Coleman, does not happen to be well represented on this slice of recordings. Al Casey's guitar solos are pedestrian, consisting unvaryingly of syncopated chordal strumming. Waller himself coasts through stride piano paraphrases of the themes with a greater frequency here than on the unaccompanied recordings discussed in Chapter 2 (of course, as mentioned there, Waller 'coasts' at a level most players never reach).

Yet some of the instrumentals reward careful attention. The rhythm section positively cooks on the dixieland-style collectively improvised final choruses of *(Oh Susannah) Dust off that Old Pianna* and *12th Street Rag*; on the former, drummer Harry Dial produces a compelling but curiously thumping beat (as if he were hitting a suitcase) by striking excessively hard with brushes, not sticks. They produce a brisk, crisp swing on many performances, including *Sweet Sue, Got a Bran' New Suit, It's a Sin to Tell a Lie*, and *Why Do I Lie to Myself about You?*, the last of which has a trumpet and clarinet riff in place of the characteristic dixieland endings.

Eugene Sedric rises above the horns' norm in solos on *Christopher Columbus* and Waller's composition *Black Raspberry Jam*, playing tenor sax in the mould of Coleman Hawkins, though with a muffled tone. Waller is by far the best soloist, when he makes the effort. Representing the thoughtful side of his piano playing is the delicate, graceful opening statement of *I'm Gonna Sit Right Down and Write Myself a Letter*; representing the bent-for-hell attitude in numerous fast syncopated choruses is his solo on *(Oh Susannah) Dust off that Old Pianna* (after he swerves out of key from tongue-in-cheek scalar exercises into stride). These are with the sextet. The main attraction of the big-band tracks is equally high-powered stride playing on *I Got Rhythm* in a battle (with no clear winner) between the orchestra's second pianist Hank Duncan and Waller, who ends his pyrotechnics by smashing the lid on the keyboard.

What elevates this material to greatness are Waller's vocals, a unique blend of jazz improvising, pop singing and comedy. Considered strictly as raw material, Waller seems an unlikely candidate for high praise. His raspy voice lacks fullness. Unable to control it well, he regularly cracks notes and sings out of tune. But like Louis Armstrong, who had an even more unlikely voice and yet turned out to be jazz's best singer, Waller has a fabulous sense of rhythmic placement and swing; listen to his remaking of the melodies of *12th Street Rag* and *I Got Rhythm*, and to the way he disconnects his voice from his hands on *What's the Reason?*, maintaining an emphatic stride piano solo while floating around the beat in a spoken reply to a woman's (unspoken) reason why he's 'not pleasin'' her. Also like Armstrong, the gruffness of his voice lent a biting attack to every syllable he uttered, imparting a special energy to his performances and thus sharply differentiating his school of jazz singing from the milky smoothness of male crooners and female songbirds in so many contemporary big bands. Unlike Armstrong, Waller does not regularly use scat singing. When he does, he seems to be copying Cab Calloway's approach, as for example in the jiving and scatting ending of *Dinah* and the vocal chorus of *I've Got my Fingers Crossed*, which emphasizes such fun and silly sounds as 'eegee weegee'. (Unfortunately, Waller also seems to have been slightly infected by Calloway's propensity for hideously ugly hollering, in the final choruses of *Dinah* and *Sweet Sue*.)

With Waller's quick wit, there was little reason for him to sing the nonsense syllables of scat. The straightforward delivery of lyrics, improvised alterations to lyrics, commentaries on lyrics, commentaries on and instructions to instrumentalists, irreverent and irrelevant asides, all are his strengths. He gives a sentimental reading of the love lyrics of I *Believe in Miracles*, just after having thrown acid in the face of *Because of Once upon a Time* by means of an interjection ('You lyin' dog – get away from here!'), a facetious cry ('whoa whoa whoa whoa') and pseudo-British pronunciation ('You cahn't be mine'). He inserts words ('. . . I love you; yes, but if you break my heart, I'll break your jaw and then I'll die'), and at the end of his chorus he repeats the tune's title and introduces clarinettist Gene Sedric with the line: 'It's a sin to tell a lie; now get on out there and tell your lie.' Clarinettist Rudy Powell is obsessed with a growling tone, and on *I Ain't Got Nobody* Waller tells him to 'make that thing sweat'. While trumpeter Herman Autrey solos on *12th Street Rag*, Waller discusses food ('. . . get them hot dogs ready, . . . get them sizzlers too, . . . potato salad'). His most off-the-wall comment comes during Autrey's solo on *Whose Honey Are You?*: 'my, they're throwing the babies out of the balcony, mercy!'

Some of the material is intentionally comic, not sentimental, providing suitable vehicles for his good-time jazz. *Fat and Greasy* is maybe a bit disgusting, and Waller put the same idea across more successfully a few years later with his big hit *Your Feet's Too Big* (1939). *Christopher Columbus*, recorded just two weeks and one week respectively after Benny Goodman and Fletcher Henderson made their hit instrumental versions, has Waller at his zaniest: silly voices (falsetto, moving down into the baritone range), silly rhymes ('world is roundo . . . safe and soundo . . . goal is foundo . . . rhythm boundo') and silly puns ('Since the crew was makin' merry, Mary got up and went home'). The excessively silly *Big Chief De Sota* (rhyming 'De Sota . . . Minnesota . . . Dakota . . . bought a boata . . . only mota . . . cannot floata') has an unusually casual band arrangement and, as it aimlessly winds down, Waller cuts off the recording in the middle of a phrase and says 'cease, cease, De Sota has went'.

For all these antics, the biggest hit in this collection and, from my experience, the one that stays longest in your mind's ear, is *I'm Gonna Sit Right Down and Write Myself a Letter*. Waller's complete sincerity brings across the feelings of a vulnerable, heartbroken man. On other songs in this vein, Waller surely would fill the space after the last note of the piece with some sort of jiving comment. Here he resists the temptation, leaving only silence.

LP

Europe: *The Indispensible Fats Waller, vols.3/4 (1935–1936),* **RCA NL 89819**

Bill Coleman (tpt), Gene Sedric (cl), Fats Waller (org, v), Albert Casey (g), Charlie Turner (sb), Harry Dial (d)

| New York | 5 Jan 1935 | **Night Wind** | |

*as **Night Wind**, but Waller (p)*   **Because of Once upon a Time**

*as **Night Wind***   **I Believe in Miracles**

*as **Night Wind**, but Waller (p)*   **You Fit into the Picture**

Herman Autrey (tpt), Rudy Powell (cl), Waller (p, v), Casey (g), Turner (sb), Dial (d)

| | 6 March 1935 | **I Ain't Got Nobody** (take 1) | 5 |
| | | **Whose Honey are You?** (take 1) | |

*as **I Ain't Got Nobody**, but Waller (celeste, v)*
                Rosetta (take 1)

*as **I Ain't Got Nobody***   **What's the Reason?** (take 1)

*as **I Ain't Got Nobody**, but Waller (p, celeste, v)*
                (Oh Susannah) Dust off that Old Pianna

as I Ain't Got Nobody
8 May 1935

Lulu's Back in Town   **10**
**I'm Gonna Sit Right Down and
   Write Myself a Letter**

*Autrey (tpt), Powell (cl), Waller (p, v), James Smith (g), Turner (sb), Arnold Boling
(d)*
Camden, NJ   24 June 1935   **Dinah**
                                          **My Very Good Friend the
                                             Milkman**
                                          Blue Because of You
                                          12th Street Rag   **15**

*as **Dinah**, but Powell (as)*   **Sweet Sue** (take 1)

*as **Dinah***   2 Aug 1935   **Truckin'**
                                          Georgia Rockin' Chair
                        20 Aug 1935   **Got a Bran' New Suit**

Autrey (tpt), Sedric (ts), Waller (p, v), Smith (g), Turner (sb), Yank Porter (d)
New York   29 Nov 1935   **I've Got my Fingers Crossed**   **20**

*Autrey, unknown (tpt), Benny Morton (tb), Emmett Mathews (ss), Powell (cl, as),
Sedric, Bob Carroll (ts), Waller (p, vb, v), Hank Duncan (p), Smith (g), Turner (sb),
Porter (d)*
                    4 Dec 1935   **Fat and Greasy** (take 2)
omit (vb)   **Functionizin'**
                                       I Got Rhythm

Autrey (tpt), Sedric (cl), Waller (p, celeste, v), Smith (g), Turner (sb), Porter (d)
                    1 Feb 1936   **Sugar Rose**

*as **Sugar Rose**, but Sedric (cl, ts), Waller (p, v)*
                                       West Wind   **25**

Autrey (tpt), Sedric (ts), Waller (p, v), Casey (g), Turner (sb), Boling (d)
                    8 April 1936   **Christopher Columbus**

*as **Christopher Columbus**, but Waller (p, celeste, v)*
                                       Cabin in the Sky

*as **Christopher Columbus**, but Sedric (cl), Yank Porter (d)*
                    5 June 1936   **It's a Sin to Tell a Lie**

| | | **Why Do I Lie to Myself about You?** | |

as **Christopher Columbus**, *but Porter (d)*

	8 June 1936	**Big Chief De Sota**	30
		Black Raspberry Jam	
		Paswonky	

Autrey (tpt), Sedric (cl), Waller (p, v), Casey (g), Turner (sb), Slick Jones (d)

| | 1 Aug 1936 | **I'm Crazy 'bout my Baby** | |

Other LPs

same contents:
  France: RCA PM 43696
plus additional tracks:
  France: *Fats Waller Complete Recordings*, on these vols.: RCA 730.571,
  730.572, 731.054, 731.055, 741.112, 741.113, FPM1-7001, FPM1-7008,
  FPM1-7025
incl. tracks 1–11:
  UK: *Dust Off That Old Pianna*, Saville SVL 189
incl. tracks 12–18:
  UK: *Take It Easy*, Saville SVL 194
incl. tracks 19–20, 24–6:
  UK: *Spreadin' Rhythm Around*, Saville SVL 204
incl. tracks 1–6:
  UK: *From the Beginning*, vol.2, JSP 1108
incl. tracks 7–8:
  UK: *From the Beginning*, vol.3, JSP 1113
incl. tracks 6, 8–10, 26, 28, 30:
  UK: *Jazz Classics in Digital Stereo: Fats Waller and his Rhythm*, BBC
  REB 684
incl. tracks 10–11, 16, 23, 28:
  Denmark: *Fats Waller*, Official 3030-1

CDs

incl. tracks 6, 8–10, 26, 28, 30:
  UK: *Jazz Classics in Digital Stereo: Fats Waller and his Rhythm*, BBC
  CD 684
incl. tracks 10–11, 16, 23, 28:
  Denmark: *Fats Waller*, Official 83030-2

Cassettes

same contents:
Europe: *The Indispensible Fats Waller, vols.3/4 (1935–1936)*, RCA NK
89819
incl. tracks 6, 8–10, 26, 28, 30:
UK: *Jazz Classics in Digital Stereo: Fats Waller and his Rhythm*, BBC
ZCF 684

* * *

Quintette du Hot Club de France: *Souvenirs*

Despite the 'hot' in its name, and associations of that word with early jazz styles, the Quintette du Hot Club de France played swing tempered by gypsy string-band music. The combo grew gradually out of jam sessions among members of the band led by Parisian string bass player Louis Vola. It took its name in 1934 as a quintet led by guitarist Django Reinhardt and violinist Stephane Grappelli (spelled 'Grappelly' at the time), with two more guitarists and Vola fleshing out the rhythm section. An anthology of recordings made in London for Decca presents the quintet a few years down the road, now in its full maturity, just before World War II; and again later, when Grappelli, having settled in England during the war, was reunited with Reinhardt for a session with a British rhythm section in 1946.

The monumental playing on this collection is by Reinhardt. Fittingly, a Belgian-born Hungarian gypsy French guitarist was the first great non-American jazz musician, and the only European player to have significantly influenced the development of Afro-American music. In my opinion he is yet to be overtaken, even when considered against the international explosion of jazz which has taken place since the 1950s. The reason is not his stinging, metallic tone, which I admire for offering an alternative to the limpid tone prevalent among jazz guitar soloists, an alternative which drew only a narrow following in swing and bop (though a wide one in blues). Nor is it his prodigious technique (notwithstanding the uselessness of two fingers on his left hand, damaged in a fire), evident in innumerable fleet lines; in passages played in octaves (foreshadowing Wes Montgomery's favourite device) at the end of his solo on *Sweet Georgia Brown* and at the start of his solo on *My Sweet*; and in his control of harmonics, played together with Grappelli momentarily at the beginning and steadily at the end of *H. C. Q. Strut*. Nor is it his imaginative use of harmony, including some wildly dissonant lower-register tremolos to begin the second half of the first chorus of the same solo on *Sweet Georgia Brown*. Nor is it his skill as a rhythm guitarist, cranking the energy and swing up several notches with his fast triplet strumming on the last chorus of *Sweet Georgia Brown*, and with his double-time strumming to wind up *My Sweet*. Great as all these things are, they do not account for his special stature. What overwhelms me about Reinhardt's playing is the way in which he spins out long, breathless improvised single-note melodies. His conception stands in opposition to that of wind players or singers, the fountainheads of jazz phrasing. He uses silence liberally, but the silences do not provide a place to breathe; rather, his phrases span silence, the end of one segment of melody being picked up and continued logically into the next. Sometimes he achieves this through simple motivic processes, repeating an idea sequentially at different levels of pitch, but usually the process is more complex: an idea breaks off without resolving, Reinhardt lets us wait for a dramatic moment until he picks it up – not to finish it off, but to carry it in a new direction and then again in yet another new direction. Ultimately this concept reaches back to baroque music, especially that of Johann Sebastian Bach, but this is heady improvised jazz, not some lightweight jazz-classical fusion. All of the solos in this collection well exemplify Reinhardt's approach, except *Daphne*. (*Daphne*, which Reinhardt and Grappelli had recorded the previous year under the leadership of violinist Eddie South, is based on the *a* section of the *aaba* theme of the jazz warhorse *I Got Rhythm*. But in place of the *b* section the piece repeats theme *a* one half step higher. In the quintet's version the soloists get tangled up, lunging gracelessly and hitting clinkers as they move back and forth between two unrelated keys.)

Grappelli, the other featured soloist, is always a happy player. An inveterate improviser, like Reinhardt he cannot wait to get rid of the themes and start making his own melodies. His style ranges more widely than Reinhardt's, embracing madcap swinging in the aforementioned strummed choruses; a lilting effect in *Honeysuckle Rose*; and romantic opening choruses to the popular song *Night and Day*, Reinhardt's 'gypsy blues' composition *Nuages* and his *Love's Melody*. Grappelli makes this last title into syrupy continental supper-club music, until Reinhardt enters to jolt the piece back into jazz with his solo.

One oddity is that both men use blue notes completely out of context, perhaps through a misunderstanding of this American idiom. Bending pitches on, for example, *Night and Day*, seems inappropriate, the resulting effect being a whine, not a lament.

Apart from Reinhardt's contributions, the rhythm sections are purely functional, laying down an adequate base and bass for swinging. Vola, who has no ability to sustain plucked notes, disastrously tries to make up for this with bowed held notes in the dreary two-beat bass line to *Souvenirs*; much more successful is his walking slap bass solo on *My Sweet*. His counterpart, expatriate Jamaican bassist Coleridge Goode, suffers more than anyone from the poorly recorded, cloudy postwar session; Goode's one brief solo on *Liza* typically is in imitation of Slam Stewart's humming while bowing, a style which Stewart had pretty well worn out by this time.

CD

UK: *Souvenirs*, London 820.591-2

Stephane Grappelli (vln), Django Reinhardt, Roger Chaput, Eugène Vées (g), Louis Vola (sb)

London	31 Jan 1938	**Honeysuckle Rose**	
		Sweet Georgia Brown	
		Night and Day	
		My Sweet	
		Souvenirs	5
		Daphne	
		Stompin' at Decca	

Grappelli (vl, p), Reinhardt (g)

	1 Feb 1938	**Nocturne**

Grappelli (p), Reinhardt (g)

		I've Got my Love to Keep me Warm	
	1 Sept 1938	**Please be Kind**	10
	10 Sept 1938	**Louise**	

Reinhardt (g)

Improvisation no.2

*as **Honeysuckle Rose**, but Roger Grasset (sb) replaces Vola*

30 Aug 1938	**Lambeth Walk**

Grappelli (vln), Django Reinhardt, Joseph Reinhardt, Vées (g), Emmanuel Soudieux (sb), Beryl Davis (v)

25 Aug 1939	**Undecided**

omit (v)	**H. C. Q. Strut**	15

add Davis (v)   **Don't Worry 'bout Me**

omit (v)   **The Man I Love**

Grappelli (vln), Django Reinhardt, Jack Llewellyn, Alan Hodgkiss (g), Coleridge Goode (sb)

London	1 Feb 1946	**Love's Melody**

Nuages
Liza   **20**

LPs

plus additional tracks:
  France: *Django Reinhardt et le Quintette du Hot Club de France*, Decca
  115.120-115.124
incl. tracks 1–7, 13, 15, 18–20: *Django Reinhardt & Stephane Grappelli with
  the Quintet of the Hot Club of France*
  UK: Ace of Clubs ACL 1158
  USA: GNP Crescendo GNP 9001
  France: Decca 168.003
incl. tracks 1–2, 7, 13–14, 19–20:
  Germany: *The Very Best of Django Reinhardt*, Decca 6.28441 DP
incl. tracks 3–6, 8–12, 15–17
  Germany: *The One and the Only*, Decca 6.28589 DP
incl. tracks 1–4, 6, 13, 15:
  UK: *Swing from Paris*, Living Era AJA 5070
incl. tracks 2–4, 6, 15:
  USA: *Swing from Paris*, London LL 1344

Cassettes

incl. tracks 1–4, 6, 13, 15:
  UK: *Swing from Paris*, Living Era ZC-AJA 5070

* * *

Billie Holiday: *The Quintessential Billie Holiday, vol.5, 1937–1938; The Quintessential Billie Holiday, vol.9, 1940–1942*

Temperamentally, singer Billie Holiday was not stable enough to keep a single group together for long, or to work happily under another leader. Musically, she was the greatest jazz singer after Louis Armstrong. The result was that, in her steady studio work from 1935 onwards, she became a freelance star around whom *ad hoc* swing combos revolved. Favouring a more mainstream style than the string-band music of the Hot Club quintet, or than the novelty and comedy songs of Waller, Holiday attracted all but a few of the most important horn and rhythm players of the era to record with her. Two clumps of sessions stand out among the extraordinary riches of her recorded legacy, though not by much; apart from the occasional failure resulting from an inability to overcome a diabolically bad song, every bit of Holiday's swing combo work is worth hearing.

The first, from the years 1937 and 1938, comprises her collaborations with five sidemen from Count Basie's orchestra: soloists Buck Clayton (trumpet) and Lester Young (tenor saxophone), and rhythm section members Freddie Green (guitar), Walter Page (string bass) and Jo Jones (drums). They were joined by several pianists, most often and most importantly Teddy Wilson, who organized many of Holiday's recording dates. They were also joined by either a distinguished clarinettist – Benny Goodman, Edmond Hall, Buster Bailey – or a trombonist drawn from Basie's ranks – Benny Morton, Dicky Wells. Volume 5 of the chronologically ordered CBS Jazz Masterpieces series provides a good sampling of their achievements.

These were neither cameo appearances by big names, playing anonymous roles subsidiary to the singer, nor the sort of all-star mish-mash heard from jazz magazine poll-winner bands, but completely integrated performances which encapsulate the very best of swing. Indeed it was normal for Holiday to sing the first chorus and then give the rest over to the instrumentalists, perhaps returning at the end to sing a half chorus, perhaps not. Perfectly matched to Holiday's approach, the instrumental work is characterized by relaxation and understatement in many respects: in the embroideries woven around Holiday's singing, in the solos, in the accompanimental riffs which occasionally appear in the background (for example, Clayton and Young at the start of *When You're Smiling*, Clayton and Morton later in the tune), and most strikingly at the end of pieces, in the mellow collectively improvised passages – the musicians' interpretation of this remnant of New Orleans jazz is the very antithesis of the wild Chicago style, with each contribution soft, cool, unintrusive.

Musically, there was an especially empathetic understanding between Holiday and tenor saxophonist Young. Always a melodic player, Young developed his ideas even more slowly and caressingly during these sessions than in his remarkable work with Basie. The very best of his playing on the Jazz Masterpieces collection is his solo on the third take of *When You're Smiling*, which for this and many other reasons, if it weren't such a dreadfully corny piece of fluff to start with, could be a candidate for Holiday's greatest recording.

Well before these sessions, Holiday had formulated her unique singing style, some elements of which proved widely influential, though no one else has come close to reproducing the whole package. What strikes first, like a hammer, is the emotional depth of her singing. Here in 1937–8, and increasingly so later, tragedy is at the centre of her experiences. She could turn around the meaning of songs, reconstructing phrases through her use of blues inflections and the lamenting timbre of her voice, to bring out the tragic side. On *He's Funny That Way*, it seems less likely that 'I got that man crazy about me', more likely that 'he'd be better off if I went away'. On *If Dreams Come True*, her droning, sad melody tells us they won't. On *When You're Smiling*, she cries out the words 'smiling' and 'smiles' over and over and over again, sending the message that these vaudeville-style smiles are the tears of a clown. She also worked with songs which were inherently tragic: *Trav'lin' all Alone*, with its grim lyrics coloured by numerous minor chords, and *When a Woman Loves a Man*, with its punch line 'tell her she's a fool – she'll say "yes, but I love him so" ', give a taste of what would later come in larger doses. Holiday brought utter conviction to a lyric. Who cannot believe her, when she sings that she's 'hoping he'll think it over, be satisfied with a simple sort of person on the sentimental side'? (Never mind that Holiday was scarcely a simple sort of person.) In marked contrast to her contemporary Ella Fitzgerald, she was never buoyantly cheerful, and one of the few unsuccessful tracks in this collection is the Fitzgerald-style ditty *Now They Call it Swing*. Looking forward with a vulnerable, guarded optimism towards a possible future love, as on *My First Impression of You* and *Back in your own Back Yard*, was about as far as she wanted to go.

The other half of the package is her musicality. The measure of a jazz singer who is not a scat singer (that is, who is not directly imitating a jazz instrument) is the ability to overhaul a given melody, and in this Holiday was superb. Usually her's was devastatingly better than the original. Though gifted with a hauntingly beautiful vocal tone and a trumpet-like articulation of notes, she had a narrow range, especially evident on *He's Funny That Way*, which is set at what is, for her, a high pitch. And so she worked on nuances of pitch and rhythm, rebuilding the contours of a song (generally flattening it out), swooping and sliding into notes in all sorts of ways, and generating a powerful sense of swing, largely by the seemingly paradoxical method of retreating further and further behind the beat. The clearest of the abundant examples is *When You're Smiling*, because, un-characteristically for a jazz musician, trombonist Benny Morton first plays the theme absolutely straight as an arrow, thus affording a structure against which Holiday's subsequent demolition and reconstruction job may be viewed. Also especially revealing from this point of view is *My Man*, re-corded during this period, but with a different group of all stars joining Clayton, Wilson and Page: pianist Wilson plays the melody while Holiday is singing, effectively wrapping her inventiveness in a rhythmic-melodic straightjacket, and dissipating the energy of the performance.

The balance had shifted by the time of Holiday's sessions of 1940–2 (all under her own name, not Wilson's). The accompaniments are still peppered with famous names – Young, Wilson, Roy Eldridge, Kenny Clarke, Eddie Heywood, Emmett Berry, Shad Collins, Jimmy Hamilton, Al Casey, J. C. Heard, Benny Carter – but there are plenty of lesser-known players as well, because the emphasis is no longer on something approaching a jam session among peers, but rather on Holiday, with her singing supported by set arrangements involving choirs of horns in sustained chords and moving lines. There is still a good deal of room for soloists, most often Heywood's restrained swinging on piano and most importantly Young's gripping double-time break on the last chorus of *All of Me*, but now the stars, Young and Eldridge, come out for briefer periods. One does not need a Lester Young for all of the horn playing here; less gifted players will do.

After several years absence from Holiday's recording sessions Young returned for that of March 1941, which proved to be one of Holiday's greatest and, for her, one of her cheeriest. Of the many recordings of Hoagy Carmichael's hit song *Georgia on my Mind*, I think that only Ray Charles's emotive soul and country version can stand up against Holiday's interpretation, which, taking a different tack from Charles, subtly lays out a spellbinding mood of wistful reminiscence. *All of Me* has a justifiably famous moment of rewriting by Holiday. She gives the song a deeper and sexier meaning by changing the words the second time around, from 'you took the part that once was my heart', to 'you took the best, so why not take the rest?'.

The next three sessions present some of the darkest moments in all of jazz. In the last, Holiday's tragic bent goes over the edge. *Mandy is Two* is an absolutely bizarre performance: a tearful lament on the occasion of a little girl's second birthday; on *It's a Sin to Tell a Lie*, I cannot help recalling Fats Waller's wonderful 'punch' line, already mentioned ('if you break my heart I'll break your jaw'), while she is singing, entirely seriously, 'if you break my heart I'll die'. But the tracks from the previous two, from May and August 1941, are profoundly beautiful, even if depressing. The outstanding performances are her own song *God Bless the Child*, a streetwise anthem to those who take care of themselves; *I Cover the Waterfront* (note, by contrast to the earlier recordings, that Holiday sings the whole way through this); and *Gloomy Sunday*, a dream about suicide.

In detailing the last two sessions, neither standard not specialist discographies have noted the extent to which the reed players use clarinets, not saxes. It is not easy to pick out the details exactly, but I believe that in the August session the musicians used clarinets, picking up their saxes only momentarily for the break on *Jim*, though there is a tenor solo, probably by Russin, on *Love Me or Leave Me*. The clarinets return, with Russin again doubling for the tenor solos, on tracks 1 and 3 from February 1942. The mere fact of reed players doubling is nothing unusual, and indeed there are plenty of places in this book where we would not presume to untangle the uncertain details of who plays which wind instrument at which moment. But here I think the clarinets have a special significance, worth hearing: the arranger has used them mainly in their low register, their dark sound adding to Holiday's dark mood.

CD

USA: *The Quintessential Billie Holiday, vol.5, 1937–1938,* **Columbia Jazz Masterpieces CK 44423**

Buck Clayton (tpt), Edmond Hall (cl), Lester Young (ts), James Sherman (p), Freddie Green (g), Walter Page (sb), Jo Jones (d), Billie Holiday (v)
New York   15 June 1937   **Born to Love**
                                      Without your Love (take 1)

Buster Bailey (cl) replaces Hall, Claude Thornhill (p) replaces Sherman
             13 Sept 1937   **Getting Some Fun out of Life**
                                        Who Wants Love?
                                        Trav'lin' all Alone   5
                                          He's Funny That Way

(Teddy Wilson:) Clayton (tpt), Prince Robinson (cl), Vido Musso (ts), Wilson (p), Allan Reuss (g), Page (sb), Cozy Cole (d), Holiday (v)
              1 Nov 1937   **Nice Work if You Can Get it**
                                        Things are Looking up
                                        My Man
                                        Can't Help Lovin' dat Man   10

(Wilson:) Clayton (tpt), Benny Morton (tb), Young (ts), Wilson (p), Green (g), Page (sb), Jones (d), Holiday (v)
              6 Jan 1938   **My First Impression of You**
                                          (take 4)
                                        When You're Smiling (take 3)
                                        I Can't Believe that You're in
                                          Love with Me (take 4)
                                        If Dreams Come True

*(Holiday:) as **My First Impression of You***
            12 Jan 1938   **Now They Call it Swing**
                                        (take 2)   15
                                        On the Sentimental Side (take 2)
                                        Back in your own Back Yard
                                        (take 1)
                                        When a Woman Loves a Man

Other CDs

same contents:
  Europe: CBS Jazz Masterpieces 465190-2

incl. tracks 2–3, 5–6, 13, 17, plus others cited below:
Italy: *Lady Day & Prez, 1937–1941*, Giants of Jazz CD 0218 AAD
incl. tracks 6, 7, 13, 15, plus others cited below:
Denmark: *The Most Important Recordings of Billie Holiday*, Official
83048-2

LPs

same contents:
USA: Columbia Jazz Masterpieces CJ 44423
Europe: CBS Jazz Masterpieces 465190-1
plus additional tracks:
Japan: *Billie Holiday*, CBS-Sony SOPH 61-SOPH 70
incl. tracks 2 (alternate take), 3, 5, 12, 14, 16 (alternate take), 17–18:
USA: *The Golden Years*, Columbia C3L 21
Europe: *The Golden Years*, vol.2, CBS BPG 62038; *The Billie Holiday Story*,
vol.1, CBS 68228
Japan: *The Golden Years*, vol.2, Columbia PMS 94
Australia: *The Billie Holiday Story*, vol.1, Avan Guard B2VL 228
incl. tracks 6–7, 9–11, 13, 15 (alternate take):
USA: *The Golden Years*, vol.2, Columbia C3L 40
Europe: *The Golden Years*, vol.2, CBS 66301; *The Golden Years*, vol.5,
CBS BPG 62815; *The Billie Holiday Story*, vol.3, CBS 68230
Japan: *The Golden Years*, vol.5, Columbia SL 1330 C
incl. tracks 3–6, 11–15, 17–18, plus alternate takes: *The Lester Young
Story, vol.2: A Musical Romance*
USA: Columbia JG 34837
UK: CBS 88263
incl. tracks 2, 5, 12–13, 15:
Italy: *Lady Day & Prez*, Giants of Jazz LPJT 45
incl. tracks 3, 6, 10, 17, plus others cited below:
Italy: *The Golden Years of 'Lady Day'*, Giants of Jazz LPJT 10
incl. tracks 6, 7, 13, 15, plus others cited below:
Denmark: *The Most Important Recordings of Billie Holiday*, Official 3048-2

Cassettes

same contents:
USA: Columbia Jazz Masterpieces CJT 44423
Europe: CBS Jazz Masterpieces 465190-4
incl. tracks 2, 5, 12–13, 15:
Italy: *Lady Day & Prez*, Giants of Jazz MCJT 45
incl. tracks 3, 6, 10, 17, plus others cited below:
Italy: *The Golden Years of 'Lady Day'*, Giants of Jazz MCJT 10

CD

USA: *The Quintessential Billie Holiday, vol.9, 1940–1942*, **Columbia Jazz Masterpieces CK 47031**

Bill Coleman (t), Morton (tb), Benny Carter (cl, as), Georgie Auld (ts), Sonny White (p), Ulysses Livingston (g), Wilson Myers (sb), Yank Porter (d), Holiday (v)
New York   15 Oct 1940   **St Louis Blues** (take 1)
                                          Loveless Love

Shad Collins (t), Leslie Johnakins, Eddie Barefield (as), Young (ts), Eddie Heywood (p), John Collins (g), Ted Sturgis (sb), Kenny Clarke (d), Holiday (v)
                   21 March 1941   **Let's do it**
                                          Georgia on my Mind
                                          Romance in the Dark   5
                                          All of Me

Roy Eldridge (tpt), Lester Boone, Jimmy Powell (as), Ernie Powell (ts), Heywood (p), Paul Chapman (g), Grachan Moncur (sb), Herbert Cowens (d), Holiday (v)
                   9 May 1941   **I'm in a Low Down Groove**
                                          God Bless the Child
                                          Am I Blue?
                                          Solitude   10

Emmett Berry (tpt), Jimmy Hamilton (cl), Hymie Schertzer (cl, as), Babe Russin (cl, ts), Teddy Wilson (p), Al Casey (g), John Williams (sb), J. C. Heard (d), Holiday (v)
                   7 Aug 1941   **Jim**
                                          I Cover the Waterfront
                                          Love Me or Leave Me
                                          Gloomy Sunday

Gene Fields (g) replaces Casey
                   10 Feb 1942   **Wherever You Are**   15
                                          Mandy is Two
                                          It's a Sin to Tell a Lie
                                          **Until the Real Thing Comes
                                               Along**

Other CDs

incl. tracks 3–6, plus others cited above:
    Italy: *Lady Day & Prez, 1937–1941*, Giants of Jazz CD 0218 AAD
incl. tracks 3–4, 8, 11, 13, plus others cited above:

Denmark: *The Most Important Recordings of Billie Holiday*, Official
83048-2

LPs

same contents:
USA: Columbia Jazz Masterpieces C-J 47031
plus additional tracks:
Japan: *Billie Holiday*, CBS-Sony SOPH 61-SOPH 70
incl. tracks 1, 3, 5, 7-8, 10, 12-13, 16-17, plus alternate takes of tracks 2, 4, 6, 9,
11, 14, 18: *God Bless the Child*
USA: Columbia KG 30782
UK: CBS M 66267
incl. tracks 4–6, 8–9, 12, 14, plus others cited above:
USA: *The Golden Years*, Columbia C3L 21
Europe: *The Golden Years*, vol.3, CBS BPG 62039; *The Billie Holiday Story*,
vol.2, CBS 68229
Japan: *The Golden Years*, vol.3, Columbia PMS 95
Australia: *The Billie Holiday Story*, vol.2, Avan Guard B2VL 229
incl. tracks 1 (alternate take), 3, 7, 10, 16–17, plus others cited above:
USA: *The Golden Years*, vol.2, Columbia C3L 40
Europe: *The Golden Years*, vol.2, CBS 66301; *The Golden Years*, vol.5, CBS
BPG 62815; *The Billie Holiday Story*, vol.3, CBS 68230
Japan: *The Golden Years*, vol.5, Columbia SL 1330 C
incl. tracks 4, 6, 9–10, 13, plus others cited above:
Italy: *The Golden Years of 'Lady Day'*, Giants of Jazz LPJT 10
incl. tracks 3–4, 8, 11, 13, plus others cited above:
Denmark: *The Most Important Recordings of Billie Holiday*, Official 3048-2

Cassettes

same contents:
USA: Columbia Jazz Masterpieces C-JT 47031
incl. tracks 4, 6, 9–10, 13, plus others cited above:
Italy: *The Golden Years of 'Lady Day'*, Giants of Jazz MCJT 10

* * *

Coleman Hawkins: *Body and Soul; The Man I Love*

During his decade with Fletcher Henderson's big band, Coleman Hawkins
more than anyone else established the tenor saxophone as a solo instrument
in jazz, but it was only after leaving Henderson in 1934 that he began to

Paris in 1937, as well as *Body and Soul* (1939) and *The Man I Love* (1943). All these are available in modern formats that are, for one reason or another, not tailored to this book. Multi-instrumentalist Benny Carter and guitarist Django Reinhardt are among Hawkins's sidemen on the Parisian session, and the excellent trumpeter Arthur Briggs solos alongside Hawkins on a session made there under Michel Warlop's direction two years earlier, but on these and other tracks from Hawkins's expatriate years the majority of his fellow players range from competent to barely adequate – Europe at the time not yet having developed a large enough pool of world-class players. How far they had yet to go may be heard on various anthologies including these sides, especially ones that also have the track *Blue Light Blues*; made in 1938 under Carter's leadership, with Alix Combelle taking Hawkins's role, it is – excepting Carter's masterful trumpet playing – filled with wrong notes and shows no sense of swing, and even Reinhardt struggles with the blues.

The masterpiece of Hawkins's career, *Body and Soul*, was made for Victor shortly after he returned to the USA from his five-year stay in Europe, but the RCA reissues I have encountered have been filled out either with too many tracks of lesser quality or with tracks representing a later phase in Hawkins's career, when he turned towards bop. *The Man I Love* is from a low fidelity session made for the little label Signature while the musicians' union was still out on strike against the major companies, and on reissues it is combined with material from other muddy sessions which are musically far less interesting. Accordingly, I feel obliged to violate the system of this book, by dealing here with the latter two titles independently, rather than in the context of anthologies, and by discussing the Parisian session in Chapter 7, in the context of Carter's album **Further Definitions**.

As the 1930s ended, Lester Young was offering a fully developed alternative to Hawkins's conception of tenor sax playing, but the generation he influenced had not yet hit the professional ranks. Hawkins, despite his absence from New York, remained the model for jazz tenor saxophone playing, and on *Body and Soul* he showed that he was still a force to be reckoned with. Some idea of its unique and revered position within the jazz community may be gained from the status of Hawkins's improvisation as the only notated solo to have been published three times in *Down Beat* magazine, so that players and listeners might study it in detail. If any performance ever demonstrated that jazz need not be integrated into a single unified whole, that an individual part can be greater than the sum of the rest, this is it. Hawkins's rhythm section is dull and the section of brass and reed instruments is abysmal, playing lethargic chords hopelessly out of tune. But Hawkins's effort is so profound, the rest doesn't matter a whit.

Hallmarks of the solo are his manipulation of timbre, volume, harmony and range. Over a slowly paced 64 bars (two choruses of the theme) his playing snowballs towards a tremendous climax. He begins softly, with a breathy sound and a small and controlled vibrato, in a moderately low register, and in at least the first sweep of the solo the opening phrase of the melody of *Body and Soul* is easily recognized. Quickly it disappears, giving way to faster-moving new lines embroidered around the song's chord progression. Hawkins gradually alters his sound, getting louder, adding an edge to his tone, growling through the instrument, widening and loosening his vibrato and aiming towards a climax which falls on a pitch just above the 'normal' range of the instrument. (After decades of screaming tenor saxes in rhythm and blues, soul music and free jazz, any young player worth his salt can hit this note cleanly; at the time Hawkins's control was authoritative.) A brief cadenza ties up the solo by spinning sequentially through a chromatic descent, in the process summarizing Hawkins's preference for creating abstract melodies by playing out chords rather than playing tunes.

By the end of 1943 Charlie Parker, playing alto sax in the style which came to be known as bop, was beginning to turn around saxophonists' notions of how jazz might be played, and Hawkins himself would soon follow in that direction, as would the bassist and drummer in the quartet which recorded *The Man I Love*, Oscar Pettiford and Shelly Manne. In fact, at that very moment Pettiford was co-leading a combo with Dizzy Gillespie. But *The Man I Love* gives no inkling that a change was in the air. It is a classic of swing combo playing. By contrast with *Body and Soul*, here the accompanists are superb, and furthermore Hawkins has adjusted the nature of the accompaniment to the florid style of his solo playing. Both tunes are meant to be slow ballads, but *The Man I Love* is in double time, with the tempo twice as fast but the harmonies moving along at their normal deliberate rate (so that the 32-bar song becomes a 64-bar song).

Even though he is using brushes, not sticks, Manne establishes a vigorous swing rhythm on the snare and bass drums. With Pettiford playing walking lines and Hawkins holding notes softly in the background, pianist Eddie Heywood, obviously inspired by the opportunity to accompany Hawkins, launches into a deep, original solo. In a few spots he refers to fragments of the melody, but he concentrates on an approach which provides a refreshing compromise between repeating riffs and spinning out ever-new melodies: his crisply articulated right hand phrases are more complicated than typical swing riffs, yet he is not reluctant to repeat a phrase, perhaps with a change in ornamentation, or at a higher or lower pitch.

The recording balance changes at the end of Heywood's choruses to capture Pettiford's solo. There was plenty of precedent by this time for a string bassist to put aside the bass line for a chorus and create a melody instead. Such players as Israel Crosby (with Gene Krupa), Milt Hinton (with Cab Calloway) and Jimmy Blanton (with Duke Ellington) had recorded solos. But, for the first time in Pettiford's agile solo (just as for the first time in Blanton's ensemble playing), everything is in place: intonation, tone quality, swing, mature ideas and melodic phrasing (the last marked by his gasping for breath, as if he were blowing a horn). Appropriately it is Pettiford, not Heywood or Hawkins, who pays close attention to the song's melody, paraphrasing a portion of it to begin the second half of his solo.

Hawkins finishes up the piece. His solo emphasizes another side of his musical personality: forthright, hard swinging, driving on top of the beat. Since Heywood and Pettiford have already started things churning there is no need to begin gently, and thus Hawkins starts at a higher intensity than on *Body and Soul*. All the other essentials of that most famous solo remain central to his aesthetic: weaving arabesques around the chord progression, widening his vibrato, and adding edge to his tone, with a special harshness reserved for climactic high notes.

CD 'single'
Europe: *Body and Soul*, **Bluebird PD 43188**

Tommy Lindsay, Joe Guy (tpt), Earl Hardy (tb), Jackie Fields, Eustis Moore (as), Coleman Hawkins (ts), Gene Rodgers (p), William Oscar Smith (sb), Arthur Herbert (d)

New York   11 Oct 1939   **Body and Soul**

Other CDs
incl. **Body and Soul:**
   USA: *Body and Soul*, Bluebird 5717-2 RB
   Europe: *Body and Soul*, Bluebird ND 85717

LPs
incl. **Body and Soul:**
   USA: *Body and Soul: a Jazz Autobiography*, RCA Victor LPV 501
   Giants of Jazz: Coleman Hawkins, Time-Life STL J06; *Body and Soul*,
   Bluebird 5658-1 RB 11
   Europe: *Body and Soul*, RCA PL 85658
   France: *Body and Soul: a Jazz Autobiography*, RCA 730.566; *Jazz Tribune no.52: the Indispensible Coleman Hawkins 1927–1956: Body and Soul*, RCA NL 89277; *His Greatest Hits*, RCA 730.625; *Coleman Hawkins, vol.1*, RCA FXM1-7325
   Germany: *Body and Soul: a Jazz Autobiography*, RCA LPM 501
   Italy: *The Bean*, Giants of Jazz LPJT 51

Cassettes

incl. **Body and Soul:**
> France: *Jazz Tribune no.52: the Indispensible Coleman Hawkins 1927–1956: Body and Soul*, RCA NK 89277
> Italy: *The Bean*, Giants of Jazz MCJT 51

CD

USA: *Classic Tenors: Coleman Hawkins and Lester Young*, **CBS Special Products AK 38446**

Hawkins (ts), Eddie Heywood (p), Oscar Pettiford (sb), Shelly Manne (d)
New York   23 Dec 1943   **The Man I Love**

Other CDs

same contents:
> USA: Doctor Jazz WK 38446

LPs

incl. **The Man I Love**
> USA: Contact CM3; Doctor Jazz FW 38446; Flying Dutchman FD 10146
> UK: Doctor Jazz ASLP 1004; Philips 6369410; Stateside SL 10117
> France: Barclay 84107; Jazz Anthology 30 CV 1252
> Italy: Joker SM 3259
> Japan: Contact LAX 3064; Flying Dutchman PG 83; Flying Dutchman RJL 2571

incl. **The Man I Love**
> France: *Saxophone Giants*, RCA FXM 3-7324
> Italy: *The Bean*, Giants of Jazz LPJT 51

Cassettes

incl. **The Man I Love**
> Italy: *The Bean*, Giants of Jazz MCJT 51

* * *

Chu Berry: *A Giant of the Tenor Sax*; Ben Webster and Don Byas: *Two Kings of the Tenor Sax*

Soon after Victor and Columbia began the widespread dissemination of jazz by recording the Original Dixieland Jazz Band in 1917, there emerged a succession of small companies recording jazz. In ever-changing combinations the independents remained a part of the jazz landscape until the depression, when they either went bankrupt or were absorbed into the majors. Their permanent return was marked by the establishment at the beginning of 1938 of the Commodore label, an outgrowth of Milt Gabler's activities as owner of the Commodore Music Shop in New York. Owing to Gabler's devotion to improvised small combo jazz and his perceptive, tasteful selection of musicians, it became one of the most important jazz labels of its era.

Among many outstanding tracks on Commodore are two sessions led by Chu Berry while he worked as the featured tenor saxophonist in Cab Calloway's big band. Although these two sessions took place in the studio, they epitomize the spirit of the swing jam sessions that were then flourishing. In the first, later in 1938, Berry teamed up with his good friend trumpeter Roy Eldridge, formerly a colleague in the big bands of Teddy Hill and Fletcher Henderson. In the second, two months before Berry's death in an automobile accident in 1941, his partner was Hot Lips Page, who had just joined Artie Shaw's big band.

This collection invites a consideration of the question of invention and repetition, since there are two versions of six of the eight tracks. I must confess that, unlike many devoted listeners, I am not automatically enamoured of alternate takes; even for someone as spectacularly inventive as Charlie Parker, I find the reward of listening to his ever-new solos on five takes of *Billie's Bounce* somewhat dampened by the drudgery of hearing the theme played again and again and again. Happily, this is not a problem on Berry's sessions. These are free-wheeling performances and most of the alternate takes are drastically altered.

Following a time-honoured tradition of musicians angling for extra money from royalties, Gabler and Page claim credit as composers for *Sittin' In* (based on the 'hold that tiger' strain of *Tiger Rag*), *Forty-six West Fifty-two* (based on *Sweet Georgia Brown*), *Blowing up a Breeze* (based on *I Got Rhythm*) and *Monday at Minton's* (a blues). The claim is not outrageous, since all that is borrowed each time is a chord progression. The players avoid familiar melodies, as they plunge right into improvising at the start, and the only remotely thematic elements are some riffs traded between Berry and Page at the end of *Blowing up a Breeze* and *Monday at Minton's*. With one exception this philosophy carries over into the other performances, in which the notion of a fixed theme never advances further than a preset piano or guitar introduction or the extremely loose paraphrase of the melodies of *Star Dust* and *Body and Soul*. The exception is Page's prearranged solo and singing on the first half of both versions of *Gee Ain't I Good to You*.

Berry was strongly influenced by Coleman Hawkins. He used a less pronounced vibrato than Hawkins, though it becomes heavy in his renditions of ballads. He was somewhat less overtly passionate, and this difference is heightened in the first session. Set against Eldridge, who is a firecracker, Berry sounds positively cool. This sense of restraint comes cross in another way on *Monday at Minton's*, with Page, in which Berry's playing points towards the emerging rhythm and blues tenor saxophone style, but without crossing over into raucousness. And these recordings suggest that Berry could not handle fast tempos as well as Hawkins. His rhythmic drive is impressive throughout, but as the tempo increases the shape of his melodies grows simpler, so that on two versions of *Sittin' In* he gets stuck repeating two-, three- or four-note figures when continuously moving lines might have provided more interest. By contrast, his melodic invention on slow tunes is creative and sophisticated. *Body and Soul*, recorded before Hawkins's famous version, begins strongly, Berry improvising at his best. Upon entering, Eldridge kicks up the tempo about two and a half times (rather than strictly double timing), with the result that Berry is hurried when he returns at half of this new tempo. There are no such glitches in *On the Sunny Side of the Street*, and the two sentimental versions afford a chance to hear Berry at his most inventive; except for a few fragments (for example, the beginning and ending of his second solo on each track, and the descent from a dramatic high point), the alternate take is entirely new and just as beautifully played.

The great tragedy of Eldridge's career was the well-publicized mid-1940s battle between the adherents of bop and the New Orleans revival, which had the side effect of forcing swing combo musicians into one camp or the other. Eldridge reluctantly abandoned swing tunes for a more traditional repertory. These earlier Commodore recordings testify how well he thrived on swing, and at the time – that is, in 1938 – he was the leading trumpet soloist in that style. On these tracks he is an exciting improviser, not at all daunted by fast tempos; indeed, on *Body and Soul*, where he throws Berry a curve, and also on *Sittin' In*, where he ignores the tempo of the introduction, he seems to be saying 'no, let's take this one faster'. Regardless of speed, he is consistently inventive, negotiating difficult leaps and fast lines which he sets against rhythmically charged repeated notes and dramatic high climaxes. He uses a mute for the opening solo on *Forty-six West Fifty-two* (in which, incidentally, about half of his solo recurs on the alternate take), but otherwise he plays with a bright, open tone, sometimes adding a burred edge to intensify his sound further.

Page is a simpler, more traditional player than Eldridge, and his improvising draws heavily from swing and blues riffs, recalling his more significant work as a soloist with the Bennie Moten and Count Basie big bands. In both sessions pianist Clyde Hart takes solos. In the main these present a functional style which provides a textural contrast to the horns' leading role; the best are on the ballad versions of *On the Sunny Side of the Street*, especially take 2. All these are fully in the swing style, with no indication as yet of Hart's involvement with bop. There are also brief drum and bass solos, but in the main the rhythm sections keep to an accompanimental role, laying down a solid, steady foundation.

The fidelity of these tracks is, for prewar technology, excellent. Throughout jazz recording, turntables have rotated at non-standard speeds, and some listeners may note that gremlins were at work on at least one track here: take 2 of *Forty-six West Fifty-two* is not merely slower than take 1, but at a lower pitch, thus indicating that something slipped in the long chain of mechanical steps between the making of the 78 rpm master and its remastering in modern formats.

The second Commodore collection, **Two Kings of the Tenor Sax**, presents the results of three sessions, two of which were originally recorded in the studio for that label in 1944: drummer Sid Catlett's quartet featuring tenor saxophonist Ben Webster, and Hot Lips Page's septet featuring tenor saxophonist Don Byas. The third segment is an excerpt from and the best part of a concert given at Town Hall in New York the following year, and it also features Byas, in duets with bassist Slam Stewart, and in a trio with Teddy Wilson added.

The four titles on the Catlett–Webster sessions were recorded during a period when the two men were working together at the Onyx Club in New York. These follow the spirit and format of Chu Berry's Commodore sessions. The few dull moments are John Simmons's walking bass solos and Catlett's tune *Just a Riff*, based largely on a plodding riff which forces the players into a long series of disconnected phrases, until Webster finally manages to build a solo in phrases which cut across the riff. The remainder of the session is magnificent, if possible surpassing Berry's. Again the emphasis is on improvised swing, with alternate and substantially new takes of the other three titles.

Catlett, who also accompanied Berry and Eldridge six years earlier, is the leader here and thus has a greater opportunity to show off his command of the swing style, particularly through his intricate snare drumming on several solos. The pianist is Marlowe Morris, whose playing here, and also with Catlett, Simmons, Lester Young and others in the film *Jammin' the Blues* this same year, marks his greatest contribution to recorded jazz. By setting fleet melodies against sparse chords in his solos, Morris suggests the growing influence of bop pianists on other New York musicians in 1944, but he displays none of the rhythmic trickiness of bop. Morris worked alone often. In this capacity he is one of the local players who might be mentioned in the same breath as Art Tatum, and here he occasionally quotes from Tatum's work (as for example in the droning figure in the second half of his solo on the first take of *Sleep*).

The star of the session is Webster. A comparison of alternate takes finds him inventing complex and convincing new melodies throughout these performances, and, unlike Berry, he is equally comfortable with the fast-tempoed *Sleep*, the medium-tempoed *Linger Awhile* and the ballad *Memories of You*. His sound is full of contrasts. These contrasts might build progressively, as on the two versions of *Sleep*. His opening statements of the melody and the solos that follow are delivered with a gentle tone and a pronounced, but not heavy, vibrato; when he returns, following Catlett's solos, he adds a growl to his tone, and this leads to ferocious climaxes on a repeated high note (which occurs earlier in take 1 than in take 2). Or the change may be sudden, as in the leap from hard-edged solo playing to a tender melodic phrase at the end of *Linger Awhile* and the explosive rip upwards inserted into the midst of the first take of his otherwise caressing version of *Memories of You*.

The remaining tracks include Page's bright, joyful blues singing and solos on *You Need Coachin'*, as well as alto saxophonist Earl Bostic's incongruous fast-running, unswinging, non-bluesy solo on that same title. But the focus is on Don Byas: his relaxed solo on *You Need Coachin'*, his soft sumptuous ballad playing on *These Foolish Things* and *Candy*, and his fleet variations on *Indiana* and *I Got Rhythm*. These last two titles, the duets with Stewart, follow an identical format. Stewart sets out a bass line, and, indeed, here the re-semblance is more literal than intended: *Indiana* begins with the first 16 bars of the bass line of *I Got Rhythm*! Byas then launches into the melody of *Indiana* and Stewart follows along in a blink. On both titles Byas plays the theme clearly before improvising in a nearly perpetual motion manner that points towards the technical facility and some of the harmonic imagination of bop saxophonists, but again, as with Morris, lacks the surprising accentuation that would be peppered throughout a characteristic bop solo. While Byas plays, Stewart keeps up a strong bass line, sometimes using a slap bass technique to add a percussive effect in the absence of drums. Sandwiched between Byas's improvisation is Stewart's melodic solo, bowed and hummed simultaneously in the humorous style which is ever present in his work. If the two ballads are far less exciting than these two duets, their melodic content is certainly far more substantial. In his gentle, breathy sound and his florid imagination, Byas here invites comparison with any of his rivals on the instrument.

CD

Germany: *A Giant of the Tenor Sax*, Commodore 8.24293

Roy Eldridge (tpt), Chu Berry (ts), Clyde Hart (p), Danny Barker (g), Artie Shapiro (sb), Sid Catlett (d)

New York	11 Nov 1941	**Sittin' In**
		Sittin' In no.2
		Star Dust

		Body and Soul	
		Forty-six West Fifty-two	5
		Forty-six West Fifty-two no.2	

Hot Lips Page (tpt), Berry (ts), Hart (p), Albert Casey (g), Al Morgan (sb), Harry Jaeger (d)

New York	Sept 1941	Blowing up a Breeze	
		Blowing up a Breeze no.2	

omit Page		On the Sunny Side of the Street	
		On the Sunny Side of the Street no.2	10

add Page		Monday at Minton's	
		Monday at Minton's no.2	

*as **Monday at Minton's**, but Page (tpt, v)*

		Gee Ain't I Good to You	
		Gee Ain't I Good to You no.2	

Other CDs
incl. tracks 1, 3–5, 7, 9, 11, 13:
   USA: *Giants of the Tenor Sax*, Commodore CCD 7004

LPs
same contents:
   USA: Commodore XFL 15353
   Germany: Commodore 6.24293 AG
plus additional tracks:
   USA: *The Complete Commodore Jazz Recordings*, Mosaic MR 23-123
incl. tracks 1, 3–5, 7, 9, 11, 13:
   USA: *The Commodore Years: the Tenor Sax: Lester Young, Chu Berry, Ben Webster*, Atlantic 2-307; *Giants of the Tenor Sax*, Commodore CCL 7004
   UK: *The Big Sound of Coleman Hawkins & Chu Berry*, London HMC 5006

LP
Germany: Ben Webster and Don Byas: *Two Kings of the Tenor Sax*, Commodore 6.24058 AG

Ben Webster (ts), Marlowe Morris (p), John Simmons (sb), Sid Catlett (d)

New York	18 March 1944	Sleep
		Sleep no.2

Linger Awhile
Linger Awhile no.2
Memories of You   5
Memories of You no.2
Just a Riff

Hot Lips Page (tpt), Don Byas (ts), Earl Bostic (as), B. G. Hammond (as), Clyde Hart (p), Al Lucas (sb), Jack Parker (d)
New York   29 Sept 1944   **You Need Coachin'**
                                       These Foolish Things

Byas (ts), Slam Stewart (sb)
New York   9 June 1945   **Indiana**   10
                                       I Got Rhythm

add Teddy Wilson (p)   **Candy**

CDs
incl. tracks 1–3, 5, 7–12:
  USA: *Giants of the Tenor Sax*, Commodore CCD 7005

Other LPs
same contents:
  USA: Commodore XFL 14938
  Germany: Commodore 6.24058 AG
plus additional tracks:
  USA: *The Complete Commodore Jazz Recordings*, Mosaic MR 23-123
incl. tracks 1, 3, 5, 7–9:
  UK: *Sax Scene*, London HMC 5004
incl. tracks 1–3, 5, 7–12:
  USA: *Giants of the Tenor Sax*, Commodore CCL 7005
incl. tracks 1, 3, 5, 7:
  USA: *The Commodore Years: the Tenor Sax: Lester Young, Chu Berry, Ben Webster*, Atlantic 2-307
incl. tracks 10–12:
  USA: *The Commodore Years: Town Hall Concert, 1945*, Atlantic 2-310
  UK: *Town Hall Concert, vol.3*, London HMC 5003

Nat 'King' Cole: *The King Cole Trio*

Nat 'King' Cole had two careers. In 1937 he founded a swing trio in which he played piano alongside guitarist Oscar Moore and string bassist Wesley Prince; all three men also sang. In 1951, after only a few changes of bassists, and up to that point still with Moore, Cole abandoned the trio to devote himself fully to an activity he had taken up a few years earlier, singing romantic popular music to the accompaniment of studio orchestras. An anthology in the Italian series Giants of Jazz focuses on his first, lesser-known career. It collects together several types of pop, jazz and blues singing and playing, and thus summarizes Cole's, and the trio's, unusually talented diversity.

A devotion to careful arrangement is a thread loosely tying together the vocal styles here. On the earliest tracks, from 1941, the three men sing perfectly in unison. This perfection is most evident in the middle of *I Like to Riff*, when they deliver a chorus of scat singing so polished that their tongues roll together as one. There is a further example of the group's coordinated unison work (now with bassist Johnny Miller having replaced Prince) on the refrain of Cole's first hit, *Straighten up and Fly Right*. His own composition, it was a pioneering performance on the rhythm-and-blues edge of swing, though the term 'rhythm and blues' was not yet in currency when he recorded the song towards the end of 1943, just as the American Federation of Musicians was beginning to settle their strike against recording companies. Ostensibly about a buzzard and a monkey, *Straighten up and Fly Right* has a harmless pop quality about it and could easily be taken for a cute animal song. But it takes no great stretch of the imagination to hear the lyric as a metaphor for race relations in the USA, and Cole pops out the climactic break with a cool, streetwise air: 'your story's so touching, but it sounds just like a lie'.

Two weeks later, he was in the studio again, blending smoothly into the mainstream of American popular music with relaxed swing versions of *Sweet Lorraine* and *It's Only a Paper Moon* and a sensuous reading of the ballad *Embraceable You*, on all of which he sticks closely to the familiar melodies in carefully enunciated performances that focus on the mellow beauty of his voice. These, together with another slow ballad recorded in 1946, *For Sentimental Reasons*, show that the equipment for his second career was already fully in place.

The remaining vocal performance in this anthology, *Route 66!*, provides a revealing contrast with the three instrumental blues, *Easy Listening Blues*, *This Way Out* and *Rhumba Azul*. I am fascinated by, and I latch right onto, blues chord progressions, and it amuses me to think how many times I heard *Route 66!* before noticing that it was based on standard 12-bar blues changes. The thematic relationship to traditional travelling blues (countless train lyrics, *Key to the Highway* and so forth) seems nothing more than coincidental: emotionally, this delightfully catchy, urbane tune is as far removed from blues as possible. Yet Cole was also capable of becoming fully immersed in the genre. This is most evident on *Easy Listening Blues*, a performance filled with classic piano blues licks which he caressingly repeats and varies. *This Way Out* – unfortunately marred by a howling feedback emanating from the guitar amplifier – has a boogie-woogie piano introduction, a riff theme (as well as other swing riffs in the choruses before the theme returns) and excellent single-note improvised blues solos in the swing style. Far less satisfying than these various blues is *Rhumba Azul*, an awkward, sloppily played blues in a minor key, with an ostinato bass line and rhythms slanted towards Latin music; this is a type of tune which Horace Silver, in his *Señor Blues*, would later make into a definitive hard-bop recording.

As instrumentalists, the members of the trio achieved a marvellous sense of swing, setting feet tapping without the aid of a drummer. Only in those passages where Cole and Moore repeatedly pound out a riff does there seem to be a need for the contrasting rhythmic patterns that a swing drummer could supply. Moore's basic approach relied heavily on the standards of tone and single-note technique set by Charlie Christian, but he also provided strong support as a strumming rhythm guitarist (which Christian did not), and harmonically he was further down the line towards bop. Cole's approach was centred around the transitional swing-to-bop manner of a fast running right-hand line accompanied by sparsely placed fragments of chords in the left. But his playing had a flexibility, and sometimes a speed, which Moore could not match. In addition to the various styles of blues playing already mentioned, and in addition to his propensity for repeating and varying tuneful ideas in taking solos on pop songs as well as blues, there is Cole's demonstration on a version of Fats Waller's *Honeysuckle Rose* that, when he wanted to, he could play with the lightning speed and clarity of touch of an Art Tatum or a Bud Powell; deceptively beginning at a cool pace, he launches into a more than double-time tempo. Also, more so than Moore, Cole had some inclination towards the jagged rhythms of bop, as heard on the second piano solo on *Bop Kick*.

The whole of *Bop Kick* is ruined by the incredibly lame bongo playing of Jack Costanzo, who betrays in his four-square, on-the-beat phrasing the same complete lack of understanding of Afro-Cuban percussion playing that drags down so many contemporary tracks by Stan Kenton's big band. As Cole and his men ranged widely through the music of their time, this track and *Rhumba Azul* are among the few things that did not work out well for them.

LP
Italy: *The King Cole Trio*, Giants of Jazz LPJT 14

Nat 'King' Cole (p, v), Oscar Moore (elg, v), Wesley Prince (sb, v)
New York   16 March 1941   **I Like to Riff**
                    23 Oct 1941   **Call the Police**

Johnny Miller (sb, v) replaces Prince
Los Angeles   30 Nov 1943   **Straighten up and Fly Right**

Cole (p, v), Moore (elg), Miller (sb)
                    15 Dec 1943   **Sweet Lorraine**
                                         Embraceable You   5
                                         It's Only a Paper Moon

omit (v)   17 Jan 1944   **The Man I Love**
                                         What is This Thing Called Love?
                    6 March 1944   **Easy Listening Blues**
                    23 May 1945   **Sweet Georgia Brown**   10
                    1 Nov 1945   **This Way Out**

*as **Straighten up and Fly Right***
                    15 March 1946   **Route 66!**

*as **Sweet Lorraine***
New York   22 Aug 1946   **For Sentimental Reasons**

*as **The Man I Love***
Los Angeles   25 June 1947   **Honeysuckle Rose**
                    Aug 1947   **Rhumba Azul**   15

Cole (p), Irving Ashby (elg), Joe Comfort (sb), Jack Costanzo (bongos)
New York   March 1949   **Bop Kick**

Other LPs
incl. tracks 3–6:
  USA: *Vocal Classics*, Capitol T 591
incl. tracks 3–4, 6, 12–13:
  USA: *Nat King Cole Story*, Capitol WCL1-1613 and SWCL1-1613
incl. tracks 7–11, 14–16:
  USA: *Instrumental Classics*, Capitol T 592
  UK: *Capitol Jazz Classics: King Cole Trio: Trio Days*, EMI One-up OU 2007

Netherlands: *Capitol Jazz Classics: King Cole Trio: Trio Days*, Capitol
5C 052.80-804

Cassettes

same contents:
  Italy: Giants of Jazz MCJT 14

* * *

Ella Fitzgerald: *Ella at Juan-les-Pins*

In a book of essays on great recordings I cannot resist beginning Ella
Fitzgerald's segment by saying that **Ella at Juan-les-Pins** is not her best
album. That honour goes to **Ella Fitzgerald Sings the George and Ira
Gershwin Song Book** (1959), a collection of faithful renditions of American
popular songs on which the singer was accompanied by a studio orchestra
under the direction of Nelson Riddle; there are few things in the world more
beautiful than her version of *Embraceable You*.

But for Fitzgerald in all her diversity as a jazz singer, this is the album.
Recorded in France at the fifth Festival Mondial du Jazz Antibes-Juan-les-
Pins in 1964, it has trumpeter Roy Eldridge at the head of a quartet that
included two longstanding members of Fitzgerald's regular trio: Gus
Johnson, formerly one of the best of Count Basie's drummers, and Tommy
Flanagan, whose extensive credentials as a bop pianist in Detroit and New
York should not deceive anyone about his appropriateness for this main-
stream swing album.

As always, popular songs are at the heart of Fitzgerald's repertory. (The
exception is *The Cricket Song*, a throwaway made on the spot in response to
the insects which were disrupting the second evening of her performance.)
What is astonishing about this album is her versatility, the breadth of interpretation which she brings to these standards. Closest to the spirit of the
studio song books are the tunes without Eldridge. *Summertime* shows off the
beauty of her voice on what is, for her, a fairly high-pitched melody; using a
languid tone which matches the lyrics, she stays close to the original tune,
modifying it with bluesy inflections and gospel melismas. By contrast, *Somewhere in the Night*, a duet with piano until the very end, affords in its opening
verse an opportunity for Fitzgerald to revel in the deep, creamy end of her
range. Eldridge also lays out on the ballad-style introduction to *I've Got You
Under my Skin*, which turns into a not entirely successful hybrid of swing
and bossa nova, and he is absent on all but the last note of *How High the
Moon*. Again in these songs Fitzgerald stays fairly close to the given

melodies. The latter is taken as a slow ballad, no doubt as an antidote to the countless up-tempo versions she had given after the success of her bop-influenced scat singing on a recording of *How High the Moon* in 1947. For one phrase of its second chorus she takes up the trumpeter's role, giving the melody over to pianist Flanagan while she weaves around it an improvised obbligato, which in a moment of reverse tone-painting dips down into her lowest range at the words 'somewhere there's heaven'.

Just as with Chu Berry's combo nearly three decades earlier, Eldridge is a firecracker here. With his support, another side of Fitzgerald's artistry opens up, revealing a hard driving, swinging, adventuresome improviser whose gritty sound is in the tradition of Kansas City blues shouters, even if her repertory is not. For the most part she avoids scat singing, preferring instead to keep to the given lyrics; but these she divorces from their melodies, supplying instead her own pitches and rhythms, while also modifying her tone with crackles and growls for emphasis. In the middle of *Day in, Day out*, she inserts *Come Rain or Come Shine* and then sings to the words 'there it is, there it is' the melody of *Mean to Me*, with Eldridge jumping right in together with her. *Just a Sittin' and a Rockin'* begins with a laid-back delivery of the opening verse, but builds through Eldridge's heated, bluesy, muted trumpet solo into Fitzgerald's most intense shout singing, as she strains at the top of her range. On the opening verse of *The Lady is a Tramp* she borrows a characteristic female vocal style from Broadway musicals, and for a few phrases sounds every bit like a New York teenager. But she moves out of this style, into her full alto voice and then into more shout singing, this time demonstrating that that intense approach can be wedded to precisely con-trolled, virtuoso improvisation; for example, after the phrase ending 'my shape is my own', she effortlessly negotiates the leaps on 'tha-hat's why-hy the la-hady is a tramp'. (This, incidentally, exemplifies the semi-scat singing which is a trademark of Fitzgerald's style, stretching out words into sounds, like 'tha-ha-ha-ha-hat' and 'suh-huh-huh-huh-humwhere'.)

St Louis Blues, the second half of which offers the only 12-bar blues pro-gression on the album, carries the leader's fervour over the boundary into crassness, with especially distorted shouting on the word 'feelin''. At the end she reveals that her heart wasn't in it: 'the only reason we sang this song, it was a request from our record'. Much more successful in this vein, though it is another popular song with a theme in the form *aaba* rather than a blues, is *They Can't Take That Away from Me*, performed at an unusually sultry pace and heavily coloured by blues phrases in Fitzgerald's recasting of the melody of the *b* section.

You'd be so Nice to Come Home to offers the most straightforward testimony to Fitzgerald's abilities as an improviser: going through the words three times, she changes the melody drastically at each repetition. But this lesson in jazz creativity is topped by *Honeysuckle Rose*. From the first note she remodels Fats Waller's familiar tune. Scarcely referring to the original, she makes new melodies on the given chord changes, while also inventing riffs in exchanges with Eldridge and scat singing. The performance is a *tour de force* in improvised swing.

LP

USA: *Ella at Juan-les-Pins*, **Verve 4065 and 64065**

Roy Eldridge (tpt), Tommy Flanagan (p), Bill Yancey (sb), Gus Johnson (d), Ella Fitzgerald (v)

Antibes, France	July 1964	**Day in, Day out**
		Just a Sittin' and a Rockin'
		The Lady is a Tramp
		Summertime
		St Louis Blues 5
		Honeysuckle Rose
		They Can't Take That Away from Me
		You'd be so Nice to Come Home to
		Somewhere in the Night
		I've Got You Under my Skin 10
		The Cricket Song
		How High the Moon

Other LPs

same contents:
   UK: Verve VLP 9083 and SVLP 9083
plus one additional track:
   France: same title, Verve GLP 3716

CHAPTER 5

We Called it Music: Dixieland and Swing

Digby Fairweather

We Called it Music was the self-effacing title chosen by guitarist Eddie Condon for his autobiography and a subsequent companion LP collection. Knowing the quality of jazz that Condon and the musicians that surrounded him always played, it's inconceivable now that anyone in our music's history could ever have called it anything else. Condon-style was a well-shaken cocktail of classic jazz freedoms stiffened with the sophistication of swing, and the swing era represents the great coming-out party for jazz – the 1930s years when she grew, instrumentally and conceptually, from rough-edged tomboyism to fully matured womanhood. Technical skills advanced, knowledge grew, and a whole bright generation from Benny Goodman to Harry James and their groundbreaking confrères established new state-of-the-art standards in some cases never to be surpassed. The sort of musicians who turn up in this chapter were – or are – contemporaries or sons of the swing era – young masters who grew up and shaped up in the generation closely following on after such true innovators as Armstrong, Noone, Hines, Teagarden and a few others. And consequently their music was technically equipped to express all the joyful new creative thoughts flooding their imagination. Bob Haggart, one of the great creators of the genre under discussion here, summed up the end-results blossoming in the music: 'What is there *not* to like?' he asked once. At that point Haggart was talking about *his* kind of 'dixieland', and the term is a controversial one, with at least two definitions, which was disliked and disowned by several of the jazz giants who turn up in these essays, notably Bobby Hackett! So, a definition: 'dixieland', for the purposes of this chapter, is neither classic New Orleans jazz nor the Euro-American tradition of revivalism. At the arranged end, it is the musical reinventions of Bob Crosby, Matty Matlock and their followers, and, at the free end, the free-for-all creativity born of sophistication applied to classic jazz principles for which Eddie Condon was the figurehead. It is the music of 'Jamboree Jones', of Muggsy's 'Great Sixteen', of Chicago and New York and of the grand jazz masters as well as their followers, from Charlie Lavere to Dick Cathcart, Billy Maxted and Rosy McHargue. They called it music – and jazz was never richer than when they did.

* * *

Bob Crosby: *Jazz Classics in Digital Stereo: Bob Crosby, 1937 to 1938*

For lovers of what is popularly (but sometimes confusingly) called 'dixieland', Bob Crosby's orchestra and small group, the Bobcats, are held in especially affectionate regard. This is logical, because Crosby's two ensembles were based on classic jazz designs and formed a dixieland oasis in the big-band years, well away from the blander trappings of swing written into the act by Tommy Dorsey, Benny Goodman or even Artie Shaw. Indeed, Crosby's band could lay some legitimate claim to having founded the American jazz revival. Much of its repertoire drew largely from classic jazz sources, and several of its cornermen – Eddie Miller, Nappy Lamare, Ray Bauduc and Irving Fazola – came from New Orleans. And even though these players – as well as others such as Yank Lawson and Bob Haggart – grew up in the swing era, their formative influences had been the classic jazz of Armstrong, Oliver, Jimmie Noone and others.

The things that set Crosby's joyful music apart from fully fledged revivalism, of course, were its technical sophistication (founder-members of his organization were ex-members of Ben Pollack's highly proficient band) and a collection of written arrangements. These served most of all to create a separate developmental heritage of dixieland, running down through Muggsy Spanier's Ragtimers, Bud Freeman's Summa Cum Laude Orchestra and the Lawson–Haggart Jazz Band, via the brilliant creations of Crosby staff arranger Matty Matlock and finally to the World's Greatest Jazz Band (again of Lawson and Haggart), which finally disbanded in 1978. This line inspired a whole coterie of international imitators (including British players Sid Phillips and Harry Gold) and created a genre for itself quite separate from the deliberate or natural archaism of Lu Watters or Bunk Johnson and George Lewis.

Perhaps the best illustration of this difference is *South Rampart Street Parade*, a brilliantly conceived sound-picture of a New Orleans street parade which sets the standard features of the genre – free clarinet, parade drums and tailgate trombone against trumpet lead – into a totally sophisticated paraphrase that achieves new effects of its own. And this unique mix of revivalism and swing sophistication, of course, carries on through producer Robert Parker's representative collection of Crosby titles. Numbers such as *Gin Mill Blues* and *Dogtown Blues*, with their catalogue of cunningly played New Orleans-isms, perfectly illustrate one of the many essential points in John Chilton's liner note: that 'the band's rule was to discard any part of a score that sounded ostentatious or superfluous – the result was tough honest music that abounded with feeling'. The coda of *Gin Mill Blues*, with its throwaway lyric diminuendo, is a fine example of the sort of minutia of dixieland composition which is now a completely lost art. *Honky Tonk Train Blues* remains the definitive big-band development of the Meade 'Lux' Lewis piano solo original, and *Squeeze Me*, with its delicate playing by Zurke and perfect performance by Eddie Miller, is a definition of big-band dixieland. Only *Swingin' at the Sugar Bowl* (featuring Nappy Lamare's likeable singing and more fine Miller tenor) reverts to standard swing formats.

Twelve of Parker's 18 tracks feature the Bobcats' state-of-the-art small-group dixieland – a sometimes indistinguishable mix of cunning scoring and flyaway ad lib, all played with unflagging intensity and conviction. A few classic highpoints among dozens are Lawson's climactic two-note lead towards the close of *Five Point Blues* (like a man too overcome with emotion to express thought); Zurke's *Big Foot Jump*, which recalls the delicate stride of Willie 'the Lion' Smith; and more perfect dixie scoring in *Slow Mood* (to which Johnny Mercer later added words as *Lazy Mood*) and *Can't We be Friends?*. The dozens of other written finesses – such as the short, potent scored passages at either end of *Who's Sorry Now?* – are Bob Crosby-style jazz at its definitively greatest.

CD

UK: *Jazz Classics in Digital Stereo: Bob Crosby, 1937 to 1938*, **BBC CD 688**

Andy Ferretti, Yank Lawson (tpt), Ward Silloway, Mark Bennett (tb), Gil Rodin, Matty Matlock (cl, as), Noni Bernardi (as), Eddie Miller (cl, ts), Deane Kincaide (ts), Bob Zurke (p), Nappy Lamare (g), Bob Haggart (sb), Ray Bauduc (d)
New York   8 Feb 1937   **Gin Mill Blues**

Zeke Zarchy, Billy Butterfield, Lawson (tpt), Silloway, Warren Smith (tb), Matlock (cl, as), Joe Kearns (as), Miller (cl, ts), Rodin (ts), Zurke (p), Lamare (g), Haggart (sb), Bauduc (d)
Los Angeles   5 Nov 1937   **Squeeze Me** (arr Haggart)

(Bob Cats:) Lawson (tpt), Smith (tb), Matlock (cl), Miller (cl, ts), Zurke (p), Lamare (g), Haggart (sb), Bauduc (d)
            9 Nov 1937   **Stumbling**

as Stumbling, but Miller (ts)

Who's Sorry Now?
Coquette   5
Fidgety Feet
You're Driving Me Crazy
Can't We be Friends?

as Squeeze Me, but Charlie Spivak (tpt) replaces Zarchy
                    16 Nov 1937   **South Rampart Street Parade** (arr
                                         Kincaide and Haggart)
                                     Dogtown Blues   10

*(Bob Cats:) as Stumbling, but Irving Fazola (cl) replaces Matlock, Haig Stephens
(sb) replaces Haggart*
New York   14 March 1938   **March of the Bob Cats**
                                    Slow Mood
                                    Big Foot Jump
                                    The Big Crash from China
                                    Five Point Blues   15

Haggart (sb, whistling), Bauduc (d)
Chicago   14 Oct 1938   **The Big Noise from Winnetka**

*Zarchy, Sterling Bose, Butterfield (tpt), Silloway, Smith (tb), Fazola (cl), Kearns
(as), Miller (cl, ts), Rodin (ts), Zurke (p), Lamare (g, v), Haggart (sb), Bauduc (d)*
                    19 Oct 1938   **Swingin' at the Sugar Bowl**

omit (v)   **Honky Tonk Train Blues** (arr
                                        Matlock)

LPs

same contents:
  UK: *Jazz Classics in Digital Stereo: Bob Crosby, 1937 to 1938*, BBC REB 688
incl. tracks 3–8, 11–14:
  Australia: *The Bob Cats 1937–1942*, Swaggie S 1245
incl. tracks 1–2, 9–10, 15, 17:
  UK: *Come on and Hear*, vol.1, Coral CP 109, and vol.2, Coral CP 110
incl. tracks 1, 9–10, 15, 17:
  France: *Those Swinging Cats*, vol.1, MCA 510.134
incl. tracks 3–6, 8, 11:
  UK: *Big Noise from Winnetka*, MCA MCFM 2695
incl. tracks 9–10, 17:
  UK: *South Rampart Street Parade*, MCA MCFM 2579

Cassettes

same contents:
  UK: *Jazz Classics in Digital Stereo: Bob Crosby, 1937 to 1938*, BBC ZCF 688
incl. tracks 1–2, 9–10:
  UK: *Bob Crosby Orchestra*, Neovox 838
incl. tracks 3–6, 10–14:
  UK: *Bob Crosby Bob Cats: 'The First 20 Tracks'*, Neovox 839

* * *

Muggsy Spanier: *At the Jazz Band Ball: Chicago/ New York Dixieland*

The sixteen titles recorded by Muggsy Spanier's Ragtime Band for RCA Victor in July, November and December 1939 are hallowed classic jazz. After their issue, critics called Spanier's band 'the greatest since King Oliver's', and time has done nothing to diminish the 'Great Sixteen'; they remain for many listeners the finest dixieland on record – a pinnacle of stylistic expression which helped refocus attention on traditional jazz values amid the swing era and which led on, within a year, to the American jazz revival. Four of Spanier's 16 titles were recorded in Chicago on 7 July 1939 while the Ragtimers were resident at the Sherman Hotel's Old Town Room, the remainder in New York after the band had moved on to Nick's club for a short residency. And every one is a cornucopia of dixieland perfection, full of dedicated musical intensity as much as of the choreographed detail which comes from nightly performance: a tightly knit ensemble, scored sustained tones behind solos (especially Spanier's), dynamic observation, and sudden texture changes in mid-performance creating the effect of electric light turned on to illuminate the dark area of a room. Spanier played the perfect lead cornet; his spare punchy phrasing, underpinned by a perfect sense of time and note-placement, was delivered in a broad, attractively sour-edged tone, and around this faithful lead his sidemen hung their ensemble lines in relaxed decorative compliment.

Just how perfectly this worked can be heard on *At Sundown*, in which it is difficult after repeated hearings to decide which parts of the ensemble opening statements were formalized and which not. *At Sundown* indeed represents one peak of the 'Great Sixteen'. It is a crafted performance which moves from fast-trot introduction to galloping ensemble; there are scored riffs behind Nick Caiazza (on tenor) and in contrary motion behind Cless (clarinet) before a bridge and key change to Bushkin's all-American piano solo, which echoes Basie for 16 bars before gambolling off into joyful dixieland expression. The great biting entry of Spanier's cornet leads to a controlled ensemble diminuendo, at which point Cless's clarinet takes over the lead for just three bars before reverting to harmony for an operatically voiced false ending. This leads the piece in near-ecstasy to a reprise capped with a mock-modest 'that's all' coda.

Were this the only side Muggsy Spanier's Ragtimers had ever recorded their reputation would be assured, but spread among the 15 others there are dozens of similarly unforgettable moments. One of them is *Relaxin' at the Touro* (named after the Touro Infirmary, New Orleans, where Spanier (just) weathered an illness in 1938), in which Joe Bushkin's solemn piano introduction ranks alongside John Lewis's opening to *Parker's Mood* as one of jazz's great scene-setters. Spanier's bitingly caustic and muted solo figures move unobtrusively into ensemble at bar 11 of the first chorus, and after Bushkin's piano solo (contemporary for its time, with its chromatic minor sevenths at bars 9 to 10) Georg Brunis's entry, voiced with the ensemble again, is a solemn funeral dirge. More of the same atmosphere turns up on *Lonesome Road*, in which Spanier's cornet, against hymn-like chords from the ensemble, creates a mock-gothic ambience. When Bushkin's piano enters after Caiazza's tenor, with ticking drum-rims in support, the effect is of a welcome *leitmotif* amid the stark blues landscape; then the humble, hushed trombone of Brunis, like a prayerful mourner, precedes 16 more bars of definitive Spanier, playing, plunger-muted, a substitute paraphrase of *Moanin' Low* in place of the original theme. Such creative thought is rare in dixieland music 50 years on, and illuminates every other track, from *Dinah* (with its dynamic introduction, irresistible out-of-tempo verse and hep Brunis vocal) to *Eccentric* (a *tour de force* for Cless) and *Black and Blue*, with Spanier's cutting solos and more definitive playing from Bushkin. The coda of this last track found its way into dixieland lore and beyond (to Count Basie's *Every Day I Have the Blues*, for one hit-making example), and there are dozens of other passages throughout the 'Great Sixteen' which – like the greatest of Armstrong, Beiderbecke or Parker – are now *de rigueur* in recreative performance. Two examples are the upward cornet climb towards the final joyful ensemble of *Big Butter and Egg Man* and the alternation of long-noted ensemble passages and solo drum breaks towards the end of *That Da Da Strain* – dixieland tablets of hot stone!

At the time of writing, the newly available Bluebird issue of Spanier's 16 tracks also includes unrelated material: two tracks by Eddie Condon from 8 February 1929, cited in Chapter 1; and four by Bud Freeman from his Summa Cum Laude orchestra's session of 19 July 1939. Track 2 is an alternate take, not the original 78 rpm master, though in this and other instances of alternate takes noted below, the versions are not very different from one another.

CD

USA: *At the Jazz Band Ball: Chicago/New York Dixieland,* Bluebird 6752-2 RB

Muggsy Spanier (c), Georg Brunis (ts, v), Rod Cless (cl), Ray McKinstry (ts), George Zack (p), Bob Casey (g), Pat Pattison (sb), Marty Greenberg (d)
Chicago   7 July 1939   **Big Butter and Egg Man** (take 1)

omit (v)   **Someday, Sweetheart** (take 1)
Eccentric (take 1)
That Da Da Strain (take 2)

Spanier (c), Brunis (tb), Cless (cl), Bernie Billings (ts), Joe Bushkin (p), Casey (sb), Don Carter (d)
New York   10 Nov 1939   **At the Jazz Band Ball** (take 2)   **5**

add Brunis (v)   **I Wish I Could Shimmy like my Sister Kate** (take 1)

omit (v)   **Dipper Mouth Blues** (take 1)
Livery Stable Blues (Barnyard Blues) (take 2)

Nick Caiazza (ts) replaces Billings
                22 Nov 1939   **Riverboat Shuffle** (take 2)
Relaxin' at the Touro (take 1)   **10**
At Sundown (take 1)
Bluin' the Blues (take 1)

Al Sidell (d) replaces Carter
                12 Dec 1939   **Lonesome Road** (take 2)
add Brunis (v)   **Dinah** (take 1)

omit (v)   **(What Did I Do to Be so) Black and Blue** (take 1)   **15**
Mandy, Make up your Mind (take 2)

Other CDs

same contents:
  Europe: Bluebird ND 86762
  UK: BBC CD 687

LPs

same contents:
  Europe: Bluebird NL 86762
  UK: BBC REB 687
same titles, but alternate takes of tracks 1–4, 7–10, 15: *The Great Sixteen*
  USA: RCA LPM 1295
  UK: RCA RD 27132
incl. tracks 5–7, 9–13 (takes unknown)
  Italy: *Muggsy Spanier*, Giants of Jazz LPJT 16

Cassettes

same contents:
  Europe: Bluebird NK 86762
same contents, but master take of track 2
  UK: Neovox 854
incl. tracks 5–7, 9–13 (takes unknown):
  Italy: *Muggsy Spanier*, Giants of Jazz MCJT 16

* * *

Bobby Hackett: *Coast Concert*

Most jazz commentators avoid critical absolutes, but a number of years ago trombonist Bill Russo advanced one that is now widely accepted: 'Jack Teagarden', he proposed, 'is *the* greatest jazz trombonist'. Place Teagarden alongside Bobby Hackett, often cited (in my view, rightly) as the most profound and musical jazz cornetist of his or perhaps any generation, and you set a level for this deeply regarded album often called (to quote Hackett on another topic) 'the best in its field'. Leaving aside the shimmering quality of the recording (Hackett and Teagarden, like their confrères here, had raw-diamond tones ready to be polished into perfection by any engineer with ears), its content is worthy of scholarly transcription – not only for the solo *chefs-d'oeuvre*, but for the relaxed perfection of what Hackett would certainly have preferred *not* to call its dixieland ensembles.

  Such perfection is heralded here with his simple five-note lead-in to *Big Butter and Egg Man*, which (like a lot of other Hackett inventions) has turned into a much-quoted adage, and carries on through gold-standard solos to an out chorus which is copybook ensemble; Hackett's flattened fifth in bar 3 is echoed with a musical friendly nod by Matty Matlock, and the root note from Abe Lincoln which follows both of them lingers like a man caught suddenly by an unexpected but beautiful view. And beneath all this genuine wit, the tuba-driven rhythm section skips along as if every member were playing jump-rope to a final 'skimmerlink' drum coda. All the glories of Hackett – sunshot tone, relaxed technical command and sophisticated guitarist's harmonic ear (he worked regularly with Glenn Miller as a rhythm guitarist) – shine out on *New Orleans*, where his bright-toned lines light up Teagarden's dark and sonorous solemnities, and on *That's a Plenty* (a favourite Hackett vehicle) you hear him swing out to the top register with feathery lip-trills like a miniaturized Armstrong. The chase chorus between Teagarden and Lincoln which follows is such skilled pecking that you can hardly tell the musicians apart bar by bar, but Lincoln is the one with the challenges, and when he turns on the heat Teagarden's gentle answers deflect the wrath like a man refusing to take part in a shouting-match. Alongside such *délices*, Matlock – the most pure-toned Goodman follower of his generation – decorates ensembles and enhances with solos, playing the perfect artistic compliment to his fellows. And such stamps of quality are the hallmark of every other up-tempo tune on the recording, including *Muskrat Ramble*, whose jokey introduction and coda have passed into dixieland jazz-lore; *Royal Garden Blues*, where Teagarden's entry reaffirms him conclusively as 'King of the Blues Trombone' while Matlock's solo recalls the suspensions of the theme of *Sobbin' Blues*; and *Fidgety Feet*, where Hackett unexpectedly but perfectly quotes from *I Could Write a Book*.

Perhaps most attention, though, should be paid to the two remaining slow tunes of the session, for both are masterpieces. First, *Basin Street Blues*, a Jack Teagarden set-piece which, like many of Louis Armstrong's, was a monument; after his ever-disarming vocal refrain Matlock's clarinet is expectant against Fatool's brush *frissons*, and then Hackett comes in. His opening motif – pivoting on suspended fourths and ninths resolving to major sevenths and sixths – is often requoted, and, as his long rambling lines unfold, each new one picked up like an afterthought, you hear all of the harmonic-melodic Hackett 'ingredients' that Louis Armstrong revered and which made the cornetist uncopiable. The other great revelation of the session is *I Guess I'll Have to Change my Plans*. After its introduction, in which Hackett improvises gently over sustained chords (a frequent trademark), Teagarden's statement of the theme over a lilting 2/4 rhythm is – like the song – rueful, wistful, somehow unfulfilled. When Hackett enters with a key change his solo is all embellishment, touching, then passing between the primary tones of Arthur Schwartz's melody like a butterfly between blooms, until the listener realizes that, by some divine process of artistic unity, the song provides the perfect structural base for the perfect Hackett solo. Throughout its 20 bars Hackett plays each and every one of Schwartz's melody tones, and the melody, thus gracefully embellished, responds to Hackett's touches like a lover in willing embrace. Teagarden's reprise of the theme is the perfect tactful capper. After his reference to *These Foolish Things* at the coda there was, on the original LP pressing, a longer-than-usual pause, as if in respect, before *Royal Garden Blues* began. It should still be there.

LP

USA: *Coast Concert*, Capitol T 692

Bobby Hackett (c), Jack Teagarden, Abe Lincoln (tb), Matty Matlock (cl), Don Owens (p), Nappy Lamare (g, bj), Phil Stevens (sb, bb), Nick Fatool (d)

Los Angeles	18–19 Oct 1955	**Struttin' with some Barbecue**
		Muskrat Ramble
		New Orleans

add Teagarden (v)   **Basin Street Blues**

omit (v)   **That's a Plenty**
                                       Big Butter and Egg Man
                                       Fidgety Feet
                                       Royal Garden Blues
                                       I Guess I'll Have to Change my Plans

CDs

plus additional tracks:
   UK: *Coast Concert / Jazz Ultimate*, Doormouse DM1 CD X02

Other LPs

same contents:
   UK: *Coast Concert*, Capitol LC 6824; *Coast to Coast*, Regal REG 2062
   Netherlands: *Coast Concert*, Capitol 038-85401

* * *

Eddie Condon: Dixieland Jam

The 1950s saw the issue of a series of LPs by Eddie Condon which were to become a recorded definition of late Chicago-style jazz. 'Chicago-style' was a genre of which Condon firmly denied the existence, but in the 1950s, as before, Condon-style jazz existed, and at this period it was made up of several elements. First, a 'modern-style' flexibility from the rhythm section. Second, a stable of Condon regulars – cornetist Wild Bill Davison, trombonist Cutty Cutshall, pianist Gene Schroeder and drummer George Wettling – who, along with visiting magicians such as Bobby Hackett, Billy Butterfield, Dick Cary, Bud Freeman and others, defined a highly individual house approach and therefore style. Third, a likeable informality on record – including Condon talking over and after the music on issued takes – which, when it was first heard, caused a sensation and matched the irreverent, often alcoholic ambience which surrounded Condon from the publication of his autobiography *We Called it Music: a Generation of Jazz* (with Thomas Sugrue) in 1947.

1950s recordings such as **Jamming at Condon's**, **Bixieland** and **The Roaring 20s** all highlighted these qualities. **Dixieland Jam** reissues eight newly mastered stereo takes from this third album (recorded in 1957) and adds six unreleased as well as one alternate take as a collectors' bonus. All three elements cited earlier are in plenteous supply, including the magnificent frank-vibratoed cornet statements of Wild Bill Davison, which made him, in Condon's view, the greatest lead in the business; placed alongside Vic Dickenson's equally motivic, deeply humorous counterpoints and young Bob Wilber's (then) underrated clarinet lines, the result is an archetypal Condon front line, as good as ever played for him.

St James Infirmary – a tune originally left unissued, perhaps because it was over-familiar then – turns into an effortless masterpiece; Davison's physico-musical flare bear-hugs the melody at its turnaround point (bars 16–17), and there are relaxed two-bar exchanges and a wonderful moment at which Condon's guitar pushes the music off into a new chorus like the swailing tail of a whale flipping away into deep water. His comments too – at track's end this time – say a lot about the true spirit in which recorded jazz is often made. On *That's a Plenty* there are more marvels; Vic Dickenson proves that – with Dicky Wells, Bill Harris and George Chisholm – he was and remains now one of the most humorous improvisers of trombone jazz; Wild Bill high-jumps two octaves and two tones from chorus 1 to chorus 2 of his solo and Wilber reminds us that reassessment of his early work is overdue. The timpani booms from Wettling after the ensemble are a further salutory reminder that Condon's men were goodtime jazzmen as well as musical curators of a style. *The Song is Ended* gives us Davison at his most sensitive, speaking through his cornet with broad Irish sentiment like all good Chicago gangsters, and a sit-down finish which sounds like a naturally completed sentence. On *Wrap your Troubles in Dreams* Billy Butterfield is heard at full power, and *When a Woman Loves a Man* (another good example of the kind of underplayed song that Condon's bands often came up with) is a perfect miniature of Condon formulae; split-led melody, tiny touches of arrangement which make all the music sound perfectly rehearsed and mid-performance key changes (to the trombone solo and final eight bars of the ensemble). Such small but vital points of finesse reveal the artistry which lay under the Condon crew's collectively bucolic exterior. They turn up again on *The Minor Drag* (a title from Condon's early recording session with Fats Waller) and elsewhere. *Why Was I Born?* – another lesser-known popular song of great value – has more archetypal Butterfield; his first three quarter notes are pure Armstrong, but the little unassuming lip-slur up a sixth at bar 10 is just as much pure Billy, and the tinkling piano of Schroeder complementing him is a historic microcosm of high jazz art. This, and other delights – Butterfield again striking out at the end of *Put 'em Down Blues*, the cheerful toddle-tempo of *Davenport Blues* and sheer dixieland exuberance of *What's the Use?* – make you realize that such music is now as rare, as precious, and as much a lost art as a late Beethoven string quartet.

CD
USA: *Dixieland Jam*, Columbia Jazz Masterpieces CK 45145

Wild Bill Davison (tpt), Vic Dickenson (tb), Bob Wilber (cl), Gene Schroeder (p), Eddie Condon (g), Leonard Gaskin (sb), George Wettling (d)
New York   19 Aug 1957   **Wolverine Blues**
                                          China Boy (take 2)
                                          China Boy (take 3)
                                          St James Infirmary
                                          That's a Plenty   5
                                          The Song is Ended
                                          Hindustan

Billy Butterfield (tpt) and Cutty Cutshall (tb) relace Davison and Dickenson
                    24–5 Sept 1957   **Wrap your Troubles in Dreams**
                                          When a Woman Loves a Man
                                          The Minor Drag   10
                                          Why Was I Born?
                                          Put 'em Down Blues
                                          Davenport Blues
                                          Apex Blues
                                          What's the Use?   15

Other CDs
same contents:
   Europe: CBS Jazz Masterpieces 465680-2

LPs
same contents:

USA: Columbia Jazz Masterpieces CJ 45145
Europe: CBS Jazz Masterpieces 465680-1
incl. tracks 1, 3–5, 10, 12–14: The *Roaring 20s*
USA: Columbia CL 1089
Europe: Philips B 07301 L

Cassettes

same contents:
USA: Columbia Jazz Masterpieces CJT 45145
Europe: CBS Jazz Masterpieces 465680-4

* * *

Vic Dickenson: *The Vic Dickenson Showcase*

There are three reasons to include these classic recordings in this chapter. First, they are the perfect embodiment of 'mainstream' – the classification invented by Stanley Dance to define a style encompassing the rhythmic flexibility of (then) modern jazz, the techno-melodic sophistication of swing and the repertoire of the pre-bebop era. Second, they celebrate the best points of extended performance first made possible by 'long-play' recording in the 1950s. And third, by consequence, they set out in unhurried exposition the talents of trombonist Dickenson and – perhaps most dramatically (on five of the tracks) – those of his young partner, cornetist Ruby Braff, alongside clarinettist Ed Hall and a Basie-based rhythm section led by pianist Sir Charles Thompson.

For Dickenson these sessions from 1953–4 provided, at last, an opportunity to parade at leisure all of his magnificently original stylistic trademarks – trademarks which had sometimes been compacted too tightly on 78s in the past. These included a repertoire of wholly motivic ideas delivered with the lazy tension of a sleepy lion, a great soft-leather sound, and a vibrato which widened regularly into something like a good-humoured turkey-gobble. Behind these basics followed on a whole catalogue of improvisational originalities: runs of tricky triple-tongued triplets like a baby bounced on the knee, sudden half-veiled windy emissions, and great shouting blues phrases erupting from rumbling asides like a man goaded from submission into a sudden shout of anger. On tracks such as *When You and I Were Young, Maggie, Old Fashioned Love, Jeepers Creepers* and the classic *Suspension Blues*, all these qualities and more show up in glorious extended exposition – sustenance enough for any jazz-hungry listener.

Yet, surprisingly at the time, they were easily matched by Ruby Braff, then aged 26, whose performance, track by track, effortlessly demonstrated new levels of facility, tonal luxury and creative synthesis which were to win the hearts of trumpeters, cornetists, their followers and most of the jazz world from then on. At every turn Braff can be heard parading his peacock gifts. In a barrelling tone, bucket-deep, he heads the ensemble with open-throated, free-breathing lead, and once in solo swaggers up and down melodic lines and chord tones, often setting whirligig-spinning flurries of centred sound against sensuous, slowed phrases like a woman stretching in the sun, and regularly placing pure-music lyric statements against huge castigating blues phrases which wrap melodic situations in a suffocating bear-hug as if to say, 'That's enough, beauty! Let's get physical!'.

This was the era of the young, hard-blowing Braff, and set against the huge sounds and conceptions of both him and Dickenson it might have been a long search to find a clarinettist of equal power, flexibility and tonal perfection. Ed Hall supplied the perfect third voice. As melodically creative and harmonically aware as his partners, Hall had a sound that was comparably mellow and meaty, and his delivery had the crackling attack of Sidney Bechet without any of the (then) more controversial aspects of Bechet's dominant style. In short Hall was a supportive sophisticate, and his contributions did much to remind a new fashionable generation of West and East Coasters that the clarinet was still hip; hear him, say, on *Nice Work if You Can Get it*, and it's plain that Hall's was a voice of classic proportions. Against the Thompson-led rhythm section (sporting rhythm guitarist Steve Jordan) the wonders of these two sessions unfold: among them the jaunty *When You and I Were Young, Maggie*, which, like much of the set, sounds like a cosy homefire chat, *Keeping out of Mischief Now*, with its majestic solos and (now standard) counter-riff, and the architectural *I Cover the Waterfront*. Only one voice is less than definitive: trumpeter Shad Collins who, on that day in the studio, sounded dry-toned and short in breath – almost as if the magnificence of the company left him shy. For the best of Collins listen elsewhere; for the best of mainstream listen here.

LP

USA: *The Vic Dickenson Showcase,* **Vanguard VRS 8520-8521**

Ruby Braff (c), Vic Dickenson (tb), Edmond Hall (cl), Sir Charles Thompson (p), Steve Jordan (g), Walter Page (sb), Les Erskine (d)

New York	29 Dec 1953	**Russian Lullaby**
		Keeping out of Mischief Now
		Sir Charles at Home
		Jeepers Creepers
		I Cover the Waterfront 5

Shad Collins (tpt), Dickenson (tb), Edmond Hall (cl), Thompson (p), Jordan (g), Page (sb), Jo Jones (d)

29 Nov 1954   **Runnin' Wild**
When You and I Were Young,
**   Maggie**
Nice Work if You Can Get it
Old Fashioned Love
Everybody Loves my Baby   10
Suspension Blues
You Brought a New Kind of Love
**   to Me**

CDs

same contents:
Japan: Vanguard 200E-6851/2

Other LPs

same contents:
USA: Vanguard T 99/100
UK: *The Essential Vic Dickenson*, Jazz Vogue VJD 551
tracks 1–5:
UK: *Vic Dickenson Showcase, vol.1*, Fontana FJL 404
tracks 6–12:
UK: *Vic Dickenson Showcase, vol.2*, Fontana FJL 406

* * *

Buck Clayton: *All the Cats Join In*

'One day', Buck Clayton recalls in his autobiography, 'towards the end of 1953, . . . I got a call from John Hammond. He wanted to know if I could make a recording session that he had planned with George Avakian for Columbia. . . . As I entered the studio I found a lot of guys there that I didn't know. I knew about half of them personally, but the others I had to be introduced to. . . . What John wanted was to record a real jam session in a studio. This is rather hard to do . . . [but] before you knew it we were all playing like we had known each other for years. . . . A few days later I was told that I had been named leader of that group and the albums are known as the *Buck Clayton Jam Sessions*. I think I must credit John Hammond for this.'

Extended jazz recording in all styles was a natural follow-on from the invention of the LP record, and the 'Buck Clayton Jam Sessions' made history as examples of a Kansas City genre which so far had been unrecordable. They received widespread critical accolade after their release – as well as discussion because of the (then) controversial use of tape editing and splicing by co-producer Avakian, which on one occasion combined sections of music recorded six months apart! In all, six sessions were recorded between 14 December 1953 and 5 March 1956, and the most famous of them – *The Hucklebuck* backed with *Robbins' Nest* on two sides of one LP – comes from 16 December 1953. **All the Cats Join In**, however, combines one track from 1953 (*Lean Baby*, recorded at the *Hucklebuck* session, but unissued as the tune was still a best-seller) with two from 1955 (featuring two definitive pairings: Buck Clayton with Ruby Braff, and Coleman Hawkins with Buddy Tate) and two more from the last Jam Session of all. This featured trumpeter Billy Butterfield teamed alongside Clayton and Braff, and untypically a singer – Jimmy Rushing – added for one title. On one album, therefore, this historic Hammond–Clayton–Avakian project is spanned from first to last, and there are other incidental virtues; tracks are not over-long (the longest, *Blue Lou*, lasts ten minutes four seconds), and occasional touches of Clayton arrangement (notably on *All the Cats Join In* and *Lean Baby*) make the soloists shine brighter in contrast. However, the prime aim of these great Columbia recordings always was to illustrate to the eager listener how jazz musicians sounded once allowed to 'stretch out' in extended solos, and, despite the problems of contending with clinical studio atmosphere, this was quickly achieved: 'we got into the best mood we could', recalls Clayton, 'and soon had a genuine session going'.

A perfect illustration is the appropriately named *All the Cats Join In* (surprisingly written by Alec Wilder and Eddie Sauter for the Walt Disney feature *Make Mine Music*), where there are perfectly in-context solos from Coleman Hawkins (supremely at home in these gently competitive surroundings), J. C. Higginbotham in fine form, Ruby Braff at his most youthfully hard-blowing, the well-matched pair of Butterfield and Clayton, Tyree Glenn commuting between vibraphone and plunger-muted trombone, Julian Dash (who had been present at the very first of the sessions) and the under-rated pianist Kenny Kersey. *Out of Nowhere* has Clayton's definitive harmon-muted lead, architectural Braff, exploratory trombone from the little-known Dickie Harris (who later worked in Broadway pit bands) set against the easy mobility of Bennie Green, and a full chorus from Hawkins (unusually) followed by a capper from the titular head. *Don't You Miss your Baby* introduces a bonus, Jimmy Rushing, and before his now highly moving sign-off ('Anyone ask you who was it sang this song / tell 'em 'lil' Jimmy Rushing, he's been here and gone!') there is a definitive solo swing segue from Braff, Higginbotham, Clayton and then Hawkins, topped in turn by a three-trumpet chase (Braff, Clayton and Butterfield) which captures all three brass voices working to one style yet parading individualities as strong as three signatures. The *Lean Baby* which follows features a few soloists (Dash, Lem Davis and Charlie Fowlkes) of less import than the stars booked for the later sessions, but also outstanding contributions from trumpeter Joe Newman, trombonist Urbie Green and Clayton; all is highly acceptable. *Blue Lou*, which concludes the album, turns the heat back up to boiling point. The whole equals indispensable mainstream history.

LP

USA: *All the Cats Join In*, **Columbia CL 882**

Buck Clayton, Joe Newman (tpt), Urbie Green, Henderson Chambers (tb), Lem Davis (as), Julian Dash (ts), Charlie Fowlkes (bar), Sir Charles Thompson (p), Freddie Green (g), Walter Page (sb), Jo Jones (d)
New York   16 Dec 1953   **Lean Baby**

Clayton (tpt), Ruby Braff (c), Bennie Green, Dickie Harris (tb), Coleman Hawkins, Buddy Tate (ts), Al Waslohn (p), Steve Jordan (g), Milt Hinton (sb), Jones (d)
                15 March 1955   **Out of Nowhere**
                                     Blue Lou

Clayton, Billy Butterfield (tpt), Braff (c), J. C. Higginbotham (tb), Tyree Glenn (tb, vb), Hawkins, Julian Dash (ts), Kenny Kersey (p), Jordan (g), Page (sb), Bobby Donaldson (d)
                5 March 1956   **All the Cats Join In**

Jimmy Rushing (v) replaces Glenn (tb, vb)
                                 Don't You Miss your Baby?

CDs
incl. tracks 1–5 (alternate takes and re-splices:) *Jam Sessions from the Vault*
    USA: Columbia Jazz Masterpieces CK 44291
    Europe: CBS Jazz Masterpieces 463336-2

Other LPs
same contents:
    UK: Philips BBL 7129
    Europe: Philips B 07163 L
    Spain: Fresh Sounds FSR 593
incl. tracks 1–5 (alternate takes and re-splices:) *Jam Sessions from the Vault*

USA: Columbia Jazz Masterpieces CJ 44291
Europe: CBS Jazz Masterpieces 463336-1

Cassettes
incl. tracks 1–5 (alternate takes and re-splices:) *Jam Sessions from the
Vault*
USA: Columbia Jazz Masterpieces CJT 44291
Europe: CBS Jazz Masterpieces 463336-4

* * *

Henry 'Red' Allen and Coleman Hawkins: *Stormy Weather*

There are not many jazz recordings which catch a player in the midst of
musical renaissance, but **Stormy Weather**, featuring trumpeter Henry 'Red'
Allen, is one. By the late 1950s the overriding European image of Allen was
of an energetic New Orleans trumpeter-entertainer whose music, at dixieland bars such as New York's Metropole, was flashy, rabble-rousing and
shallow – geared to critically unacceptable ways of pleasing a clubful of
customers drinking to the dawn of rock and roll. Around 1958, however,
when tapes of Allen recorded with Earle Warren, Coleman Hawkins and a
rhythm section began to circulate among collectors, the first seeds were
sown for the great Red Allen reassessment of the 1960s, a reassessment
based later on two great quartet recordings, one of them a live club session
titled **Feeling Good!** which bannered Don Ellis's widely quoted view of the
time that 'Red Allen is the most avant-garde trumpeter in New York'. On the
titles which were to become **Stormy Weather**, however, Allen could be
heard gloriously unveiling new creative profundities for the first time. It was
as if his style had suddenly refocused from a blurred image into sharp relief,
revealing brilliant new hues in his kaleidoscope of stylistic devices and –
above all, perhaps – a calmly unhurried authority at ballad tempo, like a
master philosopher whose last block to direct speech has been miraculously
removed. Quite suddenly – or so it seemed – a great comedian was playing
Hamlet, and magnificently, and reconsideration of his artistic status became
urgent.

All of the necessary evidence for this turns up on side 1 of **Stormy
Weather** (a transcription of the 1958 tapes), on which there are four grade-
one jazz professionals (Earle Warren, Marty Napoleon, Chubby Jackson and

George Wettling) and one usually unconquerable genius, Coleman Hawkins. But with every track the listener finds himself waiting at seat's edge for Allen's tablet-of-stone statements which, with their calm, almost stilled directness, make Hawkins sound like a lesser speaker hectoring for attention and much else of the session seem merely very good. At this point in his career Allen was cocky-lipped, cream-toned and technically equipped for every one of his revelations. And they were unique. Where, by contrast, Ruby Braff's musical statements were positive acclamation, Allen's were often more like fascinating theories half-developed, then left, sudden self-revisions or just asides – sometimes neurotic, sometimes peremptory, but always to the point. Transcribe an Allen solo of the period and you find dramatic changes in note density, bar by bar; flurries of sound are followed by pausing tones like a thoughtful speaker demurring, 'Well, yes – but on the other hand . . . !' His re-entry on *Sleepytime Gal* is a perfect example of physical technique commanding a musical response, and from then on every note of his solo, even in the fastest phrase, is perfectly sure-centred. Plainly, at this time, Allen was enjoying every idea that sprang from his trumpet bell, and in the music the listener senses urgency, discovery and delighted surprise. This leads to top-of-the-heap musical liberties such as his entry, two bars early, on *Summertime* for a solo full of physical delights; growls, glissandi, and high, cloudy, half-valved notes in the top register. The effect is mesmeric; Allen is caught in the midst of a great redefinition, and against such jubilant affirmations Hawkins sounds for once like a man blustering his way to small conclusions.

After the coming-to-flower glories of side 1, the tracks on side 2 (re-corded a year earlier) sound temporarily like a return to older, more barren lands; the arrival of J. C. Higginbotham's bucolic trombone amid a team of Metropole regulars, including clarinettist Sol Yaged, restores a dixieland format, and the band is plainly working to a different level. *Battle Hymn of the Republic*, with its hokum, features Higginbotham, all yawps and sighs, Allen playing to grandiose effect and Hawkins galloping after him like an avenging angel. This, the tension-building 'business' of *When the Saints* and the raunchy resentful-tempoed *South* embody the kind of performance that would have had Metropole habitués shouting for more drinks; Allen grandstands dutifully, but amid the industrious entertaining his emergent subtleties are easier to miss – an artfully sidestepping near-lead on *Bill Bailey* and just one veiled note on *Blues*, at the crossover from piano to trombone solo, which sounds like a perceptive onlooker slipping in a sly word unnoticed. The tactfully placed *Stormy Weather* at the end of this dixieland parade is like a second coming – as if to prove that it wasn't all a dream.

LP

UK: *Stormy Weather*, **Jazz Groove 002**

Henry 'Red' Allen (tpt), J. C. Higginbotham (tb), Sol Yaged (cl), Coleman Hawkins (ts), Lou Stein (p), Milt Hinton (sb), Cozy Cole (d)

New York	16 Dec 1957	**Battle Hymn of the Republic**
		Blues
		Won't You Come Home, Bill Bailey
		South
		When the Saints Go Marching In
		5

Allen (tpt), Earle Warren (cl), Hawkins (ts), Marty Napoleon (p), Chubby Jackson (sb), George Wettling (d)

New York	7 Aug 1958	**Mean to Me**
		Lonesome Road
		Sleepytime Gal
		Summertime
		All of Me 10
		Tea for Two
		Stormy Weather

CDs

plus additional tracks:
    USA: *Standards and Warhorses*, Jass JASS CD 2

Other LPs

incl. tracks 1–5:
    USA: *Warhorses*, Jass 10
incl. tracks 6–12:
    USA: *High Standards*, Jass 11

CHAPTER 6
The New Orleans Revival

Mike Hazeldine

The New Orleans revival began in the mid 1930s, when white middle-class Americans began to collect jazz records made by blacks. These 'race records' had been made during the previous decade and were to be found in junk shops and by canvassing black people's homes. Virtually all of these old recordings were long deleted and the difficulty in aquiring them only added to the enthusiasm of the collectors. Recordings by King Oliver, Louis Armstrong, Johnny Dodds and Jelly Roll Morton were catalogued and studied. As the personnels were rarely printed on the labels, identification of musicians became a subject of discussion – a subject which still occupies the energies of collectors today. In 1935 collectors Bill Russell and Steve Smith formed the Hot Record Exchange and began to trade the vintage records by mail. In Britain collectors met to form Rhythm Clubs, and in France the first discography was published by Charles Delaunay. Vintage jazz records began to be reissued on small collectors' labels. The Jazzman Record Shop opened in Los Angeles and the Commodore Record Shop opened in New York. Magazines devoted to New Orleans jazz, such as *Jazz Information* and *Record Changer*, began to appear.

The popular music scene had also given a nod to the New Orleans interest. Bandleader Bob Crosby had a number of notable New Orleans musicians in his orchestra and often organized them into a dixieland small group. New recordings by Johnny Dodds and Jimmie Noone were followed by the rediscovery and recording of Tommy Ladnier. Benny Goodman had a hit with Jelly Roll Morton's *King Porter Stomp*, and the composer took part in a historic series of interviews and piano solo recordings for the Library of Congress. Morton was to make several more new piano and band recordings during the next two years, but he died before he could exert any influence on the direction in which the revival was to take.

Interest in the origins and originators of jazz was growing, and in 1939 Frederick Ramsey and Charles Edward Smith edited the first book to document a history of jazz – *Jazzmen*. The importance of this book cannot be underestimated. Through his research, one of its main contributors, Bill Russell, discovered Bunk Johnson, who was to become one of the main figures of the movement. It also included a chapter on New Orleans musicians currently working in the city. The musicians discussed were to form the basis of the first revival recording in New Orleans by Kid Rena in 1940.

In San Francisco trumpeter Lu Watters formed a band to re-create the sounds and the spirit of King Oliver. The band proved to be very popular and their records sold well. Soon scores of amateur bands began to spring up throughout the USA. Some were inspired by King Oliver, others by Jelly Roll Morton; some got no further than imitating Lu Watters!

Finally, in 1940, two major record companies responded to the growing interest in New Orleans jazz. In February, Victor began a series of New Orleans-style sessions under Sidney Bechet's name. A few months later Decca issued an album entitled **New Orleans Jazz**, with new recordings by Louis Armstrong, Sidney Bechet, Johnny Dodds, Jimmie Noone and other New Orleans musicians. The American Federation of Musicians' recording ban then prevented further new recordings, and it was left to amateur enthusiasts such as Bill Russell to continue the work.

* * *

Bunk Johnson: *Bunk Johnson and his Superior Band*

Willie 'Bunk' Johnson's first recording was an important event, not only for the revival movement, but for Johnson himself. After achieving some early fame in New Orleans, he had left the city around 1914 to work with travelling shows. Had he then resided in Chicago or New York, he might well have made his recording debut during the 1920s. As for so many of his New Orleans contemporaries, the 1930s was an era of neglect for Bunk and, with no teeth and no trumpet, he retired from music. When the book *Jazzmen* was being compiled in the late 1930s, Louis Armstrong, Clarence Williams, Sidney Bechet and other prominent New Orleans musicians all singled out Bunk Johnson as the man to talk to about the early days of jazz. (Some of these musicians were later to disown him when he became famous.) His legendary reputation attracted the authors and he was found in New Iberia, a small town west of New Orleans. The veteran lost no time in impressing upon them that he still had 'what it takes to stomp trumpet yet'. Money was raised for a set of new teeth and a trumpet, and Bunk began to practise once more. He declined an invitation to record in 1940, and when he accepted in 1942 Bill Russell, Gene Williams and Dave Stuart of Jazzman Records hardly knew what to expect. The veterans Russell had interviewed for the *Jazzmen* book had either died (Jelly Roll Morton and Johnny Dodds) or were in poor health (Kid Rena and Big Eye Louis Nelson). As Bunk was not in the musicians' union, the choice of available musicians was limited. When a band was eventually assembled the members gathered at the house of pianist Walter Decou for a rehearsal. When Bunk hit the opening notes of an old spiritual, *Yes, Lord, I'm Crippled*, Russell, Williams and Stuart couldn't believe their ears. Here was no old-timer who was living on past glory, but a musician with tone and melodic ideas that were superior to any player then working in New Orleans.

After trying unsuccessfully to hire a studio for the recording, the organizers finally settled for the third floor of a piano storeroom, a borrowed portable disc-cutting machine and a box of acetates. From a recording point of view, the results were primitive. *Yes, Lord, I'm Crippled* was the first number recorded; the sound is still unbalanced and makes listening difficult at times, but moving some of the musicians around for the subsequent numbers improved the results slightly. Despite the lack of fidelity the recording still conveys all the zest and passion of New Orleans jazz at its best. None of the frictions that were later to beset the band are apparent. Bunk was an intelligent, highly articulate musician who could read, compose and arrange music. Although he had selected George Lewis and Jim Robinson to play at this session, he later found their musical shortcomings restrictive. However, here their hard-swinging style and mutual enthusiasm shows complete empathy with the leader's own ideas. All the hallmarks of his unique style are in evidence. One is the unhurried phrasing which seems to fall so far behind the beat that one feels he will never catch up, yet, by running certain phrases together or with a few carefully placed notes either side of the beat, he is back. Lewis and Robinson also placed notes around the beat, but had a more conventional melodic sense of time. Thus the effect of a free-ranging lead against a busy clarinet and a driving trombone is one of the most exciting sounds in New Orleans jazz.

In *Panama*, Robinson quickly picks up the trumpeter's love of the riff. This device had become widely used in many swing-band arrangements, yet it had been a feature of New Orleans bands since the turn of the century. The long, blue, off-scale, bent notes in the final chorus between Bunk and Robinson make this (along with the wonderful 1930 Luis Russell version) the best rendition of this much recorded tune. With the USA getting involved in the war, the spiritual *Ain't Gonna Study War No More* was released as *Down by the Riverside*, and has retained this title ever since. It later became Bunk's signature tune.

There are few solos on these recordings. Often Johnson will drop out for a chorus and then return to play a series of variations around his own imagined lead – similar to a second trumpet part. Much the same approach is employed when he does occasionally take a solo (*Bunk's Blues*). It is not a result of improvisation, but a carefully worked-out variation of the melody which he would retain every time he performed that number. Other New Orleans musicians, such as King Oliver, Kid Ory and even Louis Armstrong, had the same approach.

Weary Blues and *Moose March* match *Panama* for excitement. The band seems happiest with these tempos, and Robinson in particular is most effective. On the other hand, the trombonist seems unsure of *Ballin' the Jack*, and this is the least successful of the nine items released. The final track is made up from the three 78 rpm records of Bunk Johnson talking about his early life. In the past it has been fashionable to dismiss most of what he said as fiction, yet recent research has shown he was far nearer the truth than most of his detractors gave him credit for.

Bunk Johnson was to become even stronger during the next few years, and his playing on the 1944–5 American Music recordings is even more assured and confident. Many will argue that these are his better recordings, yet none captured the drive and the excitement of the tracks from this first session. If the revival was looking for a hero, it certainly found one in Bunk Johnson.

LP

USA: *Bunk Johnson's Superior Jazz Band*, **Good Time Jazz M 12048**

Bunk Johnson (tpt), Jim Robinson (tb), George Lewis (cl), Walter Decou (p), Lawrence Marrero (bj), Austin Young (sb), Ernest Rogers (d)

New Orleans	11 June 1942	**Yes, Lord, I'm Crippled**
		Down by the Riverside
		Storyville Blues
		Weary Blues
		Bunk's Blues 5
		Moose March
		Make me a Pallet on the Floor
		Ballin' the Jack
		Panama

Johnson (speech)	**Bunk Johnson Talking Records**
	10

same contents:
   UK: Vogue LAG 545
plus additional tracks:
   Japan: *Bunk Johnson: Memorial Scene*, Good Time Jazz SR 3134

George Lewis: *Echoes of New Orleans: George Lewis and his New Orleans Stompers, vol.2*

Following Bunk Johnson's initial two sessions in 1942 (for Jazzman and Jazz Information, the latter being issued by Commodore), the following year Bill Russell planned to visit New Orleans to record a further session with Johnson and George Lewis. In April 1943 he wrote to Johnson in New Iberia to tell him of his plans, but just as he was about to leave for New Orleans he received a telegram from San Francisco informing him that Bunk was there and playing at weekends with the Yerba Buena Jazz Band. Russell immediately wrote to George Lewis, saying that he would now like to record a band under the latter's leadership, and suggested various trumpet players to replace Johnson. When he arrived in New Orleans he began to discuss the trumpet player they might use. He had already approached Kid Shots Madison and Herb Morand without success when Lewis recommended Kid Howard. Russell expressed doubts about Howard, but Lewis assured him: 'You won't be disappointed, Mr Russell'.

Before the session, a rehearsal was organized at the home of drummer Edgar Mosley. Kid Howard and Chester Zardis were unable to attend, so the rehearsal went ahead without them. *Don't Go 'way Nobody, Let's Stay and Have a Good Time* was a number that Buddy Bolden used to feature after midnight, when respectable patrons had left, and its theme had also appeared in the Sam Morgan recording of *Everybody's Talking about Sammy*. It is a vehicle for a series of infectious breaks with everyone participating. Bassist Jim Little (Sidney Brown) dropped by the house and sat in with the group for a few numbers; his tuba playing is well featured on the sombre *Two Jim Blues*.

The following day, when the band assembled at the Gypsy Tea Room to record, some union officials were in the hall. Pianist Walter Decou had been booked and was the only band member actually in the union; seeing the officials, he declined to enter, fearing explusion. When the session was over Russell offered the best numbers to Alfred Lion of Blue Note. The American Federation of Musicians' recording ban was still in force, so Lion issued the tracks on the specially created 'Climax' label to avoid union objections. Ten titles were issued on 'Climax' 78s, but when this LP was being compiled in the 1950s Blue Note had mislaid two of the original masters, so two alternative takes were used.

After the musicians had set up and the microphone was in position, the band exploded into *Climax Rag*. Listening to it after his doubts about Howard, Russell must have felt completely reassured. The trumpeter romps through the number with tremendous spirit, and there are few recordings in all jazz which better demonstrate the sheer joy of making music. The whole band bubbles with enthusiasm, and I have met few people impervious to the excitement generated here. As in *Climax Rag*, virtually all the best takes selected for the original issue were first takes. This was occasionally on account of recording faults, but more often it was a case of the band playing with so much spirit and heart that it was often impossible for them to repeat a performance exactly the same way again. This says much for the enthusiasm with which the musicians tore into each new number.

Since the days of Buddy Bolden, New Orleans bands would often combine two or three themes of other tunes into a new number. *Dauphine Street Blues* is an example of this. This session marked the first ever recording of *Just a Closer Walk with Thee*. The number has been recorded hundreds of times since by numerous revivalist groups, yet none has come close to the haunting beauty of this version. Lewis was a little sharp throughout the proceedings, yet his delicate placement of notes and phrases around the beat make this track one of the masterpieces of New Orleans music. A second take of *Fidgety Feet* is included in place of a superb *Careless Love*, which was only on the British issue. Both these versions are completely ensemble, with the second take having to be faded out as the performance overran the disc playing time.

Chris Kelly was reputed to be the best blues trumpeter in New Orleans, though sadly his playing went unrecorded. Howard was his pupil, and something of the emotive Kelly's style can be heard on *Deep Bayou Blues*. Finally *Milenberg Joys* and *Just a Little While to Stay Here* complete one of the most satisfying LPs in any New Orleans collection.

George Lewis took part in almost 90 recording sessions, yet these tracks remain his finest achievement. Most of the numbers are completely ensemble, and where brief solos are taken they seem to grow out of the ensemble rather than be separate from it. Along with the group that recorded Kid Ory's Crescent session, this band led by George Lewis set a standard for New Orleans ensemble playing of the 1940s which was never to be achieved again. Today, at Preservation Hall in New Orleans, and in hundreds of revivalist bands around the world, ensemble playing of this quality seems to be a lost art. **Echoes of New Orleans** should be required listening for any young band wanting to play New Orleans jazz.

LP

USA: *Echoes of New Orleans: George Lewis and his New Orleans Stompers, vol.2*, Blue Note BLP 1206 and (fake stereo) BST 81206

Jim Robinson (tb), George Lewis (cl), Lawrence Marrero (bj), Sidney 'Jim Little' Brown (bb), Edgar Mosley (d)

New Orleans   15 May 1943   **Don't Go 'way Nobody**
                                      Two Jim Blues

add Kid Howard (tpt); Chester Zardis (sb) replaces Brown (bb)

16 May 1943	Climax Rag	
	Just a Closer Walk with Thee	
	Dauphine Street Blues	5
	Just a Little While to Stay Here	
	Milenberg Joys	
	Fidgety Feet	
	Fidgety Feet no.2	
	Deep Bayou Blues	10

CDs

plus additional tracks:

USA: *The Complete Blue Note Recordings of George Lewis*, Mosaic MD3 132

Other LPs

plus additional tracks:

USA: *The Complete Blue Note Recordings of George Lewis*, Mosaic MR5 132

Japan: *George Lewis and His New Orleans Stompers*, Blue Note K23P 9289
incl. tracks 2–3, 4 (alternate take), 5–8, 10:

UK: *George Lewis and his New Orleans Stompers*, Vogue LAE 12005

* * *

Kid Ory: *Kid Ory's Creole Jazz Band 1944/45*

With their high standard of musicianship and wide choice of tempos, Kid Ory's recordings are the most approachable of all those made by the latter-day genuine New Orleans bands. The trombonist had been a successful bandleader since the earliest days of jazz, and in 1921 his group (which included two musicians listed here, Mutt Carey and Ed Garland) had been the first black jazz band to record. In the 1920s his uncanny ensemble sense contributed much to the success of the classic Armstrong, Morton and New Orleans Wanderers/Bootblacks sides. But his robust tailgate style found little favour with the swing bands and he retired from music in 1933. Had he never played another note, his reputation (like that of King Oliver, who died in 1938) would have been assured. His comeback in the 1940s produced a series of brilliant recordings, all of which illustrated the leader's principles of disciplined, yet relaxed New Orleans ensemble playing.

The best of Ory's 1940s recordings were those from his four Crescent sessions, made between August 1944 and November 1945. The nucleus of the band consisted of New Orleans exiles who, like Ory, were based in Los

Angeles and had been associated with him for many years. Mutt Carey and Kid Ory were from the pioneer school of New Orleans brass players. Their occasional solos were often a straightforward statement of the main theme, but their ensemble playing, though appearing deceptively simple, always added great variety to the music, while leaving ample space for the other instruments. Although Carey was occasionally inclined to pitch sharp, his rattling lead was a perfect foil for Ory's unfailing ability to fill out the ensemble with a steady stream of perfectly placed notes and slurs. Together they formed the most exciting New Orleans brass team since King Oliver and Louis Armstrong. For the first two sessions, Ory added the New Orleans clarinettist Omer Simeon, then playing alto saxophone with Jimmie Lunceford's orchestra. As is the case with the 1926 Morton recordings, Simeon's fluent playing is ideal for this New Orleans ensemble playing. Another Ory trademark was his excellent rhythm sections. He preferred the lighter sound of Bud Scott's guitar to the banjo, and Ed Garland's light slapped bass left ample room for pianist Buster Wilson's telling support. When Minor Hall joined the band after the first session, the rhythm section became even better.

The first session produced the classic version of *Blues for Jimmie* – a tribute to the late Jimmie Noone, who had been appearing with the band when he died the year before. There are memorable solos by Simeon and Garland, plus an intense solo by Carey playing into a bucket mute. *South* is completely ensemble and, with its well spaced breaks, shows the band's real strength. It demonstrates how the best New Orleans groups could introduce subtle variations into an ensemble without losing the melody, tempo and character of a number. Ory sings in creole on his own *Creole Song*, but the track is remembered mainly for Simeon's beautifully constructed clarinet solo. *Get Out of Here* is based on the first strain of *Tiger Rag* and is claimed to be an earlier variation of the tune.

The second session was recorded just over a year later, and if it didn't quite live up to the others it still produced some memorable moments. *Panama*, a favourite of countless New Orleans revival groups, is disappointing by the band's own high standards. Simeon's solos are excellent, but Carey's uncertain square phrasing causes some uneasiness in the ensemble. *Careless Love* is taken at a brisk pace, and one feels that a slightly slower tempo would have produced a greater swing. Bud Scott's vocal on *Under the Bamboo Tree* has just the right inflections for this old vaudeville number. He is slightly under-recorded, but the whole band (particularly Minor Hall) plays with tremendous swing. *Do What Ory Say* features the leader's craggy vocal over a superb rhythm section. Simeon's solo is the best of many fine solos from these early sessions, and it is a pity that he never recorded with the band again.

Simeon was replaced for the remaining two sessions by the Chicago clarinettist Darnell Howard, who plays quite beautifully at times. The ensemble on the three rags, *1919 Rag*, *Down Home Rag* and *Maple Leaf Rag*, is magnificent. The inventive ensemble with its beautiful balance and texture compares favourably with the best of Oliver's and Morton's classic bands. This version of *Maryland, my Maryland* is probably the best jazz march ever recorded and is only a shade better their *Oh! Didn't He Ramble*, which is also excellent. *Weary Blues* also contains some brilliant ensemble playing, with fine solos by Howard and Ory. Only *Ory's Creole Trombone* and *Original Dixieland One Step*, though good by other bands' achievements, fail to match the high standard of the other tracks. Visually, their hokum strains would have been undoubted crowd pleasers, but set among so much brilliant music they often sound corny. *Ory's Creole Trombone* has some good moments, but a comparison with the Armstrong Hot Five version is inevitable.

Many who heard Ory's group live insist that it was the finest New Orleans band of the revival period. It is a pity (though understandable) that it was confined by the recording company to a dixieland repertoire, for it was also capable of playing a wide variety of popular tunes without losing its instinctive New Orleans approach.

LP
Kid Ory: *Kid Ory's Creole Jazz Band 1944/45*, Good Time Jazz L 12022

Mutt Carey (tpt), Kid Ory (tb), Omer Simeon (cl), Buster Wilson (p), Bud Scott (g), Ed Garland (sb), Alton Redd (d)
Hollywood   3 Aug 1944   **Get Out of Here**
                                          South
                                          Blues for Jimmie Noone (take 2)

add Ory (v)   **Creole Song**

omit (v); Minor Hall (d) replaces Redd
                     5 Aug 1945   **Panama**   5
                                          Careless Love
                                          Do What Ory Say

add Scott (v)   **Under the Bamboo Tree**

omit (v); Darnell Howard (cl) replaces Simeon
                     8 Sept 1945   **1919 Rag**
                                          Maryland, my Maryland   10
                                          Down Home Rag
                                          Oh! Didn't He Ramble

3 Nov 1945	Original Dixieland One Step	
	Maple Leaf Rag	
	Weary Blues	15
	Ory's Creole Trombone	

Other LPs

same contents:
  UK: Vogue LAG 12104
  France: Contemporary 68609

* * *

Wooden Joe Nicholas: *Wooden Joe's New Orleans Band 1945–1949*

In a city where so much music was played outdoors, powerful cornet players quickly gained attention and were often 'crowned' 'King' by their supporters and fellow musicians. Charles 'Buddy' Bolden (1877–1933) was the first musician to achieve this status, before he was committed to the East Louisiana State Hospital in 1907. Freddie Keppard (1889–1933) and then Joe 'King' Oliver (1885–1938) later held the crown. Both men were past their peak when they recorded in the 1920s, yet something of Keppard's power can be heard on the final choruses of *Here Comes the Hot Tamale Man*, made with Doc Cook's orchestra in 1926. Oliver's legendary power is almost totally absent on his 1923 classic recordings, although his intense solo on *Dippermouth Blues* gives an indication of what his hot style must have been like.

When the city's music began to be documented in the 1940s, there was no trumpet player more powerful than Wooden Joe Nicholas. He was older than Keppard and Oliver, but not in their class, nor was he ever crowned 'King'. But even though he was at that time over 60, he must have been close (or equal) to their power during their peak years. The strength of his lip and his endurance during 14-hour parades earned him the nickname 'Wooden' Joe. Bill Russell first heard Nicholas in 1943 and his power 'almost blew me right out on to the sidewalk'. When Russell recorded him in 1945, the acoustics of the Artesan Hall were far from ideal, yet we can get a clear indication of his powerful playing. Russell was concerned about the echo in the hall, and a few days later re-recorded Nicholas playing some of the same numbers at George Lewis's house. The small room was even less helpful in capturing his power, but Lewis's wife was concerned for the structure of the house when Nicholas began playing!

Wooden Joe Nicholas was originally a clarinettist and worked with Joe Oliver's band at the Big 25 in 1915. When Oliver began taking extended breaks to go to the pool hall, Nicholas began playing the leader's cornet to get the music started again. He took up cornet regularly in 1918. He was not a schooled musician and was limited in the keys in which he could play, yet his technique is adequate for his economical style. His musical approach was very different from that of the younger musicians such as Punch Miller, Lee Collins or Herb Morand. Possessing none of their fingering skills, he concentrated more on rhythmic drive, and notes and phrases are scattered around the beat. He displayed a greater freedom in his endless variations around the main theme, and his attack and phrasing continually change throughout a number. His single note values alter during a phrase and the phrases themselves vary in length. He constantly alters his vibrato to great effect and, with his variation of power, his playing has a considerable swing and momentum throughout this recording. On *Shake it and Break it* (not to be confused with the number that Sidney Bechet recorded in 1940, but the name often given by some New Orleans musicians to *Weary Blues*), his stabbing notes and fiery phrasing produce one of the most exciting tracks ever to be recorded in New Orleans.

The clarinettist Albert Burbank is also worthy of attention. His busy, extrovert playing is a perfect foil to Nicholas's economic style. On *Eh, La Bas* and *Up Jumped the Devil* he plays lead most of the time, allowing Nicholas even more rhythmic freedom. Trombonist Jim Robinson arrived late for the Artesian Hall date and his playing on *I Ain't Got Nobody* at the end of the session has a nice balance and provides another highlight. Baby Dodds was booked as the drummer, but he failed to appear – although he did record with the band later that week. Josiah 'Cie' Frazier was brought in as a replacement. In the 1960s Cie became the most sought-after drummer in the city, but in 1945 he was working with a navy big band. His drumming is not always in the best of taste and this band would have been better without him.

Clarinet Blues was recorded in 1949 and features Nicholas's clarinet playing. His solo, following that of Burbank, may seem crude by comparision. It owes nothing to the high standards of clarinet playing established by the Tio family (teachers of so many of the city's leading clarinettists), but it predates the rougher uptown style of John Casimir and Steve Angram.

Bill Russell had wanted to record Ann Cook since 1944, but her request of a high fee prevented it. By 1949 she had lowered her demands and she recorded two numbers with Nicholas's band. Since recording with Louis Dumaine in 1929 she had become very religious, yet *The Lord Will Make a Way Somehow* still had much of the old blues-shouter quality in evidence.

It would be a mistake to suggest that Wooden Joe Nicholas sounded like the legendary Buddy Bolden, yet his archaic and powerful playing must have had some links with the sound that poured out from the noisy uptown dance halls at the turn of the century.

LP

UK: *Wooden Joe's New Orleans Band 1945–1949*, **Storyville SLP 204**

Wooden Joe Nicholas (tpt), Albert Burbank (cl), Lawrence Marrero (bj), Austin Young (sb)

New Orleans	10 May 1945	**Shake it and Break it** (actually **Weary Blues**)

add Jim Robinson (tb)

Lead Me On
Careless Love

add Cie Frazier (d)

Artesan Hall Blues	
Tiger Rag	5
Eh, La Bas	
Up Jumped the Devil	
Don't Go Way Nobody	
I Ain't Got Nobody	

Louis Nelson (tb), Nicholas, Burbank (cl), Johnny St Cyr (bj), Young (sb), Albert Giles (d)

	21 July 1949	**Clarinet Blues** 10

as **Clarinet Blues**, *but Nicholas (tpt); add Ann Cook (v)*

The Lord Will Make a Way Somehow

Other LPs

plus alternate take of track 7:
   Japan: *Wooden Joe's New Orleans Band*, Dan VC 4010; Dan VC 7014

* * *

Mutt Carey: *Jazz New Orleans, vol.1; Jazz New Orleans, vol.2*

Thomas 'Papa Mutt' Carey was undoubtedly the most underrated of all the major New Orleans musicians. After playing in his home town with Kid Ory, in 1917 he became one of the first New Orleans pioneers in work in Chicago. Not liking the Chicago winter, he returned home the following year. Had he remained in Chicago and recorded with a variety of musicians, posterity might now place him in the same class as King Oliver and Freddie Keppard. In 1919 he left for California, where he was to remain for the rest of his career.

He immediately rejoined Kid Ory and recorded with him in 1921. The session was good, but gave Carey little opportunity to shine. When Ory left for greater fame in Chicago in 1925, Mutt Carey took over leadership of the band.

According to his pupil Buck Clayton, Carey was playing some of the most interesting trumpet to be heard in the 1930s. Early musicians never saw themselves as historical figures and paid little attention to recordings, but, sadly, musicians of his generation are today judged mainly on their recorded output from the 1920s and 1930s, and very few jazz recordings were made in California during this period. When Carey was once more reunited with Ory in the 1940s, the former was initially the leader. But by the time the band recorded commercially in 1944 he had become overshadowed by the stronger personality of Ory. His excellent recordings with Ory are discussed elsewhere, yet they do not demonstrate the quality in his playing to which all who heard him live testify. As a master of the authentic New Orleans trumpet lead he had few equals. Yet the very nature of the role in controlled ensemble playing (particularly in the short time available on a 78 rpm record) demanded an unselfish approach. He always played his part brilliantly, but his subtle contributions are often misunderstood or overlooked. His light swinging style was often capable of power (as on *Ostrich Walk*), yet according to historian Bill Russell: 'He could play so softly when the band got rocking that the shuffling beat of the dancers' feet all but drowned out the band'. Recently, some previously undiscovered 1947 live recordings of the Ory band have come to light and, when issued, these should help to rectify Carey's reputation as one of the very best lead trumpet players in New Orleans jazz. Apart from those with the Ory band, his only other recordings were a 1946 duet session with blues singer and pianist Hociel Thomas and these 1947 tracks for the Century label with his own band.

Carey left the Ory band in the summer of 1947 over a disagreement about money. He travelled to New York and formed this group using local musicians. Baby Dodds and Pops Foster had been working with Art Hodes's small band and along with Danny Barker were regulars on Rudi Blesh's weekly 'This is Jazz' broadcasts. Individually the three musicians had been part of some of the most distinctive rhythm sections on record: Baby Dodds with Bunk Johnson's 1944 band, Pops Foster with Luis Russell's 1929 group and Danny Barker with one of the best big-band rhythm sections of all – that of Cab Calloway's 1940–2 orchestra, with Milt Hinton and Cozy Cole. With the combination of Dodds's infectious drumming, Foster's slapping bass and Barker's solid, swinging guitar playing, Carey's team had already become recognized as one of the best of all small-group rhythm sections. In the broadcasts, the pianists such as James P. Johnson or Joe Sullivan did not always fit perfectly with the rhythm trio. Under Carey's astute leadership, pianists Hank Duncan or Cliff Jackson completed one of the finest small-band rhythm sections ever to have recorded.

Albert Nicholas, Edmond Hall and Jimmy Archey were also taking part in the 'This is Jazz' broadcasts. Since early 1946 Albert Nicholas had returned to small-band playing, first with Hodes, then with Kid Ory, and was at this time working at Jimmy Ryan's. He shared the broadcasts with Edmond Hall, who had been working with outstanding success in small groups since 1939. Jimmy Archey had replaced Georg Brunis in the series and, like the rhythm trio, was a fixture in the broadcasts. Unlike most of this band, Archey was not from New Orleans. Although he had worked in the big bands of King Oliver and Louis Armstrong, his small-group experience was limited. Yet he was developing a unique ensemble style that fitted well with New Orleans musicians.

The first session included a long version of *Slow Drivin'*, issued on two sides of a 78. The sides have been spliced together into one of the most satisfying blues to have been recorded during the 1940s. Nicholas's solo is superb, as is his playing throughout the session. On the second chorus of *Cake Walking Babies*, Carey and Dodds prompt him into some electrifying ensemble and solo work. Archey also has a good solo on *Slow Drivin'*. On faster numbers such as *Fidgety Feet* and *Indiana* his tone had a persuasive swing, and these recordings established his small-band reputation. Carey's understated lead pushes (rather than drives) the band and leaves plenty of room for the other voices. He reacts quickly to ideas and his choppy ragtime lead on *Shim-me-sha-wabble*, *Cake Walking Babies* and *Fidgety Feet* produces some fiery playing from the other musicians.

A few days before the second session, New Orleans clarinettist Tony Parenti recorded an album of ragtime pieces with a seven-piece band that included Archey, Barker and Dodds. The results are interesting, but were too far removed from the authentic written scores that Carey was to use. A month later Bunk Johnson was also to record many ragtime numbers using the same 'Red Back' books that Carey read from, but these latter recordings lack the swing and the joy of Carey's versions. *Joplin's Sensation* and *The Entertainer* are taken at a faster speed than versions by many of today's revival bands, but have a better swing. Like that of King Oliver, Carey's ratty tone did not record well and his lead on *Chrysanthemum* sounds clumsy. Edmond Hall performs strongly on the rags and generally solos well, but his looser ensemble style on *Fidgety Feet* and *Indiana* does not always balance the band as well as Nicholas's playing had.

Following months of inactivity during 1948, Papa Mutt re-formed his band, but he died suddenly on the eve of a season of engagements in Los Angeles and San Francisco; he was only 55. After these recordings were issued they quickly became some of the most influential of the New Orleans revival. Carey's material takes up only one side of each of the Savoy albums detailed below; the remaining tracks are by groups led by Punch Miller.

LP

USA: (Mutt Carey and Punch Miller:) *Jazz New Orleans, vol.2*, **Savoy MG 12050**

Mutt Carey (tpt), James Archey (tb), Albert Nicholas (cl), Hank Duncan (p), Danny Barker (g), Pops Foster (sb), Baby Dodds (d)

New York	18 Nov 1947	**Shim-me-sha-wabble**
		Slow Drivin'
		Ostrich Walk
		Cake Walking Babies

LP

USA: (Carey and Miller:) *Jazz New Orleans, vol.1*, **Savoy Jazz Classics SJC 415 (originally MG 12038)**

Edmond Hall (cl) and Cliff Jackson (p) replace Nicholas and Duncan

	27 Nov 1947	**Joplin's Sensation**
		Chrysanthemum
		The Entertainer
		Fidgety Feet
		Indiana

Other LPs

incl. all tracks, but alternate take of track 3: *Giants of Traditional Jazz*
    USA: Savoy SJL 2251
    UK: Esquire 32-130
    France: Savoy WL 70513

* * *

Emile Barnes and Peter Bocage: *Barnes–Bocage Big Five*

One of the unfortunate results of the New Orleans revival was that most of its well-meaning enthusiasts (particularly in Europe) have tended to restrict the music to a so-called traditional instrumentation and confine the repertoire to the blues, rags, stomps and marches issued on the 1940s recordings. This 'purist' outlook was never present among the musicians. One of the strengths of real New Orleans music is its adaptability and its acceptance of new ideas, and early New Orleans bands of between two and eight or nine musicians reveal a wide variety of instrumentation. Every instrument was regarded as a rhythm instrument: often violins or clarinets took the straight melody, and cornets, piccolos and valve trombones played their own variations. With such diverse instrumentation, and before individual roles became fixed, this must have been a highly creative period. However, the piano and the saxophone (often the most important instruments in later forms of jazz) were never included in these early bands, and the banjo (often a symbol of the New Orleans revival) was rarely used. Today, owing to the same economic conditions to which the city's musicians have always been required to adapt, there are many three-, four- or five-piece bands (the terms trio, quartet and quintet are never used in New Orleans music).

This New Orleans adaptability is nowhere better demonstrated than in the 1954 session of the Barnes–Bocage Big Five. The band (with a different drummer) had been working at Mama Lou's, an old dance hall perched precariously on the end of a wooden pier at Lake Ponchartrain, but this recording was made at the San Jacinto Hall, where the best of the Bunk Johnson American Music recordings had been made ten years earlier.

The five musicians originate from a wide variety of different musical backgrounds, yet they respond to each other's ideas without losing their own identity. Emile Barnes had grown up with Sidney Bechet and, while he possessed none of the latter's majestic ideas and technique, as a gutsy blues player he had few equals among the older clarinettists. His archaic manner stems from the earliest of New Orleans styles. Playing close to the melody, he often ends a phrase with an upward run and holds the last note before sliding into the next phrase. A similar approach can be heard in the playing of the ODJB clarinettist Larry Shields as well as of such black players as Achille Baquet and Big Eye Louis Nelson. Like Bechet, Barnes was self taught and possessed a very distinctive sound. He could not have been more different from Peter Bocage, a schooled musician whose light tone and excellent taste had been influential in many of the city's best reading bands for almost 50 years. Bocage also played the violin, xylophone, banjo and trombone and was a skilled composer and arranger. Eddie Dawson had been a member of various string bands before 1906 and had adapted to every style of music since. Homer Eugene was a younger trombonist but here plays the amplified guitar, an instrument that had not even been invented when Barnes, Bocage and Dawson had reached the veteran stage of their careers. From a strict jazz point of view, Homer Eugene is the most interesting soloist on the recording. Bocage had been used to working with steady drummers such as Louis Cottrell Sr and, latterly, Alfred Williams, and the exuberant Albert Jiles, complete with cowbells, tom-toms and chimes, was hardly to his taste. On *The Sheik of Araby* he over-punctuates the melody and his time-keeping is often erratic, yet his sheer enthusiasm produces some highly spirited playing from the band.

Neither Barnes nor Bocage had been working regularly when these recordings were made, and there is often some uncertainty in Barnes's approach. Bocage plays in a relaxed manner, mainly in the middle register and slightly behind the beat. Barnes responds by toning down some of the rougher aspects of his performance and works in a quieter, more wistful style. He often plays the first chorus straight, just behind the trumpet, before embarking on a series of simple variations and riffs. His solos are simply a more intense version of one of his variations, often presented with an increased vibrato. It was hardly a style to win a *Down Beat* award, but it was a recognized way of playing for the old New Orleans dance-hall crowd rather than pleasing the jazz record buyer.

As the band had been playing for dances, most of the tracks are taken at a fairly gentle pace. It is even possible to dance to the faster pieces such as *Toot', Toot', Tootsie, Goodbye* and *Down in Honky Tonk Town*. Some of the slower blues numbers such as *Holler Blues* are a composite of other blues themes loosely strung together. *Mama Inez*, with its spanish tinge, is played as a rumba and was a favourite in many New Orleans dance halls. Towards the end of the session, children and adults were let into the hall to enjoy the music and to dance, and their happy screams can be heard on the final tracks. As they were so uncommercial, these tracks remained unissued for many years. Eventually, Folkways issued two of the best numbers as a sampler (FA 2465) and the less interesting takes of *When my Sugar* and *Honky Tonk Town* are included here.

This recording will be the most difficult for the newcomer to New Orleans jazz to accept. It has many shortcomings, yet as the uncompromising sound of a New Orleans dance hall its study is the key to understanding the nuances and richness of New Orleans music.

LP

UK: *Barnes–Bocage Big Five*, Nola LP 9
Peter Bocage (tpt), Emile Barnes (cl), Homer Eugene (g), Eddie Dawson (sb), Albert Jiles (d)

New Orleans	9 Sept 1954	**When I Grow Too Old to Dream**
		Rat's Blues
		When my Sugar Walks Down the Street
		The Sheik of Araby
		Haltin' the Blues 5
		Toot', Toot', Tootsie, Goodbye
		I'm Gonna Sit Right Down and Write Myself a Letter
		Holler Blues
		My Blue Heaven
		Down in Honky Tonk Town 10
		Mama Inez

Other LPs

same contents:
  UK: New Orleans Jazz Society NOJS 002 (first version)
same contents, but alternate take of track 7:
  UK: New Orleans Jazz Society NOJS 002 (second version)

* * *

Louis Armstrong: *Satchmo: a Musical Autobiography*

Louis Armstrong's move back to leading a six-piece band was only partly owing to the revival of interest in New Orleans jazz; it was also an economic decision. In response to public taste, Armstrong had led a successful big band since the 1920s. By the mid-1940s, however, the public's interest in big bands began to wane, though Armstrong continued to front his orchestra until the spring of 1947. In 1944 he recorded with Jack Teagarden in a small group for V-Disc. This was a recording partnership that had brought the best out of both musicians back in 1929 and now, 25 years later, was equally successful. The following year he recorded with another small group, organized by Leonard Feather – the Esquire All-American Award Winners. By 1946 the interest in small-group New Orleans jazz was gaining momentum and Hollywood offered Armstrong a leading role in the film *New Orleans*. The film was a fictional account of how New Orleans jazz became accepted throughout the world after the closing of Storyville, and it reunited Armstrong with his former sidemen Kid Ory, Bud Scott and Zutty Singleton. Also engaged was Barney Bigard, who, like Scott, was a member of Ory's band. Under Armstrong's leadership the group recorded a dozen New Orleans numbers for the film soundtrack, then, with Ory's drummer Minor Hall replacing Singleton, re-recorded some of the pieces for Victor. When the film was released it was suggested that Armstrong should tour with the band as his regular unit. Ory declined the offer, although Bigard (who was about to leave Ory) expressed an interest. There were further small-band appearances with Edmond Hall, and Armstrong participated as a guest in a 'This is Jazz' broadcast, leading to the famous Town Hall concert in February 1947. The occasion once again reunited Armstrong with Jack Teagarden, and the partnership scaled new heights with brilliant performances such as *Rockin' Chair* and *Save it Pretty Mama*. It was only natural that Teagarden and Bigard should be the basis of the first All-Stars, a group which made its recording debut in October 1947.

The original All-Stars made many excellent recordings, though few lived

up to the promise of the Town Hall concert. In the 1950s the group underwent various personnel changes, with Teagarden and Bigard being replaced
by Trummy Young and Edmond Hall. While the decade saw the production
of many fine albums, such as the tributes to W. C. Handy and Fats Waller,
none matches the achievement of the 1956–7 boxed set entitled **Satchmo: a
Musical Autobiography of Louis Armstrong**. It was unfortunate that Decca
also included some of the tracks from previous All-Star recordings, as these
were often of lesser recording quality and the performances are generally
less interesting.

Milt Gabler had been supervising many of Armstrong's Decca sessions.
These usually featured the trumpeter fronting larger bands and singing
popular tunes. However, Gabler was also a knowledgeable jazz enthusiast
who was familiar with Armstrong's past achievements, and his suggestion
to re-record the many jazz masterpieces made between 1923–31 was eagerly
accepted by Armstrong. It was a brave decision by both participant and
recording company, for it could have had disastrous results. Unlike many
musicians, Armstrong was neither ashamed of his early recordings, nor
always fully aware of the extent to which jazz collectors lavished 'classic'
status upon them.

The **Autobiography** was recorded over several sessions between December 1956 and January 1957. Armstrong was still a great trumpet player, but
he no longer had the fertile imagination, lip agility and phenomenal strength
of his earlier years. Bob Haggart was employed to update many of the old
small-band arrangements, and he wisely lowered the keys on many numbers. But his 'modern' arrangements were often too fussy and sound today
more dated than the originals. The other arranger, Sy Oliver, was more
successful in scoring some of Armstrong's old big-band numbers for the
smaller groups. Armstrong links each track with a spoken commentary
written for him by Leonard Feather. He doesn't bother to correct some of the
mistakes in the script, and is at his best when sounding more spontaneous
with some of his own stories.

Milt Gabler persuaded Armstrong's manager Joe Glaser not to book the
band elsewhere on the recording days, and the musicians thus arrived at the
studios fresh and with an appetite for the night's work. Most of the big-band
re-creations were recorded first, during three days in mid-December, and
show that Armstrong was clearly enjoying the experience. The first session
produced a magnificent *I Can't Believe that You're in Love with Me* and *Lazy
River*, and the third a wonderful *Memories of You*, but there are many excellent moments from all three. Five weeks later Armstrong returned to the
studio for four further sessions which often produced performances of even
more breath-taking quality. His lead on *High Society* and *Everybody Loves my
Baby* displayed all the old skills, and every note he played had that New
Orleans sense of timing. *Cornet Chop Suey* and *Potato Head Blues* didn't quite

match the earlier masterpieces, though new versions of *Gully Low Blues* and *Two Deuces* came remarkably close. The original *Wild Man Blues* was also impossible to follow, yet the new version had its own poignant melancholy.

Away from the live club and concert routine, Armstrong's playing was more thoughtful, and a new urgency and intensity was present. The third of the 1957 sessions produced the unexpected: *King of the Zulus* had not been considered one of the classic recordings from Armstrong's Hot Five period, but it was better than many, and certainly in a different league from the vast majority of recordings made in 1926. This new version rolled back the years. It had the same zany humour as the original, but Armstrong's intense, imaginative and passionate playing surpasses that of the 1926 hit.

The most difficult tracks on the **Autobiography** to re-create were those from the classic blues sessions. The All-Stars' resident vocalist Velma Middleton hardly possessed the right voice for the blues of Ma Rainey, Bessie Smith, Clara Smith and Bertha 'Chippie' Hill. Her version of Ma Rainey's *See See Rider* is poor, yet she manages to project a little more composure on the other three numbers. Armstrong is magnificent. Using a straight mute to assimilate his original cornet responses, he phrases with such uncanny timing that it transforms these tracks into minor classics.

The sessions were a tremendous achievement, both for Armstrong and for Milt Gabler. The performances were the last major statement by the music's greatest figure. When Louis visited Britain in 1956, many considered that he was well past his best. Few of us could have predicted that he was still to record some of his most memorable work.

LP

USA: *Satchmo: a Musical Autobiography*, **MCA 4-10006**

Louis Armstrong (tpt), Jack Teagarden (tb), Barney Bigard (cl), Dick Cary (p), Arvell Shaw (sb), Sid Catlett (d)

| Boston | 30 Nov 1947 | **Muskrat Ramble** |

Earl Hines (p) and Cozy Cole (d) replace Cary and Catlett

New York	26 April 1950	**New Orleans Function:**
		Flee as a Bird
		Oh, Didn't He Ramble

add Armstrong (v)

| Pasadena, CA | 30 Jan 1951 | **My Monday Date** |

Armstrong (tpt), Trummy Young (tb), Bud Freeman (ts), Bigard (cl), Billy Kyle (p), Shaw (sb), Kenny John (d)
New York   19 March 1954   **Basin Street Blues**

omit Freeman (ts), Armstrong (v)   **Struttin' with Some Barbecue   5**

Barrett Deems (d) replaces John
                        21 Jan 1955   **When it's Sleepy Time Down
                                            South**

Armstrong (tpt, v), Young (tb), Edmond Hall (cl), George Dorsey (as), Lucky Thompson (ts), Dave McRae (bar), Billy Kyle (p), Everett Barksdale (g), Squire Gersh (sb), Deems (d)
New York   11 Dec 1956   **If I Could Be with You
                                          Lazy River
                                          I Can't Give You Anything but
                                            Love
                                          Body and Soul   10
                                          I Can't Believe that You're in
                                            Love with me
                                          On the Sunny Side of the Street**

omit (v); add Hilton Jefferson (as)
                        12 Dec 1956   **Mahogany Hall Stomp**

add Armstrong (v)   **When You're Smiling
                                            Some of these Days   15
                                            I Surrender Dear
                                            Georgia on my Mind
                                            Exactly like You**

Armstrong (tpt), Young (tb), Hall (cl), Kyle (p), Gersh (sb), Deems (d)
                                            High Society

*as **When You're Smiling**, but add Dorsey (fl), McRae (bass cl)*
                        13 Dec 1956   **Song of the Islands   20**

*as **When You're Smiling***   **That's my Home
                                            Memories of You**

omit (v)   **Them There Eyes**

Armstrong (tpt, v), Young (tb), Hall (cl), Kyle (p), George Barnes (g), Gersh (sb),
Deems (d)

	23 Jan 1957	**Hotter than That**	

add Young (v) — **Gut Bucket Blues** — 25

omit (v) — **Weary Blues**
Potato Head Blues
Cornet Chop Suey
**All the Wrongs You've Done to
     Me**

24 Jan 1957 — **Two Deuces** — 30
Mandy Make up your Mind
Wild Man Blues

add Armstrong (v) — **Gully Low Blues**
Everybody Loves my Baby

add Young (v) — **Heebie Jeebies** — 35

omit (v); add Armstrong, Young, Hall (speech)
25 Jan 1957 — **King of the Zulus**

omit (speech) — **Froggie Moore**

add Armstrong, Velma Middleton (v)

Georgia Grind

add Yank Lawson (tpt); omit (v) — **Snag it**

add Hall (shout) — **Dipper Mouth Blues** — 40

omit Hall (shout) — **Canal Street Blues**

Armstrong (tpt, v), Young (tb), Hall (cl), Jefferson, Dorsey (as), Seldon Powell (ts),
McRae (bar), Kyle (p), Barksdale (g), Gersh (sb), Deems (d)
28 Jan 1957 — **You Rascal You**
Hobo You Can't Ride this Train

omit (v) — **Knockin' a Jug**

Armstrong (tpt), Kyle (p) — **Dear Old Southland** — 45

Armstrong (tpt), Young (tb), Hall (cl), Kyle (p), Barksdale (g), Gersh (sb), Deems (d), Middleton (v)

See See Rider
Reckless Blues
Trouble in Mind
Courthouse Blues

CDs

incl. tracks 8, 12:
   USA: *The Best of the Decca Years, vol.1: The Singer*, MCA MCAD 31346
incl. tracks 27, 32, 33, 43:
   USA: *The Best of the Decca Years, vol.2: The Composer*, MCA MCAD 10121

Other LPs

same contents:
   USA: Decca DXM 155; Decca DL 8604, DL 8605, DL 8606, DL 8607
   UK: Brunswick LAT 8211, LAT 8212, LAT 8213, LAT 8214
   France: Brunswick 87.010, 87.011, 87.012, 87.013; Decca 2619.000 and 300.904
   Germany: MCA-Coral COPS 2619/1-4; MCA-Coral 82022-4 and 6.30014
   Italy: Fonit DL 8604, DL 8605, DL 8606, DL 8607
   Australia: Festival FAL 4-4

* * *

Kid Thomas: *Kid Thomas and his Algiers Stompers*

After the many recordings made during the 1940s by black New Orleans bands the 1950s were a lean time for a number of New Orleans collectors. Louis Armstrong, Sidney Bechet, Kid Ory and George Lewis continued to record, but most of their output was geared towards the touring circuit of younger white audiences. The Southland label in New Orleans issued numerous LPs which featured mainly white dixieland musicians and a few black musicians playing for the tourists on Bourbon Street, but produced few recordings of any distinction. However, the 1960s brought forth a new interest in black New Orleans jazz which, in sheer volume, was to more than treble the number of recordings ever made in the city. If Bunk Johnson and George Lewis were seen as the champions of the 1940s revival, then Kid Thomas and Capt. John Handy were the new heroes of the 1960s.

Kid Thomas Valentine made his recording debut for American Music in 1951, but, issued on a label that also offered Bunk Johnson, George Lewis,

Kid Shots Madison and Jim Robinson, the album received little attention and did not stay in the catalogue very long. It featured Thomas with a pick-up band. Although he was a forceful and hard-driving trumpeter, his main asset was the nucleus of musicians he had gathered together. In trombonist Louis Nelson and tenor saxophonist Emanuel Paul he had soloists who were considerably more musically literate than he was himself. This not only extended the repertoire, but added a wide range of colour to the ensemble. The constantly shifting blend of the three instruments created a sound that was distinctive and exciting. Nelson once complained that Paul's busy tenor saxophone lines often crossed into the trombone parts. This was true, but it forced the trombonist into adopting a looser and less conventional role and gave the band greater variety. Thomas frequently added a clarinet as an extra front-line voice, and Raymond Burke, Paul Barnes or George Lewis brought further variation to the solos but occasionally made the ensembles too congested. Thomas always loved to play drums and had strong ideas about New Orleans rhythm sections – the most important band members were the pianist and drummer, and he only included a banjo if it was demanded. After Joe James died in 1964 the character of the band changed, and with the death of Sammy Penn in 1969 a lot of the old drive and zest was gone. By the early 1970s, with the passing of so many veteran musicians, the band was more popular than ever, yet it was but a shadow of the group that roared into the 1960s.

The recording chosen for discussion here may not be the favourite of Kid Thomas's many followers. Opinions as to the best of his output might be equally divided among four or five LPs made over a six- or seven-year period. But, for the newcomer sampling the music of the Kid Thomas band for the first time, I believe this 1965 recording to be the most approachable and entertaining. Now without Joe James, Thomas was having difficulty getting other pianists to play in the former's simpler style. Octave Crosby was used for this session, and banjoist George Guesnon was added to try and give the rhythm some of the easy rocking movement that had been a feature of earlier Kid Thomas bands. Unlike most recorded New Orleans groups of the 1960s, this is not a pick-up band of assorted 'star' musicians, but – apart from the pianist and banjoist – a regular working unit. At the beginning of the 1960s work was scarce and the band played only about once a month, although the musicians held regular rehearsals to learn new numbers. By mid-decade they were performing regularly several times a week. Their earthy dance-hall sound and unhackneyed repertoire made an immediate appeal to collectors. Traditional pieces were mixed with waltzes, rumbas, pop tunes, blues and vaudeville numbers.

With an instinctive trumpet player such as Kid Thomas, the fact that Nelson and Paul were reading musicians probably had a lot to do with the accurate performance of many of these tunes. Often one of them will begin a piece, playing the first chorus straight and then a variation of the theme while Thomas added his own harmony. Manuel Paul opens *In the Mood* and Louis Nelson does the honours on *Summertime*. Thomas also read a little and was often capable of playing a lead with great simplicity and accuracy, as in *Star Dust* or the response parts to *In the Mood*. But it was his explosive style that was the hallmark of his playing. After outlining the melody, he roars into a broader variation with rhythmic clusters of jabbing notes, clipped phrases, a wide vibrato and a searing tone. His own composition *Algiers Strut* was an excellent vehicle for his extrovert style and will be how many thousands of his followers will remember him.

As the older neighbourhood dance-hall audience disappeared, the opening of Preservation Hall in 1961 gave the older musicians a new outlet. But the demands of the tourists who briefly visited the hall as part of their nightly tour of the French Quarter changed the character of the music. Kid Thomas and his band remained a twice-weekly attraction at Preservation Hall until the trumpeter's death in 1987 at the age of 91.

LP

USA: *Kid Thomas and his Algiers Stompers,* Jazz Crusade 2006

Kid Thomas (tpt), Louis Nelson (tb), Emanuel Paul (ts), Octave Crosby (p), George Guesnon (bj), Joseph Butler (sb), Sammy Penn (d)

New Orleans	23 April 1965	**My Blue Heaven**
		In the Mood
		Stardust
		Gettysburg March
		Clarinet Marmalade
		Alexander's Ragtime Band
		Summertime
		Algiers Strut

Other LPs

same contents:
  USA: GHB 80

CHAPTER 7

Bop and Related Styles

Mark Gardner

Bop crystallized and was perfected in New York. To be sure, many of the creators and leading exponents of this jazz form were from the American provinces. Alto saxophonist Charlie Parker, an acknowledged genius and virtuoso, came from Kansas City. Trumpeter Dizzy Gillespie, a brilliant instrumentalist, important teacher and leader of the first fully-fledged modern big band, was a son of South Carolina. Miles Davis, destined to be the most talented protégé of Parker and Gillespie, arrived in Manhattan from St Louis. His fellow trumpeter, the brilliant Fats Navarro, was an emigré from Key West, Florida. Drummers Kenny Clarke and Art Blakey were born in Pittsburgh, also the home of bass player Ray Brown. Guitarist Charlie Christian, from Texas, and bass player Jimmy Blanton, from Tennessee, died before bop flowered yet made significant contributions. The key arranger for the new sounds and one of its most melodic composers was Tadd Dameron, from Ohio.

All these men gravitated to New York in the early 1940s and found each other. They also discovered many kindred spirits who were native New Yorkers. Pianists Bud Powell, Thelonious Monk and Duke Jordan were residents, as were Walter Bishop Jr and Kenny Drew. Other New Yorkers who made substantial contributions to the style included drummer Max Roach, baritone saxophonist Cecil Payne, tenor saxophonist Sonny Rollins and alto saxophonist Jackie McLean. The bulk of the originators had worked under the disciplines of big bands from which they escaped with glee to the cramped cabarets of 52nd Street, which for half a dozen years was a unique centre of excellence.

Essentially a small-group idiom, this new music was an advance in harmonic and rhythmic complexity on the traditional and swing styles that preceded it. It became harder for two chordal instruments to agree, so more groups used a piano and dispensed with a guitar. The pianist set the chords in an understated, abstract way. Later the guitar was reintroduced, and when two closely attuned musicians such as pianist Al Haig and guitarist

Jimmy Raney, or pianist Lennie Tristano and guitarist Billy Bauer, worked together in a rhythm section, they were able to avoid clashes in accompaniment. The bass player emerged as the main time-keeper, providing a steady walking line to suit the harmonies and dovetail with the piano chords. Cymbals, especially the ride cymbal, also carried the rhythm, but otherwise the drummer was allowed a freer role which enabled him to punctuate solos with an apt commentary of his own. A key change was the elimination of the bass drum as a time-keeper, and its participation in punctuating solos came to be known as 'dropping bombs'.

Bop demanded greater facility from all instrumentalists, a feature of which was fast tempo playing to an extent not heard before. Many of the melodies, both improvised and composed, were terse and tense and had complex patterns of accentuation, this being a vital element in the rhythmic sophistication of the music. Often the composed themes were cryptic 'original' tunes written on the same chord progressions as popular songs. To confuse listeners further, groups occasionally would not even play the melody but would swiftly sail into apparently themeless improvisation, the result being more disorienting in this style than in the swing performances which had done the same thing. And it was a trademark of the boppers to end a piece on a note that sounded unresolved in conventional terms.

The rules of the game were soon assimilated and, after a period of controversy and turbulence, bop became an accepted style absorbed into the mainstream, to the considerable enrichment of the music. Originally known as bebop and also rebop, it was the basis for related styles that appeared rapidly: Afro-Cuban jazz, cool jazz, West Coast jazz, hard bop, soul jazz and bossa nova.

Bop musicians had toyed with exotic rhythms – from the Caribbean and Latin America – almost from the outset. Parker recorded with Machito's Afro-Cuban orchestra and also employed Latin percussionists on small-group sessions. He even wrote a tune, *My Little Suede Shoes*, in the Latin idiom. The use of bongos and conga drums added rhythmic spice and was also much favoured by Gillespie in combo and big-band settings. (On occasion, Latin percussionists were apt to clutter the rhythm section, especially if they had not worked regularly with the jazz drummer on the date.) Later, in the 1960s, a brief flirtation with the Brazilian samba spawned the bossa nova, which proved a god-send to melodic players who bent to its gentle beat.

Cool jazz, a reaction against the frenetic, headlong rush of bop, was more calculating and brought the arranger back into play. West Coast jazz dampened things down even further and sacrificed emotion for perfection. Hard bop brought the heat and heart back into the music, stressing not only passion and muscularity but also the value of well-conceived themes. From within hard bop came soul jazz, which took the idiom back to its gospel origins.

Bop is still heard, admired and played, although many of its finest interpreters have long departed. The present generation is learning to love this cerebral, intense and beautiful style which called for the highest musical ability. The recorded legacy is large and comprehensive.

* * *

Part 1: Bop

Dizzy Gillespie: 'Shaw 'nuff'; Jazz Tribune no.2: Dizzy Gillespie, vol.1/2 (1946–1949)

Although their names will be linked forever, Charlie Parker and Dizzy Gillespie, the twin architects of bop, worked together for only 18 months or so. They recorded in tandem on just nine occasions and on four of those they were mere sidemen. Significantly, eight of their studio sorties were compressed into 12 months in 1945–6. Our knowledge of their partnership has been expanded greatly by the release of various broadcasts, transcriptions and private tapes, but in the 1940s much of their extensive influence on other musicians was distilled from their recordings of 1945 for the Guild and Musicraft labels. These seven performances were like commandments to the faithful, tracts to be studied and analysed, copied and recycled by the most gifted of a generation of both black and white jazz players.

The music stemming from the dates under Gillespie's name included pieces which the trumpeter and his alto saxophonist had shaped up during their engagement at the Three Deuces club on 52nd Street the previous autumn. There are strong suspicions that Parker should have been part of the proceedings at the session on 9 February 1945 when *Groovin' High*, in a version initially rejected but issued many years later, and the blues *Blue 'n Boogie* were recorded by Gillespie's sextet. In the event, Gillespie and tenor saxophonist Dexter Gordon carry the solo load, with assistance from pianist Frank Paparelli and guitarist Chuck Wayne. On the blues Gillespie's bravura trumpet passage is a particularly fine example of his ability to create at speed with complete confidence.

A few weeks later, Parker was present in an entirely different sextet. Inexplicably, the two men did not use the rhythm section which had accompanied them the previous year. The line-up, essentially a compromise personnel, consists of pianist Clyde Hart, guitarist Remo Palmieri, bassist Slam Stewart and drummer Cozy Cole. Hart is a sensitive accompanist whose piano chords are cast in the modern idiom, but his solos betray his preference for swing, and this is also true of Stewart, a little of whose vocal accompaniment in unison with his improvisations goes a long way. Cole did not favour the crisp, unexpected accents employed by Roach or Clarke, and for the most part merely keeps time with brushes or, on *Dizzy Atmosphere* only, sticks. Palmieri, thoroughly a modern soloist steeped in Charlie Christian's style, is called upon to play rhythm guitar on Gillespie's compositions *Dizzy Atmosphere* and *Groovin' High*, giving the rhythm section a curious chugging quality, well distanced from the clean, fleet support that Parker certainly preferred.

Yet with all these apparent debits, the three performances are of immense musical and historical value for the sweeping, unfettered trumpet and saxophone solos and the vivid unison lines in which the two sound like a single voice. Their tones may have appeared thin and their ideas strange and uncomfortable to lay listeners in 1945 still unfamiliar with the surprising rhythms, fast tempos and original combinations of notes, but time has proved the unerring logic and beauty of these inspired creations.

Groovin' High, based on the chord progression of *Whispering*, has a call-and-response pattern established from the onset, when a unison phrase by the horns is answered by the bass and continues over into the main theme with the piano responding to the catchy phrases of alto and trumpet. The figure that they repeatedly play translates into the spoken word as 'bebop.' Parker's improvisation strikes a wonderful balance between tension and relaxation, and, following a bizarre interlude by Stewart, Gillespie punches out a muted trumpet solo of great precision and power. After the guitar solo Gillespie, removing the mute, plays his specially composed solo ending, later adapted by Tadd Dameron to fit into his melody *If You Could See Me Now*.

All the Things You Are, with its classic introduction, which was subsequently grafted on to virtually all modern jazz interpretations of the song, is a relatively straight reading. Gillespie hews fairly closely to the written melody, but Parker in his eight-bar passages improvises freely in a relaxed manner. Parker later adapted this standard as *Bird of Paradise*.

The gem of the session is the spirited *Dizzy Atmosphere* with its scene-setting opening from the trumpet, the crazy, heady dash by the horns, and the brilliance of their solos. In Parker's lissom chorus the notes seem to unravel from the saxophone with the swing and snap of an uncoiling spring. His placement of accents is continually startling yet eminently right. The same acute sense of timing, and a matching grace and guile, are present in the trumpet solo, after which Stewart's facile chorus of bowed bass and vocal comes almost as a relief. When the trumpet and saxophone return in unison it is on a smooth melodic variation of the original theme which resolves into the opening strain.

For his next assignment with Guild, Gillespie was able to present four-fifths of the Three Deuces band, including pianist Al Haig and string bass player Curly Russell. Drummer Max Roach was on the road with Benny Carter, so Gillespie chose Big Sid Catlett. The admirable Catlett had been a huge influence on Roach, Clarke, Blakey and most of the other early bop drummers. He was sympathetic to the new style and adapted to it more readily than Cole. This time there was no guitar to complicate the rhythm section.

The session was more tightly organized than its predecessor. As if to underline the atmosphere of confidence that prevailed, the musicians launch themselves immediately on a composition by Gillespie and Clarke first recorded by tenor saxophonist Georgie Auld the previous year, *Salt Peanuts*. This brusque, angular, stop-start theme was soon to become a testing ground for aspiring boppers. Jagged and dissonant, it was not intended to be pretty, and the trumpeter's vocal mugging is another strange element in this abrasive performance. Once the jarring theme, such as it is, has been despatched, the way is clear for free-wheeling solos by Haig, Parker and Gillespie, and then a meticulous drum solo by Catlett which shows in detail the influence he had on Blakey.

Catlett's drumming is also a potent ingredient of *Shaw 'nuff*, another up-tempo performance with intricate, highly charged lines. As was usually the case in fast pieces, the leader would yield to the saxophonist in the order of solos. Haig's solo benefits from its controlled understatement in the whirl-wind of music that surrounded him.

By contrast, *Lover Man*, the other undisguised song among these recordings, is an impeccable ballad read by ultra-cool singer Sarah Vaughan, who had worked with Gillespie and Parker in the Earl Hines and Billy Eckstine orchestras. Haig and the horns constantly support and embroider Vaughan's true and pure voice. Gillespie's solo subtly embellishes the melody.

Hot House, created by Tadd Dameron, is based on the chord progession of *What is this Thing Called Love?*. A bustling burst from the drums announces this medium-tempo swinger, in which Gillespie emphasizes his rapport with Parker by picking up one of the last phrases of his companion's solo to launch his own. Aside from an eight-bar intervention by Haig towards the end, this warm, relaxed, unadulterated bop performance features Parker and Gillespie, singly or together, from start to finish. Their solos became model structures for most young jazz instrumentalists.

Upon returning to New York from an uncomfortable engagement in Hollywood, Gillespie began an extended stay at the Spotlite club. Vibraphonist Milt Jackson, pianist Haig and bassist Ray Brown were still in the group, but Parker and his permanent 'deputy' Lucky Thompson had both opted to remain in Los Angeles, and drummer Stan Levey quit. Within days Gillespie was in front of the microphone for a session under the aegis of Victor, the company which would sign the trumpeter to a contract the following year.

Victor had been persuaded to record Gillespie after a certain amount of arm-twisting from critic Leonard Feather, who produced the session and also, under the pseudonym Floyd Wilson, arranged one title, *Ol' Man Rebop* (based on *Old Man River*). The company required that some of the *Esquire* magazine award winners participate. Gillespie brought in tenor saxophonist Don Byas, about to sail to Europe (whence he never returned), who had worked with Gillespie on 52nd Street in 1944; although he was a swing musician in tone and feeling, he was harmonically sophisticated and an excellent technician. Drummer J. C. Heard, another *Esquire* winner, was equally at home with mainstream jump bands as with a bop combo. For this date, the leader again called in a guitarist, the remarkably facile Bill DeArango, who had recorded alongside Gillespie at a session under Vaughan in 1945. DeArango was undoubtedly the most fluent and accomplished guitarist active at that time, but he made few recordings and none better than these tracks.

Master takes of the four titles, together with four sides by Coleman Hawkins, were rapidly issued in a 78 rpm album called **New 52nd Street Jazz**, which finished as the best-selling jazz album of 1946. In this respect, quite apart from its musical virtues, it was the most significant release in helping to attract a wide audience to the new style. Two decades later a Gillespie retrospective LP revealed alternate takes to all of the titles except Feather's contribution.

After years of contributing compositions and arrangements to various bands and collecting pieces from fellow modernists, Gillespie was virtually a walking archive of new music awaiting wider dissemination. Heard on record for the first time – pre-dating versions by Kenny Clarke, its composer Thelonious Monk and Bud Powell – was *52nd Street Theme*, built on a cunning bop riff pattern, part of which Monk borrowed from the novelty hit *Woody Woodpecker's Song*. This unwhistleable melody gained the immediate status of an anthem, invariably played at a frenetic tempo and thereby seen as a trial ground for any young bop musician. Parker adopted it as his set closer, usually launching into the turbulent contours with undisguised ferocity. Gillespie's arrangement calls for both horns along with guitar and vibes to play the main section of the melody in unison – no mean feat at a bristling tempo – but only Byas and Gillespie play the bridge. Although Jackson solos confidently, the engineering does not catch the nuances of his instrument. Byas is brusque and forthright, while DeArango executes a passage of stunning virtuosity. However, Gillespie caps them all with his invention. One senses his dissatisfaction with his own performance on the first take, which includes an uncharacteristic stumble, but no such blemish occurs in his meticulous upper-register work and cohesive integration of ideas at the second attempt. Brown also performs a bowed solo on both takes.

Gillespie wrote *A Night in Tunisia*, the first of his many 'exotic' pieces, around 1941 when he was working with saxophonist Benny Carter at Kelly's

Stable. This piece had been recorded in a vocal version by Sarah Vaughan under the title *Interlude* in 1944. Here, though, was its first, brilliant instrumental reading in an arrangement which became standard and outstripped *52nd Street Theme* in popularity. It opens with a then unusual recurring bass figure, syncopated, not walking. Gillespie's muted trumpet, assisted harmonically by the tenor sax, carries the melody, which evolved from a happy accident when Gillespie was playing thirteenth chords. The piece includes an interlude which launches Gillespie into an immaculately executed solo of enormous excitement, energy and buoyancy. He rapidly removes the mute while Byas takes a few bars. Much of Gillespie's improvisation is concentrated in the upper register, and while the tone is thinner than, say, that of Louis Armstrong or Roy Eldridge, every note is crisp and clear. Trumpet playing of such complexity and accuracy was a new element in jazz. Byas's solo and that of Jackson are inevitably anti-climactic after this precision piece of musicianship, replete with daring double-time passages and rhythmic twists. The incomplete alternate take (not included on the French **Jazz Tribune** collection) is slightly less confident than the master, but Gillespie's solo is quite different though no less brilliant. The extra take shows us that he was not a 'safe' player but would completely rethink his solo each time.

After these fireworks, *Ol' Man Rebop* seems a subdued, albeit cleverly arranged, piece. It includes 16 bars of elegant, restrained piano by Al Haig, whose accompaniment throughout this session is measured and deftly apt. Haig, who seemed incapable of putting a hand wrong, shunned the flashy and superficial, although he possessed fine technique.

Completing this momentous session was a pair of elaborations of Gillespie's composition *Anthropology*, a variation on *I Got Rhythm*. Again he uses a mute for the theme and open trumpet for his solos. More surprisingly, he chooses to unveil the tricky melody in unison with Jackson's vibraphone. Byas does not play, possibly because he was unfamiliar with the angular line. The quicker master take is far superior to the other attempt, illustrating that a speedy tempo was a necessary adjunct to certain aspects of bop. In many respects this piece is as complicated as the arrangements Lennie Tristano recorded for Capitol in 1949.

Three months later, with Jackson, Haig and Brown, Gillespie recorded four titles for the Musicraft company. Sonny Stitt, the undeniably fluent and gifted replacement alto saxophonist, had patterned his playing closely on Parker's style, and his allegiance to Parker is glaringly obvious in his solos on these recordings. Equally apparent are the differences. While Parker invariably delights with his rhythmic and melodic inventiveness, Stitt sounds rather predictable, even mechanical, by comparison. That he was able to absorb so many of Parker's lessons shows his aptitude as one of the latter's earliest disciples. Stitt was able to prevent himself being enveloped by Parker's style by switching to tenor saxophone later on.

Vibraphonist Milt Jackson, pianist Haig and bassist Ray Brown were all part of Gillespie's Hollywood line-up. Drummer Clarke was an old friend and fervent supporter of the trumpeter. On this session Gillespie shuns the mute, except for the blues track, and plays glorious open trumpet, which would be his strong suit in front of the big band he led for the following four years. By this stage he had worked hard to broaden and ripen his tone, with some success, as this date attests. Perhaps, too, he felt that his open sound blended better with Stitt's tone, which was altogether less pliant than Parker's.

As the title suggests, *One Bass Hit* features among its solos Brown's nimble and big-toned bass lines, but it is the flashing double-time passages by the trumpet that distinguish the performance. Arranger Gil Fuller was present in the studio and joined Gillespie for the vocal portion of the surreal conversation between voices and instruments on *Oop Bop Sh'bam*. *That's Earl, Brother* is a composition with more substance than many of the skeletal bop themes. Overall this date lacks the spark of the Parker–Gillespie collaborations, but it is an admirable showcase for the leader's verve and virtuosity, not to mention his skill at bandleading.

(On reissues, Gillespie's essential combo tracks appear in tandem with his big-band recordings. The latter are discussed in Chapter 3, but for convenience all details of reissues appear below and are fully duplicated in that other chapter.)

CD
USA: *'Shaw 'nuff'*, Musicraft MVSCD 53

Dizzy Gillespie (tpt), Dexter Gordon (ts), Frank Paparelli (p), Chuck Wayne (elg), Murray Shipinski (sb), Irv Kluger (d)
New York   9 Feb 1945   **Blue 'n Boogie**

Gillespie (tpt), Charlie Parker (as), Clyde Hart (p), Remo Palmieri (elg), Slam Stewart (sb), Cozy Cole (d)
                    28 Feb 1945   **Groovin' High**
                                         All the Things you Are
                                         Dizzy Atmosphere

Gillespie (tpt, v), Parker (as), Al Haig (p), Curly Russell (sb), Sid Catlett (d)
                    11 May 1945   **Salt Peanuts**   5

omit (v)   **Shaw 'nuff**

add Sarah Vaughan (v)   **Lover Man**

omit (v)   **Hot House**

Gillespie (tpt), Sonny Stitt (as), Milt Jackson (vb), Haig (p), Ray Brown (sb), Kenny
Clarke (d)
                   15 May 1946   **One Bass Hit no.1**

add Gillespie, Gil Fuller (v)   **Oop Bop Sh'bam**   10
                                              That's Earl, Brother

Gillespie, Dave Burns, Raymond Orr, Talib Daawud, John Lynch (tpt), Alton
Moore, Charles Greenlea (tb), John Brown, Howard Johnson (as), Ray Abrams,
Warren Luckey (ts), Pee Wee Moore (bar), Jackson (p), Ray Brown (sb), Clarke (d)
                   10 June 1946   **Our Delight**

add Roberts (v)   **Good Dues Blues**

Gillespie, Burns, Daawud, Kenny Dorham, Lynch, Elmon Wright (tpt), Leon Com-
egeys, Gordon Thomas, Moore (tb), Johnson, Stitt (as), Abrams, Luckey (ts), Leo
Parker (bar), John Lewis (p), Brown (sb), Clarke (d)
                   9 July 1946   **One Bass Hit no.2**
                                        Ray's Idea   15

add Jackson (vb)   **Things to Come**

add Roberts (v)   **He Beeped when He Shoulda**
                                              Bopped

Gillespie, Burns, Lynch, Wright, Matthew McKay (tpt), Thomas, Alton Moore,
Taswell Baird (tb), John Brown, Scoops Carry (as), James Moody, Bill Frazier (ts),
Pee Wee Moore (bar), John Lewis (p), Ray Brown (sb), Joe Harris (d), Kenny
Hagood (v)
                   12 Nov 1946   **I Waited for You**

add Jackson (vb)   **Emanon**

Other CDs
incl. tracks 2, 4–6, 12, 16, plus others cited below
   Denmark: *Dizzy Gillespie*, Official 83056-2

LPs
plus additional tracks:
   USA: *In the Beginning*, Prestige 24030

incl. tracks 1–11:
  USA: *The Small Groups*, Phoenix LP 2
incl. tracks 12–18:
  USA: *Dizzy's Delight*, Phoenix LP 4
tracks 1–5, 8–13, 14–16, 19: *Groovin' High*
  USA: Savoy MG 12020
  France: BYG 529.145; Savoy-Musidisc 30 SA 6037
incl. tracks 1–4, 9–11:
  USA: *Dizzy Gillespie: the Development of an American Artist, 1940–1946*,
  Smithsonian R004
tracks 1–4, 8, 10–13, 15–16, 19:
  UK: *The Dizzy Gillespie Story*, Ember EMB 3344
tracks 1, 3–4, 8–17, 19:
  USA: *Blue 'n Boogie*, Allegro LP 3083
incl. tracks 1, 4–5, 9–10, 12, 15–16, 19, plus others cited below:
  Italy: *Dizzy Gillespie: Small Combos*, Giants of Jazz LPJT 32, and
  Dizzy Gillespie and His Orchestra, Giants of Jazz LPJT 37
tracks 2–5, 8, 10–12, 14, 16–17, 19:
  UK: *Dizzy Gillespie and His Orchestra*, Saga ERO 8017
incl. tracks 2, 4–6, 12, 16, plus others cited below
  Denmark: *Dizzy Gillespie*, Official 3056-2

Cassettes

incl. tracks 1, 4–5, 9–10, 12, 15–16, 19, plus others cited below:
  Italy: *Dizzy Gillespie: Small Combos*, Giants of Jazz MCJT 32, and
  Dizzy Gillespie and His Orchestra, Giants of Jazz MCJT 37

LP

**Europe: *Jazz Tribune no.2: Dizzy Gillespie, vol.1/2 (1946–1949)*, RCA
NL 89763**

*Gillespie (tpt), Don Byas (ts), Jackson (vb), Haig (p), Bill DeArango (elg), Brown
(b), J. C. Heard (d)*

New York	22 Feb 1946	**52nd Street Theme** (take 1)	
		52nd Street Theme (take 2)	
		A Night in Tunisia	
		Ol' Man Rebop	
		Anthropology (take 1)	5
		Anthropology (take 2)	

Gillespie, Burns, Wright, McKay, Raymond Orr (tpt), Baird or Ted Kelly?, Bill

Shepherd (tb), John Brown, Johnson (as), Moody or Big Nick Nicholas?, Joe Gayles (ts), Payne (bar), Lewis (p), Ray Brown or McKibbon? (sb), Harris or Clarke? (d)

22 Aug 1947   **Ow!**

add Gillespie, Hagood (v)   **Oop-pop-a-da**

omit (v)   **Two Bass Hit**

                                      Stay on it   10

Gillespie, Burns, Elmon Wright, Lammar Wright Jr, Benny Bailey (tpt), Kelly, Shepherd (tb), John Brown, Johnson (as), Nicholas, Joe Gayles (ts), Payne (bar), Lewis (p), McKibbon (sb), Clarke (d), Chano Pozo (conga drum)

        22 Dec 1947   **Algo Bueno (Woody 'n You)**

add Gillespie, Hagood (v)   **Cool Breeze**

Pozo and band (v) replace Gillespie, Hagood

                                      Cubana Be

                                      Cubana Bop

*as **Algo Bueno**, but Gillespie (v)*

        30 Dec 1947   **Manteca**   15

omit (v)   **Good Bait**

add Gillespie, Hagood (v)   **Ool-ya-koo**

omit (v)   **Minor Walk**

Gillespie, Burns, Elmon Wright, Willie Cook (tpt), Andy Duryea, Sam Hurt, Jesse Tarrant (tb), Brown, Ernie Henry (as), Gayles, Budd Johnson (ts), Payne (bar), James Forman (p), McKibbon (sb), Teddy Stewart (d), Harris (conga drum), Sabu Martinez (bongo)

        29 Dec 1948   **Guarachi Guaro**

                            Duff Capers   20

                            Lover Come Back to Me

add Gillespie (v)   **I'm Be Boppin' Too** (take 1)

                                      I'm Be Boppin' Too (take 2)

(Metronome All Stars:) Gillespie, Miles Davis, Fats Navarro (tpt), J. J. Johnson, Kai Winding (tb), Buddy DeFranco (cl), Charlie Parker (as), Charlie Ventura (ts), Ernie

Caceres (bar), Lennie Tristano (p), Billy Bauer (elg), Eddie Safranski (sb), Shelly Manne (d)

3 Jan 1949	**Overtime**	
	Victory Ball	25

Gillespie, Little Benny Harris, Wright, Cook (tpt), Duryea, Hurt, Tarrant (tb), Brown, Henry (as), Gayles, Yusef Lateef (ts), Al Gibson (bar), Forman (p), McKibbon (sb), Stewart (d), Vince Guerro (conga drum)

14 April 1949	**St Louis Blues**
	Swedish Suite
6 May 1949	**Katy (Dizzier and Dizzier)**

add Gillespie, Joe 'Bebop' Carroll (v)

Jump Did-le-ba

Charles Greenlea, J. J. Johnson (tb) replace Hurt and Tarrant

6 July 1949	**Hey Pete, Let's Eat Mo' Meat**	30

omit (v)   **Jumpin' with Symphony Sid**

add Carroll (v)   **In the Land of Oo-bla-dee**

CDs

incl. tracks 7, 9, 11, 13–16, 19, 28, 31:
 Europe: (various artists:) *The Bebop Revolution*, Bluebird ND 82177
incl. tracks 3, 7, 11, 28, plus others cited above:
 Denmark: *Dizzy Gillespie*, Official 83056-2

Other LPs

same contents:
 France: RCA PM 42408
tracks 2–5, 9, 13–16, 18, 26, 28: *The Greatest of Dizzy Gillespie*
 USA: RCA LPM 2398
 UK: RCA RD 27242; RCA SF 5123
tracks 2–5, 7–10, 11 (alternate take), 12–22, 26–31:
 France: *Horizons du Jazz: Dizzy Gillespie Orchestra*, RCA 430.215, and
 title unknown, RCA 430.207
incl. tracks 1, 3–5, 8–16, 18, 21, 24–5, 27, 30, 32:
 France: *Dizzy Gillespie, vol.1*, RCA 731.676 and *Dizzy Gillespie, vol.2*,
 RCA 731.068
tracks 1, 3 (alternate take), 4, 11, 17, 19–21, 23, 27, 30–32: *Dizzy Gillespie*

USA: RCA LPV 530
UK: RCA RD 7827
incl. tracks 3, 7–10, 11 (alternate take), 12–17, 31, plus others cited
above:
  Italy: *Dizzy Gillespie: Small Combos*, Giants of Jazz LPJT 32, and
  Dizzy Gillespie and His Orchestra, Giants of Jazz LPJT 37
incl. tracks 2–3, 5–12, 15–17:
  Europe: *Diz Delights*, RCA CL 89804
tracks 7, 9, 11 (alternate take), 13–15, 20, 22, 26–8, 30–32:
  USA: *Dizzier and Dizzier*, RCA LJM 1009
incl. tracks 7–8, 10, 12, 29: (various leaders:) *The Be-bop Era*
  USA: RCA LPV 519
  UK: RCA RD 7827
incl. tracks 17, 19–23, 27–32:
  France: *When Be-bop Meets the Big Band (Dizzy Gillespie, vol.1, 1947–49)*
  RCA 741.095
incl. tracks 3, 7, 11, 28, plus others cited above:
  Denmark: *Dizzy Gillespie*, Official 3056-2

Cassettes

same contents:
  Europe: RCA NK 89763
incl. tracks 2–3, 5–12, 15–17:
  Europe: *Diz Delights*, RCA CK 89804
incl. tracks 3, 7–10, 11 (alternate take), 12–17, 31, plus others cited
above:
  Italy: *Dizzy Gillespie: Small Combos*, Giants of Jazz MCJT 32, and
  Dizzy Gillespie and His Orchestra, Giants of Jazz MCJT 37

* * *

Charlie Parker: *The Charlie Parker Story; Charlie Parker on Dial, vol.1*

Charlie Parker's inaugural recording session as a leader had its share of
problems. His pianist, Bud Powell, had gone house-hunting in Philadelphia.
Parker booked Dizzy Gillespie as a substitute, knowing that his trumpeter
friend was a competent piano accompanist. He also asked pianist Argonne
Thornton (Sadik Hakim) to come along. Barely had the proceedings for the
Savoy company got under way when Parker realized that his saxophone
had a defect which was causing squeaks. Later trumpeter Miles Davis

disappeared and then a union official challenged Thornton, who had no union card. Given these unsettling circumstances, it is a wonder that any music of value resulted, yet such was Parker's concentration and inspiration that 26 November 1945 is perhaps the key date in postwar jazz. For the first time, all the musicians involved were of the same stylistic persuasion. The makeshift nature of the piano accompaniment affected Parker not one jot, and he seemingly took the other distractions in his stride.

His selection of Davis, whose instrumental proficiency at this stage was far from complete, indicated Parker's perception in spotting a talent of rare promise, and the inclusion of the exemplary percussionist Max Roach foreshadowed the composition of the regular quintet he would form in 1947 with Davis and Roach as key members. Bass player Curly Russell would also be a consistent companion for recording dates, including two more with the Savoy label.

By the end of 1945, Parker's artistry was well known and widely appreciated in the jazz community, although many listeners, including some musicians, were bewildered by the speed and execution of his ideas, the rhythmic complexity of his solos and compositions and his harmonic conception. His tart tone did not find favour with those reared on the sweeter sound of Johnny Hodges or the smoother delivery of Benny Carter. It had an abrasive cutting edge which could sound shrill when Parker was not himself. Even his detractors, though, had to acknowledge that the man was a powerful blues player who, more than Gillespie, refurbished and advanced the 12-bar form.

It was in blues territory that this session began as the musicians got to grips with *Billie's Bounce*, a melodically complex theme which Parker contrived on the morning of the session. The first three takes find him struggling with the deficient saxophone, although his first solo is a good one. By take 3, when Davis has settled down, the saxophone problem is glaringly obvious, and Parker decided to give the horn a thorough test. Musicians often tackle different material after unsatisfactory takes, returning refreshed to the original later. Parker's diversion was an up-tempo improvisation on the chord sequence of the popular tune *Cherokee*. Most of this unscheduled performance, released as *Warming up a Riff*, was recorded and it indicates no obvious mechanical difficulties. With Thornton at the piano, Parker soars through an improvisation of splendid invention, relishing the stimulating chord changes and quoting from such disparate sources as *High Society* (the old New Orleans favourite), *Tea for Two*, *Irish Washerwoman* and *Cocktails for Two*. Immediately after this brilliant interlude the group returned to *Billie's Bounce*, and at the fifth attempt a successful take was accomplished. Actually, the leader's best solo is on the fourth (incomplete) take, despite some reed squeaks.

The next task was the other blues Parker had concocted at the eleventh hour, *Now's the Time* (later lifted as the basis for the pop hit *The Hucklebuck*), with a piano introduction by Gillespie that has echoes of Thelonious Monk's style. On this slower, more classical blues, Davis sounds much more confident and poised. The richness of Parker's imagination, his projection of emotion and his links with jazz tradition are all apparent in the two completed takes, which contain quite different solos, replete with double-time passages. His solo on the master take inspired Eddie Jefferson to write a fitting lyric, neatly demonstrating that the improvisation was a melody in its own right.

The most challenging business was left to the end – *Thriving on a Riff* and *Ko-ko*. The first title was rooted in the chord changes of *I Got Rhythm*. Parker would later retitle this clever piece *Anthropology*, and it was first recorded under that name by Gillespie the following year. Three surviving takes find Parker in startling form. His solo on the opening attempt is near perfect, but slight blemishes in the restatement of the theme probably led to its original rejection. The entire opening theme is dropped for the other completed take, which is a series of improvisations by Parker, Davis and Thornton, who sounds distinctly tense after the fine solos by the two horns.

With Gillespie on piano, the quartet (minus Davis) detailed a loving interpretation of one of Parker's favourite ballads, *Embraceable You*, eventually issued under the title of *Meandering*. His playing here is gentle, tender and romantic without being either rhapsodic or sentimental. Right at the end of this unscheduled warm-up, which was never intended for release, Parker reminds himself with a quotation from *You'd Better Go Now* that the saxophone had to be fixed before he could again assay the contours of *Cherokee* (this time under the title *Ko-ko*) at the blinding tempo he reserved for this speciality (on which he had been featured in the Jay McShann orchestra). At this juncture he left with producer Teddy Reig to get the recalcitrant saxophone sorted out. On their return, Davis was missing, so Gillespie was charged with doubling on trumpet and piano, with Thornton filling in at the keyboard on the theme of the first take and at the beginning of Parker's solo on the master take.

The initial try is soon whistled to a halt because Parker and Gillespie start playing the original melody of Ray Noble's *Cherokee*, which would have cost Savoy royalties. The second take is suitably themeless. Both, however, include the new intricate introduction, in unison, then with solo breaks by muted trumpet and saxophone, and again in unison. The only accompaniment for the horns on this swirling theme is the flashing brushes on Roach's snare drum. The routine serves as a propulsive launching pad for Parker's scintillating two choruses of unbroken inspiration at a crippling tempo. Its cohesive shape, fluidity and development of rapid but logical ideas mark this as one of the master works of his substantial discography. The only other soloist is Roach, whose drum passage was a landmark in technique and the controlled building of excitement.

Ko-ko, the definitive summation of all Parker had absorbed and created by the end of his 25th year, heralded his most creative and productive period. During the years 1946–8 he completed seven sessions for the Dial label and five more for Savoy. His output thereafter for Norman Granz's various labels tended to be unsatisfactory owing to the unhelpful nature of some of the contexts in which Granz placed him.

The Dials constitute his most consistent and satisfying work. Despite being treated for drug addiction and mental stress for six of the 15 months he spent in California, he functions at a highly inventive level on all but one date. Among the ensuing albums, the first volume of the Dial sides in chronological order encapsulates his highs and lows.

The opening performance, *Diggin' Diz* (based on the chord progression of *Lover*), is the only fragment to survive from a chaotic session nominally led by Gillespie. It is by a septet including tenor saxophonist Lucky Thompson and guitarist Arvin Garrison, both of whom Parker kept on when he mustered his own septet for Dial. More importantly, however, he was reunited with Davis, lately arrived in Hollywood with Benny Carter's orchestra. The brilliant, classically trained pianist Dodo Marmarosa led the rhythm section. Bass duties were assigned to Victor McMillan (his one and only studio appearance of any import), while behind the drums was the advanced and adventurous Roy Porter.

Every surviving scrap of music – ten complete performances and one edited item – detail five hours of concentrated creativity. With Parker at the peak of his form, Davis was suitably inspired to improvise with hitherto unsuspected daring. Thompson's smooth, rounded sound with its well-shaded vibrato supplied an engaging contrast to Parker's vocal tone with its keen, cutting edge. The responsive rhythm section – Garrison was exclusively a soloist, not an accompanist – maintains an insistent and unflagging pulse, with Marmarosa's percussive chording a constant source of helpful prompting to the soloists. The arrangements are precisely worked out (not always the case in Parker's sessions) and the ensembles tightly rehearsed. The understanding of producer Ross Russell, who believed in letting the musicians go about their work without interference, and the quality of the engineering also contributed to the birth of these classic sides.

To some extent preparations were as usual for Parker, who came up with the melody of *Moose the Mooche* in a taxicab on the way to the session. On the first take Davis plays open trumpet, but on the next, taken slightly faster, he inserts a mute which he used for the remainder of the date, producing a distinctive, plaintive tone closer to that of Howard McGhee than Gillespie. Parker's best flourish is on the third take, but an uncertain wobbling led to the selection of the second take for original release. The arrangement benefits from a conversational ending to which Parker, Thompson and Marmarosa each contribute two bars. Garrison lays out on these takes.

Parker had composed the melody of *Yardbird Suite*, an airy, dancing line, several years earlier. Take 1 follows a conventional pattern, with Parker playing a whole chorus, Davis, Thompson and Marmarosa halves, and Garrison a quarter. By the fourth take the routine had been altered, the net result being a performance half a chorus longer, more relaxed and of greater interest on account of the double juxtaposition of Davis and Thompson. The revised set-up runs like this: Marmarosa (8-bar introduction), unison (16 bars), Parker (8), unison (8), Parker (32), Davis (16), Thompson (8), Davis (8), Thompson (16), Garrison (16), Marmarosa (8), ensemble (8). Parker's chorus on this extended master take is a miracle of structure, unusually economical and rhythmically attuned closely to the intricacies of the design of his melody. Demonstrating his ability to conjure up a memorable phrase, the altoist, in the first eight bars of his solo, inserts the main theme of what would be recorded as *Cool Blues* almost a year later. Thus many Parker themes grew within actual improvisations – a neat reversal of standard jazz practice.

Parker had also long before composed the scintillating and serpentine melody of *Ornithology* (written down by trumpeter Benny Harris), based on the chord pattern of *How High the Moon*. The first take was clearly a run through, because Parker does not solo. The relay ending of the theme was tricky, calling for trumpet, alto, tenor, guitar and piano each to contribute one bar apiece. On take 3 they have this together at the end of the opening and closing themes. The fourth take, the master, opens with an explosive four-bar drum break from Porter and is notably quicker than its predecessors. It is the crispest cut of all.

To this trio of themes by Parker, all destined to become quintessential parts of the bop repertory, was added Gillespie's *Night in Tunisia*. Three of five takes survive, but one is a mere fragment comprising a snatch of ensemble, Parker's glorious cadenza and solo and part of Davis's solo. This was the opening sally, and Parker felt he would be unable to reproduce the soaring spontaneity in subsequent efforts, so Russell issued this 47-second miniature as *The Famous Alto Break*. Actually, Parker's forays on the two surviving complete takes are by no means anti-climactic, although on the fragment the cadenza itself is marginally more virtuosic in its ascent. The arrangement is unusual because the piano and guitar combine in unison to play the hypnotic droning line above which trumpet (in the *a* section) and alto (in the *b*) soar. Porter's strategic 'bombs' on the bass drum are most effective.

The closing four tracks, recorded just four months later, come as a deep shock. On the day of the session Parker was disintegrating, in the depths of traumatic drug withdrawal. He was not fit to play (having consumed a quart of whisky) and that he managed any coherence at all was a tribute to his innate musicianship. On one of the few occasions of his career the saxophonist flounders on fast pieces, *Max is Making Wax* and *Bebop*. His struggle is emphasized by the accurate, crackling trumpet work of Howard McGhee. *Loverman*, the first of two ballads, is sluggish and halting yet strangely moving as Parker unnaturally wrestles with an instrument of which he was a master. The same slow, deliberate manner is apparent on *The Gypsy*, which he never played again, so much did he dislike the song and its associations. Parker's fury at the release of these four sides is understandable.

LP

USA: *The Charlie Parker Story*, Savoy MG 12079

Miles Davis (tpt), Charlie Parker (as), Dizzy Gillespie (p), Curly Russell (sb), Max Roach (d)

New York	26 Nov 1945	**Billie's Bounce** (take 1)	
		Billie's Bounce (take 2)	
		Billie's Bounce (take 3)	
omit Davis		**Warming up a Riff**	
add Davis		**Billie's Bounce** (take 4)	5
		Billie's Bounce (take 5)	
		Now's the Time (take 1)	
		Now's the Time (take 2)	
		Now's the Time (take 3)	
		Now's the Time (take 4)	10

Argonne Thornton (p) replaces Gillespie

	Thriving on a Riff (take 1)	
	Thriving on a Riff (take 2)	
	Thriving on a Riff (take 3)	
*as **Warming up a Riff***	**Meandering**	

Gillespie (tpt) replaces Davis; both Gillespie and Thornton (p)

	Ko-ko (take 1)	15
	Ko-ko (take 2)	

CDs

plus additional tracks:
   USA: *The Complete Savoy Studio Sessions*, Savoy ZDS 5500
incl. tracks 4, 6, 10, 13–14, 16:

USA: *The Savoy Recording Master Tapes*, vol.1, Savoy ZDS 4402
France: *The Savoy Recordings, vol.1*, Vogue 650107
country unknown: *Bird: vol.1–2*, Savoy ACDOR 29005
incl. tracks 4, 6, 10, 13, 16, plus others cited below:
Denmark: *Charlie Parker*, Official 83011-2
incl. tracks 6, 10, 13, 16: *The Best of Bird on Savoy*
USA: Savoy ZDS 1208
France: Vogue 650109

Other LPs

same contents:
UK: *Memorial Album, vol.1*, CBS Realm LP 120; CBS Realm 52120; *Charlie Parker Memorial, vol.1*, Eros ERL 50048; *The Immortal Charlie Parker, vol.1*, London LTZ C15108; *Charlie Parker Memorial, vol.1*, Realm RM 120
France: title unknown, BYG 529.129
plus additional tracks:
USA: *The Complete Savoy Studio Sessions*, Savoy SJL 5500
France: *The Complete Charlie Parker*, BYG LP3
incl. tracks 1–13:
Japan: title unknown, CBS-Sony SOPU 21; CBS-Sony SOPL 64
incl. tracks 14–16:
Japan: title unknown, CBS-Sony SOPU 22; CBS-Sony SOPL 65
incl. tracks 1, 4, 6, 9–11, 13–15:
Japan: title unknown, CBS-Sony SOPJ 134-5 SY
incl. tracks 4, 6, 10, 13–14, 16: *Bird: The Savoy Recordings (Master Takes)*
USA: Savoy SJL 2201
France: Savoy 2C162-99010/011
Germany: Savoy 1C148-99010/011
incl. tracks 4, 6, 10, 13, 16, plus others cited below:
Denmark: *Charlie Parker*, Official 3011-2
incl. tracks 6, 10, 13, 16:
USA: *The Best of Bird on Savoy*, Savoy SJL 1208
incl. tracks 1, 9, 11:
USA: *Encores*, Savoy SJL 1107

Cassettes

incl. tracks 6, 10, 13, 16:
USA: *The Best of Bird on Savoy*, Savoy SJK 1208
incl tracks 1, 9, 11:
USA: *Encores*, Savoy SJK 1107

LP

UK: *Charlie Parker on Dial, vol.1,* Spotlite 101

Gillespie (tpt), Parker (as), Lucky Thompson (ts), George Handy (p), Arvin Garrison (elg), Ray Brown (sb), Stan Levey (d)
Glendale, CA   5 Feb 1946   **Diggin' Diz**

Davis (tpt), Parker (as), Thompson (ts), Dodo Marmarosa (p), Victor McMillan (sb), Roy Porter (d)
Hollywood   28 March 1946   **Moose the Mooche** (take 1)
                                          Moose the Mooche (take 2)
                                          Moose the Mooche (take 3)

add Garrison (elg)   **Yardbird Suite** (take 1)   5
                                          Yardbird Suite (take 4)
                                          Ornithology (take 1)
                                          Ornithology (Bird Lore) (take 3)
                                          Ornithology (take 4)
                                          **The Famous Alto Break (Night in
                                              Tunisia)**   10
                                          Night in Tunisia (take 4)
                                          Night in Tunisia (take 5)

Howard McGhee (tpt), Parker (as), Jimmy Bunn (p), Bob Kesterson (sb), Porter (d)
                  26 July 1946   **Max is Making Wax**
                                          Loverman
                                          The Gypsy   15
                                          Bebop

CDs

incl. tracks 1, 3, 5–6, 9–10, 12–16:
   USA: *The Legendary Dial Masters,* vol.1–2, Stash STCD 23 and STCD 25
incl. tracks 3, 6, 9, 12, plus others cited above:
   Denmark: *Charlie Parker,* Official 83011-2

Other LPs

plus additional tracks:
   USA: *Charlie Parker,* Warner Brothers 6BS 3159
incl. tracks 3, 6, 9, 12, plus others cited above:
   Denmark: *Charlie Parker,* Official 3011-2
incl. tracks 3, 6, 9, 12:

USA: *Bird Symbols*, Charlie Parker PLP 407;
title unknown, Charlie Parker PLP 824

* * *

Thelonious Monk: *The Complete Genius*

Of all the major contributors to shaping a course for modern jazz,
Thelonious Monk was considered the most eccentric. The pianist and composer was quickly recognized by his contemporaries for his unusual and
distinctive writing abilities. His individual perception of harmony was undoubtedly influential within the bop workshop sessions of the early 1940s,
and his themes were highly valued by Dizzy Gillespie, Charlie Parker and
others. But his instrumental work was a subject for scorn in the 1940s and his
idiosyncratic melodies were not properly explored until he indicated
through his own recordings how they should be interpreted.

His highly personal piano style evolved in a mysterious manner. His
earliest recordings, made in 1941, reveal that he was strongly under the
influence of Teddy Wilson at this stage of his career. It was also apparent
that he had listened to such stride pianists as James P. Johnson, Willie 'the
Lion' Smith and Fats Waller, but three years later, on sides with swing tenor
saxophonist Coleman Hawkins, his own keyboard concept is fully defined
in typically uncompromising fashion.

While certain critics felt that Monk's playing displayed a lack of technique, the evidence suggests he deliberately chose a brusque, percussive
stance, and consciously rejected the Wilsonian smooth sophistication which
he had earlier favoured. Monk's improvisations bristled with angular dissonance, surprising intervals and craggy runs. His wit, never far away in any
performance, often took an ironic turn; at times he was capable of tongue-in-
cheek self-parody. He would frequently insert a few bars of stride piano into
an otherwise obtuse statement. He disapproved of glib, fast 'blowing' on his
melodic structures and sought to involve his fellow musicians in deeper
exploration of what were invariably intriguing, surprising themes. Some,
notably *'Round Midnight*, were so expertly cast that even highly imaginative
players found them difficult melodies on which to improvise. The tunes
therefore added a further challenge to Monk's own unconventional
accompaniment.

Since Monk was not given to talking about his work, he left listeners to
unravel his puzzles and draw their own conclusions. Initially the majority of
musicians were certainly baffled. Even though Hawkins employed him for
nearly two years, Monk was not a popular pianist with many of the boppers.
Some simply could not play with him. So while such of his pieces as

Epistrophy, *'Round Midnight*, *52nd Street Theme* and *Well You Needn't* gained increasing currency, their composer found work scarce and little call for his keyboard style. In 1946 he was fired from Dizzy Gillespie's orchestra for persistent lateness, and he had scant reason for any optimism about the future until Blue Note Records began recording him in the autumn of 1947. His five sessions for that label, made between 1947 and 1952, are invaluable documents, showing Monk at the helm of assorted quintets and sextets and, for one date, a trio.

The performances from 1947 include 25 of his compositions. Never a prolific writer, he would recycle many of these early works throughout his career. They would be heard in solo, group and even orchestral contexts and would continue to offer provocative challenges to their creator and his numerous sidemen.

The way he played and his style of writing were closely related. Unlike Duke Ellington, he did not compose with other soloists in mind; he wrote primarily to suit his own pianistic approach. After the songs emerged from his keyboard investigations, he would cast about for suitable colleagues to lend his ideas substance. Sometimes the recruits were simply not up to the task. On his first Blue Note session, saxophonists Danny Quebec West and Billy Smith were less than satisfactory associates, whereas trumpeter Idrees Sulieman displayed sympathy and understanding. Monk's most compatible sideman was drummer Art Blakey, who perfectly understood the aims of the pianist and over many years provided the rhythmic stimulation he sought. It is no accident that Blakey is on four of the five Blue Note dates directed by Monk, who appreciated the strong rhythmic undertow and flourishing accents that he supplied. Blakey seldom played loudly in Monk's company, his accompaniment on *Humph*, a jagged up-tempo discursion on the harmonies of *I Got Rhythm*, being somewhat of an exception in this respect. The drummer on the fifth date, Shadow Wilson, was another favourite who subsequently worked alongside Monk in 1957 in the quartet which included John Coltrane.

Evonce and *Suburban Eyes*, the latter based on the chord sequence of *All God's Children Got Rhythm*, are both untypical themes, since they were written not by Monk, but by Ike Quebec and Sulieman respectively. The real gem of Monk's inaugural date was his own *Thelonious*, a telling, repetitive theme built largely around just two notes. Monk enlarges this trifle with inspired skill. The only soloist, he includes a lengthy passage of pure stride piano in his second chorus and affectionately quotes from *Salt Peanuts* in his third.

Nine days after this respectable debut, Monk returned to the same studio with the same rhythm section – veteran bass player Gene Ramey and Blakey – to perform three of his most durable compositions, *Ruby, my Dear*, *Well You Needn't* and *Off Minor*. Some nine years later, a fourth original, *Introspection*, was unearthed.

In a trio context Monk becomes noticeably more expansive and communicative, completely secure in his own structures, with no other soloists to worry about. *Ruby, my Dear* is a beautifully poignant 32-bar ballad destined to become a standard in the jazz repertory. Monk's interpretation is seminal in its economy and feeling, with Blakey's crisp brush punctuations an asset throughout. The sinewy *Well You Needn't*, another much played piece, has a most satisfying hypnotic line with a dancing contrasting melody that rises and falls through a pattern of alternating steps and leaps drawn from the opening. Monk swings hard, occasionally letting a bar or two roll by without striking a note and humming along with his improvisations; he closes with a traditional phrase from Scottish folk music. *Off Minor* also has a memorable theme, and a disconcerting second melody. *Introspection*, opening with an out-of-tempo introduction, has a more complex melody with a call-and-response pattern. In this instance, Monk only lightly embroiders his own creation. Clearly, a piece of this subtlety would have been too much for the front-line sidemen on the previous session, and even the trio required four takes before striking the mood that Monk wanted.

Possibly to show Monk at work in a context more familiar to lay listeners, he played, with unconcealed gusto and considerable distinction, the standard song *April in Paris*. Here his chord combinations and melodic embellishments are more easily comprehended, along with his personal rhythmic preferences. That Monk was part of a tradition, albeit an expander of it, is fully apparent. There is nothing weird or strange about what he plays here, but in 1947 Monk had to contend with ears and minds which were not attuned to the sounds that were the natural expression of his originality.

At his third session, again including Blakey, Monk opted for a quintet with alto saxophonist Sahib Shihab, who unlike trumpeter George Tait was an understanding interpreter of Monk's music. Monk's composition *In Walked Bud*, dedicated to his fellow pianist and protégé Bud Powell, is a clever elaboration of the chord progression of *Blue Skies* and contains a suitably optimistic piano solo. *'Round Midnight*, a dignified 32-bar ballad of classic quality, had already been recorded by the contrasting orchestras of Cootie Williams and Dizzy Gillespie before Monk delivered this masterpiece. The composer handles the melody, with a subdued commentary supplied by the horns, and he elects to improvise during the *b* section of the *aaba* melody. The piece has a late-night mood that is highly evocative of the subject.

With a completely new cast highlighting the vibraphone solos of Milt Jackson, Monk's quartet refurbished his admired *Epistrophy* and *I Mean You*, and detailed a fine new piece, *Misterioso*, at a date in 1948. Wilson replaced Blakey, and the sturdy bass playing of John Simmons was heard alongside Monk for the only time in a recording studio.

Misterioso, sounding like a pianistic exercise but played in harmony by

Monk and Jackson, reverts to a lazy beat for the solos, following the urgent theme. The vibes and piano work splendidly together, Jackson clearly enjoying Monk's sparse accompaniment. The pianist's solo is deliberate and ruminative, full of cunning phrases and wicked little runs. The jabbing punctuations he deploys when Jackson returns to the theme are gems of timing.

Epistrophy, written in collaboration with drummer Kenny Clarke, was also recorded by Williams, and it subsequently served as a closing theme for many bop groups. Through its dissonant line the *a* section of the melody builds tension which finds a vivid release in the *b* segment. Jackson's flowing manner of improvisation is by no means at odds with Monk's more rough-hewn lines.

I Mean You, earlier recorded by Hawkins, has a basic quality and a shape that appealed to the saxophonist. Again one is struck by the superior interplay of vibes and piano, a partnership that was to be revived in a famous session in 1954 at which a testy Miles Davis instructed Monk not to play during his solos. Had Davis properly listened to the way Jackson adapted to Monk's accompaniment, he might have had second thoughts. Here, as on *Epistrophy*, the solos are restricted to half choruses, but they are miniatures filled with interest and more than 40 years later still make an impact.

Monk was handicapped by his reputation as an eccentric pianist, an image he did nothing to alter by his bizarre behaviour, and his direct influence on keyboard styles was marginal. Randy Weston and Stan Tracey are two pianists who clearly are disciples, and possibly Monk's percussive touch influenced the young Horace Silver. Many others absorbed aspects of Monk's playing only via his friend Powell. Yet Monk is now seen, with hindsight, as a vital contributor to the jazz mainstream. His compositions have kept entire groups in employment, and these pieces still merit investigation by today's musicians. Monk was certainly ten years ahead of his time. Fortunately, players and listeners eventually caught up, and from the late 1950s he reaped the benefits that were his due. These Blue Notes were the brave beginnings that should not be missed.

LP

USA: *The Complete Genius*, Blue Note LA 579-2

Idrees Sulieman (tpt), Danny Quebec West (as), Billy Smith (ts), Thelonious Monk (p), Gene Ramey (sb), Art Blakey (d)

New York   15 Oct 1947   **Humph**
                                       Evonce (take 4)
                                       Suburban Eyes (take 1)
                                       Thelonious

Monk (p), Ramey (sb), Blakey (d)

24 Oct 1947	**Nice Work if You Can Get it**	
	(take 0)	5
	Ruby, my Dear (take 1)	
	Well You Needn't (take 0)	
	April in Paris (take 1)	
	Off Minor	
	Introspection	10

George Tait (tpt), Sahib Shihab (as), Monk (p), Bob Paige (sb), Blakey (d)

21 Nov 1947	**In Walked Bud**
	Monk's Mood
	Who Knows (take 0)
	'Round Midnight

Milt Jackson (vb), Monk (p), John Simmons (sb), Shadow Wilson (d), Kenny Hagood (v)

2 July 1948	**All the Things You Are**	15
	I Should Care (take 1)	

omit (v)	**Evidence**	
	Misterioso (take 1)	
	Epistrophy	
	I Mean You	20

CDs

tracks 1–14, plus alternate takes: *Genius of Modern Music, vol.1*
  USA: Blue Note CDP 7-81510-2

Other LPs

plus additional tracks and takes:
  USA: *The Complete Blue Note Recordings of Thelonious Monk*, Mosaic MR
  4-101
same contents:
  UK: Blue Note BND 4032
  Italy: Blue Note ABNST 2-36520
incl. tracks 1, 4, 6–11, 14, 18–20: *Genius of Modern Music, vol.1*
  USA: Blue Note BLP 1510; Blue Note BST 81510
  Japan: Blue Note GXF 3014; Blue Note GXK 8058; Blue Note LNJ 70090;
  Blue Note NR 8836
  Brazil: Blue Note 31C152-82836
incl. tracks 2–3, 5, 12–13: *Genius of Modern Music, vol.2*

USA: Blue Note BLP 1511; Blue Note BST 81511
Japan: Blue Note GXK 8059; Blue Note LNJ 70096

Cassettes

same contents:
USA: Blue Note LWB 00579
incl. tracks 1, 4, 6–11, 14, 18–20: *Genius of Modern Music, vol.1*
  USA: Blue Note 4BN 81510
  France: Blue Note L 81510
incl. tracks 2–3, 5, 12–13: *Genius of Modern Music, vol.2*
  USA: Blue Note 4BN 81511

* * *

Bud Powell: *The Amazing Bud Powell, vol.1* (both CD and LP)

Once the innovations of Charlie Parker and Dizzy Gillespie were out in the open during the early 1940s, jazz players of all other instruments strove to incorporate the lessons. The piano found its most advanced and accomplished modernist in Bud Powell, a young New Yorker who had hung out with Parker, Gillespie and Monk and understood and absorbed the new style completely.

By the age of 21, Powell had forged a technique of formidable proportions which enabled him to produce with his adroit right hand the incredibly fast and complex lines that Parker had achieved on the alto saxophone. Powell's left hand punched out complementary chords to suit each line. He was gifted in all areas of expression. His melodic sense was fine, his rhythmic perception acute and his harmonic knowledge, gained from close study of Art Tatum, highly advanced. Thus he became the idol of his fellow pianists. All the other early bop keyboard players, including Al Haig, Duke Jordan, Hank Jones, Dodo Marmarosa and George Wallington, adopted his procedures and borrowed from his vocabulary.

Intense is the word that best describes Powell's style. When attacking a rhythmic exercise such as *Un Poco Loco* or tearing into a bop anthem such as *52nd Street Theme* he would build almost unbearable, highly charged tension, even to a greater pitch than Parker on occasion. Powell was a man completely driven by a search for musical perfection. So involved was he in this obsession that at times his bass player George Duvivier would shine a flashlight to bring him out of a long, involved solo.

His greatest achievements emerged from the late 1940s and early 1950s when mind and hands were perfectly coordinated, when the pianist's responses allowed him to play precisely what he heard. In this highly creative period, Powell frequently recorded for the Blue Note label, for which he produced sessions of rare quality in the company of some of his peers. Just as Art Blakey was the perfect drummer for Thelonious Monk, Max Roach proved to be the ideal percussionist for Powell. Roach's presence on three of these titles is crucial. Such is the strength and flexibility of his support on *Un Poco Loco* and *A Night in Tunisia* that the presence of bass player Curly Russell is almost superfluous.

The three takes of *Un Poco Loco* (A Little Crazy) enable us to hear the evolution of a masterpiece. The first and briefest version of this hypnotic Latin jazz exercise builds broodingly, but Powell becomes increasingly dissatisfied with his own level of performance and a slight sag in tension makes him call a halt before Roach can launch into his solo. Take 2 traces the gathering improvement in the performance. A repetitive left-hand figure from Powell runs through the piece like the print through a stick of rock candy and is reflected in Roach's own figure on the cowbell. The original master take is indisputably the finest of the three. Powell probes deeper and his invention never flags as the right hand unfolds cunning thoughts.

It is beyond belief that Powell, an extremely competitive musician in certain respects, was unaware of the acclaim that had greeted Charlie Parker's 'famous alto break' on *A Night in Tunisia*, for the pianist obviously took special care to make his break of sustained interest. Again we are afforded the luxury of two takes, and the break on the shorter, alternative version is particularly memorable. Powell's fingers fly and he keeps the listener suspended with a teetering, poised pause. As for the solos, both are beautifully conceived and executed. On the longer, master take, he inserts a descending Monk-like run towards the end of the performance.

A further jewel from this important date is a charming interpretation of Powell's own *Parisian Thoroughfare*, an evocative piece that became a jazz standard. The pianist wrote it years before he ever visited Paris, yet it accurately suggests in sound the busy boulevards of that city.

The four quintet tracks, recorded nearly two years earlier, show Powell in another guise, as the leader of an unusually compatible group. Beside the dash and drive of trumpeter Fats Navarro – like Powell, a perfectionist – there are early glimpses of the fine playing of tenor saxophonist Sonny Rollins as the unit assays two of Powell's finest compositions, *Dance of the Infidels* and *Bouncing with Bud*. Powell's certainty on these performances is reflected in his compact and concise solos and firm supportive accompaniment. His solo on *Wail* is also outstanding, but his digital dexterity is at its most commanding in the swirling rapids of *52nd Street Theme*, at a testing tempo. Small wonder that enigmatic, complicated lines such as these bewildered musicians of earlier styles!

From the same session stems a relaxed trio rendition of Parker's *Ornithology*, on which drummer Roy Haynes's tidy brushwork and bass player Tommy Potter's springy lines help Powell create an improvisation of memorable design. Powell is closest to his mentor, Tatum, in the unaccompanied solo elucidation of *It Could Happen to You*, in which his regard for the older man is fully apparent as he moves with supple ease in and out of tempo. Here, surely, is a respectful tribute from one piano master to another. (Although both the new CD and the original LP have the same title, the contents of the former are substantially different from the latter; both are of great importance, however.)

CD

USA: *The Amazing Bud Powell, vol.1*, **Blue Note B21K 81503**

Fats Navarro (tpt), Sonny Rollins (ts), Bud Powell (p), Tommy Potter (sb), Roy Haynes (d)

New York	9 Aug 1949	**Bouncing with Bud** (take 0)	
		Bouncing with Bud (take 1)	
		Bouncing with Bud (take 2)	
		Wail (take 0)	
		Wail (take 3)	5
		Dance of the Infidels (take 0)	
		Dance of the Infidels (take 1)	
		52nd Street Theme	
omit Navarro and Rollins		**You Go to my Head**	
		Ornithology (take 0)	10
		Ornithology (take 1)	

Powell (p), Curly Russell (sb), Max Roach (d)

	1 May 1951	**Un Poco Loco** (take 1)	
		Un Poco Loco (take 2)	
		Un Poco Loco (take 4)	
Powell (p)		**Over the Rainbow**	15

Other CDs

USA: Blue Note CDP 7-81503-2
   Japan: Blue Note CJ28-5112; Blue Note CP 32-5241 (one of these may be
   vol.2)

LPs

plus additional tracks:
   USA: *The Complete Bud Powell Blue Note Recordings (1949–1958)*, Mosaic
   MR 5-116
tracks 3, 5, 7–8, 10, 12–14, plus others cited below: *The Amazing Bud Powell,*
   vol.1
   USA: Blue Note BLP 1503; Blue Note BST 81503
   UK: Blue Note BNS 40005
   Japan: Blue Note GXK 8071; Blue Note LNJ 70085; Blue Note NR 8832
   Brazil: Blue Note 31C152-53710
incl. tracks 9, 11, 15: *The Amazing Bud Powell, vol.2*
   USA: Blue Note BLP 1504; Blue Note BST 81504
   UK: Blue Note BNS 40006
   Japan: Blue Note GXK 8072; Blue Note LNJ 70076
   Brazil: Blue Note 31C152-53711
incl. tracks 1–8, plus others cited in the essay on Navarro and Dameron:
   (Fats Navarro:) *Prime Source*
   USA: Blue Note LA 507 HT

Cassettes

tracks 3, 5, 7–8, 10, 12–14, plus others cited below:
   USA: *The Amazing Bud Powell, vol.1*, Blue Note 4BN 81503
incl. tracks 9, 11, 15:
   USA: *The Amazing Bud Powell, vol.2*, Blue Note 4BN 81504

LP

USA: *The Amazing Bud Powell, vol.1*, Blue Note BLP 1503
incl. tracks cited above, plus:

Powell (p), Russell (sb), Roach (d)
New York   1 May 1951   **A Night in Tunisia** (take 0)
                                          A Night in Tunisia (take 1)

Powell (p)   **It Could Happen to You** (take 0)

Powell (p), Russell (sb), Roach (d)   **Parisian Thoroughfare**

Other LPs

same contents:
   see list above

Cassettes

* * *

Fats Navarro and Tadd Dameron: *The Fabulous Fats Navarro, vol.1; The Fabulous Fats Navarro, vol.2*

Two musicians of the 1940s who were inextricably linked, trumpeter Fats Navarro and composer, arranger and pianist Tadd Dameron, forged a memorable partnership. Navarro's brilliant trumpet sound provided Dameron's small groups with star quality, while the leader's melodic compositions were the ideal basis for the perfectly formed improvisations of the great brass soloist.

Navarro, who died from tuberculosis at the age of 26, was among the most accomplished of the bop instrumentalists and, unlike many of the trumpeters who worked in the style, he had a big, brassy sound, in the tradition of his relative Charlie Shavers. Such was his facility that he could compete in the fastest company, and that included Charlie Parker and Bud Powell. Dameron had proved his value as a composer and arranger with a series of commissions for big bands including those of Harlan Leonard, Georgie Auld, Count Basie and, most significantly, Dizzy Gillespie. He also contributed important pieces to the library of Billy Eckstine's bop big band. His charts incorporated both melodic appeal and harmonic challenge; sidemen enjoyed performing them because the written parts in themselves were beautiful.

The teaming of Navarro and Dameron was heard on half a dozen recording sessions for Blue Note, Savoy and Capitol as well as on numerous broadcasts from a lengthy residency at the Royal Roost club in New York. The supporting cast was apt to change but usually included Ernie Henry, Allen Eager or Charlie Rouse on saxophone, while the first choice for drummer was Kenny Clarke.

In a group that varied between quintet and septet size, Dameron was stimulated to write some of his finest lines, including *The Squirrel*, *Lady Bird*, *Jahbero* (a reworking of *All the Things You Are*) and *Symphonette*. Subtle arranging skills enabled him to make a sextet sound like a much larger ensemble. He invariably selected brass and reed players with big tones and would fully utilize them in ensembles. With a front line of only one trumpet and two saxophones at his disposal, he would assign varied roles to each in the ensemble passages. These were not confined to thematic statements alone, for Dameron also scored entirely new passages between or after solos. This technique, unusual in most bop combos (which typically proceded rigidly through a pattern of theme–solos–theme), is most strikingly employed in *Our Delight*, where the scored penultimate chorus is like a new melody, richer and more complex than the original.

Dameron's experience grafting and crafting arrangements for the big swing bands was also evident in his skilful isolation of one instrument to set up a conversation with others within a theme. He pulls off this risky process with quiet authority on *The Squirrel*, wherein he poses solo questions from the keyboard to draw responses from his front line. In miniature here is what he did with a large orchestra when contrasting his trumpet and saxophone sections, for example. He also enjoyed writing variations on his own themes and saving them up for the end of a performance, so that the listener, anticipating a restatement of the main melody, is pleasantly surprised by a fresh theme. Sometimes, as in *Dameronia*, it might be simply an eight-bar segment, but it showed the composer did not wish stolidly to retread the same ground. On the other hand, he was just as likely to pop a written sequence between solos, as on *Lady Bird*, where the two contributions from the tenor saxes are separated by eight bars of ensemble and eight of piano chords.

No soloist himself, Dameron was more than contented to have quality improvisers such as Navarro, Eager and saxophonist Wardell Gray expounding on his compositions. At the piano, Dameron restricted himself to the occasional break or brief chorded solo, but his broad, emphatic chordal accompaniment was an undervalued asset to his groups which lent them a highly distinctive sound. The riffy pattern of *The Chase* even prompts a couple of breaks by the reserved Dameron. However, it cannot be counted among his most satisfactory compositions, which are usually stronger than the average, skeletal bop original.

The items from the Blue Note sessions of 1947 and 1948 have been collected in several different packages, all issued under Navarro's name. They present Dameron's originals with alternate takes in every case, enabling the listener to make immediate comparisons between the solos. Close study reveals that the orderly, mathematical mind of Navarro invariably had his solo contours well shaped on the first cut and made only minor adjustments thereafter. This has led to his being categorized as a calculating improviser when compared with, say, Clifford Brown, whose variations would be enormous in rapid, successive takes. The truth is that Navarro's perfectionism and clarity meant he could fully deliver before his colleagues had properly got their act together. In this special ability to get things right on the first take, he was rather like Lester Young and Art Tatum.

The sides from 1947 benefit from the presence of Ernie Henry, who employed the sort of wide vibrato that Dameron loved to hear in his ensembles, and the contrasting tenor sax of Charlie Rouse, not at this point the mature soloist of Thelonious Monk's quartet, but still a worthy individual performer. However, it is Navarro's commanding lead work that sets the pace for the sextet. There are some typically complex and daring passages in his solo on *Our Delight* which Navarro executes with ridiculous ease and fluency, but these are only small effects in the meticulous construction. Navarro favours long lines and a careful attention to detail; his climaxes are always in just the right place. Henry also contributes fine solos, modern yet not too deeply cut in Parker's mould. Rouse strains slightly, no doubt finding it hard to follow the other two. He is considerably more relaxed on *The Squirrel*, but Navarro's controlled intensity and superbly cohesive contributions are in a class of their own on this chirpy blues. By the time the players reached *Dameronia*, Rouse was taking all the first solos so that Navarro did not give him an inferiority complex, and the tactic worked well. How could anyone have topped the trumpeter's scintillating entrances on either take? Indeed, Dameron discovered this was one of the problems of having Navarro in his bands – other musicians were inhibited by his brilliance.

The septet tracks are a notch or two above the sextet items because of the presence of two exceptional tenor saxophonists in Wardell Gray and Allen Eager, each of whom had the resilience and self-belief to follow Navarro. Both are in excellent fettle on *Lady Bird* (Eager is the first sax soloist) despite shimmering trumpet lessons from Navarro. *Jahbero*, with Afro-Cuban drumming supplied in tandem by Kenny Clarke and bongo player Chino Pozo, is rightly celebrated for the staggering invention of Navarro's solos and begins with one of the most electrifying entrances in the recorded annals of jazz. The trumpeter surges in with a climbing phrase of astonishing beauty. Nobody could touch Navarro in this mood.

Finally, there is the perky *Symphonette*, a somewhat neglected Dameron theme which has a more boppish opening line than many of his pieces, but a gently flowing contrasting section. Wardell Gray is most comfortable in this climate, but once again the trumpet interludes are dazzling examples of Navarro's majestic power. Eager copes with the awkward third solo spot with far more élan than anyone had a right to expect.

These sessions combine the elegance of an unusually gifted trumpeter with the perception of a marvellous melodic composer, both at their creative peak. Together they showed an intriguing route that could have been more fully explored in bop, but in the event was really never revisited, save briefly in Dameron's band in 1953.

(All issues cited include tracks from other sessions.)

CDs

USA: *The Fabulous Fats Navarro*, **vol.1–2, Blue Note B21K 81531 and B21K 81532**

(Tadd Dameron:) Fats Navarro (tpt), Ernie Henry (as), Charlie Rouse (ts), Dameron (p, arr), Nelson Boyd (sb), Shadow Wilson (d)

New York	26 Sept 1947	**The Chase** (take 0)	
		The Chase (take 2)	
		The Squirrel (take 0)	
		The Squirrel (take 1)	
		Our Delight (take 0)	5
		Our Delight (take 5)	
		Dameronia (take 0)	
		Dameronia (take 2)	

(Dameron:) Navarro (tpt), Allen Eager, Wardell Gray (ts), Dameron (p), Curly Russell (sb), Kenny Clarke (d), Chino Pozo (bongos)

13 Sept 1948	**Jahbero** (take 0)	
	Jahbero (take 1)	**10**
	Lady Bird (take 0)	
	Lady Bird (take 1)	
	Symphonette (take 1)	
	Symphonette (take 2)	

Other CDs

same contents:
   USA: Blue Note CDP 7-81531-2 and CDP 7-81532-2

LPs

incl. all tracks:
   USA: (Navarro:) *Prime Source*, Blue Note LA 507 HT
incl. all tracks: *The Fabulous Fats Navarro*, vol.1–2
   USA: Blue Note BLP 1531 and BLP 1532; Blue Note BST 81531 and BST 81532; Blue Note B11E 81531 and B11E 81532
   Japan: Blue Note GXK 8060 and GXK 8061; Blue Note LNJ 70071 and LNJ 70074
incl. one take of each title:
   Italy: *Fats Navarro*, Giants of Jazz LPJT 54

Cassettes

incl. all tracks:
   USA: *The Fabulous Fats Navarro*, vol.1–2, Blue Note 4BN 81531 and 4BN 81532; Blue Note B41E 81531 and B41E 81532
incl. one take of each title:
   Italy: *Fats Navarro*, Giants of Jazz MCJT 54

J. J. Johnson: *Mad Be Bop*

Bop presented special difficulties for jazz trombonists, almost all of whom played the slide trombone, more awkward to manipulate than valve trombone, and far more awkward than the saxophone with its keys. Adapting the trombone required a complete reappraisal of technique, so that it could negotiate the blistering tempos that were so much a part of the new style. Charlie Parker and Dizzy Gillespie caused many a trombonist to retreat to the rehearsal room to grapple with the problem. Trummy Young, a fine swing trombonist, effected a half-way style. He incorporated bop phrasing, but struggled on fast numbers. It was left to the prodigiously gifted J. J. Johnson to find the complete solutions and point the way for practically all the trombonists of his generation and those that followed.

Influenced by Vic Dickenson, Fred Beckett and Dicky Wells, Johnson also admired Jack Teagarden and John 'Streamline' Ewing, but while he was working in Snookum Russell's orchestra an even bigger influence was trumpeter Fats Navarro, whose technical facility was tremendous. While he was honing his technique in the trombone sections of the Benny Carter and Count Basie big bands, Johnson's goals were set by the solos by Parker and Gillespie he heard on records. He overcame the innate awkwardness of the instrument by developing a lightning wrist action coordinated with amazingly accurate articulation. His smooth, round, open tone was perfect in a bop context, and he also employed a variety of conventional mutes (and a bop beret) to alter that tone effectively. His legato phrasing displayed a deep admiration for Lester Young, and he invariably sounded unhurried and unflurried. Johnson's mastery of the instrument was so complete that many critics, and even fellow musicians, hearing his early recordings, believed he was 'cheating' by using a valve trombone! He never played that version of the instrument.

By 1946, when Johnson was only 22, his style was already fully formed and would show no radical departure thereafter, although his mature work of the 1950s revealed a heightened emotional involvement and depth. However, the sides from his three key sessions for the Savoy label in the 1940s possess a verve and enthusiasm that bespeak the youthful artist in the first flush of unbounded creativity, setting new boundaries for what Johnson himself once described as 'a beastly, horrid instrument' (Leonard Feather, liner notes for the Savoy double album).

For his debut as a leader, Johnson could not have wished for better companions than pianist Bud Powell and drummer Max Roach, the leading exponents of the new style on their respective instruments. Cecil Payne, soon to become a formidable baritone saxophonist but heard here on alto, played a satisfying amalgam of the approaches of Parker and Benny Carter. Bass player Leonard Gaskin was fleet of finger and sure of tone.

Johnson wrote three of the four pieces that exercised this quintet. The opening *Jay Bird* (also known as *Jaybird* and *Fly Jay*) departs from rigid conventions, following the pattern *abca* rather than the usual *aaba* bop formula and thus providing three melodic strands to make the solos more interesting. Even the title is portentous, combining the nicknames of Johnson and Parker, as if to underline the fact that the trombonist was playing in the manner of the genius of the alto saxophone. Powell's introduction to all three takes is a gem; so impressed with it was Tadd Dameron that he scored the eight-bar passage for trumpet and tenor sax and used it to introduce Navarro's recording of *Nostalgia*. The three versions differ in the order of solos. Johnson and Powell are commanding at each attempt, but Payne is not fully together until the master take, on which he sounds more boppish, infusing his solo with tension.

Max Roach composed *Coppin' the Bop*, notable for its use of suspended time and for the contrast between on-the-beat notes and typical bop phrases. Roach's drum punctuations are also a vital element, and he takes a crisp eight-bar solo during the out chorus. Payne and Johnson, who quotes from *High Society*, are both relaxed and confident, while Powell is commanding.

Johnson's helter-skelter *Jay Jay*, in three versions, is our old friend *I Got Rhythm* in new guise. Johnson really shows his mettle here with clarion clear lines and beautifully separated notes. It wasn't often that soloists could top Bud Powell, especially when he was in the consistent form evident throughout this session, but Johnson caps every one with his lithe improvisation on the master take.

Like Thelonious Monk's *Evidence* and Coleman Hawkins's *Spotlite*, Johnson's *Mad Be Bop* is based on the chord progression of *Just You, Just Me*, which is beefed up rhythmically by Gaskin and Roach. Johnson's admirable mobility and logical development of ideas are both apparent in his forthright solo on a piece that marked the conclusion of a most impressive debut.

Eighteen months later Johnson was at the helm of an entirely different quintet, drawn largely from the ranks of the band of the brothers Illinois and Russell Jacquet, with whom the trombonist was also working at the time. The roaring baritone saxophone of Leo Parker formed an effective partnership with Johnson, while the able rhythm section contained pianist Hank Jones, bass player Al Lucas and drummer Shadow Wilson.

On the ballad *Yesterdays* Johnson is heard throughout, save for eight bars of piano. Respectful of the melody, he restricts himself to a minimum of elaboration, yet it is a moving and meaningful interpretation, unmistakably the work of a jazz player of considerable sensitivity.

Johnson composed the balance of the pieces. *Boneology* has a lazy, legato quality, and in the *aaba* theme Johnson allocates the fourth bar of the *a* section to Jones, who plays a trilling bop phrase in response to the horns in unison. Always a shrewd deployer of quotations, Johnson inserts one from *'s Wonderful* in his solo, full of dash and pep, yet smoothly flowing. *Down Vernon's Alley* contrasts Parker wailing at full throttle in his most abrasive manner and Johnson, poised, urbane and perfect in an elegant solo. *Riffette* is exactly what the title implies, a repetitious riffy blues on which Johnson gets quite heated. Jones is also thoroughly involved, while Parker revels in this kind of stomping ground, inventing a few riffs of his own in a blistering example of fire-eating. This evidence suggests that Johnson and company spent a fruitful Christmas Eve in 1947, just a week before the second recording ban by the American Federation of Musicians came into effect.

The third session, held some 15 months later, was significant for several reasons. The leader's own style had been refined in the interim and by 1949 he was the complete trombonist. He chose as his front-line partner the young tenor saxophonist Sonny Rollins, who had impressed Johnson on a recording they made with singer Babs Gonzales a few weeks earlier. The choice was astute, for Rollins's rugged and jagged lines served as fitting foils to Johnson's smoothly rounded improvisations. Rollins further enhanced Johnson's selection by bringing in two original themes.

The saxophonist's *Audobahn* (also incorrectly known as *Audubon* and *Auduban*) has been released in two versions. On both Johnson placed a felt (probably his bop beret) over the bell of his trombone so that he could achieve the required blend with his saxophonist. *Don't Blame Me* is as good a ballad performance by Johnson as the earlier *Yesterdays*. Rollins's *Goof Square* is a neat bop blues which seems to suit Johnson perfectly at the medium-bounce tempo employed on all three issued takes. It is the sort of line that Charlie Parker tossed off to finish a session, and Rollins was certainly strongly under Parker's influence (instrumental and otherwise) at the time. His solos are occasionally rough in spots but consistently lively.

The trombonist had also come to know pianist John Lewis through their work with Miles Davis's cool jazz nonet and employed him on several sessions during 1949. Lewis's solo on *Goof Square* is, as ever, tidy and precise. Another blues, *Bee Jay*, this time by Johnson and much faster than *Goof Square*, concludes a sparkling date. Rollins musters his best solo on the master take, which is also enlivened by an improvisation of spry movement, wit and studied understatement by the urbane Johnson. Here was a man who knocked the abrasive corners off the instrument and substituted an undreamt-of polish and flow.

LP

USA: *Mad Be Bop*, **Savoy SJL 2232**

J. J. Johnson (tb), Cecil Payne (bar), Bud Powell (p), Leonard Gaskin (sb), Max Roach (d)

New York   26 June 1946   **Jay Bird** (take 1)
                                        Jay Bird (take 9)
                                        Jay Bird (take 11)
                                        Coppin' the Bop
                                        Jay Jay (take 1)   5
                                        Jay Jay (take 2)
                                        Jay Jay (take 4)
                                        Mad Be Bop

Johnson (tb), Leo Parker (bar), Hank Jones (p), Al Lucas (sb), Shadow Wilson (d)
                24 Dec 1947   **Boneology**
                                        Down Vernon's Alley   10
                                        Yesterdays
                                        Riffette

Johnson (tb), Sonny Rollins (ts), John Lewis (p), Gene Ramey (sb), Wilson (d)
                11 May 1949   **Audobahn** (take 1)
                                        Audobahn (take 3)
                                        Don't Blame Me   15
                                        Goof Square (take 2)
                                        Goof Square (take 4)
                                        Goof Square (take 8)
                                        Bee Jay (take 3)
                                        Bee Jay (take 5)   20

CDs

incl. 1 take of each title, plus additional tracks: *Mad Bop*
   Europe: Savoy 881919; Savoy 650119

Other LPs

tracks 3–4, 6, 8–12, 14–15, 18, 20: *Jay Jay Johnson Quintets*
   USA: Savoy MG 12106
   UK: Realm RK 195
   France: Savoy-Musidisc 30 SA 6029

* * *

Wardell Gray: *One for Prez*

The life of tenor saxophonist Wardell Gray closely paralled that of Charlie
Parker. Born just six months later in another midwestern city (Oklahoma

City), Gray survived for less than 11 weeks following Parker's death. Both men were originally inspired by Lester Young, and both worked with the big bands of Billy Eckstine and Earl Hines. Later, Gray, who recorded with Bird on two occasions, showed traces of Parker's influence in his style. Sadly, each was a victim of narcotics addiction and of racial and musical intolerance.

Few musicians had so rapidly and comprehensively digested the tonal and rhythmic lessons of Lester Young or the harmonic extensions wrought by Dizzy Gillespie and Parker as Wardell Gray, who by 1946 was probably the most modern and personal tenor saxophonist in jazz. His tone recognizably sprang from Young's sound, but Gray's was more open and he employed a subtle and unique vibrato. He had a terrific knack of creating melodic phrases, and his solos could be whistled or sung (as they were later by Annie Ross). His gift was for simplifying the complex. Like his frequent companion in tenor battles, Dexter Gordon, Gray had an engaging capacity for weaving quotations from other songs into his improvised solos. These familiar reference points were never self-consciously introduced, but formed an important part of the improvised fabric.

That Gray was technically adept and remarkably imaginative had been apparent in his early solos with Earl Hines's orchestra and was subsequently confirmed on his recordings in 1947 with Parker and Gordon. But the jazz audience at large did not fully realize just how advanced Gray was in 1946 until the systematic release of the superlative tracks from this session more than 40 years later. Supervised by Eddie Laguna after Gray had left Hines to work as a freelance in Los Angeles, the material, inexplicably, never appeared in the USA. Five of the performances were issued on small European labels and four additional tracks came out on an LP in the 1970s, but it was not until 1988 that the full wealth of 16 items from this productive date was arranged for release on CD.

For the first time it was possible to hear Gray eloquently appraising *Dell's Bells*, his lovely line based on *What is This Thing Called Love?*, in five different versions. A similar number of takes is also accorded to his tribute to Lester Young, *One for Prez*, a clever new melody based on the chord sequence of *How High the Moon*. A plethora of alternative takes can become exceedingly tedious, especially when the participants are predictable and merely polishing pet phrases until they shine to their satisfaction. But Gray was different – a thrilling off-the-top player who would create an entirely new improvisation at each attempt. This was an ability he shared with Parker and trumpeter Clifford Brown. His aptitude for instant composition is also convincingly heard in the three versions of *The Man I Love*, in none of which is Gershwin's original melody ever stated!

Laconic, erudite and composed, Gray's work carried a sense of deep inner conviction. He could suggest a wide spread of emotions. On a ballad such as

The Man I Love, he displayed a touching tenderness and humanity, and the introduction has an Ellingtonian flavour that suggests Gray was prepared to listen beyond his immediate stylistic preoccupations. At medium tempos he conveyed a jaunty optimism with an occasional ironic touch. Even at a comparatively speedy pace, preferred for *One for Prez*, he never sounds rushed. The quality of relaxation which makes his extemporizations so satisfying remains a constant.

While Gray had reason to feel bitter and angry about his lack of acclaim, neither self-pity nor frustration clouded his musical vision. Rather we turn to him for a joyous lift, a well-adjusted, happy perspective. The essence of what Wardell Gray was about is to be found on the two versions of his aptly named *Easy Swing*, which Parker recorded a couple of years later under the title of *Steeplechase*. The sequence of these chords is borrowed from *Perdido*, which Gray artfully paraphrases on each take. Possibly because this was delivered at his favourite moderate tempo, he felt the need for only two takes, each of which is a gem of pithy understatement. Unhurried and unflappable, Gray is the epitome of relaxation as he phrases fractionally behind the beat in the manner of Lester Young. Both these solos have an engaging continuity and inevitability as Gray matches long and short phrases with effective pauses in truly conversational style. The piece has a surprising, abrupt ending because he elects not to retrace the theme – a slice of boppish humour.

Gray was singularly fortunate to have the services of pianist Dodo Marmarosa for this programme. He was another brilliant individualist whose erratic lifestyle denied him the recognition his distinctive playing would have otherwise surely achieved. Marmarosa's lightning fingering in unison with Gray on the blistering theme of *One for Prez* foreshadows the complex melodic structures that Lennie Tristano would contrive for his sextet. A conservatory-trained musician, Marmarosa employed much fuller chords than were generally favoured by many of his contemporaries, and lent Gray dashing, percussive accompaniment on this occasion. His own solos reflect not only an interest in bop but an appreciation of earlier stylists, especially Art Tatum, Teddy Wilson and Earl Hines. He and Gray were wholly compatible in their approach, as they would prove on location and in other studio performances from the period.

The uncluttered drumming of Doc West and the assured bass playing of Red Callender blend cohesively, as well they might since both men regularly worked together in Erroll Garner's trio. Chuck Thompson replaces West for an impromptu version of *The Great Lie*, based on the standard *Fine and Dandy*. Once again fine playing results in what was for those times an extended recording.

CD

UK: *One for Prez*, **Black Lion BLCD 760 106**

Wardell Gray (ts), Dodo Marmarosa (p), Red Callender (sb), Doc West (d)

Hollywood	23 Nov 1946	**Dell's Bells** (take 5)
		Dell's Bells (take 4)
		Dell's Bells (take 1)
		Dell's Bells (take 2)
		Dell's Bells (take 3) 5
		One for Prez (take 5)
		One for Prez (take 4)
		One for Prez (take 1)
		One for Prez (take 2)
		One for Prez (take 3) 10
		The Man I Love (take 3)
		The Man I Love (take 2)
		The Man I Love (take 1)
		Easy Swing (take 2)
		Easy Swing (take 1) 15

Chuck Thompson (d) replaces West   **The Great Lie**

LPs

incl. tracks 2, 7, 12, 15:
   UK: *Master Swingers*, Fontana FJL 907
   Europe: *Dexter Gordon and Wardell Gray*, Fontana 683907 JCL; Fontana 883907 JCY
   Japan: title unknown, Black Lion PA 3145

* * *

Gene Ammons and Sonny Stitt: *Blues Up and Down, vol.1*

Saxophone partnerships in modern jazz enjoyed unprecedented popularity during the 1950s, when a pair of free-booting tenor players with sufficiently contrasting styles to maintain consistent interest and excitement could pack clubs and dances and make recordings for a rash of new independent labels that were springing up. The origins of these saxophone duels were the big bands. In Count Basie's orchestra, Lester Young and Herschel Evans had shown the way in the late 1930s. Norman Granz, who knew a good thing when he heard it, had encouraged saxophone battles at his earliest concerts, and the jousts between such frenetic saxophonists as Flip Phillips and Illinois Jacquet became a frenzied focus for his Jazz at the Philharmonic presentations. The two-tenor groups that cut a swinging swathe across the 1950s included Dexter Gordon and Wardell Gray, Al Cohn and Zoot Sims and above all Gene Ammons and Sonny Stitt. Companions in the saxophone section of Billy Eckstine's orchestra in 1946, Ammons and Stitt were sufficiently different stylistically to ensure listeners' attention never lapsed.

Stitt had started out on alto saxophone, but concentrated on the tenor from 1949. His fleet muscularity sat well alongside the thicker-toned Ammons, who favoured a simpler, more economical approach. The band these two formed in January 1950 was a septet of like-minded players. To balance the two reeds were the trumpet of Bill Massey and the warm, flowing trombone of Bennie Green (or the equally facile Eph Greenlea). Pianist Duke Jordan and bass player Tommy Potter had served both Charlie Parker and Stan Getz, but now found themselves in a much more basic climate.

The Ammons–Stitt band purveyed a no-frills brand of straight-ahead jazz with a repertory that was comprised of blues, the occasional standard, riffy melodies, bizarre band vocals and novelty numbers. The group was equally popular with jazz and rhythm-and-blues audiences. Dancers enjoyed the beat laid down by either swing veteran Jo Jones or the hard-bopping Art Blakey. The leaders were clearly at home with either percussionist's style. Indeed, the unit was all things to all listeners, and even after the direst vocal there was always a good saxophone solo to enjoy.

Two of the band's earliest sessions for the newly launched Prestige label were held in the spring of 1950. An archetypical tenor battle is Ammons's *Blues Up and Down*, heard here in three takes. The first shot starts well enough with Ammons opening the chases after the utilitarian theme, but Stitt has reed trouble in his first chorus and an uncertain moment in the third, and the performance ceases abruptly with Ammons still blowing. The second take is much more assured. Both men sound confident and inventive as they trade virile choruses back and forth and then indulge in some brisk four-bar breaks. Again there is a breakdown, this time in the restatement of the theme when the players were clearly signalled to halt. The third (master) take snaps along. Ammons and Stitt maintain the fluency and flow of ideas that had marked the previous attempt, and at one point both give nods in the direction of Lester Young by using a little honking phrase that was one of Young's trademarks. There are no fluffs on this occasion. The performance is a classic of the 'tough tenor' genre, characterized by hard-driving swing, a no-frills, uninhibited approach to improvisation and, in this partnership, a necessary competitive edge.

The catchy *Let it Be* verges on rhythm and blues with its hoarse vocal by the front line, swelled by the presence of Massey and Greenlea, who with the co-leaders emphasize the deliberate beat with solid hand-clapping. Stitt plays baritone saxophone on this track, and the excellent tenor solo is the work of a fecund Ammons, who also appends a vibrant ending.

Another side of the group's character is disclosed on the two takes of *You Can Depend on Me*, each briskly delivered as a tenor conversation. Ammons, with the broader tone and more pronounced vibrato, is again the first soloist; Stitt has a tighter tone and greater mobility. The two tones blend perfectly in the unison passages. Both saxophonists are in scintillating form as they speak in leaping, jaunty phrases without becoming repetitious or tired. Potter's great beat and the sure drumming of Jones drive the pair on splendidly. The second take is just a mite faster, but if anything Ammons and Stitt are even more inspired.

Touch of the Blues presents a strained vocal by Teddy Williams, who is called on to sing some ludicrous lyrics, but the arrangement is a good one in Tadd Dameron's style, and spirited ensemble work and an occasional interjection by Ammons enliven the performance. *Bye Bye*, a straightforward but effective theme, features a spirited Ammons who gains momentum as his solo unfolds. The band riffs are helpful and the first contains a snatch of *Baubles, Bangles and Beads*, showing how this band would borrow from any source if the results were justified. Massey takes an articulate 16-bar muted solo before Ammons re-enters.

The group's second session was important for its introduction of *Walkin'*, originally entitled *Gravy*, to the jazz repertory. Following Miles Davis's recording of 1954, it became a favourite blues line for jamming among hard-bop stylists. This pilot version has a fleet chorus from Duke Jordan, a master of the melodic, scene-setting piano introduction, as well as Ammons's superbly relaxed contribution and a pleasing chorus by Green. On *Chabootie*, yet another blues, Art Blakey propels Stitt into a potent baritone solo. In his chorus Stitt brings to mind the roaring tone of Leo Parker, with whom he had worked in Eckstine's band. Ammons's two choruses maintain the swaggering mood. *Easy Glide*, an apt description for the way Ammons performs on it, is a good example of the way the saxophonist tells a story with warmth and feeling. The melody and arrangement are redolent of Dameron's pieces, and the solos by Green and Jordan are inserted with appropriate consideration for the atmosphere generated by Ammons, who sounds both world-weary and hopeful. The absurdly titled *Who Threw the Sleeping Pills in Rip Van Winkle's Coffee?* borrows part of its melody from a traditional air. After a laboured band vocal and an ensemble passage Ammons breaks out with a swirling, energetic solo that compensates for the inconsequential nature of the composition.

LP

USA: *Blues Up and Down, vol.1*, **Prestige PRST 7823**

*Bill Massey (tpt), Eph Greenlea (tb), Gene Ammons (ts), Sonny Stitt (ts, bar), Duke
Jordan (p), Tommy Potter (sb), Jo Jones (d)*

New York	5 March 1950	**Bye Bye**
		Let it Be

omit Massey and Greenlea   **Blues Up and Down** (take 1)
Blues Up and Down (take 2)
Blues Up and Down (take 3)   **5**
You Can Depend on Me (take 1)
You Can Depend on Me (take 2)

add Teddy Williams (v)   **Touch of the Blues**

*Massey (tpt), Benny Green (tb), Ammons (ts), Stitt (ts, bar), Jordan (p), Potter (sb),
Art Blakey (d)*

26 April 1950   **Chabootie**
**Who Put the Sleeping Pills in Rip
Van Winkle's Coffee?**   **10**
Gravy (Walkin')
Easy Glide

Ammons (ts), Jordan (p), Gene Wright (sb), Wesley Landers (d)

28 June 1950   **I Wanna be Loved**
**I Can't Give You Anything but
Love**

Other LPs

incl. tracks 1–2, 9, 11–14:
   USA: *the Gene Ammons Story: the 78 Era*, Prestige PR 24058
incl. tracks 3–7:
   USA: *Gene Ammons All Star Sessions*, Original Jazz Classics OJC 014;
   Woofin' and Tweetin', Prestige LP 7050

Cassettes

incl. tracks 3–7:
   USA: *Gene Ammons All Star Sessions*, Original Jazz Classics OJC 5014

Stan Getz: *Stan Getz at Storyville*

Categorizing jazz soloists can be a futile and inexact pursuit, especially when the labelling is applied to a musician as versatile and adaptable as Stan Getz. After his solo on *Early Autumn* with Woody Herman, Getz was pegged as the iceman – the coolest tenor saxophonist in existence, a chilly, precise balladeer with a frosty tone. This analysis overlooked Getz's choice of Dexter Gordon as an early role model, and ignored a good deal of recorded evidence to the contrary. Getz subsequently made a nonsense of the 'deep freeze' tag by displaying his mettle in Jazz at the Philharmonic packages and jam sessions, where he took the measure of such 'hot' players as Roy Eldridge and Sonny Stitt. Getz's superficially gentle style contained a steely centre that made him a formidable adversary in a competitive blowing session. Like Lester Young, he would score by his invention and understatement.

While not strictly regarded as a bop figure, Getz used the vocabulary of Parker and Gillespie, and even shared with Parker the same rhythm section for a year or two in the early 1950s. The quintet Getz fronted briefly in the autumn of 1951 was cast in the bop mould and performed with a fire and feeling well distanced from the cool school. It remains to this day, some four decades later, the most homogeneous band Getz has led in his consistently interesting career.

With pianist Al Haig and guitarist Jimmy Raney, Getz rapidly achieved a telepathic understanding that enhanced their unity of purpose. In Tiny Kahn he found a drummer of unusual perception whose grasp of polyrhythms and ability to complement the soloist's line made him an asset in any context but especially this one. Bass player Teddy Kotick chose his notes with care and maintained impeccable time. His tone was resilient. In this responsive company Getz thrived and threw caution to the wind. The speed of his delivery evoked Parker while in his phrasing he betrayed a deep admiration for Lester Young, particularly in performances such as *Jumpin' with Symphony Sid* and *Thou Swell*.

The accommodation of the soft-toned electric guitar of Raney was achieved with the minimum of fuss. As an accompanist, Raney does not play rhythm guitar, but usually offers counterpoint to Getz's saxophone on the theme or drops into a unison role. He never gets in the way of the measured piano feeds by Haig. The additon of Raney gave the group three distinctive yet empathetic solo voices, ensuring a uniformly excellent level of improvisation. The three shared a lyrical approach to making music, so their solos were invariably melodic, yet harmonically sophisticated and rhythmically adventurous.

Recorded in front of an appreciative audience at Boston's Storyville Club, the tracks capture an electric atmosphere of creativity in which relaxation is the key. Few rhythm sections in jazz have worked together with such fluent ease as the Haig–Kotick–Kahn combination. At any tempo, they seem just naturally to fall into the groove that will be most beneficial to Getz and Raney and, of course, the splendid Haig, who shared with the tenor saxophonist a gift for understatement.

On a brisk version of *The Song is You*, Raney contrives neat contrapuntal lines to Getz's revelations on the theme. Kahn starts out with brushes but soon switches to sticks and drives along Getz's soaring work. Kahn's sticks also prod Raney, but he reverts to brushes to shade Haig's balletic mood. Saxophonist Gigi Gryce's composition *Mosquito Knees* has a boppish line, played in accurate unison by Getz and Raney, and it hurls Getz into some unexpected corners, out of which he nimbly skips. In a typically witty Haig solo there is a mellow reference to *Honeysuckle Rose*. The four-bar conversation pieces between Getz and Kahn find the saxophonist evoking Lester Young and the drummer suggesting Art Blakey.

On *Pennies from Heaven*, taken at a brisk bounce, Getz juxtaposes clipped, staccato phrases against more integrated passages, and uses Lester Young-style honks for effect. Along the way he quotes randomly from such tunes as *Fascinating Rhythm* and *How Are Things in Glocca Morra?* Apart from an eight-bar introduction by Haig, the performance is Getz's all the way, and the warmth of his solo ending is right in keeping with his amplifications of the melody that precede it.

The saxophonist's sense of order and ability to build and relate his choruses at a fast tempo is underlined by his fleet work on drummer Denzil Best's composition *Move*, on which he sails through the rapid chord changes. Raney and Kahn show similar objectivity, with Getz and Kahn again perking brightly in their exchanges. Kahn executes his drum solo beautifully, reinforcing the impression that he was rarely better captured on tape than on these sides.

Parker 51, Raney's cunning derivation from the melody of *Cherokee*, is also given express delivery, and is notable for the delightful counterpoint struck by guitar and tenor on the theme. One feels that Haig was more effective and comfortable at a gentler pace than this furious gallop. The descending contours of Getz's *Hershey Bar*, derived from *Tea for Two*, are more to Haig's liking, as he unfolds one of his neat and precise solos. The abrupt ending in the middle of the last chorus may have been the result of a tape unexpectedly running out.

On Raney's *Rubberneck*, a theme in a minor key, the tenor, guitar and piano solos are amazingly unified in style and feeling, serving as a further indicator of the close empathy between these musicians. *Signal* is also Raney's, and not surprisingly he makes the most telling contribution. Charlie Parker had lately revived the ballad *Everything Happens to Me*, performed here with restraint and sensitivity. The band plays *Yesterdays* in sturdy fashion and not at the sort of drag tempo which is apt to choke rhythmic movement. This is a feature for Getz, who carries the performance with unfailing charm, wit and vision. *Budo*, composed jointly by Bud Powell and Miles Davis, ends this invaluable set on a high, with its intricate unisons by Getz and Raney and sterling solos, including Kahn's explosive drumming.

The plum of the collection, though, is Lester Young's memorable blues *Jumpin' with Symphony Sid*, to which Getz appends an opening and closing variation also drawn from Young's phrasebook. Getz is not normally thought of as a blues player, but his eight superb choruses in this instance evince a splendid conviction and an absence of clichés. His use of double time in the sixth chorus and the Young-like honks in the eighth are climaxes placed exactly to achieve the optimum effect. After Raney and Haig take solos, Kotick in his three choruses shows a wry sense of humour by inserting a quotation, which had earlier been used by Haig, from *An English Country Garden*. These are among the most enticing and sublime seven minutes in postwar jazz.

CD
USA: *Stan Getz at Storyville*, vols.1–2, Cap. C2-7-94507-2

Stan Getz (ts), Jimmy Raney (elg), Al Haig (p), Teddy Kotick (sb), Tiny Kahn (d)

Boston	Oct 1951	Thou Swell	
		The Song is You	
		Mosquito Knees	
		Pennies from Heaven	
		Move	5
		Parker 51	
		Hershey Bar	
		Rubberneck	
		Signal	
		Everything Happens to Me	10
		Jumpin' with Symphony Sid	
		Yesterdays	
		Budo	

Other CDs
same contents:
   France: Vogue VG 651-600093
plus additional tracks:
   USA: *The Complete Recordings of the Stan Getz Quintet with Jimmy Raney*, Mosaic MD3 131

LPs

same contents: *Stan Getz at Storyville*, vol.1 (tracks 1–6) and 2 (7–13)
    USA: Roost RLP 2209 and RLP 2225
    UK: Vogue LAE 12158 and LAE 12199
    Spain: Fresh Sounds FSR 629 and FSR 630
plus additional tracks:
    USA: *The Complete Recordings of the Stan Getz Quintet with Jimmy Raney*,
    Mosaic MR4 131

* * *

Part 2: Cool Jazz, West Coast Jazz and Bossa Nova

Miles Davis: *Birth of the Cool*

The advent of the cool style in jazz was the outcome of a friendship and discussions between trumpeter Miles Davis and arranger Gil Evans as early as 1947. Davis, whose temperament and instrumental ability were not entirely suited to the torrid tempos and minimal arrangements favoured by his then employer, Charlie Parker, was thinking of a more restrained and polished setting for his low-key, economical style. He had enjoyed the unusual ensemble patterns and instrumental combinations created by Evans for Claude Thornhill's orchestra of the early and mid-1940s, and the pair worked out that, with just four brass players, two reeds and a rhythm section, they could reproduce the essential sound of Thornhill's band.

Davis's nonet began as a rehearsal band and quickly attracted musicians and composers who were thinking along similar lines. Gerry Mulligan had also written for Thornhill, while alto saxophonist Lee Konitz had been a soloist with the orchestra. John Lewis, another talented composer and an able pianist, also joined this exclusive workshop unit with some alacrity, as did trumpeter Johnny Carisi, though not in an instrumental role but as a composer and an arranger.

What lent the nonet its distinctive sound was the presence of a french horn and tuba in addition to the conventional brass and reed instruments; the tuba was in addition to, not in place of, string bass, and it functioned as a member of the brass section. None of the front line was called upon to play in a loud, strident manner. Soft unison and contrapuntal work was required to achieve the cloudy, restrained blend that Evans and Davis had in mind. The emphasis in this group was on a subtle melding of tones and a good deal of precisely scored passages for the ensemble, an area that had been somewhat neglected in the stampede of bop virtuosity.

Although Davis and Evans were the overall guiding hands, the chief writers were Mulligan, who arranged his own pieces *Jeru*, *Venus de Milo* and *Rocker* as well as *Godchild* (written by pianist George Wallington) and the ballad standard *Darn that Dream*, and Lewis, who arranged his own piece *Rouge* and also provided charts for *Move* (composed by drummer Denzil Best) and *Budo* (by Davis and pianist Bud Powell). A writer of an earlier era, Chummy MacGregor, was represented in *Moon Dreams*, arranged by Evans. Evans also supplied the framework for *Boplicity*; the piece is attributed to Cleo Henry (the name of Davis's mother), but it was co-composed by the trumpeter and Evans. Carisi wrote and scored *Israel*, and it is believed that Davis arranged his own *Deception*.

Considering that the 12 Capitol recordings involved so many writers, the oneness of feeling they achieved is a tribute to their unity of purpose and commitment to Davis's concept. The trumpeter was undoubtedly the catalyst for the band and the cool movement as a whole for, as we shall see, the leading individuals from the nonet went on to examine in other contexts the possibilities that had been opened – Davis in his own groups and through the later orchestral collaborations with Evans (discussed in Chapter 3), Lewis through the Modern Jazz Quartet, Mulligan in his quartet, tentet and Concert Jazz Band, Konitz within a series of combos and elaborations with Lennie Tristano. The influence was also spread via the orchestral compositions of J. J. Johnson and Gunther Schuller, two of the ensemble players who passed through the nonet's changing ranks. (Two decades later, the process would recur, with Davis's sidemen spreading out into the leading fusion bands.)

The band was actually a commercial disaster. Its public appearances were restricted to a couple of brief engagements at the Royal Roost and the Clique Club, and five months elapsed before Davis, through Pete Rugolo (who supervised the dates), was able to persuade Capitol to record them. But for the fact that Capitol at the time were signing up every jazz name of consequence, this music would not exist. Even when he had a contract, Davis was forced to spread the sessions over a 15-month period, which accounts for the shifts in personnel. The key constant factor, enabling the ensemble to maintain a consistency of sound, was the ever-present contingent of Davis, Konitz, Mulligan and tuba player Bill Barber.

While other musicians quickly perceived the subtle beauty of the music and set about emulating the distinctive ensemble sound and writing procedures, thereby reviving an interest in orchestration, the public was slow to catch on, although **Birth of the Cool** became a big seller when 11 of the tracks were collected on LP in 1957. Irritatingly, in repeated reissue packages, Capitol consistently omitted *Darn that Dream*, featuring a sensitive vocal by Kenny Hagood, a supple arrangement and a gem of a solo by Davis. Not until the early 1970s were all 12 pieces released together in an essential compilation by Dutch Capitol; the compact discs also include all 12.

What is immediately obvious from the improvisations of Davis, who naturally enough is the leading soloist, is the calm assurance and meticulous execution that he displays. With Parker, it seemed that the trumpeter was always fighting to keep up, struggling to compete with a soloist of unprecedented ability. This was most certainly invaluable experience, but by 1949 Davis was a considerably more confident and adept improviser. His solos brim with a new authority and his leadership is apparent within ensemble segments. He has no difficulty negotiating the tricky contours of *Move* in company with Konitz, and his solo on this item is bold and forthright. A decade later Davis would make frequent use of mutes, but with the nonet he played open horn all the way, varying the dynamics and tone by his own instrumental skill. The trumpet is the focal point of most of the writing, and Davis's solos of consistent quality illuminate every track save one. He is especially engaging in *Budo* and *Venus de Milo*.

Konitz's sound was ideally cast in this context, his thin tone blending perfectly with Davis in the unisons, and his imagination is voluminous, as can be heard in a lilting solo on *Rouge*. Mulligan, on the other hand, has a sound which is far from cool. However, he modifies his normal approach in order to knit with his colleagues, playing in gently restrained fashion. Similarly, the occasional piano solos by Lewis and the trombone interventions of Kai Winding and Johnson are in complete accord with the context. Johnson is particularly good on *Deception*.

Two of the most interesting pieces are *Israel*, a very clever treatment of the blues in a minor key, and the elegant *Moon Dreams*, a flowing, slow score by Evans, whose use of harmonies and textures indicates his originality of thought. A trifling song takes on a completely new dimension under his skilful control. Davis contents himself with an ensemble role here; Konitz and Mulligan solo briefly.

Ironically, **Birth of the Cool** even had its effect on bop's hottest soloist, Charlie Parker, who, a few months after Davis's recording was released, commissioned Mulligan to arrange *Rocker* for a string ensemble that the alto saxophonist was fronting. *Rocker* became a fixture in Parker's book with the stiff string section, and he would even play the composition with his quintet. Mulligan also recycled the tune for his 1953 tentet.

What Davis and company demonstrated, particularly in their treatments of bop originals such as *Move* and *Godchild*, was the existence of new avenues and possibilities for modern jazz. It didn't have to be fast and frantic or phrased in the astringent musical shorthand of Parker and Gillespie. Many fell in to follow Davis, but found it tough to keep up because he was already moving on.

CD

USA: *Birth of the Cool*, Capitol C21K 92862

Miles Davis (tpt), Kai Winding (tb), Junior Collins (french horn), Bill Barber (tuba), Lee Konitz (as), Gerry Mulligan (bar), Al Haig (p), Joe Schulman (sb), Max Roach (d)

New York	21 Jan 1949	**Move** (arr John Lewis)	
		Jeru (arr Mulligan)	
		Godchild (arr Mulligan)	
		Budo (arr Lewis)	

Davis (tpt), J. J. Johnson (tb), Sandy Siegelstein (french horn), Barber (tuba), Konitz (as), Mulligan (bar), Lewis (p), Nelson Boyd (sb), Kenny Clarke (d)

22 April 1949	**Venus de Milo** (arr Mulligan)	5
	Rouge (arr Lewis)	
	Boplicity (arr Gil Evans)	
	Israel (arr Johnny Carisi)	

Davis (tpt), Johnson (tb), Gunther Schuller (french horn), Barber (tuba), Konitz (as), Mulligan (bar), Lewis (p), Al McKibbon (sb), Roach (d)

9 March 1950	**Deception** (arr ?Davis)	
	Rocker (arr Mulligan)	10
	Moon Dreams (arr Evans)	

add Kenny Hagood (v)   **Darn that Dream** (arr Mulligan)

Other CDs

same contents:
  Europe: Capitol CDP 792862-2
  Japan: Capitol CP 32 5181

LPs

same contents:
  Netherlands: *The Complete Birth of the Cool*, Capitol 5C052.80798
not incl. track 12:
  USA: *Birth of the Cool*, Capitol T 762; Capitol DT 1974

Lennie Tristano: *Crosscurrents*

Few musicians in the history of jazz have prompted so much strong debate as pianist, composer and teacher Lennie Tristano. Even today, more than 40 years after these recordings were made and a decade on from Tristano's death, the arguments about his contribution to the music continue to rage. In assessing Tristano there appears to have been no middle ground of appreciation. On one side he was depicted as a man who could do no wrong, whose disciplines should have been adopted and embraced by the entire jazz community. On the other, he was portrayed as a bloodless technician, a demanding martinet whose music was over-formalized and devoid of warmth and feeling. The truth was a considerable distance from either viewpoint.

Tristano certainly preached the importance of a disciplined approach, insisting on precise ensemble playing at all times, but he also espoused the importance of pure improvisation and spontaneity within a logical framework. He did not believe in emotions ruling the head and deplored the arbitrary use of excitement and superficiality in jazz performances. He had certain idols, including Roy Eldridge (the tasteful early Eldridge, not the Eldridge who sometimes violated these very principles), Lester Young and Charlie Parker, and in getting his students and colleagues to understand the import of such soloists he would instruct them to sing the instrumental solos of Eldridge and company.

Blindness probably made Tristano more of a perfectionist when it came to music, and he was indeed a hard taskmaster. He gathered around him some extremely gifted acolytes who shared both his musical and philosophical beliefs. His two leading spokesmen were saxophonists Lee Konitz and Warne Marsh, whose light tones on alto and tenor respectively were identified with the new cool order. Indeed, Konitz, as we have already seen, was also immersed at this time in Davis's nonet and was making a copious input as a soloist to both bands.

In the first half of 1949, Tristano organized seven performances for Capitol Records which accurately encapsulated his highly personal approach to jazz. The music was difficult, spiky, introverted. It held out no easy route of understanding for the listener, who was expected to do his or her homework by concentrated listening. Here were not to be found the tonal variations, the spark, the recognizable blues phrases that were integral parts of Parker's style. Tristano's music conveyed austerity despite its complexity. Konitz and Marsh deliberately effected flat tones; it was their ideas that audiences were expected to appreciate, and these two with Tristano fashioned an abundance of intriguing melodic lines. Harmonies were also important, but rhythm in this music had a less vital role.

Tristano never yearned for inventive, dramatic percussionists such as Art

Blakey or Max Roach: he merely required steady time-keepers who would not clutter up the lines with what he heard as distracting or ephemeral accents. As a proponent of 'pure improvisation', Tristano had a natural admiration for the intricate lines of Bach, which also served as rehearsal exercises, and some of the contrapuntal forays of Konitz and Marsh have their roots in the theories of Bach rather than accepted jazz procedures. At its best, Tristano's method produced an intellectually satisfying musical outpouring. At its worst the results could sound coldly cerebral, devoid of human warmth and passion.

The Capitol sides are actually among the most fully realized of his ensemble recordings and were clearly preceded by typically thorough preparation and rehearsal. This is evident in the flawlessly synchronized playing of the themes by the two saxophonists and guitarist Bill Bauer, all three perfectly together in the twisting lines of *Wow*, *Crosscurrent* and *Marionette*. Tristano was something of a martinet about ensembles, but the drilling of his men produced the super-cool sound he was aiming for. This was by no means the first time a guitar had been placed into the front line, but never before had it blended so seamlessly. Only on *Sax of a Kind*, which as the title suggests focuses on the saxophones, does the guitar drop back into a subsidiary accompanying role.

The two pieces that were both controversial and futuristic are *Intuition* and *Digression*, since they were the first 'free' improvisations to be recorded. Without a fixed chord progression, metre or tempo, these performances were off-the-top examples of total spontaneity, but, possibly because the relationships between the participants were so close, the music is neither aimless nor chaotic. They follow each others' patterns in a controlled manner so that a definite unity of purpose prevails. Capitol failed to perceive any value in these pioneering efforts by Tristano and company, and they were released only after considerable hectoring by enthusiasts.

In a more conventional vein are the well-integrated band performances that make up the bulk of the output from these sessions. *Wow* has intense solos from all four men, while the bass and drums are as unobtrusive as they could possibly be. *Crosscurrent* is another finely tuned, intricate line in which the unified approach becomes apparent as each solo sounds like a logical continuation of the last; there is more than a hint of atonality in the running chromatic lines within all the contributions. Bauer's *Marionette* is a more relaxed, uncrowded piece which allows the composer to inspect its contours in calm fashion. Tristano is coolly detached and of the saxophones Marsh has the expressive edge here.

The Tristanoites were not averse to adopting the bop tenet of writing new melodic themes upon the chord changes of standard songs, and this is exactly what Konitz and Marsh do with *Sax of a Kind*, their joint exercise borrowed from *Fine and Dandy*. The seventh track is a quartet performance (minus the saxophones), ostensibly of Jerome Kern's *Yesterdays*, although the original melody is never stated as Tristano invents his own luminous and impressionistic variations, with some invaluable assistance from Bauer. As the piece progresses the piano and guitar lines intertwine in an extraordinary singularity of purpose, and the performance ends enigmatically without an attempt to retrace the opening atmosphere.

Here, on these recordings, is delineated a singular individualist's uncompromising attitudes to music. According to Lee Konitz, *this* was the real birth of the cool.

(The seven sides are not in themselves long enough to make an album, and reissues have been filled out with various unrelated material, not detailed below.)

LP
UK: (with Tadd Dameron and others:) *Crosscurrents*, **Affinity AFF 149**

Lee Konitz (as), Warne Marsh (ts), Lennie Tristano (p), Billy Bauer (g), Arnold Fishkin (sb), Harold Granowsky (d)
New York   4 March 1949   **Wow**
                                            Crosscurrent

omit Konitz and Marsh   **Yesterdays**

*as **Wow**, but Denzil Best (d) replaces Granowsky*
                23 April 1949   **Marionette**
                                            Sax of a Kind
                                            Intuition
                                            Digression

Other LPs
incl. tracks 1–7: (with Buddy DeFranco and others:) *Crosscurrents*
    USA: Capitol M 11060
    Netherlands: Capitol 5C052-80853
also incl. tracks 1–7:
    Japan: *Jazz Masters: Jazz of 50's Hot vs. Cool*, Capitol CR 8084;
    Cool and Quiet, Capitol ECJ 50076

Red Norvo: *The Red Norvo Trio*

Showing a commendable open-mindedness, Red Norvo, a star soloist since the 1930s on xylophone and then vibraphone, selected two young modernists as partners in a forward-looking trio that he formed in the spring of 1950. On guitar he chose Tal Farlow, a 29-year-old virtuoso from North Carolina, who had already worked with another vibraphonist, Margie Hyams, in a small group. For string bass, Norvo recruited a refugee from Lionel Hampton's orchestra, Charles Mingus, temporarily out of music and working for the US Post Office.

Norvo's style, rooted in the swing era, altered little in the context of his trio, but it sounded more modern on account of the accompaniment of Farlow and Mingus. Norvo was sophisticated harmonically, and he had found no difficulty playing with Charlie Parker and Dizzy Gillespie as early as 1945. In the trio's performances, his prodigious technique enabled him to manage comfortably tricky bop charts such as Denzil Best's *Move* and George Wallington's *Godchild*. It was only when Norvo improvised that his allegiance to older jazz tenets became obvious. His form of musical embroidery, with its skittering phrases and slight rhythmic stiffness, had its counterpart in Teddy Wilson's keyboard style. However, when accompanying Farlow's improvisations, he was invariably sensitive and unobtrusively supportive.

The sound of the trio was an interesting amalgamation of instrumental elements which had already been heard in two highly popular groups of the 1940s, the Nat Cole Trio (piano, guitar and bass) and the George Shearing Quintet (vibraphone, piano, guitar, bass and drums). With a resourceful bass in Mingus and chordal assistance from Farlow, Norvo reasoned that he did not need a drummer to disrupt a calm, orderly environment. The group turned out to be a pioneer of the 'chamber jazz' concept, and in some respects foreshadowed the establishment of the Modern Jazz Quartet a year or two later. The instrumentation undoubtedly gave Norvo's unit a cool sound. The vibraphone frequently conveys an air of detachment, even in the passionate hands of a Lionel Hampton or a Milt Jackson. The amplified guitar is not necessarily a cool instrument, but definitely so in the timbre achieved by Farlow, whose smooth round tone was in distinctive contrast to the raw tone of, say, T-Bone Walker, and certainly more melliflous than the sound of Django Reinhardt. Together, this particular combination of vibes and guitar reinforced the suspicion that studied effect was the name of the game. The sometimes overly precise, even pedantic, arrangements used by Norvo heightened that impression.

Godchild, although recorded in an exultant version by a studio band under Chubby Jackson's leadership, was perceived as one of the ultra-cool anthems; after all, it had been one of the dozen 'scriptures' handed down by

Miles Davis's Capitol band. Norvo's trio made at least three takes which afforded each man ample solo space, with Mingus making the most telling contribution in a nimble solo on the master version.

Swedish Pastry, a theme by guitarist Barney Kessel which Norvo had recorded with the composer and Swedish clarinettist Stan Hasselgård in 1947, also had a cool, smooth melodic shape which the trio delineated deftly. With its clipped contours enunciated in unison by Norvo and Farlow against Mingus's walking bass, the piece is ably developed by Norvo, Farlow and Mingus in turn. For all his reservations about the musical aims of the group, Mingus enjoyed a prominence accorded to no other bass player in modern jazz up to that time. He was truly a third solo voice rather than an occasional contributor.

The express delivery of the angular *Move* and its overt modernity are far removed from the rather old-fashioned amble through *I Can't Believe that You're in Love with Me*. Some of the arrangements, for example *I'll Remember April* and *September Song*, veer towards the writing of George Shearing at his blandest and verge on the somnolent, but then, in an unpretentious up-tempo offering such as *Zing! Went the Strings of my Heart*, everyone forgets to be cool and the music ignites. In this instance Norvo shows an aptitude for blending bop and swing phrasing, and the effect is most curious.

One case of an arrangement enhancing a performance is the dressing provided for Cole Porter's *I Get a Kick out of You*, in which fairly static unison passages by vibes and guitar are offset by running bass lines from Mingus. Norvo's slow burn approach and the intimate quality of the trio's music made the group popular not only with jazz musicians but in the smart supper clubs, where couples had no problems dancing to the friendlier tempos. *If I Had You*, taken at a real businessman's bounce, was part of that other repertory. They could even manage nifty turns to the excellent *Godchild* at a quickstep tempo! A winsome aspect of this side is Farlow's attractive rhythm-guitar stroking during the course of Mingus's solo.

Farlow's instrumental command is never in doubt. He was at that time among the most technically gifted guitarists alive, with a boundless capacity for inventing a plethora of ideas at any tempo. He would toss off the most complicated written parts with unfailing accuracy. He might have benefited, however, by some occasional percussive support other than the vibraphone. One senses his need for drums most obviously on *Swedish Pastry* when after his own solo, which cries out for a tasty backbeat, he does exactly that for Mingus, alternately plucking a held string and patting the body of his guitar, a process which helps the movement of the bass passage.

Norvo's trio was heard at its freshest in the year that Mingus was a member. After his departure it was never quite the same, although his replacement, Red Mitchell, was no mean bass player. The later Decca and Fantasy sides do not measure up to the unification that marked the material undertaken for the Discovery label. Norvo and Farlow also ultimately tired of the format, but by then their place in the development of 'chamber jazz' was assured, if sometimes perversely overlooked by many of the music's historians.

LP

USA: *The Red Norvo Trio*, **Savoy SJL 2212**

Red Norvo (vb), Tal Farlow (elg), Charles Mingus (sb)

Los Angeles	3 May 1950	**Swedish Pastry** (take 1)	
		Swedish Pastry (take 2)	
		Cheek to Cheek (alternate take)	
		Night and Day (alternate take)	
		Time and Tide	5
Chicago	31 Oct 1950	**September Song**	
		Move	
		I've Got You under my Skin	
		I'll Remember April	
		I Get a Kick out of You	10
		I Can't Believe that You're in Love with Me (alternate take)	
		Little White Lies (alternate take)	
		Have You Met Miss Jones?	
		Zing! Went the Strings of my Heart	
Los Angeles	13 April 1951	**If I Had You** (alternate take)	15
		This Can't Be Love (take 1)	
		This Can't Be Love (take 2)	
		This Can't Be Love (take 3)	
		Godchild (take 1)	
		Godchild (take 2)	20
		Godchild (take 3)	
		I'm Yours (alternate take)	
unknown place and date		**Mood Indigo**	
		Prelude to a Kiss	
		'Deed I Do	25

CDs

incl. tracks 1/2, 3–7, 10, 14, 16/17/18, 19/20/21, 22:
USA: *The Red Norvo–Charles Mingus–Tal Farlowe* [*sic*] *Trio*, vol.2, Vintage Jazz Classics VJC 1008-2

Other LPs:

same contents:
  Europe: Savoy WL 70540
tracks 2–3, 6–11, 15, 18, 21: *Move!*
  USA: Savoy MG 12088
  UK: Realm RM 158
  France: Savoy-Musidisc 30 SA 6019
incl. tracks 4–5, 12–13, 22:
  USA: (Norvo and George Shearing:) *Midnight on Cloud 69*, Savoy MG
  12093

* * *

Modern Jazz Quartet: *Modern Jazz Quartet*

The Modern Jazz Quartet is the longest-running small group in the history
of the music. It existed from 1952 to 1974, was re-formed in 1981 and is still
going strong in the 1990s. The origins of the foursome stretch back to the
1940s when Milt Jackson (vibraphone), John Lewis (piano) and Kenny
Clarke (drums) were members of Dizzy Gillespie's big band. Frequently, at
after-hours sessions, they would be joined by Gillespie's bass player Ray
Brown. This unit recorded under Milt Jackson's name for the Dee Gee label
in 1951, but it was not yet the MJQ. The music was loose and informal,
reflecting Jackson's personality.

With Ray Brown on the road with Jazz at the Philharmonic, Percy Heath,
who had worked with Lewis and Clarke in Paris in 1948, was recruited for
bass duties, and Lewis became musical director of the small cooperative.
The MJQ signed to record under that name for Prestige in 1952, and the
disciplined, shaping hand of Lewis was immediately evident in its debut
recordings. Although the band had only four instruments, Lewis created
detailed and precise arrangements for optimum effect, with frequent use of
unison lines by vibes and piano. He even wrote bass parts for Heath and had
definite instructions for his vastly experienced drummer. Lewis, who had
been a contributing arranger and pianist for Miles Davis's nonet, liked the
cool sounds and the MJQ was certainly a cool little band, a feeling enhanced
by the detached sound of the vibes and his own sparse piano style. Little
was left to chance in Lewis's careful approach, and perhaps for this reason
the quartet's music did sometimes sound a trifle too calculated for comfort.

The pianist's knowledge of and interest in European classical music was
also reflected in his compositions for the quartet, most especially in such
early pieces as *Vendome*, *The Queen's Fancy* and *Milano*. Bach-like phrases,
contrapuntal playing and echoes of Tudor melodies were apt to crop up in

Lewis's tunes. Sometimes they were incongruous, often engaging. Just when listeners might feel the atmosphere was verging towards the twee, Jackson, and occasionally Lewis, would cut loose with improvisations that proclaimed their musical origins. Lewis also wrote some splendid original melodies, not least the eminently attractive *Django*, which became a jazz standard, and the rather neglected *Delaunay's Dilemma*, a graceful and charming line which the group accorded a lightly swinging and entirely appropriate treatment.

The quartet's music was primarily cerebral. Jackson was the only passionate soloist and the tight arrangements provided him with too few chances to be his extrovert self, at least in the early life of the band when recording procedures dictated performances of limited duration. This was chamber jazz, put together with patience, precision and some dedication. By endeavouring to forge links between contemporary American jazz and European art music, Lewis and cohorts were treading new ground and anticipating by many years the later dabblings with so-called Third Stream. The neat, well-tailored nature of these sounds carried considerable appeal to a much wider audience than hard-core jazz listeners. The music was understandable and logical, with none of the raucous, spontaneous edge that is apt to frighten off middle-of-the-road concertgoers. Lewis and his companions seemingly felt more at home in concert or recital halls than in the informal atmosphere of jazz clubs. Larger, more attentive audiences provided fewer distractions than the usual patrons drinking at the bar in nightclubs.

La Ronde Suite, actually four variations on an old composition by Lewis entitled *Two Bass Hit*, was ideally cast for a concert context since it presented each member of the group in turn showing off his instrumental prowess. The tune had actually been recorded a couple of years earlier at the MJQ's inaugural session in a much less self-conscious version. *The Suite*, by contrast, places the emphasis on organization and arrangement. Lewis, for all his obsession with the classical element, did not feel hidebound by convention, particularly when he was recasting standard tunes. His frameworks for *All the Things You Are*, *Autumn in New York* and *But Not for Me* afford us new perspectives on these familiar songs by Jerome Kern, Vernon Duke and George Gershwin. *All the Things You Are* has an ethereal introduction, but soon settles into a free-wheeling groove which is to the liking of Jackson. The group gives *Autumn in New York* a slow, meditative exposition, and there is an effective striking clock sequence before the paraphrase of the theme. *But Not for Me* carries an out-of-tempo introduction but quickly moves into time, with Clarke pushing the beat forward with his immaculate brush strokes on the snare drum.

Actually Clarke, the father of modern drumming, is one of the reasons why the first edition of the quartet was so satisfying. His successor, Connie Kay, could never match Clarke's smooth, easy swing. Clarke disliked the tiny cymbals, triangles and other percussive paraphernalia which Kay readily deployed, leading some observers to suggest his drumming had too many effects and too little substance. It was no real surprise that Clarke grew tired of the MJQ's constrictions and sought more red-blooded jazz activity.

However, the MJQ undoubtedly attracted many listeners to jazz, and the members were great ambassadors for the music, earning respect and forcing listeners to take the group seriously. This was part of the trouble, for under Lewis's influence they were a shade too serious in demeanour and about their art.

LP
USA: *Modern Jazz Quartet,* **Prestige PR 24005**

Milt Jackson (vb), John Lewis (p), Percy Heath (sb), Kenny Clarke (d)

New York	22 Dec 1952	**All the Things You Are**	
		La Ronde	
		Vendome	
		Rose of the Rio Grande	
	25 June 1953	**The Queen's Fancy**	5
		Delaunay's Dilemma	
		Autumn in New York	
		But Not for Me	
	23 Dec 1954	**Django**	
		One Bass Hit	10
		Milano	
	9 Jan 1955	**La Ronde Suite**	

Connie Kay (d) replaces Clarke

	2 July 1955	**Ralph's New Blues**	
		All of You	
		I'll Remember April	15
		Gershwin ballad medley:	
		Soon	
		Love Walked in	
		Our Love is Here to Stay	
		For You, for Me, for Evermore	
		Concorde	
		Softly as in a Morning Sunrise	

CDs
incl. tracks 1–4:

USA: *MJQ*, Original Jazz Classics OJCCD 125-2
tracks 5–12: *Django*
  USA: Original Jazz Classics OJCCD 057-2
  Japan: Prestige VJD 1515
tracks 13–18: *Concorde*
  USA: Original Jazz Classics OJCCD 002-2
  Japan: Prestige VJD 1534

Other LPs

same contents:
  country unknown: Prestige 81106
tracks 1–12: *First Recordings!*
  USA: Prestige PRST 7749
  Germany: Bellaphon BJS 40157
incl. tracks 1–4: *MJQ*
  USA: Original Jazz Classics OJC 125; Prestige LP 7059
  UK: Esquire 32-134
  France: Prestige HTX 40406
  Japan: Prestige SMJ 6598
  country unknown: Prestige 68446
tracks 5–12: *Django*
  USA: Original Jazz Classics OJC 057; Prestige LP 7057
  UK: Esquire 32-124
  France: Voix de son Maitre FELP 10026; Prestige CPRX 240576
  Japan: Prestige SMJ 6502
tracks 13–18: *Concorde*
  USA: Original Jazz Classics OJC 002; Prestige LP 7005
  UK: Esquire 32-024
  France: Barclay 84028; Voix de son Maitre FELP 10017
tracks 1, 4, 7–8, 14–16, 18: *The Modern Jazz Quartet Plays for Lovers*
  USA: Prestige PR 7421
  France: Prestige CPRX 240755
tracks 2–3, 5–6, 9, 11–12, 17: *The Modern Jazz Quartet Plays Jazz Classics*
  USA: Prestige PR 7425
  Germany: Bellaphon BJS 40110
incl. tracks 2–3, 5–6, 9, 11, 17–18:
  Italy: *The Modern Jazz Quartet*, Giants of Jazz LPJT 56
details unknown: *MJQ*, Masterworks CJZLP 6

Cassettes

incl. tracks 1–4:
  USA: *MJQ*, Original Jazz Classics OJC 5125

tracks 5–12:
  USA: *Django*, Original Jazz Classics OJC 5057
tracks 13–18: *Concorde*
  USA: Original Jazz Classics OJCC 5002
  UK: Prestige Real Time PRC 7005
incl. tracks 2–3, 5–6, 9, 11, 17–18:
  Italy: *The Modern Jazz Quartet*, Giants of Jazz MCJT 56

* * *

Shorty Rogers: *Shorty Rogers and his Giants*

Several years after the release of the **Birth of the Cool** recordings, the instrumentation employed in Miles Davis's nonet began to appear in groups on the West Coast of the United States. In the case of the Gerry Mulligan tentet, which added a second trumpet to the front line, there was no real surprise, since Mulligan had been closely involved with Davis's group and simply wished to continue writing for such an ensemble. Mulligan even made a fresh recording of *Rocker*, which had figured in the nonet's repertory.

By a strange coincidence, in the same month of 1953 which saw the recording debut of Mulligan's new band, trumpeter Shorty Rogers, who had written for Woody Herman and Stan Kenton among others, took his nine-piece unit into the Los Angeles studios of Victor for two sessions which were to be influential in the evolution of West Coast jazz. Like many of his contemporaries, Rogers had been completely won over by the Miles Davis sides and wished to emulate their sound. Shorty Rogers and his Giants carried an instrumentation that differed in only one respect from the Davis blueprint: tenor saxophone was substituted for baritone. The leader's arrangements, however, were quite another matter, being slick, tidy and rather conventional. There was none of the challenge or originality to be found in the charts by Gil Evans, John Lewis and Mulligan that had made the sound of Davis's band so memorable. One or two of the compositions were attractive, but they fell short of the collective inspiration that had shaped Davis's library of tunes.

Rogers's adaptation of the cool had already been heard on six numbers recorded by Capitol in the autumn of 1951, when his octet had been lacking a trombonist. The trumpeter's tidy but slightly twee arranging methods became one of the hallmarks of the West Coast style. There was a bland, cloying quality about a Rogers ensemble that was to be repeated in so many Hollywood bands, including those of such leaders as Marty Paich and Dave Pell. The same sound would also infuse Howard Rumsey's Lighthouse All Stars and Bob Cooper's groups. A curiously flat, dead sound, the fact that it was so repetitious and ubiquitous was explained by the presence of so many of the same faces in all these bands. French horn player John Graas, for example, seemed to crop up in most Hollywood groups, along with alto saxophonist Art Pepper. Jimmy Giuffre was another who would turn up with predictable frequency. There was a definite clique of highly proficient white musicians who cornered much of the jazz market (and most of the studio assignments) in Los Angeles.

To be fair to Rogers, he equipped himself with an array of impressive soloists in the Giants, notably Pepper, later replaced by Bud Shank, and pianist Hampton Hawes, associated with a much gutsier form of jazz but adaptable to this context, although he was, on his own admission, a poor reader. Hawes, Sonny Clark and Buddy Collette were three black musicians who were occasionally used on Hollywood dates, but their musical preferences lay elsewhere. Rogers made no attempt to emulate Davis in his trumpet solos, for, while he was certainly proficient, there was no hint of Davis's beauty or clarity of thought in his efforts.

In the rather stiff version of *The Pesky Serpent* space is found for no fewer than five soloists, of whom trombonist Milt Bernhart and Pepper are the most impressive. Hawes is guilty of some misfingering and Rogers sounds bland. Giuffre is just warming to his task when he has to stop. *Diablo's Dance* is a fast-moving showcase for Hawes, who enunciates the staccato, ascending theme which the horns then repeat. The real joy, though, is Hawes's fluent improvisation, filled with the blues phrases that were such an integral part of his style. His brisk, single-note lines sound somewhat at odds with the lumbering ensemble.

Easily the most attractive of Rogers's lines is the winsome *Pirouette*, in which he uses the ensemble textures in a way reminiscent of Mulligan's writing. The melody is a good one, and the variation is cleverly related to it. Rogers interweaves ensemble passages behind segments of the solos by Pepper, the leader and Giuffre. Taking a leaf out of Tadd Dameron's book, he also presages the piano solo with an eight-bar ensemble passage. A feature of the theme's contrasting melody is one bar when the time is deliberately suspended, producing a curiously attractive effect within an otherwise smooth, even performance. Drummer Shelly Manne's meticulous brushwork and accents that are faithfully attuned to the ensemble lines are excellent examples of his thoughtful craftsmanship.

Indian Club, with a nice rising tempo set by Manne, lacks any pretence of subtlety and is a far cry from, say, *Move* by Davis's nonet. Rogers contributes an energetic opening solo, and, although Giuffre is also heard, it is the vibrant Pepper who steals the show. *Morpo* sounds contrived and is again too stiffly performed to allow for relaxed solos. Pepper gives it his best shot and Hawes is listenable, but the contributions from Giuffre and Rogers are as staid as the rhythm. The leader endeavours to make greater use of the

tonal colours available on the slow *Bunny*, which is a most effective arrangement. Pepper springs a surprise by doubling the tempo and the device is not
misplaced. The only intrusive element is the use of a triangle, which contributes nothing other than an unwelcome distraction.

Pleasantly inoffensive but hardly stirring stuff is *Powder Puff*, which finds
Bernhart and Hawes making nonsense of the twiddly arrangement and
pointed title by delivering powerfully macho solos. Pepper's unforced elegance makes one believe he could have held his own in Davis's group and
his sound would have blended as well with Davis as Konitz's did. *Mambo del
Crow* is an authentic mambo complete with excellent rhythmic percussion by
Manne, an amusing crow call, Latin style piano by Hawes and assorted
chants from the bandsmen. Manne takes a superb solo, making effective use
of timbales, and Bernhart weighs in with a virile trombone statement. But on
this track there is no justification for the chosen instrumentation.

All too often the Giants sound mechanical, yet we know that this was not
the natural stance of most of these musicians, so some of the fault must lie in
the direction. The music has not worn nearly so well as the **Birth of the Cool**
material, and that is usually the fate of blurred copies of originals. Rogers
merely adopted an instrumentation with a sound that appealed to him, but
was unable to use its pastel textures in a strikingly original way. Where the
West Coasters went wrong was their perception of cool as a fixed style
rather than as a successful experiment by some of the sharpest musical
minds who regarded the episode as a brief phase in their development.

LP

USA: *Shorty Rogers and his Giants*, **RCA LPM 1195**

*Shorty Rogers (tpt), Milt Bernhart (tb), John Graas (french horn), Gene Englund
(tuba), Art Pepper (as), Jimmy Giuffre (ts), Hampton Hawes (p), Joe Mondragon
(sb), Shelly Manne (d)*

Los Angeles	12 Jan 1953	**Powder Puff**	
		The Pesky Serpent	
		Bunny	
		Pirouette	
	15 Jan 1953	**Morpo**	5
		Diablo's Dance	
		Mambo del Crow	
		Indian Club	

Rogers (tpt), Giuffre (cl, ts, bar), Pete Jolly (p), Curtis Counce (sb), Manne (d)

10 Sept 1954	**Joycycle**	
	The Lady is a Tramp	**10**
	The Goof and I	
	My Little Suede Shoes	

CDs

incl. tracks 1–8: *Short Stops*
  USA: Bluebird 5917-2 RB
  UK: RCA CD 90209

Other LPs

same contents:
  France: RCA PM 43549
  Japan: RCA RA 5403; RCA RGP 1097; RCA RJL 2622
incl. tracks 1–8: *Short Stops*
  USA: Bluebird 5917-1 RB 11
  Europe: RCA NL 85917

Cassettes

incl. tracks 1–8: *Short Stops*
  USA: Bluebird 5917-4 RB 11
  Europe: RCA NK 85917
incl. tracks 3, 5, 11:
  Europe: *Shorty's Greatest Hits*, RCA CK 89807

* * *

Gerry Mulligan: *Gerry Mulligan Quartet*

Formed six months before the MJQ and 3,000 miles away was a quartet of a very different stripe which bestrode the West Coast and cool-jazz categories. The Gerry Mulligan Quartet was one of those happy accidents that litter the history of jazz. Mulligan, as already discussed above, had made significant contributions to Miles Davis's **Birth of the Cool**, both as an arranger and the nonet's baritone saxophonist. On arrival in Hollywood in the summer of 1952, Mulligan was keen to do more instrumental work and cast about for some suitable sidemen in the Los Angeles area.

Trumpeter Chet Baker, a 22-year-old who had already worked with Charlie Parker and was lately discharged from the army, auditioned for the assignment and was given the job. Meanwhile the leader called pianist

George Wallington in New York and asked him to come out to join his new quintet. Wallington declined and, because Mulligan could not find a suitable replacement, the famous piano-less quartet was born. Bob Whitlock was his initial choice for bass duties, and he hired Chico Hamilton as the drummer, although bassist Carson Smith and drummer Larry Bunker were the group's rhythm section later on.

This intimate environment enabled Mulligan to get through more playing than opportunities had allowed for several years. His bluff, cheery baritone formed a nicely contrasting sound to the lyrical, cool tones of Baker's trumpet. An instinctive player with a penchant for graceful, melodic lines, Baker flourished among the popular songs and catchy originals worked up by Mulligan. Neither musician was hampered by the absence of keyboard feeds, although each would often provide helpful riffs when the other was improvising. A natural outcome of this procedure was that an abundance of contrapuntal interweaving between saxophone and trumpet became one of the distinctive features of the group's recordings. The musical understanding within this partnership was remarkably close, each man seemingly able to anticipate the next thought of the other. Their personal relationship was less harmonious, yet these discords were buried when it was time to play. Mulligan has stated on more than one occasion that working with Baker provided some of the most inspired and satisfying musical experiences of his career.

The quartet existed as a working unit for just about a year, but before personal problems split it asunder an impressive collection of recordings was made for the newly formed Pacific Jazz label. Such well-shaped and neat Mulligan compositions as *Line for Lyons* and *Walkin' Shoes* produced cool, reflective performances from the principals, both of whom excelled in the unhurried climate of an even medium tempo. However, neither was averse to accelerating a few notches and Baker's staccato piece *Freeway* finds them bowling confidently along. *Carioca*, on the other hand, suggests a liking for the occasional dash of exotica, confirmed also by *Frenesi*. The slower the beat, the cooler Mulligan and Baker became, and in pieces such as *Moonlight in Vermont*, *My Funny Valentine* and *The Nearness of You* they are completely unruffled, achieving a sonorous instrumental blend that sounds like a scaled-down **Birth of the Cool**.

In contrast to these somewhat detached ballad inspections, their assessments of intrinsically hearty pieces such as *The Lady is a Tramp*, *I'm Beginning to See the Light* and *Makin' Whoopee* are brimming with bounce and bonhomie. In *Love Me or Leave Me* and *Aren't You Glad You're You?* perky, whimsical moods are struck. For such an intimate ensemble the range of textures and moods achieved was surprisingly broad.

Although a basically intuitive musician, Baker was not the poor technician depicted by some commentators. Certainly, he generally opted to play in the middle range of his instrument, but his vivid improvisation of the presto *Freeway* shows an ample technique at work and intelligent use of the trumpet's full scope, and much the same could be said of his firm contribution to Mulligan's *Bark for Barksdale*, on which the 'barking' is by no means confined to the saxophonist.

There is good reason to suppose that Baker and Mulligan in this intimate milieu, without a piano, did not welcome undue distraction, for attentive listening was one of the prerequisites for their passages of simultaneous improvisation. Perhaps this factor led them to insist that the drummer, whether Hamilton or Bunker, accompany with brushes, laying down a crispy, springy swish rather than a penetrating cymbal sizzle. No group before or since has relied so heavily on brushes, which undoubtedly contributed to the already unusual sound. Hamilton, in particular, was a master of this percussive art, and his snare-drum accents and bass-drum punctuations were always pertinent to the moment.

If Mulligan's deep-throated playing occasionally veered towards the lugubrious, it was more often robustly expressive. His rhythmic perception was different from that of many modernists; sometimes he would slip into a two-beat, dixieland feel which gave his solos a dancing quality. His liking for improvised ensemble playing also harks back to earlier jazz styles. Hear the ending of *I'm Beginning to See the Light*; it is pure dixieland.

Mulligan's compositions were usually new tunes in their own right, but he was not unwilling to follow the bop procedure of basing a piece on a popular song. Thus his *Swing House* is cut from the chord progression of *Sweet Georgia Brown.* The one direct link between the quartet and the **Birth of the Cool**, apart from Mulligan himself, was his seminal composition *Jeru*, which served to inspire Chet Baker as it did Miles Davis before him. This piece, perhaps more than any other from his early career, demonstrates Mulligan's considerable originality as a composer.

CD

Italy: *Gerry Mulligan Quartet*, Giants of Jazz CD 53027

Chet Baker (tpt), Gerry Mulligan (bar), Bob Whitlock (sb), Chico Hamilton (d)

| Los Angeles | 16 Aug 1952 | **Bernie's Tune** | |
| | | **Lullaby of the Leaves** | |

Carson Smith (sb) replaces Whitlock

San Francisco	2 Sept 1952	**Line for Lyons**	
		Carioca	
		My Funny Valentine	5
		Bark for Barksdale	

Whitlock (sb) replaces Smith

Los Angeles	15–16 Oct 1952	**Nights at the Turntable**	
		Frenesi	
		Aren't You Glad You're You?	
		Walkin' Shoes	10
		Freeway	

Smith (sb) replace Whitlock

San Francisco	3 Jan 1953	**The Lady is a Tramp**
		Turnstile
		Moonlight in Vermont

Larry Bunker (d) replaces Hamilton

Los Angeles	24 Feb 1953	**Cherry**	15
		Makin' Whoopee	
	27 April 1953	**Love Me or Leave Me**	
		Jeru	
		Swing House	
	29–30 April 1953	**I May be Wrong** (take ?)	20
		I'm Beginning to See the Light (take ?)	
		The Nearness of You	
		Tea for Two	
	20 May 1953	**Five Brothers**	

Other CDs

plus additional tracks and takes:

USA: *The Complete Pacific Jazz and Capitol Recordings of the Original Gerry Mulligan Quartet and Tentette with Chet Baker*, Mosaic MD 3-102

LPs

plus additional tracks and takes:

USA: *The Complete Pacific Jazz and Capitol Recordings of the Original Gerry Mulligan Quartet and Tentette with Chet Baker*, Mosaic MR 5-102
tracks 1–6, 10–14, 17, 19–22:

Italy: *Gerry Mulligan Quartet with Chet Baker*, Giants of Jazz LPJT 61
incl. tracks 2, 7–9, 15–16, 18–23:

USA: *Gerry Mulligan Quartet*, World Pacific 1207
incl. tracks 1–2, 7–11:

USA: *Freeway*, Blue Note LT 1101
incl. tracks 3–6, 12–14:

USA: *Gerry Mulligan/Chet Baker*, Prestige PR 24016;

Gerry Mulligan–Paul Desmond, Fantasy 3-220; Fantasy 8082; Original Jazz Classics OJC 273
France: title unknown, America 30 AM 6070
Germany: *Gerry Mulligan/Chet Baker*, Bellaphon BLST 6528
incl. tracks 1–2, 17–23:
  UK: title unknown, Vogue LAE 12050

Cassettes

tracks 1–6, 10–14, 17, 19–22:
  Italy: *Gerry Mulligan Quartet with Chet Baker*, Giants of Jazz MCJT 61
incl. tracks 3–6, 12–14:
  USA: *Gerry Mulligan–Paul Desmond*, Original Jazz Classics OJC 5273

* * *

Paul Desmond: *Bossa Antigua*

For the greater part of his career, alto saxophonist Paul Desmond was ensconced as a permanent and invariably pleasing fixture in pianist Dave Brubeck's quartet. After a 16-year run with this group, Desmond finally broke from that rather arid musical climate, and for the last decade of his life worked as a freelance and was heard in more creative contexts alongside the Modern Jazz Quartet, Gerry Mulligan and Jim Hall.

This superior album dates from a period when Desmond was seeking fresh musical stimulation in the recording studios, where he could hand-pick kindred spirits for albums under his own leadership. A most sensitive musician with a light, dry tone and a polished, melodic turn of phrase, Desmond shared certain points of style with both Lee Konitz and Art Pepper. He was fond of using the upper register of his instrument, and his solos were invariably studded with witty quotations. He was a supremely relaxed performer who swung with the ease and unhurried eloquence that are associated with such saxophonists as Lester Young, Zoot Sims and Wardell Gray. His playing was infused with a charm and gentleness rarely found in jazz. If his solos occasionally seemed a trifle too studied, this was not usually the case. On the other hand, Desmond's personality was such that he never sought to portray raw emotions but rather a calm, cool and cerebral air.

His partnership with guitarist Jim Hall was especially felicitous. Here were two men closely attuned to the same expressive wavelength, each receptive to the thoughts and moods of the other. Like Desmond, Hall favoured a quiet, restrained lyricism which had been used to excellent advantage in the groups of Sonny Rollins and Art Farmer. Perhaps as an

antidote to years of listening to crashing piano chords, Desmond deliberately dispensed with keyboards for this mellifluous session. In any event,
Hall's responsive and sophisticated accompaniment ensured a supportive
and firm cushion for the leader's invention. Bass player Gene Wright, a
longstanding companion in Brubeck's combo, was a sound choice, and
drummer Connie Kay of the Modern Jazz Quartet, playing with flexibility
and taste, completed the group.

In the early 1960s, when samba rhythms started to infiltrate jazz to an
unprecedented degree, many leading soloists were tempted to dabble in the
merger of samba and cool known as 'bossa nova', not only because the
rhythms were liltingly attractive, but also, perhaps, in the hope of register-
ing the sort of commercial success which had been enjoyed by Stan Getz.
Desmond, who with Brubeck had been playing all sorts of exotic rhythms
and in bizarre metres for years, appeared to relish the subtle, shifting beat,
and in this group of elegant performances released a torrent of beautifully
articulated improvisations. He was gifted with the instinct of perfect self-
editing, and his assured and understated contributions are felicitous, symmetrical and perfectly shaded. His feeling for Latin jazz expression is also
neatly displayed in his own idiomatic melodies, which account for five of
the eight tracks. They contain the instant appeal which is to be found in the
works of the leading Brazilian samba musicians. Desmond had suggested a
talent for composition elsewhere, but the beautifully resolved pattern of
Bossa Antigua, for example, indicates his affection for the winsome bossa
nova form. His feel for this music is authentic and as valid, though much less
well known, as Stan Getz's contributions in a similar context.

There is a mood of patient understanding between all four players as they
gently test the contours of each song. Only two standards are included, and
in the case of *The Night Has a Thousand Eyes* this was a tune already firmly
cast by tradition in a Latin climate. Jim Hall, who had previously recorded a
bossa version of the tune with Sonny Rollins, may have been responsible for
persuading Desmond to try it. It fits nicely with the originals, but so, for that
matter, does *A Ship without a Sail*, which comfortably adapts to a samba
setting, even though composer Richard Rodgers did not perceive it in this
dimension.

The danger with any enterprise of this kind is that the unchanging dance
rhythm is apt to pall and become repetitive, particularly if there are too
many of the moderate tempos which were the performance norm. Conscious of this potential trap, Desmond sought to vary the mix with pieces
such as *Alianca*, which is full of pep and noticeably less placid than some of
the other items. He and Hall also devised cunning arrangements as a way of
sustaining interest. Their unison work on *The Girl from East 9th Street* certainly enhances an already pretty melody. Hall's acute sensibility is a constant delight, whether he is playing a hypnotic, recurring figure as on *Bossa*

Antigua, limning the melody statement of *El Gato* or feeding delicate chordal assists as in *Samba Cantina*. His solos share with Desmond's an attention to detail within a brilliantly logical design.

Kay, unsatisfactory in more muscular company, is the right percussionist for this assignment, providing meticulous, punctilious rhythmic patterns with a light touch essential for the two soloists. Similarly, Wright pads along with stealth and grace, underpinning the rhythm and never clashing with Hall's chordal clusters.

Paul Desmond, in any situation, was worth listening to for the flowing, delicate lyricism that infused all his music, but with Hall and bossa nova he dispensed that quality in even more generous measures, so suitable was the context.

LP

USA: *Bossa Antigua*, RCA LPM 3320 and LSP 3320

Paul Desmond (as), Jim Hall (elg), Gene Wright (sb), Connie Kay (d)

New York	28 July 1964	Samba Cantina
		Bossa Antigua
	29 July 1964	A Ship without a Sail
		The Night Has a Thousand Eyes
	20 Aug 1964	The Girl from East 9th Street
		Curacao Doloroso
		El Gato
	8 Sept 1964	Alianca

CDs

same contents:
  Japan: RCA R25J 1045
plus additional tracks:
  USA: *The Complete Recordings of the Paul Desmond Quartet with Jim Hall*, Mosaic MD 4-120

Other LPs

same contents:
  UK: RCA RD 7701 and SF 7701
  France: RCA PL 45691
plus additional tracks:
  USA: *The Complete Recordings of the Paul Desmond Quartet with Jim Hall*, Mosaic MR 6-120

Part 3: Hard bop

Clifford Brown and Max Roach: *Clifford Brown and Max Roach*

Hard bop became a cause and a positive movement in 1954 with the formation of two quintets in which the motivating forces were pioneer bop drummers Max Roach and Art Blakey. It was appropriate that these potent percussionists should be up front in their respective bands, because the drums took on an even more definitive role as the catalyst in hard bop.

It was particularly ironic that Roach decided to form a new band in California, where for several seasons the super-cool West Coast sounds had reigned supreme. In the spring of 1954 he invited the brilliant young trumpeter Clifford Brown to join him from New York to co-lead a combo which would provide positive alternatives to the Los Angeles style. Brown had modelled his style on that of the virtuoso Fats Navarro, but, unlike the first modernists, he did not emerge from the big bands. His workshop milieu had been rhythm-and-blues groups which offered greater freedom to soloists, but as the name implied emphasized both the beat and the 12-bar form. Later, these characteristics were carried over into hard bop by a flock of other soloists from the genre – Blue Mitchell, Junior Cook, Tommy and Stanley Turrentine, Johnny Griffin and many more. Brown did work briefly with Lionel Hampton's orchestra, which synthesized big-band swing and rhythm and blues during the early 1950s. However, the trumpeter had little stomach for grinding section work and escaped from Hampton's ranks at the earliest opportunity following a controversial European tour in 1953. Thus he promptly answered Roach's request on the understanding that both men would select the rest of the personnel from the pick of the Hollywood musicians.

The Clifford Brown–Max Roach group existed for around two and a half years and left behind a body of music that encapsulated all the best virtues of hard bop. After some experiments with personnel – tenor saxophonist Teddy Edwards, pianist Carl Perkins and bassist George Bledsoe were charter members – a settled line-up emerged with tenor player Harold Land, pianist Richie Powell (brother of Bud Powell) and bassist George Morrow. Land, from Texas, had a muscular tone and a down-to-earth, unflashy style that served to complement the daring and dash of Brown's manner. Powell and the steadfast Morrow were ideal anchormen. The five points of the group were in perfect accord, which resulted in an unusually close unity of purpose. When Land eventually departed, his replacement, Sonny Rollins, although a much more inventive and original player, failed to fit in as harmoniously as his predecessor.

The numerous felicities of this tightly knit working band were seldom better displayed than in these dynamic performances. The group successfully continued a tradition of playing that had been established by Charlie Parker's quintet of 1947. There were differences, mainly to do with greater rhythmic drive, in no small measure owing to the fact that Roach was an even better drummer in 1955 than he had been eight years earlier. Brown, like Parker before him, discovered that Roach was a repository of rhythmic subtlety, a source of consistent inspiration and urgency in the act of improvisation. An almost telepathic understanding existed between them. The co-leaders projected a controlled heat, a coordinated discipline that never denied expressiveness but stopped short of an emotional deluge.

Such was the perspicacity of this wholly integrated band that they could even invest an old and creaking warhorse such as *What am I Here For?* with an agreeably surprising zest, zipping through the unpromising chord sequence at a fast clip and discovering unimagined beauty along the way. Brown made significant contributions to the repertory in the nicely turned *Daahoud*, the headlong charge that is *The Blues Walk* and, best of all, the piquant melody of *Joy Spring*, so evocative of its subject matter. Both Bud Powell's atmospheric *Parisian Thoroughfare*, on which Brown and Land skilfully simulate traffic sounds, and Duke Jordan's minor masterpiece *Jordu* had been in the group's book since its inception, while the exotic mood of *Delilah* was cleverly exploited in a very pretty arrangement on which Land plays a vamping counter-melody to Brown's muted theme statement. In Brown's sweeping solo, the commentary supplied by Roach is worthy of special study, as he seemingly anticipates every nuance of his co-leader's line. Their compatibility is further enunciated in the four-bar exchanges that flow between trumpeter and drummer. Anyone doubting the musicality of the finest jazz drummers would do well to hear Roach in this collection. His use of sticks and brushes is exemplary, his accents and fills are integral parts of each performance and his beat never falters, no matter the complexity of the cross-rhythms he compounds. His playing, ever crisp and tasteful, bespeaks an intellect of logic and clarity.

By all accounts Brown was a warm, outgoing, unaffected and humble man. His essentially optimistic outlook was reflected in an adventurous style, which was vibrant and cheerful, far removed from the moody melancholia of Miles Davis. Brown's good-natured wit was infectious and coloured the band's music. Thus, Powell humorously interjects wry quotations from *Can Can* and *The Marseillaise* into an apt arrangement of *Parisian Thoroughfare* to epitomize the happy, carefree spirit that prevailed.

Brown was a prototype hard bopper. He, together with his main influence, Navarro, combined three often unrelated streams in bop trumpet playing: beautiful timbre, super technique, creative improvisation. His playing was to affect deeply almost all the young brassmen that followed, most prominently Lee Morgan, Freddie Hubbard and Woody Shaw. Others would synthesize aspects of Brown's style with borrowings from Davis's.

The pivotal position of Brown is shown by the fact that early in 1954 he had briefly served in a short-lived edition of the Jazz Messengers (then billed as the Art Blakey Quintet) which recorded at Birdland. He could so easily have been a permanent star in that other vital unit but for Roach's offer.

CD

USA: *Clifford Brown and Max Roach*, **EmArcy 814645–2**

Clifford Brown (tpt), Harold Land (ts), Richie Powell (p), George Morrow (sb), Max Roach (d)

Los Angeles	2 Aug 1954	**Delilah**
		Parisian Thoroughfare
	3 Aug 1954	**Jordu**
	6 Aug 1954	**Joy Spring**
		Daahoud (take 1)
New York	24 Feb 1955	**The Blues Walk**
	25 Feb 1955	**What am I Here For?**

LPs

same contents:
   USA: Mercury MG 36036; Trip TLP 5540
   France: Mercury LP 7089
   Netherlands: Mercury 6336.322
   Japan: EmArcy 15 PJ 2018; EmArcy 18 PJ 2043; EmArcy EXPR 1033; Mercury IMP 10011; Mercury SFX 10550
plus additional tracks: *The Quintet*, vol.1–2
   USA: Mercury EMS 2–403 and EMS 2–407
   Netherlands: Mercury 6641.575 and 6641.644
   Japan: Mercury BT 5125/26 and BT 5139/40
   Brazil: Mercury 6643.044 and 6641.644
incl. tracks 1–5:
   UK: *Tribute to Brownie*, EmArcy EJL 1250
incl. tracks 2–5: *The Immortal Clifford Brown*
   USA: Limelight 28201; Limelight 28601
   UK: Mercury 20090–1 MCL

Horace Silver: *Horace Silver and the Jazz Messengers*; Art Blakey: *At the Jazz Corner of the World, vol.2*

A lengthy parade of superior soloists passed through the ranks of Art Blakey's Jazz Messengers in the 1950s – trumpeters Kenny Dorham, Donald Byrd, Bill Hardman and Lee Morgan, saxophonists Hank Mobley, Jackie McLean, Johnny Griffin, Benny Golson and Wayne Shorter, pianists Horace Silver, Sam Dockery, Junior Mance, Walter Bishop Jr and Bobby Timmons. Those who weren't good enough didn't last long; Blakey blew them away.

Blakey, who with Max Roach defined the rhythmic surge and intensity of hard bop, was a leader who sought out brilliant young players with fire in their bellies and an unquenchable thirst for driving swing. In Blakey's opinion, if listeners' feet were not tapping and fingers not snapping, the Jazz Messengers were not getting their message through.

Almost any of the Jazz Messengers' recordings from this period would be representative because of Blakey's huge inspirational presence and pulse. However, the quintet's first album, under Silver's leadership, shows the pianist's permanent contributions to the group's spirit and the direction it would take, while the live recordings of the 1950s have a special atmosphere of uninhibited excitement, for here was a band which ignited in the presence of a warmly responsive audience.

Silver was in the vanguard of the hard-bop movement from the outset and proved to be one of its most influential and charismatic figures. Hired by the cool and bop tenor saxophonist Stan Getz and brought to New York in 1950, he was soon recording with Miles Davis, J. J. Johnson and other leading lights. After making some spirited trio sessions for Blue Note he was asked to assemble a quintet for a further album; thus the Jazz Messengers were reborn in the autumn of 1954.

Blakey had used this group name for a Blue Note date with an octet as early as 1947, and he was the man to stir the rhythm for Silver. On bass, young Doug Watkins, a recent arrival from Detroit, was recruited. Bop veteran Dorham, a late developer whose personal sound and articulate melodic ideas had suddenly come into perfect focus, was an excellent choice to partner tenor saxophonist Mobley, still relatively unknown despite a recent stint in Dizzy Gillespie's combo. Dorham, incidentally, was a member of the original 1947 Messengers. In the group's reincarnation, Silver was clearly the motivating force in the four-sided role of composer, arranger, pianist and musical director. Then just turned 26, he possessed refreshing originality. His infectious piano style owed a debt to Bud Powell, but Silver had a bubbling, optimistic perspective, a bright, cheerful quality expressed in a percussive touch and a penchant for outrageous quotations and soulful, gospel phrases. His busy, choppy accompaniment kept soloists on their toes.

The blues had been somewhat neglected by cool and West Coast musicians, and Silver's music was a positive reaffirmation of the durability of a constant form in jazz. Similarly his use of gospel music showed how the old could inform and refresh the new. Silver wrote relatively simple melodies, often with the feel of the swing style, but juxtaposed these lines cleverly against a modern rhythm section. This effective hybrid style rapidly became the norm and was reflected in hundreds of hard-bop albums disgorged by the Blue Note, Prestige and Riverside labels. This apparent simplification made the music much more immediate than bop, which had never sought to court its audience. Silver's tunes – many of them catchy and attractive – could be whistled and danced to. Their appeal, which was neither fake nor contrived, opened the way for a much wider appreciation of jazz.

Silver and his colleagues also restored red-blooded emotion, excitement and the importance of the individual soloist to jazz after a period of arch, over-arranged confections. All members of the group were gifted, resourceful soloists, and in Silver's compositions there was a vigour that infused their playing. In his seven pieces and one by Mobley (*Hankerin'*) the level of invention is high.

Hankerin' is notable for the particularly nimble solos by Mobley and Dorham as they lightly ride a rhythmic switchback supplied by Blakey. *Room 608*, taken at a fast bop tempo, illustrates Silver's concern for detail as he inserts neatly arranged riffs between the solos. His own pair of vibrant choruses are matched by a molten drum break by the dynamic Blakey. *Creepin' in* explores a more sinuous, slow mood. The theme is in a minor key, a feature by no means new to jazz, but one which with hard bop for the first time became a regular element of the music. Dorham indicates how well suited he was to this setting. Silver's emphatic touch and deliberate use of repetitious, bluesy phrases makes his a potent solo, wholly in keeping with the spirit of the piece.

To Whom it May Concern, with a staccato melodic line and an attractive Latin contrasting theme, finds Silver developing clear, well-resolved phrases in his first solo, but he cannot resist an amusing reference to *The Donkey Serenade* along the way. The composer's ready wit is also displayed on *Hippy*, which sounds as if it will have a conventional *aaba* structure, but has a tag to extend the composition in *ccdc* fashion, giving the impression of two tunes in one. It is a delightful piece of writing. In keeping with the happy atmosphere, Silver launches his solo with a hilarious borrowing from *Bye Bye Blackbird*.

The piece from this session which became an instant jazz standard is *The Preacher*, subsequently in the repertory of all manner of bands, large and small. It inspired Eddie Jefferson to write an eminently suitable lyric. An adhesive 16-bar theme, it is littered with blues and gospel phrases but stands as a memorable melody. The solos are in keeping with the atmosphere, and again Silver has the two horns play unison passages where another solo might be expected. The blues *Doodlin'* is as attractive in its way as *Creepin' in* and *The Preacher*. The soul phrasing that Silver employs in his solo became overdone and exaggerated by some of his lesser imitators, but in his hands it sounds unpretentious and unforced.

The pattern of Horace Silver's future development and substantial recorded output was firmly established on this exceptional album, brimming with zest, vitality and music that has withstood the test of time quite superbly. In little over a year he was following this course with his own quintet, after having left the cooperative Jazz Messengers in Blakey's firm hands.

The selection from Blakey's live recordings features a transitional personnel which briefly brought back charter Messenger Mobley in a positively electrifying parnership with trumpeter Lee Morgan. Mobley, a consistently inventive soloist, tended to be over-shadowed during his most creative years by such contemporary saxophonists as Sonny Rollins, John Coltrane and Johnny Griffin. His even, unflashy tone made his work superficially less distinctive than that of those three, but his great rhythmic perspicacity and improvised lines of unfailing logic and clarity were revealed on closer acquaintance. Undoubtedly a 'musician's musician', Mobley, rather like Wardell Gray before him, remained largely unappreciated by a wider audience throughout a career notable for a consistency of craftsmanship.

The unsuppressed vivacity of trumpeter Morgan provided a most satisfying counterbalance to Mobley's dark and sinuous lines. Blakey's barrage provoked Morgan to fashion his most durable improvisations when in the drummer's company; his crackling delivery was never quite so crisp when other drummers were feeding the beat. The same would be true, to a slightly lesser extent, of Morgan's successor, Freddie Hubbard, who also thrived on the pulsations of this extraordinary drummer.

At this stage of their existence the Messengers had no current musical director – a role first taken by Silver and later ably filled by Benny Golson and Wayne Shorter – so Blakey commissioned compositions by writers outside the band's ranks. Pianist Ray Bryant came up with the delightfully catchy *Chicken an' Dumplins*, a chuckling theme eminently suited to the potent ensemble. Pianist Gildo Mahones supplied the minor-keyed *Art's Revelation*, and from pianist Randy Weston Blakey borrowed the attractively melodic original *Hi-Fly*. Mobley, not renowned for composition, contributed the sturdy *M and M* (standing for Mobley and Morgan), a good blowing line with an arrangement that showed the saxophonist had learned a lesson or two from Silver's methods. As for *The Theme*, this bop riff pattern had been claimed by many composers, but was most probably written by Wardell Gray, although authentication is now virtually impossible and the matter will surely remain an unsolved jazz mystery. On this album the piece is uncredited.

The live atmosphere of these recordings made at Birdland in New York is apparent in not only the applause, but the shrill huckstering of pint-sized MC Pee Wee Marquette and the occasional verbal exhortations of Blakey himself. Fortunately a fine recording balance was achieved and the only slight drawback is the rather casually tuned piano with which Bobby Timmons had to deal.

Chicken an' Dumplins, wherein Blakey lays down a powerful backbeat, sets the proceedings aflame with its comical, stuttering line, which proves to be a launching pad for earthy solos by Mobley and Morgan. Timmons feeds a steady supply of broad chords for the strutting soloists, and then immerses himself in an infectious gospel groove. Blakey takes a typically potent and pithy break before the quiet, stalking ending. After this leisurely stroll, the band hurls itself into a frightening charge tempo on *M and M*. Mobley, despite having trouble with an unresponsive reed, keeps his cool and builds a solo of admirable cohesion. Morgan deploys a host of vocal effects and displays his ultra-fast technique in a scintillating solo. Timmons has a tough row to hoe in following such virtuosity but struggles to keep up, while Blakey appends a series of eight- and four-bar explosions in a rushing, climactic conversation with the horns. Allowing the temperature to cool somewhat following this fervid flourish, the Messengers play *Hi-Fly*, and in his solo Timmons indicates his admiration for Bud Powell. The piece was neatly arranged by trombonist Melba Liston, whose pleasant scored interlude allows Blakey time for tension-building accents on his snare and even four bars by bass player Jymie Merritt before the thematic reprise.

A rapid burst of *The Theme* is merely an appetizer for a much more detailed and lengthier exploration of the piece, this time at a medium tempo. Mobley shows his harmonic understanding in some unexpected twists. Horn riffs assist the penultimate chorus of Timmons's cogent solo, and Morgan's little growling phrases provide a delicious touch in the closing statement of the theme. *Art's Revelation* employs another scorching tempo which once again finds Morgan and Mobley highly inventive and Timmons striving, but the joy of this track is Blakey's richly detailed and enormously stimulating solo, his only extended workout of the set.

Blakey's own volcanic playing and the style and general approach of his groups in the three decades after this album was recorded did not really change one jot. While others were diverted to new stylistic areas, Blakey hewed closely to the hard-bop sound with which he was so closely identified. In the process he succoured many young talents who went on to make important contributions to jazz, including trumpeters Woody Shaw, Chuck Mangione and Wynton Marsalis, saxophonists Branford Marsalis and Gary Bartz, pianists Keith Jarrett and JoAnne Brackeen, and many others. All found that a spell with the Messengers was helpful and educational. Blakey's commitment to fostering good, young players certainly enriched the music. Without his dedication it is unlikely that hard bop would have become such a potent force.

CD

USA: *Horace Silver and the Jazz Messengers,* **Blue Note B21K 46140**

Kenny Dorham (tpt), Hank Mobley (ts), Horace Silver (p), Doug Watkins (sb), Art Blakey (d)

Hackensack, NJ	13 Nov 1954	**Room 608**
		Creepin' in
		Doodlin'
		Stop Time
	6 Feb 1955	**Hippy**
		To Whom it May Concern
		Hankerin'
		The Preacher

Other CDs

same contents:
    USA: Blue Note CDP 7046140–2
    Germany: Blue Note 746140.2
    Japan: Blue Note CP 32–5223

LPs

same contents:
    USA: Blue Note BLP 1518; Blue Note BST 81518
    Japan: Blue Note GXK 8062; Blue Note NR 8837

Cassettes

same contents:
    USA: Blue Note 4BN 81518

LP

USA: *At the Jazz Corner of the World, vol.2,* **Blue Note BLP 4016 and BST 84016**

Lee Morgan (tpt), Hank Mobley (ts), Bobby Timmons (p), Jymie Merritt (sb), Blakey (d, speech)

| New York | 15 April 1959 | **Chicken an' Dumplins** |

omit (speech)	**M and M** **Hi-Fly**
add Pee Wee Marquette (speech)	**The Theme (short version)** **The Theme (long version)**
omit (speech)	**Art's Revelation**

Other LPs

same contents:
  Japan: Blue Note K18P 9202
  Brazil: Blue Note 31C152–82847

* * *

Miles Davis: *'Round about Midnight*

Despite the artistic success and considerable influence of his **Birth of the Cool** recordings, Miles Davis had some lean times in the early 1950s. Without a group of his own and struggling with personal problems, he was forced to take jobs as a guest soloist, and but for recordings on the independent Blue Note and Prestige labels we would know little of his progress during that period of temporary public eclipse. Fortunately, those sessions provide a faithful account of his development and interest in the burgeoning hard-bop style which was being embraced by all the rising young talents in New York and Detroit, a centre for a seemingly inexhaustible supply of gifted jazz players. Davis was the first to give alto saxophonist Jackie McLean a chance to record, and subsequently employed such hard boppers as Horace Silver, Art Blakey, Sonny Rollins and drummer Philly Joe Jones on his dates.

After Davis's career was buoyed by a standing ovation at the 1955 Newport Jazz Festival, he cast about for personnel to fit a quintet he was forming. Pianist Red Garland and Philly Joe Jones had impressed Davis on a quartet recording and were both engaged for the new group. The trumpeter then recruited 20-year-old Paul Chambers, one of the most promising young bass players. As a front-line partner he selected tenor saxophonist John Coltrane, who had worked with Dizzy Gillespie, Earl Bostic and Johnny Hodges without making much of an impression.

Thus one of the most important small groups of the decade was born. Typically, Davis adapted hard bop to his own ends. The rhythm section was certainly in the hard-swinging mould associated with the style, but neither

Davis nor Coltrane favoured the overtly declarative manner of the horn players operating in the genre. Neither did Davis embrace the catchy original themes or soulful, gospel influence introduced by Horace Silver, Hampton Hawes and others. Davis's book consisted largely of older popular standards, bop originals, compositions by Thelonious Monk and the occasional line from the leader's own pen. In this unit, possessing the same instrumentation as the classic bop group, Davis skilfully merged his cool perception with the heat of hard bop in a unique blend.

The cool overlay stemmed largely from Davis's own trumpet style, which increasingly was projected through a Harmon mute. His leisurely readings of ballads with long, held notes in the middle register occasionally suggested a frosty detachment in his solos. Coltrane's rough and jagged improvisations with a steely centre were a surprisingly apt contrast to the leader's work. Another positive factor was Garland's unobtrusive piano, with solos that balanced single-note lines with personally framed passages of block chording. However, the source of much of the band's momentum was drawn from the explosive yet meticulous drumming of Jones, whose high-octane performances Davis rightly regarded as crucial. Neither should the perceptive and lean bass lines of Chambers be undervalued in this context. He was considerably more mobile than the bop bass players. Whether 'walking' or 'running', Chambers had an infectious time feel, and his choice of notes was not as predictable as that of the majority of bass players. Davis's regard for him is indicated by the fact that the trumpeter employed him for well over seven years, longer than any of his other sidemen, excepting drummer Al Foster.

While still working out his contract with Prestige, Davis unveiled this quintet for the first time at a session for Columbia Records, with which he would be affiliated for the next three decades. It was fitting that the debut title should have been *Ah-leu-cha*, an intricate theme by Charlie Parker which Davis had recorded with his erstwhile employer some eight years earlier. In a clever arrangement, its repeated eight-bar theme on which the horns play contrapuntal lines is divided by punching breaks by Jones. Davis's open horn solo is flowing and outgoing, and a bold spirit also infuses Coltrane's effort. Garland sounds spry and there isn't a block chord to be heard. Jones's dynamic drumming lifts everyone. Davis also eschews the mute for a rapid inspection of Tadd Dameron's *Tadd's Delight* (also known as *Sid's Delight*), which has the melodic appeal and harmonic interest that one associates with this composer's works. The brisk nature of the performance has as much to do with Jones's percussive urgency as the involvement of the soloists.

Elsewhere, though, on this thoughtful and ingeniously conceived album, Davis opts for the mute as a device to help express his calm, order and sparse ideas. Never a man aimlessly to fill up every bar with the maximum number of notes, Davis would often let several measures ride before continuing his improvisation. By contrast, Coltrane's solos were positively verbose and at this juncture lacked the incisive execution of which Davis was now possessed.

Davis's rhythmic certainty was such that his clipped treatments of hoary old standards such as *Bye Bye Blackbird* and *All of You* became the accepted manner of dealing with the compositions, which rapidly found their way into the repertory of many other bands of the day. Both pieces, incidentally, remained as regularly inspected components of the trumpeter's repertory for five or six years, suggesting that he found their melodic contours and chord progressions consistently stimulating.

Among the most moving tracks on this inaugural set by the quintet is Davis's emotive exploration of Thelonious Monk's distinctive composition *'Round Midnight,* as perfect a reading of the tune as you could hope to find. The trumpeter's melody statement is spare and pristine in quality. Coltrane elects to double the tempo for his solo, into which he is launched by a tension-building insert where Davis removes the mute for eight biting notes. Such felicitious touches in the arrangements were a carryover from his discoveries with the earlier nonet.

Saxophonist Stan Getz had introduced a jazz version of a Swedish folk melody, *Dear Old Stockholm,* several years earlier, and Davis redefined the brooding theme with the aid of an excellent arrangement. Chambers is prominent in both the theme and the solo roster. Surprisingly, he is the opening soloist and this platform provides an ideal view of his nimble elasticity. Undoubtedly this was one of the most satisfying bass solos put on record up to that time, and his contemporaries studied it with the sort of attention that the previous generation had reserved for Jimmy Blanton's improvisations. Listening to this and the other sides, it is not difficult to understand why, once again, many would follow where Davis led.

CD
USA: *'Round about Midnight,* Columbia Jazz Masterpieces CK 40610

Miles Davis (tpt), John Coltrane (ts), Red Garland (p), Paul Chambers (sb), Philly Joe Jones (d)

New York	27 Oct 1955	**Ah-leu-cha**
	5 June 1956	**Dear Old Stockholm**
		Bye Bye Blackbird
		Tadd's Delight
	10 Sept 1956	**All of You**
		'Round Midnight

Other CDs
same contents:
  Europe: CBS CD 62323; CBS Jazz Masterpieces 460605–2
  Japan: CBS 32 DP 510

LPs
same contents:
  USA: Columbia CL 949; Columbia CS 8649; Columbia PC 9849; Columbia
  Jazz Masterpieces CJ 40610
  UK: Philips BBL 7140
  Europe: CBS BPG 62323; CBS Jazz Masterpieces 460605–1; Philips
  B 07198 L
  Germany: CBS 88029
  Japan: CBS-Sony SOPC 57139; CBS-Sony SOPL 151

Cassettes
same contents:
  USA: Columbia Jazz Masterpieces CJT 40610
  Europe: CBS Jazz Masterpieces 460605–4

* * *

Phil Woods: *Woodlore*

Of the second wave of alto saxophonists who took Charlie Parker as their
starting point, Phil Woods and Jackie McLean were perhaps the two most
creative and influential. Although they developed along contrasting lines,
each has stayed the course and remains a model for younger musicians.
Both were employed by pianist George Wallington in editions of his
mid-1950s quintet, and they were affiliated to the Prestige label for several
years. Whereas McLean effected an even more biting tone than Parker's and
infused his playing with a searing 'cry', Woods revealed a love for the
bubbling exuberance which was another aspect of Parker's multi-layered
musical personality. Cannonball Adderley was another of the 'second wave'
who took an optimistic stance, though he lacked Woods's resilience.
    Woods had, and still has, the ability to elate with his fierce attack, devo-
tion to the beat and love of medium-fast sorties through standard tunes and
compositions of his own creation. The boldness and vibrancy of his leaping

improvisations carry the listener along. He revels in swinging lithely, never holding back, ever becoming emotionally involved.

First works are not invariably prescient in informing listeners of the course of a jazz musician's career, but Woods's first album for Prestige proved to be a reliable and extremely impressive pointer to his artistic progress. Made in 1955 on his 24th birthday, the quartet album entitled **Woodlore** showed Woods to be an inventive soloist of considerable ability and sure technical accomplishment. Excitement is endemic to his music, but even at this early juncture he showed himself well capable of projecting all kinds of emotional moods. *Falling in Love All Over Again* is an infinitely tender and perceptive study in the ballad form. Yet on *Be my Love*, previously associated with the theatrical voice of Mario Lanza, Woods strips away the song's sentimentality and substitutes a bustling, extrovert sense of optimism. Woods's winsome way with show tunes is also apparent on his fast inspection of *Get Happy*, but the gem of this rewarding set is his jaunty and uninhibited canter through the chords of the unlikely *On a Slow Boat to China*, a pop melody that Charlie Parker also used on occasion. Tearing into the piece with unconcealed pleasure, Woods unleashes four choruses of perfectly symmetrical improvisation, his dry tone and spry, limber phrasing combining to memorable effect above the choppy chord pattern laid down by pianist John Williams. Who, after hearing this track alone, could doubt the allegiance of Woods to hard bop? His mercurial solo on *Get Happy* reinforces the conclusion, as at a flying tempo he inserts some positively shouting 'vocal' effects and gets increasingly heated as the choruses flash by. His instrumental command on this track is quite remarkable, and shows how far jazz had travelled in terms of technique by 1955.

Strollin' with Pam is an impressive example of Woods's blues playing. When a pianist was advised to 'stroll' it meant he didn't play, and Woods's first three choruses are to an accompaniment of bass and drums – hence the title. Woods laces his neatly developed statement with the smearing blues phrases which had been heard in this idiom many years earlier, but they come out sounding newly minted, and the saxophonist builds tension by an economical use of double-time passages in his fifth chorus. Much of his playing in this instance is what used to be termed 'funky' – earthy and basic – and it is all delivered with a deceptive ease.

His other original composition from this date, *Woodlore*, is of considerably more substance, and its interestingly structured chord changes enable Woods to deploy his harmonic knowledge, but his undoubted skill in this area and his rhythmic flexibility do not disguise that he is also a melodic player of considerable sensitivity.

While primarily a style associated with young black musicians, hard bop was not exclusively their domain. Woods and his colleagues here play four square in that manner. They clearly regarded it as the natural style to adopt,

316 Bop and Related Styles

the contemporary music of their time. Pianist Williams had unashamedly listened to Horace Silver and adapted the idea of laying down a jumpy, highly percussive accompaniment which particularly suited Woods's stream of long-lined phrases in *On a Slow Boat to China* and elsewhere. Drummer Nick Stabulas and bass player Teddy Kotick had worked with Woods in Wallington's band and were closely attuned to his rhythmic needs. Their presence helps explain Woods's supremely confident air throughout this satisfying recital. Stabulas sounds as assured as Arthur Taylor, and like that drummer tends slightly to accelerate during a performance, but this tendency in no way detracts from the performance; it actually enhances it. Kotick, having worked extensively with Charlie Parker, would later slot into Silver's quintet. On *Get Happy* he contributes an excellent running solo and dancing support lines. He was also a fine walking-bass player, as he is able to show on *Strollin' with Pam*.

Phil Woods went on to create music of richer texture and greater variety in the years that followed, but the freshness, involvement and devil-may-care mood of this set retain an appeal that transcends time and style.

CD

USA: *Woodlore*, Original Jazz Classics OJCCD 052–2

Phil Woods (as), John Williams (p), Teddy Kotick (sb), Nick Stabulas (d)
New York   25 Nov 1955   **Be my Love**
                                       Woodlore
                                       Falling in Love All Over Again
                                       Get Happy
                                       Strollin' with Pam
                                       On a Slow Boat to China

LPs

same contents:
  USA: Original Jazz Classics OJC 052; Prestige PRLP 7018
  UK: Esquire 32–020
  Japan: Prestige SMJ 6515

Cassettes

same contents:
  USA: Original Jazz Classics OJC 5052

Sonny Rollins: *Saxophone Colossus*

If ever there was a career turning-point in the life of tenor saxophonist Sonny Rollins it was this remarkable recording. To be sure, Rollins already had a growing reputation and at the age of 26 was certainly no novice, having salted away invaluable learning experience with such seminal modernists as Charlie Parker, Miles Davis, Thelonious Monk, J. J. Johnson and Max Roach, but the quality of his pre-1956 recordings had been decidedly uneven and inconsistent. Rollins was a comparatively late developer, despite his taking part in sessions with Bud Powell and Johnson when he was only 19.

His raw, rumbustious talent received its final polish during the first half of 1956 when he was the front-line partner of trumpeter Clifford Brown in the Brown–Roach quintet. Aside from the challenge of measuring up to Brown's exhilarating solos, Rollins discovered anew in this unit the inspirational drumming of Roach, the most disciplined, musical and commanding percussionist of that time. Roach knew how to fire and control a soloist of Rollins's potential; his polyrhythms extracted consistently adventurous playing from the tenorman. To place the album in its historical context, it was recorded just four days before the horrific road accident which claimed the lives of Brown and the band's pianist Richie Powell and effectively ended one of the most important hard-bop combinations.

Although by this juncture Sonny Rollins had outgrown his obsession with the style of Coleman Hawkins, his approach and gruff, even brusque, tone owed more to Hawkins than to Lester Young. In his reappraisal of Hawkins's innovations, Rollins offered new alternatives to his contemporaries. Hawkins had been unjustifiably neglected during the 1950s; Rollins's enthusiasm for him would revive interest in the work of the older man.

The close collaboration between Rollins and Roach is apparent throughout this programme, and the drummer is a potent solo voice in the proceedings, but it should also be noted how skilfully pianist Tommy Flanagan and bass player Doug Watkins slot into the quartet with the two New Yorkers. Flanagan and Watkins were two of the able exports from a flourishing bop scene in Detroit, and both rapidly established their credentials on the East Coast. Flanagan's neat, melodic and understated manner was suitable to all manner of contexts, and his thoughtful accompanying chords allowed soloists a multiplicity of options. Rollins disliked being confined by over-emphatic leads from the keyboard, and it would be no surprise when, in later years, he frequently shunned pianistic support, preferring to operate with strong drummers and resilient bass players. However, he suffered no constriction from the thoughtful and sympathetic presence of Flanagan. Yet, in *Strode Rode*, for example, one senses a soaring surge from Rollins in the choruses on which Flanagan lays out.

A number of elements that were to become associated with Rollins are displayed here. His own *St Thomas* vividly demonstrates his love for the intoxicating rhythms and cheerful melodies of calypso. The music of the West Indies is part of his heritage, and in later years he would consistently evaluate these roots in such pieces as *Don't Stop the Carnival*, *Hold 'em Joe*, *Mangoes* and *The Everywhere Calypso*. Both Parker and Dizzy Gillespie had found Caribbean rhythms fertile fields for improvisation, but for Rollins harnessing that droning beat to the demands and disciplines of jazz proved especially stimulating.

A penchant for unlikely, at times bizarre, popular melodies was another of his trademarks. In this case the man who had already energetically sifted the contours of *No Business like Show Business*, *Love is a Many-Splendoured Thing*, *Sonny Boy* and *Count your Blessings*, casts an ironic eye over *Moritat* (*Mack the Knife*). Granted this piece had provided a pop-chart hit for Louis Armstrong, it was hardly the stuff of the modernists' repertory until Rollins indicated the possibilities with a loosely swinging exploration. After his close inspection, though, the song was quickly embraced by many of his contemporaries.

Rollins also took the opportunity to exhibit his strong allegiance to the blues form in the deceptively casual *Blue Seven*, which affords him the space to structure two solos of irresistible fluency. There is nothing condescending or superficial about his probings of this traditional structure. Like the majority of the great creative improvisers, he seeks to enlarge that tradition, regarding the blues framework as a challenge to his powers of invention. Between Rollins's solos, Roach gives one of the finest demonstrations of how a drum solo may be musical rather than technical. Keying the various rhythms and timbres of his drums and cymbals to the 12-bar blues structure, he plays percussion phrases which build up into a succession of 12-bar patterns. The walking bass of Doug Watkins opens this minor key blues and is a constant hypnotic thread that runs through the fabric of Rollins's studied extemporizations. Watkins, a back seat musician of rare quality, had few peers at this particular game. Only Leroy Vinnegar and Paul Chambers had the necessary patience for such an unselfish yet vital role. Fittingly he is the final soloist.

On the two briefer selections from this delightfully informal but quintessential session, *You Don't Know What Love Is* and *Strode Rode*, Rollins invests the former with a stern masculinity, deploying a broad sweep of tonal inflections with frequent double-time passages to spice what in other hands can lapse into a dreary dirge. Rollins blows away the self-pitying atmosphere of the song, substituting a hard-edged realism. The Rollins–Roach blend is at its best on *Strode Rode*, where tenor sax and drumsticks punch out in a staccato duet an electrifying insert within the theme and later indulge in a two-way dramatic conversation. Rollins has a genuine swagger in his rhythmic step here – a self-belief engendered by his ability and the assurance of his companions. His vocal and mobile approach was certainly an attractive alternative to the mesmeric messages of his contemporary and fellow saxophonist John Coltrane.

CD

USA: *Saxophone Colossus*, **Original Jazz Classics OJCCD 291–2**

Sonny Rollins (ts), Tommy Flanagan (p), Doug Watkins (sb), Max Roach (d)
New York   22 June 1956   **You Don't Know What Love Is**
                                          St Thomas
                                          Strode Rode
                                          Blue Seven
                                          Moritat

Other CDs

same contents:
  Japan: Prestige VDJ 1501

LPs

same contents:
  USA: Original Jazz Classics OJC 291; Prestige PRLP 7079; Prestige PRLP 7326
  UK: Esquire 32–045; Stateside SL 10164
  France: Barclay 84–084; Prestige CPRX 240857
  Germany: Bellaphon BJS 40104
  Italy: Musica LPM 2048
  Japan: Prestige SMJ 6501
plus additional tracks:
  USA: *Saxophone Colossus and More*, Prestige PR 24050

Cassettes

same contents:
  USA: Original Jazz Classics OJC 5291

John Coltrane: *Blue Train*

John Coltrane, a standard-bearer for change in the 1960s, had a contradictory relationship with hard bop. He could perform fluently in this branch of the idiom; but whether he was wholly comfortable in this climate is open to question. Sometimes he seemingly ignored his accompanists to unravel long, steely, multi-noted solos that were stretching for a different context.

Between 1955 and 1959 the tenor saxophonist participated in scores of recording sessions, most frequently for Prestige, with Miles Davis, with all-star ensembles, or with quartets and quintets of his own choosing. He made only four appearances on the rival Blue Note mark, two of which were jam sessions and another a favour for his bass player friend from Davis's group, Paul Chambers. **Blue Train** was to be his solitary Blue Note date as a leader, and the cohesive and satisfying nature of the music it produced makes it a matter for regret that there were no successors.

The sombre, intense, almost puritanical voice that Coltrane favoured in the late 1950s needed companions of a sunnier disposition to offset a single-minded abrasiveness that could be overwhelming. In this respect, bright and bubbly trumpeter Lee Morgan and underrated trombonist Curtis Fuller, whose round tone and cliché-free solos were always plus factors, served to frame Coltrane's saxophone in a genial setting.

Members of the rhythm section – pianist Kenny Drew, bassist Chambers, drummer Philly Joe Jones – were anything but strangers to the saxophonist. Chambers and Jones had been colleagues with him in the Miles Davis Quintet and would be again in the later sextet. With Drew at the keyboard, Chambers and Jones had also backed the tenorman at a notable quartet session in Los Angeles the previous year. Drew's nimble and witty contributions provided another welcome dimension to the roster of soloists, a light leavening absent from so many of Coltrane's offerings from the period.

In the autumn of 1957 Coltrane was still engaged in a stimulating spell of employment with Thelonious Monk. It was a challenging and instructive assignment for the saxophonist as he grappled with the gripping but nourishing material of the master composer and wayward pianist. On **Blue Train** one senses a new awareness of form in Coltrane's improvisations and perhaps a feeling of release from the particular disciplines imposed by Monk. On the title track, for example, there is a brilliant buoyancy about his double-time runs, and the blues unison riffs of Morgan and Fuller spur him forward. If humour is largely absent from Coltrane's perception, there is no shortage of spirit or resilience. His austere tone has an edge that demands attention, and he executes ideas, no matter how complex, with a technical perfection that bespeaks a serious musician.

A driving passion infuses Coltrane's monumental solo on *Moment's Notice,* which shows his harmonic sophistication and his sheer patience in building the interlocking flurries of notes that would be accurately dubbed 'sheets of sound'. Coltrane does not make listeners smile, but in this mood he creates an air of exultation. Conversely, Morgan's daring and limber statement is warmingly agreeable; his dashing cut and thrust is the epitome of youthful expression, as affecting and effective in its way as the messianic mood struck by the leader. Both men are well served by the energizing current that flows from Philly Joe Jones's drum kit. It is too bad that Morgan and Coltrane recorded together on only one other occasion, because each seemed to play with unusual fire.

In the up-tempo blues *Locomotion*, both men construct dashing solos, but the palm here really goes to Fuller, who defies the physical limitations of his instrument in an immaculately designed improvisation. Coltrane evinced his most satisfying projection of emotion on slow ballad performances, and his reading of *I'm Old Fashioned* has a sublime poignancy and tenderness that are not to be found in the saxophonist's presto exercises. He would explore this side of his musical character many times, most notably in an entire programme of songs with singer Johnny Hartman some years later.

Lazy Bird is the composition by Coltrane from this set which made the greatest impact on his fellow musicians, and in short order it became a jazz standard, much relished by other saxophonists. Its attractive chord changes certainly suited the leader's colleagues in this instance. Morgan sets the temperature soaring with a contribution of great ferocity. Fuller, by contrast, opts for a cool interlude before Coltrane holds sway with a logical compilation of precisely chiselled notes. In this mood, Coltrane's control over his material was positively awesome.

It is possible to hear, within this sophisticated expression of hard bop, the move by Coltrane to the harmonic testing grounds of his 1959 recording of *Giant Steps* and even the course his work would take beyond that milestone. He was a man restless for change and thirsty for fulfilment. He felt he had absorbed all that he could of his predecessors and contemporaries, and after the years with Dizzy Gillespie, Johnny Hodges, Davis and Monk he was ready to strike out in pursuit of a wholly personal objective. So while belonging to the hard-bop movement for several years, his long-term commitment lay elsewhere.

Coltrane's purposeful, even calculating, approach was actually the antithesis of that adopted by Dexter Gordon, one of his early idols. Perhaps the most notable omission from Coltrane's perception was a sense of humour. His progress towards far horizons allowed no time for the jocularity of Gillespie or the hip amusement of Charlie Parker. And in truth Coltrane's time afforded scant reason for mirth. However, in a hard bop setting he never made a better recording than **Blue Train**, which proved to be among the highlights of his extensive output in the East Coast studios.

CD

USA: *Blue Train*, Blue Note B21K 46095

Lee Morgan (tpt), Curtis Fuller (tb), John Coltrane (ts), Kenny Drew (p), Paul Chambers (sb), Philly Joe Jones (d)
Hackensack, NJ   15 Sept 1957   **Lazy Bird**
Moment's Notice
Blue Train
Locomotion
I'm Old Fashioned

Other CDs
same contents:
  USA: Blue Note CDP 7–46095–2
  Japan: Blue Note CP 35–3088

LPs
same contents:
  USA: Blue Note BLP 1577 and BST 81577
  UK: Blue Note BNS 40009
  Japan: Blue Note LNJ 80067; Blue Note GXK 3010; Blue Note GXK 8055
  Brazil: Blue Note 31C152–53712

Cassettes
same contents:
  USA: Blue Note 4BN 81577; Blue Note TC-BST 81577
  UK: Blue Note K 81577
  France: Blue Note K 81577
  Japan: Blue Note AF 6004; Blue Note ZR 23–1065

* * *

Lee Morgan: *Leeway*

Carrying the identical instrumentation to that of Charlie Parker's classic quintet of a decade earlier, this homogeneous Lee Morgan unit exemplified the changes wrought in the jazz mainstream during the immediate post-Parker period. Gone are the astringent bop themes. The new compositions are rounder and more melodic. The music is more relaxed. And the rhythms these men danced to were set to emphasize the beat –

especially when Morgan's then employer, Art Blakey, was providing the propulsion.

That bop was already one step removed was apparent from the playing of trumpeter Morgan, who had absorbed the influences of Dizzy Gillespie and Fats Navarro via the work of Clifford Brown, even though he had become a trumpet soloist in Gillespie's big band in the 1950s; in the blazing context of that crew, Morgan's solos showed him to be much closer in conception to Brown than to his employer.

Pianist Bobby Timmons had drawn considerably on the inspiration of Bud Powell, but with half an ear cocked to Horace Silver's keyboard delineations. Utilizing blues and gospel motifs, Timmons, a much maligned musician, wrote some catchy tunes that helped instigate the brief fad for 'soul jazz'. This aspect of his work certainly helped the record sales of his current group, again the Jazz Messengers, as well as Cannonball Adderley's combo, in which Timmons served from 1959 to 1960.

The easier sense of swing induced by groups like this one was also due in part to the improving ability of the new young bass players, of whom Paul Chambers was one of the finest. Only in the playing of alto saxophonist Jackie McLean are to be found the astringency and concentrated tension that were omnipresent ingredients in the first phase of modern jazz. Six years older than Morgan and already a youthful veteran of service with Miles Davis, the Jazz Messengers and George Wallington, McLean brought his experience and challenging attack to these proceedings. His harsh, acidic tone and biting, jagged lines made for difficult initial listening. But familiarity with his sound and methods invariably provided rewards to listeners. A strongly emotional player, McLean uses a searing 'cry' without affectation.

The material from this date includes a pair of compositions by the trumpeter and brilliant writer Calvin Massey, from Philadelphia. The first, *These Are Soulful Days*, is a minor key, 24-bar *aaba* pattern of some charm, and it contains one typical soul phrase that appears right at the end of the melody, taken at a purposeful march tempo. Reversing the expected order, Chambers has the first solo. Blakey is particularly restrained behind Chambers and Timmons, but articulates appropriate rim shots and press rolls in the course of the statements by McLean and Morgan.

Morgan, albeit the composer and arranger of *The Lion and the Wolff* (named after the owners of the Blue Note label), was not an especially assertive leader, and on this sinewy blues he again yields the first solo spot, this time to McLean. In his own solo Morgan occasionally creates riffs for himself to answer in following phrases. Chambers has an especially effective solo, and Blakey's artfully constructed exercise, building in intensity, is a model of its kind. The fashionable fade out to end the piece is, for once, wholly justified: the closing Latin phrase is only partially resolved, but its repetition by the horns induces a satisfying hypnotic effect as engineer Rudy Van Gelder reduces the volume to a distant echo.

McLean's functional 12-bar *Midtown Blues* provides more scope for Morgan to conduct his own inner conversation with musical queries and equally personal responses. By this time McLean had moved well clear of Charlie Parker's shadow, and only the occasional characteristic trill betrays his profound admiration for Parker. Blakey bears down heavily on this track, but in tandem with Chambers spreads the firmest of bases for McLean's long, impassioned solo. Timmons's keyboard passage includes a portion played in the two-handed, block chord style popularized by Milt Buckner, George Shearing and Red Garland, with the chords spelled out in Garland's manner.

The plum of the session is unquestionably Massey's *Nakatini Suite*, not in fact a suite at all but a striking *aaba* composition of 66 measures, with the *b* section 18 bars long, rather than the usual 16. Massey had written this a decade earlier, and it was certainly an advanced work for 1948. The tune seems to lie perfectly for Morgan, probably because it was created by a fellow trumpeter, and it inspires him to unleash his finest solo of the set, a leaping, lithe improvisation that shows his resilience and control. A splendid achievement this, for a man only just turned 20. *Nakatini Suite* is a tantalizing fragment from a genuine composer whose output, slender though it was, suggested he was a melodic writer in Tadd Dameron's mould. Massey's works were also admired and recorded by John Coltrane and others, but unfortunately he made only a single album of his own pieces with a somewhat ill-assorted personnel. The two tracks here are more fitting reminders of his ability, brought to life by the quicksilver trumpet of Morgan and a band that existed for just this one revealing recording.

LP

USA: *Leeway*, Blue Note BLP 4034 and BST 84034

Lee Morgan (tpt), Jackie McLean (as), Bobby Timmons (p), Paul Chambers (sb), Art Blakey (d)

Englewood	28 April 1960	**Nakatini Suite**
Cliffs, NJ		**These Are Soulful Days**
		The Lion and the Wolff
		Midtown Blues

Other LPs

same contents:
   Japan: Blue Note GXK 8133

Freddie Redd: *The Music from 'The Connection'*

A watershed year for hard bop was 1960, when so many exponents of the style seemed to hit a creative peak. One thinks especially of the work of Donald Byrd, Kenny Dorham, Hank Mobley, Tina Brooks, Kenny Drew, Sonny Clark, the entire Jazz Messengers and the two principals on this album, pianist Freddie Redd and Jackie McLean, who never sounded better than in their 1960 collaborations.

McLean, of the biting, searing sound and highly personal stance in the music, and Redd, a restless wanderer and one of the hardest swinging pianists of his generation, were perfectly matched associates who each eschewed compromise and imbued their music with an urgent excitement. The pair were able to work together for many months in the Off-Broadway production of Jack Gelber's hard-hitting play *The Connection*, about junkies and their preoccupations. Redd and McLean not only played this music on stage as an integrated part of the action, they also took acting roles in the drama. They later transferred with the company to the West End of London, where the play had a brief and controversial season. For British audiences, though, *The Connection* was important chiefly because it enabled them to hear these dynamic players for the first time.

Redd had made a number of recordings before 1960, but none did him real justice until this Blue Note session of his vibrant score for *The Connection* which, incidentally, was also made into a movie featuring Redd and company. McLean took to the pianist's richly melodic compositions with glee, and his tone and attack became inextricably identified with these songs. When Redd made another version of exactly the same material with a different personnel, without McLean, much of the magic was missing. Both soloists were immensely helped by the surging power of two relatively little-known musicians, bassist Michael Mattos and drummer Larry Ritchie, who with Redd formed a rhythm section of unflagging energy and sure swiftness.

McLean completely immersed himself in Redd's clever chord changes, churning rhythms and satisfyingly resolved melodic lines, which he found a constant challenge and source of renewal. The results are positively explosive, as an emotional torrent of notes poured from the bell of his saxophone. Similarly inspired was Redd himself. Influenced by Bud Powell and Horace Silver, he favoured a firm touch and chordal clusters which put a solid underfelt beneath the soloist. Redd was never the most technically accurate of pianists, but his playing was notable for its bustling impatience and sheer verve. He was daring and uninhibited, and a joyous, casual air infused his unpredictable solos. His willingness to take chances in a disarming and invariably vigorous manner made his improvisations infinitely more exciting than those of pianists gifted with far greater technical expertise. Glib boredom has no place in Redd's jazz.

His seven pieces for *The Connection* hang together as clearly the stylistic work of one composer, yet each serves to clarify a different mood, and just how well can be fully appreciated only by seeing the movie. However, without any visual aids this fine music exists in its own right. Redd was one of the most direct and felicitous of the hard-bop composers, and such is the sincerity and strength of his themes that many listeners will have regretted that writing has been only a sporadic pursuit for him over the past 30 years. He never found a more fitting interpreter for his music than McLean.

The fast action of this recital is set by *Who Killed Cock Robin?*, a rollicking, fluid melody that features cohesive, expressive work by McLean, who barely pauses for breath in the onrush of improvisation. Redd plays in a warmly relaxed manner with his fulsome chords counteracted by some lively interjections from his mobile right hand. *Wigglin'*, a soulful blues shuffle, is lit by emphatic yet appropriate contributions in a succinct statement by McLean and Redd, both of them excellent interpreters of the blues, and Mattos, who sticks to basics and reveals the wonderful tone of his instrument.

Redd's joyous spirit is most effectively expressed in the heated climate of *Music Forever*, another fast exercise coupled with a winsome melodic line. McLean boosts the tension by enunciating the theme in half time while his accompanists lay down a mercurial four beat. Redd has fun with the beat at several points in his intense solo, riding on and behind the feverish rhythm by turn. It is an exhilarating experience. This piece seems to capture the very essence of Redd's musical persona.

Time to Smile is much more relaxed, and, as he punches out the melody, the pianist brings Erroll Garner to mind. McLean compiles a solo of stunning design in which his tone, dynamics and vocal effects are all melded into an unwavering line that conveys a bittersweet feeling. Redd's touch here is particularly percussive and his broken accompaniment is truly enhancing. *Theme for Sister Salvation* introduces a gospel march tempo that is redolent of its Salvation Army subject, but the piece is cleverly cast in two moods, because the meat of the composition is an entirely different slow melody. This allows McLean and Redd to fashion tender ballad solos before the brisk march is reinstated and played to a fade ending.

Jim Dunn's Dilemma has an edgy, neurotic line, encapsulating a glorious contrasting theme. There is concentrated ad-libbing by an inspired McLean who loves moving through minor keys at such insinuating tempos. Redd floats with the time, his forward momentum being generously assisted by the whirling percussive patterns worked by Ritchie. *O.D.* is a fittingly declamatory statement, opening with a menacing tribal 'cry' which leads into the sinewy melody. McLean's playing, passionate and intense, is closer than usual to Charlie Parker here, but the keening tone remains wholly distinctive. The emotion is so strong it almost overwhelms. Redd follows this with equal fervour but no flamboyance. His playing is occasionally reminiscent of Sir Charles Thompson; the two share a penchant for pungent chords.

None of this music is for the timid; it has a compelling, turbulent atmosphere, but it informs and rewards in generous measure. Here is undiluted honesty, raw, uplifting and occasionally disturbing.

LP

USA: *The Music from 'The Connection'*, **Blue Note BLP 4027 and BST 84027**

Jackie McLean (as), Freddie Redd (p), Michael Mattos (sb), Larry Ritchie (d)

Englewood	15 Feb 1960	**Time to Smile**
Cliffs, NJ		**Jim Dunn's dilemma**
		Wigglin'
		Music Forever
		Theme for Sister Salvation
		Who Killed Cock Robin?
		O.D.

CDs

plus additional tracks:
  USA: *The Complete Blue Note Recordings of Freddie Redd*, Mosaic MD2–124

Other LPs

same contents:
  UK: Boplicity BOP 4
  Japan: Blue Note GXK 8144
plus additional tracks:
  USA: *The Complete Blue Note Recordings of Freddie Redd*, Mosaic MR3–124

* * *

Harold Land: *The Fox*

West Coast jazz coexisted on the West Coast with other jazz styles. Alongside the white musicians playing neat and precise arrangements by the likes of Shorty Rogers and Marty Paich in the 1950s was the continuing revival of traditional jazz as played by white musicians and centred in the San Francisco Bay Area, and, somewhat less prominently, a few white musicians (including Art Pepper) and a large contingent of gifted black players who were closely attuned to the hard-bop camp in the East.

Among these last were tenor saxophonist Harold Land, pianist Elmo Hope and drummer Frank Butler, all of whom were more advanced than many of their better-known brothers in New York. Land at least had a fairly wide reputation, via his years with the Clifford Brown–Max Roach group. Hope, however, despite a boyhood association with Bud Powell and several excellent albums, was unfamiliar to most listeners. Butler, once hailed by Jo Jones as 'the greatest drummer in the world', was also an obscure figure. Yet the three were all long on ability, and their work together in the group led by bassist Curtis Counce gave them at least some sort of platform to show their mettle. When Land was invited to make this album for the short-lived Hifi-jazz label, he pulled in Hope and Butler, and added the obscure trumpeter Dupree Bolton and an 18-year old bass player, Herbie Lewis.

If this sounds an unpromising cast, the music they made exhibited a quality and originality that defied those who would pass hasty judgements. Hope, a quirky, unpredictable player who enjoyed manufacturing themes of off-beat complexity, was one of the main reasons for the electrifying atmosphere that exists on this date. Four of the six provocative pieces are his, and one suspects he also had a hand in arranging the two originals by Land. All the writing is distinctive and unhackneyed. It seems to say: 'Hard bop is understood, but here's another way of phrasing it.'

In the centre of this jazz maelstrom is the solid professionalism of Harold Land, a man who could play anything that was put in front of him. His dark-hued tenor sound blended with Bolton's tart trumpet tone to create memorable textures, and swirling behind them were the tempestuous but precise rhythms of Butler and the curious and questioning chords of Hope. For young Lewis this intense and idiosyncratic music must have seemed a daunting assignment, but he shows both insight and feeling and copes with the tricky twists and turns of charts that call for high technical accomplishment.

The challenging nature of the material is set by *The Fox*, taken at a blinding, blurring tempo that never flags for an instant. Among the soloists, Hope finds unsuspected combinations of notes in a minimalist approach. Hope's *Mirror-Mind Rose* is performed in the deliberate manner of Thelonious Monk. On *One Second, Please*, probably Hope's most conventional piece in this collection, Butler's astute placement of crisp accents helps the soloists to take wings. *Sims-a-Plenty* has by contrast the jagged edges and chordal shifts that formed so many of Hope's musical minefields. Besides being tough to execute, Hope's tunes make for hard listening. They are not pieces the layman would whistle readily, and their order and logic are revealed only on repeated auditions. That they served to refresh the imaginations of Land and Bolton is obvious from the verve that illuminates their solos. Hope was undoubtedly the best interpreter of his own originals, but he never again mustered men who understood his music so deeply.

Land's *Little Chris* contains echoes of *Broadway* and the soul-jazz fad in its whimsical melody. The suspended time breaks build up and then release tension, making the soloists' task more absorbing. The performance elicits from Bolton a statement of acute melodic sensibility. What a shame that we subsequently heard so little from him and nothing to rival the quality of his accomplished work on this programme.

One Down is a satisfying exploration of a flowing structure by Hope. As Land once observed of his esteemed colleague, Hope's compositions expressed a sure sense of form while his playing was loose and free. Hope shared with Land a background of apprenticeship in rhythm-and-blues bands, which presupposed an ability to swing that neither man ever lost or sacrificed in the cause of complexity.

Thus this album has great intellectual appeal but at once provokes body movement. Coming right at the end of the decade, it shakes a fist at the pallid fare peddled by the makers of musical mediocrity in the Los Angeles of the 1950s.

CD
USA: *The Fox*, Original Jazz Classics OJCCD 343–2

Dupree Bolton (tpt), Harold Land (ts), Elmo Hope (p), Herbie Lewis (sb), Frank Butler (d)

Los Angeles	Aug 1959	**The Fox**
		Mirror-Mind Rose
		One Second, Please
		Sims-a-Plenty
		Little Chris
		One Down

LPs
same contents:
USA: Contemporary S 7619; Hifijazz 612 and S 612; Original Jazz Classics OJC 343
UK: Vogue LAE 12269

Cassettes
same contents:
USA: Original Jazz Classics OJC 5343

Art Pepper: *Intensity*

Alto saxophonist Art Pepper lived dangerously in music and in life. All improvising jazz musicians take risks every time they perform in front of an audience or a microphone. By exposing so honestly the emotions they feel, they make themselves vulnerable. But the act of instantaneous composition also produces a stimulus to excitement. Pepper seemed to thrive on high risk, and often created some of his finest music under the most severe strain, when, to compound the contradiction, his playing would be supremely relaxed.

This album, for example, was made while he was on bail awaiting what he knew would be a lengthy term of imprisonment, yet Pepper performs with total composure, icy professionalism and sustained artistry in the most taxing of circumstances. In this respect at least, he was able to show remarkable resolve and strength of character by shutting out the most intrusive aspects of a chaotic lifestyle when music-making was on the agenda.

Pepper, a graduate of the orchestras of Benny Carter and Stan Kenton, had won admiration for his deft and driving solos with Kenton. In the 1950s he emerged as a potent small-group leader and a busy guest soloist in the Hollywood studios. Through his work with Shorty Rogers, Marty Paich, Chet Baker, Dave Pell and Shelly Manne, he became closely identified with the West Coast jazz movement. He was by far the most distinguished improviser to emerge from that amorphous grouping. Pepper favoured a cool tone, drawn from Lester Young and his early mentor Carter, and his style owed nothing to Charlie Parker, although he certainly drew in some measure from the latter's vocabulary. His sound was deceptive. At first hearing apparently lightweight and thin, it revealed on closer acquaintance a hard edge. When buried in larger ensembles with heavily arranged orchestrations, Pepper's flame burned only intermittently. While no listener could dispute the precision and clarity of his work in such settings, he was properly ignited only by an intimate context with a mobile rhythm section and one or two brass or reed players of similar persuasion.

Pepper shared with Young an instinct for recasting tunes to extract the optimum melodic appeal. Superficially sophisticated and definitely accomplished in the area of harmonic knowledge, he was actually an intensely emotional player, capable of expressing and communicating deep feeling. He could play the blues with genuine conviction, his ability to swing was unquestionable and his well-shaded and powerfully personal solos were invariably beautifully resolved. Pepper had previously shown a liking for assertive accompanists and had made two stunning albums with Miles Davis's rhythm sections, along with a recording in the company of the individualistic and quirky pianist Carl Perkins. However, while the supporting cast for **Intensity** may be lesser known, its members formed a unit of considerable flexibility and ability.

Pianist Dolo Coker, possibly because he elected to live and work in California, had a small reputation, yet he was a musician of manifest sensitivity and stylistic awareness whose solos and accompaniment here are a revelation. Only many years later, in the last chapter of his life, did he enjoy deserved recognition. Similarly, Jimmy Bond, a close companion of Coker's, was a bass player of accomplishment and drive. As for drummer Frank Butler, he gave Pepper the same resourcefulness and supportive swing that he had brought to Harold Land's **The Fox**.

Because of the hurried nature of the session, standard songs that would be familiar to all four participants were chosen. That they sound so satisfyingly integrated is testimony to the superb professionalism of these men who thrived in each other's company and the impromptu atmosphere that was established.

Bond's fleet bass line introduces *I Can't Believe that You're in Love with Me*, and Bond and Pepper handle the entire melody, save for the bridge when Butler joins in, so when Coker does enter the performance there is a pleasant surprise. Pepper's use of blues phrases imbues the piece with qualities not implicit in the tune. Coker's compact chorus is in accord with the mood, and the stimulating four-bar trades between saxophone and drums are punchy and pertinent.

Pepper was fond of Latin rhythms, and the arrangement of the theme of *I Love You* is in this vein, but the treatment for the ad-libbing is at a heady swing tempo. Butler is alive to every twist of Pepper's subtle improvisation, and his reflexes are such that at one point he repeats in the following instant the shape of a rhythmic phrase played by the leader. Coker's carefully controlled solo benefits from an interlude when Butler pauses for part of a chorus to leave the pianist to run with the bass.

A master of the slow ballad performance, Pepper made *Come Rain or Come Shine* into one of his masterpieces in the genre. Tender, deeply affecting yet unsentimental, it enshrines Pepper's awesome integrity. As with all the great players, even when performing the melody, Pepper recomposes it by tone, inflection and note placement.

Long Ago and Far Away delineates the fierce, concentrated exhilaration of which Pepper was capable at fast tempos. His command of instrument, material and ideas is complete in this agile exercise. By virtue of his technique, he makes it all sound easy and relaxed. Coker nibbles at the keys in a cryptic solo which somehow fits after the elegance of the alto.

The group adopts a medium-tempo shuffle rhythm for a cool account of *Gone with the Wind*, in which Pepper deploys his personal vibrato and singing sound to brilliant effect, sparingly using double-time runs and snatches of blues phrasing in his deft design. Showing how the band was thinking on its feet, instead of following the solos with the conventional exchanges between sax and drums, Pepper this time begins by trading ideas with the bass. Another variation in treatment is the statement of the first segment of *I Wished on the Moon* by drums and saxophone. Pepper's solo is heated and he repeats a riff-like motif to raise the tension, clearly enjoying Butler's off-beat contributions at every stage.

Even in an unpromising tune such as *Too Close for Comfort* Pepper finds unsuspected quality, as he unfolds an improvisation brimming with crisp, cutting ideas that transform the trite melody. Using the whole range of his instrument, he creates a solo of unerring logic and unwavering interest – Pepper personified.

CD
USA: *Intensity*, Original Jazz Classics OJC CD 387–2

Art Pepper (as), Dolo Coker (p), Jimmy Bond (sb), Frank Butler (d)

Los Angeles	23 and 25 Nov 1960	**I Can't Believe that You're in Love with Me**
		I Love You
		Come Rain or Come Shine
		Long Ago and Far Away
		Gone with the Wind
		I Wished on the Moon
		Too Close for Comfort
		Five Points

Other CDs
not incl. track 8:
   USA: Contemporary JCD 720–7607
   Japan: Contemporary VDJ 1581

LPs
not incl. track 8:
   USA: Contemporary M 3607 and S 7607; Original Jazz Classics OJC 387
   UK: Vogue LAC 533

Cassettes
not incl. track 8:
   USA: Original Jazz Classics OJC 5387

Jimmy Smith: *Crazy! Baby*

Organist Jimmy Smith's debut as a Blue Note recording artist early in 1956 was ideally timed for him to add to the growing momentum which hard bop was gathering as it became the dominant international jazz style of the late 1950s. A native of Pennsylvania, Smith had studied both piano and bass, which made him well qualified to exploit the duality of the electric Hammond organ, supplying his own bass lines on the foot pedals while giving full expression to his copious ideas on the keyboard. Smith transferred the conventions of bop piano playing to the organ with a horn-like use of his right hand, fashioning fast, single-note lines while his left hand punched out appropriate chords. He favoured a bright, sharp sound and avoided the instrument's muddier reaches.

His preference was for either the organ-guitar-drums trio, to which he would frequently add a tenor saxophone, or loose blowing sessions featuring a queue of good soloists. The trio was his perfect vehicle, for of the organ he was able to make an entire orchestra of his own. Smith's energy was inexhaustible. He could improvise daringly and satisfyingly for chorus after chorus. As an interpreter of blues he was earthy, authentic and hugely adventurous. Indeed, blues phrases are a recurring motif in all his work. He also had a prodigious sense of swing and built excitement through his use of sustained and repeated riff patterns at strategic points in his driving solos.

Crazy! Baby, his first album of the 1960s, contains several selections that certainly must be counted among his outstanding recorded performances. He is to be found at the peak of his musical potency on *When Johnny Comes Marching Home* in the archetypal trio format. This surging, uninhibited exercise gives Smith an opportunity to display his fecund preaching while always showing his rhythmic flexibility and astuteness. In many respects guitarist Quentin Warren and drummer Donald Bailey were the most appropriate of sidemen. Each works hand in glove with the organist and helps to maintain the intensity of this dramatic performance, which opens with a clever combination of bagpipe drone and Middle Eastern commentary by Smith – bizarre, but effective! Bailey's lithe ad-libbing sets things up considerably for the leader's torrid outpouring, which stops just the right side of frenzy. His astute and snappy rim shots, his tom-tom raps and his shimmering cymbal patterns are the spurs for Smith's inspiration. After the excitement has passed, the organist allows the atmosphere to calm, gently and naturally.

Smith's playing assumes a muted quality for a perky passage through *Makin' Whoopee*, a hoary standard that he infuses with a spry, bluesy air. In this attractively trilling performance, he occupies the entire solo space and justifies the decision with some bubbling, staccato lines.

Tackling a bop express exercise like *A Night in Tunisia* holds no terrors for

Smith, who unzips a sparkling and original introduction before warming to the task of enlarging Dizzy Gillespie's composition in a highly personal manner. The neat and sparse solo by Warren shows the poise of this under-valued performer.

Smith brings equal fervour to Sonny Rollins's blues *Sonnymoon for Two*, allowing his guitarist to fire the opening shots before homing in himself with a solo rich in pungent organ effects and rhythmic variety. Towards the close of a vividly exciting, blues-drenched improvisation, he builds the tension to fever pitch by holding a sustained note for four entire choruses!

Mack the Knife takes on a new life as Smith tosses it around playfully but with just a touch of dark humour, deploying his monstrous technical facility to excellent purpose in a running improvisation of considerable guile. It was tracks of this quality that persuaded all the organists that followed to use Smith's style as the blueprint.

The pent-up physical energy that seems to permeate most of Smith's performances is held in check for a good-natured assessment of *What's New*, but even here Smith is not content to recline and opt for a smoochy slow ballad offering. Instead he brings into play crashing chords and shrill piping effects which are certainly lively, if a trifle over-emphatic. Any sentimentality that may have been lurking in the song is well and truly wrung out.

Smith's only original composition of this set, *Alfredo*, is an attractive minor-key melody which prompts Warren to yield up his most refreshing solo of the date. As if in appreciation of his sideman, Smith takes up Warren's last phrase to launch himself into a steely-fingered contribution of compelling swing and sureness.

Smith's style has altered very little since those first mind-blowing, ear-tweaking debut albums caused a justifiable sensation. The validity of that style and its architect's strength are never in doubt for one instant in this definitive example of his work. Thanks to Smith and the Blue Note label, the organ trio became a fixture in jazz for which only the most snobbish purist can find no room.

CD

USA: *Crazy! Baby*, **Blue Note B21K 84030**

Jimmy Smith (org), Quentin Warren (elg), Donald Bailey (d)

Englewood   4 Jan 1960   **Alfredo**
Cliffs, NJ   **Mack the Knife**
                                                    Makin' Whoopee
                                                    What's New
                                                    Sonnymoon for Two
                                                    **When Johnny Comes Marching
                                                         Home**

A Night in Tunisia
If I Should Lose You
When Lights Are Low

Other CDs

same contents
   USA: Blue Note CDP 7–84030–2
   Japan: Blue Note CJ 28–5133

LPs

not incl. tracks 8–9:
   USA: Blue Note BLP 4030 and BST 84030
   Japan: Blue Note GXK 8145

Cassettes

not incl. tracks 8–9:
   USA: Blue Note 4BN 84030
   France: Blue Note K84030

* * *

Dexter Gordon: *Doin' Allright*

Dexter Gordon, a forceful influence from the early years of pure bop, found little difficulty in adjusting to the somewhat differing demands of the hard-bop idiom. It is regrettable, therefore, that for much of the 1950s the tenor saxophonist was musically inactive, making only a handful of recordings during the decade. When he eventually resumed his career in 1960 he made an arguably greater impact than during his first emergence 15 years earlier. An initial album, recorded in Los Angeles, indicated that his ebullience and rhythmic certainty were undiminished. His harmonic knowledge had deepened and his lengthy solos continued to evince a bountiful stock of melodic touches. These hints of a well-developed and wholly personal style were fully displayed in the first recording session he completed under a productive association for the Blue Note label. The music flowed from him with an ease and purpose which eclipsed the long years of denial. Gordon, fairly bursting with ideas and inventiveness, strongly signalled that he intended to make up for lost time. His solos have a breadth and shape which confirm a satisfying inner logic, yet they are at once packed with emotion and coloured by a personable wit. A musical vocabulary which had always been rich showed a positive expansion. In a sojourn remote from the epicentre of jazz, Gordon had kept abreast of innovations, and his work on **Doin' Allright** shows an awareness of the styles of both John Coltrane and Sonny Rollins. Not that he was overly swayed from either quarter, for an intense conviction in his own ability was an enduring characteristic.

The supporting cast for a dynamic debut on Blue Note was of the high calibre calculated to bring out the best from the saxophonist. The bright brashness of Freddie Hubbard's trumpet provided the ideal foil to Gordon's powerful voice. Each man draws inspiration from the other. It was a memorable first meeting of minds from two generations. The addition of a supple, loose-jointed, working rhythm section was probably the critical factor that ensured the success and durability of the date. Pianist Horace Parlan, bass player George Tucker and drummer Al Harewood had functioned as a regular unit for several seasons. With saxophonist Booker Ervin they were integral components of the Playhouse Four, and they had recorded as a trio and with horns. A funky sense of swing was their special forte and they possessed a mutual understanding which enabled them to conjure up an irresistible groove immediately. This they achieved in most telling fashion on Gershwin's standard *I Was Doing All Right*, where the course of the performance is determined by the jogging, relaxed medium tempo set by Parlan, Tucker and Harewood. On this track the responsive and flexible underfelt they supply is trodden with gleeful confidence by Gordon in his assertive opening statement. Hubbard's crisp contribution takes its cue from Gordon's relaxed delivery. Hubbard does not feel obliged, as on some outings elsewhere from this period, to crowd notes into every available space, but instead uses rests to enhance the cascading runs and occasional held notes. Parlan is the epitome of laid-back assurance, as he begins sparsely and then switches to rolling block chords for the closing measures of a lucid solo. While fadeout endings could be a feeble way of not knowing how to finish, the suspended final phrases and fade in this instance are the perfect exit for the mood of *I Was Doing All Right*.

In the terrain of the jazz ballad Gordon has few peers, and his majestic exploration of *You've Changed* carries an authority seldom achieved in this type of slow performance. Gordon's deployment of a wide range of tonal effects, including a pronounced vibrato on low notes, enhances his unsentimental but romantic statement, while his harmonic astuteness is consistently in evidence. With Harewood using brushes, Tucker's sonorous and unfussy bass lines assume some significance here. Gordon's confidence is underlined by his unaccompanied passage at the close.

The thematic variety to be found in hard bop certainly appealed to Gordon, and his ability to write in the idiom was amply illustrated by his compositions *For Regulars Only* and *Society Red*. The stuttering phrasing of the opening of *For Regulars Only*, counterbalanced by its joyous contrasting theme, make for an intriguing composition. Gordon's penchant for humour in the shape of an apt quotation is never more apparent than in his solo here. He also uses such devices as the honk and the shake to spice up his improvisation, but these shots from his locker are fired with judicious placement – never overdone. The alternate take of this piece, eventually made available some 27 years later, proffers an entirely different solo by Gordon with only a couple of similar reference points, showing he was definitely an off-the-top player with awesome inventive power.

The vigorous *Society Red*, the longest performance from the session, is an almost archetypal hard-bop composition with more than a few touches of Horace Silver's soul style gleaming in the melody. In this instance Gordon redistributes the solo routine, giving Hubbard first bite, and his arrangement includes catchy breaks for the two horns between solos. The leader is decidedly earthy in his swaggering passages on this item, and his dramatic flair is apparent in a series of beautifully sustained choruses which are never repetitive.

Mounting the popular warhorse *It's You or No One*, Gordon imbues it with a distinctive flavour in a neat arrangement. At a brisk tempo, the ideas tumble in a deluge from Gordon's horn in a cohesive display that marks him as a virtuoso. The occasional bagpipe drone set by Parlan at strategic points is a refreshing means of heightening the tension.

Another composition by Gordon, unknown until its appearance on the CD compilation in 1988, is *I Want More*, an attractive melody on which the leader's work is as spirited and buoyant as on the remainder of the material. It completes the picture of a highly original musician, at the peak of his powers, who had drawn on the language of Lester Young and Charlie Parker without for one moment submerging or sacrificing his individuality.

CD

USA: *Doin' Allright*, Blue Note B21S 84077

Freddie Hubbard (tpt), Dexter Gordon (ts), Horace Parlan (p), George Tucker (sb), Al Harewood (d)

Englewood	6 May 1961	**I Was Doing All Right**
Cliffs, NJ		**You've Changed**
		For Regulars Only (take 1)
		For Regulars Only (take 2)
		Society Red
		It's You or No One
		I Want More

Other CDs

same contents:
USA: Blue Note CDP 7–84077–2
Japan: Blue Note B21S 84077

LPs

not incl. tracks 4, 7:
USA: Blue Note BLP 4077 and BST 84077; Applause APP 2322
UK: Blue Note BNS 40014
Japan: Applause BNJ 71072; King K18P 9247

Cassettes

not incl. tracks 4, 7:
USA: Blue Note 4BN 84077

* * *

Sonny Clark: *Leapin' and Lopin'*

Pianist Sonny Clark was perhaps the classic case of a musician to whom genuine recognition came many years after his death. Of course there are others, including his fellow pianists Carl Perkins and Herbie Nichols, but those two perhaps lacked the lyricism and ability to communicate that are characteristic of Clark's entire discography. His early career was spent on the West Coast, where his employers included Buddy DeFranco, Oscar Pettiford, Wardell Gray and Howard Rumsey. Although he was hampered by a chaotic lifestyle, in 1957 he moved to New York, and in the last six years of his short life he recorded for the Blue Note label around 30 sessions yielding a remarkably consistent and fine level of performance.

Leapin' and Lopin' dates from his final flush of creativity, and it was the last date he undertook as a leader. Clark, bass player Butch Warren and drummer Billy Higgins formed the last great Blue Note house rhythm section in the early 1960s, and their intelligent support was lent to such diverse soloists as Jackie McLean, Dexter Gordon, Kenny Dorham and Grant Green. They were a supremely relaxed and responsive team with a loosely swinging unity which afforded soloists a wide choice of options. In this congenial company, Tommy Turrentine, a small-toned but expressive trumpeter, and tenor saxophonist Charlie Rouse, already embarked on a lengthy stay with the group of Thelonious Monk, were moved to deliver some of the most luminescent playing of their respective careers.

Clark is the fulcrum of their inspiration, not only through his attentive and considerate accompaniment and beautifully resolved solos, but also in the crafting and texture of his melodic compositions, *Somethin' Special*, *Melody for C* and *Voodoo*. Warren's piece *Eric Walks* is in perfect accord with his leader's writing, and rehearsal time was clearly fruitful in perfecting the neat arrangements. *Midnight Mambo*, by Turrentine, is arguably the weakest of the originals, but the standard of improvisation compensates for the rather corny line. In its incarnation on compact disc a further gem by Clark, *Zellmar's Delight*, was revealed. Only the time limits of the LP format can have led to its original exclusion.

Clark's chief influence was Bud Powell, but his playing also displayed an awareness of Horace Silver and Hampton Hawes, a close friend, in its earthy quality. In solo recordings he invariably paid homage to Art Tatum, the pianist revered by all the modernists for his harmonic depth and rhythmic richness, and on slow ballads he would occasionally adopt the deliberate, emphatic approach of Powell. He had a strong right hand which fashioned lightning, single-note lines, and his left hand provided soft and sparing chordal commentary. He possessed a firm, distinctive keyboard touch, and even if his fingering was not always precise it did not seem to matter, such was the spirit of adventure in his improvisations, which were mercurial and inevitably betrayed his gift for the creation of melodic phrases. His liking for minor-key excursions is evident in the dark-hued blues *Somethin' Special*, and his improvisational powers are displayed in two strikingly different solos on the takes of *Melody for C* which have been released.

On record, at least, Sonny Clark seldom enjoyed the opportunity to work alongside musicians from an earlier era, so his relatively few sessions with tenor saxophonist Ike Quebec, a devotee of the Coleman Hawkins–Ben Webster school of influence, are especially valuable and clearly afforded the pianist much pleasure. For the opulent, romantic ballad *Deep in a Dream*, Clark sidelined Turrentine and Rouse, bringing in Quebec as a special guest. This was a masterstroke of planning, for Quebec's sensuous and breathy style suits the song's beauty. Clark limns a pretty introduction and then quietly unfolds the touching melody. Just when it seems this is to be a gently restrained trio performance, Quebec makes his moving entrance. His blend of sophistication and emotion recalls Webster, but the saxophonist had a singularly personal voice and in this solo conveys a vulnerability which is implicit in the song itself. Aside from any other considerations, this tender treatise emphasizes the unimportance of stylistic divisions and indicates how effectively men of different generations could work together. (By one of those strange strokes of fate, both Clark and Quebec died within three days of each other in January 1963.) The common ground existing between the best swing players and post-bop musicians was far greater than many commentators appreciated. Here is a pertinent example of how varied elements could comfortably meld in the jazz mainstream.

There may be more brilliant samples of Clark's piano playing available, not least his illustrious trio sessions for the Blue Note and Time labels, but none that provides a better picture of the leader, composer, arranger, accompanist *and* improviser than **Leapin' and Lopin'**.

CD
USA: *Leapin' and Lopin'*, Blue Note BCT 84091

Tommy Turrentine (tpt), Charlie Rouse (ts), Sonny Clark (p), Butch Warren (sb), Billy Higgins (d)

Englewood	15 Jan 1961	**Voodoo**
Cliffs, NJ		**Somethin' Special**
		Midnight Mambo
		Melody for C
		Eric Walks
		Melody for C (alternate take)
		Zellmar's Delight

omit Turrentine and Rouse; add Ike Quebec (ts)
Deep in a Dream

Other CDs
same contents:
  USA: Blue Note CDP 7–84091–2
  Japan: Blue Note CP32 9524

LPs
not incl. tracks 6–7:
  USA: Blue Note BLP 4091 and BST 84091
  Japan: Blue Note LNJ 80156; Blue Note GXK 8216

* * *

Roland Kirk: *Rip, Rig & Panic*

Jazz is truly the art of the impossible, as its more adventurous practitioners have proved consistently – none more so than the late lamented extrovert virtuoso Roland Kirk. Like Art Tatum, Kirk was blinded from an early age but overcame this handicap and developed into one of the most individualistic, vital forces in music during the 1960s. Not content with being arguably the leading flute stylist in jazz, Kirk was also a resilient tenor saxophonist. But his most amazing feat involved a technique which enabled him to play three saxophones simultaneously. At the age of 16 he dreamed that this was possible and promptly acquired a pair of antique saxophones, the stritch (a straight sax but a rough equivalent of the alto) and the manzello (a hooked instrument that sounded like the soprano). These curious reeds were added to his tenor sax, and, having worked out a clever pattern of false-fingering that enabled him to produce a blend of three-part harmony, Kirk astonished listeners and fellow musicians with his unique invention.

Some sceptics, choosing to overlook Kirk's impelling work on single instruments, dismissed his discovery as a gimmick. Sour words failed to deflect him from continued research into multi-instrumental technique, and by the mid-1960s he was including the oboe in his triple deliveries. In *Mystical Dreams* on this set, he deploys the oboe alongside stritch and tenor sax, a combination that posed unprecedented problems since the embouchure for the two single-reed saxophones is scarcely compatible with that required for the oboe's double reed. Inevitably, with his inquisitive mind and ready facility operating in tandem, Kirk was able to resolve the difficulty and manage a most convincing three-part ensemble.

It was frequently stated when Kirk was alive that he combined the energy and enthusiasm of the untutored street musician with the knowledge and skill of the modern jazz player. This unusual amalgam meant that he was always open to a wide range of influences and, with his broadminded outlook, was capable of fitting in with all manner of bands and styles. His appreciation of jazz encompassed such early individualists as Sidney Bechet, Duke Ellington, Fats Waller and Barney Bigard, yet his admiration also extended through Lester Young and Don Byas to Thelonious Monk, Clifford Brown and John Coltrane. His own work reflected no single, overwhelming influence, since Kirk was one of a kind and matched any strand he may have adopted with something of his own.

This hugely entertaining and enjoyable recording affords an invaluable introduction to Kirk in some of his numerous guises – as superb flute soloist, warm tenor saxophonist, multi-instrumentalist, experimenter with electronic sound (years before synthesizers came into use), composer, and master of those obscure reeds manzello and stritch. Sharing in his delights are three players who also took risks to innovate. Pianist Jaki Byard, another man of many instruments, found fun in music, as did Kirk. The fierce originality of drummer Elvin Jones, architect of many a percussive barrage behind Coltrane, and the technically adroit bass playing of Richard Davis were pooled to serve Kirk's expansive imagination.

Two pieces in the set utilize pre-recorded backing tracks devised by Kirk himself and made up of all manner of sounds, including chimes, his own voice amplified, his baby screaming. Some of the sounds were slowed down before being played together. On *Rip, Rig and Panic*, another element is Kirk's 'live' tenor sax which he makes creak and vibrate with shuddering intensity. He ends the electronic introduction by smashing a glass on the studio floor. In the closing segment the human cries can be heard. In between these experimental episodes there lies an oblique theme and a driving tenor sax solo of wild and uninhibited scope.

Slippery, Hippery, Flippery also mixes a manifest of effects to which Byard contributes by plucking the piano's strings. Kirk used a cycle of notes from a computer to make the line. His darting stritch solo is followed by a startling keyboard excursion from Byard, who between fast, intricate lines actually bangs the keys at several points to obtain an explosive effect.

Kirk delivers his flowing waltz *Black Diamond* on the sonorous manzello, which has a slightly more colourful tone than the soprano. Performances like this show his melodic sensibility and superior instrumental command. The same might also be said of his exceptionally passionate interpretation of *Once in a While*, inspired by trumpeter Clifford Brown. Kirk uses his three saxophones as textural devices but feelingly delivers the body of his improvisation on tenor, where more than a hint of his early idol, Byas, may be detected. At the close he hits top notes that few people realized were within the tenor's range.

From Bechet, Byas and Fats is a tribute on which Kirk plays both manzello and tenor while Byard recalls Waller's style, both in his stride piano accompaniment behind Kirk and in his solo, which astutely quotes from Waller's piece *Jitterbug Waltz*. Jones enriches the serpentine theme through his use of chimes, and Kirk tosses off his multi-noted and complex tenor passage with incredible élan.

Many listeners regretted that Kirk's preoccupation with the saxophone did not allow him more time to devote to the flute, because his control of this instrument, often in the wrong hands too thin and watery for jazz, was exceptional. Jazz flute enjoyed considerable popularity in the 1950s following recordings by Frank Wess with Count Basie's orchestra, but only a handful of musicians were able to give it sufficient body and expertise to sustain serious examination. James Moody, Yusef Lateef and Sam Most all achieved individual styles, but none of them quite managed the true, strong sound that Kirk seemed to obtain with an effortless ease. There is an excellent example of his flute playing on *Mystical Dreams*, a fast piece which draws a solo of wit, beauty and free-wheeling momentum from Kirk. His tone is firm and clear and the vibrato expertly controlled. Occasionally, Kirk would use a buzzy throat growl to accompany the flute line, but he shuns that procedure in this instance.

Sirens and whistles, castanets and numerous other devices for making unusual sounds – all had a place in the turbulent, creative world of Roland

Kirk, a musician who was fascinated by everything he heard and often recycled effects from the most unlikely sources in his solos and compositions. To Kirk the seemingly impossible was always within his grasp, yet he was essentially a modern traditionalist with a keen appreciation of both the music's history and its contemporary strivings. His catholicity of taste and eclecticism were the signs of an ever open mind.

LP

USA: *Rip, Rig & Panic*, **Limelight 82027 and 86027**

Roland Kirk (ts, manzello, stritch, oboe, castanets, siren, v), Jaki Byard (p), Richard Davis (sb), Elvin Jones (d)

Englewood	13 Jan 1965	**No Tonic Pres**
Cliffs, NJ		**Once in a While**
		From Bechet, Byas and Fats
		Mystical Dreams
		Rip, Rig and Panic
		Black Diamond
		Slippery, Hippery, Flippery

CDs

plus additional tracks:
   USA: EmArcy 832 164-2

Other LPs

same contents:
   UK: Mercury LML 4015

* * *

Wes Montgomery: *Wes Montgomery Live in Paris, 1965*

Wes Montgomery was a self-taught virtuoso who pushed the guitar to limits which the instrument had not experienced since the experiments of Charlie Christian some 20 years earlier. By unravelling the mysteries of the instrument by himself, Montgomery stumbled on techniques that came easily to his nimble, responsive fingers. He learned to play simultaneously in octaves to perfection, a procedure first engineered by Django Reinhardt. He also reintroduced four-note chording, used by earlier guitarists, to lend texture to his work. Unlike most jazz guitarists he did not pick the strings with the fingers or a plectrum but employed an unusually mobile right thumb.

Although he was a member of Lionel Hampton's orchestra from 1948 to 1950, few listeners had any idea of his exceptional facility until his emergence a decade later in a group which included his brothers, electric bass guitarist Monk and vibraphonist Buddy. A contract with Riverside Records enabled him to reveal his mature talent on a series of sparkling albums. He was heard to good effect with such pianists as Tommy Flanagan, Hank Jones and especially Wynton Kelly, a real kindred spirit. Montgomery's career at the top encompassed only the last ten years of his life, which was ended by a heart attack in 1968. European audiences enjoyed the benefit of only one tour, in the spring of 1965, and this admirable recording on location at the Théâtre des Champs-Elysées, Paris, stems from that all-too-brief visit.

For this concert, the guitarist was faithfully served by his regular rhythm section of pianist Harold Mabern Jr, bassist Arthur Harper and drummer Jimmy Lovelace. And somebody had the creative idea of adding tenor saxophonist Johnny Griffin, with whom Montgomery had worked in the USA. The presence of Griffin on two tracks is a further delight and allows listeners to savour two virtuosos for the price of one. These vivid recordings, far superior in most respects to Montgomery's studio output, which suffered from dead sound quality, were scarcely known beyond a small group of French cognoscenti until the late 1980s, when they were finally cleared for release, greatly enhancing the available knowledge of the guitarist. Possibly inspired by the appreciative audience and fired by the rare chance to combine with Griffin, Montgomery was moved to muster some of his most plangent playing on four extended performances comprising 50 minutes of pure, concentrated inspiration.

Never one to linger over lachrymose ballads, here Montgomery's concerns are his own compositions and a blues by Dizzy Gillespie. The atmosphere is hard swinging and tensile, as guitarist and saxophonist improvise in uninhibited style with useful solo support from pianist Mabern. Montgomery's *Full House*, a bright and bubbly waltz, sidesteps the polite mood this time is apt to engender. Indeed, the guitarist gives the piece a 6/8 feel while sounding perfectly at ease swinging in either metre. He drops into octaves for his second chorus and stays there for the remainder of a dramatic solo. Griffin, revelling in the rhythmic impetus, opens in fragmented manner, gradually pulling together his ideas and reaching an electrifying, double-time climax in his penultimate chorus. The muted out chorus in which everyone paraphrases the melody is attractively executed, as is the subdued suspended ending. No wonder the audience roared its approval.

Jingles, also by Montgomery, features a stop-time procedure on the main melody with a fast contrasting section. It is taken at a presto tempo which the guitarist uses to deploy some of his fleetest single-note lines in the first part of his solo. The expected octaves come as a pleasant contrast, stalked by Mabern's urgent piano chords. Montgomery also inserts a passage of running rhythm guitar which is both agreeable and adventurous at this kind of pace. Mabern takes a solo in McCoy Tyner's manner, with dense, off centre chords punctuating his busily modal right hand. His emphatic verbosity becomes a shade too heavy in his final chorus. There are some crisp eight-bar exchanges between guitar and drums which segue into a percussive barrage by Lovelace before the nifty theme resumes.

Griffin sits out *Jingles* and also the perky *Twisted Blues*, the third of the guitarist's functional compositions. This one has a soul phrase inserted in the melody line. Montgomery improvises his first chorus against the support of bass and drums. Then Mabern joins the fun as Montgomery's earthy extemporisation unravels. It is noticeable in this performance that he plays squarely on top of the beat and uses riff patterns to squeeze the tension. Like Horace Silver, Montgomery enjoyed tossing quotations from gospel music into his mixture. It must be admitted that the temperature drops considerably when Mabern shifts to the fore and gets hung up on some corny keyboard runs. However, a solid solo by Harper helps to repair this flaw in the treatment.

Although first recorded at the onset of the bop era, Gillespie's *Blue 'n Boogie* was very popular among musicians of the 1950s, especially after its revival by Miles Davis in 1954. It is meat and drink to Montgomery and Griffin, who each assay the riffy blues with unconcealed delight. Montgomery even quotes extensively from the counter-melody often used in arrangements of the piece. His is a busy, precariously balanced solo. Griffin finds the insistent pulse to his taste and elects to navigate without the aid of either piano or guitar for much of his adroit exercise in forward motion. Actually his flow is slightly disrupted when Mabern eventually enters the picture. He picks it up again, though, in a remarkable unaccompanied passage that brings the house down at the close of a tremendously stimulating set which ends with a smidgeon of *West Coast Blues* and the crowd stamping for more. This is the best possible way to remember the glowing gift of Wes Montgomery.

CD

France: *Wes Montgomery Live in Paris, 1965*, France's Concert FCD 108

Johnny Griffin (ts), Harold Mabern (p), Wes Montgomery (elg), Arthur Harper (sb), Jimmy Lovelace (d)

| Paris | 27 March 1965 | **Full House** |
| | | **Blue 'n Boogie** |

omit Griffin		**Jingles**
		Twisted Blues
		West Coast Blues

Johnny Griffin: *Blues for Harvey*

No other jazz tenor saxophonist sounds remotely like Johnny Griffin, whose breathy, vocal, bluesy and ultra-fast lines have a unique flavour, redolent of highly spiced but delicious cuisine. Griffin embarked from his native Chicago at the age of 17 with the frenetic Lionel Hampton Orchestra, which already had a tradition for saxophone hysteria. From there he jumped into Joe Morris's rhythm-and-blues combo, which boasted such sterling assets as pianist Elmo Hope and drummer Philly Joe Jones. Griffin's career really blossomed in the 1950s when he moved to New York and enjoyed two productive spells in the group of Thelonious Monk and a stint with the Jazz Messengers. He later co-led a quintet with fellow saxophonist Eddie 'Lock-jaw' Davis before emigrating to Europe.

Griffin became renowned for his dexterity in up-tempo exercises, but in his case technique was used as a means to an end; his bubbling personality sought expression with the rhythmic accelerator pressed hard down. In excessive moments this can be positively exhausting to the listener, but at his best Griffin brings a splendid sense of exhilaration to his music, pouring out great smears of notes that form a logical pattern. His penchant for breakneck gallops and the pressure they put him under should not disguise the fact that Griffin is also a most capable interpreter of slow ballads and the most basic of blues, to which his edgy tone is best suited.

While many observers have cited John Coltrane's collaboration with Monk as being of particular significance, there can be little doubt that Griffin also brought a fine appreciation to the pianist's compositions. His rhythmic fluidity lent Monk's spiky, angular pieces a feeling not previously indicated, and Griffin's sly and ready wit matched that of his keyboard employer. The experience with Monk made a lasting impact on Griffin who, for many years thereafter, used Monk's melody *Rhythm-a-ning* as an opening and closing theme in club performances. Indeed, on this album he appends a flashing fragment of Monk's tune at the very end.

The album stems from a relaxed and happy stage of Griffin's career and was recorded on location in one of his favourite haunts, the Jazzhus Montmartre in Copenhagen. He had been a European resident for a decade, and his frequent partner for engagements of this kind was fellow expatriate Kenny Drew, a seasoned and accomplished bop-inspired pianist. Griffin and Drew, having worked and recorded together extensively in New York years before, were intimately versed in each other's styles. Drummer Ed Thigpen, a former cohort of Oscar Peterson, was a more recent arrival in Europe, but was a welcome addition to Copenhagen's jazz community of the early 1970s. His alert, responsive drumming is a continual source of refreshment to both Griffin and Drew in the four extended performances that form the backbone of this energizing set, and he conceives an especially fecund solo on *Blues for*

Harvey after trading a series of snappy eight-bar breaks with Griffin. Mads Vinding typifies the new breed of European bass player, highly competent as soloist or accompanist, and more than capable of holding his own in celebrated company.

Griffin's occasionally brash but always breezy outlook infuses the music, not only through his exhilarating playing but also via his own compositions. The tone is set by the righteous blues *That Party Upstairs*, in which Griffin paints a convincing picture of a good-time gathering with his shouting, keening and wobbly phrases. Long before the advent of the jazz new wave, Griffin had used shrieks, barks, waspish smears, squealing honks and shrill top notes as parts of his arsenal of diverse effects to colour a performance; these were the stock-in-trade of a good booting rhythm-and-blues saxophonist. This performance is laced with such devices, and his tonguing technique has rarely been heard to better advantage. A solo by Griffin is never a smooth ride, but invariably a provocative, surprising jaunt. The steadfast rhythm also proves to be to the taste of Drew, whose flowing solo juxtaposes earthy blues phrases with darting and complex single-note runs. Unrepressed joy is the order of the day in this derivative from an earlier blues, Gene Ammons's *Red Top*.

Alone Again explores a more subdued mood, but the stately tempo does not preclude Griffin from doubling up when he feels the need. The piece is gentle and tender without being maudlin, and the leader's commitment to honest emotion is never in doubt during the course of his delineation. The tune bears a passing resemblance to *The Nearness of You*.

Soft and Furry, a stealthy, slow piece, is one of Griffin's most memorable originals, with its expressive theme stated by bowed bass and tenor in unison with creeping assists from the piano. Opening in restrained fashion, Griffin imperceptibly raises the heat but remains fully controlled. Somehow, he is even more exciting when keeping some of his virtuoso power in reserve. ·

Blues for Harvey is a repetitious riffy opus that allows Griffin to unleash a torrent of extrovert ideas, operating initially without pianistic support and demonstrating the full gamut of his stimulating vocal style and rhythmic sophistication. This is the Griffin that, once heard, is never forgotten, the archetypal jazz improviser, bursting with enthusiasm and preaching with uninhibited zeal.

CD

Denmark: *Blues for Harvey*, **Steeplechase SCCD 31004**

Johnny Griffin (ts), Kenny Drew (p), Mads Vinding (sb), Ed Thigpen (d)
Copenhagen   4–5 July 1973   **That Party Upstairs**
Alone Again
Soft and Furry
Blues for Harvey
Rhythm-a-ning

LP

same contents:
   Denmark: Steeplechase SCS 1004

CHAPTER 8

Swing–Bop Combos

Barry Kernfeld

Swing and bop combos have their own identities. In archetypal performances, there can be no mistaking, say, Roy Eldridge and Chu Berry with Sid Catlett for Dizzy Gillespie and Charlie Parker with Max Roach. Earlier chapters have surveyed characteristics of each, but it may be useful to add one grand overview: in crossing over, the greatest challenge for swing musicians was the rhythmic complexity of bop; for bop musicians, it was the tunefulness of swing. Those uninterested in meeting, or unable to meet, either challenge have kept their separate traditions through what has now become generations of players. But the two styles have much in common – a basic instrumentation, walking bass lines, swinging cymbal rhythms, a common foundation of pop songs and blues, a devotion to solo improvisation – and many musicians have wanted to bring them together.

Having followed this thread through big bands in Chapter 3, and having introduced Don Byas's special blend of bop speed and swing accentuation, Nat 'King' Cole's unsatisfying bop pieces within an eclectic and otherwise highly successful body of recordings, Jo Jones's drumming with Gene Ammons and Sonny Stitt, Red Norvo's swing-style solos within the framework of his cool jazz trio, the book now introduces performers who achieved a deeper fusion in their work with small groups. For Erroll Garner, whose music falls mainly on the swing side of the equation, it was a matter of his having grasped, in his improvisations, the rhythmic jaggedness which lies at the heart of bop. For Benny Carter, a veteran swing musician, it meant not only absorbing elements of bop into his personal improvisatory style, but also working with musicians who had grown up with the new music. For Sarah Vaughan, it meant a less common blend of swing, cool jazz and singing, while Eddie 'Lockjaw' Davis and Shirley Scott took a more common path, bringing bop's complexity to the rhythm-and-blues edge of swing. And for Oscar Peterson and Clark Terry, it was a matter of being completely comfortable in either style, and consequently jumping fluently between them, piece by piece, chorus by chorus, phrase by phrase.

It must be said that chronology, a crucial consideration for other selections, is not terribly important in the union of swing and bop combo styles, except of course that bop needs to have been around long enough for the musicians to have comprehended it. The five recordings here represent, I think, the leaders' (and organist Scott's) very best work, and though they happen to span the years 1955 to 1964, that particular span does not carry special significance.

* * *

Erroll Garner: *Concert by the Sea*

In 1955, in the midst of a long and successful career touring as the leader of a trio, Erroll Garner recorded his deservedly best-known album, **Concert by the Sea**. At the time of this performance, in a building situated on the northern California coast, his assistants were bass player Eddie Calhoun and drummer Denzil Best, who has already figured prominently in this book as a member of Lennie Tristano's group, as well as, in a different way, for having composed the bop and cool jazz theme *Move*.

In an idiom which attracts players clumped around a popular technique – the busy stride of Johnson and Waller, a Basie-like sparseness, the relentless boogie-woogie bass lines of Albert Ammons and Meade 'Lux' Lewis, the fast-running single-note lines of Powell – Garner, like Thelonious Monk, was off in a room of his own. Most original was his use of the left hand, which on this and other trio sessions (he also recorded unaccompanied) is carefully integrated with the roles of his sidemen. With the touch of a cat pawing at a pillow, Garner plays soft, gentle, steady, swinging chords on each beat, producing an effect which frequently has been described as a pianistic equivalent to a swing guitarist's four-beat strum. Rhythmically intertwined with this strumming, but sharply differentiated in loudness and energetic attack, are unpredictably placed notes played with the same hand (sometimes it seems as if he must have an extra hand!), producing a pianistic equivalent to a drummer 'dropping bombs' on the bass drum. In using his left hand this way for so much of the concert, Garner depends on Calhoun to provide the bass line; at the same time, Best stays well out of Garner's way, playing swing and swirling patterns with brushes on the snare drum and cymbals, and (except in arranged passages) leaving to the pianist the job of providing random rhythmic punctuations.

One aspect of his right-hand technique also stands out, in those passages where he duplicates the melody an octave lower, or harmonizes it. This technique is not unusual in itself, but Garner's mastery of it is noteworthy:

he nimbly articulates long, fast stretches of two- or three-part lines, his right hand more or less locked into position.

By combining these devices with more conventional ones – single-note lines, two-handed block chords and (infrequently on this album) flowery arpeggios – Garner creates several distinct textures, invariably linked to changes in volume and characterized by a tremendous sense of swing. The first track, *I'll Remember April*, is representative of the procedures he follows (not necessarily in this order) on much of the album. It begins with pounding chords and a dissonant, twisted version of the opening melody. (Garner's propensity for inventing long, fanciful introductions, a general element of his style, is only hinted at during the issued portions of this recorded concert.) The theme comes in softly, harmonized in the right hand, as the strumming left hand keeps time together with the bass and drums. To delineate the structure of the tune, left-hand bombs intensify at the end of a phrase, then fall away suddenly as a new phrase quietly emerges. When he has finished presenting the theme and begins to improvise, Garner changes the texture, his right hand keeping now mainly to a fast-running, single-note line. The third time through this *aaba* tune, the trio's arrangement makes differentiations within and between the sections: the first half of each *a* section draws them together, hammering out a syncopated rhythm, two notes to every three beats; the second half is at a moderate level of volume, akin to that during Garner's improvisation; and the *b* section is soft, in a breath-taking manner that elicits applause. Unusually among jazz musicians, Garner uses softness for emphasis.

On one piece, *Autumn Leaves*, these sorts of contrasts go too far. Garner plays a fine solo in the middle of the piece, but the unaccompanied introduction is mawkish and the ending leaps back and forth between bombastic chords and soft tremolos. By contrast, in the blues *Red Top* he shows impeccable taste. Here too, at the end, the theme returns in the guise of chords and tremolos, but these Garner plays at a moderate volume, which in the context proves to be a delightful surprise.

Garner's improvising is an amalgam of swing and bop techniques, a reflection of experiences and associations from his formative work in the mid-1940s, when he deputized for Art Tatum and then later recorded with Charlie Parker. His continuously changing single-note lines approach the bop style in their jaggedness and irregular accentuations, but he also commonly repeats ideas, either swing riffs or motifs of a more abstract nature. He is fond of inserting quotations. Fittingly, he places the most swing-like of Parker's blues themes, *Now's the Time*, into his version of *Red Top* and refers to *The Last Time I Saw Paris* at the end of *April in Paris*.

Prospective buyers should be forewarned that the fidelity, without being anywhere near as bad as that of King Oliver's Gennett recordings from 1923, is not anywhere near the standards of a good 1955 studio recording. The sound is murky, the concert having been given in an echoic building that had formerly been a church. Also, Garner, like many of the great jazz pianists, moans and grunts while he plays, and the microphone has managed to pick up these sounds better than some of the instrumental ones. But the murkiness and vocalizing are easily ignored, the music is so good.

CD

USA: *Concert by the Sea*, **Columbia Jazz Masterpieces CK 40589**

Erroll Garner (p), Eddie Calhoun (sb), Denzil Best (d)

Carmel, CA	19 Sept 1955	I'll Remember April	
		Teach Me Tonight	
		Mambo Carmel	
		Autumn Leaves	
		It's All Right with Me	5
		Red Top	
		April in Paris	
		They Can't Take That Away from Me	
		How Could You Do a Thing like That to Me?	
		Where or When	10
		Erroll's Theme	

Other CDs

same contents:
   Europe: CBS Jazz Masterpieces 451042–2
   Japan: CBS 32 DP 660

LPs

same contents:
   USA: Columbia CL 883; Columbia CS 9821; Columbia Jazz Masterpieces CJ 40589
   UK: Philips BBL 7106
   Europe: CBS Jazz Masterpieces 451042–1; Philips B 07170 L
   France: CBS 62310
   Japan: Columbia PL 5044; Columbia PMS 67
   Australia: SBP 234108
plus additional tracks:
   Netherlands: *This is Erroll Garner, vol.2*, CBS 68219

Cassettes

same contents:
  USA: Columbia Jazz Masterpieces CJT 40589
  Europe: CBS Jazz Masterpieces 451042–4

* * *

Eddie 'Lockjaw' Davis: *The Cookbook*

The rhythm-and-blues edge of jazz carries with it connotations of particular and deep connections to black-American religion, the toughness of inner-city life and macho swaggering. But music and humanity are quirky, always reminding us to beware of stereotypes. Thus it is that on the albums originally issued individually as volumes of **The Eddie Lockjaw Davis Cookbook**, the tough tenor saxophonist Davis, who is in excellent form, is upstaged by the incredibly great playing of Hammond organist Shirley Scott, who comes across as one of the 'baddest', most 'virile' players in jazz. Her gospel roots run deep, but her gentle personality belies the toughness of her playing, and clearly it's not safe to presume that you need to be male to translate virility into sound.

This album also brings to the fore an entirely different issue. Jazz need not be consistent. As with Coleman Hawkins's *Body and Soul*, the success of the whole is often unimportant, especially in improvised jazz. On these performances, the intensity and interest plummet when Davis and Scott stop playing: the other soloists are either competent or downright poor, and the compositions and their arrangements are commonplace – conventional renditions (theme, solos, theme) of blues, ballads and unremarkable bop melodies. When Davis and Scott re-enter, the level shoots right back up to where it was, and this is so high that the rest does not matter much. It is nice to imagine a perfect album without the unexciting segments, but even with its faults **The Cookbook** should fall onto any short list of the very best jazz.

The drummer is Arthur Edghill (not Edgehill, by the way), whose experience in swing, hard-bop, and rhythm-and-blues groups made him the ideal accompanist on an album which brings together these three styles. Bassist George Duvivier was an even more wide-ranging accompanist, comfortable with players as different as Benny Carter and Eric Dolphy. His solos on these tracks do not indicate what a marvellous melodic improviser he could be, and it is strictly as a time-keeper that he makes his critical contribution to the group's success. The weak link is Jerome Richardson, who later went on to hold a respected position as the lead alto saxophonist in the Thad Jones–Mel Lewis Orchestra. He is a good jazz musician, but being matched up against someone as strong as Davis was a mistake. Richardson's flute sounds absurdly delicate in the context of this gutbucket music, and when he tries to add body to the sound by flutter-tonguing the result is not the gruff tone that flautist Roland Kirk was able to make, but an annoying buzz. To compound these problems, his disconnected improvisations cannot stand up against the competition. This is most painfully obvious when Richardson takes up his tenor saxophone for the hard bop tune *Three Deuces*, ostensibly a duel following in the tradition of improvised tenor sax battles between Dexter Gordon and Gene Ammons, Gordon and Wardell Gray, Ammons and Sonny Stitt. The contest is over after Davis's first shot. Following the theme, Davis's solo opens the piece. Richardson enters after the organ solo, and a minute later Davis jumps in after him, initiating a series of quick exchanges. As a soloist with Count Basie's big band in 1952–3 and again in 1957, Davis had been well prepared for such battles, and it was not until 1960, when he formed a quintet with Johnny Griffin, that he found a suitable tough tenor to serve as his partner.

On most parts of **The Cookbook**, Davis charges ahead, playing bop lines or swing and rhythm-and-blues riffs with a hard, vibratoless tone that moves frequently into grittiness; this is especially effective on repeated high notes, as for example during his solos on *Have Horn, Will Blow* and *In the Kitchen*, where his intentional distortion of the tone lends character to what otherwise would be a thin squeal. He shows his versatility on such ballads as *But Beautiful*, playing pretty melodies with a warm, breathy, sensuous tone and a pronounced but soft vibrato.

Scott, having taken up the organ in 1955, shortly after Hammond organist Jimmy Smith made a dramatic impact upon Philadelphia jazz musicians, was in the midst of a five-year association with Davis at the time of this recording. By comparison with Smith, there is an old-fashioned quavering quality to her sound, as she keeps the mechanical vibrato of the organ's Leslie speaker horn literally whirling on its fastest setting. Like Smith, she prefers a deep tone, but places this against biting, trebly percussive attacks. She lacks Smith's ability to keep a convincing bass line going on the foot pedals, but when string bassist Duvivier is a member of your group this is not an issue.

Block chords are central to Scott's accompanying and improvising. She may present them in fundamental rhythm-and-blues chord progressions (for example, at the conclusion of her solo on the slow blues *In the Kitchen*, leading into Davis's entrance) or coloured by the harmonic complexities of bop.

Scott has a complete command of blues formulas. Owing to her keen sense of how to build a melody, she uses these in a traditional way which is neither trite not boring, no matter how familiar the material may be. On the contrary, her blues improvising is exhilarating, and Davis, who disposes of Richardson quickly, more than meets his match on these tracks.

LP
USA: *The Cookbook*, **Prestige PR 24039**

*Eddie 'Lockjaw' Davis (ts), Jerome Richardon (fl, ts), Shirley Scott (org), George
Duvivier (sb), Arthur Edghill (d)*

New York	20 June 1958	The Chef	
		Have Horn, Will Blow	
		In the Kitchen	
		But Beautiful	
		Three Deuces	5
	5 Dec 1958	The Broilers	
		Star Dust	
		Skillet	
		I Surrender Dear	
		The Rev	10

Other LPs
tracks 1–5, as *The Eddie 'Lockjaw' Davis Cookbook, vol.1*
   USA: Prestige 7141; Prestige 7660
   UK: Esquire 32–104
tracks 6–10, as *The Eddie 'Lockjaw' Davis Cookbook, vol.2*
   USA: Prestige 7161; Prestige 7782
   France: Bel Air 331002

* * *

Sarah Vaughan: *The Divine One*

Sarah Vaughan's **The Divine One** is an album of romantic ballads and cool
swing. It was produced by Roulette, a label notoriously casual about clerical
matters, so all we know is that it was made in 1961 (maybe 1960) in three
segments, each with a rhythm section headed by her pianist and arranger
Jimmy Jones. The first segment is with trumpeter Harry 'Sweets' Edison,
who improvises muted accompaniments to Vaughan's singing, as does an
unidentified electric guitarist. On the second segment the five players are
joined by three unidentified woodwinds (these turn out to be flutes and
clarinets) which take the group's sound over the sugary edge. Edison

continues his improvising here and on the third segment, in which he also plays Jones's arranged cool-jazz passages, leading a section containing an anonymous tenor saxophonist, baritone saxophonist and trombonist; in this last capacity, Edison plays with a tone so gentle that his trumpet might be mistaken for a flute, were it not for the occasional bite as he attacks notes.

Perhaps the frustration of not knowing details of the session does not matter a lot, because in any event the musical focus is entirely upon Vaughan. She delves into scat singing, blended into the lyrics, on the central portion of *Have You Met Miss Jones?*, but otherwise this is an album of popular songs with the lyrics kept reasonably intact. Nonetheless, Vaughan's abilities as a jazz musician shine through. Depending upon the tempo, the songs cycle through at least one and a half times, sometimes more than twice, and on any of these tunes a comparison of the ways in which she renders the repeated material demonstrates the extent to which she can fluently improvise new melodies. The clearest example of this is on *You Stepped Out of a Dream*. The first time through, she sings repeated notes with a clean leap down to 'like yours' in the questions 'Could there be eyes like yours? Could there be lips like yours? Could there be smiles like yours?'; the second time through, she redistributes the relationship between the words and the leaps up and down.

Her main approach is to enunciate lyrics clearly and to sing in a rich alto voice, perfectly in tune, with a classical vibrato at the end of held notes. But this too she plays with gracefully. For example, on the last note of *Have You Met Miss Jones?* she begins the word 'I' with a gritty tone, then clears it and adds a classical vibrato. On *Ain't No Use* she throws European intonation out the window and adopts an Afro-American approach, sliding between pitches and hammering out a sultry repeated blue note on the words 'you been gone and you been wrong so many times'. On this same tune she shows off her contralto voice, dropping down to say 'take your love and go away', and on the second time through the lyrics she lets her voice break to underscore the meaning of 'so many tears'. She moves in and out of a breathy tone on the first lines of *Every Time I See You* and a nasal tone on 'ain't cha thrilled' in *Jump for Joy*, while the repeated descents from a delicate climax at the end of *I'm Gonna Laugh You Right Out of my Life* effectively begin with a female falsetto sound (though technically there is no such thing).

Having and using these virtuosic devices, Vaughan suffered from accusations that she sacrificed meaning for musical effect. This is true sometimes; for example, the text of *Wrap your Troubles in Dreams* suffers from her agile leaps the second time through the words 'castles may tumble, that's fate after all'. But there is not much of this sort of conflict on this album. She sets most of the text entirely appropriately. Most successful are her delightful interpretation of *Have You Met Miss Jones?* and the lamenting *Ain't No Use*. It was somewhat daring of Vaughan to take on a song closely associated with Billie Holiday, *Gloomy Sunday*. Holiday, as she often did, intentionally warps the text, adding an emotional punch by bringing out the gloominess. What would the critical reaction have been if Vaughan had taken the same liberties? Instead she stays true to the original, keeping a lightly bouncing undertone through the gloomy parts and bursting into a double-time swing feeling in the middle section, which tells us that the gloominess was just a dream.

LP
USA: *The Divine One*, Roulette R 52060 and RS 52060

Harry Edison (tpt), Jimmy Jones (p), unknown (g, sb, d), Sarah Vaughan (v)
New York   ?1961   **Ain't No Use**
                                          When your Lover Has Gone
                                          Gloomy Sunday
                                          Somebody Else's Dream

add unknown (three woodwinds: variously clarinets and flutes)
                                          Every Time I See You   5
                                          What Do You See in Her?
                                          I'm Gonna Laugh You Right Out
                                          of my Life
                                          Trouble is a Man

(woodwinds replaced by tb, ts, bar)
                                          Have You Met Miss Jones?
                                          You Stepped Out of a Dream   10
                                          Jump for Joy
                                          Wrap your Troubles in Dreams

Other LPs
same contents:
  Spain: Fresh Sounds FSR 659

* * *

Benny Carter: *Further Definitions*

What is being defined further on Benny Carter's album **Further Definitions** are two of his arrangements recorded by an octet under Coleman Hawkins's leadership in Paris in 1937, *Honeysuckle Rose* and *Crazy Rhythm*. Here, in 1961, are eight of Carter's arrangements for an octet of the same instrumentation – two alto saxes, two tenor saxes and rhythm section – including new versions of *Honeysuckle Rose* and *Crazy Rhythm* which draw upon aspects of the original ones. Martin Williams's liner notes to this album are tremendously informative, outlining the circumstances of the session, identifying the sources of borrowed material, describing each player's style and Carter's arranging, and detailing the order in which the soloists appear on each track. It seems most sensible, then, to leave these central topics to Williams and address the album from other angles.

The Parisian and New York sessions have quite different strengths. Hawkins's solos on the 1937 recordings are landmarks in his career. On *Honeysuckle Rose* – substantially slower than Carter's remake – Hawkins locks into the groove and concentrates more on swinging variations of a small number of simple figures than on the continuous and harmonically oriented spinning-out of ever-changing lines for which he is best known; interestingly, to accompany Hawkins's second chorus, Carter arranged a sax riff which would become, a week short of 16 months later, the main idea of Count Basie's *Jumpin' at the Woodside*. The most renowned of Hawkins's solos from this date is that on *Crazy Rhythm*. The tempo is fast – substantially faster than the remake, in fact – and Alix Combelle, the first tenor saxophonist to take a solo, seems frantic and scattered trying to keep up; after Carter's alto sax solo intervenes, Hawkins shows how it is done, driving through the song with such energy that guitarist Django Reinhardt urges him on to an unplanned second chorus. The other two titles from this acclaimed swing-era session have a different instrumentation, with multi-instrumentalist Carter switching from alto sax to trumpet. Hawkins plays just as well. After the muted trumpet states the melody of *Out of Nowhere*, Carter's arrangement features the tenor sax all the way, and he begins with a relaxed solo, not nearly as busy as the previous ones, before moving into his usual double-time feel. On *Sweet Georgia Brown* Hawkins plays florid and swinging choruses, entering for his second solo with a spectacular upward swoop which must have had a lot of tenor players scratching their head, wondering how to keep up with this man's originality. As well as Hawkins was still playing in 1961, this early work couldn't possibly be improved upon.

The rhythm section is driven by Reinhardt, whose sparkling chordal work at the beginning of *Crazy Rhythm* is sorely missed in the remake. But John Collins is a respectable rhythm guitarist, and in the rest of the rhythm section the decision goes hands down to the modern players: pianist Dick Katz rather than Stephane Grappelli (Grappelli is a great violinist, but as a piano accompanist he provides little better than a clumping beat); bassist Jimmy Garrison rather than Eugene d'Hellemmes; drummer Jo Jones rather than the expatriate American Tommy Benford. It is worth noting as a curiosity that at this time Garrison was a member of John Coltrane's group and less than two weeks earlier had made Coltrane's radical series of recordings released under the rubric **Live at the Village Vanguard**. With Carter the bassist shows his versatility by suppressing all his impulses towards modal and free-jazz bass playing and instead provides rock-steady walking lines, as if he were, say, John Simmons or Leroy Vinnegar.

A trademark of Carter's arranging is his scoring for saxophone sections playing melodies harmonized in block chords, and again the advantage goes to the tighter American version, where Carter and Hawkins are joined by alto saxophonist Phil Woods and tenor saxophonist Charlie Rouse, rather than André Ekyan and Combelle. They work in this fashion on the opening theme and closing riffs of *Honeysuckle Rose*, the theme and ensemble chorus of *Cottontail* (borrowed from Duke Ellington's recording of 1940), the opening of *Body and Soul* (a four-part harmonization of the first phrases of Hawkins's famous improvisation on this piece, from the recording of 1939 discussed in Chapter 4), and the section work on *Blue Star*, newly written for this performance. Especially characteristic of Carter's practice is the sort of intricate section work that gives the impression of a solo improvisation harmonized for a group of saxes, though his melody lines were usually written anew, rather than borrowed as on these recordings. A further excellent example occurs on Carter's arrangement of *Happy as the Day is Long* (1934) from among the recordings by Fletcher Henderson's big band cited in Chapter 3.

Yet another advantage of the 1961 tracks is Carter's solo playing, which is drastically different in style – in the interim he had moved significantly in the direction of bop – and, I would argue, much better. At the risk of being the Grinch who stole Christmas, I must confess that I do not at all like the early alto sax solos by the man who, at the time of writing, has been feted widely as the dean of surviving swing musicians. His improvisation on the Parisian version of *Crazy Rhythm* is oddly mannered and unswinging, with untuneful lines incorporating a weird selection of pitches, with too many notes placed squarely on the beat and with no sense of phrasing, each note being detached from the next. His improvising on this and all other tracks of **Further Definitions** is not so idiosyncratic, yet just as individually creative, and more elegant.

Finally, there is a largely irrelevant matter too interesting to ignore. On some reissues the material from 1937 is paired with tracks from an excellent swing session that the same French label, Swing, recorded in New York on 23 August 1946 under Carter's direction, with tenor saxophonist Ben Webster and drummer Sid Catlett among his sidemen. Some discographies and reissues (including a recent CD which offers a different slice of recordings, entirely of Swing's sessions in the USA) do not acknowledge that there is a singer on *Out of my Way*; those that do mention it agree that Catlett is the singer, and indeed the drum part falls away into a simple, quiet cymbal beat when the singing begins, and picks up again when it ends. If indeed he was not covering up for someone else, then it is a shame we do not have many more tracks from someone who had as handsome a baritone voice as Billy Eckstine, just as clear-toned, just as full, just as warm, just as well in tune, just as articulate. But then, of course, the record companies would have done what they did to Nat 'King' Cole, luring Catlett into syrupy pop, and jazz would have lost one of its best drummers, so perhaps it's a good thing that not many people paid attention to this cut.

In addition to these tracks with Catlett, the Swing collection includes other tracks unrelated to Carter's **Further Definitions**: only the four relevant tracks, from 28 April 1937, are listed below.

LP
USA: *Coleman Hawkins and Benny Carter in Paris*, Swing SW 8403

Benny Carter (as, arr), André Ekyan (as), Alix Combelle, Coleman Hawkins (ts), Stephane Grappelli (p), Django Reinhardt (g), Eugene d'Hellemmes (sb), Tommy Benford (d)
Paris   28 April 1937   **Honeysuckle Rose**
                                                 Crazy Rhythm

*as **Honeysuckle Rose**, but Carter (tpt, arr), Combelle (cl)*
                                                 Out of Nowhere
                                                 Sweet Georgia Brown

CDs
incl. tracks 1–4:
   Italy: *Coleman Hawkins in Europe*, Jazzup 317/18/19
incl. track 1: *Django Reinhardt Memorial 1910/1953*
   UK: EMI CZ 135
   France: Jazz Time 790560–2
incl. tracks 2–4:
   France: *Americans in Paris, vol.2*, Jazz Time 251277–2

Other LPs
incl. tracks 1–4:
   USA: *Django Reinhardt and American Jazz Giants*, Prestige PR 7633
   UK: *Django & his American Friends*, HMV CLP 1890
   The Hawk in Europe 1934–1937, Living Era AJA 5054

The Genius of Django, 3, World SM 643
France: *Django, vol.III*, La Voix de son Maître FELP 174
Django Selection, vol.3. La Voix de son Maître HTX 40159
Django et ses Amis Americains, La Voix de son Maître CHTX 240552
Djangologie 4, Pathé 2 C054–16004
Australia: *Django and his American Friends*, HMV OCLP 1890
Django Rhythm, Swaggie S1251
not incl. **Out of Nowhere**
USA: *Giants of Jazz: Coleman Hawkins*, Time-Life STL J06

Cassettes

incl. tracks 1–4:
USA: *Coleman Hawkins and Benny Carter in Paris*, Swing SWC 8403
UK: *The Hawk in Europe 1934–1937*, Living Era ZC AJA 5054

CD

USA: *Further Definitions*, MCA Impulse! MCAD 5651

*Benny Carter (as, arr), Phil Woods (as), Coleman Hawkins, Charlie Rouse (ts), Dick
Katz (p), John Collins (g), Jimmy Garrison (sb), Jo Jones (d)*

New York	13 Nov 1961	**Honeysuckle Rose**
		The Midnight Sun Will Never Set
		Cherry
		Crazy Rhythm
	15 Nov 1961	**Doozy**
		Blue Star
		Cottontail
		Body and Soul

LPs

same contents:
USA: Impulse! A 12 and AS 12; MCA Impulse! 29006
UK: HMV CLP 1624 and CSD 1480; Impulse! IMPL 8037; Jasmine JAS 14;
World Record Club T 864
Japan: Impulse! YP 8519; King SH 3002; MCA Impulse! JVC 460

Cassettes

same contents:
UK: Jasmine JASC 14

Oscar Peterson: *The Oscar Peterson Trio + One: Clark Terry*

This joyous album, made in August 1964, brings together men who were already jazz veterans, though still young. Trumpeter and flugelhorn player Clark Terry had sandwiched stints with Count Basie and Quincy Jones around an eight-year stand as the featured soloist with Duke Ellington's big band. Now he was concentrating on studio work, while he and trombonist Bob Brookmeyer also led a combo which aimed for the same seamless blend of swing and bop styles heard on this album. Pianist Oscar Peterson, bassist Ray Brown and drummer Ed Thigpen were into their sixth year as a trio, Peterson having previously worked for years with Brown and a guitarist. Too often I find myself disappointed by this sort of all star session, because reputation (hence guaranteed record sales) often takes precedence over compatibility in bringing together the principals. On this occasion the outcome was nothing short of magnificent.

Peterson is regularly mentioned and not infrequently damned as a follower of Art Tatum. Among all the pianists who have come along after Tatum, he is best equipped to match the latter's prodigious technical command of the keyboard. But the consequent assumption, that having this ability he would use it, turns out not to be true. In a music filled with close relationships between innovators and imitators (followers of Louis Armstrong, of Charlie Parker, of John Coltrane, etc.), Tatum and Peterson are distantly removed from one another. This observation is no novel idea on my part. Listeners who have thought about what Peterson plays have noted that his greatest strengths – group playing and hard-driving swing – are not Tatum's. But the notion of the connection remains so pervasive that it seems worth while to challenge it once again. Indeed, Peterson himself encourages the idea in his own liner notes to the original issue, which mention his debt to Tatum with regard to the younger man's unaccompanied introduction to the ballad *They Didn't Believe Me*, an introduction which then proves to have none of the swooping arpeggiated interruptions which Tatum certainly would have supplied.

Peterson's concentration on swinging takes several forms. He improvises abstract, lightning-quick bop lines (*Squeaky's Blues*), but also plays more tuneful melodies. For example, his solos on *Brotherhood of Man* and *Roundalay*, laced with flashy lines, include soul jazz licks and, on the latter, passages in block chords. On *Jim* his touch and tone are sumptuous as he plays standard bluesy phrases in two-part harmony, using tremolos to hold out the ends of phrases, as if he were singing his ideas. At some points, as for example in portions of Peterson's solo on the jump tune *Blues for Smedley*, the microphone picks up the pianist grunting out melodies in unison with his fingers, like some of the earthier jazzman with whom he might not be immediately associated.

Like his first inspiration, Oscar Pettiford, Ray Brown has all of the equipment to be a major soloist – perfect time and intonation, clean articulation, mature melodic ideas – but Brown is more content than Pettiford was to remain an accompanist. In fact, his greatest moment on this album is not the three-chorus solo on *Blues for Smedley*, but his accompaniment to Terry in the sections of *Mack the Knife* where Peterson lays out. He deftly varies the style of his bass line, playing a rocking two beat, walking deliberately from beat to beat, dancing about in broken triplet rhythms, all the time keeping the trumpeter's harmonic support crystal clear. And in the more usual segments of the album, when Peterson is playing, the pianist uses his left hand sparingly and in the middle register of the keyboard, thus staying respectfully out of Brown's domain.

All these actions in the interest of discretion and taste, tunefulness and swing apply equally to Terry, who has the technique to hit high notes (*Blues for Smedley*) and to articulate with speed (*Mack the Knife*, *Squeaky's Blues*) and the good sense not to overdo either. One of his main concerns is tone colour. He plays flugelhorn and trumpet, uses several types of mutes and sings (well, mumbles) in different 'voices'. On *Jim*, his burnished, open flugelhorn, played in its low-to-middle register, contrasts with his tightly muted trumpet, played in its middle-to-high register, in a series of four-, two- and one-bar internal dialogues, culminating in downward glisses for which he moves between the two horns note by note to the end of the piece. He also uses flugelhorn (again unmuted) in a bop-oriented solo on *Roundalay* and an uncluttered reading of the pretty melody of *They Didn't Believe Me*, played with a warm tone and a pronounced vibrato which recalls jazz brass from an earlier era.

Playing trumpet, he either keeps the mute on or plays wa-wa melodies by moving between open and muted sounds. This does not mean, though, that the two instruments are always easy to distinguish. Forays into the high register and a slight lack of ease in the low register are the only clues to reveal that he is playing trumpet on the ballad *I Want a Little Girl*, which otherwise pours out with such a gorgeous, full-bodied, mellow sound that the instrument could easily be mistaken for a flugelhorn.

Mumbles (which became Terry's nickname) and *Incoherent Blues* mark the start of Terry's recording career as a hilarious singer who simultaneously celebrates and pokes fun at down-home blues. As the titles suggest, he intentionally sings in a poorly enunciated manner which confuses the non-sense syllables of scat singing with the characteristic love-life lyrics and the black-American dialect of blues songs. *Mumbles* leans towards the scat singing side of the line, while *Incoherent Blues* is a surrealistic conversation between an impressionable woman (portrayed in a mousy falsetto voice) and a self-assured man, whose boasting descends at the very end into a gravelly leer.

CD

USA: *The Oscar Peterson Trio + One: Clark Terry*, **EmArcy 818840–2**

Clark Terry (tpt, flugelhorn), Oscar Peterson (p), Ray Brown (sb), Ed Thigpen (d)
New York   17 Aug 1964   **Brotherhood of Man**
                                               Jim
                                               Blues for Smedley
                                               Roundalay

*as **Brotherhood of Man**, but Terry (v)*

                                               Mumbles   5

*as **Brotherhood of Man***

                                               Mack the Knife
                                               They Didn't Believe Me
                                               Squeaky's Blues
                                               I Want a Little Girl

*as **Brotherhood of Man**, but Terry (v)*

                                               Incoherent Blues   10

Other CDs

same contents:
   Europe: EmArcy 818840
   Japan: EmArcy 32 JD 96

LPs

same contents:
   US: Mercury MG 20975 and SR 60975
   UK: Mercury 20030 MCL
   Japan: EmArcy number unknown

CHAPTER 9

Leaving Hard Bop

Barry Kernfeld

As quickly as hard bop became the dominant jazz style in the mid-1950s, so quickly did it fall away from the cutting edge of innovation. After all, the parent style, bop, had been well established a decade earlier, which is a long time in this ever-searching genre of music, and the rules governing hard bop, if considered from anything but the closest distance, seem not drastically different from those governing its parent. Thus it was that, even as hard bop was inspiring into the 1960s the many notable new albums cited in Chapter 7, groups of musicians were searching for new styles, to avoid feeling that their playing was sounding conventional. The radical results of these searches – free jazz and fusion – broke away as no previous style had done and in the process eventually served by contrast to consolidate all earlier forms, from New Orleans to hard bop, into a broader than ever notion of the mainstream.

At the turn of the 1960s free jazz was already well established, but fusion would have to wait another decade while blues and rock musicians showed the way. Miles Davis, Charles Mingus, John Coltrane and Herbie Hancock would later embrace one or other of these approaches. For the time being, they, together with Bill Evans (who never took the final stylistic step away from hard bop), were extending rather than breaking away from the mainstream, retaining some aspects of hard bop while leaving others behind. In the process these five leaders made albums which are landmarks in the history of jazz. Perhaps it was the very ambiguity of their situation, their desire to remain in touch with tradition and yet also to invent new sounds on an *ad hoc* basis, which pushed them to the limits of their creativity. And when players such as these are at the top of their game, the results are nothing short of astonishing.

Miles Davis: *Kind of Blue*

The album **Kind of Blue** is as accessible and beautiful as it is creative and important. By 1959, when his sextet recorded it, Davis was only beginning down the path that would lead a decade later to jazz-rock. But **Kind of Blue** offered a new approach which has come to be known as modal jazz, or modal playing. It is easy to get tied up in knots trying to figure out what 'modal' means, and a crucial mistake in Bill Evans's liner notes to the original LP issue (referring to 'a few modal changes') tightens the knots further (more on that below).

It seems best to use the word simply because everybody else does, but to ignore its meaning, vaguely tied to the modes of medieval church music, or the major-minor modes of classical music, or some scalar pattern used in the music of India, China, Bulgaria, West Africa, Spain, etc. The key element of modal jazz is a single and, for its time, profound idea: the slowing of 'harmonic rhythm'; that is, the slowing of the rate at which chords change. In hard bop and related styles, harmony moves along at a good clip, the chords usually changing at least once every one or two bars, and sometimes as fast as once every beat; to accord with the accompaniment, the typical soloist consequently plays a fast-moving and ever-changing line. Davis did not want to play early jazz or swing, both of these being predominantly tuneful styles, but he wanted to create an environment in which he could invent tuneful melodies. For much of the album, he simply slowed down the harmony. This is modal jazz.

The album was recorded at two sessions a month apart, with (according to Evans) little rehearsal, although to my ears Cannonball Adderley's vastly improved playing at the second session suggests that at least he had thought about this new musical situation for a while, and figured something out. Davis plays brilliantly throughout, and it didn't hurt a bit to have the equally brilliant John Coltrane among his sidemen. Paul Chambers, a rock-steady, conservative player, was the perfect man to maintain the inevitably restrictive bass lines which the new style required. Jimmy Cobb, far less fiery than Davis's former drummer Philly Joe Jones, was right for the relaxed rhythms on every track. The sessions begin chronologically (not in the order on the album) with Wynton Kelly playing piano on *Freddie Freeloader*. The most conventional track, this is a blues in a toe-tapping rhythmic groove, but still there is a considerable nod in the direction of modal playing, in that the blues progression is less complex than that of the usual hard-bop theme. The sighing motif played at the start by the trumpet and saxes underscores this simplicity.

Evans replaces Kelly for the remainder of the tracks. Like *Freedie Freeloader*, *So What* has a relaxed groove, and its song form (a 32-bar *aaba* pattern) is equally as familiar as the blues. But, following a rhythmically free and harmonically wandering introduction, the harmony is static, the *a* section resting on one sound corresponding, essentially, to the white keys of the piano, the *b* section moving that sound one pitch upwards. After the theme's 'melody', such as it is, Davis plays a lyrical solo. Coltrane discovers Davis's method for himself: confronted with the challenge of playing without the supporting crutch of fast-moving harmonies, he repeats and varies a series of ideas, rather than just 'running the changes'. He came to like this approach so much that it became the backbone of his most famous work while leading a quartet throughout the early 1960s; his *Impressions*, from 1962, is based directly on *So What*. Adderley fails to meet the same challenge and never quite locks into the feeling of the piece. Evans's contribution before the return of the theme is unremarkable. He is mainly filling the spaces between the trumpet and sax riff.

Blue in Green, on which Adderley does not play, shares the subdued atmosphere of the album as a whole, but harmonically it is diametrically opposed to modal jazz. What I find remarkable are the pretty melodies which Davis (playing with his patented brooding sound, produced with a stemless Harmon mute) and Coltrane fashion from the tortuous theme. It moves through an obscure, complex chord progression at a slow ballad tempo when Davis and Coltrane take the lead, then doubles into a moderately swinging pace whenever Evans has it. The best way to learn this theme is to listen to the ending, where Evans repeats it above Chambers's bowed bass notes. This sort of tonally ambiguous writing probably influenced the compositional style of two of Davis's future sidemen in the mid-1960s, Herbie Hancock and Wayne Shorter.

Endless confusion arises from the disagreement between the original liner notes and record label as to the respective identities of *Flamenco Sketches* and *All Blues*. All subsequent recordings of *All Blues* (not to mention good old common sense) confirm that it is, indeed, a blues, but unfortunately this has the uncomfortable result that the label is right and Evans's notes are wrong. The confusion has been carried widely into the literature, including Benny Green's notes for the LP issue in the UK (CBS BPG 62066). *All Blues*, then, is a 12-bar blues in 6/8 rhythm; repetition of the opening pattern stretches some of the choruses to 16 bars. Cobb plays bop waltz patterns with brushes during the theme and with sticks during the solos, and Chambers, foreshadowing jazz-rock, eschews walking bass lines in favour of a repeated figure closely synchronized with the drum accents. The harmony is even simpler than that of *Freedie Freeloader*, and, for those interested, Evans's cryptic comment that the form 'produces its mood through only a few modal changes' means that, in bars 1 to 8 and 11 to 12 of each chorus, the harmony sits on the pitches G–A–C–D–E–F, the only change being from the major mode (with B) to the minor mode (with B flat, in bars 5 to 6). By this session there is outstanding solo playing from all four men, including

Adderley, who has picked up some ideas about this new method; instead of trying to insert bursts of hard-bop playing, he spends much of his bouncy solo developing motifs that move up and down three steps.

Flamenco Sketches is, Evans obliquely tells us, 'a series of five scales, each to be played as long as the soloist wishes until he has completed the series'. This isn't quite true: each segment is either four or eight bars long. But it is true that the number is not exactly fixed, and on more than one occasion Chambers is fooled by a soloist who does or does not move on to the next segment when Chambers expects him to. This open-ended approach was a first step towards Coltrane's modal albums and towards jazz-rock, with its extended improvisations on chordally static patterns. I think this ethereal performance is one of the most beautiful recordings in all of jazz, with the soloists at their very best. Davis, with an eye to his album **Sketches of Spain** (recorded soon afterwards), deliberates over the half-step oscillations characteristic of flamenco music. Coltrane plays with the tender warmth which he was increasingly bringing to performances at ballad tempos. Adderley contributes a complex solo, in part romantic and singing, in part dashing and complex. Evans presents his unique sense of chordal voicing, spreading out and clustering together the piano keys in combinations all his own. Although all the compositions are credited to Davis, at least the first segment of *Flamenco Sketches* comes directly from Evans, who had recorded it as *Peace Piece* in 1958.

CD

USA: *Kind of Blue*, **Columbia Jazz Masterpieces CK 40579**

Miles Davis (tpt), Cannonball Adderley (as), John Coltrane (ts), Wynton Kelly (p), Paul Chambers (sb), Jimmy Cobb (d)
New York   2 March 1959   **Freddie Freeloader**

Bill Evans replaces Kelly   **So What**

omit Adderley   **Blue in Green**

Davis, Adderley, Coltrane, Evans, Chambers, Cobb
                22 April 1959   **Flamenco Sketches**
                                         All Blues

Other CDs

same contents:
    USA: CBS CK 08163
    Europe: CBS Jazz Masterworks 460603–2
    Japan: CBS 32 DP 513

LPs

same contents:
   USA: Columbia CL 1355; Columbia CS 8163; Columbia PC 8163; Colum-
   bia C6X 36976; Columbia Jazz Masterpieces CJ 40579
   UK: CBS BPG 62066; Fontana TFL 5072; Fontana STFL 513; Philips BBL
   7430; Philips SBBL 600
   Europe: CBS PC 8163; CBS 32109; CBS Jazz Masterpieces 460603–1; Fon-
   tana 682 059 TL; Fontana 855 133 TY; Philips BL 47047; Philips B 47047
   Netherlands: CBS S 63620
   Japan: CBS Sony SONP-S 0027; CBS Sony SOPL 155; CBS Sony 18 AP 2057;
   CBS Sony 23 AP 2556; CBS Sony 25 AP 755

Cassettes

same contents:
   USA: Columbia Jazz Masterpieces CJT 40579
   Europe: CBS BPG 62066; CBS Jazz Masterpieces 460603–4

* * *

Charles Mingus: *Mingus Ah Um; Charles Mingus Presents Charles Mingus*

Among the giants of jazz, composer, bandleader and string bass player
Charles Mingus ranged the furthest stylistically. While focusing on bop,
especially hard bop, his performances explored all of the other main cur-
rents in jazz – the New Orleans style, swing, free jazz and fusion – and other
genres as well – blues, rhythm and blues, boogie-woogie and gospel music.
Two albums recorded a year and a half apart, **Mingus Ah Um** and **Charles
Mingus Presents Charles Mingus**, exemplify all these interests excepting
fusion, which occupied Mingus in the last three years of his life (he died at
the beginning of 1979) and which, I think, yielded the least successful results
from among the diverse areas he touched. **Mingus Ah Um** (a pun on Latin
declension), recorded by a five- to seven-piece band in a Columbia studio in
1959, is a virtual catalogue of his great compositions. **Charles Mingus Presents Charles Mingus** shows off his talent for improvisation alongside that of
the formidable alto saxophonist and bass clarinettist Eric Dolphy, the two
men together as part of a quartet which simulated a nightclub performance
for the Candid label in 1960.
   Better Git it in your Soul is a revised version of a gospel-influenced soul-
jazz piece which Mingus had recorded a few months earlier as *Wednesday*

Night Prayer Meeting. The theme, shouted out in a medium-fast 6/8 rhythm by the reed and brass congregation, is in song form (*aaba*), but the body of the piece consists of blues improvisations of changing character. During these a one-note riff intoned by the horns either alternates with or accompanies first a boppish sax solo; second, oscillating piano chords in a pattern not far removed from that of Miles Davis's *All Blues*; third, stop-time choruses in which Booker Ervin's preaching on the tenor sax is accompanied by rhythm only (hand-clapping, bass drum, hi-hat cymbal); finally, before the theme returns, Dannie Richmond's drum solo, which maintains the 12-bar blues pattern in a rhythmic and timbral analogy to it.

Bird Calls, a vehicle for hard-bop improvisation, is notable for the moments of free jazz in the introduction, where the saxes imitate bird calls over atonal piano and bass lines and random drum accents, and at the end, where Mingus adds his shrieking bowed bass to the soft, squeaking saxes. During the main theme, the saxophones are not quite together. This may be one of many examples of Mingus's reputation for rehearsing insufficiently, but I find the push and pull exciting and wonder if it isn't intentional.

Fables of Faubus exists here in two versions, the second one being 'Original', because, according to Nat Hentoff's liner notes for the Candid LP, the biting and satirical lyrics protesting against racism in America were suppressed for the Columbia LP (Orval Faubus was the notoriously racist governor of Arkansas). The other side of the coin is that Columbia had the good sense to omit Mingus and Richmond's singing, which is horribly incompetent, however noble their intentions. The version from 1959 is well polished and exemplifies one of the ideals of the groups Mingus had been leading under the rubric Jazz Workshop: the interweaving saxophones and trombone move between playing composed material and improvising in a way that obscures boundaries between the two processes. Strictly, as a composition, *Fables of Faubus* is one of Mingus's great achievements, a rare success among attempts in jazz to create substantial structures without losing touch with what makes the music tick. The theme, a 71-bar structure (regularized to 64 bars to accommodate the soloists in the ensuing improvisations), lasts for over two minutes and takes a complex approach to conventional song form, subdividing each part of the familiar *aaba* pattern into an *aabc* pattern. Separate phrases have a markedly different character, including an eerie chord which builds up in the last subsection of each *a*; a double-time bop passage in the second subsection of *b* and a taunting oscillating figure in the last subsection of *b*; a machine-gun-like attack by the combined bass and drums in the first part of *a* during the improvisations; and a breaking up of the theme's double-time passage into two separate segments during the improvisations.

Pussy Cat Dues and *Jelly Roll* pay homage to earlier styles. The former is a slow blues, and, except in the theme, clarinet replaces alto sax, both for solo work and to participate in the earthy, relaxed riffs accompanying other solos. The latter, recorded earlier the same year as *My Jelly Roll Soul*, has a charming old-fashioned theme. Mingus sets the saxes and piano, playing together in harmony, against trombonist Jimmy Knepper, who improvises and plays composed counter-melodies. There is unfortunately a crude parody of early jazz, with Mingus's slap bass accompanying a ricky-ticky alto sax. Once again the body of the piece is hard bop, which has been lurking just around the corner throughout the album. The final series of false endings and solo breaks again recalls early jazz.

Mingus was fond of Duke Ellington's orchestra and frequently performed pieces from its repertory. *Open Letter to Duke*, Mingus's own composition, has a more tangential relationship to Ellington. After a hard-bop tenor sax solo and a drum interlude which moves into a Latin-jazz rhythm, a theme emerges. It begins in the Latin mood, but slows to a ballad which suggests Ellington as seen through Mingus's curved mirror. Imitating Johnny Hodges, one of the alto saxophonists takes the lead, scooping up to notes in a sensuous manner. But the harmony intentionally goes haywire, with stark dissonances peppered throughout this section. The ballad segues back into the Latin-jazz rhythm and then to a calypso beat beneath a happy alto sax solo; this last part might well have been called 'Open Letter to Sonny Rollins'.

Other references to past styles occur in *Boogie Stop Shuffle* and *Goodbye Pork Pie Hat*. On the former, trombonist Willie Dennis uses a wa-wa mute in the theme and for a riff beneath the alto saxophone's bop blues solo. On the latter, dedicated to Lester Young and his preferred style of hat, the saxophonists recall Young's cool, pure, vibratoless timbre. The theme, one of Mingus's most singable tunes, is built on a completely original 12-bar pattern with a bluesy feeling, yet not strictly the blues.

The album **Charles Mingus Presents Charles Mingus**, as Hentoff's liner notes explain, was recorded just as trumpeter Ted Curson and reed player Dolphy were leaving the Jazz Workshop, after it had held a long residency at the Showplace in New York. This album captures the spirit of their performances, complete with Mingus's instructions to the audience (don't talk, don't rattle your glasses, don't applaud) and his arguments with band members. And it captures Mingus's unmatched skills as a bass player: his roaring, vocalized string tone; his driving time-keeping, on top of the beat; his ability to provide a solid, sophisticated harmonic foundation for the others, without the help of a chordal instrument; his inventiveness and quickness as a melodic improviser.

The form of *Folk Forms, No.1* is a standard 12-bar blues, which this performance carries far from its folk roots, but without losing touch with a blues feeling. Largely disregarding traditional divisions into soloist and accompanists, the four men improvise collectively and take turns in playing solos, duos and trios, textural contrast being a key element in the conception of the piece. The harmonic pattern of the blues moves along steadily, as does the beat. Intermittently Richmond maintains swinging hard-bop cymbal patterns and occasionally, especially during the climactic ending, Mingus maintains a walking-bass line, but for the most part the beat is implicit, the compelling rhythmic drive determined more by the interlocking lines of the four men than by any single time-keeper's contribution. Notable features are, on the one hand, the many variations on basic blues riffs and, on the other, a nearly free-jazz passage in which the alto saxophone and trumpet stab out points of sound (following the bass solo). As he had done on *Better Git it in your Soul* and *Boogie Stop Shuffle*, Richmond follows the 12-bar blues pattern in his solos here; the first one is an especially clear example which breaks into a series of percussive calls and responses.

Original Faubus Fables is much rawer than the Columbia version. The theme is by necessity reduced to a skeletal four-part arrangement, with voices supplying, in addition to the previously unheard lyrics, only a few of the extra lines evident on the fuller version from the previous year. There is one fine new accompanimental figure: during the trumpet (later alto saxophone) solo, Mingus sings in falsetto voice a haunting line which moves either along with or in contrary motion to the accompanying alto sax (later trumpet). The high point of this version is Dolphy's fantastically original improvisation, putting together wide leaps, smeared fast-running bop lines, squeals, simple little motifs repeated at different pitches, and a distorted quotation from *When Johnny Comes Marching Home Again*, all played with a quavering, cutting timbre and a non-Western conception of pitch.

All the Things You Could Be by Now if Sigmund Freud's Wife was your Mother and *What Love* are based loosely on the popular songs *All the Things You Are* and *What is This Thing Called Love?*, but Mingus claims credit as composer on both tunes. The claim is a reasonable one. Unlike many mainstream performances of pop songs, these are radical transformations of the originals.

A motif which had the same shape (not the same rhythm) as that heard in Sergei Rachmaninoff's *Prelude in C sharp minor* found its way into bop versions of *All the Things You Are*. Mingus had put the two together in his 1955 recording *All the Things You Are in C Sharp Minor*, with Rachmaninoff's motif pounded out in a dreary and too-cute trombone counterpoint to Jerome Kern's melody. By 1960 the piece had evolved in a different direction. On the subjunctive *All the Things You Could Be . . .* Mingus completely recomposed the theme. Curson's bop-oriented solo generally follows the chord progression of Kern's original, but only listeners truly familiar with it will be able to keep their place, and I am not sure what the point of that would be. In *Folk Forms, No.1* the players make blues the focus of their esoteric performance, but here they mean to blow apart the underlying form. There are extreme changes of tempo, and Mingus regularly leaves the song altogether to invent counter-melodies to Curson's line. Dolphy's solo carries things further away. He was known for his ability to play 'outside', that is to improvise lines which are not in accord with the accompanying harmonies. Playing mainly fast-running lines, he demonstrates this approach, although the notion of 'outside' gradually loses its meaning, because the accompanists, excepting Richmond, get freer and freer. Ultimately, before Mingus's new theme returns, there is a dissonant passage in which Curson again and again repeats a grating three-note riff against Dolphy's wild melody.

What Love departs even further from the original song. There is little reason to classify this interpretation as anything but free jazz. Again Mingus has composed a new theme, which the four men play at a freely varied slow tempo. In the context Curson's solo is somewhat conservative, with the borrowed chord progression peeking out regularly, but portions of it move into free collective improvisation, and a flamenco-like drone recurs where the opening chords of the popular song might have been.

After the theme Curson begins to improvise while Dolphy switches from alto sax to bass clarinet. He single-handedly made this instrument into a viable jazz voice, his style of severe contrasts being well suited to the inherent sound of the bass clarinet, round and full-bodied in its lowest range, harshly edgy at the top. Dolphy begins by doodling in the background. There follows a bass solo, in which Mingus humorously quotes the song *Oh What a Beautiful Morning* and overtly plays the opening melody of *What is This Thing Called Love?*. Dolphy's entrance marks the beginning of a bizarre, hilarious free-jazz duet, in which the two men conduct an argument in an instrumental parallel to street talk, each insulting the other. At one point, just before Dolphy begins an incredible series of growling popping sounds, Mingus intones his playfully obscene speech patterns with the precision of *Pygmalion*'s Professor Higgins.

CD

USA: *Mingus Ah Um*, Columbia Jazz Masterpieces CK 40648

Jimmy Knepper (tb), John Handy (as), Shafi Hadi, Booker Ervin (ts), Horace Parlan (p), Charles Mingus (sb), Dannie Richmond (d)
New York   5 May 1959   **Better Git it in your Soul**

omit Knepper; Hadi (as)   **Bird Calls** *add Knepper; Hadi (as)*   **Fables of Faubus**

*as **Better Git it in your Soul**, but Handy (cl)*
                                            Pussy Cat Dues

*as **Better Git it in your Soul***   **Jelly Roll**

Willie Dennis (tb), Handy (as), Hadi, Ervin (ts), Parlan (p), Mingus (sb), Richmond (d)

12 May 1959   **Open Letter to Duke**
                     Boogie Stop Shuffle
                     Self Portrait in Three Colors
                     Goodbye Pork Pie Hat

Other CDs

same contents:
  Europe: CBS Jazz Masterpieces 450436–2
  Japan: CBS 25 DP 5304

LPs

same contents:
  USA: Columbia CL 1370; Columbia CS 8171; Columbia PC 8171; Columbia Jazz Masterpieces CJ 40648
  UK: CBS 66290; Philips BBL 7352; Realm 52364
  Europe: CBS Jazz Masterpieces 450436–1
  France: Philips B 07556 L
  Japan: CBS Sony SOPM 145; CBS Sony 20 AP 1454
plus additional tracks:
  USA: *Nostalgia in Times Square*, Columbia JG 35717

Cassettes

same contents:
  USA: Columbia Jazz Masterpieces CJT 40648
  Europe: CBS Jazz Masterpieces 450436–4

CD

USA: *Charles Mingus Presents Charles Mingus*, Candid CD 9005

Ted Curson (tpt), Eric Dolphy (as), Charles Mingus (sb), Dannie Richmond (d)
New York   20 Oct 1960   **Folk Forms, No.1**

add Mingus, Richmond (v)   **Original Faubus Fables**

*as **Folk Forms, No.1**, but Dolphy (bass cl)*
                                    What Love

*as **Folk Forms, No.1***   **All the Things You Could Be by
                                     Now if Sigmond Freud's Wife
                                     was your Mother**

Other CDs

same contents:
    USA: Candid CCD 79005
plus additional tracks:
    USA: *The Complete Candid Recordings of Charles Mingus*, Mosaic MD3–111

LPs

same contents:
    USA: Barnaby Z 30561; Candid CJM 8005; Candid CJS 9005; Jazzman JAZ
    5048
    France: America 30 AM 6082
plus additional tracks:
    USA: *The Complete Candid Recordings of Charles Mingus*, Mosaic MR4–111

* * *

Bill Evans: *The Village Vanguard Sessions*

After leaving Miles Davis's sextet in 1959, pianist Bill Evans mainly led trios.
The best of these, with bassist Scott LaFaro and drummer Paul Motian,
recorded at the Village Vanguard in New York on 25 June 1961, just ten days
before LaFaro died in an automobile accident. Two albums resulted. These
remain available both separately and under one cover. I think the single
album **Sunday at the Village Vanguard** is slightly stronger than the other
(**Waltz for Debby**), but no one who opts to buy the results of the whole
session should be disappointed.

Five of the selections are closely associated with Davis: the bop theme
Solar, the popular song *All of You*, the modal theme *Milestones*, and two
excerpts from *Porgy and Bess*, *My Man's Gone Now* and *Porgy* (this last is an
additional title not on either of the single albums). The remainder consists of

four pop songs, the waltz *Alice in Wonderland* (taken from the Walt Disney production), Evans's own *Waltz for Debby* (the body of which is not in waltz time) and two themes written by LaFaro. One, *Gloria's Step*, well captures the esoteric side of the trio's playing, with its oblique chord progression and its unusual length of 20 bars (in phrases of five plus five plus ten, rather than the usual four plus four plus eight); the other, a lugubrious tune entitled *Jade Visions*, offers the only dull moment (no doubt the musicians were tired by this time after a day-long marathon of recording 23 pieces, including alternate takes). The trio perform all these extremely quietly at slow to moderate tempos, and they might collectively be described as playing the coolest of cool jazz, were it not for the intensity generated by the looseness and extraordinary creativity of Evans and LaFaro's improvising above Motian's light bop rhythms, as well as the lovingly romantic interpretations of the ballad themes of *My Foolish Heart*, *Some other Spring* and *Detour Ahead*.

Solar summarizes much of the trio's approach and achievements. After Davis recorded this piece in 1954, it became a jazz standard. In straightforward little segments it moves quickly and endlessly through four keys (D minor – G – F – E flat – D minor – G – F – E flat . . .) and thus it has the potential to be treated as an exercise, with mechanical melodies and bass lines resulting from a key-by-key run through sequential patterns. But Evans and LaFaro avoid this trap. In part this is on account of a general notion which was then coming into free jazz – conceiving of the string bass as a melodic instrument rather than as a keeper of time and harmony – but more directly it derives from their personal styles. After playing the theme twice Evans lets his left hand rest, and one of the distinctive textures of the trio emerges: two interweaving melody lines supported by the drums. LaFaro, who not coincidentally was also recording with Ornette Coleman at the time, restlessly moves throughout the range of his instrument, from a soft boom at the bottom to a plaintive quiver at the top. He plays perfectly in tune and with great dexterity in a manner which engages Evans in a dialogue more than supporting his solo playing. This dialogue is mostly improvised, although just after the start LaFaro plays the melody of *Solar* against Evans's new line. At times *Solar* seems to disappear altogether, with nothing but the bop cymbal patterns separating this performance from a highly accessible type of free jazz. Finally Evans brings the chords back in to accompany his own melody and the beginning of LaFaro's solo. Later, another convention is slightly altered: we might expect normally to hear the three players together, then bass with drums, then briefer segments with the three alternating with the drums alone; but here, when this improvised trading back and forth begins, the irrepressible LaFaro keeps right on playing through the drum 'solos'. Here and elsewhere this enthusiasm also comes through on endings, where he is the last to stop playing. On *Milestones* someone (Evans?) starts laughing at LaFaro's refusal to quit.

All the tracks from this session demonstrate Evans's original conception of harmony. His playing is at one and the same time cutting, in his use of two- or three-note clusters within chords; precise, in his careful working out of the logical movement of individual notes; and smooth, in his use of the pedal to build overlapping pyramids of sound, as well as reiterating notes (usually from within the clusters) to obscure the boundaries between one chord and the next. Examples include the chordal rendition of the theme of *Milestones* (compare Red Garland's playing with Davis on the album of the same name from 1958), the opening of *Some other Spring* (borrowed from Evans's previous recordings of *Peace Piece*, made under his own name, and *Flamenco Sketches*, on Davis's album **Kind of Blue**) and his reharmonization of the theme of *All of You*.

It may not be surprising, given Evans's tremendous concentration on an imaginative approach to harmony and voice leading, that he sometimes neglects one aspect of rhythm, the independence between his hands. There are sections of boppish playing, with jabbing left-hand chords irregularly accentuating, or filling spaces between, the right-hand melodies. But far more often the two hands attack simultaneously, not in the locked-hands style of such pianists as Milt Buckner, George Shearing and Erroll Garner, but in a disappointingly undifferentiated presentation of melodic and accompanimental rhythms.

Evans's trio was enormously influential. Most specifically, in all but one way (namely that there are no gentle rock rhythms here) these performances foreshadow and define what would become more than a decade later the house style of the recording company ECM. If this session had taken place, say, in Oslo in 1980, no doubt we would be reading in lots of reviews and interviews about the perfect musical manifestation of nordic winter!

LP

USA: *The Village Vanguard Sessions*, Milestone M 47002

Bill Evans (p), Scott LaFaro (sb), Paul Motian (d)

New York	25 June 1961	**My Foolish Heart**	
		My Romance (take 1)	
		Some other Spring	
		Solar	
		Gloria's Step (take 2)	5
		My Man's Gone Now (take 2)	
		All of You (take 2)	
		Alice in Wonderland (take 2)	
		Porgy	
		Milestones	10

Detour Ahead (take 2)
Waltz for Debby (take 2)
Jade Visions (take 2)

Other LPs

same contents:
France: Milestone CA 271 68.101
plus additional tracks:
USA: *The Complete Riverside Recordings*, Riverside R 018
not incl. **Porgy**:
Italy: *The Golden Bill Evans Trio*, Riverside / Fonit Cetra RIV 4003–4004
tracks 1–3, 10–12:
USA: *Waltz for Debby*, Original Jazz Classics OJC 210; Riverside RLP 399;
Riverside RLP 9399
Japan: Riverside SMJ 6118
tracks 4–8, 13:
USA: *Sunday Evening at the Village Vanguard*, Original Jazz Classics OJC
140; Riverside RLP 376; Riverside RLP 9376;
USA: *Live at Village Vanguard*, Riverside ST 3006
Japan: *Sunday Evening at the Village Vanguard*, Riverside SMJ 6201

CDs

plus alternate tracks:
USA: *The Complete Riverside Recordings*, Riverside 12RCD 018–2
tracks 1–3, 10–12, plus alternate takes:
USA: *Waltz for Debby*, Original Jazz Classics OJCCD 210
tracks 4–8, 13, plus alternate takes:
USA: *Sunday Evening at the Village Vanguard*, Original Jazz Classics
OJCCD 140

Cassettes

tracks 1–3, 10–12:
USA: *Waltz for Debby*, Original Jazz Classics OJC 210
Japan: Riverside VCW 534
tracks 4–8, 13:
USA: *Sunday Evening at the Village Vanguard*, Original Jazz Classics OJC
140
Japan: Riverside VCW 535

John Coltrane: *A Love Supreme*

The 1960s witnessed repeated efforts to wed jazz with an explicitly religious programme: Lalo Schifrin's *Jazz Suite on the Mass Texts*, Mary Lou Williams's *Black Christ of the Andes*, Duke Ellington's first two sacred concerts, Michael Garrick's *Jazz Praises at Saint Paul's*, and, by far the most successful one, John Coltrane's *A Love Supreme*. The spiritual inspiration for the piece dates from 1957, when a strengthening of his religious convictions helped Coltrane overcome the debilitating effects of drug addiction and alcoholism. But the music dates from 1964, by which time he was nearly at the end of a decade-long search after creativity and perfection which led him from hard bop to free jazz. At this point he was playing with his quartet – pianist McCoy Tyner, bassist Jimmy Garrison, drummer Elvin Jones – in a manner which consolidated elements of both styles together with a droning approach to accompaniment derived from Miles Davis's modal jazz (described above).

A Love Supreme is a suite in four movements of widely differing character, the pairs on each side linked by bass solos. Coltrane's opening fanfare and solo in *Acknowledgement* summarizes the salient features of his mid-1960s style on his principal instrument, tenor saxophone (he also played soprano sax). There is his tone: hard, penetrating and metallic in the main range of the horn, it becomes edgy, harsh and sometimes distorted (breaking into two or more simultaneous pitches) in the highest register; he avoids vibrato. This has become a widely imitated sound, though many imitators have developed a facile ability to pop out the highest pitches, not realizing that Coltrane's harshness connects his sound to traditional gritty-voiced black-American timbres, and moreover his very struggle to reach these high notes yields some of the strongest emotional content in his music. There is also his manner of improvising melody by repeating and embellishing motifs. Several plain three- and four-note ideas form the basis for large segments of his playing. Garrison states one of these after the fanfare. Coltrane picks it up in the midst of his solo. The two men restate it together in various keys (without any intention of settling at the same time on the same key). Finally the group chants this motif in gruff voices, to the words 'a love supreme'. Throughout the body of the piece, Jones maintains a samba rhythm, not of the meek bossa nova variety, but rather an eruption of accents, as if a whole corps of Brazilian street drummers had been stuffed into his four limbs. Although Garrison and Tyner have some freedom, Garrison improvising counter-melodies to Coltrane's lines and Tyner following Coltrane into distant keys and higher levels of dissonance, both men return regularly to anchor the piece through drones and simple repeated patterns. Taken together, this combination of factors make the quartet's playing at once esoteric and accessible.

Garrison intermittently plays walking-bass lines on *Resolution* and

Pursuance, but these two movements of the suite are driven by Jones, who plays hard-bop rhythms in an ever-changing manner which is, if possible, even more effusive than Art Blakey's. Both pieces include piano solos partially indebted to the hard-bop style, but both are based more on drones and slithering blocks of chords than on boppish harmonies, and *Pursuance* has freer elements. It begins with a drum solo emphasizing colour and speed, not the beat. The theme, based on the blues, uses one of the main motifs heard in *Acknowledgement*, and Tyner develops this motif during a good portion of his solo, thus helping to unify the whole. Coltrane's solo is highly charged and at its intense climax the bop rhythms break apart. The movement concludes with Jones and Garrison improvising simultaneously; Jones drops out, leaving Garrison to prepare the calm finale.

Coltrane always had a fondness for ballads. If on one track he was playing at a mile a minute, on the next he might be giving a caressing rendition of a song associated with Frank Sinatra and Tommy Dorsey. In 1963 he invented a new equivalent to the standard jazz ballad, accommodating the idea of a ballad to the aesthetics and emotion of his non-standard style: *Alabama* was a meditative piece dedicated to black schoolchildren killed in the state. *Psalm* follows in this new path and carries it one step further by supplying a text. As Coltrane himself explains in his liner notes, *Psalm* is literally that, a musical narration of the prayer 'A Love Supreme' printed there. (At one point I purchased a reissue which had no liner notes. Did complaints over this omission lead to the appearance of a sticker on later reissues, stating 'all original liner notes & photos appear on inner sleeve'?) *Psalm* proceeds at a free rhythm, as would be appropriate for the singing of a psalm by a church choir, and accordingly the accompaniment is colouristic, with Jones using soft mallets rather than sticks. At the very end an unidentified second saxophonist plays two notes (a musical 'amen') and Coltrane restates at a higher pitch level a bit of the opening fanfare of *Acknowledgement*, thus neatly tying things up.

CD

USA: *A Love Supreme*, **MCA Impulse! AS 77 and ASC 77**

John Coltrane (ts, v), McCoy Tyner (p, v), Jimmy Garrison (sb, v), Elvin Jones (d, v)

New York   9 Dec 1964   **Acknowledgement**

omit all (v)   **Resolution**
                                                Pursuance
                                                Psalm

Other CDs
same contents:
    USA: MCA Impulse! MCAD 5660
    UK: MCA Impulse! DMCL 1648

LPs
same contents:
    USA: Impulse! A 77; Impulse! AS 77; MCA Impulse! 29017; MCA Impulse!
    MCA 5660
    UK: HMV CLP 1869; HMV CSD 1605; Impulse! IMPL 8001
    Japan: Impulse! IMP 88060; Imp! YP 8527

Cassettes
same contents:
    USA: Impulse! M 50077; MCA Impulse! MCAC 5660

* * *

Herbie Hancock: *Maiden Voyage*

In 1965, when the three men were finishing their second year as the rhythm
section of Miles Davis's quintet, pianist Herbie Hancock brought bassist Ron
Carter and drummer Tony Williams into the studio to record the album
Maiden Voyage. Fleshing out his quintet were tenor saxophonist George
Coleman, who had been their companion in Davis's group from 1963 to
1964, and trumpeter Freddie Hubbard. Over a decade later, this widely
influential album provided the inspiration for Hancock's taking a break
from jazz-rock and pop music to tour and record with his group VSOP (also
known as '*the* quintet'), with Wayne Shorter taking Coleman's place.

The quintet recorded five of Hancock's compositions. Like Davis's *So
What*, the theme of the title track *Maiden Voyage* has a conventional song
form (32-bar *aaba*) but fills this out with slow-moving, lush chords (two in
each section) which have no strong harmonic interrelationships. The piece is
glued together by a reiterated rhythm which shows Hancock's talent for
making something new out of a cliché. He takes the stereotypical bossa nova
rhythm, accented as on the first line, but turns the accents around, as on the
second:

ONE and two AND three and FOUR and / one and TWO and three AND four and
ONE and TWO and three AND four and / one and two AND three and four and

The esoteric theme of *The Eye of the Hurricane*, while taking hard-bop rhythm as a point of departure, has changing metres and dense harmonies. The theme of *Little One* has an introspective line played slowly but loosely, accompanied in part by a droning bowed bass, and it recalls such pieces as Ornette Coleman's dirge *Lonely Woman*. But these pieces take no further steps towards free jazz. The body of *The Eye of the Hurricane* is a fast hard-bop blues. The body of *Little One* is a moderately paced hard-bop waltz, but with oblique harmonies.

Survival of the Fittest is a more complex composition without such inconsistencies between the theme and the improvisations. In the first part, a Latin-jazz rhythmic vamp and a fanfare led by Hubbard announce a short, colouristic, unmetred drum solo by Williams. This segues into a trumpet solo, which builds over fast hard-bop rhythms and droning harmony before moving into free collective improvisation among Hubbard, Hancock, Carter and Williams. The cycle begins again, without the opening Latin rhythm: fanfare, drum solo (exploring a different part of the drum kit) and now saxophone. George Coleman is a more conservative player than the others. His solo never moves closer to free jazz than the playing of a dissonant trill, and so Hancock returns to the more comfortable drone. The fanfare announces the second part, an improvised duet between Williams's impressionistic drumming and Hancock's ethereal, atonal piano playing. It is astounding that Hancock has the ability both to create chart-topping pop music videos and to play free jazz in this rarefied manner.

The final piece, *Dolphin Dance*, again shows off Hancock's ability to combine the accessible with the esoteric. A light-hearted melody (constructed largely from a few simple motifs) twists its way gracefully through a tortuous succession of harmonies, juxtaposing aspects of blues, bop chord progressions, sweet static pop chords and bitonal conglomerates of sound, supported by Carter's nimble, dancing bass line and Williams's crisp swinging ride cymbal.

George Coleman takes John Coltrane's tenor saxophone tone as his point of departure, but draws his ideas from the blues end of the hard-bop style. He builds a majestic solo on the open form of *Maiden Voyage*, charges through standard hard-bop lines on the blues section of *The Eye of the Hurricane*, and perhaps proceeds cautiously in negotiating the more difficult pieces. It may be unfair, however, to judge Coleman against the company he is keeping at this moment. I think this is the finest album that Hubbard ever made. As always, following in the footsteps of Fats Navarro and Clifford Brown, his tone is beautiful and his technique impressive. But he has a bad habit of letting technical displays get in the way of music-making. Here for once that does not happen, and Hubbard, for his tasteful inventions, earns the right to be viewed as Miles Davis's substitute in this quintet. His impressive solos on *Maiden Voyage* and *Dolphin Dance* are far more complex than the usual 'well-constructed' jazz solo (that is, start slow and low and soft, end fast and high and loud), and he subtly varies speed, tunefulness and volume throughout.

Then there is the exemplary playing of the Hancock–Carter–Williams rhythm section, renowned as the best of its era. It should be clear from the description of Hancock's compositions that no single style of harmony, no moment-by-moment transition between styles, is beyond his and Carter's abilities. The three men together are equally at ease with rhythm, dancing around the beat with great flexibility while maintaining a metronomically precise internal pulse. They listen intensely to one another and to the horns, and react instantly. Some examples of their fluid work on *Maiden Voyage* are as follows. After establishing the 'warped' bossa nova rhythm, Williams increasingly departs from and ornaments it, such that his playing (especially from Hubbard's solo onwards) is more of a drum solo than accompanimental time-keeping. As Hubbard varies the loudness of his playing the three men follow suit immediately, and when Hubbard (towards the end of his solo) develops a swirling motif, Hancock echoes it (and later repeats the idea in his own solo) while Williams swirls around the drums. Hancock, to start his solo, begins to emphasize groups of three eighth notes, and Carter and Williams join in, not in a simple juxtaposition of three against four, but in an elastic, broken manner which creates an ambiguity between the two rhythms. At the end, as the piece is about to fade out, Williams, having played with a beat that is no longer Latin jazz but not quite yet jazz-rock, introduces a touch of swing rhythm.

CD

USA: *Maiden Voyage***, Blue Note B21K 46339**

Freddie Hubbard (tpt), George Coleman (ts), Herbie Hancock (p), Ron Carter (sb), Tony Williams (d)

Englewood	17 March 1965	**Maiden Voyage**
Cliffs, NJ		**The Eye of the Hurricane**
		Dolphin Dance
		Survival of the Fittest
		Little One

Other CDs

same contents:
   USA: Blue Note CDP 7–46339–2
   Japan: Blue Note CP 32–9535

LPs

same contents:
  USA: Blue Note BLP 4195 and BST 84195
  UK: Blue Note BNS 40020
  Portugal: Blue Note 1827861 (8E074–82786)
  Japan: Blue Note GXF 3020; Blue Note GXK 8050; Blue Note LNJ 80077;
  Blue Note BNJ 71057

Cassettes

same contents:
  USA: Blue Note 4BN 84195
  Japan: Blue Note AF 6003; Blue Note ZR 23–1080

CHAPTER 10

Free Jazz

Ekkehard Jost

At the end of the 1950s Ornette Coleman made a startling statement: 'Let's play the music and not the background' (in Martin Williams: *The Jazz Tradition*, New York, 1970, p. 207). With this sentence, Coleman, who was then one of the pioneers of a new form of music that was soon to be called free jazz (after one of his recordings), proclaimed an aesthetic programme that paved the way for one of the most radical moves in the stylistic evolution of jazz, which until then had flowed comparatively smoothly. By 'background' Coleman obviously meant the traditional framework of jazz improvisation which had been established in the music's early years and which had never before been questioned seriously. This background consisted of a couple of rules and agreements that more or less controlled the individual means of expression of improvising musicians and that regulated musical interaction within a group: the elementary formal framework of a jazz piece (theme – improvisation – theme), its harmonic and metric structure (derived from the theme) and the normative character of a constant fundamental beat. Whereas most of the preceding stylistic developments manifested themselves in gradual changes of technical and expressive means of creation, and sometimes also in the growing complexity of the structure of the background, in the years around 1960 the background itself started to disintegrate. The break from a traditional system of rules led to a precarious situation full of contradictions and insecurity, for with the liberation *from* old norms the question arose what this liberation should be *for*.

The musicians who set out to find their ways through the stylistic mazes of the new music developed a large repertory of expressive means and principles of creation which, in its broadness, proved to be unique in jazz. The repertory not only concentrated on the new and unheard, but also encompassed blues, many traditional forms of jazz, musics of the Third World, and the European avant garde. To free oneself from the norms of strict formal patterns, a common harmonic and rhythmic language and a fundamental beat did not mean that all this was now and forever forbidden, but that it was not automatically required.

Free jazz as a stylistic term is therefore only valuable when the freedom promised by the little word 'free' is understood as a freedom of choice among an infinite number of alternatives and not merely as a rebellion against tradition. And this of course means that free jazz cannot be understood as a compact style of jazz with definite characteristics and sharply drawn borders, but rather as a stylistic conglomerate, the most essential feature of which is its potential diversity. A few central points among the vast variety of musical changes and innovations that came along with free jazz are as follows:

The questioning (not the abolition) of any kinds of rules.

The growing importance of spontaneous interaction among players and, connected with this, the partial nullification of traditional divisions between soloists and accompanists, and a growing tendency toward collective instead of solo improvisation.

The emancipation of sound colour, which becomes an independent means of creation and consequently opens the possibility of improvising amelodically.

The importance of energy and intensity as communicative elements and sources for collective ecstasy.

A turn towards musical cultures of the Third World and thereby the integration of diverse 'exotic' elements into jazz.

A growing consciousness of social, political and economic problems among musicians and the consequent development of a new form of self-understanding.

All these points mark tendencies and are, taken together, not to be related to one single musician or group. Their individual relevance during the evolution of free jazz should become apparent in the following essays.

* * *

Ornette Coleman: *The Shape of Jazz to Come; Free Jazz*

Ornette Coleman grew up – musically speaking – near the roots of jazz. Born in the black ghetto of Fort Worth, Texas, he spent his years of apprenticeship in the rough atmosphere of tent shows, where musicians played the blues in a rude and original way that was untouched by the polish of jazz. When, around 1955, Coleman left rhythm and blues and turned to jazz, he adapted his playing to the established principles, but only partly and not for long.

The first recordings that Coleman, after years of hunger and frustration, recorded with his partner, trumpeter Don Cherry, in Los Angeles in 1958–9 show a hesitating revolutionary, hampered by an inadequate rhythm section and by the image of a record label, Contemporary, attached to the then contemporary West Coast jazz style. Coleman's aesthetic programme, the abolition of the 'background', was not to be solved in these surroundings.

The turning-point came in 1959 with a six-month engagement at the Five Spot in New York and with recording a couple of albums for Atlantic Records. In the meantime Coleman had settled upon some appropriate partners who, together with Cherry, not only followed his concept of playing freely but also made their own decisive contributions: bassist Charlie Haden and drummer Billy Higgins, both of whom had earlier played with Coleman in Los Angeles.

Coleman's musical innovations, and their shock effect on jazz listeners at the time, proceeded mainly from the negation of a quasi-axiomatic prerequisite of late 1950s jazz: the use of a predetermined harmonic framework as a formal element and as a basis for improvisation. This negative definition alone does not, of course, capture the character of Coleman's music, but it is important to realize that it was mainly the *lack* of these features that collided with the listening habits of jazz audiences. What Coleman had to offer in place of the rules which he threw overboard was less apparent and became evident only with intensive listening. His compositions, the themes or 'heads' of his pieces, are no longer functioning just to supply a set of chord changes to the improvisers, but in fact in most of his pieces there is a much deeper unity of theme and improvisation. The nature of that unity is more emotional than formal insofar as the expressive character of his themes often determines the emotional content of his improvisations, as is apparent from the lamenting character of *Lonely Woman* and the boppish *Chronology*. A most interesting relationship between composition and improvisation is represented by *Congeniality*, which would become a model for many other of Coleman's themes. The expressive content of this rather complex thematic structure is happy, sad and hectic, all three together, and it is up to the improviser to choose from the reservoir of emotional content. *Congeniality*, therefore, is a free jazz theme in the truest sense.

Both Coleman's themes and his improvisations reveal a peculiar mixture of complexity and simplicity. Both reflect a definite blues character, which by means of an extremely angular phrasing often becomes distorted without ever losing its identity. And, as in archaic blues singing, Coleman ignores not only the border lines of established formal frameworks but also the norms of intonation, especially those following the laws of equal temperament. Nevertheless, his improvisations are by no means so 'disorderly' as they appeared to audiences at the time. On the contrary, independent from the limiting structures of chord changes, his solos reveal a fascinating inner logic: one musical thought develops from another, becomes transformed, distorted, and leads into another one – a process of motivic improvisation in which the details very often show a rather simple, folksong-like character and yet the total structure gives the impression of high complexity. One is reminded of Bix Beiderbecke's notion of the 'correlated chorus', but with the 'chorus' left out!

In his notes to **Change of the Century** (recorded in October 1959), Coleman wrote: 'Perhaps the most important new element in our music is our conception of free group improvisation'. Considering the time it was written, this should be appraised as a plan whose realization still had to wait some time. To be sure, by that time Coleman's music was already free from norms previously held to be inviolable. But he had not given up the dominating role of the *soloist* and the resultant auxiliary role of the *accompanists*. The bassist had been liberated from playing chord progressions, but he and the drummer still had to mark the beat. The universally common sequence of composed ensembles and improvised solos was only rarely broken by fainthearted free collective improvisation.

This all radically changed in December 1960 with *Free Jazz*, a performance that named a whole musical era. To record it, two quartets gathered in the Atlantic studio: with Coleman were Cherry, Haden, and drummers Higgins and Ed Blackwell (all members of his groups), plus bass clarinettist Eric Dolphy, trumpeter Freddie Hubbard, and string bass player Scott LaFaro. These eight musicians carried Coleman's conception of 'free group improvisation' to a degree of completeness such as had never been heard before in jazz. In terms of freedom, as it was understood in 1960, the outer framework of this 36-minute piece is infinitesimal. Transitional ensemble passages link single complexes, each led by a different 'soloist'. Some of the ensembles are written out and have the character of Coleman's typical lines. Others are partially improvised structures which he misleadingly calls 'harmonic unisons'; here he provides the players with tonal material, the timing of which is not fixed. This procedure was to be highly important as a compositional technique in later developments of free jazz.

The players have obviously agreed on a tonal centre and the tempo, to which they adhere from start to finish. Coleman also allotted roles: Haden and Blackwell are responsible for the fundamental rhythm, which LaFaro and Higgins constantly challenge and consciously 'endanger'. The music played on the basis of these agreements depends for coherence almost exclusively on the players' readiness to interact. Within a traditional framework, an uninspired collective improvisation with no interactions among the players might be hard to take, but would not end in a musical catastrophe. The same unrelated simultaneity within the boundlessness of free jazz could only end in chaos. Coleman and his musicians must have been aware of this danger. They avoided it by a method that had already given shape to Coleman's solo improvisations: motivic chain associations. In *Free Jazz* these are evolved by the group as a whole, not just by a single improviser. Ideas introduced by the 'soloist' of a given section are spontaneously paraphrased by the other players, developed further, and handed back to the originator in altered form. Despite an abundance of motivic interaction, the overall character of *Free Jazz* must be called static rather than dynamic. Only rarely do emotional climaxes occur, and there is hardly any differentiation of expression. The wealth of musical ideas and the continuous exchange of thoughts takes place on an unvarying expressive level. Now and then there are passages in which folksong-like phrases by Coleman suggest a kind of bucolic peacefulness; and Dolphy's rumbling, vocalized bass clarinet sound adds an occasional humorous touch. But these passages are both short and relatively incidental.

Thirty years later, one can only speculate about the causes of this emotional – not musical – sameness. Perhaps Coleman and his musicians were too occupied articulating a newly acquired vocabulary and conquering a musical terra incognita to devise a palette of moods and temperaments in the process. It may also be that Coleman set out to create a static, homogeneous whole, his main point being the integration of individual ideas to form an interlocking collective. His later music would seem to support the latter theory.

CD

USA: *The Shape of Jazz to Come*, **Atlantic 1317–2**

Don Cherry (pocket c), Ornette Coleman (as), Charlie Haden (sb), Billy Higgins (d)
Hollywood   22 May 1959   **Focus on Sanity**
                                            Chronology
                                            Peace
                                            Congeniality
                                            Lonely Woman

Other CDs

same contents:
  USA: Atlantic 19238–2
  Europe: Atlantic 781339–2
  Japan: Atlantic 30 XD 1032

LPs

same contents:
    USA: Atlantic LP 1317; Atlantic SD 1317
    UK: Atlantic 587 022; Atlantic S588 022
    France: Atlantic 40441; Atlantic 332 010
    Japan: Atlantic P 6004; Atlantic P 7510

CD

USA: *Free Jazz*, Atlantic 1364–2

Cherry (pocket c), Hubbard (t), Coleman (as), Eric Dolphy (bass cl), Haden, Scott LaFaro (sb), Ed Blackwell, Higgins (d)
New York   21 Dec 1960   **Free Jazz**

Other CDs

same contents:
    Europe: Atlantic CD 1364–2
    Japan: Atlantic 30 XD 1031

LPs

same contents:
    USA: Atlantic LP 1364; Atlantic SD 1364
    France: Atlantic 40232; Atlantic 50240; Atlantic 412 008
    Japan: Atlantic P 6059

* * *

Cecil Taylor: *Unit Structures*

'Call Ornette the shepherd and Cecil the seer.' In these words tenor saxophonist and poet Archie Shepp characterized the two musicians who are at once the true initiators of free jazz and its musical and psychological antipodes ('A View from the Inside', *Down Beat Music '66*, Chicago, 1966, pp. 39–44). One side of the coin is the 'shepherd' Coleman, with a new and almost folkloristic simplicity of expression whose roots – for all Coleman's abrogation of traditional norms – go back to the blues, the bedrock of jazz. The other side is the 'seer' Cecil Taylor, whose music is marked by unremitting tension between emotionality and a structural complexity that is due in part to assimilating tendencies of contemporary European and American new music into the language of free jazz.

Born in New York and raised in a middle-class milieu, Taylor attended the New England Conservatory in Boston, where he became familiar with the music of Bartók, Stravinsky and Schoenberg. Clearly it was there that he developed the idea of trying 'to consciously utilize the energies and techniques of European composers, and to blend them with the traditional music of the American Negro, and in this way create a new energy' (Shepp, op. cit.).

Two aspects are essential to an understanding of Taylor's music: his rhythmic approach and his attitude towards musical form. His music generally has no fixed tempo and therefore most of the time lacks the elementary quality of mainstream styles, swing. Nevertheless, his music generates an immense drive, a phenomenon that is sometimes called by contemporary theorists 'rhythmic energy'. 'Energy', of course, is a metaphor whose terminological virtues are problematic. In any event, energy is not to be misunderstood as loudness, measured in decibels, but it is – in the sense of kinetic energy – a variable of time. It creates motion or results from motion, in a process by which the level of loudness is just one variable and by no means a constant. Taylor's concept of rhythmic energy was very influential on younger free-jazz musicians, especially in Europe.

Similarly, Taylor creates *ad hoc*, open forms which nonetheless follow certain creative principles. He organizes many pieces in three parts, and he may repeat the second and third, each time with a different content. He calls these formal units *Anacrusis*, *Plain* and *Area*. The title of the first part is taken from antique prosody and means 'upbeat'. Its purpose, then, is to lay down a general 'programme' rather than to provide material for improvisatory elaboration. That happens in the section called *Plain*. There the actual thematic (or motivic) material evolves. In the process of improvisation the players state, juxtapose and reshape predetermined structures. New melodic and rhythmic patterns grow out of given patterns. As Taylor obscurely explains in his own liner notes, 'content, quality and change growth in addition to direction found [*sic*]'. In the third part, *Area*, 'intuition and given material mix group interaction.' An 'unknown totality, made whole through self analysis (improvisation), the conscious manipulation of known material.' The realization of this method of spontaneous formal construction in his compositions proves to be extremely flexible. What happens is not that traditional formal schemes are replaced by others whose novelty lay only in an unorthodox terminology; the formal disposition of *Anacrusis*, *Plain* and *Area* does not create boundaries, but directions, not predictable structures, but progressive developments.

Taylor's principles may be deduced very well from his composition-improvisation *Unit Structures*, a piece which draws its title from the large repertory of structural units which build its substantial material. The *Anacrusis* here is a brief (one minute long) episode in which the production of sound colour plays the dominant role. *Plain 1* follows, in which collective improvising presents and develops the different structural units. The two reedmen, Ken McIntyre and Jimmy Lyons, dominate *Area 1*, which is freely improvised. In the rather brief *Plain 2* again some structural units are established and transformed. *Area 2* follows, in which trumpeter Eddie Gale Stevens Jr and finally Taylor himself step into the foreground. The whole ensemble then joins in, improvising into the finale.

What Taylor does in *Unit Structures* illustrates several things that are of great importance to free jazz as a whole. Beneath the emotional impact of his music, which is what the listener primarily responds to, is an intricate network of formal relationships. These inner formative aspects – created by composition and agreement, as well as by spontaneous interaction on the part of the players – are utterly independent of traditional schematic demarcations and thus have only a low degree of predictability for the listener. The German jazz critic Manfred Miller correctly states that a first unprepared encounter with Taylor's music usually causes complete confusion ('Cecil Taylor: Schlüsselfigur der Avantgarde', *Neue Musikzeitung*, xix/1, Feb/March 1970, 10). And, especially at live performances by his group, again and again one meets listeners who are willing but irritated. Overwhelmed by the energy and intensity of the music, they are rarely able immediately to grasp the inner structures. But it is precisely the formative details – which become apparent only after several listenings – that set Taylor's music apart from that of his many cluster-clumping emulators. By demonstrating that spontaneity and structure need not be mutually exclusive, Taylor shows that the freedom of free jazz does not mean complete abstention from every kind of organization. Freedom lies, first and foremost, in the opportunity to make a conscious choice from boundless material. Further, the idea is to shape this material in such a way that the end result is not only a psychogram of the musicians involved, but a musical structure, balancing in equal measure emotion and intellect, energy and form.

CD

USA: *Unit Structures*, **Blue Note CDP 7–84237-2**

Jimmy Lyons (as), Ken McIntyre (as), Cecil Taylor (p), Henry Grimes, Alan Silva (sb), Andrew Cyrille (d)
Englewood   19 May 1966   **Steps**
Cliffs, NJ

Eddie Gale Stevens Jr (tpt), McIntyre (oboe), Taylor (p and bells), Grimes, Silva (sb), Cyrille (d)

**Enter Evening (Soft Line
Structure)**

Stevens (tpt), Lyons (as), McIntyre (bass cl), Taylor (p), Grimes, Silva (sb), Cyrille (d)   **Unit Structures (As of a Now; Section)**

Taylor, Grimes, Silva, Cyrille   **Tales (8 Whips)**

Other CDs

same contents:
  USA: Blue Note BCT 84237
  UK: Blue Note BNZ 217

LPs

same contents:
  USA Blue Note BLP 4237 and BST 84237
  UK: Blue Note BNS 40023
  Japan: Blue Note GXK 8147; Blue Note BNJ 71047

* * *

John Coltrane: *Ascension*

In 1965 the evolution of free jazz received a new central figure and thus a new stylistic focus. John Coltrane, who had worked his way from the rhythm-and-blues sounds of Earl Bostic's group, through hard bop, Miles Davis's modal concept and his own harmonic adventures (*Giant Steps*), now joined the young generation of free players. This step not only had far-reaching musical consequences but also a strong symbolic value: Coltrane, the established artist, demonstrated his solidarity with a group of socially underprivileged young musicians of the New York scene.

The first and, at the same time, most famous musical document of this coalition is an approximately three-quarter-hour piece, *Ascension*, recorded on 25 June 1965 in the Impulse! studios in New York, in two takes of uncertain order. (Confusingly, both takes were released at one time or another under the original catalogue number, Impulse! 95; they were distinguished by the order of solos, listed below, and by the words 'Edition I' or 'Edition II', stamped on the vinyl near the LP label.) Taking part were trumpeters Dewey Johnson and Freddie Hubbard, alto saxophonists Marion Brown and John Tchicai, tenor players Coltrane, Pharoah Sanders and Archie Shepp, pianist McCoy Tyner, string bassists Art Davis and Jimmy Garrison, and drummer Elvin Jones.

From the list of players alone, it is clear that this session meant a great deal more than just another free-jazz recording. But what is really special about *Ascension* goes beyond the personnel of the group and the length of the piece. 'This is possibly the most powerful human sound ever recorded', began the review of *Ascension* by jazz theorist and critic Bill Mathieu in *Down Beat* (5 May 1966, p. 25). His words are just as valid today as they were in the mid-1960s, a significant reflection of the emotional impact *Ascension* had on listeners at the time.

Even while *Ascension* was being made, that is, during the recording session, the musicians must have been aware that they were involved in an experience of total communication and that the product could never match that experience completely. Marion Brown said later: 'We did two takes, and they both had that kind of thing in them that makes people scream. The people who were in the studio *were screaming*' (liner notes to **Ascension**, HMV CSD 3543, by A. B. Spellman). Here we arrive at a problem that looms ever larger as free jazz develops: being in on the act of creation, the 'now', becomes at least as significant as the musical end-product, the 'after'. Whether or not the acoustical result, the recording, transcends the event of total communication is, likely as not, of secondary interest to the musicians themselves. Nevertheless, one of the most apparent features for the listener is the extraordinary emotion of *Ascension*. This very intensity may obscure the fact that the piece has thoroughly traditional elements, and, where one might assume that each man is playing exactly what he pleases, there is actually a definite musical organization.

As many listeners have pointed out, the construction of *Ascension* has parallels to that of Ornette Coleman's double quartet recording from 1960, *Free Jazz*. In both, the formal framework is an alternation of collective improvisations and solos, and there is a minimum of preset material and a maximum of spontaneous, free creation. But although the two show a similar radical stance in their renunciation of convention (and thus similarly triggered the development of jazz in ensuing years), their internal structure and their emotional content represent fundamentally different dialects of the same language.

In *Ascension*, the formal disposition into collective improvisations and solos has a second framework superimposed on it, which is a source of structural differentiation, especially during ensemble passages. It consists of systematic changes of modal levels, and occurs with only slight deviations in all eight collective improvisations. Such an organization – however elementary it may be – naturally needs a certain amount of steering, especially when, as in *Ascension*, organization occurs spontaneously, being subject to no schematic breakdown with a fixed timing. Usually the steersman is Coltrane. He gives signals for changing modes by holding tones related to the modal level towards which the music is moving. In the collective improvisations, changes thus initiated are then usually defined by complete scales or scale fragments – played as a rule by Hubbard – and stabilized by chordal patterns from Tyner.

The melodic nucleus of *Ascension*, a short motif played by Coltrane to open the first collective improvisation, doubtless has a symbolic character; its similarity to the main theme of his suite *A Love Supreme* cannot be missed. But this motif has only a secondary function in the piece. The principal model used to steer the group improvisations consists of descending lines which both define the mode and create a distinct body of sound. These lines, often scalar fragments or broken chords drawn from the modal framework, are obviously prearranged only as to the general course they take, not as to their melodic shape or exactly where they occur.

Thus a large number of rhythmically independent lines are set against one another by seven wind instruments, with resultant overlapping. This super-imposition produces rapidly moving sound-fields whose rhythmic differen-tiation is provided as a rule by the rhythm section, rather than coming from within. When seven independent lines coincide, the relationships among them lose clarity, fusing into a field of sound enlivened by irregular accen-tuations. On the other hand, there are passages in *Ascension* in which indi-vidual musicians, by incessantly repeating short rhythmic motifs, create a driving, drilling rhythm whose impulses, when taken up by the other im-provisers, awaken associations with the energetic rhythms of Cecil Taylor's groups.

In spite of the variety and density of sound and the occasionally dissonant cutting edge of these group improvisations, it is evident that their elements, namely what the various musicians play, are less 'revolutionary' melodically than the sum of those parts. Whereas in the group improvisations of Cole-man's *Free Jazz* every melody has a clearly drawn intervallic structure (the result of motivic give and take between the musicians), the horn lines in *Ascension*, taken singly, are relatively simple in shape.

Here we can lay hold of one of the essential differences between these two recordings, whose consequences are probably the most important and far reaching in the evolution of free jazz. In the collective improvisations of *Free Jazz* the contributions of each and every improviser have a certain melodic life of their own; motivic connections and dove-tailing of the various parts create a polyphonic web of interactions. In *Ascension*, on the other hand, the parts contribute above all to the formation of changing sound-structures, in which the individual usually has only a secondary importance. Quite plainly, the central idea is not to produce a network of interwoven indepen-dent lines, but dense sound complexes.

The musical significance of *Ascension* for the further course of jazz history lies in part in its chronological position. Coming five years after Coleman's piece, it signals a second phase of free collective improvisation: the chamber-music dialogue between musicians, which was Coleman's principal aim, is succeeded by orchestral sound structures. No longer does the whole take its meaning from the constituent elements. Just the reverse: the elements now cannot be understood except by reference to the whole.

CD

USA: *Ascension*, **MCA Impulse! AS 95. Edition II, with solos by Coltrane, Johnson, Sanders, Hubbard, Brown, Shepp, Tchicai, Tyner, basses.**

Freddie Hubbard, Dewey Johnson (tpt), Marion Brown, John Tchicai (as), John Coltrane, Pharoah Sanders, Archie Shepp (ts), McCoy Tyner (p), Art Davis, Jimmy Garrison (sb), Elvin Jones (d)

Englewood   28 June 1965   **Ascension**
Cliffs, NJ

Other CDs
Edition I, with solos by Coltrane, Johnson, Sanders, Hubbard, Shepp,
    Tchicai, Brown, Tyner, basses, Jones:
    Europe: Impulse! 254745–2
    Japan: Impulse! 32 XD 584

Edition II, as above:
    Europe: Impulse! 254618–2
    Japan: Impulse! 32 XD 577

LPs
Edition I:
    USA: Impulse! A 95; Impulse! AS 95
    UK: HMV CLP 3543 and CSD 3543
    France: EMI 9563
    Japan: King SR 3026/28; MCA VIM 4666

Edition II:
    USA: Impulse! A 95; Impulse! AS 95; MCA-Impulse! 29020
    UK: Jasmine JAS 45
    Japan: Impulse! IMP 88119; Impulse! YP 8529; MCA VIM 4624

Cassettes
Edition II:
    UK: Jasmine JASC 45

Don Cherry: *Eternal Rhythm*

Don Cherry first became known on the jazz scene as the trumpeter of the original Ornette Coleman quartet. (Actually he did not play trumpet but a pocket cornet.) After he left Coleman's group in the early 1960s Cherry played with Sonny Rollins, Archie Shepp and Albert Ayler, among others. In 1965 he moved to Europe, where he formed his own groups and started developing a new concept for the integration of composition and improvisation into large suites, exemplified on his albums **Complete Communion** (1965) and **Symphony for Improvisers** (1966). At the same time, Cherry became involved in non-Western musics, especially those of India, Turkey and North Africa. From these sources he not only adapted different stylistic means (rhythmic patterns, circular melodies) but also expanded his own instrumental scope by learning to play wooden flutes, conch horns, berimbau, and a large array of percussion instruments.

The first recorded document of this evolution is an LP Cherry made in Berlin in 1968, **Eternal Rhythm**. It was made in the wake of a concert during the Berlin Jazztage, for which he was given the chance to assemble an orchestra in line with his own ideas. At the concert, between the big bands of Maynard Ferguson and Count Basie, Cherry's orchestra ultimately demolished everything the Berlin audience was accustomed to thinking about big bands as an institution. Cherry accomplished this by employing his ten musicians not as members of sections, not as players who either lead or accompany, but as the individualists they were.

The musicians he brought together in the studio to record the suite *Eternal Rhythm* on 11 and 12 November 1968 were among the best available on the European free-jazz scene at that time: trombonists Albert Mangelsdorff and Eje Thelin, saxophonist Bernt Rosengren, pianist Joachim Kühn, bassist Arild Andersen and drummer Jacques Thollot; Karl Berger, a former member of Cherry's groups then working in New York, played various metallophones. The American guitarist Sonny Sharrock also came over to work with this ensemble.

A necessary point in understanding *Eternal Rhythm* is that, despite its *ad hoc* assembly, put together for Berlin, the piece is by no means all a product of spontaneous ideas organized and laid down in a few rehearsals, but rather an extract of Cherry's previous work with his European groups. The group conception of *Eternal Rhythm* consists of a composed or agreed-upon system of references, within which the musicians have a maximum amount of individual freedom and where Cherry acts as the catalyst: 'Don is a natural conductor of music through his playing', said Berger in the programme notes for the festival ('Das Don-Cherry-Märchen', *Berliner Jazztage 1968*, p. 12).

Themes occur at strategic points of the piece. They create structural differentiation and formal articulation, but they hardly figure as motivic material in the improvisations. All in all, the work seems to be designed from the outset for evolving sounds and rhythms rather than for developing motivic and melodic interconnections. Part of this shift of emphasis is the fact that the solos are relatively few and short; collective improvisation predominates. When solo instruments do emerge, they are almost always surrounded by a dense web of sounds, partly diffuse and partly accentuated, which provide a constantly changing background. Occasionally, as in Kühn's piano solo, the background gradually heightens in dynamics, intensity and density until it becomes the foreground and submerges the solo.

A new element in Cherry's music underscores the dominance of tone colour and rhythm: third-world music. The most obvious indications of its influence are the many instruments which are in addition to each man's main horn. Cherry, for instance, plays a whole assortment of differently tuned flutes and recorders of Eastern origin. Rosengren plays a normal Western oboe, but he uses it more like an Indian sanāī. The percussion section makes the chief contribution to the oriental coloration of the orchestra. Its arsenal includes gongs, chimes and the Balinese gamelan instruments gender and saron; the latter are metal idiophones resembling the xylophone in form and owe their special sound to the tuned bamboo resonators fixed below the metal bars.

Don Cherry's *Eternal Rhythm*, with its own particular emphasis on Near and Far Eastern musical elements, by no means stands alone in the history of free jazz. It must be viewed together with similar ventures undertaken by musicians such as John Coltrane, Pharoah Sanders, Archie Shepp, Sunny Murray, Sun Ra, etc., as the consequence of a growing sympathy for the musical cultures of Africa and Asia. Within this stylistic metamorphosis, *Eternal Rhythm* has the status of an individual variant. On no account should it be placed in the same category as the **Jazz Meets the World** recordings made about the same time in Germany, which signalled (sometimes in a very self-conscious way) that the Third World was in vogue, just as bossa nova or Baroque jazz before it, and jazz-rock later. For Cherry, as opposed to most of the European musicians riding the oriental wave, occupation with African and Asian music signified more than just a short-lived fad. *Eternal Rhythm* should be considered as one long stride in a march which gradually increased the distance between Cherry and the rules of the game of the free-jazz mainstream.

LP

Germany: *Eternal Rhythm*, **Saba MPS 15204**

Don Cherry (c, bamboo fl, bengali fl, metal fl, plastic fl, gender, saron, northern

*bells, Haitian gourd, v), Albert Mangelsdorff, Eje Thelin (tb), Bernt Rosengren (cl,
ts, fl, oboe), Joachim Kühn (p), Sonny Sharrock (g), Arild Andersen (sb), Jacques
Thollot (d, saron, bells, gong, v), Karl Berger (vb, p, gender)*

Berlin	11–12 Nov 1968	**Baby's Breath**	
		Sonny Sharrock	
		Turkish Prayer	
		Crystal Clear (exposition)	
		Endless Beginnings	5

Cherry unaccompanied	**Baby's Breath**	
full orchestra	**Autumn Melody**	
	Lanoo	
	Crystal Clear (development)	
	Screaming	10
	Always Beginnings	

Other LPs

same contents:
  Germany: BASF 21 20680–7; MPS 15007; Saba MPS 68225

* * *

Art Ensemble of Chicago: *A Jackson in your House*

There is hardly any other group of individuals in free jazz as tightly
enclosed by a classification as those Chicago musicians who banded together in the mid-1960s under the heading of the Association for the Ad-
vancement of Creative Musicians (AACM) and who later, in several
formations, spread throughout the world the tidings of a new kind of
Chicago jazz.

   The specific nature of Chicago free jazz can be explained partly by geo-
graphical location and the nature of the jazz community in the city, where
the music arose relatively unaffected by what was happening musically in
New York. In New York, constantly increasing competition led jazzmen to
do their own thing, that is, to strive for uniqueness and individuality. Chicago was different. There was a unifying bond from the outset, in that the
musicians were members of a larger organization and renounced all claims
to individual fame. This ultimately had an effect on the stylistic evolution of
their music. When we speak of Chicago free jazz, then, we have to describe
not only a certain group of musicians and a certain kind of music, but also an

interdependence of social and musical factors to which that music owes its individual status within the stylistic conglomerate of free jazz.

The first musical core of Chicago free jazz became the Experimental Band, led by pianist Muhal Richard Abrams. Practically every AACM member played in this ever-changing orchestra, which thus became a kind of school for upcoming Chicago avant-gardists. During the second half of the 1960s a number of bands within the band emerged from Abrams's workshop. Proceeding from a common musical basis but employing different means, these smaller groups consolidated knowledge gained in the experimental workshop of the big band into the specific Chicago style of free jazz. The most prominent group within this context became the Art Ensemble of Chicago, consisting of Lester Bowie, Joseph Jarman, Roscoe Mitchell and Malachi Favors. Building on a distinct jazz foundation, this quartet expanded and consolidated into an unmistakable musical language the experience gained in the various AACM groups. Their music represents the maturity of Chicago free jazz.

One of the most important stylistic factors in AACM music from the very beginning was an exploration of tone colour, which led to the use of an unusual quantity of diverse instruments and also had a direct effect on creative principles, such as the development of static sound-fields. When the quartet went to Europe in 1969 it took along more than 500 musical instruments. A first impression of what that array included can be gained by summarizing the instruments listed on recordings made by the group in France:

Lester Bowie: trumpet, flugelhorn, cowhorn, bass drum.
Roscoe Mitchell: soprano, alto and bass saxophone, clarinet, flute, cymbals, gongs, conga drums, logs, steel drum, gongs, bells, siren, whistles.
Joseph Jarman: soprano, alto and tenor saxophone, clarinet, oboe, bassoon, flutes, marimba, vibraphone, guitar, conga drums, bells, gongs, whistles, sirens.
Malachi Favors: double bass, Fender bass, banjo, zither, log drums, other percussion.

Some recordings also have piano and accordion. (Later, in 1970, while still in Paris, Don Moye, playing drums and a wide variety of percussion, joined the group, making it a quintet.)

Considering the quantity of equipment and the availability of a wide range of sounds and colours, there is an astounding economy in their use. One of the decisive achievements of the Art Ensemble lies precisely in turning away from every kind of musical muscle-flexing. What creates the impression of intensity and enhancement is not decibels, but density and drive. Moreover, the music gains greatly in transparency by dispensing with a drummer. Actually, what is dispensed with is jazz percussion of the traditional kind, for each of the musicians plays several percussion instruments. However, by spreading the instruments over the quartet, by a division of labour into bass drum, cymbals, melodic percussion (marimba and vibraphone) and other struck devices, they employ percussion selectively and to a considerable degree as a means of structural differentiation. It is not constantly present as a matter of course.

Isolating the various elements of conventional jazz percussion goes hand in hand with a partial rejection of customary ways of playing other instruments. The piano, for example, which the Art Ensemble paradoxically puts in the 'little instrument' category, generally provides just a background of sound. The accordion does not play melodies – its traditional function – but produces long, sustained, static tones. Favors does not pluck the strings of the zither, but strikes them with a stick to produce either sharply accentuated clusters of indeterminate pitch or a rhythmic continuum. These and other examples of denatured sound rarely appear for their own sake and should not be understood as isolated occurrences sufficient unto themselves. In general, each stands in a dialectical relationship to the music around it, complementing some other musical element. For example, the interpolation of denatured sounds and noises sometimes deliberately disrupts standard themes, such as Dexter Gordon's *Dexterity*. Similar things happen during some lyrical trumpet solos by Bowie, whose beauty of melody and tone contrasts with the rattle and click of little instruments. This confrontation of various levels of expression and style, in which the expressive power of one level relativizes the other, is an important part of the Art Ensemble's basic conception, even though the passages in question may not be preplanned in detail but result from spontaneous interactions among the musicians.

Compared with the music of other AACM groups up to 1968, there is a considerable expansion in the Art Ensemble's thematic material. The group shows a partiality for traditional elements from all conceivable musical and cultural areas. The LP **A Jackson in your House** provides excellent examples of this. The title piece, a suite, begins with a pompous overture whose baroque grace is considerably impaired by percussive interjections and laughter. There follows a dixieland piece with slapped bass and a clarinet whose syncopated phrasing is insistently corny. Finally, an episode imitates the swing style. *Get in Line* goes at an unmilitary headlong pace until it ends in the total pandemonium of a collective cymbal-crashing session. The Viennese charm of *The Waltz* is rather adversely affected by the bass's hacking accentuations.

Without a doubt, this is music about music, for the 'historical' material appears unfiltered only in the rarest instances. Otherwise, the Art Ensemble shapes it to match the group's specific stylistic features. Clichés remain recognizable by allusion and occasionally by ironic overstatement, but they are never brought directly into play. Many of these pieces are funny (to use a word that is taboo in jazz criticism) and are doubtless meant to be. Others, such as the album **Message to our Folks** (included in the double album BYG 529.204, cited below), are obviously tied up with the socio-critical message of the Art Ensemble, which takes a much more direct and aggressive line than was the case in earlier AACM productions; ideology, no longer disguised as poetry, appears as a sermon (*Old Time Religion*). On the album **Certain Blacks**, from 1970, open agitation replaces metaphorical trappings on the title track *Certain Blacks Do What They Wanna! – Join Them!*. Getting these messages across in a medium as non-political as music necessarily means going back to models whose meaning the listener can decipher. But reversion does not unavoidably have to end in triviality. The Art Ensemble's 'traditional' themes demonstrate this conclusively. To measure them exclusively by an aesthetic yardstick, however, would be just as senseless as to interpret the group's improvisations in sound as protest.

LP

France: *A Jackson in your House*, **BYG Actuel 2**

Lester Bowie (tpt, flugelhorn, bass drums, horns, v), Roscoe Mitchell (as, ss, bass s, cl, fl, cymbals, gongs, conga drums, logs, bells, siren, whistle, steel drums, v), Joseph Jarman (as, ss, cl, oboe, fl, marimba, vb, conga drums, bells, whistles, gongs, siren, v), Malachi Favors (sb, elb, bj, log drums, zither, perc, v)

Paris	23 June 1969	**A Jackson in your House**
		Get in Line
		The Waltz
		Ericka
		Song for Charles

Other LPs

same contents:
  UK: Affinity AFF 9
  France: BYG 529.302
  Japan: BYG YX 8027; Toho TX 8027
plus additional tracks:
  France: *Art Ensemble of Chicago*, BYG 529.204

Sun Ra: *The Heliocentric Worlds of Sun Ra*

One of the most controversial personalities within the history of free jazz is pianist, composer and bandleader Sun Ra. Scolded as a charlatan by one faction of the jazz community, he is celebrated as a charismatic figure and genial innovator by another. Reasons for this discrepancy are more easily found in his intergalactic philosophy than in the musical output of his orchestra (which he calls 'Arkestra'), which was very convincing from the outset.

Like the AACM groups, Sun Ra developed his musical language in Chicago during the early 1960s. But before the mid-1960s his music could not be called free jazz. The first step in this stylistic direction is represented by two LPs recorded in 1965, **The Heliocentric Worlds of Sun Ra**, volumes 1 and 2. It is difficult to subject the albums to objective musical analysis. When one hears them today, they suggest comparisons with things that originated at the same time, or just before or after, in adjacent stylistic areas of free jazz. One is reminded of the monumental collective improvisation in Coltrane's *Ascension* (recorded the same year), of the unorthodox tone colours and the courageous use of silence in the AACM's music, of the collective composing in Cecil Taylor's groups. But beyond all musical and technical parallels – and having nothing to do with the extent to which tradition is overcome – there is a component in Sun Ra's music, at the time of **Heliocentric Worlds**, that distinguishes it from every other kind of free jazz: creative principles of composition and improvisation interweave with programmed emotional qualities.

On **Heliocentric Worlds**, one can hardly speak of composition in the customary sense. Not one of the ten pieces has fixed thematic material; there are no written-out horn arrangements; there is not even a tiny unison melodic line. Abstaining in this way from everything that can be prefabricated in the form of notes does not, however, lead to disorganization. On the contrary, the music on these two LPs has extraordinary clarity of structure and a broad range of emotional levels. This circumstance can presumably be traced to three different factors: the use of programmes to establish musical processes; a specific kind of communication between Sun Ra and his sidemen; and the high standard of these musicians.

There are clear indications in **Heliocentric Worlds** that Sun Ra's real 'thematic material' is found in the titles of his pieces, that the 'themes' are thus formulated verbally and not musically. Numerous interviews with Sun Ra and his musicians testify that he has always been concerned with translating ideas into music, illustrating emotional states or sketching pictures. The titles of his pieces function in that process as captions or mottos. During the 1950s translation of a verbal programme was more or less accomplished in the composition (that is, the arrangement, instrumentation, etc.), while improvisation by the soloists – who were still playing hard bop – was for the most part untouched by the programmatic aspects of the thematic material. Now, in 1965, the transformation of figurative or emotional ideas no longer occurs by writing out a composition. Instead, the motto expressed in the title of a piece directly intervenes in the process of improvisatory creation.

(With a good conscience, one may call this programme music, but one should not overlook the fact that in highly emotional music like jazz the expression of something, be it happiness, sadness, anger, sex, loneliness, peace, or whatever, has always been one of the triggers of musical creation. Renouncing emotion does not necessarily result in bad music, but it often does result in dull jazz.)

So that these theoretical considerations do not remain as mysterious and cryptic as Sun Ra's own explanations of his music generally are, I shall illustrate the translation of programmatic ideas into musical form in three pieces from the first volume of **Heliocentric Worlds**.

Outer Nothingness: the group translates the 'emptiness' of space into a musical context by coupling two expressive ideas: a strong emphasis on low instrumental registers, and tonal and rhythmic indeterminacy. Timpani, bongos and bass marimba (the last played by Sun Ra) provide a rhythmic background that is lively but diffusely accentuated. Against it, trombone, bass trombone, bass clarinet and baritone saxophone play long, sustained, dissonant, loud sounds in their lowest registers. The entrances do not all occur at once; sounds overlap, creating an impression of turgid, narrow clusters. The combination of bass register, atonality, rhythmic diffuseness and aggressive dynamics sets off that magical and threatening atmosphere which is present as an emotional basis in the ensemble passages. The collective improvisations in this piece, then, are as it were verbally pre-programmed, and some of the solos also realize the motto. A good example of the latter is John Gilmore's tenor saxophone solo, in which he suggests 'nothingness' in a significant way: he dispenses with melodic evolution. There are fragmentary phrases in half-steps, irregular single accents, and a great deal of 'space' (rests). He takes the solo at a free tempo and plays against a rhythmically unorganized, diffuse backdrop of drums, cymbals and bass marimba. He ends with overblown multiphonics (producing several pitches simultaneously in the highest register).

Dancing in the Sun: rhythm translates the title into music. This is the only piece on **Heliocentric Worlds** that has a continuous beat, and the improvisations swing in a traditional manner.

Nebulae: this is a solo improvisation by Sun Ra on celeste, an instrument whose timbre is relatively thin and yet diffuse. The sound itself is enough to awaken associations with something 'nebulous' and indeterminate, and therefore Sun Ra frequently uses the instrument in ensemble passages to create a quasi 'spheric' background of sound. The way Sun Ra improvises augments the non-transparency of the celeste's timbre: atonal lines in free tempo criss-cross, becoming interwoven into a dense melodic web, while irregularly interjected dissonant chords or clusters contribute to rhythmic insecurity.

The relationships between verbal theme and musical structure in **Heliocentric Worlds** are not all as easy to pin down as in these three examples. In particular the longer compositions – *Sun Myth*, *House of Beauty* and *Cosmic Chaos* – contain a profusion of forms and a diversity of emotional levels which can hardly be reduced to a single programmatic theme. The tendency to translate ideas or emotional states into music is nevertheless noticeable almost throughout. And that translation of thoughts or feelings proves to be what really governs the progress of Sun Ra's music. 'My rule is that every note written or played must be a living note. In order to achieve this, I use notes like words in a sentence, making each series of sounds a separate thought' (Barry McRae: 'Sun Ra', *Jazz Journal*, xix, August 1966, 15–16).

LP
USA: The *Heliocentric Worlds of Sun Ra, Vol.I: 'Other Worlds'*, ESP 1014

Chris Capers (tpt), Teddy Nance (tb), Bernard Pettaway (bass tb), Danny Davis (as, fl), Marshall Allen (as, fl, piccolo, per), John Gilmore (ts, timpani), Robert Cummings (bass cl, woodblocks), Pat Patrick (bar, per), Sun Ra (p, electric celeste, bass marimba, per, arr), Ronnie Boykins (sb)
New York   20 April 1965   **Heliocentric**

*as **Heliocentric**, but Gilmore (ts), Sun Ra (timpani)*
                                    Outer Nothingness

*as **Heliocentric**, but Gilmore (ts) and add Jimhmi Johnson (per)*
                                    Other Worlds

*as **Heliocentric**, but Allen (spiral cymbal), Gilmore (ts), Johnson (per, timpani)*
                                    The Cosmos

*as **Heliocentric***   **Of Heavenly Things**

Sun Ra unaccompanied (p, electric celeste)
                                    Nebulae

*as **Heliocentric**, but Gilmore (ts)*

                                    Dancing in the Sun

Other LPs

same contents:
   UK: Fontana STL 5514
   Germany: Rosy 1014
   Italy: Base 1014
   Japan: Phonogramm BT 5055
   countries unknown: Boots 2404; Happy Bird B 90131

LP

USA: *The Heliocentric Worlds of Sun Ra, Vol.II: 'The Sun Myth'*, **ESP 1017**

Walter Miller (tpt), Allen (as, fl, piccolo, per), Gilmore (ts), Patrick (bar, per),
Cummings (bass cl, per), Sun Ra (p, clavoline, per, tuned bongo), Boykins (sb),
Roger Blank (per)

New York   16 Nov 1965   **The Sun Myth**
                                        A House of Beauty
                                        Cosmic Chaos

Other LPs

same contents:
   UK: Fontana STL 5499
   Germany: Rosy 1017; Happy Bird B 90132
   Italy: Base 1017
   countries unknown: Boots 2406; ESP Explosive 538.108

* * *

Charlie Haden: *Liberation Music Orchestra*

Charlie Haden's 'liberation music' can be understood as the musical expression of a growing tendency towards political consciousness among jazz
musicians during the 1960s and early 1970s, a tendency that of course had its
roots in the general social and political upheavals and the mental climate of
that time. Political ideas infiltrated the work of such musicians and groups
as Charles Mingus, Sonny Rollins, Max Roach, Archie Shepp and the Art
Ensemble of Chicago. Haden, in explaining his motives for the production of
this liberation music, wrote in the liner notes: 'The music in this album is
dedicated to creating a better world; a world without war and killing, without racism, without poverty and exploitation; a world where men of all
governments realize the vital importance of life and strive to protect rather

than to destroy it. We hope to see a new society of enlightenment and wisdom where creative thought becomes the most dominant force in all people's lives.'

The problem with any kind of political music is how to get the message across by means of such an abstract art. The most common and not always very convincing solution seems to lie in adding titles or texts to the music. Haden, with the help of pianist, arranger and composer Carla Bley, took another path. He avoided the direct meaning of texts and instead used a musical material with political connotations that, at least potentially, communicate indirectly by memory and historical experience. The nucleus of the liberation music consists of socialist songs from the Spanish Civil War (1936–9). In addition, Haden uses the *Song of the United Front*, written by Hanns Eisler; the unofficial hymn of the American civil rights movement, *We Shall Overcome*; Ornette Coleman's *War Orphans*; and his own graceful *Song for Ché* (as well as a functional introduction, mid-point ending and interlude composed by Bley). Thus the political meaning establishes itself through the use of the music within a certain political context, and listeners who do not know anything about this context will hardly be able to decipher Haden's political concerns. And so once again, despite the path Haden has taken, one has to have recourse to titles, commentaries and explanation.

The general aesthetic problems of political music notwithstanding, Haden's **Liberation Music Orchestra** is a most important document for the specific mental climate of jazz in the 1960s. It is also a very convincing example of the integration of historical musical material into the context of free jazz. Arranging for an ensemble drawn from the ranks of the Jazz Composer's Orchestra, which she had headed with trumpeter Mike Mantler since 1966, Bley tackled the challenge of finding a balance between scored big-band passages and free improvisation, the result being a combination of rowdy ensemble work and fiery solos, with recurring and essentially unaltered references to the borrowed songs.

CD

USA: *Liberation Music Orchestra,* **MCA Impulse! AS 9183**

Mike Mantler (tpt), Roswell Rudd (tb), Bob Northern (french horn, bells, crow call, whistle, woodblocks), Howard Johnson (tuba), Gato Barbieri (ts, cl), Dewey Redman (ts, as), Perry Robinson (cl), Carla Bley (org, p, tambourine, v), Sam Brown (g, Tanganyikan guitar, thumb piano), Charlie Haden (sb), Paul Motian (d, per)
New York   27–9 April 1969   **The Introduction**

omit Brown   **Song of the United Front** *add Don Cherry (c, flugelhorn, Indian bamboo fl, Indian wood fl) and Brown*

                        El Quinto Regimiento (The Fifth Regiment)

                        Los Cuatro Generales (The Four Generales)

                        Viva la Quince Brigada (Long Live the Fifteenth Brigade)   5

omit Cherry   **The Ending to the First Side**

add Cherry   **Song for Ché**

omit Cherry   **War Orphans**

                        The Interlude (Drinking Music)

omit Brown and Cherry; add Andrew Cyrille (per)

                        Circus '68, '69   10

omit Cyrille   **We Shall Overcome**

Other CDs

same contents:
   USA: Impulse! MCAD 39125
   Europe: Impulse! 254633–2
   Japan: Impulse! 32 XD 619

LPs

same contents:
   USA: Impulse! AS 9183
   UK: Jasmine JAS 55; Probe SPB 1037

Cassettes

same contents:
   USA: Impulse! MCAC 39125

Anthony Braxton: *Five Pieces 1975*

Like the Art Ensemble of Chicago, multi-instrumentalist reedplayer and composer Anthony Braxton came out of the ranks of the AACM, Chicago's musicians' cooperative. But whereas the Art Ensemble took its main impulses from traditional Afro-American music as well as from musical cultures of the Third World, Braxton drew much of his inspiration from studying the works and concepts of the Second Viennese School, and of John Cage and Karl-Heinz Stockhausen. These different points of reference in fact mark what might be called different schools of the Chicago jazz avant garde: one down to earth, colourful and extroverted, the other intellectual, austere and introspective (which does not mean that Braxton's music cannot be highly emotional at times).

For the development of contemporary jazz Braxton's role as a composer and conceptualist is of equally high importance as his role as an instrumentalist. In his compositions, which show a great variety of constructive principles, he often draws from mathematical concepts and graphic schemes, most of the time leaving large parts for the improvising musicians to fill out with their ideas. As an instrumentalist, using the whole consorts of saxophones, clarinets and flutes, he is a true virtuoso, with a distinctive style.

The LP **Five Pieces 1975** features Braxton as a composer and improviser with one of his most coherent groups of the 1970s, consisting of Canadian trumpeter Kenny Wheeler, who in England became at home in many contemporary jazz idioms; bassist Dave Holland, who came out of the English free-music scene, turned towards jazz-rock upon being 'discovered' by Miles Davis, and developed into one of the most inspiring free-jazz players; and American drummer Barry Altschul, an extremely sound-conscious percussionist and a master of playing 'free time'.

The **Five Pieces** each show a distinct character demonstrating a different principle of collective creation. *You Stepped out of a Dream* of course is not by Braxton, but an old standard. Braxton performs it in a duet with Holland, the latter playing the changes conventionally, whereas Braxton constantly moves in and out of the harmonic framework, thus accepting the traditional formal structure of the tune but at the same time filling it with new content.

The second piece starts out with an extended multi-part thematic structure, leads into a drum solo focusing on sound colour, and ends with a short reprise of the initial thematic motifs. It is a heterogeneous piece in which the parts are linked without any attempt to create a whole. The third piece is conventional in its framework (theme – improvisation – theme) and adventurous in its content. It opens with a typically angular Braxton theme in even (non-swinging) eighths and with a complex, wide intervallic structure, played by the horns in unison over an intricate rhythmic foundation laid out synchronically by bass and drums. Braxton's improvisation, in correspondence with the thematic material, is mostly in staccato, even eighths and seems purposefully to avoid any association with the rhythmic substance of conventional jazz.

The fourth piece shows the most stratified structural approach. It again starts with a unison line with dodecaphonic allusions, which develops peacefully over a second layer, a slow bass drone. The ensuing collective improvisations aim towards different goals: a gradual intensification and then reduction of rhythmic energy and structural density, and a constant change of register and instrumental sound colour. In the course of a few minutes Braxton moves from sopranino saxophone via B flat clarinet and flute to contrabass clarinet.

Five Pieces 1975 is an important album in Braxton's career. Although it by no means represents the vast scope of his musical world, this recording suitably demonstrates the possibilities of integrating the spontaneity of improvisation with structural processes of composition.

LP
USA: *Five Pieces 1975*, **Arista AL 4064**

Anthony Braxton (as), Dave Holland (sb)
New York   1 July 1975   **You Stepped out of a Dream**

Braxton (as, sopranino s, cl, contrabass cl, fl, alto fl), Kenny Wheeler (tpt, flugelhorn), Holland (sb), Barry Altschul (d)
2 July 1975

Alexander von Schlippenbach: *Globe Unity*

A united effort to imitate creative developments in the United States marks the history of jazz in Europe up to the middle of the 1960s. European musicians readily absorbed the changing aesthetics of Afro-American music, the development of new structural patterns and a gradual expansion of musical material. The closest possible imitation of the respective American original was a standard for musical quality. It was probably not only the lack of self-assurance concerning their own creative capacity that caused European musicians to produce such a decade of epigons and imitations; the range of expectations put up by audiences and jazz critics added to this development. To them, the prophet was esteemed in his own country only when interpreting the message sent by the American gods.

Towards the middle of the 1960s there was a gradual change in the way European musicians related to their American models. The development of American jazz itself may have caused this, but so may have the change in the way European musicians perceived themselves. Like their American models, they broke with the routine of harmonic-metrical schemes, dissolved the beat into an irregular series of accentuations and concentrated on musical sound instead of improvisations oriented towards melody. At the same time, however, they began to drift from the direct influence of American musicians. They created their own manners of expression and structural patterns, making these points central to their music. Thus, towards the end of the decade, a specific European type of free jazz found its way to the public.

What were the causes of this unexpected emancipation? At least two factors are worth mentioning, one inherent in the music itself, the other ideological or, if you will, political. The first is that, with the origin of free jazz, European musicians for the first time were confronted with a style that was not definite, not bound by a system of relatively limited standards, but comprising a variety of individual and group styles, one hardly comparing with the next. The development of a personal style within this conglomerate of styles called 'free jazz' was easier than ever before.

The second cause has much to do with the social and political atmosphere among young people during the late 1960s. The students' movement in Germany and France had come to a climax in 1968, and numerous young musicians sympathized with it. Above all two essential characteristics of this movement might have influenced the young free-jazz phalanx's self-perception: a distaste for any kind of authority and an underlying anti-Americanism which was intensified by the cruel consequences of the Vietnam War. For the first time since World War II, the position of the USA as the 'lodestar' had been thoroughly questioned. Despite the common cliché of jazz musicians as romantic outsiders (of course there have been a few, such as Thelonious Monk), jazz musicians do not exist outside society, but are part of it. Certainly in the 1960s European jazz musicians were very much inside what was happening around them, and consequently these tendencies found shape in their perceptions of self and – in a mediated way – in their music.

One of the first and most important documents for the emancipation of European jazz is a recording by the Globe Unity Orchestra. Founded in 1966, the orchestra owes its existence to RIAS Berlin having requested Alexander von Schlippenbach to write a composition for the Jazzfest Berlin of that year. Schlippenbach successfully created a compositional framework that allowed for a great number of free-jazz players. Without falling back on old big-band clichés, he organized a structural variety while still leaving enough space for individual creative exertion and spontaneous interaction.

The nucleus of the Globe Unity Orchestra was made up of members of the Manfred Schoof quintet and the Peter Brötzmann trio, to whom were added five horn players and vibraphonist Karl Berger. Schlippenbach wrote two compositions of distinct character for the orchestra's performance and the recording sessions that followed: *Globe Unity* and *Sun*. *Globe Unity* is characterized by an intensive rhythmic power play, with parts for solos and collective ensemble organized according to given scalar material, clusters or tonally undefined chords. The basic conception shows similarities to Coltrane's *Ascension*, although a direct influence is unlikely. (Call-and-response patterns are a common way to organize orchestral free jazz.) Still, a comparison with *Ascension* is instructive. It reveals certain essential characteristics of European free jazz, already formed in this early phase of its existence. The basic rhythmic posture of *Globe Unity* – compared with the music of Afro-American musicians – is more hectic, nervous, at times violent. The improvisations presented by the horns concentrate more on sound and energy than on melodic continuity; they are consequently so anti-melodic that not even the 'screamers' in *Ascension* (Pharoah Sanders and Archie Shepp) can compare.

Even more impressive than the approach to composition and improvisation in *Globe Unity* is the systematic exploration of sound in *Sun*. Compared with *Globe Unity*, *Sun* is looser in its musical structure, more contemplative in its emotional substance and more concentrated on colour than on energetic power. The instrumentation emphasizes this. 'Little instruments', as the Art Ensemble of Chicago later dubbed them, such as rattles, triangles, lotus flutes, flexatones, etc., play a dominant role. Also, the way the horns are played shows a differentiated treatment of sound patterns, particularly in the trumpet solos by Claude Deron and Schoof; both solos involve undefined pitch (generated by the technique of half-valving, that is, depressing the pistons half way) and distorted sounds.

When the Globe Unity Orchestra's first production was presented to the public, it met strong resentment and caused many a misunderstanding. Newspaper headlines ran 'Odd men playing jokes at the Philharmonie' and 'A blend of jazz and chamber music'. Neither of these quotations underline the clear-sightedness of contemporary jazz critics. In any case, resentment against the Globe Unity's music and its classification as part of the hybrid 'third stream' had a result: public performances became rare. Only since 1972 has the ensemble performed on a regular basis, gradually stabilizing their musical language. This in no way diminishes the standing of the first Globe Unity Orchestra within the historical development of original European free jazz. It proved there was a musical substance in the making that could do without prefabricated patterns. It helped make clear that there was a growing potential for European musicians, in and apart from Globe Unity, to make this substance come alive.

LP
Germany: *Globe Unity*, **Saba MPS SB 15109**

Claude Deron (tpt, lotus fl), Manfred Schoof (flugelhorn, triangle), Willie Lietzmann (tuba, marimba), Peter Brötzmann (as, gurke), Gerd Dudek (ts, duck call), Kris Wanders (bar, zorna as, lotus fl), Willem Breuker (bar, ss, ratchet), Gunter Hampel (bass cl, fl, pandeira), Buschi Niebergall (sb, siren), Peter Kowald (sb, bells), Jacki Liebezeit (d, per, durbuka), Muni Neumeier (d, gongs, per), Alexander von Schlippenbach (p, tam tam, clocks, gongs, knives, flexatone)
Cologne 6–7 Dec 1966 **Globe Unity**

add Karl Berger (vb) **Sun**

* * *

Peter Brötzmann: *Machine Gun*

Since 1968 the mainstream of West German free jazz has been represented mainly by Brötzmann and Schlippenbach. There was a growing tendency towards working in large ensembles and an ever-increasing internationalization of the scene, involving principally English and Dutch musicians. 'In retrospect', Brötzmann stated in an interview with Didier Pennequin ('Allemagne – Pays Bas', *Jazz magazine*, no.220, March 1974, 19–21), 'the year of 1968 was the year of big bands, where we met with friends to play like crazy.'

One of the most striking examples of the work of the large ensembles is Brötzmann's LP **Machine Gun**. (The title is not meant to express any military program; 'like a machine gun' was the way that Don Cherry described

Brötzmann's playing, as reported in Bert Noglik: *Jazzwerkstatt International*, Berlin, 1981, p. 199.) **Machine Gun** may be seen as the product of what bassist Peter Kowald once called the 'kaputt-play' era: 'The main objective was to really and thoroughly tear apart the old values, this meaning: to omit any harmony and melody; and the result wasn't boring only because it was played with such high intensity . . . In a way, that 'kaputt-play' time has made anything 'playable', equally playable, that is possible in music . . . Today, for the first time, it becomes clear that our generation can do without the musical influence of most Americans' (Dirk Fröse: 'Freiheit wovon – Freiheit wozu? Peter Kowald Quintett,' *Jazz Podium*, xxi, Dec 1972, pp. 22–5). What kind of musical results were achieved in that period of 'kaputt-play', a period which not only Kowald considers to have been transitional? In the context of **Machine Gun** some general characteristics can be listed.

Composing is generally limited to a minimum. By and large without themes, the music presents riff-like attacks and interjections, at times directed only in their movement up or down. There is a tendency to use distorted thematic quotations. The players abandon definite pitch as a stable element of musical organization in favour of unstable sound patterns. Structural distinctions result mainly from collective variations of register, density and loudness. Developmental processes lead, somewhat inevitably, towards a limit where individual musical events cannot be strictly identified as such, but combine to become a diffuse, intensive totality. Sometimes homogeneous and low-pitched instrumentation, frequently used by Brötzmann's ensembles, supports this process. In general, the musicians have a restless attitude towards time. Even when density and intensity diminish and the structures open up, the basic tempo (not necessarily played, but felt) remains hectic. In fact, at that stage of development there is something like a standard tempo, probably on account of physiological reasons: a majority of recordings show an identical metrical basis, moving at 240 to 270 beats per minute. This means that a four-beat measure approximately corresponds to human pulsation, and thus the kind of free jazz we are dealing with here is body-related to a much higher degree than is generally assumed.

Not immediately touching upon the structural characteristics of this music, but upon its reception, is the problem of instrumental technique. From conversations, I have gathered that many listeners, especially those 'well-acquainted' with jazz, wonder whether those who make all that noise on stage just cannot play, whether they really do master their instruments. It seems relatively easy to dub it 'kaputt-play' as Kowald did, yet it is not that simple. Most musicians working in the ensembles of Brötzmann, Schlippenbach and Schoof had developed individual techniques enabling them not only to demolish conventions but also to develop, in a constructive way, new personal techniques. Someone who argues that Evan Parker's sound nuances, or Brötzmann's overblown sounds, have nothing to do with technique, someone arguing that Gerd Dudek's and Alan Skidmore's almost classical virtuosity is the sole acceptable quintessence of technique, simply reveals a narrow conception of technique. Technique in music means, at least to me, the ability to do what I want to do. Brötzmann expressed it more pointedly: 'I'm not what you would call a "good technician". To me, technique taught by conservatories is bullshit. To make a music like ours, you have to develop your own technique first and then make your own music. The objective of our music is not to play "right" or "wrong", that doesn't mean a thing. What really counts is to know what one's playing' (Pennequin, op. cit.).

LP

Germany: *Machine Gun*, **BRO 2**

Peter Brötzmann (ts, bar), Willem Breuker (ts, bass cl), Evan Parker (ts), Fred van Hove (p), Peter Kowald, Buschi Niebergall (sb), Han Bennink (d), Sven Johansson (d, per)

Bremen, West	May 1968	**Machine Gun**
Germany		**Responsible – for Jan De Ven**
		Music for Han Bennink

Other LPs

same contents:
   Germany: FMP 0090

* * *

Music Improvisation Company: *The Music Improvisation Company 1968–1971*

During the early phase of its existence European free jazz developed a number of different schools or regional styles, and it was quite common to speak of German energy play, Dutch comical music or British sound research. This last is represented by the work of the Music Improvisation Company (MIC), founded in 1968. The essence of its work lies in the idea of non-idiomatic music, as formulated by guitarist Derek Bailey. A freely improvised music, independent of all existing musical languages, would follow the individual techniques and preferences of the players exclusively.

   Of course this idea is probably based on an illusion, for although the mere avoidance of any idiomatically fixed means of creation must not automatically result in a new musical idiom (it could, as with John Cage, lead into the dominion of chance), the practical results of the MIC's work make it quite clear that this music can easily be identified as a particular and unmistakable form of musical creation – in other words, as a music idiom. Obviously *style*, under certain preconditions, may be established when any associations with existing musical languages are forcefully avoided. One of the most important preconditions is that the improviser acts as a conscious ego and does not follow only the generative energy of chance. And this is obviously the case with the members of the MIC.

To describe the group's conceptual guidelines, it seems easier to identify features it does not exhibit rather than those it does: no tonality, no repetition, no melodic continuity, no periodicity, no system. On the other hand there is one feature obvious at first hearing: the emancipation of noise as an independent means of creation, 'noise' meaning sound with a dense structure of non-harmonic frequencies whose amplitudes and phases change randomly.

The most efficient noise-producer in the group, of course, is Hugh Davies. With his electronics he brings to the music a vast repertory of noise: static noise, like buzzing or humming, pulsating noise, like crackling or clapping, variable noise, like gliding frequency bands, etc. Also, guitarist Bailey uses his instrument to produce aperiodic sound structures by rubbing the strings with his fingers or other devices, and by working with variable string tension. And Parker finds a number of ways to produce non-harmonic and also percussive sounds on his saxophone. Thus the conscious manipulation of noise is one dominating feature of the MIC's work. The other is interaction. Because any written score or even verbal arrangements are taboo, the group relies exclusively on spontaneous actions and reactions among all four players. This interaction within the group converges most of the time, for although both Davies and Bailey speak of a tendency towards 'mutual subversion', meaning that one player might irritate the other by non-participation or contrary action, such situations occur only rarely, at least in the group's recordings. This form of agreement should not be confused with harmony and linear development, for the overall sound structure is predominantly dissonant and discontinuous.

LP

UK: *The Music Improvisation Company 1968–1971*, **Incus 17**

Evan Parker (ss, electric autoharp), Hugh Davies (org, synthesizers), Derek Bailey (g), Jamie Muir (per)

London   4 July 1969   **Painting**
                                                          Untitled 3

Untitled 4
Bedrest
18 June 1970   Its Tongue Trapped to the Rock
by a Limpet, the Water Rat
Succumbed to the Incoming
Tide
In the Victim's Absence

* * *

Michel Portal: *Michel Portal Unit à Châteauvallon*

The French multi-instrumental reed player Michel Portal is an exceptional musician. Many listeners praise him as a brilliant interpreter of Mozart's Clarinet Concerto; others know him as an experimenter with sound who worked his way through Stockhausen's intuitive music as well as through Pierre Boulez's *Domaines*; still others saw him in the band that accompanied Edith Piaf at the staging of *Sheherazade*; and still others find him one of the most important improvisers in European contemporary jazz.

A musical chameleon? Although Portal's work is highly competent in all these areas, his main focus of interest – his love – is jazz: 'Jazz, for me, really offers the only possibility to be free, to float, to dream' (Philippe Carles and Francis Marmande: 'Michel Portal ou la parole au present', *Jazz magazine*, no.210, April 1973, 11–14, 32–6). In 1966 he was a member of the first French free-jazz group, led by pianist François Tusques. He worked with German pianist Joachim Kühn in 1969 and with English baritone saxophonist John Surman in 1970. In 1972 he appeared with his own group at the jazz festival at Châteauvallon. The concert was recorded and produced by the small French label Chant du Monde, and is, I believe, one of the most stimulating recordings to which European free jazz gave birth during the 1970s.

A cursory listening reveals a music that is as far away from American free jazz as from the diverse regional branches of the European avant garde. The music at first gives the impression of being raw and unhewn, with sound complexes resembling square tones and rudimentary melodic contours resembling signals more than songs. There is no trace of French elegance and refinement. In fact the central creative dimensions of this music are to be found in neither melody nor harmony, but in rhythm and sound. That is, the structural and formal work of the group manifests itself essentially in a conscious stratification and junction of sound and rhythm and not in a sequence of melodic inventions or harmonic turns. One of the most important preconditions for the success of this work seems to lie in a distinct and collectively adapted sense for the significance of time and for the economy

of material. In both respects the musicians, notwithstanding their drive towards ecstasy, show some quasi-bourgeois virtues: they are patient, in that
they do not jump hectically from one event to another, but take their time to
let processes and situations slowly grow; they are thrifty, in their concentration, over long stretches of time, on the exposure or variation of a rather
narrowly confined repertory of sound structures, on certain forms of
groundwork, on certain patterns or variations of intervallic constellations or
phrases. All in all this is a collective enterprise of high sensibility, which,
unfortunately, never found the acclaim that it deserved.

LP

France: *Michel Portal Unit à Châteauvallon*, Chant du Monde LDX 74526

*Bernard Vitet (c, tpt, vln), Michel Portal (bass cl, contrabass cl, as, ss, taragot),
Léon Francioli, Beb Guérin (sb), Pierre Favre (per), Tamia (v)*
Châteauvallon,   22 Aug 1972   **No, No But it May Be**
France

CHAPTER 11

Fusion

Mark Gilbert

Fusion might be the youngest of jazz idioms, but it is not the first hybrid that jazz has produced. Jazz owes its very existence to a confluence of different elements, and almost every stage of its development has been marked by the absorption of some kind of alien influence. Nevertheless, in the early 1970s the term 'fusion' acquired a relatively specific meaning. Since then it has been used in the main to signify a union between jazz and rock or funk. However, there are exceptions, and a fully comprehensive definition remains elusive; even within the area described above, there are as many varieties of fusion as there are types of jazz.

The dominant form of fusion is most easily distinguished from mainstream jazz by its rhythms. Many fusion groups copied the heavily syncopated rhythmic patterns used by the bands which backed such soul artists as the Temptations, Sly Stone and James Brown in the 1960s. Herbie Hancock's Headhunters and the Brecker Brothers borrowed rhythm and much else from such bands; others, such as Bruford and the Mahavishnu Orchestra, had a closer similarity to white rock bands. Still others, like the Pat Metheny Group, Weather Report and Chick Corea's Return to Forever, employed rock and funk mannerisms but also made wide use of Latin American rhythms. However, one thing unified these different types of fusion: all were dominated by repetitive 'straight eighth' rhythms. Funk, rock and Latin music are based on an even division of the beat into two or four, which creates the firm march-like effect so typical of the fusion rhythm section. Swing and bop, on the other hand, divide the beat into three, and the result is a lighter, more flowing pulse. These are 'jazz eighth' rhythms. Funk, rock and Latin rhythms also tend to be more emphatic than swing and bop rhythms; the incisive sound of the snare drum, often produced by a synthesizer, became a hallmark of much 1980s funk-orientated fusion.

Along with the adoption of non-swing rhythms came the use of the instruments and sonorities found in 1960s rock and soul music. The highly amplified electric guitar, piano and bass became staple instruments in the fusion ensemble, as did the synthesizer once it became widely available in the early 1970s. Later, other wind and string instruments were amplified and played through signal processors such as the wa-wa pedal and the phase shifter. By the late 1980s, conventional instruments were able to interface with synthesizers. Many bands also carried Latin and African percussion.

Fusion received a mixed reaction from critics and consumers. Purists tended to see it as diluted jazz; others resented what they perceived as blatant commercialism. Indeed, the energetic marketing of much mediocre material helped to give good fusion a bad name. The genre's detractors dwelt on these artistic failures and ignored, or were ignorant of, the music's many triumphs. However, their cynicism was not shared by audiences – fusion is the most popular jazz form since swing and more than two decades after its emergence it continues to flourish and develop.

* * *

Miles Davis: *In a Silent Way*

A key figure in fusion's development has been the trumpeter Miles Davis, who is still working in the idiom in the 1990s. Five of the nine record dates discussed in this chapter were led by Davis's ex-sidemen, and the first by Davis himself.

Davis has always shown a readiness to change direction, and during the 1960s, partly as a result of pressure from his record company, he became interested in rock and soul music. In February 1969 he recorded **In a Silent Way** and soon after abandoned the bop-derived style he had embraced since the mid-1940s.

In a Silent Way borrows extensively from rock music. One of the most important players on the recording is bassist Dave Holland, whose short, repetitive lines virtually define the structure of two of the three tracks and reflect Davis's interest in the sustained 'grooves' found in soul music. Except for a few brief variations, Holland plays the same two- or three-note figure throughout the entire 18 minutes of *Shhh/Peaceful*, while *It's About That Time* is built around two simple bass riffs. The second of these features a combination of notes which are characteristic of rhythm and blues, the music from which soul grew: major and minor thirds and a minor seventh. The bare frameworks of these pieces are also a reminder of Davis's modal work of the late 1950s, which, in reaction to the rapid chord changes of bop, featured tunes with as few as two chords.

Drummer Tony Williams is similarly economical. Except for a brief passage at the climax of *It's About That Time*, he confines himself to relentless, clock-like rhythms on snare drum and hi-hat. His playing here is rudimentary by comparison with his work in Davis's 1960 quintet, but no less dramatic.

In a Silent Way is dominated by haunting, dream-like moods. The playing is generally restrained, and the repetitive figures in the rhythm section combine with the floating textures produced by the three keyboard players to create a trance-like atmosphere which is disturbed only during the climaxes of *It's About That Time*. There were numerous precedents for this impressionist style in Davis's reflective work of the 1950s and in such of his 1960s quintet pieces as *Nefertiti*, and it was to find continued life in Weather Report, the fusion band formed in 1970 by Joe Zawinul and Wayne Shorter.

In typical jazz style, **In a Silent Way** was an impromptu session. Zawinul and guitarist John McLaughlin knew of the date only hours before, and Zawinul's *In a Silent Way* underwent radical revision in the studio. The spontaneity of the meeting can be sensed in the music, which often sounds as if it was arranged as it was performed. The arrangements, like the themes, have none of the complexity of later fusion, and, since the recording contains few preset harmonic progressions, the music often proceeds by other means. For example, *Shhh/Peaceful*, anchored throughout by a terse bass riff, progresses through simple variations of instrumental texture and moments of rest. However, the suspenseful bass motif begs for a resolution which never arrives, and leaves *Shhh/Peaceful* seeming like an unfinished blueprint for the more rounded *It's About That Time*.

The title track, which acts as a prelude to *It's About That Time*, illustrates Davis's attitude to music at that time. Keen to get away from complex chord changes and into groove-based playing, Davis took Zawinul's densely harmonized melody, discarded most of the chords and set it over a simple bowed bass drone and E major triad – the first sound heard from McLaughlin's guitar. The result is an elegiac tone poem which forms an effective contrast with the dark menace of *It's About That Time*.

It's About That Time is a masterpiece of dynamic control and development which inspires the best solos on the recording. It is built on two alternating bass figures, the first creating a sense of suspension which is both relieved and intensified by the increased mobility of the second. The first substantial solos are by McLaughlin, whose nervous, scurrying runs and brittle tone perfectly match the mood of the piece, and by Wayne Shorter, who made his debut on soprano saxophone on this album. The brooding tension which has been mounting during the first part of the piece finally explodes during Davis's solo. Tony Williams, long restricted to urgent but restrained rim shots and hi-hat cymbal patterns, finds joyous liberation in splashing cymbals and cracking snare-drum accents before the recording draws to a peaceful conclusion with a literal repetition of the title track.

CD

USA: *In a Silent Way*, **Columbia Jazz Masterpieces CK 40580**

Miles Davis (tpt), Herbie Hancock, Chick Corea (elp), Joe Zawinul (org), Wayne Shorter (ss), Dave Holland (sb), John McLaughlin (elg), Tony Williams (d)
New York   18 Feb 1969   **Shhh/Peaceful**
                  20 Feb 1969   **It's About That Time**

as **It's About That Time**, *but Zawinul (elp)*
                                   In a Silent Way

Other CDs
same contents:
   Europe: CBS Jazz Masterpieces 450982–2
   Japan: CBS 32 DP 730

LPs
same contents:
   USA: Columbia CS 9875; Columbia KCS 9875; Columbia PC 9875; Columbia Jazz Masterpieces CJ 40580
   UK: CBS 63630
   Europe: CBS Jazz Masterpieces 450982–1

Cassettes
same contents:
   USA: Columbia Jazz Masterpieces CJT 40580
   Europe: CBS Jazz Masterpieces 450982–4

* * *

Mahavishnu Orchestra: *The Inner Mounting Flame*

By the late 1960s, Miles Davis was a long-established and respected figure in the pre-rock jazz world, and his fusion experiments caused a considerable stir. However, while his high visibility meant that he became a focal point for the new movement, there is scant evidence to support the view that he founded it. He provided a platform for younger players who subsequently became leaders in the idiom, but in many cases these players had investigated rock and other non-jazz music before joining Davis. Furthermore, much of the music they produced after leaving Davis bore little resemblance to either **In a Silent Way** or its successor, **Bitches Brew**. Perhaps the most radical departures were made by one of the first of the **In a Silent Way** personnel to lead his own fusion band – John McLaughlin.

In his Mahavishnu Orchestra, McLaughlin sought to merge a wide range of influences, including rock, rhythm and blues, European concert music, Indian music and jazz. This was one of the most self-consciously eclectic and hard rocking of the early fusion bands. In fact, the group's 1971 debut album, **The Inner Mounting Flame**, seems not so much jazz-rock fusion as rock-classical, rock-raga, rock-folk or even rock-rock fusion. Though many listeners have heard jazz elements in McLaughlin's guitar solos with the Mahavishnu Orchestra, and though, like drummer Billy Cobham, electric bass guitarist Rick Laird and keyboard player Jan Hammer, he had had experience with jazz, his sympathy with rock guitarists is stronger, and not just because he employs a distorted tone and such effects as wa-wa and flanging: the structure and harmonies of his compositions for the Mahavishnu Orchestra are generally more redolent of rock than jazz.

The Inner Mounting Flame reflects the heightened sense of spiritual awareness McLaughlin had developed while studying with the guru Sri Chimnoy in the months before he formed the Mahavishnu Orchestra. It was Chimnoy who had suggested the name Mahavishnu, meaning 'divine compassion, power and justice', for his disciple's new band. McLaughlin had long taken an interest in all aspects of Indian culture, including its music, and this is plainly audible in the sonorities and irregular metres of **The Inner Mounting Flame**. His choice of electric violinist Jerry Goodman as a second melody voice confirmed this interest, and also brought occasional touches of country and folk to the orchestra's music.

One of the most striking aspects of **The Inner Mounting Flame** is its relentless intensity. Tracks such as *Meetings of the Spirit*, *The Noonward Race* and *Awakening* have incredibly fast and varied thematic lines, the likes of which had never been heard before in jazz or rock. By today's standards the ensembles sound ragged, but at the time they represented a huge technical advance. Nowhere is this more apparent than in the work of Billy Cobham, whose mastery of irregular metres and fast tempos set the standard for jazz-rock drumming. *Awakening* provides an especially formidable example of his prowess: using the snare drum, he phrases along with a theme that moves at something around ten notes per second. This is somewhat faster than march tempo, but proves that Cobham's early years as a military bandsman were not wasted.

The players' virtuosity is further tested by the abrupt way in which new themes, time signatures and tempos are introduced. Precipitate transitions are especially apparent in *Dawn*, *Vital Transformation* and *The Dance of Maya*. In *Dawn*, an awkward double-time shift from 7/4 to 14/8 is accompanied by a radical change of key, with the only link between the two sections a dubiously pitched common tone from the guitar. *Vital Transformation* alternates without preparation between a lopsided 9/8 and a slow waltz interlude, while *The Dance of Maya* butts a grotesque guitar theme in 20/4 against an atrophied rhythm-and-blues shuffle in 17/8. The last two are, however, finally woven into the kind of polytonal blend which might have delighted Charles Ives. Perhaps McLaughlin had some sort of cod surrealism in mind when he wrote these pieces, or perhaps he was recalling a particularly bizarre LSD experience, but it is hard to avoid the suspicion that they were formulated in a rather arbitrary manner. Instead of an evolution of logically related ideas, many of them present a series of unconnected episodes spliced into an uneasy montage.

McLaughlin takes a similar approach to improvising, particularly during up-tempo passages. His solos display a remarkable technical facility, but their turbulent energy does not disguise vagaries of pitching and timing and at best haphazard melodic development. They feature more repeated riffs than continuous melodies and closely mirror the harmony of the compositions, which are based chiefly on exotic minor and pentatonic scales. Apart from Jan Hammer's solo on *The Noonward Race* there is little evidence in **The Inner Mounting Flame** of the chromaticism found in modern jazz. Furthermore, for someone who is often classed as a jazz-rock player, McLaughlin the soloist makes surprisingly little use of the blues. Even in *The Noonward Race*, which opens with the funky dominant ninth chord beloved of soul musicians from James Brown (*Sex Machine*) to Prince (*Kiss*), McLaughlin's solo makes only the briefest of references to the blues.

The Mahavishnu Orchestra's fusion of disparate elements may be viewed as one which only partially coalesced. There are exceptions, as in the lyrical *A Lotus on Irish Streams* and *You Know You Know*, but variety is rarely balanced by unity in McLaughlin's writing. However, it should be remembered that **The Inner Mounting Flame** was the product of an era which placed a special value on experimentation. By that token, it is one of the most authentic – and most dated – of 1970s fusion albums.

CD

USA: *The Inner Mounting Flame*, **Columbia CK 31067**

John McLaughlin (elg), Jan Hammer (elp), Rick Laird (elb), Billy Cobham (d), Jerry Goodman (vln)

New York	1971	**Meetings of the Spirit**
		Dawn
		The Noonward Race

McLaughlin (g), Hammer (p), Goodman (vln)
                                        A Lotus on Irish Streams

as Meetings of the Spirit   **Vital Transformation**
                                        The Dance of Maya
                                        You Know You Know
                                        Awakening

LPs
same contents:
  USA: Columbia KC 31067; Columbia PC 31067
  UK: CBS 64717

Cassettes
same contents:
  USA: Columbia PCT 31067

* * *

Chick Corea's Return to Forever: *Hymn of the Seventh Galaxy*

The innovations of the Mahavishnu Orchestra were widely admired and imitated, not least by one of McLaughlin's fellow sidemen from **In a Silent Way**, Chick Corea, who gives more credit to Mahavishnu than to Miles Davis for inspiring his band Return to Forever. He debunked the myth of Davis's influence in conversation with Josef Woodward: 'that's Disneyland ... John's band, more than my experience with Miles, led me to want to turn the volume up and write music that was more dramatic' ('Chick Corea: Piano Dreams Come True', *Down Beat*, lv, September 1988, p. 19). There were other factors too. Around 1970 Corea had become involved with Scientology, the quasi-religious philosophical movement which, among its many tenets, holds that art should concern itself with communication rather than the pursuit of aesthetic perfection. He duly abandoned his explorations of free improvisation with the group Circle and assembled the first edition of Return to Forever, a mostly acoustic quartet which specialized in a gentle fusion of jazz and Brazilian music. His subsequent discovery of the Mahavishnu Orchestra encouraged him to regroup Return to Forever as an all electric band.

 Hymn of the Seventh Galaxy, the 1973 debut album by the new Return to

Forever, contains many reminders of **The Inner Mounting Flame**, but also much that is new. Like the Mahavishnu Orchestra, Return to Forever featured high levels of amplification, intricate, rapidly executed themes and the sound of the overdriven electric guitar. It also used irregular time signatures (in *Hymn of the Seventh Galaxy* and the central section of *Theme to the Mothership*), but there the similarity ends. A constant tempo is maintained on all the tracks, and this not only makes them more accessible, but also illustrates Corea's concern with continuity. He had long admired the way in which Béla Bartók avoided the classical compositional formula of theme, development and recapitulation, and he applied similar methods to the construction of *Hymn of the Seventh Galaxy*, *Captain Señor Mouse*, *Theme to the Mothership*, *Space Circus part 2* and *The Game Maker*. These pieces are all continuously developed, and although they feature only a limited degree of repetition they are highly unified. Even separate tracks are linked by suite-like connections. The electronic white noise which ends *Hymn of the Seventh Galaxy* is echoed by the gong which opens *After the Cosmic Rain*, and the two tracks use closely related keys and tempos. Similar links of key and mood unite the last three tracks, *Space Circus parts 1 and 2* and *The Game Maker*.

Although Return to Forever inherited its thicker textures from the Mahavishnu Orchestra, much of Corea's writing reflects his interest in lighter weaves and sunny, optimistic moods. Where McLaughlin favours dour minor modes and airless arrangements, Corea is not averse to writing simple melodies in major keys, as in *Captain Señor Mouse* and *Theme to the Mothership*, or letting his music breathe, as in *After the Cosmic Rain*, *Space Circus parts 1 and 2* and *The Game Maker*. Even McLaughlin substitute Bill Connors cannot help but sound lyrical in such settings.

Hymn of the Seventh Galaxy is also marked by its use of Latin rhythms, which add to the buoyant, dancing quality of the music. Latin, or, to be more precise, Hispanic influences pervade most of Corea's work here, but especially his solos on *After the Cosmic Rain* and *Captain Señor Mouse*. The latter is built on a favourite of Corea's, the Phrygian mode, which has a characteristically Spanish flavour. Corea's longstanding involvement with jazz is also evident, both in the harmonic depth of his writing and in the extraordinary ideas expressed in his solo on *Theme to the Mothership*, where he appears to overdrive his amplifier in order to extract a singing synthesizer-like tone from the Fender–Rhodes piano. Although he had yet to employ a synthesizer, Corea's interest in novel sonorities is further evident in the use of harpsichord on *Captain Señor Mouse* and the 'fuzz bass' solo on Stanley Clarke's *After the Cosmic Rain*.

The funk and soul side of popular music provided yet another influence upon this album. Clarke is responsible for the funky bass rhythms which underpin the central theme of *After the Cosmic Rain* and the long groove sections of *Theme to the Mothership* and *Space Circus part 2*, although he had yet to develop the slapping percussive attack which became his trademark. Corea has credited soul singers Sly Stone and Stevie Wonder as inspirations for his funkier passages, and his overdriven Rhodes is a forceful reminder of the clavinet sound heard in Wonder's *Superstition* from the 1972 album **Talking Book**.

LP

USA: *Hymn of the Seventh Galaxy*, **Polydor 5536**

Chick Corea (org, elp, gongs), Bill Connors (elg), Stanley Clarke (elb), Lenny White (d, per)

New York	August 1973	**Hymn of the Seventh Galaxy**

add Clarke (fuzz bass, bell tree)

After the Cosmic Rain

*as **Hymn**, but add Corea (harpsichord)*

Captain Señor Mouse

*as **Hymn**, but Corea (elp)*

Theme to the Mothership

Corea (elp, p, org, harpsichord)

Space Circus part 1

*as **Hymn**, but Corea (elp)*

Space Circus part 2

*as **Hymn**, but Connors (g, elg)*

The Game Maker

Other LPs

same contents:
  UK: Polydor Super 2310 283
  France: Polydor 2302028

Cassettes

same contents:
  USA: Polydor CF 5536

Herbie Hancock: *Headhunters*

If Chick Corea was partially influenced by funk, his ex-Davis colleague Herbie Hancock adopted it wholesale. Although he came to international notice playing bop-based jazz in Davis's quintet of the mid-1960s, the pianist grew up in Chicago, surrounded by rhythm and blues. As early as 1963 he had had a pop hit with *Watermelon Man*, a naive gospel-flavoured tune which that year reached the Top 20 in a version by Mongo Santamaria and was later covered on record in more than 200 versions. After leaving Davis, Hancock formed an often esoteric sextet which was eventually dissolved due to poor record sales and Hancock's own misgivings about the material. His rhythm-and-blues muse was returning, and in 1972 he set about devising something like the music he had heard on James Brown's *Papa's Got a Brand New Bag*, Sly Stone's *Thank you falettinme be mice elf agin* and Stevie Wonder's **Talking Book**. The result was **Headhunters**, a million-seller and the archetypal jazz-funk album.

Hancock conceived **Headhunters** as a set of funk tunes directed at the charts, and, sure enough, the opening track, *Chameleon*, became a disco hit. However, in *Chameleon*, and in **Headhunters** as a whole, Hancock inadvertently produced something more than a model for much subsequent commercial funk writing: he created a musical masterpiece with enough substance to satisfy the most discriminating of jazz listeners.

Headhunters has its share of less than original elements, among them a predominance of 4/4 dance metres, simple harmonic schemes (most of *Chameleon*'s 15 minutes are occupied by two chords) and, unlike much of Return to Forever's **Hymn of the Seventh Galaxy**, the use of song structures in which the opening theme is repeated at the end. *Chameleon*, for all its modernity, has that feature in common with the Broadway and Tin Pan Alley songs which form the greater part of the swing and bop repertory.

However, two elements set Hancock's funk apart from its inspirations: one is its remarkably sophisticated rhythmic fabric, the other a wealth of jazz improvisation on the highest level. Regarding the former, Hancock told Bret Primack: 'In the popular forms of funk, which I've been trying to get into, the attention is on the interplay of rhythm between the different instruments. The part the Clavinet plays has to fit with the part the drums play and the line that the bass plays and the line that the guitar plays. It's almost like African drummers where seven drummers play different parts' ('Herbie Hancock: Chameleon in his Disco Phase', *Down Beat*, xlvi, 17 May 1979, p. 12). Nowhere is this principle better illustrated than in *Chameleon*, where the five elements that make up the rhythm section – an ARP synthesizer bass line, a guitar-like electric bass figure, drums and two keyboards – are introduced successively, gradually combining to form an artfully syncopated rhythmic counterpoint. Each part – basically a two-bar riff pattern – has its own space and rarely duplicates the movement of its neighbours; each remains individually audible in the ensemble. *Watermelon Man*, a funky reworking of the 1963 classic with a new eight-bar section and an array of exotic percussion, is similarly constructed. The two other tracks on the album, *Sly* and *Vein Melter*, both use funk rhythms, but feature less of the complex interplay found in *Chameleon*. The restful *Vein Melter* contains echoes of **In a Silent Way** in its atmospheric use of Fender–Rhodes electric piano and its repetitive bass line, although Hancock has said the tune was modelled on his composition *Maiden Voyage*, recorded in 1965.

Although the **Headhunters** band created some tightly arranged funk, it also jammed at length, with the result that the album contains more sustained improvisation than most of its contemporaries. *Chameleon* and *Sly* are built on mostly static harmony and thus provide ideal vehicles for extended modal improvisation. Keyboard solos from Hancock take up almost half of the 15-minute *Chameleon*. The first, on synthesizer, is unremarkable, perhaps because Hancock was feeling his way on the new instrument or was keen to sustain a populist flavour. However, a second, on Fender–Rhodes over a new bass figure, is full of jazz phrasing and ideas. The trio of Hancock, Paul Jackson and Harvey Mason produce three minutes of inventive Latin-flavoured jazz, and eventually, in the best jazz manner, Hancock trades licks, not with another soloist but with a lyrical, synthesized string section that plays rapid chord changes in triple time; the effect is to throw the staccato funk sections into sharp relief. The clamorous Latin-funk rhythms of *Sly* prompt even wilder improvisations; seven of its ten minutes are filled with undiluted jazz from the Wayne Shorter-like soprano saxophonist Bennie Maupin and a ferociously creative Hancock.

CD
USA: *Headhunters*, Columbia CK 32731

Bennie Maupin (ss, ts, saxello, bass cl, alto fl), Herbie Hancock (syn, clavinet, elp, pipes), Paul Jackson (elb, marimbula), Harvey Mason (d), Bill Summers (conga, shekere, balafon, agogo, cabasa, hindewho, tambourine, log drum, surdo, gankoqui, beer bottle)

San Francisco   1973   **Chameleon**
                                               Watermelon Man
                                               Sly
                                               Vein Melter

Other CDs
same contents:
  Europe: CBS CD 69528
  Japan: CBS 32 DP 438

LPs

same contents:
  USA: Columbia KC 32731; Columbia PC 32731
  UK: CBS 32008

Cassettes

same contents:
  USA: Columbia CT 32731; Columbia PCT 32731

* * *

Weather Report: *Heavy Weather*

As Hancock strove to produce highly structured funk arrangements, two others of his colleagues from **In a Silent Way**, Joe Zawinul and Wayne Shorter, were exploring the opposite extreme. The first two albums by their band Weather Report (formed in 1970 and so named by Shorter because of the ever-changing character of the music) were born largely of collective improvisation. In contrast to the repetitive funk bass lines, infectious riffs and hot solos of **Headhunters**, early Weather Report dealt in haunting, impressionistic textures and fierce, up-tempo interaction which often seemed like an extension of the early fusion experiments of Miles Davis. However, Zawinul's dominance of the band and appetite for larger audiences brought a marked move towards accessibility in the mid-1970s. Free improvisation was replaced by formal composition, often irregular time by imaginatively deployed Latin and funk rhythms, frequent atonality by lyrical melody. The culmination of this development, **Heavy Weather**, was recorded in 1976. It became the group's best-selling album and helped turn Weather Report into the most durable and influential of fusion bands. The new style was no better exemplified than by the celebratory *Birdland*, the disco hit which fuelled a thousand aerobics sessions.

Zawinul was inspired to write *Birdland* by hearing Count Basie's band at the New York club of the same name, and, apart from having many strikingly original features, the piece is a faithful tribute to the swing bandleader. Its rhythm – a crisp straight eight on the hi-hat cymbal – and much of its harmony are plainly of a later vintage, but the sustained use of bluesy riff figures is pure 1930s Kansas City jazz, while the bridge brings idiomatic swing-style chord changes. Zawinul was even able to mimic the warm sound of a big-band horn section by using his recently acquired Oberheim Polythonic synthesizer, an instrument which became central to the orchestral sound that typified Weather Report's music from this point on. (On the later album **8:30** the look back was carried still further in a live version of *Birdland* which replaces the straight eighth-note rhythm with a shuffle beat, though the older style beat does not work well for this piece.)

The full-time appointment of electric bass guitarist Jaco Pastorius (he had recorded only briefly on the preceding album, **Black Market**) not only enriched the orchestral resources of Weather Report but also transformed its sound and repertory. In Pastorius's hands, the electric bass became the complete instrument (as he had shown in *Portrait of Tracy* on **Jaco Pastorius**, his debut album as leader from the same year). He used it to play sustained pedal tones which had the depth and volume of a dozen double basses, traditional walking lines (though not on **Heavy Weather**), Latin and funk figures which had the complexity of an entire Latin American percussion ensemble, chords, and fluent high-register solos and front-line melodies (most conspicuously in the first theme of *Birdland*, where he uses harmonics and string bending like a guitarist). He did all this with a clarity and agility previously unknown on the electric bass.

Pastorius also drew on sound harmonic knowledge to enliven the most routine chord structures. His accompanying lines and fills in *Birdland* invigorate an already strong composition, as does his raw, penetrating tone, achieved by playing his fretless bass very close to the instrument's bridge. The fretless fingerboard also enabled him to play the kind of glissandi heard in the riff to *Palladíum* and in *Harlequin*, where he slides an entire chord.

Pastorius contributed two compositions to **Heavy Weather**, both of which used the bass as a melody instrument and introduced a new rhythmic vitality to the band. The devices found in his solo on *Havona* are typical of much of his playing and were imitated by a generation of electric bassists. Indeed, although composition theoretically took precedence over improvisation in the new Weather Report, Pastorius became a major soloist. Even when he was accompanying, his lines were so forceful they often dominated the ensemble.

By contrast, Wayne Shorter's role as a soloist in Weather Report gradually diminished. However, a composition like *Palladíum* shows that he had lost none of the writing skill which brought him recognition as one of the most original jazz composers of the 1960s.

CD

USA: *Heavy Weather*, **Columbia CK 34418**

Wayne Shorter (ss, ts), Joe Zawinul (syn, p, v, melodica), Jaco Pastorius (elb, mandocello), Alex Acuña (d), Manolo Badrena (tambourine)

Hollywood   1976   **Birdland**

Shorter (ts), Zawinul (syn, elp), Pastorius (elb), Acuña (d)
A Remark You Made

Shorter (ss), Zawinul (syn, elp, melodica), Pastorius (elb), Acuña (d),
Badrena (conga)   **Teen Town**

*as **Teen Town**, but Zawinul (syn, elp, p), Badrena (v)*
Harlequin

Acuña, Badrena (timbales, conga, tom toms, v)
Rumba Mamá

Shorter (ss, ts), Zawinul (syn, elp), Pastorius (elb, steel drums), Acuña
(d), Badrena (conga, per)   **Palladíum**

Shorter (ss), Zawinul (syn, p, g, tabla), Pastorius (elb, mandocello),
Acuña (d), Badrena (per)   **The Juggler**

Shorter (ss), Zawinul (syn, p), Pastorius (elb), Acuña (d)
Havona

Other CDs
same contents:
  UK: CBS CD 81775
  Europe: CBS 462525–2
  Japan: CBS 35 DP 131

LPs
same contents:
  USA: Columbia PC 34418
  UK: CBS 32358

Cassettes
same contents:
  USA: Columbia PCT 34418
  UK: CBS 40–32358

Bill Bruford: *Feels Good to Me*

While American fusion was drawing explicitly from such pan-American popular idioms as funk, soul and Latin music, a somewhat different situation pertained across the Atlantic. Many budding young British fusion musicians absorbed the influence of soul music, but they took perhaps greater account of that peculiarly British phenomenon, art rock, as exemplified by such groups as Yes and King Crimson. Perhaps the most creative of British fusion bands was Bruford, led by a former member of both those groups, drummer Bill Bruford. At a time when much early fusion has dated badly, Bruford's 1977 debut album, **Feels Good to Me**, remains a timeless masterpiece, its many achievements unsurpassed.

Bruford conceived **Feels Good to Me** as a rock album, notwithstanding its many virtues as a fusion recording. There is, however, a complexity of rhythm, harmony and form, not found in hard rock, which suggests borrowing from jazz and European concert music. There are funky elements, but no **Headhunter**-type grooves, and only passing reference to rhythm and blues and the blues; if ever there were a 'jazz-rock' as opposed to 'jazz-funk' fusion, this is it.

Feels Good to Me smoothly dovetails high velocity ensemble lines which have the harmonic and rhythmic complexity of bop (*Beelzebub* and *If You Can't Stand the Heat . . .*) with echoes of art rock (*Sample and Hold* and *Feels Good to Me*), jazz-inflected ballads (*Seems Like a Lifetime Ago* and *Either End of August*), heavy rock passages, a romantic piano and flugelhorn duet (*Springtime in Siberia*), Eastern folk flavours which long predate the 1980s world-music boom (the introduction to *Adios a la Pasada*) and impressionism reminiscent of **In a Silent Way** (passages in *Seems Like a Lifetime Ago* and *Sample and Hold*). Although Bruford told this writer that he 'felt like an amateur' when making the album, it is full of highly detailed arrangements, executed with astonishing precision. It displays a wide range of tone colour, mood, rhythm and metre (the first theme of *Beelzebub*, for example, is polymetric, using different metres for the rhythm section and lead instruments), but all the pieces evolve organically and virtually all are supported by a constant or at least regular pulse; there are none of the cut-and-paste arrangements found in the work of the Mahavishnu Orchestra.

Nobody in the band had a classical background; even Dave Stewart, the keyboard player who did much to flesh out the harmonies of Bruford's tunes, was largely self-taught. But, true to its art-rock antecedents, **Feels Good to Me** abounds in classical references. Several of the pieces are continuous suites rather than songs, and the themes to *Feels Good to Me*, *Either End of August* and *Springtime in Siberia* are all classically flavoured. On many tracks the sound of organ, synthesized brass and strings and the pure, uninflected tone of Kenny Wheeler's flugelhorn reinforce the impression;

and on *Springtime in Siberia*, in his duet with Wheeler, Stewart supplies measured block chords which often recall Chopin or Debussy.

Jazz, meanwhile, is nowhere more apparent than in the highly chromatic playing of Allan Holdsworth, who since the early 1980s has been one of the most influential jazz-rock guitarists. A former reed player and disciple of Coltrane, Holdsworth employs the overdriven sound of the rock guitarist, but only because the sustained tones it generates allow him to emulate the phrasing of a saxophone. In pursuit of a reed-like sound, he has redrawn the boundaries of guitar technique and created a novel, unclichéd syntax for his instrument. Though much imitated, his agility, fluidity and lyricism have rarely been matched. **Feels Good to Me** contains some of his best playing, not least on *If You Can't Stand the Heat* . . ., where he makes uniquely expressive use of the guitar's vibrato bar.

Feels Good to Me also benefits from three appearances by singer Annette Peacock, whose mixture of suppressed hysteria and whispered passion is a delight, and from the bass playing of Jeff Berlin, who, while not as innovative as Pastorius or Stanley Clarke, matched both for virtuosity.

CD
USA: *Feels Good to Me*, **EG CD 33**

Dave Stewart (syn, org), Allan Holdsworth (elg), Jeff Berlin (elb), Bill Bruford (d, vb or xylophone)
London   August 1977   **Beelzebub**

add Annette Peacock (v)   **Back to the Beginning**

Kenny Wheeler (flugelhorn), Stewart (syn, elp), Holdsworth (elg), Berlin (elg), Bruford (d), Peacock (v)   **Seems Like a Lifetime Ago**
                                                        (part 1)

omit Wheeler; add Bruford (vb or xylophone)
                                               Seems Like a Lifetime Ago
                                                        (part 2)

omit Peacock; add Stewart (org, p)   **Sample and Hold**

Stewart (syn, org, p), Holdsworth, John Goodsall (elg), Berlin (elb), Bruford (d, tambourine)   **Feels Good to Me**

Wheeler (flugelhorn), Stewart (syn, p), Holdsworth (elg), Berlin (elb), Bruford (d, per)   **Either End of August** as *Beelzebub*, but Stewart (elp, p)   **If You Can't Stand the Heat . . .**

Wheeler (flugelhorn), Stewart (p)   **Springtime in Siberia**

as *Back to the Beginning*, but Stewart (syn, p), Bruford (d)
                                             **Adios a la Pasada (Goodbye to
                                             the Past)**

Other CDs
same contents:
   Japan: VJD 28051

LPs
same contents:
   USA: Polydor 6149
   UK: Polydor Deluxe 2302 075

Cassettes
same contents:
   USA: Polydor CT1–6149

* * *

Brecker Brothers: *Heavy Metal Bebop*

If Bruford and the Mahavishnu Orchestra provide typical examples of jazz-rock, the Brecker Brothers, a band led by saxophonist Michael and trumpeter Randy Brecker between 1974 and 1982, was the definitive jazz-funk fusion band. It used heavy rock amplification and wailing electric guitar, but its rhythms, all in 4/4 time, followed the examples of James Brown and Motown. The brothers had been fascinated by funk and soul ever since arriving in New York in the late 1960s, although both had a solid background in jazz and toured and recorded with Horace Silver in the early 1970s. In 1969 they formed one of the first fusion bands, Dreams, a group which made much use of rhythm and blues. It recorded two albums but was only a modest commercial success, and the brothers moved into session work, eventually joining the studio elite. By the late 1980s Michael Brecker had played on more than 400 record dates, frequently supplying just brief eight-bar solos. However, in many instances he played astonishingly inventive, virtuosic full-length improvisations, and on the strength of this work he became probably the most widely imitated saxophonist of the 1980s.

The brothers' talents as jazz soloists can be heard clearly on their mostly live release **Heavy Metal Bebop**, recorded in 1978. This was the fourth of six albums by the Brecker Brothers, and in many ways it forms a 'best-of' collection. It not only features some of the brothers' strongest writing, but the live setting, at My Father's Place on Long Island, seems to draw out some of their most inspired playing. It is also free of the commercial excesses which blight many of their albums. It seems incredible that the pen which produced such sublime charts as *Some Skunk Funk* and *Squids* should also create such utter banalities as *Oh my Stars*, *Finger Lickin' Good* and *Lovely Lady*. This stylistic schizophrenia, which resulted from pressure from their record company, is happily absent from **Heavy Metal Bebop**.

Rarely has an album been more appropriately named. **Heavy Metal Bebop** presents a potent synthesis of the brothers' favourite musics, a distinctive blend of the sonorities and attitudes of heavy metal with the dance rhythms of funk and the harmonic depth of postwar jazz. The rhythmic flavour is very much straight eighths, with slapped funk bass lines and staccato horn ensembles phrased in the Motown manner. However, the punching, breakneck ensembles of *Some Skunk Funk*, a tune which encapsulates the main features of the Breckers' style, illustrate not only the brothers' technical virtuosity but also the harmonic sophistication of Randy's writing. They feature highly dissonant, deftly syncopated sixteenth-note lines played together at a speed of around 126 beats per minute (about eight notes a second). Here and elsewhere, the mood is intensified by the use of 'quartal' harmony (the suspended sound associated with pianist McCoy Tyner), astringent altered chords and volatile tone clusters.

There are some storming solos, especially from trumpeter Randy, who took credit for most of the Brecker Brothers' tunes. Apart from displaying his authoritative mastery of both bebop and rhythm and blues, his solos make much use of such electronic processing as wa-wa and harmonizer: the wa-wa makes his tone not unlike that of Miles Davis around the same time, while the harmonizer duplicates his trumpet sound at other pitches, creating lines in parallel harmony. Randy had used these effects on a number of the group's albums before this, but on **Heavy Metal Bebop** Mike made his debut with them. Like Randy, he demonstrates a confident mastery of both hard bop and rhythm and blues, and uses the harmonizer to produce rich chords reminiscent of a gospel choir. He makes especially effective use of the device in the long preaching cadenza which closes the soulful rock ballad *Funky Sea, Funky Dew*.

Other aspects of the Breckers' work are found in the much modified 12-bar blues that is *Inside Out* and in *Squids*, where riffs are combined to produce the kind of layered arrangement heard in Herbie Hancock's *Chameleon*.

LP

USA: *Heavy Metal Bebop*, Arista 4185

Randy Brecker (tpt), Michael Brecker (ts), Barry Finnerty (elg, guitorganizer), Neil Jason (elb), Terry Bozzio (d)

Long Island   1978   **Inside Out**

add Randy Brecker (kbd); omit (guitorganizer)

                                     Some Skunk Funk
                                       Sponge

add Sammy Figueroa, Rafael Cruz (per)

                                       Funky Sea, Funky Dew
                                       Squids

add Paul Schaeffer (elp), Alan Schwartzberg (d), Jason, Jeff Schoen, Roy Herring (v), Kash Monet (v, per, handclaps), Bob Clearmountain and others (handclaps)

New York   1978   **East River**

CDs

same contents:
    Japan: Victor B20D 51001
incl. tracks 1, 6: *The Brecker Brothers Collection, vol.1*
    USA: RCA Novus 3075-2
    Europe: RCA Novus ND 90442
incl. tracks 2–5: *The Brecker Brothers Collection, vol. 2* (forthcoming)

Other LPs

same contents:
    UK: Arista SPART 1070
incl. tracks 1, 6: *The Brecker Brothers Collection, vol.1*
    Europe: RCA Novus NL 90442
incl. tracks 2–5: *The Brecker Brothers Collection, vol.2* (forthcoming)

Cassettes

same contents:
    USA: Arista ATC 4185
incl. tracks 1, 6: *The Brecker Brothers Collection, vol.1*
    USA: RCA Novus 3075-4
    Europe: RCA Novus NK 90442
incl. tracks 2–5: *The Brecker Brothers Collection, vol.2* (forthcoming)

John Scofield: *Still Warm*

The piquant combination of funk and post-bop harmony favoured by the Brecker Brothers is also evident in the work of guitarist John Scofield, a player who made his mark in both fusion and bop as early as the mid-1970s, but only came to widespread notice following a stint with Miles Davis in the mid-1980s. Like two earlier sidemen with Davis, Herbie Hancock and Chick Corea, Scofield had studied the great bop players, and his ability in this idiom is well documented on two recordings from the late 1970s which he made for the Enja label. But he also absorbed the rock and rhythm-and-blues sounds which were a part of his childhood in the 1960s, and these have taken their place in his style. An album from 1979, **Who's Who**, announced his interest in playing jazz in a rock and funk setting, and by the mid-1980s, thanks perhaps to his contact with Davis, his ideas in this area had acquired even stronger focus. The result was a series of electric albums recorded for Gramavision between 1984 and 1987, among which the 1985 **Still Warm** represented a peak of development. It confirmed the arrival of a composer and soloist of striking individuality.

Scofield's originality is most apparent in his improvisations. It was obvious enough in his earliest recordings, but it finds especially powerful expression in **Still Warm**. His special combination of blues, rock and post-bop elements has resulted in a new and highly idiosyncratic language not only for his instrument but for jazz at large. As far as bop goes, Scofield tends to avoid the continuous eighth-note lines which typify the playing of many bop guitarists, preferring to emulate the breath-punctuated phrasing of the horn player. From guitarists such as Otis Rush and Jimi Hendrix he has borrowed typical blues and rock techniques to produce such effects and sounds as note-bending, muting, harmonics and an overdriven tone. These are to be heard throughout **Still Warm**, but especially in *Rule of Thumb*.

However, rather more characteristic of Scofield the soloist than either personalized bop or blues licks is an extremely dissonant harmonic vocabulary, often expressed in wide intervallic leaps. This approach can be heard in the theme of *Protocol*, which also makes use of diminished scales. Towards the end of the piece, Scofield uses the blues technique of string bending but applies it to pairs of dissonant intervals rather than the usual blue notes. In the coda to *Rule of Thumb*, he takes risks which, in the hands of a lesser player, might result in gross errors. On one occasion he strikes, perhaps by accident, a highly dissonant interval, but makes it good by paraphrasing it a few moments later in a higher register. He then compounds the outrage by bending two highly dissonant and distinctly non-bluesy notes before resolving back into the home key.

Scofield has often been unreasonably modest about his abilities as a composer, claiming that he has only three or four ideas which are perpetually recycled. However, the handful of compositional formulas he reworks are distinctly his own, and often reflect the vocabulary found in his solos. **Still Warm** offers two tunes, *Techno* and *Protocol*, which are based on up-tempo funk dance rhythms. However, in this case 'funk' refers only to the powerful rhythmic groove set up by bassist Darryl Jones and drummer Omar Hakim. Harmonically and melodically, these pieces have the complexity of modern jazz, especially when Scofield solos. Another song type – slow with a lyrical melody – is heard in several pieces here, especially *High and Mighty* and *Rule of Thumb*. The latter in particular illustrates Scofield's idea about limited song types, since its mood and structure are highly reminiscent of *Holidays*, a piece from Scofield's trio album **Out Light a Light**, recorded in 1981. Along with *Techno* and *Protocol*, it is a highlight of **Still Warm**. At its centre is a simple 16-bar chord cycle over which Scofield builds an increasingly jubilant solo, creating a burgeoning sense of confirmation with the arrival of each new chorus.

CD

USA: *Still Warm*, Gramavision R2 79401

Don Grolnick (kbd), John Scofield (elg), Darryl Jones (elb), Omar Hakim (d, per)

New York	June 1985	Techno
		Still Warm
		High and Mighty
		Protocol
		Rule of Thumb
		Picks and Pans
		Gil B643

Other CDs

same contents:
  UK: Gramavision 18–8508–2
  Germany: Gramavision 971.028
  Japan: Gramavision D22Y 0306

LPs

same contents:
  USA: Gramavision R1 79401
  UK: Gramavision 18–8508–1

Cassettes

same contents:

USA: Gramavision R4 79401
UK: Gramavision 18–8508–4

* * *

Pat Metheny: *Still Life (Talking)*

If John Scofield is one indication of the continuing health and growth of fusion, his fellow guitarist Pat Metheny is another. Both were bop fanatics in their teens and both have developed distinctly individual voices. However, Scofield and Metheny's mature styles sit at opposite ends of the jazz spectrum. Where Scofield is preoccupied with angular, urban idioms and plays the blues in virtually everything, Metheny takes a markedly more lyrical, pastoral approach. Many listeners have discerned a country-and-western flavour in his music, and he has acknowledged the effect of a childhood near Kansas City in this respect. He has also shown an abiding fascination with another type of folk music – that of Latin America, in particular that of Brazil. Ornette Coleman's free jazz is yet another strong influence, and, although some observers have found it difficult to reconcile the typically smooth contours of Metheny's music with the angularity of much of Coleman's, Metheny has described the appeal of Coleman's music as being essentially melodic. Although the key elements of his style have been apparent since the late 1970s, Metheny's distinctive mix of North and South American vernaculars found particularly full expression in the Grammy Award-winning recording made in 1987, **Still Life (Talking)**.

Metheny had an early passion for the bossa novas of Antonio Carlos Jobim, and later for the work of Milton Nascimento, whom he credits as the inspiration for the wordless vocals which are heard throughout **Still Life (Talking)**. They are especially effective when carrying the soaring melodies of (*It's Just*) *Talk*. The explicit Latin rhythms which had been a novel feature of the group's previous album, **First Circle** (1984), are also revisited. These are not, however, the kind of rhythms associated with Machito or Tito Puente. These are muted, lightly dancing pulses rather than the strident grooves of the Cuban school.

A similarly muted quality distinguishes Metheny's guitar playing. Unlike Scofield, McLaughlin and other guitarists associated with fusion, he shows little evidence of a debt to rock or rhythm and blues, either in his writing or his playing. Among his early models were Wes Montgomery and Jim Hall, but Metheny's guitar sound is even darker than Montgomery's and further softened by the use of digital delay. Only a residue of his influences now remains; he has developed into a quite distinctive voice, recognizable after a few notes and much imitated by the late 1980s.

Still Life (Talking) marked the beginning of a return to extensive straight-ahead solo playing for Metheny – something which became fully apparent on the next album he made, in spring 1989, **Letter from Home**. Here, in 1987, he is particularly striking in *Third Wind*, where he takes a remarkable unaccompanied break and solo which recalls the example set by Charlie Parker's 1946 recordings of *Night in Tunisia*. This is an unequivocal bop solo, full of chromatic lines and delivered with enormous velocity and drive. His solo in the second section of this piece is played on a Roland guitar synthesizer, with the signature sound Metheny has made his own. He also takes a substantial guitar solo on *Minuano (Six Eight)*.

Metheny's partner of more than 15 years, keyboard player Lyle Mays, delivers solos which contrast dramatically with Metheny's. His considered piano outings on *So May it Secretly Begin* and *(It's Just) Talk* are masterpieces of understatement and appropriately recall Jobim's sparse piano solos. A similar subtlety is apparent in Mays's deployment of synthesizers, which are used mainly for unobtrusive string and horn sounds. Synthesized, almost funk-like horn riffs are heard towards the close of *(It's Just) Talk*, but these are virtually the only hint of rhythm and blues in the music of the Pat Metheny Group. The folky, banjo-like twang of Metheny's guitar synthesizer on *Last Train Home* says much more about the group's style.

CD
USA: *Still Life (Talking)*, **Geffen GHS 24145–2**

Lyle Mays (syn, p), Pat Metheny (g, elg, ?g syn), Steve Rodby (sb), Paul Wertico (d), Armando Marçal (per, v), David Blamires, Mark Ledford (v)

New York	March–April 1987	**Minuano (Six Eight)**

omit (g)   **So May it Secretly Begin**

*as **Minuano**, but Metheny (g syn), Rodby (?elb), omit (per)*
                                                Last Train Home

*as **Minuano**, but Metheny (elg)*   **(It's Just) Talk**

*as **Minuano**, but Mays (syn), Metheny (g, g syn)*
                                                Third Wind

Mays (syn), Marçal (per)   **Distance** *as **Minuano**, but Metheny (g), omit (d), omit (v)*

In her Family

Other CDs

same contents:
  UK: Geffen 924 145–2

LPs

same contents:
  USA: Geffen GHS 24145
  UK: Geffen 924 145–1

Cassettes

same contents:
  USA: Geffen M5G 24145
  UK: Geffen 924 145–4

Compact Disc Supplement

In the 15 months since the original publication of the *Guide* a number of the contributors' selections have been issued on compact disc, either to be more widely distributed or – better still – for the first time. The approach taken in this appendix should be self-evident, as it follows the book's format exactly.

p. 4: Original Dixieland Jazz Band

same contents:
   USA: Bluebird CD 61098

p. 8: New Orleans Rhythm Kings

incl. tracks 1-21, plus additional take of *Shim-me-sha-wabble* (take B):
   Germany: *New Orleans Rhythm Kings*, Village VILCD004-2
not incl. alternative takes:
   USA: *New Orleans Rhythm Kings*, Milestone MCD 47020-2

p. 13: King Oliver

same contents:
   Germany: *Louis Armstrong with King Oliver, vol. 1*, Village VILCD003-2;
   vol. 2, Village VILCD012-2
incl. tracks 1-9, 17-20, 33-7, plus Red Onion Jazz Babies, cited below:
   USA: *Louis Armstrong and King Oliver*, Milestone MCD 47017-2
incl. tracks 1-9, 17-20, 40-1:
   UK: *The Classic New Orleans Jazz of the King & Mister Jelly Lord*, Parade
   PAR2303
incl. tracks 5-6, 10-13, 21, 33, 36-7, 40:
   UK: *King Oliver, vol. 1, 1923-1929*, BBC RPCD787
incl. tracks 10-16, 25-32:

France: *King Oliver Jazz Band 1923*, Jazz Archives ZET746
incl. tracks 1-34, 37:
  France: *Louis Armstrong, Vol. 1, 1923*, Masters of Jazz MJCD 1; *Vol. 2, 1923-1924*, Masters of Jazz MJCD 2

p. 16: Red Onion Jazz Babies

same contents:
  USA: *Louis Armstrong and King Oliver*, Milestone MCD 47017-2
plus additional tracks:
  Germany: *Louis Armstrong 1924-25*, Village VILCD009-2

p. 22: Jelly Roll Morton's piano solos

plus additional tracks, incl. p. 14, tracks 40-1:
  USA: *Jelly Roll Morton*, Milestone MCD 47018-2
plus additional tracks:
  France: *The Complete Piano Solos 1923-1939*, Virgin 34000
incl. tracks 1-2 (or 3), 4-6, 9, 11-12, 15-16:
  USA: *The Pianist and Composer*, Smithsonian RD 043
incl. tracks 1-2, 4-16:
  France: *Jelly Roll Morton 1923-1924*, Classics 584

p. 23: Jelly Roll Morton's bands

plus additional tracks: *The Jelly Roll Morton Centennial: His Complete Victor Recordings*
  Europe: Bluebird ND82361
incl. tracks 1-21:
  UK: *Jelly Roll Morton*, vol. 1, JSP CD321; vol. 2, JSP CD322; vol. 4, JSP CD324; vol. 5, JSP CD325
  France: *Jelly Roll Morton 1924-1926*, Classics 599; . . . *1926-1928*, Classics 612; . . . *1928-1929*, Classics 627
incl. tracks 1, 3, 7-10, 12-16, 19, 22-3:
  Italy: *Red Hot Peppers, New Orleans Jazzmen & Trios*, Giants of Jazz CD53018
incl. tracks 1-11, 14-15:
  France: *The Complete Jelly Roll Morton Red Hot Peppers, 1926-1930*, Music Memoria 30380
incl. tracks 1, 3, 5, 7-8, 15, 19:
  Australia: *Jazz Classics in Digital Stereo*, ABC CD38416, ABC 836.199

p. 29: Louis Armstrong

same contents:
   France: *Louis Armstrong and his Orchestra 1925-1926*, Classics 600;
   . . . *1926-1927*, Classics 585; . . . *1928-1929*, Classics 570
plus additional tracks:
   UK: *Louis Armstrong Hot Fives & Sevens*, Vol. 1, JSP CD312;
   vol. 2, JSP CD313; vol. 3, JSP CD314
incl. tracks 1-22, 24-6, 28-49:
   Germany: *Louis Armstrong: the Span of the Years (1925-1950)*, vol. 1,
   Bellaphon 625.50.004; vol. 2, Bellaphon 625.50.009; vol. 3, Bellaphon
   625.50.013; vol. 4, Bellaphon 625.50.018
incl. tracks 1-3, 6-7, 10, 20-1, 38, 40, 42-5:
   Italy: *The Essential Hot Five Sides*, Suisa JZCD324
incl. tracks 2, 4, 7, 10, 20, 25-6, 28-35, 37-8, 40, 44-5, 48, 50, 58:
   Italy: *Hot Five and Hot Seven (1925-1928)*, Giants of Jazz CD0242, CD53001

p. 35: Johnny Dodds

plus additional tracks:
   France: *Johnny Dodds 1926*, Classics 589; . . . *1927-1928*, Classics 617
incl. tracks 1 8, 14 15:
   Germany: *Johnny Dodds, Volume 1*, Village VILCD002-2
incl. tracks 1-8:
   UK: *Johnny Dodds 1926-1940, part 1*, Affinity CDAFS1023-3
incl. tracks 1-3, 10 or 11, 14-18, 22:
   Italy: *Johnny Dodds: the Myth of New Orleans*, Giants of Jazz CD53077

p. 39: Jimmie Noone

plus additional tracks, incl. additional alternative takes:
   UK: *Jimmy Noone: the Complete Recordings, Vol. 1*, Affinity CDAFS1027-3
incl. tracks 1-4 (take B of *Four or Five Times*), 6-13:
   France: *Jimmie Noone 1928-1929*, Classics 611
unknown contents:
   Japan: *Apex Blues*, WEA WMC5-332

p. 42: Bix Beiderbecke

plus additional tracks:
   Italy: *The Complete Bix Beiderbecke in Chronological Order*, vol. 2 IRD
   BIX2; vol. 3, IRD BIX3
incl. tracks 1, 3, 5-7, 12, 14, 16, 20:

UK: *The Golden Age of Bix Beiderbecke*, Music for Pleasure CDMFP6046, 791439-2
incl. tracks 3-7, 9:
 Italy: *The Bix Beiderbecke Collection*, Deja Vu DVCD2049
incl. tracks 1-2, 4-7:
 Italy: *The Bix Beiderbecke Story*, Deja Vu RECD14
incl. tracks 1, 3-7, 12:
 Italy: *Bixology*, Giants of Jazz CD53017

p. 58: Sidney Bechet

plus additional tracks:
 USA: *Sidney Bechet: the Victor Sessions, Master Takes, 1932-43*, RCA 2402-2 RB
incl. tracks 1-2, 5-6:
 France: *Sidney Bechet 1923-1936*, Classics 583; . . . *1940*, Classics 619

p. 67: James P. Johnson

incl. tracks 8-11:
 UK: *Feelin' Blue*, Halcyon CHDL107

p. 70: Fats Waller

incl. tracks 1-21, 24-33: *Turn on the Heat: the Fats Waller Piano Solos*
 USA: Bluebird 2482-2 RB
 Europe: Bluebird ND82482(2)
incl. tracks 3, 13, 18, 24-5 (and alternative takes of tracks 8 & 31), plus tracks cited below for listing re p. 158:
 Japan: *Fats Waller*, Bluebird BVCJ9023, BVCJ9024 (2-CD set)
incl. tracks 14-21, 24-8:
 France: *Piano Masterworks, Vol. 2, 1929-1943*, Hot 'n Sweet FDC5113
incl. track 1, plus material cited below for listing re p. 158:
 UK: *The Cream Series: Fats Waller*, Flapper PASTCD9742
incl. tracks 2-3, 10, 14:
 UK: *You Rascal, You*, Living Era CDAJA5040
incl. tracks 29, 31, plus tracks cited below for listing re p. 158:
 UK: *Diamond Series: Fats Waller*, RCA CD90117

p. 73: Earl Hines

plus additional tracks:
 France: *Special Earl Hines 1928-1965*, Jazz Time 253.624-2

p. 76: Art Tatum

incl. tracks 1-7, 9-10, 12-13:
   France: *Art Tatum, 1934-1940*, Classics 560

p. 78: Thelonious Monk

plus additional track:
   USA: Columbia Jazz Masterpieces CK 47854
   Europe: CBS Jazz Masterpieces, number unknown

p. 85: Fletcher Henderson

incl. tracks 3-9:
   France: *Fletcher Henderson and his Orchestra, 1926-1927*, Classics 597;
   . . .*1927*, Classics 580; . . . *1927-1931*, Classics 572

p. 92: Duke Ellington, 1927-34

incl. tracks 10-16:
   France: *Duke Ellington and his Orchestra 1929*, Classics 569; . . . *1930, Vol.
   2*, Classics 596; . . . *1930-1931*, Classics 605; . . . *1931-1932*, Classics 616
incl. tracks 1-7, 10-14, 16 (unknown takes):
   Italy: *Duke Ellington and his Orchestra 1927-1931*, Giants of Jazz CD53030

p. 95: Duke Ellington, 1940-2

incl. tracks 2-4, 11-12, 15, 20, 22, 26-7, 29, 33, 35, 39:
   Italy: *Duke Ellington: the Jimmy Blanton Era 1939-1941*, Giants of Jazz
   CD53048

p. 106: Count Basie in Bennie Moten's band

same contents (but take 3 of *Small Black*):
   France: *Bennie Moten's Kansas City Orchestra 1929-1930*, Classics 578; . . .
   1930-1932, Classics 591
plus additional tracks:
   France: *Count Basie, vol. 1, 1929-30, Count Basie, vol. 2, 1930-32*, Masters of
   Jazz MJCD 3, MJCD 4
incl. track 15, plus tracks cited below:
   UK: *Count Basie Volume One 1932-1938*, BBC RPCD785

p. 109: Count Basie, 1937-9

plus additional tracks: *The Original American Decca Recordings*
  USA: MCA, number unknown
  Europe: MCA GRP36112
incl. tracks 1-18:
  Germany: *One O'Clock Jump*, MCA 872.081
incl. tracks 1, 3, 5-7, 10-15, plus track cited above:
  UK: *Count Basie Volume One 1932-1938*, BBC RPCD785
incl. tracks 4-5, 8, 12-13, 16-17, 23-4, plus tracks cited below:
  Italy: *Count Basie with his Orchestra and his Rhythm Section 1937-1943*,
  Giants of Jazz CD53072
incl. tracks 1-3, 5-6, 10-11, 18:
  UK: *Blue and Sentimental*, Jazz Collection OR 0097

p. 112: Count Basie, 1936 & 1939-40

incl. tracks 4-6, 7-9, 12, plus first takes of tracks 10-11 and tracks cited on p.
111:
  France: *Count Basie and his Orchestra, 1939*, Classics 513; . . . *1939 Vol. 2*,
  Classics 533; . . . *1939-1940*, Classics 563
incl. tracks 7, 9, 10 (unknown take), plus tracks cited above:
  Italy: *Count Basie with his Orchestra and his Rhythm Section 1937-1943*,
  Giants of Jazz CD53072

p. 114: Count Basie, 1955-6

same contents:
  Japan: Verve POCJ1826

p. 118: Chick Webb, 1929-36

incl. tracks 11-13, plus tracks cited below:
  France: *Chick Webb and his Orchestra, 1935-1938*, Classics 517
incl. tracks 13-14, plus tracks cited below:
  France: *The Best of Ella Fitzgerald and Chick Webb*, Virgin 34002
incl. tracks 8, 14, plus tracks cited below:
  UK: *Ella Fitzgerald with the Chick Webb Band*, Flapper PASTCD9762

p. 119: Chick Webb, 1937-9

incl. tracks 1-5, 8, 10-11, plus tracks cited above:
  France: *Chick Webb and his Orchestra, 1935-1938*, Classics 517

incl. tracks 1-2, 4-14, plus tracks cited above:
France: *The Best of Ella Fitzgerald and Chick Webb*, Virgin 34002
incl. tracks 4-5, 8-9, 11, plus tracks cited above:
UK: *Ella Fitzgerald with the Chick Webb Band*, Flapper PASTCD9762

p. 123: Jimmie Lunceford

incl. tracks 7-14:
France: *Jimmie Lunceford and his Orchestra, 1937-1939*, Classics 520; . . .
1941, Classics 622

p. 152: Benny Goodman Trios & Quartets

incl. tracks 1-7, 11, plus tracks cited below:
Italy: *Small Combos 1935-1941*, Giants of Jazz CD53039
incl. tracks 8-12: *Avalon: the Small Bands, Volume 2 (1937-1939)*
USA: Bluebird 2273-2-RB
Europe: Bluebird ND82273

p. 154: Benny Goodman, 1935-41

incl. tracks 1, 5, plus tracks cited above:
Italy: *Small Combos 1935-1941*, Giants of Jazz CD53039
incl. tracks 2-4, 6-12:
Italy: *Charlie Christian, Genius of the Electric Guitar*, Giants of Jazz
CD53049

p. 158: Fats Waller's bands

incl. tracks 1-11:
UK: *Dust off that Old Pianna*, The Compact Selection TQ202
incl. tracks 3, 11, 13, 20, 28, 33:
UK: *Fats & His Rhythm*, Stagedoor SDC8085
incl. tracks 5, 12, 15-16, 20, 23, 29, 33:
Italy: *Ain't Misbehavin' 1934-43*, Giants of Jazz CD53078
incl. tracks 5, 10-12, 28:
Italy: *Fats Waller: the Pop Singer*, Suisa JZCD349
incl. tracks 15, 23, 26:
Italy: *Fats Waller: the Jazz Singer*, Suisa JZCD350
incl. tracks 6, 8, 10, 16, 26:
Spain: *Ain't Misbehavin'*, Rockin' Chair CD25
incl. tracks 11-13, 16-17, 28, 31, plus track cited above for listing re p. 70:
UK: *The Cream Series: Fats Waller*, Flapper PASTCD9742

incl. tracks 11-16, 23:
  UK: *Fats at his Finest*, Parade PAR 2003
incl. tracks 10, 13, 33, plus tracks cited above for listing re p.70:
  UK: *Diamond Series: Fats Waller*, RCA CD90117
incl. tracks 22, 26, 28, 30-31, plus tracks cited above for listing re p.70:
  Japan: *Fats Waller*, Bluebird BVCJ9023, BVCJ9024 (2-CD set)
incl. tracks 5, 8-10, 26, 28, 30:
  UK: *Fats Waller Jazz Classics in Digital Stereo*, BBC CD684

p. 163: Quintette du Hot Club de France

incl. tracks 1-4, 6, 13, 15:
  UK: *Swing in Paris*, Living Era CDAJA5070

p. 168: Billie Holiday, 1937-8

incl. tracks 1-4:
  France: *Billie Holiday and her Orchestra, 1933-1937*, Classics 582
incl. tracks 5-7, 9, 13, 18, plus tracks cited below: *The Legacy (1933-1958)*
  USA: Columbia Jazz Masterpieces C3K-47724
  Europe: CBS Jazz Masterpieces 469049-2

p. 170: Billie Holiday, 1940-2

incl. tracks 3, 6, 8, 14, 18, plus tracks cited above: *The Legacy (1933-1958)*
  USA: Columbia Jazz Masterpieces C3K-47724
  Europe: CBS Jazz Masterpieces 469049-2

p. 174: Coleman Hawkins

incl. *Body and Soul*:
  USA: *Three Great Swing Saxophones*, Bluebird 9683-2 RB
  UK: *Coleman Hawkins 1927-1939*, BBC CD698
  Europe: *Three Great Swing Saxophones*, Bluebird ND90405
  France: *Coleman Hawkins 1926-1940*, Jazz Archives 997.582; *Coleman Hawkins 1939-1940*, Classics 634

p. 175: Coleman Hawkins with Lester Young

incl. *The Man I Love*:
  France: *Great Tenor Saxophones*, Jazz Archives 999721; *Coleman Hawkins, Ben Webster, Julian Dash*, Doctor Jazz FDC5008

p. 179: Chu Berry

plus additional tracks cited below:
 Germany: *Classics in Swing: Ben Webster–Chu Berry*, Commodore
 9031-72726-2

p. 180: Ben Webster and Don Byas

incl. tracks 1-7, plus tracks cited above:
 Germany: *Classics in Swing: Ben Webster–Chu Berry*, Commodore
 9031-72726-2
incl. tracks 8-9:
 Germany: *Classics in Swing: Buck Clayton–Jonah Jones–Hot Lips Page*,
 Commodore 9031-72735-2
incl. tracks 10-12:
 Germany: *Classics in Swing: Town Hall Concert*, Commodore 9031-72739-2

p. 184: Nat 'King' Cole

incl. tracks 3-16:
 USA: *The Complete Capitol Recordings of the Nat King Cole Trio*, Mosaic MD
 18-138
incl. tracks 1, 3-4, 6, 8, 11-16:
 Italy: *Nat King Cole Trio (and Guests)*, Giants of Jazz CD0231, CD53005
incl. tracks 3-6, 8, 12-13:
 USA: *Jumpin' at Capitol: the Best of the Nat King Cole Trio*, Rhino R2 71009
incl. tracks 3-4, 6, 12-23: *The Nat King Cole Story*
 USA: Capitol C21Y-91529
 UK: Capitol 795129-2
incl. tracks 7-11, 14-16:
 USA: *The Best of the Nat King Cole Trio*, Capitol CDP 7-98288-2

p. 211: Bunk Johnson

same contents:
 USA, Europe: *Authentic New Orleans Jazz*, Good Time Jazz GTJCD12048-2

p. 216: Kid Ory

same contents:
 USA: Good Time Jazz GTJCD 12022-2

p. 219: Wooden Joe Nicholas

plus additional tracks:
  USA: American Music AMCD-5

p. 242: Dizzy Gillespie, 1946-9

incl. tracks 7, 9, 11, 13-16, 19, 28, 31: *The Bebop Revolution*
  USA: Bluebird 2177-2 RB

p. 250: Charlie Parker

same contents:
  Japan: *The Charlie Parker Story*, Savoy SV0105
plus additional tracks: *The Complete Savoy Studio Sessions*:
  Europe: Savoy 886421
incl. tracks 4, 6, 10, 13-14, 16:
  USA: *Bird: the Savoy Original Master Takes*, Savoy ZDS8801
incl. tracks 4, 6, 10, 13, 16: *Savoy Master Takes*
  Europe: Savoy ZD70737
  Japan: Savoy 240E-6802

p. 256: Thelonious Monk

same contents:
  USA: Blue Note B21Y 81510
incl. tracks 4, 6-8, 12, 14, 17-20:
  USA: *The Blue Note Years: the Best of Thelonious Monk*, Blue Note CDP 7-96636-2

p. 264: Fats Navarro and Tadd Dameron

same contents:
  USA: Blue note B21Y 81531-2, B21Y 81532-2

p. 278: Stan Getz

same contents:
  UK: Roulette CDP 7945072

p. 305: Clifford Brown and Max Roach

plus additional tracks:
  Japan: *Brownie: the Complete EmArcy Recordings of Clifford Brown*, EmArcy
  838306-2 (10-CD set)

p. 310: Horace Silver

same contents:
  USA: Blue Note B21Y 46140

p. 322: John Coltrane

same contents:
  USA: Blue Note B21Y 46095

p. 334: Jimmy Smith

same contents:
  USA: Blue Note B21Y 84030

p. 337: Dexter Gordon

same contents:
  USA: Blue Note B21Y 84077

p. 343: Roland Kirk

plus additional tracks: *Rahsaan: the Complete Mercury Recordings of Roland
Kirk* (10-CD set)
  USA, Germany: Mercury 846630-2
  Japan: Mercury PHCD4001-4010

p. 355: Eddie 'Lockjaw' Davis

tracks 1-5, as *The Eddie 'Lockjaw' Davis Cookbook, Vol. 1*:
  USA: Original Jazz Classics OJCCD652
tracks 6-10, as *The Eddie 'Lockjaw' Davis Cookbook, Vol. 2*:
  USA: Original Jazz Classics OJCCD653

p. 357: Sarah Vaughan

same contents:
  Japan: Roulette TOCJ5387

p. 364: Oscar Peterson

same contents:
  Japan: Mercury EJD3016

p. 402: Art Ensemble of Chicago

same contents:
  UK: Charly CDCHARLY78
incl. tracks 1-2, 4-5:
  UK: *A Jackson in your House (Message to our Folks)*, Affinity AFF752

p. 405: Sun Ra

same contents:
  Italy: *Cosmic Equation*, Magic Music 30011-CD

p. 427: Chick Corea

same contents:
  USA, Germany: Polydor 825336-2

p. 437: Brecker Brothers

same contents:
  Japan: Novus BVCJ5029
incl. tracks, 1, 6: *The Brecker Brothers Collection, Vol. 1*:
  Japan: Victor BVCJ5011
incl. tracks 2-5: *The Brecker Brothers Collection, Vol. 2*:
  USA: RCA Novus 3076-2
  Europe: RCA Novus ND83076

Index to Names and Places

Index to Titles